Dodger Classics

Dodger Classics

**Outstanding Games
From Each of the
Dodgers' 101 Seasons
1883-1983**

Robert L. Tiemann

Baseball Histories, Inc.

St. Louis

Published by:
Baseball Histories, Inc.
P.O. Box 15168
St. Louis, Missouri 63110

Typeset by: Marc Zasada

Printed by: McNaughton-Gunn, Inc., Saline, MI

ISBN 0-9608534-1-3

To my Mother,

whose love means so very much to me

Acknowledgements & Bibliographical Note

HAVING PUBLISHED A BOOK CALLED *CARDINAL CLASSICS* IN COLLABORATION WITH my father and mother, R. L. and R. K. Tiemann, and my brother-in-law John M. Howard, it was decided to use the same format for a book about the Dodgers. Being based in St. Louis, as much of the research as possible was done in the St. Louis Public Library and in the archives of *The Sporting News.* At *The Sporting News,* the director of historical research, Paul Mac Farlane, took my project under his wing and offered valuable advice and encouragement as well as access to the wide variety of research materials. And Steve Brener and the publicity department of the Los Angeles Dodgers offered photographs, score sheets, and encouragement.

Journeys were made to libraries in New York and California. The New York Public Library, the Brooklyn Public Library, the University of California Library at Berkeley, the Stanford University Library, the University of Missouri Library, and the University of Illinois Library were the sources of a hundred pounds of copies from microfilms. The microtext librarians at all these libraries were unfailingly helpful.

My brother Jonathan Tiemann was not only a generous host, he also turned out to be an invaluable research assistant on the East Coast. On the West Coast, my research was greatly facilitated by the multi-faceted resources of the Fife Institute of Palo Alto.

IN RESEARCHING THIS BOOK, A WIDE RANGE OF BASEBALL SOURCES WAS USED. AT least the score of every Dodger game ever played was researched using daily newspapers, the baseball weeklies *The Sporting News* and *Sporting Life,* and official baseball guides put out by Spalding, Reach, and *The Sporting News.*

These same sources were used again for information and statistics about the specific games chosen for this book.

For background material, old histories of the Brooklyn Dodgers were read. Of these, *Dodger Daze and Knights* by Tommy Holmes was the most useful. Roger Kahn's *The Boys of Summer* provided excellent insights into a short period of Dodger history and into the craft of writing about baseball. Interview books with old-timers by Lawrence S. Ritter and Donald Honig were also culled for pertinent facts. And many baseball autobiographies were read. These included *Koufax* by Sandy Koufax, *One Year at a Time* by Walter Alston, *The Dodgers and Me* by Leo Durocher, *I Never Had it Made* by Jackie Robinson, *It's Good to Be Alive* by Roy Campanella, and even *Charley Hustle* by Pete Rose.

The majority of the box scores were checked against the National League's official statistic sheets, which are listed by player in day-to-day form. And Henry Chadwick's scoresheets, now in the possession of the New York Public Library, were an incomparable source for play-to-play information on more than a dozen of the early games chosen.

But by far the most material came directly from daily newspapers, and the accounts in this book were made possible by the working sportswriters who covered the Dodgers over the last century.

There follows a complete list of the newspapers consulted in the preparation of this book:

Brooklyn: *Daily Eagle, Citizen, Daily Times, Standard-Union, Times-Union.* **Los Angeles:** *Times, Evening Herald and Express, Herald-Examiner, Mirror, Mirror-News, La Opinión.* **New York:** *Times, Herald-Tribune, Herald, Tribune, The World, Evening Telegram, World-Telegram, World-Telegram and Sun, American, Evening Journal, Journal-American, Daily News, Daily Mirror, Sun, Post.* **Boston:** *Daily Globe, Herald.* **St. Louis:** *Globe-Democrat, Star, Star-Times, Missouri Republican, Republic, Post-Dispatch.* **Philadelphia:** *Evening Bulletin, Inquirer.* **Montreal:** *Gazette.* **Louisville:** *Courier-Journal.* **Baltimore:** *The Sun.* **Chicago:** *Tribune, Herald, Herald-Examiner, Daily News, Record-Herald.* **Milwaukee:** *Journal, Sentinel.*

Introduction

THIS BOOK EXPLORES THE FIRST 100 YEARS OF DODGER HISTORY BY FOCUSING ON ONE game from each season, starting when Brooklyn gained a franchise in the minor league Interstate Association in 1883. This club shifted to the major league American Association in 1884 and to the National League in 1890. All through these moves, the team's ownership remained the same, and the player rosters were carrried over from one league to the next. Then in 1958, the club moved to Los Angeles after 75 years in Brooklyn.

Rather than present a complete overview of the various ownership, player, and financial developments in the history of the club, the reader is invited to peruse the various stages of the club's evolution through the examination of one game per season. This format, first used in the book *Cardinal Classics,* allows the reader to get some idea of what was happening to the Dodgers each year without having to refer back to too many previous pages on trades, management changes, etc. These issues are dealt with in a cursory manner in introductions to the 17 chapters into which the games are divided.

Each game story in the book stands by itself, making the book well-suited for placement in the living room or bathroom for perusal during the occasional pauses in each day's routine. Yet each game is chosen and written about in the context of the season in which it took place.

Having researched at least the score of every game played by the Dodgers, the games in the book are chosen with a set of priorities in mind. First of all, one game is included from every season, with additional games added for each round of playoffs and World Series that the Dodgers were involved in. In years in which the Dodgers were involved in close pennant races, key games from the races take precedence. If the team was not a pennant contender, the game for that year may be chosen because it was exciting in its own right; or it was somehow representative of the team's fortunes for the season; or some outstanding individual or team record was set in the game.

Happily, these criteria sometimes coincide nicely. In 1951, for example, the Dodgers were tied for first place on the last day of the regular season, and they won an extremely exciting game to force a playoff. But in other years the choice was more difficult. Like 1962, when the Dodgers opened the new Dodger Stadium in April, set a new all-time attendance record in September, and blew the pennant in a playoff. That year Sandy Koufax struck out 18 batters in one game and hurled a no-hitter in another. Maury Wills thrilled the baseball world by breaking Ty Cobb's stolen base record. And rookie Pete Richert struck out the first six men he faced in his major league debut. Since the loss of the pennant would be dealt with in the game from the playoff, a game in mid-September in which the Dodgers extended their lead to the maximum that year using base stealing as a key ingredient was chosen. And Koufax's and Richert's record performances were unfortunately passed over.

There were, however, three records which were so outstanding that I could not pass them over even though the Dodgers were involved in exciting pennant races in the same year. These were: 1) A 26-inning tie game played by Brooklyn in Boston on May 1, 1920; 2) four home runs in one game by Gil Hodges on August 31, 1950; and 3) Sandy Koufax's perfect game on September 9, 1965. These three games are included in the book along with a pennant-race game in each of those years.

Of course, each fan has his or her favorite games, and they will not always agree with my choices. But it is hoped that the games included here will illuminate Dodger history for both the casual fan and the serious historian of the team.

In keeping with the aim of giving the reader some of the flavor of baseball at the various stages of the Dodgers' development, each game is written about as if it was just completed using the terminology of the era in which it took place. Some of the terms and rules of the 1880's are no longer used, but it is hoped that they can be understood in the context of the story. Thus, the word *cranks* is used before the turn of the century to refer to what are now called *fans*. The word *Pittsburg* is not spelled with an *h* on the end until around World War I, when the nation's sports pages adopted the present, less Germanic spelling. And terms like *grand slam* and *beanball* are not used until they became contemporaneous.

The game was rather different in the 1880's than it is a century later. Most of the fielders played barehanded, and the catchers generally wore two gloves, one on each hand. These gloves were much more similar to today's batting gloves than to modern fielder's gloves, i.e., they were tight-fitting and unpadded. Substitutions were not allowed without the consent of the opposing teams until 1891, although one could switch the players already in the game from position to position. The top salary on the Brooklyn club in 1884 was probably around $2,000 for the full season, and a crank could buy a ticket into the park for 25¢, 50¢, or 75¢.

But it was still baseball, with three strikes for an out and three outs to the inning. And teams played for nine innings with nine men playing the very same positions as they do today, even if the outfielders and infielders play much deeper now.

I trust that the reader will be intrigued by the subtle evolution of the game and by the various developments of the Brooklyn and Los Angeles club. And of course, by the games which are presented here.

A Note about Nicknames

NOWADAYS, WHENEVER A NEW SPORTS FRANCHISE INTO EXISTENCE, ONE OF THE first orders of business is to choose a nickname for the team. But a century ago, there was no such thing as official nicknames for baseball clubs. Some clubs had names such as *The Athletic Club of Philadelphia,* and the team was called *the Athletics* in the sports reports. But most clubs were simply named after their cities. Thus, the official name in 1883 for the club that became the Dodgers was the *Brooklyn club.*

However, sportswriters seeking variations often referred to the teams in terms of the colors of their uniforms or socks. This usage generated names like the Boston *Red Stockings* and the St. Louis *Browns.* Since the Brooklyn team originally wore gray uniforms, they were sometimes called the *Grays.*

In 1887, the team abandoned gray, and the team was without a nickname until the following year. It seems that during the winter of 1887-88, several members of the team got married. So sportswriters dubbed the team the *Bridegrooms,* sometimes shortened to *Grooms.* This name enjoyed widespread popularity through the rest of the 19th century.

When the Brooklyn club moved to Eastern Park in 1891, the team picked up another nickname, the *Trolley Dodgers.* This was because of the maze of streetcar and railroad tracks that fans had to cross to get from public transportation to the entrance to the park. This name, of course, was shortened to the *Dodgers.*

In 1899, the Brooklyn club merged with the Baltimore club and acquired an array of established stars led by the famous manager Ned Hanlon. At the same time, there happened to be a vaudeville act around called "Hanlon's Superbas." So the sporting press soon adopted this name for the revamped Brooklyn team. The name *Superbas* pretty much supplanted *Bridegrooms. Superbas* was used in some Brooklyn papers as late as the mid-1920's. But when Hanlon left the club in 1906, the older nickname *Dodgers* enjoyed a revival.

When Wilbert Robinson became manager in 1914, the Brooklyn team picked up yet another nickname, *Robins.* The *Robins* were referred to collectively as *the Flock* upon occasion. So in the late 1910's and the early 1920's, there were three competing nicknames: *Superbas, Dodgers,* and *Robins.* Each newspaper had its own favorite, and none was official.

When Robinson was finally replaced as manager in 1932, the name *Robins* was dropped, although the squad was still sometimes called *the Flock.* The name *Superbas* having fallen by the way in the twenties, so *Dodgers* was the winner by default.

It was also in the 1930's that the newspapers picked up on *Bums* as a nickname. This was adopted straight from the Ebbets Field fans, who often called the Brooklyn players bums for their poor work. As the team's fortunes improved, it came to be something of a term of endearment. Although *Dodgers* was more less the official nickname of the team by the 1940's, a cartoon character dressed like a bum became widely accepted as the unofficial mascot of the team.

The name *Dodgers,* of course, was carried with the club to Los Angeles in 1958. But the *Bums,* the *Flock,* and the cartoon character did not survive the move.

In this book, the nickname or nicknames current to the time of the game are used. This often leads to use of two or more nicknames in the same story. The reader is forgiven for being confused, and it is hoped that this practice will not detract too much from the enjoyment of the reporting. But that is the way some newspapers did it at the time, just as today one can see the New York American Leaguers referred to as both the *Yankees* and the *Bronx Bombers* in the same article.

Explanation of the Box Scores

THE BOX SCORES IN THIS BOOK ARE PROVIDED AS AN ADJUNCT TO THE NARRATIVE. The figures in them are not necessarily official.

List of Abbreviations:

Names: The last name of the players and umpires are preceded by the initial of their most commonly used first name or nickname. Example: "D. Vance" is Dazzy Vance.

Positions: Standard abbreviations are used for the nine fielding positions and for pinch-hitters and pinch-runners. If a player did not start the game, or he changed positions during a game, the inning he entered the game or changed positions follows the abbreviation. Example: "pr8-rf-lf12" means that a player entered the game as a pinch-runner in the eighth inning, stayed in the game to play right field, then switched to left field in the twelfth inning.

ab: at bats, as counted in the year that the game took place.
h: hits
r: runs scored
bi: runs-batted-in. Calculated using today's rules. This statistic is estimated for the 1904 game.
o: putouts
a: assists
e: errors
ip: innings pitched. If a pitcher pitched part of an inning without retiring a batter, that fact is noted below the pitching summary.
h: hits allowed
r-er: runs allowed and earned runs allowed. Earned runs are calculated by applying modern rules.
bb: bases on balls allowed
so: batters struck out
WP: wild pitches
PB: passed balls
HBP: hit by pitch. Listed by pitcher, with the name of the batter hit in parentheses.
(W 1-0): The winning pitcher and his new record are listed
(L 0-1): The losing pitcher and his new record are listed
(sv #1): The pitcher getting official credit for a save (since 1969) and the number of saves for the season are also listed.

Game-Winning RBI: The player whose run-batted-in put his team ahead in the game is listed. If the winning run was scored on an error or wild pitch, etc., for which there was no RBI, that fact is also noted.

2B: two-base hits (doubles)
3B: three-base hits (triples)
HR: home runs
BB: bases on balls. Listed only for 1887, the only year in which walks counted as at bats and hits
SH: sacrifices. Listed only in years in which sacrifices were officially recognized.
SF: sacrifices flies. Also listed only when they were an official statistic
SB: stolen bases.
CS: caught stealing.
LOB: number of runners left on base
BE: number of runners who were allowed to reach first base because of errors.
DP: double plays. Defensive players who were involved in the play are listed in sequence, connected by hyphens. Names of players grounding into double plays are shown in parentheses. This is done only for double plays involving two force outs on ground balls.
TP: triple plays

Time, Attendance, and Umpires: are also listed, when available.

In the line score, runs scored are listed by innings. The team which batted first is always listed on top. If the winning run was scored in the bottom half of the ninth inning or of an extra inning, the number of outs at the time is noted.

In cases of doubleheaders, a full box score is provided for one game, and a line score is provided for the other. To this line score, each team's final total of runs, hits, and errors are added. The player making the Game-Winning RBI is listed. Also provided are listing of the batteries for each team. The pitchers are followed by the number of innings pitched, and the winning and losing pitchers, plus their records, are noted. The catchers are listed following the symbol "&."

In the "Today's Results" tables, the scores of all games involving teams in the Dodgers' league or division on that day are listed. If there were games postponed ("ppd.") or cancelled, that is also noted.

In the "Standings" tables, the standings following all of the day's games are listed. W-L is for games won and lost thus far during the season. Pct. is the winning percentage. And GB is for games behind the first-place club. In a very few cases, a team in second place (by percentage) is ahead in "games behind." In those cases, the second place club has its number listed in parentheses with a plus (+) before its number.

Table of Contents

Prologue **Baseball in Brooklyn Before the Dodgers** 1

Chapter I **Three Leagues & Three Pennants** 2

1883	September 29th	Brooklyn Wins Interstate Pennant on Final Day
1884	October 4th	A 10-Inning No-Hitter
1885	June 18th	Owner Byrne Chews Out His Players
1886	June 24th	Brooklyn Romps to 25-1 Victory
1887	April 16th	Beat Mets on Opening Day, 14-10
1888	July 10th	Bridegrooms Sweep Series from Browns
1889	September 7th	St. Louis Forfeits Key Game in Brooklyn
1889	**World Series Game No. 1**	Brooklyn Beats Giants in Opener
1890	September 1st	Brooklyn Wins a Tripleheader
1890	**World Series Game No. 7**	Series Called Off Due to Cold

Chapter II **Sojourn in Eastern Park** 25

1891	June 22nd	No-Hitter for Brooklyn's Lovett
1892	July 19th	Flat Bat Helps Win Double Shutout
1893	June 12th	Brooklyn Wins 14-13 to Take 1st Place
1894	August 11th	Home Run in 9th Wins Seesaw Game
1895	June 26th	13-Inning Duel Goes to Dodgers 1-0
1896	August 6th	Brooks Trail 10-0, Then Win 11-10
1897	July 31st	Kennedy Throws the Ball at the Umpire
1898	May 6th	Trolley Dodgers Score 6 in 9th to Win

Chapter III **Hanlon's Superbas** 44

1899	September 4th	''Brooklyn Finishes'' on Both Sides of the River
1900	June 21st	Superbas Rally to Win, Grab League Lead
1900	**Cup Series**	Brooklyn Wins the Cup
1901	September 23rd	Two Bases-Loaded Home Runs in 25-6 Win
1902	May 13th	Donovan Loses One-Hitter
1903	August 27th	Superbas Win with 17 Walks
1904	April 24th	Three Players Arrested at Sunday Game
1905	September 1st	Errors Keep Superbas in Last Place

Chapter IV **The Ex-Superbas** 64

1906	August 1st	McIntire Has No-Hitter for 10 Innings, Then Loses
1907	April 20th	Nap Rucker Loses Brooklyn Debut
1908	September 5th	Rucker Hurls No-Hitter
1909	April 15th	No-Hit for 9, Brooklyn Wins Opener in 13
1910	June 15th	Cy Barger Pitches and Bats Dodgers to Victory
1911	July 8th	Fans Bombard Umpire
1912	September 17th	Stengel Makes 4 Hits in Debut
1913	April 5th	Opening of Ebbets Field Draws 30,000

Chapter V Uncle Robbie Arrives 84
1914 July 4th Daubert Knocked Unconscious Scoring Winning Run
1915 September 9th Dodgers Win on One Scratch Hit
1916 October 3rd Brooklyn Clinches the Pennant
1916 **World Series Game No. 3** Dodgers Hold Off Red Sox, 4-3
1917 September 26th Robins Slip to 7th
1918 August 7th Zack and Mack Wheat Star
1919 May 15th Lose 10-0 in 13th Inning
Chapter VI Ups and Downs in the Twenties 102
1920 May 1st Robins and Braves Play 26-Inning Tie
1920 September 10th Two Big Rallies Keep Dodgers in 1st Place
1920 **World Series Game No. 3** Robins Take 2-1 Lead in Series
1921 May 2nd Brooklyn Pulls Out 11th Consecutive Victory
1922 July 1st Ruether Stars in 1-0 Victory
1923 May 7th At Least Johnston Wanted to Win
1924 September 7th Big Mob Sees Robins Lose Key Game
1925 September 13th Dazzy Gets a No-Hitter
Chapter VII The Daffiness Boys....................................122
1926 August 15th Three Dodgers on Third Base
1927 May 1st Carey's Daring Dash Wins for Brooklyn
1928 June 12th Uncle Robbie Shakes Up Lineup & Wins 13-1
1929 May 17th Nail-Biter Ends Losing Streak
1930 September 15th League-Leading Flock Wins 11th Straight
1931 April 15th Alta Cohen's Strange Debut
Chapter VIII "Is Brooklyn Still in the League?" 138
1932 September 12th Frederick Hits 6th Pinch Homer
1933 May 14th Pinch Grand Slam by Hack Wilson
1934 September 30th Brooklyn IS Still in the League!
1935 July 22nd Dodgers Win a Wild One, 14-13
1936 April 16th "Once a Dodger, Always a Dodger"
1937 August 31st Dodgers Blow the Game, Grimes Blows a Fuse
Chapter IX Larry and Leo 154
1938 June 15th No-Hitter in First Brooklyn Night Game
1939 June 1st Triple Play & Steal of Home Win for Dodgers
1940 April 30th Flock's Record 9-0 After No-Hitter
1941 September 25th Bums Clinch Pennant
1941 **World Series Game No. 4** Mickey Owen Misses the Third Strike
1942 August 4th Wartime Curfew Robs Dodgers of a Win
Chapter X Rickey Builds a Winner 170
1943 July 10th Dodgers Almost Go On Strike, Then Win 23-6
1944 July 16th Bums Snap 15⅝ Game Losing Streak
1945 July 8th Babe Herman Returns with a Hit
1946 September 14th Leo Plays a Hunch & Branca Stars
1946 **Playoff Game No. 2** Dodgers Lose Pennant as Desperate Rally Fails

Chapter XI **The Incredible Era Begins** 184

1947 July 31st Win 13th Straight, Lead League by 10
1947 **World Series Game No. 4** Spoil No-Hitter in 9th and Beat Yanks
1948 July 4th Campanella's First N.L. Home Runs
1949 October 2nd Win Pennant in Extra Innings on Last Day
1949 **World Series Game No. 2** Roe Stops Yankees 1-0
1950 August 31st Hodges Hits 4 Home Runs
1950 October 1st Tenth-Inning Homer Ends Pennant Hopes
1951 September 30th Robinson's Heroics Force a Playoff
1951 **Playoff Game No. 3** Thomson's Homer Kills Dodgers

Chapter XII **Triumph and Twilight** 206

1952 September 8th Dodgers Whip Giants, 10-2, amidst Beanballs
1952 **World Series Game No. 5** Bums Top Bombers in Classic Struggle, 6-5
1953 September 6th Furillo & Durocher Brawl
1953 **World Series Game No. 3** Erskine Fans 14 Yankees
1954 August 8th Score 12 Runs With Two Out
1955 May 10th Newcombe's One-Hitter Gives Brooklyn 22-2 Record
1955 **World Series Game No. 7** "Next Year" Finally Arrives!
1956 September 30th Duke & Newk Lead Dodgers to Pennant
1956 **World Series Game No. 6** Stay Alive with 1-0 Victory
1957 September 24th The Last Game at Ebbets-Field

Chapter XIII **The Golden State** 230

1958 April 18th Big League Baseball Comes to Los Angeles
1959 September 19th Dodgers Win Two to Catch Giants
1959 **Playoff Game No. 2** Dodger Comeback Wins Pennant
1959 **World Series Game No. 6** Los Angeles Wins the World Series
1960 April 12th Essegian's Pinch Homer Wins Opening Game
1961 August 16th Dodgers Shut Out Twice, Drop from 1st

Chapter XIV **Flying Feet + Golden Arms = Glorious Years** 246

1962 September 15th Lead by 4 Games after Triple Steal
1962 **Playoff Game No. 3** Giants "Walk Away" with the Pennant
1963 September 18th Dodgers Sweep Big Series from Cardinals
1963 **World Series Game No. 4** Dodgers Sweep Yankees!
1964 June 28th Lose 1-0 & Fall to 9th Place
1965 September 9th Koufax Hurls Perfect Game
1965 October 2nd Win on 2 Hits to Clinch Flag
1965 **World Series Game No. 7** Sandy's 3-Hitter Nails Down the Series
1966 October 2nd Koufax Wins Last Game to Save Pennant
1966 **World Series Game No. 4** Dodgers Shut Out in World Series

Chapter XV **The Wilderness Years** 270

1967 September 15th 1-0 Wins for Singer and Drysdale
1968 June 4th Six Shutouts in a Row for Drysdale
1969 September 3rd Willie Davis's Hitting Streak Up to 31 Games
1970 July 22nd Grand Slam by Pinch-Hitter Haller

1971 September 14th Manny Mota's Biggest Pinch Hit
1972 September 30th Osteen Bats His Way to Win #19
Chapter XVI **Alston Finds That New Infield** 286
1973 September 3rd Blow 8-1 Lead, Lose League Lead, Too
1974 September 15th Wynn's Grand Slam Finishes Reds
1974 **League Championship Series Game No. 4** Crush Pirates 12-1 for Title
1974 **World Series Game No. 2** Pick Off A's to Even Series
1975 April 17th Win 4th Straight Thriller from Reds
1976 May 5th Dodgers Win Chicago Windfest, 14-12
Chapter XVII **Lasorda's Dodger Bluebloods** 302
1977 August 8th Tommy John Hits a Home Run
1977 **League Championship Series Game No. 3** Miracle Rally Tops Phils
1977 **World Series Game No. 2** Beat Yanks with Hooton & Homers
1978 September 4th Five-Run Rally Turns Giants Back
1978 **League Champ. Game No. 4** Russell's Single Follows Error to Win Flag
1978 **World Series Game No. 2** Cey Drives in 4, Welch Fans Jackson
1979 May 25th Seven L.A. Homers & One Fight with Cincinnati
1980 October 5th Another Great Comeback Forces a Playoff
1980 **Playoff** Dodger Pennant Dream Collapses
1981 May 14th Fernando Wins 8th Straight
1981 **Div. Champ. Series Game No. 5** Shutout by Reuss Completes Comeback
1981 **League Champ. Series Game No. 5** Monday's Homer Wins League Title
1981 **W. S. Game No. 6** ''Comeback Dodgers'' Crush Yanks for Championship
1982 August 8th Eighth Straight Win over Braves
Chapter XVIII **Retooling a Winner in 1983** 336
1983 September 11th 4-Run Rally Sends Braves Reeling
1983 **League Champ. Game No. 2** Fernando & Dodgers Even Series with 4-1 Victory
Appendices 346

Prologue Baseball in Brooklyn Before the Dodgers

THE CITY OF BROOKLYN WAS ONE OF THE ORIGINAL HOTBEDS OF BASEBALL. WHEN various bat-and-ball games were being refined, it was the rules perfected in New York City, Brooklyn, and vicinity that were adopted to become the national sport.

Many of the early baseball clubs in the City of Churches were distinctly social in character; but from the first, Brooklyn sported some top-flight teams. For one period of nine years (1857 through 1865) the metropolitan championship was held by one club or another from Brooklyn. These early powers were the Atlantics, the Eckfords, and the Excelsiors.

The first known instance of admission being charged to a baseball game came in 1858 when a team of Brooklyn All-Stars played a squad of New York stars in a series of games out on Long Island. Brooklyn lost two games out of three. In 1862, one William Cammeyer put a fence around a playing field for the first time with the object of charging spectators for the right to see a game. This field, the Union Grounds, was located at the corner of Lee and Rutledge in the Williamsburg section of Brooklyn.

Already, Brooklyn fans had shown the type of behavior which would make them famous for a century. In 1860 during a game between the Atlantics and the Excelsiors, the backers of the former hurled so much verbal abuse at the players on the latter team that the game broke up into fist fights.

When the first professional league, the National Association of Professional Baseball Players, was organized in 1871, there were no Brooklyn clubs in the circuit. But the Mutuals of New York were members, and they played their games at the Union Grounds. The Eckfords and the Atlantics joined the association the following year, but the Eckfords dropped out after just one season. The Atlantics stuck through 1875, even though their record that year was a dismal 2 victories and 42 defeats.

The National League supplanted the National Association in 1876, and one of the new organization's objectives was to limit the number of franchises in any city to one. The Mutuals entered the league and got the New York and Brooklyn territories, since they represented Manhattan but played across the river in Brooklyn.

After the "Mutes" were expelled from the circuit during the first year, the Hartford club decided to play its games in 1877 at the Union Grounds. Their team was variously called "the Hartfords," "the Brooklyns," and "the Brooklyn Hartfords." They disbanded after the 1877 season.

Brooklyn was without a professional baseball club until 1883.

At the time, Brooklyn was a separate city from New York. In May, 1883, the world-famous Brooklyn Bridge was opened, directly linking Manhattan and Brooklyn for the first time. That was also the month that the team which evolved into the Dodgers played its first games. By itself, Brooklyn was the third-largest city in the nation and had been one of the great centers in the growth of baseball.

In those days a century ago, more fielders played barehanded than wore gloves. Catchers, pitchers, and first basemen might wear gloves that were more similar to today's batting gloves than to modern fielders' gloves. Back then the ball was softer and it was kept in play for as long as possible.

The rules were basically the same with a few differences. The pitchers had to throw the ball from below the hip, and it took seven balls for a walk. A batter could be retired if his foul ball or tip was caught on the first bounce (as well as on the fly, of course). But fouls were not counted as strikes. Still, it took three strikes for an out and three outs for an inning; pitchers usually relied upon speed mixed with curves; righthanded hitters generally hit the ball to left field; and so forth.

There were already two established major leagues, the National League and the American Association. And minor leagues were springing up across the land.

Chapter I Three Leagues & Three Pennants

1883 September 29th
Brooklyn Wins Interstate Pennant of Final Day

1884 October 4th
A 10-Inning No-Hitter

1885 June 18th
Owner Byrne Chews Out His Players

1886 June 24th
Brooklyn Romps to 25-1 Victory

1887 April 16th
Beat Mets on Opening Day, 14-10

1888 July 10th
Bridegrooms Sweep Series from Browns

1889 September 7th
St. Louis Forfeits Key Game in Brooklyn

1889 World Series Game No. 1
Brooklyn Beats Giants in Opener

1890 September 1st
Brooklyn Wins Tripleheader

1890 World Series Game No. 7
Series Called Off Due to Cold

THE CLUB THAT BECAME THE LOS ANGELES DODGERS, NOW ARGUABLY THE MOST SUCcessful franchise in professional sports, had its origins as a minor league club in Brooklyn, New York, in 1883.

The owners of the new club were Charles H. Byrne, Joseph J. Doyle, and Ferdinand Abell, with Byrne serving as president. From the start they pursued a policy of heavily investing in playing talent to strenghten the team on the field.

They also built a new ballpark in the Park Slope neighborhood of Brooklyn. It was located between Fourth and Fifth Avenues and Third and Fifth Streets. It was called "Washington Park" because George Washington had reputedly slept in the building on one side of the lot in 1776.

After the team started slowly, Byrne made his first big player purchase in mid-season. He acquired five players from the league-leading Merritt club of Camden, which was folding due to financial woes. The new men were good enough to bring the pennant to Brooklyn, although the flag was not clinched until the Grays beat second-place Harrisburg in the final game of the season.

After this initial success, the club moved up to the American Association, which was then considered a major league. The going was rougher at this level, and the Brooks struggled to finish ninth in 1884. The only highlight of the year came late in the season when Sam Kimber pitched a ten-inning no-hitter. Unfortunately, his teammates could not score, and the game ended as a 0-0 tie.

In an effort to improve the team for 1885, Byrne acquired five new men from the defunct Cleveland National League team. These included George "Germany" Smith and George Pinckney, both of whom were to be mainstays of the team for many years. But the arrival of the "Cleveland clique" caused problems that first season. Manager Charlie Hackett failed to unify the team, and he resigned in mid-June. A few days later the Brooklyns made 28 errors in one game, and president Byrne had to step in with a firm hand. Threatening heavy fines and suspension, he established some control over the team, which played errorless ball the next day. Eventually the Grays finished tied for fifth.

In 1886, the Brooks were improved enough to finish the third with a .555 winning percentage. On June 25th, they knocked the best pitcher in the Association (Baltimore's Matt Kilroy) out of the box and won the game by a record margin of 25-1. Exactly one month later, pitcher Bill Terry hurled a thrilling, 1-0 no-hitter against the powerful St. Louis Browns.

The 1887 season started on a promising note when Brooklyn beat the Mets of New York in a ten-inning thriller on opening day, 14-10. But the season was a big disappointment. The team fell all the way to sixth place, 34½ games behind the pennant-winning Browns.

So the owners went back to their policy of expenditures. First of all, they bought the entire Mets' roster for $25,000. Then they bought three of St. Louis's star players for around $18,000.

These moves made a contender out of the Brooklyn team in 1888. And the squad also picked up a new nickname. It seems that several of the players had gotten married over the winter, so the sportswriters dubbed them the "Bridegrooms." This name still appeared in some newspapers as late as the turn of the century. In the pennant struggle with the Browns, Brooklyn's finest moment came in early July, when the Bridegrooms swept four games in a row in St. Louis. But the champions were still too strong, and Brooklyn lost the lead by July 20th. The team slipped all the way to fourth place by late August. President Byrne made three late-season acquisitions, getting Tom "Oyster" Burns, John "Pop" Corkhill, and Hub Collins, enabling the team to finish second.

By 1889, the team was ready to go over the top. The 'Grooms got off to a slow start and trailed St. Louis through much of the summer. But on August 31st, Brooklyn finally caught up. The big confrontation between the two teams began on September 7th. That day the teams were engaged in an exciting game until St. Louis, which led 4-2, began delaying for darkness. The umpire obstinately refused to call the game, however, and the Browns ended up by walking off and forfeiting. They also refused to play the following day, forfeiting again but depriving the Brooklyn management of thousands of dollars in gate receipts. The last two games of the series were rained out, costing still more money.

Against a background of acrimonious haggling with St. Louis owner Chris Von der Ahe, the Bridegrooms held on and won the pennant. They also won three of the first four games of the World Series against the National League champion New York Giants. But the Giants rallied and won the series, 6 games to 3.

Brooklyn set a new attendance record in 1889 by drawing 353,690 customers to their home games. But the hassles with St. Louis and a revolt by the Players' Brotherhood convinced Byrne and the other owners to quit the American Association for the more stable National League. The League had a higher minimum admission charge than the Association (50¢ as opposed to 25¢), and it did not allow Sunday games. For four years the Bridegrooms had played Sunday games just over the county line in Ridgewood, Queens, and had always drawn very well there.

The League policies and the presence of a strong Players' League team in Brooklyn caused the Bridegrooms' attendance to drop 66% in 1890. But they did win the National League pennant in their first year in the circuit. They took over first place to stay on August 2nd and upped their lead to 5½ games with a big tripleheader victory on September 1st. Their final margin was 6 games.

Ignoring the Players' League champions, Brooklyn arranged a best-of-nine game World Series against the A. A. champions from Louisville. The series was plagued by cold weather and poor attendance, however, and it was called off after each team had won three games.

1883 SATURDAY, SEPTEMBER 29TH, AT WASHINGTON PARK, BROOKLYN

Brooklyn Wins Interstate Pennant on Final Day

Grays Defeat Second-Place Harrisburg 11-6
President Byrne's Investments Prove Successful

THE NEW BROOKLYN CLUB CLOSED OUT its first season successfully by winning the pennant in the Interstate Association. The title was gained by defeating second-place Harrisburg in the final game of the year, 11-6. A defeat would have dropped the Brooks to second place.

Today's Results			
BROOKLYN 11-Harrisburg 6 (8 innings)			
Trenton 14-Anthracite 2 (7 innings)			
no other game scheduled			

Standings	W-L	Pct.	GB
BROOKLYN	44-28	.611	—
Harrisburg	43-30	.589	1½
Active	37-32	.536	5½
Trenton	33-36	.478	9½
Anthracite	25-50	.333	20½
Quickstep	24-49	.328	20½
*Merritt	27- 8	—	*

*team disbanded July 20th

Brooklyn club president Charles H. Byrne spared no expense to put a championship team onto the field this season. When the players who began the year did not turn out to be a winning combination, he sent manager George Taylor out to find replacements. William J. Terry, who pitched today's game for Brooklyn, was recruited from his native western Massachusetts in June. The most important acquisitions came in July, when Byrne signed the pick of the Merritt Club of Camden. The Merritts were leading the Interstate race by a goodly margin but were forced to disband due to lack of money. Byrne stepped in and signed five of their top players. These men were pitcher Sam Kimber, catcher John Corcoran, and infielders Bill Greenwood, Charlie Householder, and Frank Fennelly.

In all, only two men in the lineup at the end of the season today were with the Grays on opening day in Wilmington on May 1st.

At the beginning of the season, the club did not even have a ballpark. The first "home" game for Brooklyn was played in Newark and the second was played in the open spaces of Prospect Park in Brooklyn. The club's own Washington Park was finally opened on May 12th. The largest crowd of the year, about 6,000 persons, was on hand for the dedication ceremonies.

The team was still a distant third in the standings with a 15-17 record when the Merritts disbanded on July 20th. Then the new men led the Grays to the top. They swept four games from Harrisburg as August turned to September and took the league lead. But Harrisburg stayed close on Brooklyn's heels. On Friday they beat the Brooks, 8-5, to set up a final-game showdown today.

The pitchers in Friday's game were Kimber for Brooklyn and Jack Schappert for the visitors. For today, the Brooks still had a good boxman, Terry, left. But Harrisburg had to go with Tom "Oyster" Burns, a versatile outfielder-third baseman who sometimes pitched.

The home team knocked Burns out of the box with seven runs in the first three innings, and this early lead proved decisive. The visitors made it close at one point, trailing only 7-6, before the Grays began to hit substitute pitcher Jimmy Say and assure themselves of victory. The game was called after eight rounds on account of darkness with the Brooks winning 11-6.

Harrisburg won the coin toss and sent Brooklyn to bat first. Greenwood started the Grays on their way by beating out a tap to shortstop. John Doyle's single moved him to second, and a walk to Edgar Smith loaded the bases. Frank Fennelly's fly out to center field scored Greenwood. Oscar Walker struck out. Householder then came through with a long triple to right, and Doyle and Smith romped home. Billy Geer popped out, leaving Householder on third.

Harrisburg loaded the bases in the bottom half of the first when the first three batters singled. But a brilliant play by catcher John Farrow defused the potentially explosive situation. With John Shetzline at bat, Farrow purposely dropped the third strike, and Shetzline stupidly ran toward first base, forcing the other runners. Farrow picked the ball up, stepped on home plate to force one man out, then threw to first to retire Shetzline for a double play. Harrisburg captain Henry Myers was so peeved that he immediately fined Shetzline $50 for running. Dennis Casey flied out to second base to end the inning.

Brooklyn scored two more runs in the second inning on hits by Farrow, Terry, Greenwood, and Doyle, along with two wild pitches. Greenwood's ball was counted as a hit only because Farrow allowed himself to be struck by the sphere, thusly preventing a potential double play.

Triples by Fennelly and Farrow, a walk, and a fly out gave the Brooks two more tallies in the third.

Harrisburg pushed its first run across in its third inning on a walk, two hits, and a throwing error by Smith.

Say switched positions with Burns in the fourth, and his pitching held Brooklyn at bay through the next three rounds.

Harrisburg, meanwhile, rallied in the fourth and fifth innings. In the fourth, they were presented with three runs on three errors, a passed ball, a base on balls, and just one clean hit. In the next frame, they made two hits and scored two runs with the aid of a wild pitch, a passed ball, and a muffed fly. With the score 7-6 and the tying run on third base, Terry struck Shetzline out for the third time in the game.

Brooklyn then batted out three runs in the seventh on three hits and a balk by Say. Two errors gave the home team its last run in the eighth.

Harrisburg put two men on base in each of the last two rounds but could not bat them home.

After the eighth inning was completed, umpire Griffiths called the game due to darkness, and the Brooklyn Grays were undisputed champions of the Interstate Association. Not bad for the club's first year.

Brooklyn	ab	r	h	bi	o	a	e
B. Greenwood, 2b	5	3	2	0	3	1	0
J. Doyle, rf	5	1	2	0	0	0	0
E. Smith, lf	3	1	1	1	0	0	2
F. Fennelly, 3b	4	2	2	1	0	1	0
O. Walker, cf	4	1	2	2	2	0	1
C. Householder, 1b	4	1	2	2	10	0	1
B. Geer, ss	2	1	0	0	0	5	2
J. Farrow, c	4	0	2	1	8	1	1
B. Terry, p	4	1	1	0	1	5	2
	35	11	14	7	24	13	9

Harrisburg	ab	r	h	bi	o	a	e
M. Cline, 2b	4	3	2	0	2	1	0
J. Reccius, lf	4	1	3	0	1	1	0
H. Myers, ss	5	1	3	2	2	2	0
J. Shetzline, 1b	5	0	0	0	6	0	1
D. Casey, cf	5	0	1	1	3	0	0
T. Burns, p-3b4	4	0	0	0	0	0	2
J. Say, 3b-p4	4	0	1	0	2	1	2
G. Miller, rf	4	1	1	0	2	0	0
B. McCloskey, c	4	0	0	0	5	3	0
	39	6	11	3	23	8	5

(Farrow out for not running)

Brooklyn	322 000 31	= 11
Harrisburg	001 032 00	= 6

game called on account of darkness

	ip	h	r-er	bb	so
Terry (W 16-9)	8	11	6-1	7	7
Burns (L 5-8)	3	9	7-6	2	2
Say	5	5	4-3	1	2

Balk: Say
WP: Terry, Burns 2, Say 2
PB: Farrow 3, McCloskey
Umpire: Griffiths

Game-Winning RBI: Fennelly
LOB: Brooklyn 3, Harrisburg 9

BE: Brooklyn 5, Harrisburg 7
DP: Farrow-Householder
Reccius-Shetzline
2B: Casey
3B: Householder, Fennelly, Farrow
SB: Reccius, Fennelly
CS: Cline, Geer
Picked Off: Smith
Time—1:55
Attendance—3,000

The Interstate Association broke up after just one year. The Brooklyn club was able to secure a franchise in the American Association, a major league at that time, for the 1884 season.

1884 SATURDAY, OCTOBER 4TH, AT WASHINGTON PARK

A 10-Inning No-Hitter

And Still Brooklyn Cannot Win the Game
Kimber Pitches Brilliantly, But His Teammates Don't Score

Today's Results

BROOKLYN 0-Toledo 0 (TIE) (10 innings)
St. Louis 5-Mets 4
Columbus 15-Allegheny 4 (7 innings)
Athletics 7-Louisville 0
Cincinnati 7-Virginia 5 (8 innings)
Baltimore 7-Indianapolis 3 (1st game)
Baltimore 6-Indianapols 2 (6 innings)(2nd)

Standings	W-L	Pct.	GB
Metropolitan	70-31	.693	—
Columbus	66-36	.647	4½
Louisville	64-36	.640	5½
St. Louis	63-38	.624	7
Cincinnati	64-39	.621	7
Baltimore	58-40	.592	10½
Athletic	56-44	.560	13½
Toledo	42-57	.424	27
BROOKLYN	38-61	.384	31
Allegheny	30-73	.291	41
Indianapolis	29-71	.290	40½
Virginia	22-76	.224	46½

THE BROOKLYN CLUB, WHICH WON A minor league pennant in the Interstate Association in 1883, moved into the major-league American Association in 1884 and fell flat on its face. The team lost its first championship game on May 1st to Washington by the one-sided score of 12-0. Four days later the Grays won their home opener, 11-3 over the same Washington team. But thereafter Brooklyn sank fast. In the twelve-team Association race, the Brooks were in eighth place from May 20th until September 16th, when they fell into ninth. At least they did better than Washington, which dropped out of the league in August and was replaced by the Virginia club.

With the season winding down and the Brooks needing a victory over Toledo to maintain some hope of finishing eighth, Sam Kimber hurled a great game today, no-hitting Toledo for ten innings. Kimber had pitched a seven-inning no-hitter for the Grays in 1883 against the Actives of Reading, but this was Brooklyn's first big league no-hitter. Unfortunately, today his teammates could not push a run across against Toledo's pitcher, Tony Mullane, and the game ended as a 0-0 tie.

Both pitchers relied heavily on speed, and the batters looked most reluctant to stand up in the batter's box and take their cuts. Kimber hit three Toledo batsmen with his pitches. Mullane, who was well-known for hitting batters, did not connect with any bodies today. Kimber also gave two men their bases on balls, while three strolled against Mullane. Each hurler unfurled one wild pitch.

The two catchers, Tug Arundel for Toledo and John Corcoran for Brooklyn, gave their batterymates fine support. Arundel stood out by catching one foul bound, one foul fly, two foul tips, and five third strikes. He also threw a man out at first after dropping a third strike, tagged a man out at home, and threw to Mullane to nip another man at home who tried to score on a short passed ball.

The other fielders did well, too. There was only one error in the game: a muff by Brooklyn shortstop Billy Geer.

Because of the dominance of the pitching, the game had very little real excitement. The Brooklyn players did complain that Mullane's delivery was illegal. They contended that Tony released the ball from above his hip and that the rules prohibited such high-armed pitching. But the umpire did nothing about it.

The first base runner was Toledo's Curt Welch. With two out in the first inning, he reached when Geer muffed his easy fly. Tom Poorman ended the inning by flying out to third baseman Jim Knowles.

Brooklyn got two runners in the bottom of the first. Bill Greenwood led off by going out on a foul that Arundel snared on the first bound. Geer and John Cassidy followed with bases on balls and moved to third and second on a wild pitch. Brooklyn's best hitter, Oscar Walker, was at bat. Arundel saved the day for Mullane by making a fine catch of a foul tip to retire Walker. Jack Remsen then flied to center, and the rally fell short.

Toledo's best chance to score came in the second inning. With two out, Arundel was hit by an inside pitch. He moved to second on a wild pitch. Trick McSorley walked behind him. But Frank Olin grounded out, third to first.

Kimber set the Toledos down in order in five of the remaining innings. The only other visitors to reach base did so in the fourth, fifth, and ninth rounds. In the fourth, Mullane got a base on balls but was doubled off first after Geer snared John Meister's fly. In the fifth, Arundel led off and was again hit by a pitch. But two force outs and a runner caught stealing ended the inning. Kimber hit Joe Miller with a pitch with one out in the ninth. He was left on base.

Mullane had no more difficulty until the fifth. Then Charlie Householder hit a long double to left field with one out. He moved to third on an infield out. When a pitch rolled away from Arundel, Householder brazenly tried to score. But the catcher threw to the pitcher, who was covering home, and Householder was tagged out.

Another desperate dash by Brooklyn went for naught in the sixth. Geer walked with two out. When Cassidy bounced a hit to right field, Geer tried to come all the way around to score. Unfortunately, second baseman Sam Barkley threw him out at home.

Householder opened the home eighth with a hit, but good defense cut the rally off quickly. First of all, Corcoran was retired on another fine capture by Arundel of a foul tip. Then Kimber's drive to right was caught in fine style by Poorman, who passed the ball to first to nip Householder before he could get back to the bag.

Geer singled to right with one out in the ninth, but he was left on base. Arundel ended the inning by making yet another fine play, this a catch of Walker's foul fly.

With the autumn sun already set, the two righthanded speedballers looked invincible in the tenth inning. Each pitcher struck out two batters in that last round. After Arundel dropped the third strike on the last man and threw to first base for the out, umpire John Dyler had to call the game on account of darkness.

So, despite the record-setting, ten-inning no-hit pitching of Sam Kimber, Brooklyn could not win the game. The first year in the American Association was indeed a tough one for Brooklyn.

Toledo	ab	r	h	bi	o	a	e
S. Barkley, 2b	4	0	0	0	3	3	0
J. Miller, ss	3	0	0	0	0	4	0
C. Welch, cf	4	0	0	0	1	0	0
T. Poorman, rf	4	0	0	0	2	1	0
T. Mullane, p	3	0	0	0	2	2	0
J. Meister, 3b	4	0	0	0	0	0	0
T. Arundel, c	2	0	0	0	10	2	0
T. McSorley, 1b	2	0	0	0	12	0	0
F. Olin, lf	3	0	0	0	0	0	0
	29	0	0	0	30	12	0

Brooklyn	ab	r	h	bi	o	a	e
B. Greenwood, 2b	4	0	0	0	3	2	0
B. Geer, ss	2	0	1	0	3	5	1
J. Cassidy, rf	3	0	1	0	0	0	0
O. Walker, lf	4	0	0	0	2	0	0
J. Remsen, cf	4	0	0	0	1	0	0
J. Knowles, 3b	4	0	0	0	1	4	0
C. Householder, 1b	4	0	2	0	13	0	0
J. Corcoran, c	3	0	0	0	7	1	0
S. Kimber, p	3	0	0	0	0	0	0
	31	0	4	0	30	12	1

Toledo	000 000 000 0	=	0
Brooklyn	000 000 000 0	=	0

game called on account of darkness

	ip	h	r-er	bb	so
Mullane	10	4	0-0	3	6
Kimber	10	0	0-0	2	6

WP: Mullane, Kimber
Umpire: J. Dyler

LOB: Toledo 4, Brooklyn 4
BE: Toledo 1
DP: Geer-Householder
Poorman-McSorley
2B: Householder
CS: Olin, Householder
HBP: by Kimber 3 (Arundel 2, Miller)
Time—2:00
Attendance—1,200

On the following Tuesday, Kimber and Mullane met again, and again the game ended as a tie. That time the score was 4-4 when rain halted play in the fifth inning.

After the season ended, the American Association reduced to twelve teams. Toledo dropped out, but Brooklyn remained in the circuit.

The rules allowing an out on a caught foul bound and prohibiting high-arm pitching were abolished by the Association early in the 1885 season.

1885 THURSDAY, JUNE 18TH, AT WASHINGTON PARK

Owner Byrne Chews Out His Players

Levies a Total of Over $500 in Fines
Brooks Respond With a Victory Over St. Louis, 3-1

Today's Results

BROOKLYN 3-St. Louis 1
Cincinnati 5-Mets 4
Athletics 6-Pittsburg 5
Baltimore 11-Louisville 2

Standings	W-L	Pct.	GB
St. Louis	30-11	.732	—
Cincinnati	26-18	.591	5½
Pittsburg	25-18	.581	6
Louisville	20-23	.465	11
Baltimore	19-22	.463	11
Athletic	19-24	.442	12
BROOKLYN	16-25	.390	14
Metropolitan	14-28	.333	16½

PRESIDENT CHARLES H. BYRNE AND THE Brooklyn club went to a great deal of expense to acquire a team that would challenge for the American Association pennant this season. Six new players were purchased at the end of the 1884 season from the Cleveland National League club at a cost of around $9,000. In addition, four other players were acquired from as many different clubs. Together with three holdovers from last year's Brooklyn squad, the revamped team had much talent.

But the team performed very poorly in the early stages of this season's pennant race. Cliques were formed which harmed the team's overall efforts. The old Cleveland players seemed to have banded together to support each other but not the other players. "Adonis Bill" Terry, one of the Brooklyn players retained from 1884, complained of poor support when he had his turns in the pitcher's box. The figures appeared to bear him out. In the games he had pitched thus far this year, the team had made more errors and scored fewer runs, on the average, than it had in games pitched by Henry Porter and John Harkins, both new men.

When Byrne made inquiries about the team's problems, he was told by several of the players that manager Charlie Hackett was to blame. When Hackett was told this, he resigned his post effective last Saturday. Since he left, the situation had not improved a bit, with the Brooks losing five games out of seven.

Matters came to a head yesterday. Byrne gave a new pitcher, John Smith from the Allentown (Eastern League) club, a trial. One clique appeared to lay down entirely behind him. Shortstop George "Germany" Smith committed seven errors. Two other former Cleveland players contributed bad misplays. Catcher John "Jackie" Hayes, a Brooklyn holdover, added seven more errors. With the unsettled J. Smith adding ten errors himself, Brooklyn totalled an unbelievable 28 errors and lost the game to St. Louis, 18-5.

Newspaper observers and cranks who were present at the game were unanimously convinced that the erring players had thrown the game away to keep the new man from making a decent showing. Apparently Mr. Byrne felt the same way. After the game, he went to the dressing room and calmly but firmly told the players that there would be a meeting in the morning and that everyone's presence was required.

When the appointed hour arrived this morning, all the players were gathered. Although he spoke calmly, Byrne obviously had fire in his eyes. He first told the men that he did not make it a habit to interfere in the conduct of the club, since that was the province of the manager and the captain. He also pointed out that he had treated each man fairly and had always been prompt and generous in paying the players. And, in case anyone had forgotten, he read from the standard player contract that each man was paid on the supposition that he would give his best effort on the field.

Then he addressed the subject of Mr. Hackett's resignation. Since the players had been almost unanimous in blaming the failure to win on him, and since Hackett had resigned, Byrne expressed curiosity as to why the team continued to play so poorly. He especially wondered about the reason for "the dirty piece of work at the hands of a minority of the team yesterday."

Without naming names, he demanded that every man play up to standard, and he threatened expulsion from the club to anyone who did not. Hitting home, Byrne continued that "no further leniency" would be shown. As regards to the disgraceful exhibition on Wednesday, he told the men that a total of over $500 in fines had been deducted from the team's pay. Again he did not name names or amounts, saying that each man would find out at the end of the month when he got his paycheck. Byrne closed his speech by telling the men that from here on out they would have to "play ball," or they would be expelled from the team and from baseball.

What wonders the president's talk worked on the team's play! Facing the leaders in the Association race, the St. Louis Browns, Brooklyn played superb baseball today. The Grays made no error at all, although pitcher Porter did issue four bases on balls. The Brooks banged out eleven hits, while Porter held St. Louis down to four. The result was a 3-1 victory for Brooklyn.

That Hayes and G. Smith were intimidated by Byrne's speech seemed most obvious. Whereas each man had made seven errors yesterday, today both played perfect ball in the field. In addition, Hayes made two safe hits, and Smith made one.

St. Louis made three errors, and each one led to a Brooklyn run. The game was scoreless until the sixth inning. Then Ed Swartwood was given a life on a fumble by St. Louis second baseman Sam Barkley. A bobble by shortstop Bill Gleason allowed Bill Phillips to reach safely, too. George Pinckney promptly brought the two men home with a triple.

The Browns made their run in the bottom of the sixth. Gleason walked and stole second. After Charlie Comiskey went out, Barkley hit safely to drive Gleason home.

Brooklyn got the final run of the game in the eighth. John Cassidy reached on a fumble by first baseman Comiskey. Singles by Pinckney and Smith brought him around.

Backed by fine fielding, Porter held the Browns safe and won the game 3-1. Most of the 1,500 patrons had come to the park to boo the home team's players for yesterday's work. But they had to cheer today's effort, instead.

From an 18-5 defeat to a 3-1 victory, and from 28 errors to none at all! President Byrne's little talk about fines and expulsions certainly seemed to have put a new life into the boys.

Brooklyn	ab	r	h	bi	o	a	e
P. Hotaling, cf	5	0	1	0	0	0	0
B. McClellan, 3b	5	0	0	0	1	2	0
E. Swartwood, lf	5	1	1	0	3	0	0
B. Phillips, 1b	4	1	2	0	16	0	0
J. Cassidy, rf	4	1	0	0	2	0	0
G. Pinckney, 3b	3	0	2	2	3	2	0
G. Smith, ss	4	0	1	1	0	6	0
J. Hayes, c	4	0	2	0	2	1	0
H. Porter, p	4	0	2	0	0	5	0
	38	3	11	3	27	16	0

St. Louis	ab	r	h	bi	o	a	e
A. Latham, 3b	4	0	0	0	0	2	0
B. Gleason, ss	2	1	1	0	0	3	1
C. Comiskey, 1b	4	0	0	0	14	0	1
S. Barkley, 2b	4	0	1	1	4	4	1
H. Nicol, rf	3	0	0	0	2	0	0
Y. Robinson, lf	3	0	0	0	1	0	0
C. Welch, cf	4	0	0	0	3	0	0
B. Caruthers, p	3	0	1	0	0	4	0
D. Bushong, c	3	0	1	0	3	3	0
	30	1	4	1	27	16	3

Brooklyn	000 002 010	=	3
St. Louis	000 001 000	=	1

	ip	h	r-er	bb	so
Porter (W 8-6)	9	4	1-1	4	1
Caruthers (L 16-4)	9	11	3-0	0	2

WP: Porter PB: Bushong

Game-Winning RBI: Pinckney
LOB: Brooklyn 9, St. Louis 6
BE: Bkn 3
3B: Bushong, Pinckney
HBP: by Caruthers (Pinckney)
Time—1:45 Attendance—1,500
Umpire: J. Connell

The Brooklyn team continued to do rather poorly on the road. But at home, under the watchful eye of President Byrne, it played good ball in the latter part of the season. The result was an improvement to a tie for fifth place by the end of the season. Brooklyn's final record was 53-59.

1886 THURSDAY, JUNE 24TH, AT WASHINGTON PARK

Brooklyn Romps to 25-1 Victory

Baltimore's Kilroy Can't Find a Catcher and Goes to Pieces
All Nine Brooklyn Players Score at Least Two Runs Apiece

IN THE MOST ONE-SIDED VICTORY IN THE club's history, Brooklyn buried Baltimore by a score of 25-1. All nine Brooklyn players scored two or more runs, and eight of the nine made three or more hits. The one recalcitrant batter, Jimmy Peoples, made only one safe hit. But at least that was a home run with the bases loaded.

Today's Results

BROOKLYN 25-Baltimore 1
St. Louis 2-Pittsburg 1
Mets 7-Athletics 6 (12 innings)
Cincinnati 12-Louisville 5

Standings	W-L	Pct.	GB
St. Louis	33-20	.623	—
BROOKLYN	28-21	.571	3
Pittsburg	27-24	.529	5
Athletic	24-22	.522	5½
Louisville	26-28	.481	7½
Metropolitan	21-26	.447	9
Baltimore	19-27	.413	10½
Cincinnati	23-33	.411	11½

Baltimore presented its new pitching phenomenon, Matt Kilroy, at the start of the game. But the Orioles' regular catcher, Chris Fulmer, had sore hands and could not hold Kilroy's tremendous speed. When the lefthander slowed down his pitches, the Brooklyns batted his stuff for ten hits and eleven runs in less than three innings. And when Kilroy used his best velocity, six wild pitches zipped back to the grandstand wall. Kilroy was replaced in the box by outfielder Joe Sommers, against whom the Brooks ran up fourteen more runs and nineteen more hits.

They could have scored more, but it started to rain in the fourth inning. Since they already had a big lead, the Brooklyn players tried to make outs to insure that five innings were played to make the game official. They scored only one run each round in the fourth and fifth innings. After the game reached the required five innings and the threat of rain subsided, Brooklyn pounded out twelve runs in the next two rounds. Then, apparently bored with the run-getting, the Brooklyn men allowed themselves to be put out in the final two innings without scoring.

The victory today kept Brooklyn 3 games behind the front-running St. Louis Browns in the American Association standings.

The hapless Orioles contributed ten errors, eight wild pitches, and four bases on balls to the Brooklyn cause. Baltimore scored just one run. That came on two walks, a single, and a wild pitch. Brooklyn pitcher Bill "Adonis" Terry limited the visitors to just five hits. He received errorless support from his fielders.

Kilroy's troubles started in the top half of the first inning. The home team chose to bat first, and the first Brooklyn batter, George Pinckney, beat out an infield hit and advanced to second on a throwing error by the Baltimore pitcher. He went to third on an out and scored on Kilroy's first wild pitch. A hit, a walk, and two stolen bases had put men on second and third when the inning was ended.

In the second inning, Kilroy struck out the first and last batters. But in between, five men scored. After Peoples opened by fanning, the next three men all singled and stole second against the fumbling Fulmer. After a wild pitch had cleared the bases, Bill McClellan hit safely and got second on a wild throw by the catcher. He scored on a double by Jim McTamany, who in turn scored on an infield out and another wild pitch.

Mike Muldoon scored for Baltimore in the bottom of the second, making the score 6-1.

In the top of the third, the Baltimore battery came apart completely. Terry led off with a hit, took second on a wild pitch. At this point, Fulmer gave up as catcher and switched places with left fielder Sommers. The change did not help. The next hitter, Bob Clark, walked. Then Ernie Burch and Pinckney both doubled. After another wild pitch moved Pinckney to third, Kilroy was removed from the pitcher's box. He went to left field, while Sommers went from catcher to pitcher, and Ed Greer (usually an outfielder) came into the game to catch. A substitution required the assent of the opposing team, but Brooklyn magnanimously allowed the sore-handed Fulmer to retire to the bench.

The new catcher dropped a third strike, allowing McClellan to reach first. But then he nabbed a foul tip to retire McTamany and doubled McClellan off first with a quick throw. Bill Phillips struck out.

With rain threatening, Brooklyn limited its offense to just three hits in the fourth and fifth innings. Baltimore added two throwing errors, a passed ball, and a muffed fly, giving the Grays one run in each round.

Meanwhile, the Orioles were being dispatched with ease by Terry. He struck out one man in the fourth and two in the fifth, the last out making the game official.

In the sixth, Brooklyn got two more runs on three two-out singles and a walk.

In the seventh, Sommers collapsed under the home team's renewed batting onslaught. Phillips, Smith, and Terry opened the round with hits, loading the bases. Peoples then hit a long one to the right field stands and scored behind the three runners when the ball was lost among the spectators. The next two men went out, but the attack resumed with five straight hits, followed by a throwing error on a grounder and yet another single. By the time Burch had fouled out to end the inning, Brooklyn had tallied ten times, and the score of the game was 25-1.

In the eighth inning, McClellan singled with one out. But he was put out at third base trying to take two bases on a ground out.

In the ninth, Phillips led off with a triple. But he allowed himself to be doubled off the base on a pop to third baseman Muldoon.

Baltimore threatened to score in the seventh when Milt Scott hit a two-out triple. But the unhappy Kilroy followed with a strikeout.

The Orioles went out quickly in the eighth and ninth, and Brooklyn won with the greatest ease ever, 25-1.

Brooklyn	ab	r	h	bi	o	a	e
G. Pinckney, 3b	6	3	3	3	1	0	0
B. McClellan, 2b	7	2	4	1	3	3	0
J. McTamany, cf	7	3	4	1	4	0	0
B. Phillips, 1b	6	2	3	2	10	0	0
G. Smith, ss	7	3	2	0	3	4	0
B. Terry, p	7	3	3	1	1	1	0
J. Peoples, rf	5	2	1	4	0	0	0
B. Clark, c	5	4	5	1	5	2	0
E. Burch, lf	6	3	3	4	0	0	0
	56	25	28	17	27	10	0

Baltimore	ab	r	h	bi	o	a	e
J. Manning, rf	4	0	0	0	1	0	2
J. Sommer, lf-cf-p3	4	0	0	0	1	1	1
J. Farrell, 2b	4	0	2	0	1	1	1
S. Houck, ss	4	0	1	0	1	3	0
M. Muldoon, 3b	3	1	0	0	6	2	1
C. Fulmer, c-lf3	1	0	0	0	2	0	1
E. Greer, c3	3	0	0	0	2	1	2
J. Clinton, cf	3	0	1	0	3	0	0
M. Scott, 1b	3	0	1	0	10	1	1
M. Kilroy, p-lf3	2	0	0	0	0	1	1
	31	1	5	0	27	10	10

Brooklyn	155 112 (10)00 =	25
Baltimore	010 000 0 00	1

	ip	h	r-er	bb	so
Terry (W 5-5)	9	5	1-1	2	7
Kilroy (L 15-9)	*2	10	11-1	3	2
Sommer	7	18	14-8	1	1

*faced five batters in third
WP: Kilroy 6, Sommer 2, Terry
PB: Clark, Greer
Time—2:15
Attendance—1,700
Umpire: J. Kelly

Game-Winning Run Scored on wild pitch
LOB: Brooklyn 8, Baltimore 5
BE: Brooklyn 3
DP: Greer-Scott
Smith-McClellan-Phillips (Muldoon)
Houck-Scott-Muldoon
Muldoon unassisted
2B: McTamany, Burch, Pinckney, Clark, McClellan
3B: Phillips
HR: Peoples
SB: McClellan, Smith, Clark 3, Burch, Pinckney, Clinton, Kilroy, Terry

The next time Kilroy faced Brooklyn, he had a healthy catcher and shut the Brooks out.

Brooklyn was unable to mount a serious bid to overtake first-place St. Louis. The team spent the rest of the season contending with Pittsburg and Louisville for second. Pittsburg won out, with Brooklyn coming in third with a 76-61.

1887 SATURDAY, APRIL 16TH, AT WASHINGTON PARK

Beat Mets on Opening Day, 14-10

Big Crowd Celebrates the Beginning of the Season
Errors and Excitement Featured

THE AMERICAN ASSOCIATION CHAMPionship season of 1887 began in Brooklyn today with as exciting a game as one could hope to see on any day of the year. The home team beat the Metropolitan club of New York in ten innings, 14-10.

The Brooklyn nine got out to an early lead of 5-1, only to see the Mets tie the game 5-5. After the home team regained the lead at 7-5, the visitors rallied to grab a 10-7 advantage. But Brooklyn delighted the cranks by scoring three runs in the ninth inning to tie the game. Then the Brooks scored four times in the tenth inning to win out.

Today's Results

BROOKLYN 14-Mets 10 (10 innings)
Louisville 8-St. Louis 3
Cincinnati 16-Cleveland 6
Baltimore 8-Athletics 3

Standings	W-L	Pct.	GB
BROOKLYN	1-0	1.000	—
Louisville	1-0	1.000	—
Cincinnati	1-0	1.000	—
Baltimore	1-0	1.000	—
Metropolitans	0-1	.000	1
St. Louis	0-1	.000	1
Cleveland	0-1	.000	1
Athletics	0-1	.000	1

The weather was very favorable this afternoon, and a large crowd of about 7,000 came out to Washington Park. Included among the spectators was a large contingent of baseball magnates, whom Brooklyn club president Charles Byrne entertained in his personal box. The entire assemblage was well-behaved, and it cheered the good plays by both nines. As the game progressed, a strong northwest wind came up, causing a chill to fall upon the players and spectators.

Both squads appeared in brand-new uniforms. The Mets wore suits of brown and gray, while the Brooklyns had new white and maroon outfits. Both teams were cheered loudly when they appeared on the field for the first time.

The crowd also got its first taste of the new rules adopted for this year. The biggest change, of course, was the increase in the number of strikes for an out from three to four. The decrease in balls for a base from seven to five also favored the hitters, and twelve men were given first base by the pitchers. With a change in scoring rules that counted walks as hits, a total of thirty-six hits were made today.

Brooklyn chose to bat first, and they were given two quick runs on the wildness of the Mets' pitcher, John Schafer. He walked four of the first six batters in the game.

Paul Radford scored for the Mets in the last of the first on a walk, two wild throws by catcher Jack O'Brien, and John Meister's base hit.

Brooklyn started to hit the ball in the second. Henry Porter walked with one out and scored on a double by George Pinckney. Bill McClellan got another base on balls, and Will Terry's out moved the runners up. Bill Phillips delivered a bouncing hit to left to drive the two runners home. Another hit and a hit batsman loaded the bases. But catcher Bill Holbert ended the inning by capturing a difficult foul off the bat of George Smith.

Brooklyn's 5-1 lead lasted only for one inning. The Mets rallied for four runs in the bottom of the third thanks to miserable fielding by the Brooks. Radford got a life on a fumble by Smith, and Frank Hankinson tripled him home. Two more errors by Smith allowed both Meister and Dave Orr to reach. Dude Esterbrook hit down to third, and Pinckney fell down fielding the ball. Then he threw wildly to home, and when the dust cleared, the score was tied.

Brooklyn quickly regained the lead in the fourth on a two-run home run by Ernie Burch. Jim McTamany was on base courtesy of a throwing error by Esterbrook. Burch then sent a low liner between the right and center fielders and circled the bases. He was wildly cheered by the cranks.

Easterbrook scored a run in the fifth on a hit-by-pitch and throwing errors by

Porter and O'Brien. That cut the Brooklyn lead to 7-6.

Two more runs in the seventh gave the Mets the lead for the first time in the game. Orr led off by waiting for a base on balls. He quickly stole second. After a foul out, Jon Morrison singled Orr to third. Darby O'Brien's infield out sent Orr home. Schafer drove Morrison home with a hit to left, putting the Mets into the lead.

The Mets added two more runs in the eighth to increase their lead to 10-7. Radford, who played a fine game in his debut with the Mets, opened with a hit and a steal. With two gone, Orr shot a double past third base for a run and took third on a fumble by outfielder Burch. After Esterbrook watched five balls and strolled, Morrison sent Orr home with a single to center.

The home team came to bat in the ninth needing three runs to tie. As Schafer had settled down in the previous four innings, things did not look promising. But McTamany bounced a double to left to start the inning. Burch made a similar two-bagger to plate one run. Smith lifted an easy fly to center, but Morrison muffed it. Jack O'Brien cracked a hit to left, scoring Burch. And when Darby O'Brien fumbled the hit and followed with a wild throw to third, Smith scored the tying run. With none out and the lead run on second base, Brooklyn's chances looked excellent. But Schafer turned them back on a strikeout and two flies.

Pitcher Porter disposed of the Mets quickly in the bottom of the ninth, and the regulation innings ended with the score tied 10-10. Met captain Orr wanted the game called on account of darkness, but umpire McQuade ordered play to go on.

The first batter in the tenth, Terry, was given first base on a fumble by shortshop Esterbrook. He moved to second on Phillips's sacrifice hit. McTamany sent a grounder up the middle for a hit, and Terry scored. Burch singled. Smith doubled two more runs across. After a long fly to right, Porter singled Smith home, and Brooklyn had a 14-10 lead.

Hankinson opened the Mets' tenth with a double. But the next three men were easy outs, and the Brooklyns had won. The fine rally in the ninth and tenth innings especially had given their supporters hope for an improvement over last year's third-place finish.

Brooklyn	ab	r	h	bi	o	a	e
G. Pinckney, 3b	6	2	3	1	1	4	2
B. McClellan, 2b	6	2	3	0	3	4	1
B. Terry, lf	6	1	0	1	0	0	0
B. Phillips, 1b	6	0	2	2	16	0	0
J. McTamany, cf	6	3	3	2	1	0	1
E. Burch, lf	5	3	5	3	2	0	1
G. Smith, ss	6	2	2	2	1	8	3
J. O'Brien, c	6	0	2	1	6	1	2
H. Porter, p	6	1	2	1	0	2	1
	53	14	22	13	30	19	11

Metropolitan	ab	r	h	bi	o	a	e
P. Radford, rf	6	3	2	0	4	0	0
F. Hankinson, 3b	6	1	2	1	2	3	0
J. Meister, 2b	6	1	1	1	1	3	1
D. Orr, 1b	6	3	2	1	14	0	0
D. Esterbrook, ss	5	1	2	1	0	3	4
J. Morrison, cf	5	1	3	1	2	0	1
D. O'Brien, lf	5	0	1	1	3	0	2
J. Schafer, p	5	0	1	1	0	4	0
B. Holbert, c	5	0	0	0	4	1	1
	49	10	14	7	30	14	9

Brooklyn	230	200	003	4	=	14
Mets	104	010	220	0	=	10

	ip	h	r-er	bb	so
Porter (W 1-0)	10	14	10- 3	4	4
Schafer (L 0-1)	10	22	14-10	8	3

WP: Schafer
PB: Holbert
HBP: by Schafer (Burch)
by Porter (Esterbrook)
Time—2:30
Attendance—7,053

Umpire: J. McQuade

Game-Winning RBI: McTamany
LOB: Brooklyn 10, Mets 10
BE: Brooklyn 3, Mets 5
DP: Hankinson-Meister-Orr (Porter)
2B: Pinckney 2, Esterbrook, Orr, McTamany, Burch, J. O'Brien, Smith, Hankinson
3B: Hankinson
HR: Burch
BB: Pinckney, McClellan 3, Phillips, Burch, Radford, Porter, Morrison, J. O'Brien, Orr, Esterbrook
SB: Pinckney, McClellan, Orr, Radford, J. O'Brien, Porter
CS: Meister

Brooklyn won six of its first seven games but then slipped slowly through the season to a sixth-place finish. The four-strike rule benefitted teams with good hitting, which did not include Brooklyn. And the reduction to five balls also hurt the Brooks, since their pitchers walked more batters than any other staff in the Association.

Brooklyn finished the year with a 60-74 record.

1888 TUESDAY, JULY 10TH, AT SPORTSMAN'S PARK, ST. LOUIS

Bridegrooms Sweep Series from Browns

Rally With Three in 9th to Tie, Win in 10th, 5-4
Increase First-Place Lead to 4½ Games

Today's Results			
BROOKLYN 5-St. Louis 4 (10 innings)			
Cincinnati 5-Athletics 4 (11 innings)			
Baltimore 12-Kansas City 1			
Louisville 7-Cleveland 4			
Standings	**W-L**	**Pct.**	**GB**
BROOKLYN	45-20	.692	—
St. Louis	37-21	.638	4½
Athletics	36-24	.600	6½
Cincinnati	37-25	.597	6½
Baltimore	28-32	.467	14½
Louisville	22-40	.355	21½
Cleveland	19-41	.317	23½
Kansas City	18-39	.316	23

CHARLIE BYRNE'S HIGH-PRICED BROOKlyn team has taken on the look of a pennant winner. By rallying to tie and then defeat the defending-champion St. Louis Browns, the Brooklyn Bridegrooms today completed a four-game sweep of the series. The victories vaulted Brooklyn from .013 behind in the percentage column to .054 ahead.

The games were all the more satisfying for Byrne since three of the heroes of the series were bought from St. Louis last winter. One of the new players, Bob Caruthers, pitched three of the four games, including today's. Also today, Caruthers drove in two runs, including the winning run. The two other men purchased from St. Louis by Brooklyn, first baseman Dave Foutz and catcher Al "Doc" Bushong, also contributed key hits today. In addition, Foutz was a hitting star in two of the other three games in the series.

Byrne and his associates with the Brooklyn club paid St. Louis owner Chris Von der Ahe a total of $18,000 for those three men. They also paid out $25,000 for the entire Metropolitan franchise after the close of the 1887 season. This transaction yielded three starting players: Paul Radford, Darby O'Brien, and Dave Orr. Brooklyn recovered some of the money, however, by selling eight players, including four old Mets, to the new Kansas City franchise that replaced the Mets in the American Association. Radford got the key hit in today's ninth-inning rally that tied the game.

For Von der Ahe, the defeats, especially at the hands of men like Caruthers, were agonizing. Angrily he lashed out in the press at both Byrne and the umpire in the series, Bob Ferguson.

The charge against Byrne was of tampering with the Browns' top hitter, Tip O'Neill. Byrne denied any dealings with O'Neill, although he was aware of the fact that Brooklyn's Bushong had written a letter to his former teammate. The letter reputedly said that Brooklyn would like to secure O'Neill's contract. Today St. Louis captain Charlie Comiskey kept O'Neill on the bench.

Freguson was accused of unfairly favoring the visitors, a charge which could not be substantiated. Nevertheless, the most controversial call of today's game went against St. Louis and helped set up a Brooklyn run.

The game was scoreless until Brooklyn came up in the bottom of the third. With two out and Bushong on second base, Foutz hit a bouncer along the first base line. Comiskey made a fine stop of the ball and flipped to pitcher Charley King, who was running to cover the base. Although even the Brooklyn press contingent thought that King beat Foutz to the bag, ump Ferguson called the batter safe. Comiskey blew his cork at this and argued at length about the ruling. But, of course, Ferguson did not change his mind. Caruthers then came up and pulled a hit to right field to drive Bushong home from third.

Other than that inning, King kept the Brooklyn hits well scattered until the ninth.

Caruthers got good support in the early innings, and St. Louis did not score until the seventh. Their first run finally came when the Brooklyn defense broke down. With one out, Yank Robinson reached second on a wild throw by shortstop George Smith. He went to third on a ground out and scored on a two-out fumble by third baseman George Pinckney.

The score was still 1-1 going into the ninth. After the first two St. Louis batters were retired, Robinson sent a corker to left field for two bases. Harry Lyons hit a safe one to right, and Robinson rounded third. But Arlie Latham, coaching the base, went half way down the line to stop the runner. As Bill McClellan's throw home was perfect, it was a good thing for St. Louis. Lyons stole second. Ed Herr, who was taking O'Neill's place in the lineup, then fouled the old ball out of the park. A new ball was put into play. Herr caught it on the fat part of his bat and sent it into the left field seats for a three-run home run.

So Byrne's men found themselves trailing 4-1 when they came to bat in the last of the ninth. When the first two batters were retired on infield grounders, the visitors began packing up their bats. Bob Clark hit another grounder to second baseman Robinson, but the fielder obligingly fumbled it. McClellan kept the Brooklyn hopes alive with a clean hit to right, sending Clark to third. McClellan was allowed to steal second.

Now it was up to Radford, one of the weakest hitters on the team. To everyone's surprise, he connected with one of King's shoots and lined it into center field. Lyons came charging in and, instead of playing it safe, he inexplicably tried for a shoestring catch. He missed, and the ball rolled toward the fence. Clark and McClellan scored, and Radford was rounding third when Latham juggled the throw from the outfield. This error allowed Radford to score the tying run without a play.

King and Comiskey were fit to be tied by this turn of events, and the whole St. Louis team seemed greatly demoralized. They were retired with ease in the top of the tenth.

Latham muffed Pinckney's liner to open the bottom of the round. The runner stole second, but Foutz flied out to center. Caruthers then strode to the plate. He waited for King to serve up an easy one, then he smacked the ball into the seats in right. He hit it far enough for a home run, but he stopped running when Pinckney scored from second, Caruthers was credited with a double.

The Browns dejectedly shuffled off to the clubhouse, while Von der Ahe fumed. A few of the St. Louis fans directed their frustrations at umpire Ferguson, who had to beat a hasty retreat under a barrage of beer mugs and seat cushions. But the Bridegrooms were oblivious to this, as they were busy congratulating each other and pounding Caruthers on the back.

St. Louis	ab	r	h	bi	o	a	e
A. Latham, 3b	5	0	1	0	3	6	2
T. McCarthy, rf	5	0	0	0	2	1	0
E. Herr, 1f	5	1	2	3	2	1	0
C. Comiskey, 1b	5	0	0	0	14	1	0
Y. Robinson, 2b	3	2	1	0	1	3	1
H. Lyons, cf	5	1	3	0	2	0	1
B. White, ss	5	0	0	0	1	0	0
J. Milligan, c	4	0	1	0	2	0	1
C. King, p	4	0	0	0	1	2	1
	41	4	8	3	28	14	6

Brooklyn	ab	r	h	bi	o	a	e
G. Pinckney, 3b	4	1	0	0	3	4	1
D. Foutz, 1b	5	0	1	0	14	1	0
B. Caruthers, p	5	0	3	2	1	5	1
G. Smith, ss	4	0	0	0	0	4	1
J. Burdock, 2b	4	0	1	0	0	3	0
B. Clark, 1f	4	1	0	0	4	0	0
B. McClellan, rf	4	1	1	0	1	2	0
P. Radford, cf	4	1	1	1	2	0	0
A. Bushong, c	4	1	2	0	5	0	0
	38	5	9	3	30	19	3

St. Louis	000	000	103	0	= 4
Brooklyn	001	000	003	1	= 5

one out when winning run scored

	ip	h	r-er	bb	so
King (L 17-10)	9⅓	9	5-1	1	1
Caruthers (W 19-6)	10	8	4-3	1	3

WP: King 2 PB: Milligan
HBP: by Caruthers (Robinson)

Game-Winning RBI: Caruthers
LOB: St. Louis 9, Brooklyn 6
BE: St. Louis 3, Brooklyn 3
DP: Pinckney-Foutz-Pinckney
2B: Herr, Caruthers 2, Robinson
HR: Herr
SB: Bushong, Lyons, Pinckney
Time—1:50
Umpire: B. Ferguson

St. Louis rebounded to win nine of its next eleven to regain first place. The Bridegrooms fell all the way to fourth place, 11 games behind by the end of August. Brooklyn then finished strongly, but it was too late. St. Louis won the pennant by 6½ games. The Bridegrooms finished second with an 88-52 record.

1889 SATURDAY, SEPTEMBER 7TH, AT WASHINGTON PARK

St. Louis Forfeits Key Game in Brooklyn

Ump Refuses to Call Game After Browns Delay for Darkness
Brooklyn is Trailing 4-2 When St. Louis Walks Off Field

Today's Results			
BROOKLYN 9-ST. LOUIS 0 (Forfeit)			
Cincinnati 5-Baltimore 5 (Tie) (9 inn.)			
Athletics 4-Louisville 4 (Tie) (9 inn.)			
Columbus 5-Kansas City 0			
Standings	**W-L**	**Pct.**	**GB**
BROOKLYN	76-37	.673	—
St. Louis	72-40	.643	3½
Baltimore	64-45	.587	10
Athletics	61-47	.565	12½
Cincinnati	59-55	.518	17½
Kansas City	46-66	.411	29½
Columbus	47-68	.409	30
Louisville	23-90	.204	53

IT BEGAN AS THE BIGGEST GAME OF THE year, and it ended with the biggest row with an umpire all season. The Brooklyn Bridegrooms were all but beaten by the St. Louis Browns in the game, but the umpire handed Brooklyn the victory by forfeit when St. Louis walked off the field. The Browns claimed, with some reason, that it was too dark to finish the game. But they had done everything imaginable to delay the game in the previous innings, and umpire Fred Goldsmith obstinately refused to call the game.

Today's contest was the first of three games scheduled between the two teams, who were fighting for the American Association pennant. As the games promised to be decisive in the race, over 15,000 Brooklyn cranks came to today's battle. An even larger crowd was expected to see the Sunday game at Ridgewood Park, but St. Louis owner Chris Von der Ahe told the press and the Brooklyn management that he would refuse to let his team play any more games in Brooklyn unless today's disputed contest was played over. Brooklyn president Charles Byrne, of course, refused to allow that. The feud cost both sides big money, since St. Louis was subject to a $1,500 fine for each forfeit (and faced with possible expulsion from the Association), and Brooklyn was deprived of up to $8,000 in gate receipts.

The two nines played an exciting game today, running the bases with abandon and trying to force the defense into mistakes. Although eleven errors were made, the fielders were up to the challenge in most cases, and no fewer than five players were tagged out trying to score. Four other men were thrown out stealing, three by Brooklyn catcher Bob Clark.

Today's crowd was the second-largest of the year here. The grandstand was filled entirely, and the overflow ringed the outfield.

Play was called at 4 o'clock, with Brooklyn choosing to bat first. The Bridegrooms opened with two runs, then did not score again. An error by the shortstop, a passed ball, a double by Hub Collins, and a single by Dave Foutz brought the runs in. A great throw from right field to third base by St. Louis's Tommy McCarthy cut the rally short.

The excitement was intense in the fourth inning, when two men on each team were thrown out at home.

St. Louis finally scored in its half of the fifth. Charlie Duffee led off with a sharp single to left. He allowed himself to be hit by a wild return throw and took second. Brooklyn claimed that he had intentionally interfered, but Goldsmith allowed Duffee to stay on second. He scored on an infield out and a hit by Jocko Milligan.

St. Louis took the lead in the sixth with two runs on three hits and a throwing error by the center fielder.

Now that they led, the Browns started delaying in the seventh inning. Although it was only 5:40 p.m. when the inning started, it was an overcast day and growing dark. Brooklyn played into St. Louis's hands by also arguing with the umpire. First, Bob Caruthers, who was batting, disputed a called strike. When he finally got a base on balls, catcher Milligan railed at Goldsmith's eyesight. George Smith was hit by a pitch, but Goldsmith (goaded by St. Louis captain Charlie Comiskey) ruled that Smith had not tried to get out of the way and ordered him to bat again. Brooklyn argued about this for a while. Caruthers stole second, but St. Louis claimed Smith had interfered with the catcher's throw. Comiskey argued for so long that Goldsmith pulled his watch out and threatened to forfeit the game to Brooklyn if the Browns did not go back to their positions. Finally play resumed, and the side was retired.

St. Louis scored another run in their half of the seventh on two errors and a hit by Tip O'Neill. Before going out onto the field, McCarthy dunked the ball into a bucket of water. But Goldsmith found out and put a new ball into play.

The eighth inning witnessed more harsh words and more delays. Von der Ahe humored the crowd by distributing lighted candles to be placed in front of the St. Louis bench. This was the last straw for Goldsmith, who was now determined to play the game out even if it took until midnight.

When Brooklyn came to bat in the ninth, it was very dark. The first batter could not see the ball and struck out. But the catcher could not see either and missed the third strike, allowing the batter to reach first. When the next pitch got away and the runner advanced, Comiskey refused to play any longer and ordered his men off the field.

Umpire Goldsmith pulled out hs watch and ordered the Browns to return to their positions. The St. Louis players, however, were walking off to the dressing room. Some of the cranks in the outfield threw bottles, and a few Browns were hit. McCarthy was struck in the mouth.

When the required five minutes had elapsed, Goldsmith forfeited the game to Brooklyn. So what had been a fine game was turned into a disgraceful display of umpire-baiting and hot-headed umpiring. Out of it all, Brooklyn was given an undeserved victory in the most important game of the year.

Brooklyn	**ab**	**r**	**h**	**bi**	**o**	**a**	**e**
D. O'Brien, 1f	4	1	1	0	2	0	1
H. Collins, 2b	4	1	2	1	4	4	2
D. Foutz, 1b	4	0	2	1	11	0	0
T. Burns, rf	4	0	0	0	1	0	0
G. Pinckney, 3b	4	0	1	0	1	1	1
P. Corkhill, 3b	3	0	0	0	0	0	1
B. Clark, c	4	0	1	0	4	4	1
B. Caruthers, p	2	0	0	0	0	5	0
G. Smith, ss	2	0	0	0	1	4	0
	31	2	7	2	24	18	6

St. Louis	**ab**	**r**	**h**	**bi**	**o**	**a**	**e**
A. Latham, 3b	4	1	1	0	2	3	0
T. McCarthy, rf	4	0	0	0	3	1	1
T. O'Neill, 1f	4	1	3	1	1	0	0
C. Comiskey, 1b	4	0	0	0	3	2	0
Y. Robinson, 2b	4	1	1	0	0	3	1
C. Duffee, cf	4	1	1	0	4	0	1
S. Fuller, ss	4	0	1	1	3	1	1
J. Milligan, c	3	0	2	1	7	2	1
E. Chamberlain, p	3	0	1	0	1	1	0
	34	4	10	3	24	13	5

Brooklyn	200 000 00*	=	9
St. Louis	000 012 10	=	0

*Game forfeited to Brooklyn with one man on and no one out in the top of the ninth.

	ip	**h**	**r-er**	**bb**	**so**
Caruthers	8	10	4-1	0	3
Chamberlain	†8	7	2-1	3	4

†faced two batters in ninth
WP: Chamberlain
PB: Milligan 2, Clark
Time—2:25
Attendance—15,143

LOB: St. Louis 6, Brooklyn 8
BE: St. Louis 3, Brooklyn 3 (includes one batter who reached on a missed 3rd strike)
DP: McCarthy-Latham
2B: Collins, Pinckney, O'Neill, Fuller
SB: Corkhill
CS:Latham, O'Neill, Collins, Corkhill
Umpire: F. Goldsmith

At a special American Association meeting on September 23rd, the league reversed the umpire's decision and ruled this game a 4-2 St. Louis victory, much to the disgust of Brooklyn president Byrne. The September 8th forfeit, however, was upheld. The ruling reduced Brooklyn's lead to 3½ games.

The Browns put on a great stretch drive, winning twelve games in a row. But the Bridegrooms won eleven of their final fourteen to hold on and win the pennant by 2 games. Brooklyn's final record was 93-44. And the team set a new all-time attendance record by drawing 353,690 paying customers.

1889 FRIDAY, OCTOBER 18TH, AT THE POLO GROUNDS, NEW YORK
World Series—Game #1

Brooklyn Beats Giants in Opener

ON THIS DATE THE BROOKLYN CLUB PLAYED IN ITS FIRST WORLD SERIES GAME. BROOKlyn beat the New York Giants at the Polo Grounds, 12-10, in the opening game of the 1889 world championship. The ownership of the two clubs arranged for a best-of-eleven series with the games alternating between New York and Brooklyn daily except Sundays.

The Giants won the 1888 World Series, defeating the St. Louis Browns, and were generally favored to win again this year. Today, backers of the New York club lost heavily to Brooklyn partisans who came over the bridge. The game was decided by a four-run rally in the last half of the eighth inning by the 'Grooms. It was too dark to play the ninth inning.

Both teams were nervous and played poorly. And the umpiring was just as bad. To start with, one of the two men engaged to work the game failed to show up. Old Bob Ferguson was chosen out of the crowd, and his work was poor. The other arbiter, John Gaffney, made two controversial calls that hurt Brooklyn. Then he refused to call the game while New York was ahead, giving Brooklyn a chance to win in the twilight.

New York presented its star pitcher, Tim Keefe, but he was decidely off in his form. The visitors hit his delivery almost at will in the first and last stages of the game, collecting a total of 16 hits. "Adonis" Bill Terry, the Brooklyn hurler, was also hit hard, and the Giants connected for 11 safe blows. Terry received poor fielding support, especially from his outfielders, and eight Brooklyn errors helped the New York scoring.

Giant captain Buck Ewing chose to bat his team first, and Terry disposed of the first three batters quickly.

Brooklyn came in and ran up a lead of five runs. Capt. Darby O'Brien started things with a safe hit just past second baseman Danny Richardson's reach. Hub Collins pasted a double all the way to the left field fence. Tom Burns sent a long hit to right, driving home the first two runs of the game. The next two men went out. But Bob Clark kept the rally going with a hit to right. Burns came home on the drive, and Clark took second on a throwing error by Mike Tiernan. Terry followed with a bouncing hit to right. Pop Corkhill's long double sent two runners across the pan. Before they knew what hit them, the Giants found themselves behind 5-0. Their partisans in the stands were mute and disgusted.

But the National League champions began to catch up immediately, scoring two runs in the second. John Ward began by taking a base on balls. Roger Connor hit an easy grounder to second base. There Collins, in his haste to make a double play, fumbled the ball, and both runners were safe. They tried a double steal, but catcher Clark's good throw retired Ward at third. Richardson bounced a hit to right field, and Burns missed the ball completely. Connor scored and Richardson got all the way to third. He came home on Jim O'Rourke's fly to center.

Brooklyn countered with one run on Collins's drive into the seats in deep left field. It yielded a home run before O'Rourke could find the ball and return it to the infield.

After a runless third inning, New York scored two in the fourth. The first three batters reached safely, but Clark threw two of them out trying to steal third. With one man still on base, Richardson sent a fly over Corkhill's head in deep center. The outfielder made a somersaulting lunge and came up with the ball, but umpire Gafney ruled it a safe hit. Corkhill, stunned and injured and thinking that he had caught the ball, lay on the ground while two Giants circled the bases. Brooklyn argued Gaffney's call, but the runs were counted.

New York pulled to within one run, 6-5, with another tally in the fifth. Keefe scored it on a walk, an error by Collins, a passed ball, a hit by Ward, and an error by Joe Visner in center.

After neither side scored in the sixth, New York rallied for five runs in the seventh to take the lead. George Gore and Tiernan made hits with one out. Ewing lifted a twister near third, which third baseman George Pinckney dropped. He quickly picked the ball up and stepped on third, forcing Gore. But Gaffney ruled that the drop was intentional, and he declared Ewing, not Gore, out. This was fair enough, except that Gaffney allowed the runners to stay on second and third, rather than first and second, where they had started. Somehow, Brooklyn could not convince the arbiter to send the men back. Both scored on a single by Ward. A muffed fly, a single by Richardson, and a triple by O'Rourke (misplayed by O'Brien) ran the New York lead to 10-6.

Brooklyn came back with two runs in the bottom of the seventh on a throwing error by Ward and hits by Burns and Dave Foutz.

When the inning ended, captain Ewing tried to convince the umpires to call the game. Although the argument consumed some minutes, the umps declared that one more inning could by played.

The Giants were held scoreless in the top of the eighth, despite two hits.

The Bridegrooms, needing two runs to tie, came to bat. Terry went out on a tap to Keefe. Visner hit safely to left and took second on O'Rourke's fumble, the outfielder complaining that he could not see the ball. Germany Smith fouled out, and Brooklyn was down to its final out. O'Brien kept his team's hopes alive with a hit that Richardson failed to stop, and Visner scored. Collins delivered a long two-bagger to left, and O'Brien tallied the tying run. Burns lifted a fly into the gloaming, and it fell between O'Rourke and Gore, allowing Collins to score the go-ahead run. Foutz hit a liner past the unsuspecting third baseman, and Burns came home.

That was all Ewing could stand, and he demanded the game be called. Foutz, meanwhile, ended the controversy by wandering off second base and allowing himself to be tagged out. That ended the inning, and the umpires sent everyone home.

The Brooklyn team and their supporters went home happy, while the New Yorkers left wondering what exactly had gone wrong.

New York (NL)	ab	r	h	bi	o	a	e
G. Gore, cf	5	1	1	0	2	0	0
M. Tiernan, rf	5	1	2	0	0	0	1
B. Ewing, c	4	0	1	0	2	0	0
J. Ward, ss	2	1	2	3	3	2	1
R. Connor, 1b	3	3	0	0	12	0	0
D. Richardson, 2b	4	3	2	1	3	3	0
J. O'Rourke, lf	4	0	2	2	1	1	1
A. Whitney, 3b	4	0	0	0	0	2	0
T. Keefe, p	3	1	1	0	1	4	0
	34	10	11	6	24	12	3

Brooklyn (AA)	ab	r	h	bi	o	a	e
D. O'Brien, lf	5	2	2	1	2	0	2
H. Collins, 2b	5	4	3	2	2	2	2
T. Burns, rf	5	3	4	3	1	0	1
D. Foutz, 1b	5	0	2	2	5	0	0
G. Pinckney, 3b	4	0	1	1	5	1	1
B. Clark, c	4	1	1	1	3	3	0
B. Terry, p	4	1	1	0	1	1	0
P. Corkhill, cf	2	1	1	2	2	0	1
J. Visner, cf4	2	0	1	0	1	0	1
G. Smith, ss	4	0	0	0	2	3	0
	40	12	16	12	24	10	8

New York	020 210 50	=	10
Brooklyn	510 000 24	=	12

game called on account of darkness

	ip	h	r-er	bb	so
Keefe (L 0-1)	8	16	12-10	0	2
Terry (W 1-0)	8	11	10- 3	5	3

PB: Clark

Time—2:10 Attendance—8,848

Umpires: J. Gaffney & B. Ferguson

Game-Winning RBI: Burns
LOB: New York 5, Brooklyn 4
BE: New York 3, Brooklyn 1
DP: Smith-Pinckney-Foutz
2B: Collins 2, Burns 2, Corkhill, Ewing, Foutz
3B: O'Rourke
HR: Burns
SB: Connor 2, Ward, Ewing
CS: Ward 2, Ewing

With the series alternating sites, the Giants won the second game (played in Brooklyn), 6-2.

The Bridegrooms won the next two contests, 8-7 and 10-7 in six innings, to take a 3-1 lead in the best-of-eleven series.

But after that it was all New York. The Giants won the last five games to take the series, 6 games to 3. The scores were 11-3, 2-1 in 11 innings, 11-7, 16-7, and 3-2. New York's second-line pitchers Hank O'Day and Ed Crane were credited with all the Giant victories.

1890 LABOR DAY, MONDAY, SEPTEMBER 1ST, AT WASHINGTON PARK

Brooklyn Wins a Tripleheader

Poor Pittsburgs Lose Three Times, 10-9, 3-2, & 8-4
First-Place Bridegrooms Extend League Lead by 2½ Games

Today's Results			
BROOKLYN 10—Pittsburg 9 (1st-morning)			
BROOKLYN 3—Pittsburg 2 (2nd-afternoon)			
BROOKLYN 8—Pittsburg 4 (3rd-afternoon)			
Chicago 4—Boston 1 (morning)			
Chicago 15—Boston 11 (afternoon)			
Philadelphia 2—Cincinnati 1 (morning)			
Cincinnati 8—Philadelphia 5 (afternoon)			
New York 4—Cleveland 0 (morning)			
New York 5—Cleveland 1 (afternoon)			
Standings	**W-L**	**Pct.**	**GB**
BROOKLYN	74-36	.673	—
Boston	69-42	.621	5½
Cincinnati	65-42	.607	7½
Philadelphia	66-44	.600	8
Chicago	63-47	.573	11
New York	51-60	.459	23½
Cleveland	31-75	.292	41
Pittsburg	19-92	.171	55½

THE BROOKLYN BRIDEGROOMS WENT A long way toward winning the National League pennant today. They defeated the lowly Pittsburgs in three games, while the second-place Boston Beaneaters were losing two games to the Chicago Colts. That increased Brooklyn's lead from .031 to .051 in the percentage chart, and moved them from 3 games ahead to 5½ in front.

The hapless visitors won only once in August, while losing 27 times. And today they began the new month with an unprecedented three defeats on one day! Still, they did not go down easily. In the morning game, the tailenders were trailing 10-0 before rallying in the ninth inning for nine runs. The last out was made at home plate when George Miller tried to stretch a triple into a home run. In the second game of the day, the tying run was again thrown out at home in the ninth, and Pittsburg lost 3-2. Brooklyn jumped to a quick 7-0 lead in the final game, and Pittsburg did not get closer than 7-4 behind. The final score was 8-4.

Despite the fact that the Bridegrooms were pennant-bound in their first year in the National League, the 1890 season was not as successful for Byrne's club as 1889 had been. This was mainly due to the Brotherhood revolt and the presence of a Players' League team in Brooklyn. The American Association had also put a new club into the territory, but it folded on August 26th. Attendance at Washington Park was way down from the previous season.

But the Brooklyn situation was among the best for the National League in its "war" with the Brotherhood. Pittsburg, on the other hand, represented the worst. Totally outclassed on the field due to defections to the rival circuit, the Pittsburg League team has had to transfer most of its home games to other cities.

Not wishing to miss any easy victories over the cellar-dwellers, the Brooklyn management added a postponed game from May to the scheduled Labor Day doubleheader. The extra game was added to the afternoon contest, giving the cranks a rare chance to see two games for one admission.

Only 915 persons chose to come to the morning game. For eight innings, they were not given much in the way of excitement. The home players ran the bases with impunity and built up a 10-0 lead. But the visitors staged a great rally in the ninth to make the game exciting, and they came within an ace of tying the score.

The Bridegrooms started the day with four runs in the first inning. Hub Collins was first up, and he was given first base on balls and second on a wild pitch. George Pinckney sacrificed him to third, and he scored when right fielder Fred Osborne dropped Darby O'Brien's fly. Osborne then compounded his error by throwing so wildly that O'Brien circled the bases. After Dave Foutz fanned, Bill Terry singled and went to third on a wild throw by the catcher. Tom Burns was hit by a pitch and stole second. Bob Clark drove the two runners in with a hit to left.

The Groom added two runs in the third, one in the fourth, another in the sixth, and two more in the seventh to run the score to 10-0.

Going into the ninth, Brooklyn pitcher Bob Caruthers was working on a three-hit shutout. Pittsburg finally got its first runs on a two-out single by Guy Hecker. And they continued to bat around until the score was 10-6, the bases were loaded, and their best hitter, Miller, was up at the plate. Dog-faced George smacked a hit to deep center. Three runs were already across the plate when shortstop George Smith got the throw from the outfield. Miller had rounded third under a full head of steam, but Smith's fine relay nipped him at home and saved the game for Brooklyn. The final score was 10-9.

A much larger crowd was on hand for the afternoon games. Brooklyn scored in the first inning on a hit and steal by Pinckney and a hit by O'Brien. Three Pittsburgh singles tied the count in the third. Pinckney scored again in the fourth after tripling. And Burns tripled and scored in the fifth.

Pittsburg rallied in the ninth on a single by Hecker and a one-out triple by Ed Sales. Mike Jordan grounded to short, and Smith threw home to retire Sales. Jordan stole second. But pitcher Tom Lovett struck out Dave Anderson to end the game.

In the third game of the day, the home team was never threatened. They scored three runs in the first inning and four in the second, O'Brien batting home three and scoring one and Collins scoring twice and knocking home two men. Burns added a home run in the seventh. Pitcher Bill Terry was hit for four runs but held onto the lead. The final score this time was 8-4.

For the first time in big-league history, one team had won three games in one day.

FIRST GAME (morning)

Pittsburg	ab	r	h	bi	o	a	e
E. Burke, cf	3	2	1	0	1	0	0
G. Miller, 3b	5	1	1	3	2	3	1
T. Berger, 2b	3	1	0	0	1	0	0
B. Wilson, c	4	0	1	0	4	2	1
G. Hecker, 1b	4	1	1	2	9	0	0
F. Osborne, rf	3	1	0	0	2	0	2
E. Sales, ss	4	1	1	1	2	4	0
M. Jordan, 1f	4	1	2	2	3	1	0
K. Baker, p	4	1	2	0	0	0	2
	34	9	9	8	24	10	6

Brooklyn	ab	r	h	bi	o	a	e
H. Collins, 2b	4	2	1	0	6	7	1
G. Pinckney, 3b	4	0	1	1	1	2	0
D. O'Brien, cf	4	2	2	1	0	1	0
D. Foutz, 1b	3	1	0	0	15	0	0
B. Terry, 1f	4	1	1	0	3	0	0
T. Burns, rf	3	2	1	1	0	0	0
B. Clark, c	4	1	3	4	1	2	0
G. Smith, ss	4	0	1	1	1	1	0
B. Caruthers, p	4	1	1	0	0	1	1
	34	10	11	8	27	14	2

Pittsburg	000 000 009	= 9
Brooklyn	402 101 20x	= 10

	ip	h	r-er	bb	so
Baker (L 2-19)	8	11	10-3	4	3
Caruthers (W 21-11)	9	9	9-0	2	0

PB: Wilson 2
WP: Baker
HBP: by Baker (Burns)
by Caruthers 2 (Osborne, Burke)
Time—1:32 Attendance—915

Game-Winning Run scored on a muffed fly ball
LOB: Pittsburg 2, Brooklyn 5
BE: Pittsburg 1, Brooklyn 2
DP: Collins unassisted
Sales-Wilson-Hecker
2B: Clark, Baker, O'Brien, Burke
3B: Clark, Miller
SB: Burns, O'Brien, Foutz 2, Collins, Jordan
CS: Smith
Umpire: G. Strief

SECOND GAME (afternoon)

			r	h	e
Pittsburg	001 000 001	=	2	8	1
Brooklyn	100 110 00x	=	3	5	2

Game-Winning RBI: O'Brien

Batteries: D. Anderson (L 1-4) & H. Decker.
T. Lovett (W 26-7) & T. Daly

THIRD GAME (afternoon)

			r	h	e
Pittsburg	000 103 000	=	4	6	2
Brooklyn	340 000 10x	=	8	11	2

Game-Winning RBI: O'Brien

Batteries: D. Anderson (L 1-5) & H. Decker
B. Terry (W 22-13) & T. Daly
Afternoon Attendance—7,194

The next day, the Bridegrooms rallied for three runs in the bottom of the ninth to beat the poor Pittsburgs, 5-4.

Brooklyn held onto its lead without too much trouble and won the National League pennant by 6 games over second-place Chicago. The 'Grooms had a final record of 86-43.

1890 TUESDAY, OCTOBER 28TH, AT WASHINGTON PARK World Series—Game #7

Series Called Off Due to Cold

THE PENNANT-WINNING CLUBS OF THE NATIONAL LEAGUE AND AMERICAN ASSOCIAtion, the Brooklyn Bridegrooms and the Louisville Colonels, had arranged for a best-of-nine game series to determine the "World Championship." But after playing the seventh game today in bitter cold, the series was called off by mutual consent. Louisville won the last game, 6-2, and the aborted series ended tied at three victories apiece with one game having been tied.

Perhaps it was just as well to leave the series undecided. The rival Players' League was not invited to compete, and its champion Boston club was thought by many to have the strongest team in the land.

The Louisville-Brooklyn series got off to a bad start when the first game was delayed for two days by rain in Louisville. When the opening game was finally played, the Bridegrooms won in a walk, 9-0, with their Adonis, Bill Terry, pitching a shutout. Tom Lovett hurled Brooklyn to victory in the second game, 5-3. At that point the series looked like a walkover for the Brooks.

The third game was the most exciting of the series. In it the Colonels rallied for three runs in the eighth inning to tie the score, 7-7, just before the game was called due to darkness. Louisville finally scored a victory in the fourth and final game played in the Falls City, 5-4. Red Ehret was the pitching star for the winners.

The series shifted to Brooklyn for five games, if necessary. But the rain and chill were so bad on October 23rd and 24th that no baseball could be played. The series finally resumed on Saturday the 25th, but only about 1,000 spectators braved the elements to see it. Those who came saw a fine Brooklyn victory, 7-2. Lovett pitched a five-hitter, and Tommy Burns opened the scoring with a two-run home run. Patsy Donovan did some remarkable base running.

Louisville finally hit its stride in the sixth game played, winning 9-8. A shivering gathering of no more than 600 saw this contest. The Colonels blew a 5-1 lead, then moved ahead again 9-5. Brooklyn rallied valiantly, but relief pitcher Ehret stopped them short of victory.

The two managers, Bill McGunnigle of Brooklyn and Jack Chapman of Louisville, met this morning and agreed that further play in the frosty weather would be futile. The game announced for today was played as scheduled, but before it started it was announced that there would be no additional games. Since neither side could gain the fifth victory required to win the championship, today's contest had little significance.

Although he had pitched three innings the day before, Ehret occupied the pitcher's box for the visitors today. He did excellent work, holding Brooklyn to just four hits and two runs despite some poor fielding support. He faced the minimum number of batters over the final five innings.

Brooklyn was not at full strength today. Terry and George Pinckney were both ill and unable to play. Bob Caruthers played left field despite a lame ankle. Tom "Oyster" Burns, normally an outfielder, was at third base, where he did a splendid job. George "Germany" Smith also played well at shortstop. Brooklyn made only one error, compared to six by Louisville. But the visitors won on long hits off of Brooklyn pitcher Tom Lovett.

Harry Taylor opened the game with a safe hit, and he scored on two sacrifices and a passed ball.

Brooklyn came in and scored two runs in their first ups. the first two hitters went out on infield chances. Burns then hit safely. Dave Foutz followed with a long double, and Burns scored. Smith walked. Tom Daly hit to second baseman Tim Shinnick, whose fumble and wild throw allowed Foutz to come home. The other runners were left stranded when Donovan grounded out third to first.

Shinnick singled with two gone in the Louisville second but was thrown out by Donovan trying to stretch the hit into a double. Hub Collins tripled with two out in the Brooklyn half, and O'Brien walked and stole behind him. But Burns flied out to left.

Louisville took the lead with a three-run rally in the third. With one out, Ehret helped his own cause with a triple over Donovan's head. Taylor popped to the catcher. Harry Raymond, however, knocked another long triple, and Ehret scored. Farmer Bill Weaver went to first on called balls and stole second. Then Jimmy "Chicken" Wolf scooted a ground single up the middle to drive both Raymond and Weaver home.

Ehret pitched out of trouble in the bottom of the third. A walk, a muff, and two throwing errors put men on second and third with none out. But Daly was retired on a fly to shortstop, and center fielder Weaver threw Foutz out at home when that runner tried to score after a fly out.

Thereafter, Brooklyn got only two men to first. Caruthers walked to open the fourth but was left on first. And Foutz hit safely with one out in the eighth, only to have Smith ground into a double play behind him.

Louisville added two runs in the eighth on a double by Taylor, a muff by Caruthers, and a one-base hit by Ed Daily.

The final score was 6-2 and the series ended with the standings even. The two teams solemnly promised to finish the championship when the weather was better, next spring.

Louisville (AA)	ab	r	h	bi	o	a	e
H. Taylor, 1b	4	2	2	0	14	0	1
H. Raymond, ss	4	1	1	1	3	4	0
F. Weaver, cf	3	2	0	1	3	1	0
C. Wolf, 3b	4	0	1	2	0	2	1
E. Daily, rf	4	0	1	1	0	0	0
C. Hamburg, lf	4	0	0	0	1	0	0
T. Shinnick, 2b	4	0	1	0	0	4	3
N. Bligh, c	0	0	0	0	0	0	0
P. Weckenbecker, c2	4	0	0	0	6	2	1
R. Ehret, p	4	1	2	0	0	1	0
	35	6	8	5	27	14	6

Brooklyn (NL)	ab	r	h	bi	o	a	e
H. Collins, 2b	4	0	1	0	1	1	0
D. O'Brien, cf	3	0	0	0	0	0	0
T. Burns, 3b	4	1	1	0	2	6	0
D. Foutz, 1b	3	1	2	1	19	0	0
G. Smith, ss	3	0	0	0	1	6	0
T. Daly, c	4	0	0	0	3	1	0
P. Donovan, rf	4	0	0	0	1	1	0
B. Caruthers, lf	3	0	0	0	0	0	1
T. Lovett, p	3	0	0	0	0	5	0
	31	2	4	1	27	20	1

Louisville	103	000	020	=	6
Brooklyn	200	000	000	=	2

	ip	h	r-er	bb	so
Ehret (W 2-0)	9	4	2-1	4	5
Lovett (L 2-2)	9	8	6-4	1	2

PB: Daly
Time—1:30
Attendance—300

Game-Winning RBI: Wolf
LOB: Louisville 3, Brooklyn 6
BE: Louisville 1, Brooklyn 2
DP: Weaver-Weckenbecker
Shinnick-Raymond-Taylor (Smith)
2B: Foutz, Taylor
3B: Collins, Ehret, Raymond
SB: O'Brien, Weaver 2, Foutz, Smith
Umpires: W. Curry & J. McQuaid

Over the winter, the Brotherhood "war" was settled. In Brooklyn, the Bridegrooms were consolidated with the Brooklyn Players' League club, managed by John M. Ward.

The settlement engendered a contract "war" between the National League and the American Association, and the Louisville-Brooklyn series was never resumed.

The Brooklyn Bridegrooms of 1889

Chapter II Sojourn in Eastern Park

1891 June 22nd
No-Hitter for Brooklyn's Lovett

1892 July 19th
Flat Bat Helps Win Double Shutout

1893 June 12th
Brooklyn Wins 14-13 to Take 1st Place

1894 August 11th
Home Run in 9th Wins Seesaw Game

1895 June 26th
13-Inning Duel Goes to Dodgers 1-0

1896 August 6th
Brooks Trail 10-0, Then Win 11-10

1897 July 31st
Kennedy Throws the Ball at the Umpire

1898 May 6th
Trolley Dodgers Score 6 in 9th to Win

AFTER THE 1890 SEASON, BOTH THE NATIONAL LEAGUE AND THE PLAYERS' LEAGUE were exhausted financially. In Brooklyn, the owners of the two rival clubs agreed to a merger. Although Byrne, Doyle, and Abell still retained the controlling interest in the club, the team on the field took on a Players' League look.

First of all, Washington Park was abandoned for the Players' League's newer Eastern Park, built in 1890. This field was located way out in the East New York district of Brooklyn, on the blocks bounded by the present-day Pitkin and Sutter Avenues and Van Sinderen and Powell Streets. This site was far from the center of Brooklyn population, but it was well served by streetcars and elevated railroad lines. Unfortunately, to get to the park from the nearest trolley and "el" stops, one had to get across the tracks of the New York & Manhattan Beach Railroad, which ran excursion trams from a ferry in Greenpoint to the resorts on Jamaica Bay and Coney Island. The maze of tracks and trains led to the coining of a new nickname for the team: the "Trolley Dodgers." This was, of course, later shortened to the "Dodgers."

The managerial reins of the team were taken out of the hands of old Bill McGunnigle, who had led the Bridegrooms to two consecutive pennants, and given to John Montgomery Ward, who had been the guiding spirit of the Players' League and its Brooklyn franchise. That team, which had not been rated very highly at the beginning of the season, had finished a strong second in 1890.

With Ward's team combined with the champion Bridegrooms, Brooklyn appeared to have a strong team for 1891. But the age of the veterans worked against the team. Every one of the regular players fell off in batting average. Even more important was the breakdown of the pitching. Bill Terry fell from 25-16 in 1890 to 7-17 in 1891. Bob Caruthers slipped from 23-11 to 17-17. And Tom Lovett went from 32-11 to 21-20. Lovett did, however, provide the high note of the year by no-hitting the Giants on June 22nd. The Bridegrooms slid all the way to sixth place in the final standings.

In 1892, Brooklyn picked up several key players from the now-defunct American Association. These included pitcher George Haddock and infielders Dan Brouthers, Bill Joyce, and Tommy Corcoran. Pitcher Ed Stein was lifted out of the Western Association to become the leader of the staff along with Haddock. With the National League expanded to twelve teams, it was decided to split the season into two halves. Despite the sudden death of Hub Collins, Ward's remodelled team made a strong bid late in the first half to overtake first-place Boston. But Brooklyn could only finish second. In the second half, Brooklyn started strongly but could not maintain a good pace. The Grooms finished a distant third behind Cleveland and Boston.

After this disappointment, Ward decided that he had had enough of Brooklyn, and he demanded to be sent to New York. The Giants were eager to get him, but they had no players of Ward's caliber to trade, and they had very little money. A deal was finally worked out by which Ward was sent to the Giants in exchange for a share of New York's gate receipts in 1893.

Meanwhile back at Eastern Park, veteran Dave Foutz was put in charge of the Trolley Dodgers. The team started the 1893 campaign well and was involved in a very close race for first place through June. But the team declined badly over the final three months and finished tied for sixth place. Leg and arm troubles reduced Haddock's production from 31 wins in 1892 to only 8 in 1893. Several other veterans also fell off. The Bridgrooms did acquire a lefthanded third baseman named Willie Keeler from the Giants on July 27th. But Brooklyn traded him and slugger Brouthers to Baltimore the following winter for third baseman Billy Shindle and outfielder George Treadway.

The pitching distance was increased in 1893 by about 5 feet to the present distance of 60½ feet. This helped the hitters greatly. Brooklyn did not show a big improvement, however, until 1894. Then the team scored 1021 runs, which is still a club record. But that total was only fifth best in the league that year. With everyone slugging the ball, Brooklyn was desperate for pitchers. One recruit, Con Lucid, gave up ten runs in his first game and was thought to be a success, especially since he beat the defending champion Boston Beaneaters. Overall, the Trolley Dodgers improved a little over 1893, moving up to fifth place.

Given the high-scoring nature of the games in those days, it was considered quite a sensation when Brooklyn had to go 13 innings to beat Washinton 1-0 on June 26th, 1895. Ed Stein, then in his fourth year with the Grooms, was the winning pitcher. But both Stein and Bill Kennedy, the other leader of the staff, had disappointing years. And the team batting average of .282 was only tenth best in the League.

John M. Ward

Mike Griffin

Dave Foutz

"Roaring Bill" Kennedy

Only in fielding, where shortstop Tommy Corcoran was a standout, were the Dodgers above average. Still, the team was good enough to finish fifth again.

In 1896, Corcoran remained near the top of the list in fielding average, but the team batting continued to be bad. As the pitching did not improve, the Trolley Dodgers were never in the pennant race. Although they were in seventh place for most of August, their age showed at the end, and the team finished in a tie for ninth. The two highlights of an otherwise dismal season were a game in which Brooklyn beat Pittsburg 25-6 (May 20th) and a game in which they overcame a 10-0 deficit to beat the Phillies 11-10 (August 6th).

In 1897, the Brooks were still well down the list in batting average (ninth with .279), and their winning percentage was only slightly improved over 1896 (.462 as opposed to .443). But somehow they moved up three spots in the final standings to a tie for sixth. Still, they were never in the pennant race, and the club lost over $10,000 with an attendance of 220,000. On the field, the frustration was typified by a game against the Giants on the last day of July. Pitching ace "Roaring Bill" Kennedy blew a 2-0 lead in the ninth and allowed a fourth run to score when he threw the ball in anger at the umpire. That became the decisive run when the Bridegrooms scored once in the bottom of the ninth and lost 4-3.

Aging Charles H. Byrne resigned the club presidency in December, 1897, and he died shortly thereafter. He was succeeded by young Charles Hercules Ebbets, who had started with the club as an office boy in 1883. Ebbets's first decision was to move the club from distant Eastern Park back to the Park Slope district. A new ballpark, called Washington Park after the original park which had stood a few blocks away, was opened on April 30th. It was located on a plot bounded by Fourth Avenue, Third Street, Third Avenue, and First Street. The Phillies spoiled the opening game by winning, 6-4. But the Trolley Dodgers won the next five games at home, three with dramatic late rallies.

Unfortunately for Ebbets and the other shareholders, the public was more concerned with the war with Spain than it was with baseball. Furthermore, Brooklyn had a very poor team, which finished a weak tenth in the twelve-team standings. Attendance fell all the way to 122,514. The club was in serious financial trouble.

But an ingenious scheme was soon hatched to save baseball in Brooklyn.

1891 MONDAY, JUNE 22ND, AT EASTERN PARK, BROOKLYN

No-Hitter for Brooklyn's Lovett

Giants Beaten 4-0 Through Scientific Baseball
Sacrifice Hitting, Good Fielding, and Great Pitching

Today's Results			
BROOKLYN 4-New York 0			
Chicago 4-Cleveland 3			
Boston 6-Philadelphia 2			
Pittsburg 4-Cincinnati 3			
Standings	**W-L**	**Pct.**	**GB**
New York	29-19	.604	—
Chicago	28-21	.571	1½
Boston	29-22	.569	1½
BROOKLYN	25-26	.490	5½
Cleveland	25-27	.481	6
Philadelphia	23-27	.460	7
Pittsburg	20-27	.426	8½
Cincinnati	20-30	.400	10

ALTHOUGH THIS HAD BEEN A RATHER disappointing season for the Brooklyn club and its followers, today the team played a nearly perfect game of ball and defeated its metropolitan rivals, the New York Giants, by a score of 4-0.

After the collapse of the Player's League last winter, the strong Brooklyn team from that organization was merged with the pennant-winning Brooklyn National League club. The amalgamated team seemed to have everything needed to win another pennant. But the team's pitching and batting both fell far below its previous standards, and Brooklyn has never been high in the pennant race in 1891.

The poor showing on the field also contributed to poor attendance. The team moved out to Eastern Park, located well away from the center of Brooklyn's population. The park had been built in 1890 for the Players' league team and was deemed more modern and commodious than Washington Park by the ownership of the merged club.

Eastern Park did have one pleasant aspect to it. Brisk breezes from Jamaica Bay made it the coolest park in the National League. Today many spectators took advantage of the park's location to escape from the heat of the city. As they enjoyed the cool breeze, they were treated to a red-hot demonstration of winning baseball by the home team.

The outstanding feature of the game was the fast pitching of Tom Lovett, who shut New York out wihout a hit. And the Bridegrooms also showed great form in the field, on the basepaths, and at bat. They stole five bases, advanced runners with five sacrifice hits of one sort or another, made eight base hits, and played errorless defense.

In marked contrast, the visiting New Yorkers tried only to knock the ball out of the park and succeeded in hitting easy fly balls to the Brooklyn fielders, instead. No fewer than six of their batters were retired on foul pops, while two more went out on foul tips caught by catcher Tom Daly. Lovett struck out three men. Only one ball hit by the Giants came close to falling safely, and that ball was caught in fine style by right fielder Tom Burns. The Bridegrooms made several other fine catches, but they mostly came on foul flies.

Mike Tiernan of the visitors opened the game by grounding out from second to first. Captain John Ward went far from his shortstop position to capture Danny Richardson's foul fly. And George Gore fanned on a "home run" swing.

Brooklyn then came in and scored a run without making a safe hit. Hub Collins led off with a hot grounder that was fumbled by the third baseman. He quickly stole second and went to third on Ward's neat sacrifice bunt. Mike Griffin was retired on a difficult grounder to third as Collins scored.

Lovett walked Roger Connor to start the second. But the next two batters popped out, and Lew Whistler struck out.

Brooklyn added a run in its second ups on smart base running. Darby O'Brien beat out a perfect bunt toward third. George Pinckney was hit on the shoulder by a pitch. Dave Foutz moved the men up with a bounder to shortstop. Pinckney took a big lead off second. When catcher Archie Clark threw behind him, O'Brien stole home cleanly.

In the third, Ward was caught trying to duplicate the steal of home.

Richardson made New York's closest bid for a hit leading off the fourth. He hit a low liner to right, but Burns raced in and caught the ball just before it hit the ground. Gore and Connor then fouled out.

Whistler was walked with two out in the top of the fifth, but he was forced out by Clark on a grounder to Ward.

In the Brooklyn half, the Trolley Dodgers added another run. Collins's short fly dropped in front of Jim O'Rourke, and Hub got a double on hard running. He took third on a wild pitch and eventually scored on Griffin's fly out.

After John Ewing opened the New York sixth by striking out, Tiernan worked Lovett for a base on balls. He was running toward second when Richarson hit a fly to short right field. While Collins was running out to catch the pop, shortstop Ward was acting as if he were getting ready for a throw to second base. Tiernan was fooled by Ward's decoy into thinking the ball had fallen in, and he was easily doubled off first.

The home team scored its final run in the sixth. O'Brien opened with a safe bounder and stole second on a throwing error by Clark. He came around on outs by Pinckney and Foutz.

Collins and O'Brien made hits and stole around to third in the seventh and eighth innings, respectively, but neither could score.

New York went out in order in each of the last three innings. The fielding feature of these frames was Daly's running catch of O'Rourke's foul right at the wall in the seventh. The hitters continued to play into Lovett's hands by trying to slug out long hits. Four of them were retired on outfield flies in the last three innings, and another went out on an infield pop. Only one man grounded out, while two others were retired by Daly on pretty catches of foul tips.

So Lovett completed his no-hit game easily. And Brooklyn showed, for one day at least, the form which had been expected of the team this season.

New York	ab	r	h	bi	o	a	e
M. Tiernan, rf	3	0	0	0	1	1	0
D. Richardson, 2b	4	0	0	0	3	2	0
G. Gore, cf	3	0	0	0	2	0	0
R. Connor, 1b	2	0	0	0	10	0	0
J. O'Rourke, 1f	3	0	0	0	0	0	0
C. Bassett, 3b	3	0	0	0	1	1	1
L. Whistler, ss	2	0	0	0	0	4	0
A. Clark, c	3	0	0	0	6	1	1
J. Ewing, p	3	0	0	0	1	3	1
	26	0	0	0	24	12	3

Brooklyn	ab	r	h	bi	o	a	e
H. Collins, 2b	4	2	2	0	2	4	0
J. Ward, ss	4	0	1	0	2	0	0
M. Griffin, cf	4	0	1	2	1	0	0
T. Burns, rf	4	0	0	0	4	0	0
D. O'Brien, 1f	4	2	3	0	1	0	0
G. Pinckney, 3b	3	0	0	0	2	1	0
D. Foutz, 1b	4	0	0	1	7	0	0
T. Daly, c	3	0	1	0	8	0	0
T. Lovett, p	3	0	0	0	0	1	0
	33	4	8	3	27	6	0

New York	000 000 000	=	0
Brooklyn	110 011 00x	=	4

	ip	h	r-er	bb	so
Ewing (L 7-3)	8	8	4-3	0	4
Lovett (W 10-7)	9	0	0-0	3	4

WP: Ewing
PB: Clark
HBP: by Ewing (Pinckney)
Umpire: J. McQuaid

Game-Winning RBI: Griffin
LOB: New York 2, Brooklyn 6
BE: Brooklyn 1
Base on Missed 3rd Strike: Brooklyn 1
DP: Collins-Foutz
2B: Collins, O'Brien
SB: Collins 2, O'Brien 3
CS: Ward, Collins
Time—1:35
Attendance—4,194

In his next game, Lovett was rocked for 15 hits and lost to the Giants, 9-2. He finished the year with a 21-20 record. Unfortunately for Brooklyn, there were no other pitchers as good. The Bridegrooms never got above .500, and they faded badly in the last six weeks of the season. They finished in sixth place with a 61-76 record.

1892 TUESDAY, JULY 19TH, AT EASTERN PARK

Flat Bat Helps Win Double Shutout

Haddock Pitches First Game and Drives in Only Run
Grooms Beat Browns Twice, 1-0 & 13-0

Today's Results			
BROOKLYN 1-St. Louis 0 (1st game)			
BROOKLYN 13-St. Louis 0 (2nd game)			
Cleveland 6-Baltimore 3 (6 innings)			
Philadelphia 7-Chicago 0			
Cincinnati 3-New York 1			
Washington 7-Louisville 6 (6 innings)			
Pittsburg 4-Boston 3			

Standings	W-L	Pct.	GB
BROOKLYN	4-0	1.000	—
Cleveland	3-1	.750	1
Cincinnati	3-1	.750	1
Philadelphia	3-1	.750	1
Washington	3-1	.750	1
Pittsburg	2-1	.667	1½
New York	1-2	.333	2½
Boston	1-3	.250	3
Baltimore	1-3	.250	3
Louisville	1-3	.250	3
St. Louis	1-3	.250	3
Chicago	0-4	.000	4

WITH PITCHER GEORGE HADDOCK USING a flat-sided bunting bat to smack the winning hit in the first game, Brooklyn today won doubleheader from St. Louis by scores of 1-0 and 13-0. The victories gave the Bridegrooms a 4-0 record in the early stages of the second half of the National League's split-season pennant race.

Haddock had held out for the first month of the season, but the Brooks were still able to finish a strong second to the Boston Beaneaters in the first-half standings. Today he showed great pitching speed and raised his 1892 record to 17 wins and 3 losses. With Haddock around for the rest of the campaign, Brooklyn player-manager John M. Ward was confident that his team would win the second-half championship and be able to defeat Boston in the post-season championship series.

Indeed, Ward's pitching was looking very strong of late. Ed Stein pitched a two-hit shutout in the second game this afternoon for his second victory in the first week of the second half. And old Dave Foutz had come out of the outfield to pitch three tough, extra-inning victories in a row at the close of the first half.

Ward's other players had almost all proven themselves to be winners in recent years. Three of the four regular infielders, all three starting outfielders, and one of the three catchers had played for pennant-winning teams within the last three seasons.

Ward and third baseman Bill Joyce were out of the lineup today due to various ailments, and their absences caused a shift of the other players. Tom Burns was brought in from the outfield to fill in for Joyce, and catcher Con Daily took Burns's position in right. Another catcher, Tom Daly, filled in for Ward at second base. T. Daly did very well, especially considering that he used his catcher's glove in the infield.

Today's victories were against a tough St. Louis team. Although the Browns finished ninth in the first half, they won a majority of games played against the top three teams, including the Bridegrooms. Indeed, today's doubleheader was made necessary by a 4-4 tie in the 14-inning thriller played on Monday.

Today's first game, which matched the 25-year-old Haddock against 36-year-old Jim Galvin in the pitching box, was a classic pitchers' duel. Each hurler allowed six hits, and in only one half inning did either side get more than one safe blow. That inning, not surprisingly, yielded the only run of the game.

Galvin, whose old-time speed left him many years ago, had good success against the home-team hitters by varying his deliveries and speeds. Haddock, on the other hand, relied mainly on his fast pitching, as usual. Each man was successful in his own way. And each was backed up by steady fielding. Only one man from each side was given a life at first by an error. And only one other error allowed a runner to advance.

The game's only run came in the fifth inning. Tom Kinslow led off by timing one of Galvin's slows and driving it to farthest center field. Anyone but the slow-footed catcher would have had a home run, but Kinslow only got as far as third base. Haddock then walked up to the plate carrying a bunting bat, i.e., one that was flat on one side. Since the strategy was obvious to all, the St. Louis infielders crept very close to the plate. Sizing up this situation, Haddock took a little uppercut swing and lofted a looper over the shortstop's head. It fell safely, and Kinslow trotted home with a run.

Haddock scattered six St. Louis hits, and Brooklyn won the game, 1-0.

In the second game, the home team pounded veteran Charlie Getzein at will and walked away with a 13-0 victory. Old Dan Brouthers was the leading hitter in the game for Brooklyn, getting two singles, a double, and a triple. He drove in three runs and scored three others. Con Daily, Tom Burns, and Tom Daly all made three hits.

By contrast, the Browns could do nothing against Stein's slants. Ed allowed hits in the first and second innings, but none thereafter. And he retired the last 14 batters in a row. The net result was a lopsided victory for the home team and a sweep of the two games.

The Bridegrooms used their big round bats to good effect in the second game. But it had taken a hit with a flat bat to win the opener.

FIRST GAME

St. Louis	ab	r	h	bi	o	a	e
J. Crooks	3	0	1	0	4	2	0
C. Carroll, 1f	4	0	1	0	1	0	0
P. Werden, 1b	4	0	1	0	8	0	0
J. Glasscock, ss	4	0	0	0	2	2	0
S. Brodie, cf	4	0	0	0	2	0	0
B. Caruthers, rf	2	0	1	0	0	0	0
G. Pinckney, 3b	4	0	2	0	0	1	1
D. Buckley, c	3	0	0	0	6	0	1
J. Galvin, p	3	0	0	0	1	2	0
	31	0	6	0	24	7	2

Brooklyn	ab	r	h	bi	o	a	e
D. Foutz, cf	3	0	1	0	1	0	0
C. Daily, rf	4	0	0	0	1	0	0
T. Corcoran, ss	4	0	1	0	4	7	0
T. Burns, 3b	4	0	0	0	0	2	1
D. Brouthers, 1b	4	0	0	0	13	0	0
D. O'Brien, 1f	4	0	0	0	3	0	0
T. Daly, 2b	2	0	1	0	3	5	0
T. Kinslow, c	3	1	2	0	2	2	0
G. Haddock, p	3	0	1	1	0	2	0
	31	1	6	1	27	18	1

St. Louis	000 000 000	= 0
Brooklyn	000 010 00x	= 1

	ip	h	r-er	bb	so
Galvin (L 9-9)	8	6	1-1	2	5
Haddock (W 17-3)	9	6	0-0	2	2

HBP: by Haddock (Crooks)
Time—1:34
Attendance—3,579

Game-Winning RBI: Haddock
LOB: St. Louis 7, Brooklyn 8
BE: St. Louis 1, Brooklyn 1
DP: Corcoran-Brouthers (Galvin)
2B: Kinslow
3B Kinslow
SB: Haddock
CS: Carroll, Buckley
Umpire: J. McQuaid

SECOND GAME

		r	h	e
St. Louis	000 000 000	0	2	4
Brooklyn	032 034 01x	13	19	1

Game-Winning Run scored on throwing error

Batteries: C. Getzein (L 5-8) & D. Buckley, B. Moran.
E. Stein (W 12-8) & T. Kinslow

After the good start in the second half, Brooklyn was unable to put together a sustained drive for the second-half pennant. But by winning 17 of the last 24 decisions, the Bridegrooms were able to finish third in the second half, 9½ games behind the Cleveland Spiders, who won out.

Brooklyn was 51-26 in the first half and 44-33 in the second.

1893 MONDAY, JUNE 12TH, AT EASTERN PARK

Brooklyn Wins 14-13 To Take 1st Place

Come From Behind Three Times to Overtake Cincinnati
Stovey's Long Hit in 9th Finally Sends the Cranks Home Happy

THE BROOKLYN TOOK POSSESSION OF first place in the National League pennant race today by defeating Cincinnati in a thriller, 14-13.

The game featured big rallies and changes in the lead. After the visiting Reds had opened the game with three runs in the first inning, the Trolley Dodgers pounded the ball for seven runs in the second and looked like sure winners. But then the Brooklyn bats fell silent for five innings, and Cincinnati regained the lead, 11-7, with a five-run rally in the seventh round. The home players finally shook themselves out of their batting slumber in the eighth inning and scored five runs to go on top, 12-11. Cincinnati was not through yet, however. Their pitcher, Tony Mullane, smacked a two-run home run, and the Reds led again. But the home team had chosen last bats, and the Brooks made good with two runs of their own in the bottom of the ninth to win the game, 14-13.

Today's Results

BROOKLYN 14-Cincinnati 13
Boston 7-Pittsburg 4
St. Louis 3-Philadephia 2
Cleveland 13-Baltimore 12
New York 13-Louisville 3
Washington 7-Chicago 6

Standings	W-L	Pct.	GB
BROOKLYN	23-14	.622	—
Boston	24-15	.615	—
Pittsburg	23-15	.605	½
Philadelphia	21-16	.568	2
Cleveland	17-14	.548	3½
New York	20-18	.526	4
Baltimore	20-18	.526	4
Washington	18-19	.486	5½
St. Louis	15-20	.429	7½
Cincinnati	16-22	.421	8
Chicago	15-21	.417	8
Louisville	4-24	.143	15

Each captain had replaced his pitcher in the ninth inning, but the relievers, Mike Sullivan for Cincinnati and Bill Kennedy for Brooklyn, were not effective, each giving up two runs.

The triumph was the sixth in a row for the Trolley Dodgers, and it moved them past Pittsburg and into a clear lead in the race.

The veteran Mullane essayed to pitch for captain Charlie Comiskey's Reds. He was hit hard in two innings, the second and the eighth, but was effective in the other rounds. He hit a home run to put his team ahead in the ninth inning, but the exertion of rounding the bases at top speed was such that Comiskey took him out of the game when Brooklyn came to bat. The Dodgers then batted out victory against Sullivan.

George Haddock pitched for the home team, but he was adversely affected by a lingering leg injury, which hurt his control. He walked seven men and added a wild pitch. After he had scored a run in the home half of the eighth, he was replace in the box by "Brickyard" Bill Kennedy. The new pitcher was touched for a double and Mullane's homer in the ninth. But he then contributed a key hit in the bottom of the ninth, driving home the tying run and eventually scoring the winning run himself.

Haddock began the game by sending the first two visiting batters to first base on balls. When he finally got the ball over the plate, Bug Holliday ripped it past the third baseman for a hit, loading the bases. One batter popped out, but Jimmy Canavan sent the first two runs of the day home with a clean hit. Another walk and a bad error by shortstop Tommy Corcoran sent another man home. The side was then retired on a quick double play from third to home to first. After Brooklyn went out without a hit in the bottom of the first, it looked like Cincinnati's game easily.

But the home team put together a long strong of hits in the second inning to earn a 7-3 lead. A bad bounce helped their cause in the early stages of the rally after a leadoff hitter had walked. The next two men went out, then six batters in a row hit safely. Harry Stovey (with a triple) and George Shoch (with a double) got the biggest blows.

Cincinnati was able to cut into the Brooklyn lead. In the third inning they scored once and in the fourth they counted twice to cut their deficit to 7-6.

In the seventh inning, Cincinnati apparently broke the game open with five runs. Once again, a walk started things off. Four singles, a fielders choice, and two stolen bases followed, giving the Reds an 11-7 advantage.

There was one out in the home eighth when Haddock got his second hit of the day. Mullane then took up the free-pass game by walking Dave Foutz and Stovey to load the bases. Big Dan Brouthers shot a long drive between the outfielders, and the hometown cranks suddenly came to life. Three runners scored, but the lumbering Brouthers could only make third. Tom Kinslow came to the rescue with another shot past center fielder Holliday, and this one rolled so far that the turtle-paced Kinslow was able to score a home run, giving Brooklyn the lead.

With a one-run lead and one inning to go, Kennedy was inserted into Haddock's place. With one out, Morgan Murphy jumped on a pitch for a double. Mullane then astonished all observers by sending a tremendous drive to left center for a home run.

Cincinnati was now in the lead, and the Brooklyn partisans and club president Byrne were beside themselves with dismay.

But Brooklyn, like Cincinnati, got a chance to hit against a new pitcher in the ninth. The Reds' hurler, Sullivan, quickly sent Danny Richardson to first on balls. Corcoran sacrificed him to second. Kennedy bounced a hit to left, and Richardson raced home with a tying run. Kennedy further redeemed himself for his poor pitching by stealing second. He advanced to third on an infield out. Harry Stovey then smashed a drive to the outer reaches of the outfield, and Kennedy loped home with the winning run.

The crowd was ecstatic, for not only had their team won the most exciting game of the year, it had moved into first place in the pennant race. And the biggest smile of all was on the face of Charlie Byrne.

Cincinnati	ab	r	h	bi	o	a	e
A. Latham, 3b	5	1	2	2	1	2	1
B. McPhee, 2b	3	2	0	0	7	4	0
B. Holliday, cf	4	3	2	0	2	0	0
F. Vaughn, lf	5	1	2	0	3	0	0
J. Canavan, rf	4	2	3	2	1	0	0
C. Comiskey, 1b	4	0	1	1	9	0	0
G. Smith, ss	5	1	1	3	1	3	1
M. Murphy, c	5	2	1	0	2	0	0
T. Mullane, p	5	1	1	2	0	2	0
M. Sullivan, p9	0	0	0	0	0	1	0
	40	13	13	10	26	12	2

Brooklyn	ab	r	h	bi	o	a	e
D. Foutz, cf	5	2	2	0	2	0	1
H. Stovey, 1f	5	2	2	3	5	0	0
D. Brouthers, 1b	4	2	3	4	9	0	0
T. Kinslow, c	5	2	2	3	4	2	0
G. Shoch, 3b	4	1	1	1	2	4	0
T. Burns, rf	5	1	2	0	1	1	1
D. Richardson, 2b	3	1	0	0	2	1	0
T. Corcoran, ss	5	0	0	0	1	2	1
G. Haddock, p	4	2	2	2	1	0	0
B. Kennedy, p9	1	1	1	1	0	0	0
	41	14	15	14	27	10	3

Cincinnati	301 200 502	= 13
Brooklyn	070 000 052	= 14

two out when winning run scored

	ip	h	r-er	bb	so
Mullane	8	13	12-12	5	2
Sullivan (L 0-2)	⅔	2	2-2	1	0
Haddock (W 3-5)	8	11	11-8	7	0
Kennedy	1	2	2-2	0	2

WP: Haddock, Mullane
Time—2:00 Attendance—3,000
Umpire: B. Emslie

Game-Winning RBI: Stovey
LOB: Cincinnati 7, Brooklyn 7
BE: Cincinnati 1, Brooklyn 2
DP: Shoch-Kinslow-Brouthers (Murphy)
McPhee-Comisky (Corcoran)
Latham-McPhee-Comiskey (Burns)
Burns-Brouthers
2B: Brouthers, Shoch, Foutz, Murphy
3B: Stovey, Brouthers
HR: Kinslow, Mullane
SB: Latham, Canavan, McPhee, Comiskey, Vaughn, Smith, Murphy, Foutz, Kennedy

The Bridegrooms were tied for first place as late as the end of June. But they lost 15 of their first 16 decisions in July to drop out of the race.

Poor offense was the biggest reason for the team's failure. Whereas every other club in the league showed a big increase in runs scored per game in 1893 because of the lengthening of the pitching distance to 60½ feet, Brooklyn's offensive output remained practically unchanged.

The Bridegrooms finished exactly in the middle of the league: tied for sixth place. Their record was 65-63.

1894 SATURDAY, AUGUST 11TH, AT EASTERN PARK

Home Run in Ninth Wins Seesaw Game

Lead Changes Hands Six Times
LaChance's Homer Defeats Beaneaters, 11-10

THE BRIDEGROOMS OF BROOKLYN DEfeated the defending-champion Beaneaters of Boston in a thrilling 11-10 game at Eastern Park today. The lead changed hands in the game six times, and on two other occasions the score was tied but the team that had been ahead regained the advantage. Boston tied the game for the final time with two runs in the first half of the ninth inning. Then Brooklyn came to bat and won on a dramatic home run by George "Candy" LaChance.

The game also marked the debut of Brooklyn's newest pitcher, Con Lucid. He hurled a credible game against the high-powered champs, allowing thirteen hits. He gave five bases on balls, hit one batter, and made a costly error. He also hit a key double in the game. In all, it was not too bad a showing in his first game since Brooklyn signed him from the Haverhill minor league club.

Today's Results

BROOKLYN 11-Boston 10
Baltimore 20-New York 1
Cleveland 11-Chicago 9
Pittsburg 3- Louisville 2
Philadelphia 10-Washington 7 (1st game)
Philadelphia 16-Washington 4 (7 inn.)(2nd)
Cincinnati 7-St. Louis 6

Standings	**W-L**	**Pct.**	**GB**
Boston	59-32	.648	—
Baltimore	57-32	.640	1
New York	55-36	.604	4
Cleveland	51-37	.580	6½
Pittsburg	50-42	.543	9½
Philadelphia	46-41	.529	11
BROOKLYN	47-44	.516	12
Cincinnati	42-48	.467	16½
Chicago	41-50	.451	18
St. Louis	38-55	.409	22
Louisville	31-61	.337	28½
Washington	27-66	.290	33

Both Lucid and Boston pitcher Jack Stivetts were somewhat handicapped by the erratic work of umpire John Gaffney, who was off in his calling of balls and strikes. At least he did not favor either side.

An enthusiastic crowd of over 6,000 enjoyed the game, especially the thrilling finish. After LaChance had crossed the plate with his home run, he was surrounded by admiring cranks who slapped his back all the way to the clubhouse. Lucid made the same journey escorted by a covey of admirers.

Brooklyn scored the game's first run in the bottom of the first inning. Mike Griffin opened with a three-base hit to left. Tommy Corcoran followed with a grounder that was fumbled, and Griffin scored.

Boston came in and took a 2-1 lead in the second. Tommy Tucker began with a scratch hit and a stolen base. The crowd cheered when Lucid struck out Billy Nash. But it moaned when Jimmy Bannon and Charley Ganzel followed with long hits to drive in runs.

There was no more scoring until the fifth inning.

In the Boston fifth, the Beaneaters were held scoreless with the aid of a controversial decision by the umpire. Frank Connaughton doubled with one out, and Fred Tenney strolled behind him. Tommy McCarthy hit a double-play ball to shortstop Corcoran. He fielded it and threw to Tom Daly for a force at second base. Daly pivoted to throw to first, but Tenney ran into him in such away as to prevent a throw. Ump Gaffney ruled this to be interference and declared McCarthy out at first. The Brooklyn partisans loved the ruling, while the Beaneaters were inspired to argue at length.

Buoyed by the decision, the Trolley Dodgers came to bat and took the lead with two runs. Two walks, a hit by Corcoran that was fumbled by the center fielder, and a throwing error on a double steal gave Brooklyn its tallies.

Boston got two in the sixth to regain the advantage, 4-3. Tucker, Bannon, and Stivetts singled around a pass to Nash.

By good running, Daly got Brooklyn a run in its half to tie. He beat out a bunt, stole second and continued to third on a wild throw, and came home on a wild pitch.

Boston got two more in the seventh for a 6-4 margin. Tucker's three-bagger drove in Tenney, who had walked. Tucker then scored on a fumble by Lucid.

As was the pattern of the day, the home team stormed back into the lead with three tallies in its half. Corcoran hit, stole, and scored on a hit by George Treadway. George Shoch tripled a run home and tallied himself of a bingle by Daly.

Boston bounced back on top in the eighth, 8-7, on a two-run home run by Tenney. He hit a ball that rolled under the right field fence as was lost.

The Grooms responded in kind, counting three runs in their eighth. Lucid started the rally with a two-out double. Griffin singled him home. Corcoran hit safely to left, and Griffin scored when outfielder McCarthy threw wildly past third base. Corcoran also kept running for home, and he counted when catcher Ganzel, who had chased the ball down, threw it over the pitcher's head at home.

Boston came up in the ninth trailing 10-8. The first batter, Tucker, was hit in the back by a pitch. Nash grounded out to third. Bannon hit safely to left and outraced the throw to second, while Tucker scored. Bannon boldly stole third and came home on a long fly out by Ganzel, tying the game at 10-10.

Billy Shindle, batting first for the home team, opened the ninth by fouling out. Up stepped LaChance. He had had one hit, one base on balls, and two strike outs in his previous appearances. This time he caught the ball with the thick part of the bat and sent it exactly halfway between the left and center fielders. He propelled his legs around the bases as McCarthy was running the ball down. The throw toward the infield was just being made as LaChance rounded third, and it seemed a sure home run. But the big first baseman was running out of steam, and he stumbed and fell about six feet from home. As he rolled and crawled to the pan, the catcher got the relay. But LaChance touched the rubber just before the tag could be applied, and Gaffney called him safe with the winning run.

Before the exhausted hero had any opportunity to regain his composure, he was surrounded by adoring fans and teammates and swept to the dressing room in glory. It had been quite a game, and LaChance had ended it with quite a flourish.

Boston	ab	r	h	bi	o	a	e
B. Lowe, 2b	4	0	0	0	2	3	0
F. Connaughton, ss	5	0	1	0	1	2	1
F. Tenney, cf	3	2	2	2	0	0	1
T. McCarthy, 1f	5	0	0	0	1	0	1
T. Tucker, 1b	4	4	3	1	10	3	0
B. Nash, 3b	3	1	0	0	0	1	2
J. Bannon, rf	5	2	3	3	2	0	1
C. Ganzel, c	5	0	2	3	6	2	3
J. Stivetts, p	5	1	2	0	3	2	0
	39	10	13	9	25	13	9

Brooklyn	ab	r	h	bi	o	a	e
M. Griffin, cf	4	3	2	1	1	0	0
T. Corcoran, ss	5	2	3	0	1	6	0
G. Treadway, 1f	4	1	1	1	3	0	0
G. Shoch, rf	5	1	2	1	2	0	1
T. Daly, 2b	5	1	2	1	7	3	0
T. Kinslow, c	5	0	1	0	1	0	0
B. Shindle, 3b	4	0	0	0	0	4	0
G. LaChance, 1b	4	2	2	1	10	0	0
C. Lucid, p	4	1	1	0	1	0	1
	40	11	14	5	*26	13	2

*McCarthy declared out on Tenney's interference

Boston	020 002 222	=	10
Brooklyn	100 021 331	=	11

one out when winning run scored

	ip	h	r-er	bb	so
Stivetts (L 18-10)	8⅓	14	11-5	4	5
Lucid (W 1-0)	9	13	10-9	5	1

WP: Stivetts, Lucid
HBP: by Lucid (Tucker)
Time—2:35 Attendance—6,256
Umpire: J. Gaffney

Game-Winning RBI: LaChance
LOB: Boston 8, Brooklyn 8
BE: Boston 1, Brooklyn 3
DP: Corcoran-Daly-LaChance (Stivetts)
2B: Ganzel, Tenney, Connaughton, Lucid, Bannon
3B: Griffin, Bannon, Tucker, Shoch
HR: Tenney, LaChance
SB: Tucker 2, LaChance, Daly 3, Nash, Corcoran, Bannon
CS: Shindle, Corcoran

LaChance hit five home runs in 1894 and totaled 39 in 12 years in the majors.

Lucid posted a 5-3 record for the season with Brooklyn.

The Bridegrooms pushed their way into fifth place in late August and finished there with a 70-61 record.

1895 WEDNESDAY, JUNE 26TH, AT EASTERN PARK

13-Inning Duel Goes to Dodgers 1-0

Ed Stein Pitches 5-Hitter and Scores Winning Run
Anderson's Mental Lapse Gives Victors Their Run

BREAKING THE TREND OF RECENT YEARS, Brooklyn and Washington gave the cranks at Eastern Park a rare treat by staging a red-hot pitchers' battle. It took until the 13th inning for either team to get a run across the pan. Brooklyn finally scored when Varney Anderson, the Washington pitcher, cut off a throw to the plate as the winning run was trying to score.

Today's Results

BROOKLYN 1-Washington 0 (13 innings)
Boston 15-Philadelphia 5
Baltimore 5-New York 2
Chicago 6-Pittsburg 2
Cincinnati 12-St. Louis 5
Louisville at Cleveland, ppd., rain

Standings	W-L	Pct.	GB
Boston	32-17	.653	—
Baltimore	28-19	.596	3
Chicago	33-23	.589	2½
Cleveland	31-22	.585	3
Pittsburg	31-22	.585	3
Cincinnati	27-23	.540	5½
BROOKLYN	27-24	.529	6
Philadelphia	27-24	.529	6
New York	26-26	.500	7½
Washington	21-29	.420	11½
St. Louis	17-36	.321	17
Louisville	7-42	.143	25

That was Anderson's only bad mistake of the day, but it was fatal. By battling through twelve scoreless innings, Anderson and Brooklyn's Ed Stein engaged in the longest 0-0 duel in the National League in over three years. Since the pitcher's box was replaced by the pitcher's plate (or rubber) and the pitching distance was increased to 60½ feet in 1893, the hitters had dominated the league, and 1-0 games became a rarity.

Neither the Trolley Dodgers nor the Senators were ranked among the best hitting teams in the league. But then again, neither were Stein nor Anderson ranked among the top pitchers in the league this year. Today, however, both pitched gilt-edged ball and were loudly applauded by the crowd. Stein used mostly his fastball to hold the Washington bats at bay. He won his third straight game after losing his first six decisions this season. Anderson relied on a deadly slow ball to frustrate the Bridegrooms inning after inning. Both pitchers got splendid fielding support, with Brooklyn shortstop Tommy Corcoran being especially brilliant.

There was only one hit in the first three innings. That was a single in the first by George LaChance of Brooklyn. A dubious call by umpire Bob Emslie in the third helped keep the Senators off base. Batting with two out, Anderson hit a sharp grounder to second base, where Tom Daly juggled the ball before throwing. First baseman LaChance let the ball slip out of his grasp, but Emslie somehow ruled the batter out. Even the Brooklyn partisans razzed the ump for the call.

The first Washington hit came with one out in the fourth when Bill Joyce beat out an infield safety. Moments later, he was caught napping off first base, much to the delight of the crowd.

Brooklyn got another hit in the fifth round. Bill Shindle led off with a soft pop that fell safely in short left field. He was left on second base.

The first man to reach third was Washington's Kip Selbach, who smashed a long triple over the center fielder's head with two out in the sixth. Stein fell behind Joyce, three balls and one strike, before Bill fanned with two mightly swings. The cranks jeered the batter loudly for his efforts.

Brooklyn wasted a walk in the bottom of the sixth.

In the home half of the seventh, George Treadway bunted and reached first safely with a great slide past first baseman Ed Cartwright. Treadway was later caught stealing.

Jack Crooks of the Senators got a hit in the eighth, but he was thrown out trying to steal as well. In the same round, Charlie Abbey walked and was left on.

Tom Burns hit safely in the Brooklyn half but was stranded on second.

Joyce's safe bunt in the ninth was likewise wasted.

Crooks singled with two down in the tenth but was again nabbed trying to pilfer second. Shindle opened the Brooklyn tenth with a hit and stole second with two out only to be left there.

Three good infield plays retired the Washingtons in the eleventh, although Selbach reached first base on balls. For Brooklyn, Griffin was given first on a fumble by shortstop Jack Glasscock. But Bill Hassamaer made two brilliant catches in right field to rob Corcoran and LaChance of extra bases and save the game for Washington.

A hit, a sacrifice, and an intentional pass with two outs put two Brooklyn runners on base for the first time in the game in the twelfth. But Con Daily ended the inning with a fly out to left.

The Senators again got a man to third in the top of the thirteenth. Cartwright walked to lead off. Crooks's sacrifice bunt and Abbey's ground out put him on the far corner. Anderson then made a bid to win his own game with a looper in back of third. The left fielder and the third baseman had no chance to get it, but shortstop Corcoran angled over and made a desperate stab to catch the ball just before it fell to earth. The run-saving play elicited loud applause from the gallery.

Stein also got a fine hand when he came to bat to open the bottom of the thirteenth. He responded with a solid hit to center. Griffin's safe hit to right sent him to second. Corcoran then pushed a pretty baser to right, and Stein raced around third. The throw from Hassamaer was cut off by Anderson, who seemed to have a fine chance of catching Stein at the plate. But Corcoran rounded first, and Anderson stupidly threw the ball to second base. The surprised second baseman dropped the throw, but it made no difference since Stein had scored the run which won the game.

Anderson quickly realized his mistake and gave a wounded look to the heavens. All that great pitching ruined by an instant of bad headwork! His teammates shared his chagrin. But the Brooklyn cranks left the ground with their heads held high. It had been one of the few great pitching duels in recent years, and their team had emerged victorious.

Washington	ab	r	h	bi	o	a	e
K. Selbach, 1f	4	0	1	0	3	0	0
B. Joyce, 3b	5	0	2	0	2	5	0
B. Hassamaer, rf	4	0	0	0	4	0	0
J. Glasscock, ss	5	0	0	0	0	2	1
J. McGuire, c	5	0	0	0	5	1	0
E. Cartwright, 1b	4	0	0	0	17	1	0
J. Crooks, 2b	4	0	2	0	1	5	0
C. Abbey, cf	4	0	0	0	1	0	0
V. Anderson, p	5	0	0	0	2	1	0
	40	0	5	0	*35	15	1

*LaChance out for running out of base line

Brooklyn	ab	r	h	bi	o	a	e
M. Griffin, cf	5	0	1	0	3	0	0
T. Corcoran, ss	6	0	1	1	4	4	0
G. LaChance, 1b	5	0	1	0	22	0	0
G. Treadway, rf	5	0	2	0	0	0	0
B. Shindle, 3b	4	0	2	0	2	5	0
T. Daly, 2b	5	0	0	0	4	7	0
T. Burns, 1f	4	0	1	0	1	0	0
C. Daily, c	4	0	0	0	3	2	0
E. Stein, p	5	1	1	0	0	3	0
	43	1	9	1	39	21	0

Washington	000 000 000 000 0	= 0
Brooklyn	000 000 000 000 1	= 1

none out when winning run scored

	ip	h	r-er	bb	so
Anderson (L 3-1)	†12	9	1-1	2	4
Stein (W 3-6)	13	5	0-0	4	1

†faced three batters in thirteenth

Umpire: B. Emslie

Game-Winning RBI: Corcoran
LOB: Washington 6, Brooklyn 10
BE: Brooklyn 1
3B: Selbach
SH: Crooks, Shindle, Daily
SB: Shindle 2
CS: Treadway, Crooks 2
Picked off: Joyce
Time—2:23 Attendance—1,700

Stein pitched well for most of the rest of the year and finished with a 15-13 record. Still, that was a disappointment after he had averaged 24 wins in the previous three seasons.

Overall, the Brooklyn pitching was below average, as was the team's hitting. But the fielding was good enough to keep the Bridegrooms in the middle of the league. A good spurt in late August got Brooklyn as high as fourth place. The team finished tied for fifth with a 71-60 record.

1896 THURSDAY, AUGUST 6TH, AT EASTERN PARK

Brooks Trail 10-0, Then Win 11-10

Rally in Last 5 Innings Against Taylor & Phillies
George Harper Pitches Great Ball in Relief

IN AN UNPRECEDENTED COMEBACK, THE Brooklyn National League team today rallied from a 10-0 deficit to defeat the Philadelphia team, 11-10. The Phillies pounded two Brooklyn pitchers for ten runs and sixteen hits in the first five innings. Then they were held hitless for the last four innings by the third Brooklyn hurler, George Harper. The Philadelphia pitcher, Jack Taylor, retired the Bridegrooms without a hit through the first three innings and allowed only one scratch hit in the fourth. Then he fell apart, and the home team knocked out fourteen hits and eleven runs in the final five frames to win the game.

Today's Results			
BROOKLYN 11-Philadelphia 10			
Baltimore 9-New York 6			
Cincinnati 4-Pittsburg 2			
Chicago 5-St. Louis 3 (5 innings)			
Boston 1-Washington 0			
no other game scheduled			
Standings	**W-L**	**Pct.**	**GB**
Baltimore	59-27	.686	—
Cincinnati	63-29	.685	(+1)
Cleveland	57-31	.648	3
Chicago	54-40	.574	9
Boston	48-39	.552	11½
Pittsburg	49-40	.551	11½
BROOKLYN	41-47	.466	19
Philadelphia	39-49	.443	21
New York	36-52	.409	24
Washington	34-51	.400	24½
St. Louis	28-61	.315	32½
Louisville	22-64	.256	37

The comeback led the cranks, especially those in the bleachers, to throw propriety out the window. They had become a bunch of raving fanatics by the end of the contest, shouting everything they could think of to rattle poor Taylor and to inspire the home team. When the victory was finally achieved, the spectators regained their proper manners. Still, they were quite animated with the wonder of it all, and enthusiastic recollections of fine plays and hard hits filled the air as the throng skipped across the train tracks and headed for the streetcars and for home.

At the beginning of the game, the only solace for the cranks was the pleasant breeze which cooled the heat of the sun. Down on the field, the visitors provided all the hot stuff in the early going.

The Phillies opened right up with four runs in the first inning. Duff Cooley led off with a safe hit to center field. Pitcher Bert Abbey gave Bill Hulen a base on balls. Sam Mertes sacrificed the runners along. And Ed Delahanty drove them home with a double to left center. Sam Thompson plated Delahanty with a one-baser to right. Bill Hallman and Lave Cross added singles to score Thompson.

Abbey was dismissed after the first inning, and Danny Daub took over the pitching duties at the start of the second. Thanks to good support, he shut the Phillies out for three innings. Catcher Jack Grim did the best work by throwing out two men trying to steal.

Taylor, meanwhile, had set the Trolley Dodgers down in order through the first three innings. Mike Griffin broke the string with a bloop hit to open the fourth, but he was left on base.

The Phillies finally broke through against Daub in a big way in the fifth, scoring six times. After Delahanty opened with a ground out, Thompson, Hallman, and Jack Clements all hit safely, bringing the first two runs in. A force play on Cross's bouncer provided the second out. But the third out was a long time coming. Taylor kept the inning going with a hit, and Cooley's single scored Cross. Daub passed Hulen to load the bases for Mertes. "Sandow" Sam smacked a two-run single to left. Delahanty followed with a one-run hit to the same garden, and the score was 10-0. Thompson flied out to end the inning.

At this point the game seemed assuredly lost to Brooklyn. But Dave Foutz's men did not give up. George LaChance got them going with an infield hit with one gone in the bottom of the fifth. George Shoch made the second out. But Grim singled, and the runners moved to second and third on a fumble in the outfield. Daub drove them both in with a hit to right. A force out ended the inning with the Grooms trailing 10-2.

Manager Foutz decided that this would be a good chance to see his new pitcher Harper work. George had been recently recalled from Scranton and had been waiting for a spot to pitch in. He responded to his chance today with a brilliant performance, allowing no hits and only one base on balls in four innings.

While Harper was cooling the Philly bats, the Brooklyn sticks began to warm up. Two more runs were scored in the sixth on four hits and two errors. Harper, however, ended the rally by flying out with the bases loaded.

When the Dodgers scored three more times in the seventh, the cranks began to believe that the game could be won. Griffin opened this round with a hot shot through third. Bill Shindle dropped a triple down the right field line and scored on a throwing error by Cross. John Anderson and LaChance then singled to bring another run home.

The Grooms pulled to within one run with two more tallies in the eighth. Griffin was on base with a one-out walk when Shindle duplicated his triple of the previous inning with another shot to the same spot. Shindle scored as Fielder Jones bounced out.

Brooklyn needed only one to tie and two to win when the team came to bat in the ninth. Anderson opened with a long drive off the wall in left field for three bases. By now the cranks were all screaming, and the game seemed as good as won. LaChance put a slight damper on the crowd by fouling out to the catcher. But Shoch started the raving again with a clean hit to right to send home the tying run. The noise continued as Shoch stole second and Grim was hit by a pitch. Harper hit a difficult grounder to short, and Hulen threw wildly to load the bases. Taylor kicked the dirt on the mound furiously and muttered under his breath. Captain Mike Griffin stepped to the pan, and the crowd screeched in anticipation. Mike lifted a long fly to left, which allowed Shoch to score after the catch, and the game was won!

The rejoicing by the Brooklyn fans was as great as anything seen since the glory days of '89. From ten runs behind, their Dodgers had come back to win.

Philadelphia	ab	r	h	bi	o	a	e
D. Cooley, 1f	4	2	3	1	2	0	0
B. Hulen, ss	3	2	1	0	3	9	3
S. Mertes, cf	4	0	2	2	1	0	1
E. Delahanty, 1b	5	1	2	3	15	0	0
S. Thompson, rf	5	2	2	1	1	0	0
B. Hallman, 2b	5	1	3	0	0	4	0
J. Clements, c	5	0	1	2	2	0	0
L. Cross, 3b	5	1	1	1	2	1	2
J. Taylor, p	4	1	1	0	0	3	0
	40	10	16	10	26	17	6

Brooklyn	ab	r	h	bi	o	a	e
M. Griffin, cf	5	2	2	1	5	0	0
B. Shindle, 3b	5	2	2	2	1	4	0
F. Jones, rf	5	1	1	1	1	0	0
T. Corcoran, ss	5	1	0	0	1	5	0
J. Anderson, 1f	5	2	2	0	1	0	0
G. LaChance, 1b	5	1	3	2	10	1	1
G. Shoch, 3b	5	1	2	1	2	1	0
J. Grim, c	4	1	2	0	5	2	0
B. Abbey, p	0	0	0	0	0	0	0
D. Daub, p2	2	0	1	2	1	0	0
G. Harper, p6	3	0	0	0	0	1	0
	44	11	15	9	27	14	1

Philadelphia	400 060 000	= 10
Brooklyn	000 022 322	= 11

two out when winning run scored

	ip	h	r-er	bb	so
Taylor (L 16-13)	8⅔	15	11-5	1	1
Abbey	1	5	4-4	1	1
Daub	4	11	6-6	1	1
Harper (W 2-6)	4	0	0-0	1	2

HBP: by Taylor (Grim)

Game-Winning RBI: Griffin
LOB: Philadelphia 8, Brooklyn 9
BE: Philadelphia 1, Brooklyn 3
2B: Delahanty
3B: Shindle 2, Anderson
SH: Mertes, Cooley
SB: Mertes, Shoch
CS: Hulen, Cooley
Time—2:00 Attendance—1,200
Umpire: T. Hurst

Brooklyn stayed ahead of Philadelphia and New York for most of August, then collapsed in September and barely avoided a tenth place finish. By winning 13-10 on the final day of the season, the Bridegrooms were able to tie the Senators for ninth. Their record was 58-73, the club's worst season since 1884.

1897 SATURDAY, JULY 31ST, AT EASTERN PARK

Kennedy Throws the Ball at the Umpire

That Cost Brooklyn a Run, and the Dodgers Lose 4-3
O'Day's Decision Aids Giants in 4-Run Rally in 9th

UMPIRE HANK O'DAY MADE HIMSELF SO unpopular with the Brooklyn players today that the pitcher, Bill Kennedy, threw the ball at the arbiter's backside as he was bending to brush off the plate. The incident occurred in the ninth inning of the game, just after the visiting New York Giants had scored three runs to take the lead. Kennedy's heave missed its target, and the error allowed another run to score. When the Trolley Dodgers came up with one run in the bottom of the ninth, the run that scored on Kennedy's throw turned out to be decisive.

Today's Results

New York 4-BROOKLYN 3
Boston 7-Washington 6
Baltimore 8-Philadelphia 2
Cleveland 6-Cincinnati 3
Louisville 11-St. Louis 6 (1st game)
St. Louis 7-Louisville 6 (8 inn.)(2nd)
Chicago 7-Pittsburg 6

Standings	W-L	Pct.	GB
Boston	56-24	.700	—
Baltimore	52-26	.667	3
Cincinnati	50-27	.649	4½
New York	47-31	.603	8
Cleveland	44-35	.557	11½
Philadelphia	40-44	.476	18
Pittsburg	37-43	.462	19
Chicago	37-47	.440	21
Louisville	36-48	.429	22
BROOKLYN	34-46	.425	22
Washington	29-50	.367	26½
St. Louis	21-62	.253	36½

O'Day had materially aided the New York rally by calling a man safe at first even though he appeared to have been beaten by the throw. The go-ahead run then scored on a fly out that otherwise would have ended the inning. Kennedy lost his temper at this point and tried to make the ump pay. When Kennedy's throw went to the backstop, the runner who had been safe on the controversial call scored from second base.

Here is how the ninth inning went in detail. Jouett Meekin opened the inning with a clean single to center, only the fourth hit of the day against Kennedy. George Van Haltren kept fouling pitches off until Kennedy finally came over with a fat one. Van Haltren knocked it into center field for another hit, sending Meekin to third. This brought a roar from the New York fans in attendance. Mike Tiernan hit a hard bounder down to first baseman George LaChance, who could not stop it. Second baseman George Shoch got it, however, but Kennedy failed to cover first and Tiernan got a hit. Meekin scored on the play. The Giants' partisans, who had come across the river in force, increased their cheering to a deafening level. They were so loud that umpire O'Day could not make himself heard, and he had to indicate the count of balls and strikes by holding up the proper number of fingers. Bill Joyce sacrificed to the first baseman, moving the runners to second and third.

Then came the fateful call. George Davis hit one back to the box. Kennedy deflected it to shortstop George Smith, who fumbled, recovered, and threw to first. The play was close, though even some of the New York sportswriters thought Davis was out. O'Day, however, called him safe. Immediately the entire Brooklyn squad surrounded the umpire and reviled him for his decision. Safe or out, the tying run had scored on the play. But the situation was now men on first and third and one out, instead of just a man on third with two out. The argument lasted until O'Day threatened to forfeit the game to New York if the Dodgers did not return to their positions.

When play resumed, Kid Gleason delivered a long fly to the bicycle track in right field. Fielder Jones made a magnificent catch and a strong throw to second. But Davis slid safely into second as Tiernan was crossing the plate with the run that put New York ahead.

Rattled by this turn of events and by the screaming of the Giant fans, the home team's battery could no longer control its anger. Catcher John Grim began arguing stridently with O'Day, while "Roaring Bill" Kennedy was fuming on the mound.

Finally O'Day dismissed Grim's entreaties and picked up the broom to sweep off the plate. When O'Day's back was turned to the pitcher, the distraught Kennedy could not resist the inviting target, and he let fly with a fastball. It missed the umpire by an inch and went to the backstop. Kennedy later alibied that he had seen a runner break from third to home, and he threw to head him off. But the only Giant near third base was Van Haltren, who had gone to the coaching line after scoring on Gleason's fly. As it happened, Van Haltren did notice the wild throw home, got Davis's attention at second base, and nearly dragged him around third to score. Davis crossed the plate before catcher Grim was aware that the ball was past him.

This further incited the New Yorkers in the stands, and it caused more complaining by the Brooklyn manager, Bill Barnie. Captain Mike Griffin came all the way in from the outfield to try and argue that Davis should be sent back to second. But O'Day would have none of it, and New York now led 4-2.

The Trolley Dodgers made a game effort to tie the score in the bottom of the ninth. Grim opened with a long two-bagger to left, bringing a cheer from the Brooklyn half of the crowd. But the next two men went out. Griffin kept his team's hopes alive with a single to center, scoring Grim. Jones followed with a drive to deep center field. For a moment it looked like a home run to win the game. But Van Haltren raced back and caught the ball for the final out.

The Giants had won, but the Bridegrooms were inclined to credit the umpire with defeating them. Manager Barnie kept haggling with O'Day all the way to the dressing room, where the beleaguered umpire was finally able to escape the whining.

Up until the eventful ninth, the game was marked by fine pitching and great fielding. Only eight hits were made in the first eight innings. Five errors were also made, but these were offset by five fancy double plays. Brooklyn right fielder Jones started two of the twin killings with great catches. And New York shortstop Davis started the other three on ground balls.

Brooklyn's first run came in the first inning. Griffin and Jones opened with singles and John Anderson walked to load the bases. Griffin then scored on the first twin-killing of the game. In the fourth inning, Brooklyn added another tally on a walk to Shoch, a hit by Grim, and a force out by Kennedy. That was all the scoring until the last inning.

Then the game was decided by controversy and an ill-tempered and ill-advised attempt to injure the umpire with the baseball. It was not a game for Kennedy and the Trolley Dodgers to be proud of.

New York	ab	r	h	bi	o	a	e
G. Van Haltren, cf	4	1	1	0	2	0	0
M. Tiernan, rf	4	1	1	1	2	0	0
B. Joyce, 3b	3	0	1	0	2	2	1
G. Davis, ss	4	1	1	1	4	8	0
K. Gleason, 2b	4	0	0	1	1	2	0
D. Holmes, 1f	4	0	0	0	0	0	0
W. Clark, 1b	3	0	0	0	11	1	2
J. Warner, c	3	0	0	0	5	1	0
J. Meekin, p	3	1	2	0	0	2	0
	32	4	6	3	27	16	3

Brooklyn	ab	r	h	bi	o	a	e
M. Griffin, cf	4	1	2	1	3	0	0
F. Jones, rf	4	0	1	0	4	2	0
J. Anderson, 1f	3	0	0	0	0	0	1
B. Shindle, 3b	3	0	0	0	0	0	0
G. LaChance, 1b	4	0	0	0	17	2	0
G. Shoch, 2b	3	1	0	0	1	6	0
J. Grim, c	4	1	2	0	1	0	0
B. Kennedy, p	4	0	1	1	1	4	1
G. Smith, ss	3	0	1	0	0	0	1
	32	3	7	2	27	14	3

New York	000	000	004	=	4
Brooklyn	100	100	001	=	3

	ip	h	r-er	bb	so
Meekin (W 12-6)	9	7	3-3	3	1
Kennedy (L 13-15)	9	6	4-2	0	1

HBP: by Meekin (Shindle)

Time—2:05
Attendance—11,197
Umpire: H. O'Day

Game-Winning RBI: Gleason
LOB: NY 2, Bkn 8
BE: NY 3, Bkn 3
DP: Davis-Clark (Shindle)
Jones-Grim
Davis-Clark-Warner-Joyce
Jones-LaChance
Davis-Clark (Anderson)
2B: Grim
SH: Jones, Griffin, Joyce
SB: Davis

Despite lackluster pitching and a nine-game losing streak in mid-August, the Trolley Dodgers managed to finish tied for sixth. Their final record was 61-71.

1898 FRIDAY, MAY 6TH, AT THE NEW WASHINGTON PARK

Trolley Dodgers Score 6 in 9th to Win

LaChance Switches Sides of Plate and Drives in Winning Run
Washington Senators Beaten, 10-9

BROOKLYN WON ANOTHER GAME IN ITS new ballpark today, rallying for six runs in the ninth inning to defeat the Washington Senators 10-9. The victory was the fourth in a row for the Trolley Dodgers in the new Washington Park.

They had opened the season on the road with four triumphs and three defeats. The new park was inaugurated on April 30th with a 6-4 defeat at the hands of the Philadelphia Phillies. After that, the Dodgers beat the Phils and the Senators twice each. The first victory at home came on May 2nd, when the Bridegrooms scored five runs in the eighth to win 10-9. They came from behind again the following afternoon to beat the Phillies again, 9-6. In the opening game of the Washington series, the Grooms won with ease, 11-2. Yesterday they were rained out.

Today's Results

BROOKLYN 10-Washington 9
New York 7-Boston 5
St. Louis at Cincinnati, ppd.—rain
Louisville at Cleveland, ppd.—rain
Philadelphia at Baltimore, ppd.—rain
Chicago at Pittsburg, ppd.—rain

Standings	W-L	Pct.	GB
Baltimore	8- 2	.800	—
Cincinnati	11- 3	.786	(+1)
Cleveland	10- 5	.667	½
BROOKLYN	8- 4	.667	1
Chicago	8- 5	.615	1½
Boston	8- 8	.500	3
New York	6- 7	.462	3½
Pittsburg	7- 9	.438	4
Philadelphia	5- 7	.417	4
Louisville	5-11	.312	6
Washington	3-10	.231	6½
St. Louis	2-10	.167	7

Today they rallied to victory yet again. The big heroes in this triumph were catcher Alexander "Broadway Alec" Smith (who hit a three-run triple) and George "Candy" LaChance (who knocked in the final two runs with a long hit). A switch-hitter, LaChance had previously been hitless in five attempts against southpaw pitcher Morris "Doc" Amole. In the ninth he decided to try batting from the left side of the plate. But after one pitch, captain Mike Griffin convinced LaChance to switch back to righthanded. He did and soon delivered the game-winning hit into the right field corner.

Amole was hit hard through much of the game. But he was able to get the home team out with men on base until the ninth. Jack Dunn, who pitched for Brooklyn, was not so effective in the pinches, and Washington hit him for fourteen hits and eight runs in seven innings. Ralph Miller pitched the last inning for the Bridegrooms, and he was touched for one run.

Brooklyn scored two runs in the first inning but could have gotten more. Griffin led off with a two-bagger to left, and Fielder Jones drove him home with a safe bouncer to right. A muff by the third baseman put LaChance on, and a walk to Jimmy Sheckard loaded the bases with none out. But a double play and a ground out ended the rally with only one more run counting.

Singles by Jim "Deacon" McGuire and Tom Brown, followed by two outs, gave Washington its first run in the second inning. A two-run home run into the bleachers in center field by Zeke Wrigley in the fourth put the Senators ahead.

Brooklyn tied the score briefly in the bottom of the fourth on consecutive hits by Billy Hallman, Alec Smith, and Jack Dunn.

But Washington regained the lead in the fifth. Kip Selback tripled and came home on a soft hit past short by Jack Doyle.

The visitors pulled away with three runs in the sixth, aided by an error by LaChance and a disputed call at the plate by umpire Charley Snyder. Hits by Tom Leahy, Heinie Reitz, and Kip Selbach didn't hurt the rally, either.

A double by McGuire led to another Washington run in the seventh.

A walk, a steal, and a hit by Wrigley gave Washington its final run in the ninth.

The Trolley Dodgers came in for their final chance needing five runs to tie the game and six to win it. With the prospects that poor, many of the 3,000 spectators were already heading for home when Sheckard led off with a looping hit to left center. He was forced out on Billy Shindle's grounder, and more people got up to leave. Tommy Tucker then smashed a hit to left. Catcher McGuire muffed a chance to catch Hallman's pop foul, and Billy took advantage of the favor by cracking a shot that was too hot for the third baseman to handle.

The bases were now loaded for Smith. Alec delivered a tremendous blast over the center fielder's head and earned three bases, while three runners scored.

John Anderson was sent up to bat for pitcher Miller. The cranks called for a home run but only got a tap to the pitcher. Anderson was retired as Smith scored.

Things looked dim. One run was still needed to tie the game, no one was on base, and two were out. But Griffin brought the remainder of the crowd to life with a solid single to right. More cheering followed a base on balls to Jones.

LaChance was up next. George had looked very weak batting righthanded against Amole all afternoon. So he switched over to the left side of the plate this time. The crowd seemed to think this was a good idea. But Amole's first pitch was a curve that broke over the plate while LaChance was jumping out of the way. Griffin then yelled in from second base ordering George to go back to batting righthanded. The captain knows best, it would seem. LaChance crossed over and smashed a ball hard past first base. It zipped past the first baseman and went all the way to the outfield fence. Both Griffin and Jones scored easily, and Brooklyn had won the game.

As Jones crossed the plate, he became the center of a crowd of jubilant players and spectators. Hugging and backslapping continued as the mob followed the players across Fourth Avenue into the dressing room. And many of the fanatics waited for nearly an hour to cheer the players again when they emerged in their street clothes. That was some way to win a game!

Washington	ab	r	h	bi	o	a	e
T. Leahy, 3b	5	1	1	1	1	5	1
J. Gettman, rf	4	0	1	1	0	0	0
K. Selbach, 1f	5	1	3	1	2	0	0
J. Doyle, 1b	5	0	2	1	15	1	0
J. McGuire, c	5	2	2	0	1	0	1
T. Brown, cf	4	1	1	0	4	0	0
H. Reitz, 2b	4	2	2	1	2	2	1
Z. Wrigley, ss	5	1	2	4	0	4	2
D. Amole, p	5	1	1	0	1	4	1
	42	9	15	9	26	16	6

Brooklyn	ab	r	h	bi	o	a	e
M. Griffin, cf	6	2	3	1	6	0	0
F. Jones, rf	4	2	2	1	1	0	0
G. LaChance, ss	6	0	1	2	2	1	1
J. Sheckard, 1f	4	0	2	0	4	0	0
B. Shindle, 3b	5	1	1	0	5	0	1
T. Tucker, 1b	5	2	2	0	4	0	0
B. Hallman, 2b	5	2	2	0	0	2	0
A. Smith, c	5	1	2	3	5	4	1
J. Dunn, p	3	0	1	1	0	0	0
R. Miller, p8	1	0	0	0	0	0	0
J. Anderson, ph9	1	0	0	1	-	-	-
	45	10	16	9	27	7	3

Washington	010	213	101	=	9
Brooklyn	200	100	016	=	10

two out when winning run scored

	ip	h	r-er	bb	so
Amole (L 0-4)	8⅔	16	10-4	3	1
Dunn	7	14	8-7	0	2
Miller (W 1-0)	2	1	1-1	1	2

HBP: by Dunn (Gettman)
Time—2:15
Attendance—3,000

Game-Winning RBI: LaChance
LOB: Washington 9, Brooklyn 12
BE: Washington 2, Brooklyn 4
DP: Wrigley-Reitz-Doyle (Shindle)
2B: Griffin, McGuire, LaChance
3B: Selbach, Smith
HR: Wrigley
SH: Reitz
SB: Brown 2, Wrigley
CS: Gettman, Selbach
Umpires: C. Snyder & W. Curry

The opening of the new park was about the only good feature of the season for Brooklyn. The Bridegrooms spent much of the summer in ninth place, then slipped to tenth in late August. They finished there with a 54-91 record and the worst percentage any Brooklyn club had yet had. Even the attraction of a new ballpark could not keep attendance from dropping over 40%.

Chapter III Hanlon's Superbas

1899 September 4th
"Brooklyn Finishes" on Both Sides of the River

1900 June 21st
Superbas Rally to Win, Grab League Lead

1900 Cup Series—Game #4
Brooklyn Wins the Cup

1901 September 23rd
Two Bases-Loaded Home Runs in 25-6 Win

1902 May 13th
Donovan Loses One-Hitter

1903 August 27th
Superbas Win with 17 Walks

1904 April 24th
Three Players Arrested at Sunday Game

1905 September 1st
Errors Keep Superbas in Last Place

AFTER THE DISASTROUS 1898 SEASON, PRESIDENT CHARLES H. EBBETS AND THE BROOKlyn club were deeply in debt, saddled with a tenth-place team, and had little prospect of improving their position.

The Baltimore club was also in a financial bind at the time. But at least Baltimore had a strong team. The mighty Orioles had won three pennants in 1894–95–96 and had just missed out in 1897. In that year a very close pennant race had kept Baltimore's home attendance above the 250,000 mark for the fourth straight season. But in 1898, their patronage fell all the way to 123,000, despite another second-place finish.

Baltimore owner Harry Von der Horst decided his good team would be better supported in a larger city. So he hatched a deal with Ebbets to merge the Brooklyn and Baltimore clubs. Under the agreement, Von der Horst and his manager, Edward "Ned" Hanlon, were given 50% ownership of both clubs, while the Brooklyn owners, principally Ebbets and Ferdinand Abell, got the other 50% of both clubs.

The joint ownership then transferred manager Hanlon and the pick of the Oriole players to Brooklyn, with Baltimore getting what was left over. Only two prominent Oriole stars refused to make the switch. They were third baseman John McGraw and catcher Wilbert Robinson. They were allowed to remain in Baltimore (where they had a profitable saloon), and McGraw became manager of the denuded Orioles. Hanlon remained connected with Baltimore in the capacity of club president.

By coincidence, there was a prominent acrobatic act on the vaudeville circuit in those days called "Hanlon's Superbas." Sportswriters picked up this name and applied it to the new Brooklyn manager and his greatly strengthened team. The name Superbas remained with the Brooklyn ball club long after it was no longer superb and long after Hanlon had left Brooklyn.

The stars who accompanied their manager from Baltimore to Brooklyn included pitchers James "Doc" McJames and Jimmy Hughes, first baseman Dan McGann, infielder Hugh Jennings, and outfielders Joe Kelley and Willie Keeler. Jennings, Kelley, and Keeler had been the heart of the Oriole lineup during its championship years. For Wee Willie, this was finally a chance to play in his home town after having been traded by the Trolley Dodgers in 1894. In addition to these stars, Baltimore had recently acquired Bill Dahlen, a fine shortstop, from Chicago, and he was also transferred to Brooklyn.

Ned Hanlon

These players were melded with the better Brooklyn players: speedy center fielder Fielder Jones, veteran second baseman Tom Daly, first baseman John Anderson, and pitchers Jack Dunn and Bill Kennedy. The combination was formidable.

Ten days after the season started, Hanlon further strengthened the team by trading three minor leaguers to Washington for catcher Charles "Duke" Farrell and third baseman Jim "Doc" Casey. This deal made the Superbas the class of the league, and they moved into first place for good on May 22nd.

After surviving an eight-game losing streak in late June and early July, Hanlon decided he needed another top catcher. So he traded McGann to Washington for veteran Jim "Deacon" McGuire, one of the finest receivers in the league. He tried to send Alec Smith from Baltimore to Washinton as part of the deal, but the Orioles' McGraw blocked the transfer. When McGraw acquired shortstop Gene DeMontreville for Baltimore in August, Hanlon tried to move the new man directly to Brooklyn. But once again, McGraw was able to balk the move.

The Orioles also gave the Superbas trouble on the field. Although his team was supposedly low on talent, McGraw managed to keep the Orioles in the first division all year. And they beat Brooklyn six times in fourteen games over the course of the season. Only one team did better against the champion Superbas.

Against their metropolitan rivals, the New York Giants, Hanlon's men did much better. They won ten of twelve, including two come-from-behind victories on Labor Day, one in Brooklyn and one over in New York.

Late rallies were the trademark of the veteran Brooklyn squad, and the newspapers came to call them "Brooklyn finishes." Despite some controversy about the signing of an infielder also claimed by New York, the Superbas won the championship easily.

In 1900, the National League reduced its size from twelve clubs to eight. Baltimore was one of the clubs eliminated, and its players became Brooklyn property. This gave Hanlon some more fine players, including pitchers Joe McGinnity, Harry Howell, Jerry Nops, and Frank Kitson, shortstop DeMontreville, and outfielder Jimmy Sheckard. Sheckard and Howell had been with the Trolley Dodgers before the merger, but had been transferred to Baltimore in 1899. McGraw and Robinson still steadfastly refused to play in Brooklyn, and they were sold to St. Louis.

The new pitchers were especially welcome, since two of Hanlon's aces of 1899, Hughes and McJames, did not pitch in 1900. Hughes stayed in California all summer, and McJames, who had earned a medical degree, stayed in South Carolina to begin his career as a doctor. But McGinnity pitched brilliantly for Brooklyn and led the Superbas to another pennant. Brooklyn took over first place with a come-from-behind victory over the Phillies on June 21st and held onto the top spot the rest of the way.

Pittsburg provided the stiffest opposition down the stretch, finishing 4½ games behind Brooklyn. Since the Pirates had won the season series from the Superbas, 11 games to 8, a Pittsburg newspaper arranged a challenge series between the two teams after the close of the season. The Superbas defended their claim to superiority by winning the series handily, 3 games to 1. The victory cup was given to McGinnity, whom the other players deemed to be the team's top star. Each player also received about $400 for the series.

In 1901, the upstart American League began raiding the National League for players. Brooklyn was hard hit, losing outfielder Jones, third baseman Lave Cross, and pitchers McGinnity and Howell. These losses were only partially offset by the return of both McJames and Hughes. Another new pitcher, Bill Donovan, emerged as the ace of the staff. But the weakened Superbas fell to third in the final standings, 9½ games behind the pennant-winning Pirates.

In 1902, Joe Kelley and Tom Daly jumped to the A.L., and Brooklyn's percentage continued to decline. Although they finished second, the Superbas wound up a whopping 27½ games behind the Pirates. Donovan continued to pitch well. But sometimes, like the day in May in which he pitched a one-hitter and lost 2-0, it was not good enough.

Donovan led the jumpers in 1903. Willie Keeler, Cozy Dolan, and Frank Kitson also signed with the American League. This really decimated Hanlon's team, as only Bill Dahlen and Jimmy Sheckard were left from the 1900 champs.

To counteract these losses, Hanlon raided the California League for talent, signing pitchers Oscar Jones and Henry Schmidt (who combined for 41 victories in 1903). But even gift games like the one of August 27th, when the Phillies presented the Dodgers with 17 walks and an 11-10 victory, could not keep Brooklyn in the first division. Hanlon's Superbas finished fifth.

Although the "war" with the American League was over, the West Coast teams, now formed into the Pacific Coast League, signed Schmidt and second baseman Tim Flood away from Brooklyn in 1904. Hanlon was also the owner of the minor league

Charles H. Ebbets

club in Baltimore, and the P.C.L. raids also threatened his holdings there. So he led a movement that negotiated a "peace treaty" with the western circuit. One good development that arose from the settlement was the acquisition by Brooklyn of Seattle slugger Harry Lumley.

With his money tied up in Baltimore, Hanlon did not have the resources to buy additional stock in the Brooklyn club when first Abell and then Von der Horst sold out. President Ebbets, on the other hand, borrowed heavily from furniture manufacturer Henry W. Medicus and acquired as much stock as he could. This undermined Hanlon's position in Brooklyn and a feud developed between him and Ebbets.

Meanwhile, the team continued to decline on the playing field, finishing sixth in 1904 with a dismal .366 percentage. To keep attendance up, Ebbets tried to institute Sunday baseball at Washington Park. Although it was against the state law to charge admission to games on Sundays, he got around this by admitting the fans for free, then charging them for scorecards according to the price of the seat they were occupying. The police winked at this practice the first time, then made token arrests of players and scorecard vendors the next time to test the practice in court. Church organizations finally stopped the Sunday games in the appeals courts after seven games had been played in 1904.

Ebbets kept trying, however, and in both 1905 and 1906 he staged games on Sundays for a few months before adverse legal decisions caused him to stop.

By 1905, Ebbets had gained a controlling interest in the club. He raised his own salary to $10,000 and offered Hanlon a cut from $12,500 to $6,500. A compromise was reached, but Ned could see the writing on the wall pretty clearly.

On the field, Hanlon's old magic was gone. Having built a reputation on making winning pitchers out of other clubs' rejects, he picked up Elmer Stricklett and Mal Eason from amongst the American League discards. But they had a combined record of 13-39 for Brooklyn in 1905. The team's only winning pitcher was Dr. William Scanlon, a practicing physician in the off-season. "Doc" was not enough to keep the team out of the cellar all by himself. And on September 1st, Scanlon even made a bad error to help the Superbas miss their last chance to get out of last place.

As it was, Brooklyn finished eighth with a 48-104 record, 2 games behind seventh-place Boston and 56½ games out of first place. Their percentage of .316 remains the lowest in the history of the franchise, and 1905 was the only year in the club's first 100 in which the team finished last. After the season, Hanlon left the team. But the nickname Superbas lingered on for twenty years or so.

Wee Willie Keeler

Iron Man Joe McGinnity

1899 LABOR DAY, MONDAY, SEPTEMBER 4TH, AT BROOKLYN AND NEW YORK

"Brooklyn Finishes" on Both Sides of the River

9th-Inning Rally Wins the Morning Game at Washington Park
4-Run 8th Gives Superbas Afternoon Game at the Polo Grounds

THE PENNANT-BOUND BROOKLYN Superbas beat the New York Giants twice today with late rallies on both sides of the bridge. In the morning game at Washington Park in Brooklyn, the home team rallied for two runs in the bottom of the ninth to win out, 3-2. In the afternoon game at the Polo Grounds in New York, the Superbas pulled out a 5-4 victory with four runs in the eighth inning.

Today's Results
BROOKLYN 3-New York 2 (morning game)
BROOKLYN 5-New York 4 (afternoon)
Boston 4-Baltimore 1
Philadelphia 3-Washington 2 (10 inn.)(a.m.)
Philadelphia 17-Washington 0 (p.m.)
Cincinnati 6-Cleveland 3 (1st game)
Cincinnati 8-Cleveland 1 (2nd game)
Louisville 14-St. Louis 2 (1st game)
St. Louis 2-Louisville 1 (8 inn.)(2nd)
Pittsburg 7-Chicago 2 (1st game)
Chicago 4-Pittsburg 4 (Tie)(9 inn.)(2nd)

Standings	W-L	Pct.	GB
BROOKLYN	80-36	.690	—
Boston	73-44	.624	7½
Philadelphia	75-46	.620	7½
Baltimore	66-48	.579	13
St. Louis	69-54	.561	14½
Cincinnati	66-52	.559	15
Pittsburg	60-58	.508	21
Chicago	60-60	.500	22
Louisville	53-65	.449	28
New York	49-67	.422	31
Washington	41-76	.350	39½
Cleveland	19-105	.153	65

Late rallies had become so commonplace for Ned Hanlon's league-leaders that they had come to be called "Brooklyn finishes." Today's victories were the Superbas' 17th and 18th in the last 20 games, and they increased the team's first-place margin to 7½ games.

Heroes abounded in the double victory today. Pitchers Bill Kennedy and Jim Hughes each pitched a fine game. Catcher Duke Farrell and outfielder Joe Kelley each had a game-winning hit. And substitute John Anderson scored a key run in each contest.

A good morning crowd came to Washington Park for the first game. The spectators saw a pitchers' duel between Kennedy and Charlie Gettig, with only five hits being made in the first seven innings.

Brooklyn scored the first run of the game on a fluke in the fourth inning when George Van Haltren lost a ball in the sun. It fell safely, allowing a man to score.

Brooklyn's 1-0 lead held up until the top of the eighth, when New York scored twice. With two out Tom O'Brien sent a deep one to the center field fence. Van Haltren scored on the triple and O'Brien came home as center fielder Fielder Jones was fumbling the ball. That put the visitors ahead, 2-1.

The Superbas got down to their last out before coming back to win. In the bottom of the ninth, Doc Casey opened with an easy ground out, and Jim McGuire fouled out. Anderson was sent up to hit for Kennedy, and the pinch-batter drew a base on balls. Jones kept Brooklyn alive with a single to left. Willie Keeler dropped a well-placed poke in back of third to load the bases. Hugh Jennings came through with a hot blast that third baseman Mike Grady could only knock down. That tied the game. Kelley then hammered a clean hit to center, and the winning run trotted across the plate, much to the delight of the Brooklyn crowd.

The afternoon crowd at the Polo Grounds was delighted when pitcher Cy Seymour turned slugger in the second inning and tripled two runs home. The Giants scored two more runs in the third on a double by O'Brien, a sacrifice, two stolen bases, and two errors by catcher Farrell. They might have scored more in the round had not one man been picked off base and another caught stealing.

Brooklyn scored in the fifth on hits by Farrell and Jennings around a walk.

But New York still led, 4-1, going into the eighth. Keeler opened with a scratch hit just beyond the pitcher, but he hurt his leg running to first and had to leave the game. Anderson went in as a substitute runner and quickly stole second. Jennings walked. Kelley was called out on strikes. Tom Daly then was given a base on balls to fill the sacks. Bill Dahlen was nicked by an inside pitch, and Anderson walked home with an easy run. Casey hit into a force out, and Jennings scored. Casey stole second. Farrell then sent out a long two-run double to put Brooklyn into the lead, 5-4

New York left the bases loaded in both the seventh and eighth innings. In the ninth, New York tried hitting the ball to Anderson, who was in an unfamiliar postion in right field. O'Brien led off and reached first on Anderson's muff of his fly. Clarence Foster sent another fly to Anderson, which was misjudged but finally caught. Jack Doyle hit cleanly to right, and Anderson's quick return held O'Brien at second. Kid Gleason sent a difficult fly to right, and Anderson did a fine job of catching it. John then tried to get fancy and double Doyle off first base. His throw was poor and got past first baseman Jennings. With O'Brien already on third, catcher McGuire boldly ran over to back up the overthrow. Doyle, having tagged up at first by now, made an ill-advised dash for second. He was retired by a strong throw from McGuire before O'Brien could score the tying run. So Anderson's overthrow was turned into a game-ending double play.

That final play made the double defeat especially hard for New York to swallow. On the other side, Hanlon's men took the victories in stride. After all, they didn't call them "Brooklyn finishes" for nothing.

MORNING GAME
at Washington Park, Brooklyn

			r	h	e
New York	000 000 020	=	2	7	0
Brooklyn	000 100 002	=	3	6	2

Game-Winning RBI: Kelley

two out when winning run scored
Batteries: C. Gettig (L 4-4) & P. Wilson
B. Kennedy (W 17-7) & J. McGuire

Attendance—6,100

AFTERNOON GAME
at the Polo Grounds, New York

Brooklyn	ab	r	h	bi	o	a	e
F. Jones, cf	4	0	0	0	0	0	0
W. Keeler, rf	3	0	1	0	2	0	0
J. Anderson, pr8-rf	1	1	0	0	2	0	1
H. Jennings, 1b	4	1	1	1	8	0	1
J. Kelley, 1f	4	0	1	0	0	0	0
T. Daly, 2b	2	1	0	0	3	4	1
B. Dahlen, ss	3	0	0	1	1	0	0
D. Casey, 3b	4	1	1	1	4	0	0
D. Farrell, c	4	1	2	2	7	5	2
J. Hughes, p	4	0	1	0	0	4	0
	33	5	7	5	27	13	5

New York	ab	r	h	bi	o	a	e
G. Van Haltren, cf	4	0	0	0	0	1	0
T. O'Brien, 1f	5	1	2	0	1	0	0
C. Foster, rf	3	0	0	0	0	0	0
J. Doyle, 1b	3	0	1	0	8	0	0
K. Gleason, 2b	4	1	1	0	2	2	1
P. Wilson, c	2	0	1	0	12	1	0
F. Martin, 3b	4	1	1	0	2	4	1
S. Hardesty, ss	4	1	2	0	2	0	0
C. Seymour, p	4	0	2	2	0	5	0
	33	4	10	2	27	13	2

Brooklyn	000 010 040	=	5
New York	022 000 000	=	4

	ip	h	r-er	bb	so
Hughes (W 22-4)	9	10	4-2	6	8
Seymour (L 10-13)	9	7	5-5	6	10

HBP: by Hughes (Foster)
by Seymour (Dahlen)
PB: Wilson
Time—2:35
Attendance—7,200
Umpires: B. Emslie & J. Dwyer

Game-Winning RBI: Farrell
LOB: Brooklyn 8, New York 10
BE: Brooklyn 2, New York 2
DP: Martin-Doyle (Dahlen)
Anderson-Farrell-Daly
2B: O'Brien, Farrell, Gleason
3B: Seymour
SH: Doyle
SB: Casey 2, Gleason 2, Wilson, O'Brien, Anderson
Picked Off: Jones, Seymour, Foster
CS: Doyle, Wilson

The Superbas had no trouble holding onto their league lead and winning the pennant. Their final margin was 8 games. They had a record for the season of 101-47, although a ruling by the league later threw out some 15 games because of the use of an illegally signed player. Still, Brooklyn was declared the National League champion.

1900 THURSDAY, JUNE 21ST, AT PHILADELPHIA PARK

Superbas Rally to Win, Grab League Lead

Great Batting Gives Brooklyn 5 Runs in 9th for 8-6 Win
Tenth Victory in Eleven Games for Champs

Today's Results			
BROOKLYN 8-Philadelphia 6			
Boston 5-New York 1			
Cincinnati at Chicago, ppd.—rain			
no other game scheduled			
Standings	**W-L**	**Pct.**	**GB**
BROOKLYN	31-17	.646	—
Philadelphia	31-18	.633	½
Pittsburg	25-27	.481	8
Chicago	23-25	.479	8
Boston	22-24	.478	8
Cincinnati	20-26	.435	10
St. Louis	20-27	.426	10½
New York	19-27	.413	11

THE BROOKLYN SUPERBAS DID IT AGAIN today. They rallied late to pull a victory out of the jaws of defeat. This time they seized the game from the grasp of the first-place Philadelphia Phillies and grabbed the league lead with it. Hanlon's men ran their current hot streak to ten victories in eleven games. And four of those triumphs have come with rallies in the eighth, ninth, or eleventh innings. Today it was a ninth-inning string of six hits and a base on balls that yielded five runs and turned a 6-3 deficit into an 8-6 lead.

Aside from the winning rally, the feature of the game was the work of Brooklyn center fielder Fielder Jones. The swift fly hawk grabbed eight fly balls, several of them on difficult chances. One of his catches resulted in a double play. Jones also made three hits and scored two runs on offense. It was his double that started the winning rally in the ninth.

In the final inning, Brooklyn routed pitcher Al Orth, then completed the scoring against the top Philly pitcher, Bill Bernhard. For the Superbas, lefthander Jerry Nops pitched good ball for eight innings but received poor support (except from Jones). He left the game for a pinch-hitter, and Frank Kitson pitched the bottom of the ninth.

The visiting Superbas were sent to bat first, and they were retired without a run or hit. Billy Keeler was given a base on balls but was caught stealing.

The Phillies were handed two runs in their half of the first. With one out, Jimmy Slagle poked a fly into short center for a hit. Ed Delahanty followed with a double-play grounder to third. But second baseman Tom Daly dropped Lave Cross's throw, and both runners were safe. After an infield out, "Klondike" Bill Douglass lifted a high fly to left field. Joe Kelley misjudged it at first, then ran under it just in time to drop it for a two-run error.

Brooklyn got one run back in the second. Bill Dahlen led off with a hit. Cross sent a hot shot through Joe Dolan's legs at third for another safety. Daly was hit by a pitch. With the bases loaded and no one out, it seemed like the champs would have a big rally. Jim McGuire drove in one run with a fly out. Nops then flied to right, and Cross, through stupid base running, was doubled off second to end the inning.

Brooklyn had a single and a triple in the third but did not score because Jones, who had the single, was caught stealing.

Philadelphia upped its lead with three runs in the bottom of the third. Slagle started with a bad-hop hit over shortstop. He stole second. Delahanty raised an easy foul, but catcher McGuire muffed it. Given another chance, Ed cracked a hit to right, sending Slagle home. Flick smashed one off poor Nops's shins for a hit. Douglass followed with another baser to score Delahanty. After Flick was caught stealing, Douglass eventually scored on a bingle by Dolan.

Daring work on the basepaths got the Superbas two runs in the fifth. Jones led off with a pop-fly single over third base. He moved to second on an infield out and to third on a passed ball. Hugh Jennings was given a walk. On the double steal, Hughie broke for second, and Jones made for home when the catcher threw the ball. Jones was safe on a great slide around Douglass's tag after the return throw, and the Phillies put up a kick with the umpire. While they were arguing, Jennings brazenly raced to third, getting credit for two stolen bases on one pitch! He came home on Kelley's ground out to shortstop.

That made the score 5-3, but the Phils added another run in the seventh to make it 6-3. A great catch by Kelley on the bicycle track kept the home team from scoring a couple of more runs.

So the stage was set for the big rally in the ninth. Jimmy Sheckard, batting for Nops, went out on an easy pop to third. Jones came through with a slashing double to right. Keeler beat out a beautiful bunt along the third base line. Jennings's smash into center scored Jones. Willie and Hugh advanced a base on a short passed ball.

With the tying runs now on second and third, captain Joe Kelley found a fastball to his liking and sent it to deep center for two bases and two runs. A wild return throw gave Kelley third.

In a desperate attempt to save the game, Philadelphia manager Bill Shettsline removed Orth and brought in his hottest pitcher, Bill Bernhard. Bernhard did not have his "good stuff" today. Dahlen greeted him with a clean single to center, sending Kelley home with the go-ahead run. Two wild pitches moved Dahlen to third, and L. Cross was given a walk. Daly put the icing on the cake with a hit that scored Dahlen.

After the Brooks had finally been retired, Frank Kitson was sent to the mound in the bottom of the ninth. He retired three batters in a row, thanks to some excellent outfielding. Flick, up first, sent a high one to right that Keeler ran under and caught. Douglass hit a dangerous liner to short center, but Jones got to it with some hard sprinting. Pearce Chiles then slammed a deep drive over Jones's head. Fielder stumbled as he started back, but he recovered quickly and overtook the ball for the final out.

The Philadelphia fans left the park mumbling about Brooklyn's luck. But the Superbas also played some fine baseball. They deserved to be in first place and were there on talent not on luck.

Brooklyn	ab	r	h	bi	o	a	e
F. Jones, cf	5	2	3	0	8	1	0
W. Keeler, rf	4	1	3	0	4	0	0
H. Jennings, 1b	3	2	1	1	5	1	0
J. Kelley, 1f	5	1	1	3	4	0	1
B. Dahlen, ss	5	2	2	1	0	0	0
L. Cross, 3b	4	0	2	0	2	2	0
T. Daly, 2b	3	0	2	1	1	1	2
J. McGuire, c	5	0	0	1	2	1	1
J. Nops, p	3	0	0	0	1	1	0
J. Sheckard, ph9	1	0	0	0	-	-	-
F. Kitson, p9	0	0	0	0	0	0	0
	38	8	14	7	27	7	4

Philadelphia	ab	r	h	bi	o	a	e
R. Thomas, cf	3	0	1	0	0	0	1
J. Slagle, 1f	5	2	2	0	4	0	0
E. Delahanty, 1b	5	1	1	1	7	0	0
E. Flick, rf	5	2	3	0	1	1	0
B. Douglass, c	4	1	1	1	4	2	1
P. Chiles, 2b	3	0	0	0	1	1	0
J. Dolan, 3b	4	0	1	2	2	4	0
M. Cross, ss	4	0	0	0	8	2	0
A. Orth, p	3	0	0	0	0	0	0
B. Bernhard, p9	0	0	0	0	0	0	0
	36	6	9	4	27	10	2

Brooklyn	010	020	005	=	8
Philadelphia	203	000	100	=	6

	ip	h	r-er	bb	so
Nops (W 2-2)	8	9	6-1	5	2
Kitson	1	0	0-0	0	0
Orth (L 3-5)	8⅓	12	7-5	3	2
Bernhard	⅔	2	1-1	1	0

HBP: by Orth 2 (Daly, Jennings)
PB: McGuire, Douglass 2
WP: Bernhard 2
Umpire: H. O'Day

Game-Winning RBI: Dahlen
LOB: Brooklyn 9, Philadelphia 9
BE: Brooklyn 0, Philadelphia 4
DP: Flick-M. Cross
Jones-Daly-Jennings
2B: Jones, Kelley
3B: Keeler
SH: Thomas
SB: Keeler, Slagle, Jennings 2, Jones, Thomas, Flick, Douglass
CS: Jones, Flick, L. Cross
Time—2:42 Attendance—7,405

Brooklyn won its next four games to build up a 4-game lead. Although Pittsburg made a run at first place in early September, the Superbas won the pennant with relative ease. Their final record was 82-54, which left them 4½ games ahead of the Pirates.

1900 THURSDAY, OCTOBER 18TH, AT EXPOSITION PARK, PITTSBURG
Cup Series—Game #4

Brooklyn Wins the Cup

THE NATIONAL LEAGUE CHAMPION BROOKLYN SUPERBAS TODAY CEMENTED THEIR claim to the title of "World Champions" by winning a post-season series against the second-place Pittsburg Pirates, 3 games to 1. The score of today's final game was 6-1.

The Pirates had beaten Brooklyn in the season series this year, 11 games to 8, although the Superbas had finished ahead of Pittsburg in the final standings. Hoping to show that the hometown Pirates were better than the Superbas, a Pittsburg newspaper, the *Chronicle-Telegraph,* had offered a $500 loving cup to the team that won a post-season series between the two rivals. Since the players were to split the gate receipts in the best-of-five-game series, the Brooklyn accepted the challenge. All the games were to be played in Pittsburg, where fan interest was still high at the end of the season.

With pitching star Joe McGinnity leading the way (as he had all season long), the Superbas won the series easily.

On Wednesday night, a team meeting was held to determine how the men would dispose of the trophy. It was there unanimously decided to give it to the Superbas' star performer and most popular member, "Iron Man" Joe McGinnity. The ever-obsequious McGinnity reminded his teammates that their success was the joint effort of all the players, but he was quite honored by their gesture.

Joe was not present at the presentation ceremony on Thursday night. It seems that he was in quite a hurry to get back to his iron-working business in McAlester, Indian Territory, and he left Pittsburg right after winning the final game. At the banquet, captain Joe Kelley accepted the cup on behalf of the players, and he was to see that it got to McGinnity. Each member of both teams received nearly $400 from the receipts.

McGinnity had begun his National League career with Baltimore in 1899. This year he was transferred to Brooklyn when the Baltimore franchise was eliminated in the reduction of the circuit from twelve teams to eight. Pitching for the Superbas, he led the league in games won, innings pitched, and winning percentage. And he was the man Hanlon relied upon to win the most critical games in the pennant race.

He also set the tone for the *Chronicle-Telegraph* Cup Series by pitching and winning the first game over Pittsburg's Rube Waddell, 5-2. Joe was in command all the way, and the Pirate runs did not come until the ninth inning.

Frank Kitson pitched a four-hitter for Brooklyn in the second game, and the Superbas won, 4-2, with the aid of six Pirate errors.

With his team ahead in the series by two games, captain Kelley could afford to give 22-year-old Harry Howell a chance to pitch in the third game. Handsome Harry was hit all over the yard, as the Pirates scored ten runs. Meanwhile, Deacon Phillipe shut the Superbas out. But the 10-0 victory for Pittsburg had little effect other than to give the Smoky City bettors a chance to regain some of their losses from the previous two days.

Today it was all Brooklyn again. Although they were out-hit, the Superbas scored as they pleased in the early going. McGinnity kept the Pirate hits well scattered. And the champions were far superior in the field, making many fine plays. Lave Cross at third base was particularly brilliant, making four difficult plays.

Sam Leever, who had pitched and lost the second game of the series, was touched for a run in the first inning today. Fielder Jones hit the first pitch of the game past the second baseman for a base. He stole second, went to third on a perfect sacrifice bunt by Billy Keeler, and came home on a ground out by Hugh Jennings.

In the bottom of the second, the champion pitcher, McGinnity, had a classic confrontation with the league's champion batsman, Hans Wagner. The big Dutchman fouled off half a dozen of the Iron Man's famous underhanded curveballs before connecting solidly. But the line drive went straight into the hands of outfielder Jones, much to Wagner's chagrin. Jimmy Williams and Tom O'Brien singled with two out. But Fred Ely ended the inning with an easy fly to center.

Brooklyn all but won the game in the fourth, when they scored three runs. Cross slashed a single down the left field line for starters. Tom Daly followed with a double to the same spot. Bill Dahlen's single to left brought the two men home. After a fly out, Leever fumbled McGinnity's bunt, putting men on first and third. Dahlen then scored on Jones's long fly to right.

G. Edward "Rube" Waddell and Charles "Chief" Zimmer took over as the Pittsburg battery in the fifth. Brooklyn was given a run in that inning on a base on balls, an infield out, a wild pitch, and a hit by Cross.

The visitors' final run came in the bottom of the sixth. Jones got a life on a wild throw by Ely, and Jennings sent him home with a long two-bagger to left.

Pittsburg's run came in the bottom of the sixth. Claude Ritchey doubled with one out. Wagner's hit was knocked down by Cross, but no play could be made. O'Brien's infield out scored Ritchey. A fine play by Cross on Williams's hot grounder ended the inning.

The Pirates got four hits in the last three innings, but McGinnity kept them from scoring.

The happy Superbas left the grounds shouting their team cheer, "Brooklyn rah, Brooklyn ha-ha, ha-ha-ha, Brooklyn, Brooklyn, Brooklyn!" The cheer was repeated at the train depot, where the whole team went to give McGinnity a rousing second send-off.

Brooklyn	ab	r	h	bi	o	a	e
F. Jones, cf	5	2	1	1	4	0	0
W. Keeler, rf	4	0	0	0	1	0	0
H. Jennings, 1b	4	1	1	2	10	0	0
J. Kelley, lf	5	0	1	0	2	0	0
L. Cross, 3b	4	1	2	1	0	6	0
T. Daly, 2b	3	1	1	0	1	2	0
B. Dahlen, ss	4	1	1	2	3	0	0
D. Farrell, c	4	0	1	0	6	0	0
J. McGinnity, p	3	0	0	0	0	3	0
	36	6	8	6	27	11	0

Pittsburg	ab	r	h	bi	o	a	e
T. Leach, lf	5	0	0	0	3	0	0
G. Beaumont, cf	4	0	1	0	1	0	0
C. Ritchey, 2b	4	1	1	0	2	1	0
H. Wagner, rf	4	0	2	0	3	0	0
T. O'Brien, 1b	4	0	0	1	9	0	0
J. Williams, 3b	4	0	1	0	1	0	0
J. O'Connor, c	1	0	1	0	0	0	1
C. Zimmer, c5	2	0	0	0	4	0	0
F. Ely, ss	4	0	1	0	3	6	1
S. Leever, p	1	0	1	0	1	1	1
R. Waddell, p5	2	0	1	0	0	1	0
P. Schriver, ph9	1	0	0	0	-	-	-
	36	1	9	1	27	9	3

Brooklyn	100 311 000	– 6
Pittsburg	000 001 000	= 1

	ip	h	r-er	bb	so
McGinnity (W 2-0)	9	9	1-1	1	4
Leever (L 0-2)	4	6	4-3	1	0
Waddell	5	2	2-1	1	5

WP: Waddell 2
Umpires: E. Swartwood & T. Hurst

Game-Winning RBI: Jennings
LOB: Brooklyn 7, Pittsburg 9
BE: Brooklyn 2
Base on Missed 3rd Strike: Brooklyn 1
2B: Daly, Jennings, Ritchey, Ely
SH: Keeler, McGinnity
SB: Jones, Leever, Cross, Dahlen, Zimmer, Ely
Time—2:03 Attendance—2,335

Over the winter, McGinnity accepted an offer from the rival American League and left the Brooklyn club. Lave Cross, Fielder Jones, and Harry Howell also jumped to the A.L.

1901 MONDAY, SEPTEMBER 23RD, AT LEAGUE PARK, CINCINNATI

Two Bases-Loaded Home Runs in 25-6 Win

Kelley and Sheckard Hit the Big Home Runs
Jimmy Hughes Pitches and Hits Well

NED HANLON'S BROOKLYN SUPERBAS tied a club record by scoring 25 runs in a game today. They also tied a major league record by hitting two home runs with the bases loaded. The slugging feats, however, provided precious little comfort for the defending champions from Brooklyn, who have been all but eliminated from a chance at a third straight pennant. While they may not be champions much longer, today the Superbas looked like world-beaters against the last-place Cincinnati Reds.

Today's Results			
BROOKLYN 25-Cincinnati 6			
Pittsburg 5-New York 4 (10 innings)			
Philadelphia 3-Chicago 1			
St. Louis 9-Boston 3			
Standings	**W-L**	**Pct.**	**GB**
Pittsburg	83-45	.648	—
Philadelphia	74-54	.578	9
BROOKLYN	74-55	.573	9½
St. Louis	68-61	.527	15½
Boston	65-64	.504	18½
New York	51-76	.402	31½
Chicago	51-81	.386	34
Cincinnati	47-77	.379	34

The Brooklyn club had had two previous games in which the team scored 25 runs. The first time was back in 1886 in an American Association game in which Baltimore was trounced 25-1. The other time was on May 20, 1896, at Pittsburg, when the Trolley Dodgers crushed the Pirates 25-6.

The feat of two four-run home runs in one game had been accomplished twice before in the major leagues. The first time was back in 1890 when the Chicago National League team did it. The second time was earlier in 1901, when it was done by the Chicago American Leaguers.

Today's massacre came after the Superbas had spotted the Red two runs in the first inning. The Brooklyn hitters went to work in the second, scoring seven times. The last four came on a four-bagger by Joe Kelley. After two scoreless rounds, the Brooklyns put the game away with eleven runs on eleven hits and an error in the fifth. The biggest blast of that round was another bases-loaded home run, this one off the bat of Jimmy Sheckard. After the fifth inning, the Superbas slowed down a bit, counting "only" five runs in the sixth and two in the seventh. By that time they were exhausted, and they went without scoring in each of the final two rounds.

Kelley led the slugging with two homers and a single. Sheckard also had a single to go with his round-tripper. But there were batting stars all up and down the lineup. Tom Daly had the most hits, five, including two doubles. Jimmy Hughes had four singles. And four other Superbas had three hits each.

Hughes's hitting almost outweighed his pitching today. With four base knocks, he had half as many as the entire Cincinnati squad had for the day. And by scoring twice and driving in four runners, he equalled the total run production of the Reds.

It was Hughes's own error that helped the home team to an early 2-0 lead. In the bottom of the first, Harry Bay led off with a safe hit. Dick Harley bunted for a sacrifice, and both runners were safe when first baseman Kelley threw to second too late for a force out. Jake Beckley also bunted, and Hughes threw the ball so far past first that two runners scored.

But the Cincinnati lead did not last long. Pitcher Archie Stimmel, who had retired the Superbas on just one hit in the first inning, was rocked for seven runs in the second. Daly opened with a two-baser to left. Second baseman Pete O'Brien missed Bill Dahlen's grounder, and Daly scored. Charlie Irwin dropped a safe hit into short left. Duke Farrell bunted and reached first on an error. Dahlen was forced at home on Hughes's grounder. Willie Keeler's fly out allowed Irwin to score. Sheckard then put Brooklyn ahead with a single to right, scoring Farrell. Cozy Dolan walked to fill the bases. Captain Kelley then knocked a long drive over the center fielder's head for a home run.

The score remained 7-2 until the fifth. Then Daly started an eleven-run rally with another double. Dahlen bounced out, but Irwin hit past short, sending Daly home. Farrell, Hughes, and Keeler all reached on infield taps, plating Irwin and loading the bases ahead of Sheckard's home run to deep right field. Dolan fanned for the second out, but a muff by right fielder Sam Crawford kept the inning going. Six consecutive hits followed, sending five runs home before Sheckard finally made the third out. The total damage was reckoned at eleven runs, making the Brooklyn lead 18-2.

A bad error by Keeler gave Cincinnati one run in their half of the fifth.

Reds' manager Bid McPhee mercifully took Stimmel out of the game and sent Jack Suthoff out to pitch in the sixth. The visitors greeted him warmly, pounding out six hits and five runs. Suthoff started his own troubles by walking the first man he faced. The Brooklyn bats did the rest.

The final two runs for the Superbas came in the seventh. Kelley hit his second home run of the day, and Daly got his fifth hit and eventually scored.

That made the score 25-3. In the last two innings, Hanlon called his men off the attack, and they went out in order.

Hughes also let up in his pitching. After allowing only three hits in the first six innings, he gave up five in the last three. Four of the hits came in the eighth, when Cincinnati scored three runs. That made the score 25-6, which was the final count.

The victory enabled the third-place Superbas to keep pace with the second-place Phillies. But the league-leading Pirates also won, and Brooklyn's slim mathematical chances at the pennant were diminished even further.

Still, it was a great game for slugging records and a great day for the Brooklyn team. The Cincinnati fans, on the other hand, were none too pleased with their afternoon's entertainment.

Brooklyn	ab	r	h	bi	o	a	e
W. Keeler, rf	7	1	3	1	3	0	1
J. Sheckard, 1f	6	2	2	5	1	0	0
C. Dolan, cf	5	2	1	0	3	0	0
J. Kelley, 1b	7	4	3	5	12	0	0
T. Daly, 2b	6	5	5	1	2	5	0
B. Dahlen, ss	6	2	2	3	2	5	0
C. Irwin, 3b	6	3	3	2	1	3	0
D. Farrell, c	5	4	3	3	3	0	0
J. Hughes, p	6	2	4	4	0	1	2
	54	25	26	24	27	14	3

Cincinnati	ab	r	h	bi	o	a	e
H. Bay, cf	4	2	1	1	3	0	1
D. Harley, 1f	4	1	0	0	7	0	0
J. Beckley, 1b	4	1	3	0	5	1	0
S. Crawford, rf	3	1	1	2	4	0	1
T. Corcoran, ss	4	0	0	1	0	5	0
H. Steinfeldt, 3b	3	0	1	0	2	2	0
P. O'Brien, 2b	4	0	2	0	2	1	1
P. Hurley, c	4	1	0	0	4	0	1
A. Stimmel, p	2	0	0	0	0	0	1
J. Suthoff, p6	2	0	0	0	0	0	0
	34	6	8	4	27	9	5

Brooklyn	070 0(11)5 200	=	25
Cincinnati	200 0 1 0 030	=	6

	ip	h	r-er	bb	so
Hughes (W 16-12)	9	8	6-3	2	1
Stimmel (L 4-11)	5	18	18-7	1	1
Suthoff	4	8	7-6	1	1

HBP: by Hughes (Crawford)
WP: Stimmel
Time—2:00
Attendance—900

Game-Winning RBI: Sheckard
LOB: Brooklyn 6, Cincinnati 5
BE: Brooklyn 3, Cincinnati 1
DP: Daly-Dahlen-Kelley (O'Brien)
Daly-Kelley (Hurley)
2B: Daly 2, Farrell, Steinfeldt
3B: Crawford
HR: Kelley 2, Sheckard
SH: Harley, Farrell, Sheckard
SB: Daly
Umpires: B. Nash & T. Brown

On the next afternoon, the Superbas again crushed the Reds, this time by a 16-2 score. Sheckard hit another four-run home run. Brooklyn also won the final game of the series, 9-2.

The Superbas never did catch the Phillies and finished third with a 79-57 record.

1902 TUESDAY, MAY 13TH, AT WEST SIDE PARK, CHICAGO

Donovan Loses One-Hitter

Cubs Win 2-0 on a Walk, Wild Bill's Error, and Their Only Hit
Hidden Ball Trick Ends Superbas' Best Chance to Score

BROOKLYN'S PITCHING ACE, WILD BILL Donovan, pitched a one-hit game today. Unfortunately, that one hit was combined with a walk and two errors to give Chicago two runs and a 2-0 victory over Donovan and the Superbas. The Brooks managed five hits off of Cub pitchers Walter "Pop" Williams and John "Jocko" Menefee but could not score. The only Brooklyn runner to get as far as third base was quickly eliminated by the old hidden ball trick.

Today's Results

Chicago 2-BROOKLYN 0
New York 3-St. Louis 1 (10 innings)
Cincinnati 24-Philadelphia 2
Boston at Pittsburg, ppd.—rain

Standings	W-L	Pct.	GB
Pittsburg	19-3	.864	—
Chicago	11-7	.611	6
New York	12-9	.571	6½
Boston	9-10	.474	8½
Philadelphia	9-11	.450	9
BROOKLYN	9-13	.409	10
Cincinnati	7-15	.318	12
St. Louis	6-14	.300	12

So Ned Hanlon's once-proud Superbas continued to struggle in the early stages of the pennant race. And the Chicagos, under Hanlon's old managerial rival Frank Selee, showed further signs of emerging from three years in the lower depths of the league.

Selee stole a march on Hanlon today by removing Williams after just two innings. Although he had not allowed any runs, Williams had been found for three hits, and Selee felt that he would do worse as the game wore on. Menefee, the relief hurler, held the Trolley Dodgers to just two hits over the final seven innings of the game.

Donovan outdid the Chicago pair in the matter of fewest hits allowed. "Wild Bill" gave up only one safety. But he lived up to his nickname by giving three bases on balls and making a critical throwing error. That error was bunched into the same inning with the only other error of the game, one of the walks, and the only Chicago hit to yield the only two runs of the day.

Brooklyn's five hits were not supplemented by any free passes or defensive lapses, and the Superbas were shut out as a result.

The game started promisingly for the visitors. After Cozy Dolan led off by flying out, Wee Willie Keeler beat out a bunt to the right side. Jimmy Sheckard followed with a clean hit to left, putting men on second and first. But Tom McCreery hit an easy fly to right, and Bill Dahlen grounded out, second to first, to end the inning.

Charlie Irwin smacked a two-base hit for Brooklyn with one out in the second inning. But once again, the subsequent batters could not move him around. This time Duke Farrell went out on a foul pop to third, and Donovan fanned the air three times.

The early hitting convinced Selee that today was not Williams's day. So rather than lose the game with a weak pitcher, he called Jocko Menefee into a game for the first time in ten days. Menefee was obviously fresh, and the Dodgers did not make a hit against his delivery until the seventh inning.

In the meantime, Donovan kept Selee's Colts from threatening for the first five innings. The first Chicago runner was Bobby Lowe, who walked with two out in the second. He was quickly erased trying to steal second by a fine throw by Farrell. Hal O'Hagan opened the third by strolling, and Joe Tinker sacrificed him to second. But Menefee flied out, and Jimmy Slagle struck out.

The break in the game finally came in the bottom half of the sixth. Donovan started well, getting two quick strikes on Tinker, the leadoff batter. But then his control went out the window, and four wide ones put Tinker on first. Menefee, to no one's surprise, bunted. Donovan pounced on the ball and had enough time to get a force out at second. But Wild Bill threw wide and pulled shortstop Dahlen off the base for an error, allowing both runners to be safe. Slagle continued the bunting game, and Donovan once again threw badly, this time to first. But this time first baseman McCreery made a fine stretch and catch to retire the batter. Tinker and Menefee advanced a base on the sacrifice. At this opportune moment, Dakin Miller delivered the only hit for Chicago, a line single over shortstop. It sent Tinker home and put Menefee on third. Charlie Dexter hit a bouncer to third, where Irwin fumbled the chance and allowed Menefee to score and Dexter to reach first. After Bunk Congalton flied out, Dexter stole second. He was left there when Johnny Kling grounded out.

Trailing 2-0, the Superbas came up in the seventh determined to score. Although McCreery opened by popping out, Dahlen hit safely past the second baseman and stole second. Tim Flood hit a long drive to center. Outfielder Slagle caught the ball, but Dahlen challenged his arm and beat the throw to third. While Bill was dusting himself off after his slide, third baseman Dexter was hiding the ball in his glove. Pitcher Menefee went through the motions of preparing to pitch, and Dahlen edged off third base. He was taken completely by surprise when Dexter snuck up and tagged him out. "Bad Bill" was in a blue funk at this turn of events, but all the profanity in the world could not keep him from being out and having to go pick up his glove for the Chicago half of the inning.

In the Brooklyn eighth, Irwin led off with a hit to left. But Farrell and Donovan hit easy flies, and Dolan struck out.

In the ninth, Menefee induced Keeler to pop to short. Sheckard hit a hard liner, but it went directly to first baseman O'Hagan for the second out. And second baseman Lowe ran under McCreery's fly to end the game.

Although he had been nearly unhittable, Donovan had beaten himself through his own wild pitching and wild throwing to the bases. But he was not entirely to blame. After all, you can't win if your team gets shut out.

Brooklyn	ab	r	h	bi	o	a	e
C. Dolan, cf	4	0	0	0	1	0	0
W. Keeler, rf	4	0	1	0	3	0	0
J. Sheckard, 1f	4	0	1	0	1	0	0
T. McCreery, 1b	4	0	0	0	11	0	0
B. Dahlen, ss	3	0	1	0	4	3	0
T. Flood, 2b	3	0	0	0	1	1	0
C. Irwin, 3b	3	0	2	0	0	5	1
D. Farrell, c	3	0	0	0	3	1	0
B. Donovan, p	3	0	0	0	0	2	1
	31	0	5	0	24	12	2

Chicago	ab	r	h	bi	o	a	e
J. Slagle, cf	3	0	0	0	3	0	0
D. Miller, 1f	4	0	1	1	3	0	0
C. Dexter, 3b	3	0	0	0	3	0	0
B. Congalton, rf	3	0	0	0	1	0	0
J. Kling, c	3	0	0	0	3	0	0
B. Lowe, 2b	2	0	0	0	2	4	0
H. O'Hagan, 1b	2	0	0	0	8	0	0
J. Tinker, ss	1	1	0	0	1	1	0
P. Williams, p	0	0	0	0	1	0	0
J. Menefee, p3	3	1	0	0	2	2	0
	24	2	1	1	27	7	0

Brooklyn	000 000 000	=	0
Chicago	000 002 00x	=	2

	ip	h	r-er	bb	so
Donovan (L 1-4)	8	1	2-0	3	2
Williams	2	3	0-0	0	1
Menefee (W 3-0)	7	2	0-0	0	2

Umpire: B. Emslie

Game-Winning RBI: Miller
LOB: Brooklyn 4, Chicago 3
BE: Chicago 2
2B: Irwin
SH: Tinker, Slagle
SB: Dexter, Dahlen
CS: Lowe
Time—1:25 Attendance-1,100

After their slow start, Donovan and the Superbas gradually improved their records. Wild Bill wound up the season with a 17-15 log. The team reached second place by mid-June, although they had to battle with Boston the rest of the way for the runner-up slot. Brooklyn finished with a 75-63 record, which got them second, 1½ games ahead of the Beaneaters but 27½ behind the pennant-winning Pirates.

1903 THURSDAY, AUGUST 27TH, AT WASHINGTON PARK

Superbas Win with 17 Walks

Brooklyn Makes only 7 Hits but Beats Philadelphia 11-10
Wild Hurling and Key Errors Beat Phillies

Today's Results			
BROOKLYN 11-Philadelphia 10			
Cincinnati 8-Chicago 1			
Boston 3-New York 1 (1st game)			
New York 7-Boston 1 (2nd game)			
St. Louis at Pittsburg, ppd.—rain			
Standings	**W-L**	**Pct.**	**GB**
Pittsburg	72-37	.661	—
Chicago	65-45	.591	7½
New York	66-46	.589	7½
Cincinnati	59-49	.546	12½
BROOKLYN	54-55	.495	18
Boston	46-60	.434	24½
St. Louis	38-73	.342	35
Philadelphia	33-68	.327	35

TODAY THE BROOKLYN FANS GOT A chance to see why the Philadelphia Phillies were on the bottom of the National League standings. Although the Phils scored ten runs by pounding out sixteen hits, they gave the game to the Superbas by walking seventeen of the home team's batters. The visitors overcame a Brooklyn lead in the sixth inning, only to hand the game right back in the eighth.

The seventeen bases on balls represented a National League record, tying the mark set in 1887. Today the Phillies used two hurlers, Fred Mitchell and Bill Duggleby. Mitchell did worse, walking twelve in five innings of work. Duggleby passed five in three innings.

Brooklyn used three pitchers, and none of them gave a base on balls. But the Superba moundmen were hit hard, and the Brooklyn fielders made five errors and a passed ball to help the Phillies score ten runs in all.

The Phils made three errors. And Brooklyn mixed five of its seven hits in with the myriad walks to come up with eleven runs and victory. Jimmy Sheckard was the hitting star for the winners. He had two singles and his team's only extra base hit, a double. His last hit drove in the game-winning run in the eighth inning.

The Phillies opened the game with two quick hits off of Henry Schmidt. But the California German then got a double play and a fly out to stop the threat.

In the second inning, however, Schmidt was rocked for four hits and four runs. He started his own troubles by hitting the first batter, Shad Barry, with a pitch. Klondike Bill Douglass singled Barry to third, and Rudy Hulswitt's sacrifice fly sent him home. Roy Thomas sent a screamer to center, which John Dobbs misplayed into a triple, Mitchell scoring. Thomas came home on a hit up the middle by Kid Gleason.

Mitchell had walked his first batter in the opening inning, but that man had been thrown out trying to steal second. Mitchell's wildness cost him a run in the second, however. With one out, Bill Dahlen looked at four wide ones. As the runner was stealing second, Mitchell pitched one back to the screen, allowing Dahlen to go all the way to third. Harry "Doc" Gessler got nicked by a pitch. Tim Jordan hit a grounder to shortstop, forcing Gessler. But Jordan beat the attempt at a double play, and Dahlen counted a run.

The Superbas got two bases on balls in the third but did not score.

The Phillies were given a run by the bad play of the Brooks in the fourth. Dooin singled with one out. He moved to second on a passed ball. Then he stole third and came home off a wild throw by catcher Fred Jacklitsch.

Trailing 5-1, the Superbas rallied to tie the game in their fourth by getting three hits to go with three walks. Jack Doyle and Dahlen opened with hits, and catcher Dooin's wild pickoff throw to first moved the runners to second and third. They scored on two infield outs. Mitchell then went up in the air like a balloon and walked three men to load the bases. Sheckard picked this spot to knock a double to right field, tying the game. Dobb's grounded out ended the inning.

But the Phils quickly grabbed the lead again with two runs in the fifth. Doubles by Gleason and Barry around a fumbled bunt got the runs home.

Undaunted, Mitchell proceeded to hand the lead to the Superbas in the bottom of the fifth by giving five free tickets to first base. Shortstop Hulswitt contributed an error, and the Dodgers got three runs without a single hit.

Pitcher Schmidt had been removed for a pinch-hitter in the rally, and Bill Reidy took over the pitching duties in the sixth. Aided by an error, the Phillies got two runs off him in that inning to go back on top, 9-8.

Philadelphia captain Chief Zimmer decided to try a new pitcher, too, and Duggleby took the mound in the bottom of the sixth. He walked two men in his first inning of work, but they did not score.

The Phillies got another run in the seventh on a hit by Douglass, a force out, a wild pitch, and a single by Duggleby.

Then the Superbas scored three times in the eighth to take the winning lead. Doyle opened with a safe hit, but Dahlen and Gessler flied out. Hulswitt then fumbled away a chance to end the inning, and Jordan reached first on the error. Upset by the poor support, Duggleby lost his control. Jacklitsch walked to load the bases. Tom McCreery, batting for Reidy, also strolled, forcing a run home. And Sammy Strang waited out his free pass to bring home the tying run. Sheckard singled Jacklitsch home to put Brooklyn ahead.

Manager Ned Hanlon sent Virgil Garvin to the mound to protect the lead in the ninth. Douglass greeted the new pitcher with a single to right. Hulswitt also hit the ball hard. But his liner went directly to first baseman Doyle, who ran to the bag to double Douglass off base. Dooin got a hit, but Duggleby fanned to end the game.

Brooklyn had the victory, 11-10, thanks to all those walks and a few strategically placed hits and errors. It was not the sort of game to be especially proud of, but it was a victory nonetheless.

Philadelphia	**ab**	**r**	**h**	**bi**	**o**	**a**	**e**
R. Thomas, cf	5	2	2	1	5	0	0
K. Gleason, 2b	5	2	4	1	1	4	0
H. Wolverton, 3b	4	1	1	2	0	0	0
B. Hallman, rf	4	0	1	1	0	0	0
S. Barry, 1f	4	1	1	1	3	0	0
B. Douglass, 1b	5	1	3	0	8	1	0
R. Hulswitt, ss	5	1	0	1	3	2	2
R. Dooin, c	5	1	2	0	3	3	1
F. Mitchell, p	3	1	1	1	1	2	0
B. Duggleby, p6	2	0	1	1	0	0	0
	42	10	16	9	24	12	3

Brooklyn	**ab**	**r**	**h**	**bi**	**o**	**a**	**e**
S. Strang, 3b	3	0	0	1	1	1	2
J. Sheckard, 1f	4	0	3	4	2	0	0
J. Dobbs, cf	4	0	0	0	3	0	1
J. Doyle, 1b	3	3	2	0	10	0	0
B. Dahlen, ss	3	3	1	0	3	2	0
D. Gessler, rf	2	0	0	2	1	0	0
D. Jordan, 2b	5	1	0	2	1	4	1
F. Jacklitsch, c	2	3	1	0	6	1	1
H. Schmidt, p	0	1	0	0	0	1	0
T. Flood, ph5	1	0	0	0	-	-	-
B. Reidy, p6	1	0	0	0	0	0	0
T. McCreery, ph8	0	0	0	1	-	-	-
V. Garvin, p9	0	0	0	0	0	0	0
	28	11	7	10	27	9	5

Philadelphia	040	122	100	=	10
Brooklyn	010	430	03x	=	11

	ip	**h**	**r-er**	**bb**	**so**
Mitchell (L 8-12)	5	3	8-6	12	0
Duggleby	3	4	3-0	5	1
Schmidt (W 17-13)	5	9	7-5	0	3
Reidy	3	5	3-1	0	2
Garvin	1	2	0-0	0	1

HBP: by Schmidt (Barry)
by Mitchell (Gessler)
WP: Mitchell, Duggleby, Reidy
PB: Jacklitsch

Game-Winning RBI: Sheckard
LOB: Philadelphia 8, Brooklyn 12
BE: Philadelphia 3, Brooklyn 2
DP: Jordan-Doyle (Wolverton)
Doyle unassisted
2B: Mitchell, Sheckard, Gleason
3B: Thomas
SH: Gessler, Wolverton, Hallman
SB: Dahlen, Dooin, Gleason
CS: Sheckard, Doyle
Picked Off: Schmidt
Time—2:14 Attendance—1,200
Umpire: H. O'Day

Seventeen bases on balls remains the National League record for one game 80 years later.

Brooklyn got over the .500 mark and ended the season with a 70-66 record. That was still only good enough for fifth place.

1904 SUNDAY, APRIL 24TH, AT WASHINGTON PARK

Three Players Arrested at Sunday Game

Three Scorecard Vendors Also Arrested to Test Sunday Blue Law
Game is Then Played and Brooklyn Wins 8-6

Today's Results			
BROOKLYN 8-Philadelphia 6			
St. Louis 4-Chicago 3			
Cincinnati 6-Pittsburg 5			
no other games scheduled			
Standings	**W-L**	**Pct.**	**GB**
New York	6-1	.857	—
St. Louis	5-3	.625	1½
Cincinnati	6-4	.600	1½
BROOKLYN	5-4	.556	2
Pittsburg	4-6	.400	3½
Boston	3-5	.375	3½
Chicago	3-5	.375	3½
Philadelphia	2-6	.250	4½

CHARLIE EBBETS'S PLAN TO CIRCUMVENT the state law prohibiting ballplaying on Sunday was put to the test today. Since the law made selling tickets to amusements on the Sabbath illegal, last Sunday Ebbets staged a game at Washington Park with ostensibly free admission. But the patrons were then expected to purchase scorecards at a price equal to the cost of a ticket for the seats they occupied. For example, the grandstand customers were "offered" scorecards for 50¢, while the bleacherites were given scorecards for 25¢.

The police observed the proceedings but did nothing last Sunday. And just yesterday, police commissioner McAdoo had said that the game scheduled for this Sunday would not be interfered with. But Saturday afternoon a delegation from the Kings County Sabbath Observation Association called upon the commissioner to protest the Sunday games. In response, McAdoo this morning sent orders to Captain White of the Bergen Street Police Station to make arrests "in good faith."

Captain White called upon club president Ebbets and secretary Harry Von der Horst early in the afternoon to tell them of the impending action. When the first fans were admitted, three policemen in plain clothes were amongst them. When they were sold programs, they duly arrested three different scorecard vendors.

Since the managers had been warned of planned arrests in advance, substitutes were used at the start of the game. When the umpire called "Play Ball," Frank Roth was the Philadelphia batter, and Ed Poole was the Brooklyn pitcher. After Poole had thrown two pitches to Roth, Captain White marched onto the field and placed Roth under arrest. He also took Poole and catcher Fred Jacklitsch into custody and seized the ball and bat as evidence. The players were allowed to change into their street clothes before being taken off to the station house.

The players were charged under Section 265 of the Penal Code, which prohibited hunting, fishing, shooting, and playing of games on the first day of the week. The vendors were charged under Section 267, which related to selling tickets to games played on Sundays. All six men were quickly bailed out.

Meanwhile back on the field, the game was allowed to go on. Hugh Duffy took Roth's place after the arrests, and Grant Thatcher and Lou Ritter formed a new battery. It had all happened so quickly that many of the spectators were unaware that any arrests had been made at all.

Captain White returned to the grounds and watched most of the game. Afterwards he stated the opinion that, "Personally, I saw no grounds for police interference. I have seen many crowds at many ball games in my day, but a finer-looking, better-behaved crowd than that at Washington Park this afternoon I have never seen." But orders were orders, so he had made his arrests.

Young Thatcher, pitching his first game of the season, started off poorly. The Phillies pounded his deliveries for eight hits and six runs in the first four innings. Then the righthander settled down and limited the visitors to just one hit and no runs in the last five frames.

The highlight of the early going was an unusual play in the third inning. Harry Wolverton had singled home a run and was on first base with two out. John Titus got a hit to right field, and Wolverton tried to make third. Outfielder Harry Lumley's throw had him beaten by twenty feet, but the ball hit the runner in the back of the head. Wolverton stumbled to the base safely, then staggered off and collapsed to the ground, only semi-conscious. Doc Marshall, coaching at third base, tried to drag the body back to the base, but third baseman Dude McCormick recovered the ball and tagged Wolverton before Marshall could get him back to third. However, umpire Bob Emslie would not allow the out, ruling that Wolverton had reached the base safely before passing out. Kid Gleason, who had just made an out, was put in to run in Wolverton's place, and he eventually scored a run. The tally was credited to Wolverton in the box score. By the time the third out had been made, Wolverton was sufficiently revived to resume his position, and he finished the game.

Brooklyn trailed 6-0 going into the bottom of the fourth. Jimmy Sheckard got the Superbas started on the road back to victory with a single. Lumley beat out a bunt. Both runners moved up on a sacrifice and scored on a hit by Charlie Babb.

Another Brooklyn run was made in the fifth to make the score 6-3. This tally came on a bunt single by Sammy Strang, a stolen base, and a bingle by Lumley.

The Brooks won the game with a five-run rally in the seventh. Ritter led off with a long drive to left field, which Shad Barry misjudged and allowed to go for a triple. Thatcher singled Ritter home. Pitcher Bill Duggleby then got two quick outs. But he laid a fat one in to Lumley, and Harry slammed out a terrific triple to the center field fence to make the score 6-5. John Dobbs doubled to left to tie the game. Babb hit safely to right, and Dobbs beat the throw home to put Brooklyn into the lead. Frank Dillon doubled Babb home with the final run of the game.

At this juncture, a young man in the grandstand became so enthused with swinging his arm about that he dislocated his shoulder and had to be taken away for medical treatment. The rest of the big crowd went home happy after Thatcher completed the victory by shutting the Phillies out in the final innings.

If Ebbets and his attorney could win the cases against the arrested players and vendors, Brooklyn could look forward to many more enjoyable Sunday afternoons at the ballpark.

Philadelphia	ab	r	h	bi	o	a	e
F. Roth, cf*	0	0	0	0	0	0	0
H. Duffy, ph1-cf	3	1	2	1	2	0	0
K. Gleason, 2b	3	0	0	0	3	3	0
H. Wolverton, 3b	4	2	2	2	2	0	0
J. Titus, rf	4	0	1	0	1	0	0
S. Barry, 1f	3	0	0	0	1	0	0
B. Hall, 1b	4	1	2	1	8	0	0
R. Hulswitt, ss	4	1	1	0	1	4	0
R. Dooin, c	3	0	0	0	6	0	0
B. Duggleby, p	3	1	1	0	0	1	1
J. Lush, ph9	1	0	0	0	-	-	-
	32	6	9	4	24	8	1

Brooklyn	ab	r	h	bi	o	a	e
S. Strang, 2b	5	1	2	0	6	0	1
J. Sheckard, 1f	4	2	1	0	1	0	0
H. Lumley, rf	4	2	3	2	0	0	0
J. Dobbs, cf	3	1	1	1	6	0	0
C. Babb, ss	4	1	2	3	1	3	0
F. Dillon, 1b	4	0	1	1	6	2	0
D. McCormick, 3b	4	0	1	0	1	3	0
F. Jacklitsch, c*	0	0	0	0	0	0	0
L. Ritter, c1	4	1	1	0	6	2	0
E. Poole, p*	0	0	0	0	0	0	0
G. Thatcher, p1	4	0	1	1	0	1	0
	36	8	13	8	27	11	1

*Roth, Jacklitsch, and Poole arrested at the start of the game.

Philadelphia	202	200	000	=	6
Brooklyn	000	210	50x	=	8

	ip	h	r-er	bb	so
Duggleby (L 1-2)	8	13	8-8	0	4
Poole	*0	0	0-0	0	0
Thatcher (W 1-0)	9	9	6-4	2	4

WP: Thatcher
PB: Ritter
Time—1:50 Attendance—13,614

Game-Winning RBI: Babb
LOB: Philadelphia 4, Brooklyn 5
BE: Philadelphia 1, Brooklyn 0
DP: Ritter-Babb
2B: Wolverton, Dobbs, Dillon
2B: Ritter, Lumley
SH: Duffy, Gleason, Dooin, Dobbs
SB: Strang, Sheckard, Titus, Duffy
CS: Titus
Umpire: B. Emslie

After more "test-case" arrests and much legal action by the club and the religious organizations, the Sunday games were finally ruled illegal at the end of June.

The games helped boost the club's attendance, but the team on the field was still quite weak. It managed to avoid the cellar by 2½ games, but finished seventh, 52 games behind the pennant-winning Giants. Brooklyn's record was 55-98.

1905 FRIDAY, SEPTEMBER 1ST, AT THE SOUTH ENDS GROUNDS, BOSTON

Errors Keep Superbas in Last Place

Scanlan Pitches Fine Game Except for One Terrible Throw
Errors Give Boston 3 Runs in Second and 4-2 Victory

Today's Results			
Boston 4-BROOKLYN 2			
New York 4-Philadelphia 1			
Pittsburg 6-St. Louis 0			
Chicago 3-Cincinnati 0			
Standings	**W-L**	**Pct.**	**GB**
New York	84-34	.712	—
Pittsburg	80-43	.650	6½
Chicago	71-50	.587	14½
Philadelphia	63-56	.529	21½
Cincinnati	61-58	.513	23½
St. Louis	46-77	.374	40½
Boston	40-83	.325	46½
BROOKLYN	37-81	.314	47

NED HANLON'S "SUPERBAS" TODAY HAD a chance to escape last place in the National League standings, but they failed to do so. They lost a game to the seventh-place Boston Beaneaters, 4-2, although Brooklyn outhit Boston, eight to six. The difference in the game was two errors by Brooklyn in the second inning, which gave Boston three runs and a lead which the Beans never lost.

Dodger pitcher William "Doc" Scanlan pitched credibly, but he was in no position to complain about poor fielding support. It was he who made the worst error of the game, throwing away an easy chance and allowing two runners to score on what should have been the third out of the inning. The other error in the second was made by third baseman Charlie Babb, who booted a grounder. A third error was made by Brooklyn in the eighth inning, but it did not result in any Boston runs.

Brooklyn also ran the bases poorly, thereby losing a couple of chances to score.

The Beans played errorless ball behind their hurler, Irving "Young Cy" Young. Each team turned a neat double play.

The two clubs, who were the class of the league five or six years ago, have struggled all season to stay out of the cellar. But one was certain to finish in last place for the first time in its history. Although St. Louis was in eighth place briefly in May, it was a two-team "battle" between Brooklyn and Boston all summer. The Superbas, who had lost all claim to being superb some time ago, were last throughout June. Boston dropped to last a couple of times in July, but Brooklyn fell to the bottom for most of August. On August 28th, the Trolley Dodgers nosed their way back up to seventh. But two days later, the Beaneaters went back ahead.

Before today's game, Brooklyn needed a victory over Boston to move back into seventh place. Manager Hanlon had his only winning pitcher on the season, Scanlan, primed and ready to "bring home the bacon." Boston's player-manager, Fred Tenney, however, countered with his only hurler with a winning record, Young. Neither pitcher was at his best, but both did reasonably well.

Young yielded three hits in the first inning, but fast fielding and poor base running kept the Dodgers from scoring. John Dobbs opened the game with a hit to center. Jimmy Sheckard hit sharply to first baseman Tenney, who turned one of his famous first-to-short-to-first double plays. Bob Hall then hit safely to center. Harry "Doc" Gessler rapped a single to right, and Hall tried to take third only to be retired by a fine throw from Cozy Dolan to Allie Strobel. So the three of the four Brooklyn batters in the inning had hit safely, but the side was retired with no runs and only one man left on base.

Tenney whacked a double to left with one out in the Boston first. He tried to come all the way home as Scanlan was throwing Dolan out at first base, and Gessler threw to the catcher in time to nab Tenney at the plate, completing Brooklyn's double play.

Babb got in the way of one of Young's outshoots to lead off the second inning. Phil Lewis attempted to sacrifice but popped out instead. Babb did get to second on Charlie Malay's tap to the mound and took third on a wild pitch. Then the game was interrupted by an unusual occurrence. A foul tip off of the bat of Bill Bergen got stuck in umpire George Bausewine's mask. It took several players, but the ball was finally pried loose. The delay only postponed the inevitable for a few minutes, and the weak-hitting Bergen soon struck out, leaving Babb on third.

Then came the fateful bottom of the second. Jim Delahanty led off with a short pop fly that fell safely in front of left fielder Sheckard. Rip Cannell tried to sacrifice, but his bunt forced Delahanty at second. Fred Raymer grounded down to Babb at third, and Charlie made a rank fumble, putting men on first and second. Scanlan got Strobel to pop out. But Pat Moran hit a long double to the fence in left, and Cannell scored the first run of the game. Young followed with an easy bouncer to Scanlan. Doc had plenty of time to throw to first and retire the side, but he inexplicably threw wildly past Gessler, and Raymer and Moran scored before the ball could be retrieved. That gave Boston a 3-0 lead.

The Superbas quickly got two runs back in the third. Scanlan struck out to lead off. Dobbs then dropped a Texas Leaguer into left for a base. Sheckard slipped a grounder under Young's fingers for another single. Hall flied to center for the second out. Then Gessler delivered a long drive over Cannell's head in center, driving two men home and earning three bases himself. Gessler was left on third when Babb flied out to right.

After getting the first two out in the Boston third, Scanlan lost his control and walked Delahanty. Cannell blooped one over the shortstop's head, and Delahanty raced to third, with Cannell taking second on the late throw. Raymer was walked to get to rookie Strobel, whom Scanlan struck out.

The Beaneaters managed to score the game's final run in the fifth. With one man gone, Dolan bunted safely. After the second out, Cozy stole second and scored on Cannell's hit to left.

The Superbas got only one hit off of Young from the fourth inning through the eighth. That was a two-out single by Babb in the sixth.

Going into the ninth inning, Brooklyn still trailed by two runs. Gessler led off with a safe hit to left, but he stupidly tried to stretch it into a double and was thrown out by Delahanty. With their already sagging spirits thusly deflated further, the Brooklyns made the final two outs quickly.

The game ended with Boston winning, 4-2, and the hapless Superbas just a little deeper in last place. By giving games away like they did today, Hanlon's men could have an easy time staying there for the rest of the season.

Brooklyn	ab	r	h	bi	o	a	e
J. Dobbs, cf	4	1	2	0	2	0	0
J. Sheckard, 1f	4	1	1	0	3	0	0
B. Hall, rf	4	0	1	0	2	0	0
D. Gessler, 1b	4	0	3	2	6	1	0
C. Babb, 3b	3	0	1	0	2	2	1
P. Lewis, ss	4	0	0	0	2	1	0
C. Malay, 2b	3	0	0	0	0	2	1
B. Bergen, c	3	0	0	0	7	0	0
D. Scanlan, p	3	0	0	0	0	2	1
	32	2	8	2	24	8	3

Boston	ab	r	h	bi	o	a	e
E. Abbaticchio, ss	4	0	0	0	2	3	0
F. Tenney, 1b	4	0	1	0	10	2	0
C. Dolan, rf	4	1	1	0	2	1	0
J. Delahanty, 1f	3	0	1	0	0	1	0
R. Cannell, cf	4	1	2	1	3	0	0
F. Raymer, 2b	3	1	0	0	1	3	0
A. Strobel, 3b	4	0	0	0	1	0	0
P. Moran, c	3	1	1	1	5	0	0
I. Young, p	3	0	0	0	3	4	0
	32	4	6	2	27	14	0

Brooklyn	002 000 000	=	2
Boston	030 010 00x	=	4

	ip	h	r-er	bb	so
Scanlan (L 10-10)	8	6	4-1	2	5
Young (W 17-15)	9	8	2-2	0	4

WP: Young
HBP: by Young (Babb)
Umpire: G. Bausewine

Game-Winning RBI: Moran
LOB: Brooklyn 4, Boston 6
BE: Boston 3
DP: Tenney-Abbaticchio-Tenney (Sheckard)
Scanlan-Gessler-Bergen
2B: Tenney, Moran
3B: Gessler
SB: Dolan
Time—1:40 Attendance—1,406

The next day, the Superbas lost to the Beaneaters again, this time 1-0. Brooklyn never did catch Boston and finished last for the only time in history. The Superbas' record was a dismal 48-104, which was 3 games worse than the Beans'.

Chapter IV The Ex-Superbas

1906 August 1st
McIntire Has No-Hitter for 10 Innings, then Loses

1907 April 20th
Nap Rucker Loses Brooklyn Debut

1908 September 5th
Rucker Hurls No-Hitter

1909 April 15th
No-Hit for 9, Brooklyn Wins Opener in 13

1910 June 15th
Cy Barger Pitches and Bats Dodgers to Victory

1911 July 8th
Fans Bombard Umpire

1912 September 17th
Stengel Makes 4 Hits in Debut

1913 April 5th
Opening of Ebbets Field Draws 30,000

AFTER NED HANLON'S "SUPERBAS" FELL TO LAST PLACE IN 1905, HANLON QUIT THE Brooklyn club and signed to manage in Cincinnati. His conflicts with Brooklyn owner Charles Ebbets surfaced from time to time over the next few years in the form of lawsuits against Ebbets concerning the liquidation of the old Baltimore franchise.

After Hanlon left, some sportswriters altered the nickname of the team to "ex-Superbas." The team was certainly far from superb, but the name Superbas remained in use well into the 1920's.

Hanlon's successor as manager was Patsy Donovan, who had played for the Bridegrooms briefly in 1890. Since then, Donovan had been around the big leagues as an outfielder and player-manager. When he came to Brooklyn, it was strictly as a bench manager. But his playing background and easygoing manner made him popular with his players.

To try and get out of the cellar, the club also added several new players. Chicago made an offer that could not be refused, and the Dodgers got four players for Jimmy Sheckard, the leading Brooklyn hitter in 1905. Three of the players received from the Cubs (Doc Casey, Bill Maloney, and Jack McCarthy) became regulars for Donovan. But they were all past their primes and had to be replaced within a year or two. Two minor leaguers also broke into the lineup, second baseman Charles "Whitey" Alperman and first baseman Tim "Big City" Jordan. One pitcher of note, lefthander John Pastorious, was also acquired.

The revamped squad got off to a terrible start and was in last place until Memorial Day. Then the team improved enough to creep up in the standings. Shortstop was still a problem, but the defense in general was much improved. Pitchers Harry McIntire and Mal Eason each pitched a nine-inning no-hitter in the middle of the summer, although McIntire lost his no-hitter in the eleventh inning and lost the game in the thirteenth. But the Superba offense was still woefully weak.

By the end of the season, Donovan's first year at the helm looked like a positive success, especially when the Superbas won their final four games to overtake Hanlon's Reds and finish in fifth place. Sunday crowds early in the season helped the club turn a modest profit. But for the third year in a row, Sunday games were ruled illegal, and this time the Sunday experiments were ended until World War I.

Nap Rucker

In 1907, Brooklyn fielded pretty much the same team as it had in 1906. The only notable additions were pitchers George Bell and Nap Rucker. Brooklyn had drafted Bell from the Amsterdam-Johnstown-Gloversville club of the New York State League in the fall of 1904. But he was not interested in Brooklyn's salary offers, even when the club went as high as $1500 for the season. He had pitched in the "outlaw" Tri-State League in 1906, but he finally came to terms with Brooklyn in 1907. Bell pitched some good ball for the next four years, although he had a lot of hard luck.

George Napoleon Rucker had been the property of the Atlanta Crackers, who had farmed him to the Augusta, Ga., team. With the Dodgers, he pitched well in each of his first three games but lost. That would be the story of his career. A lefthander with a great fastball and a fine curve, Rucker became the mainstay of the franchise for the next half dozen seasons, although his lifetime record was a dead-even 134-134.

In the 1907 season, Patsy's Superbas once again got off to a horrid start, winning only 1 or their first 17 decisions. Thereafter, they were not much worse than a .500 team. By August 5th, they had established themselves permanently in fifth place. Both Jordan and Alperman suffered broken ankles, and only three players hit over .250. But Rucker and Pastorious posted winning records. The team as a whole wound up with a 65-83 slate.

In 1908 it was more of the same except that the lineup was older and less effective now. Jordan led the team in hitting with a microscopic .247 average. The team average shrank all the way to .213, the lowest in the history of the franchise. And the average of 2.4 runs scored per game was the second-lowest in the history of the major leagues.

Things got to be very bad in early September, when Brooklyn won only 1 of its first 17 games in the month. That one victory was on a no-hit, 14-strikeout performance by Rucker. After Nap's gem, the Dodgers lost three straight games by scores of 1-0. Luckily, the St. Louis Cardinals were even worse than the Superbas, and Brooklyn finished seventh despite 101 losses. Donovan was fired after the season.

Ebbets tried hard to get Bill Dahlen from Boston to be the new Brooklyn manager, but the asking price was too high for Ebbets's limited budget. Eventually captain Harry Lumley was appointed as manager. A chubby, easygoing fellow, Lumley was well respected by his teammates for his hitting ability. But he was not well-suited to be a manager. His managerial debut, at least, was a day to remember. The team opened against the Giants in New York and was no-hit for nine innings. But Irvin "Kaiser" Wilhelm pitched a shutout for the Superbas, too. Finally in the thirteenth

(left) Bill Dahlen
(right) Patsy Donovan

inning, Lumley himself started a rally with a big triple, and Brooklyn won, 3-0.

In the next game, Lumley broke his finger and was out for over a month. Later in the year he suffered from leg and shoulder miseries. The disillusioned Brooklyn fans were booing Lumley, a one-time hero, by the end of the season. A knee injury to Jordan hurt the team in June, and it dropped to seventh place. To fill a couple of big holes in the outfield, Ebbets purchased a couple of minor leaguers in late August who were destined to become stars in the outfield for Brooklyn. One, Hi Myers, needed more seasoning and did not crack the regular lineup until 1914. But the other, purchased from Mobile, arrived on September 11, 1909, and remained a fixture in left field until 1926. His name was Zack Wheat.

Thanks to another late swoon by St. Louis, the Superbas wound up in sixth place, ½ game ahead of the Cardinals and 55½ games behind the first-place Pirates.

After the 1909 season, Boston released Dahlen, and Ebbets was able to sign him as manager for 1910. Nicknamed "Bad Bill," Dahlen was a scrapper who got along poorly with the press and even worse with the umpires. But Ebbets liked him and kept him for four years.

Dahlen inherited the same problems that had plagued Donovan and Lumley before him, i.e., anemic hitting, poor shortstopping, and not enough Nap Ruckers on the pitching staff. But there were some useful additions to the team in 1910. Eros Bolivar "Cy" Barger was bought from Rochester. He was a good pitcher who could also hit. He proved that on June 15th, when he hit two RBI doubles and beat the mighty Chicago Cubs in 14 innings. He wound up 15-15 on the season. Rucker was 17-18. Poor George Bell was 10-27, losing more games than any Brooklyn pitcher since 1884.

Rookie first baseman Jake Daubert hit a modest .264 in 1910 but later blossomed into a great ballplayer. Catcher Otto Miller also joined the team in 1910, and he stayed with the Dodgers for 13 years.

Once again it was a dogfight with St. Louis for sixth place. And once again the Cardinals lost out by ½ game. Brooklyn's record of 64-90 was an improvement of 8½ games over 1909.

As usual, the Superbas started the 1911 season in last place. They moved into seventh on May 17th, and this year they stayed there. Although Rucker had his only 20-win season (22-18) and Daubert emerged as a solid hitter (.307), the fans had little to cheer about. The bleacherites at Washington Park had long before established themselves as the most obnoxious in the league, and the umpires always had a rough time in Brooklyn. On July 11th, one umpiring recruit threw the entire Brooklyn bench (including the batboy) out of the game, and he was showered with bottles from the stands in response. Although the team finished with a slightly improved record compared to 1910, no amount of fuming on Dahlen's part could get it out of seventh place.

Over the winter of 1912, Charles Hercules Ebbets unveiled the plans for his greatest dream, a new baseball palace. The park was appropriately named Ebbets

Field. The club owner had quietly been acquiring one square block in Flatbush for some years. By the time he had bought the entire plot, however, he did not have enough money left to build a first-class park. So he sold a one-half interest in his club to the McKeever brothers, Steve and Ed, who were Brooklyn construction contractors. The new park, which was designed by architect Clarence Van Buskirk and heavily influenced by Ebbets's ideas of the ideal stadium, cost over $700,000 to build. Ground was broken in March, 1912, with completion scheduled for early 1913.

Meanwhile back at Washington Park, life was as raucous as ever. On opening day, the club sold nearly 30,000 tickets, and the place was completely packed. Fans ringed the outfield so tightly that there was barely room to play a game. In the grandstand the crowding was incredible. All the aisles were filled and no one could move. Luckily no mob panic broke out, although the Giants slaughtered the Dodgers on the field, 18-3. A week later in New York, Dahlen got into a fist fight with an umpire at the end of the game.

With only one steady pitcher (Rucker was 18-21), the Superbas finished seventh again. But there were some optimistic notes. Otto Miller became the number-one catcher. Rookie George Cutshaw provided stability at second base. And a recruit outfielder from the Montgomery club had an auspicious big league debut in September with four hits in his first game. His name was Charles D. "Casey" Stengel.

Ebbets Field was ready for use in 1913. Nearly 30,000 came out to the first game played there, an exhibition against the Yankees on April 5th. The Dodgers won that one but lost the regular-season opener to the Phillies four days later. In the first season at the new park, the Superbas had a losing record. But it would be another ten years before Brooklyn had another losing season at home.

For the first time in years, the team had a reasonably set lineup, and the hitting was finally getting good. Jake Daubert won the batting title and the Most Valuable Player award. The Dodgers were in second place for much of May and were in third as late as July 3rd. But then the bottom fell out, and the team plummeted to a sixth-place finish. The Superbas lost nine out of ten 1-0 games over the course of the season. And the second-half slide convinced Ebbets that Dahlen would finally have to be replaced.

After much speculation, Wilbert Robinson of old Baltimore Oriole fame was hired as the new manager. He remained with the club through 1931 and even succeeded Ebbets as president.

at the Opening of Ebbets Field
(left to right) Charles Ebbets, Jr., Stephen W. McKeever, Charles Ebbets, Edward J. McKeever, Henry Medicus, and Clarence Van Buskirk

1906 WEDNESDAY AUGUST 1ST, AT WASHINGTON PARK

McIntire Has No-Hitter for 10 Innings, then Loses

Leifield Pitches for Pittsburg and Wins, 1-0, in 13 Innings
First Pirate Hit Comes after Short Rain Delay in 11th

HARRY MCINTIRE PITCHED THE GAME OF his life today. He stopped the slugging Pittsburg Pirates without a hit for ten innings. But he was pitching for the Dodgers, and his effort, great as it was, was not good enough to win the game. His teammates could not score a run, and eventually McIntire went down to defeat, 1-0, in 13 innings.

The no-hitter was the second of the season by a Brooklyn pitcher. The first was turned in by Mal Eason on July 20th against the St. Louis Cardinals. Luckily Eason got a couple of runs in support and won, 2-0.

Today's Results

Pittsburg 1-BROOKLYN 0 (13 innings)
Philadelphia 5-Chicago 3
New York 7-St. Louis 1
Boston 6-Cincinnati 1

Standings	W-L	Pct.	GB
Chicago	66-29	.695	—
Pittsburg	59-32	.648	5
New York	59-32	.648	5
Philadelphia	43-51	.457	22½
Cincinnati	41-54	.432	25
BROOKLYN	38-54	.413	26½
St. Louis	36-61	.371	31
Boston	32-61	.344	33

Only two Pirates reached first base safely against McIntire through the first ten innings today. One walked, and the other reached on a muffed pop fly. In the eleventh inning there were two out when a downpour interrupted play.After a delay of less than five minutes, McIntire went back to work against Claude Ritchey. With two strikes on the batter, he barely missed the outside corner twice (according to the umpire, at least). Then Ritchey hit one through the box and into center field for the first Pittsburg hit.The Pirates got three more hits in the thirteenth to push the game's only run across the plate.

For Pittsburg, Albert "Lefty" Leifield pitched a brilliant game. The Superbas were able to get only one man to third base against him, and of course, none to home. He received flawless support from his fielders. Shortstop Hans Wagner and second baseman Claude Ritchey were the fielding stars.

For Brooklyn, shortstop Phil Lewis and catcher Bill Bergen stood out with their glovework. Jack McCarthy was the goat of the game, twice getting caught napping off first base.

Pittsburg's Jim Nealon was given a free pass with one out in the second. Then McIntire gloved Tommy Sheehan's grounder and started a double play to end the inning.

Second baseman Whitey Alperman muffed Ritchey's fly to start the third, allowing the batter to reach second. But McIntire muscled up and struck the next two batters out and got Tommy Leach on a pop to first base.

Thereafter, Harry had the Pirate batters eating out of his hand. His side-armed curve and underhand riser were unhittable.

On the other side, Brooklyn could do little with Leifield's speed.

Wagner spoiled bids for runs in the seventh and ninth innings. Alperman started the seventh with a hit to center and moved to third on two infield outs. Bergen then lined one toward left field, but Wagner leaped high and snared the ball for the final out. In the ninth, Harry Lumley led off with a double to left. Tim Jordan missed two bunts then flied out. Alperman also flied out. Then McCarthy looped one over the third baseman for an apparent game-winning hit. But the great Wagner raced over and caught the ball with a desperate, sideways leap.

Through the first ten innings, the Brooklyn fielders had made two fine plays to keep the no-hitter intact. In the sixth, Lewis made a one-handed circus catch of Eddie Phelps's dangerous pop fly in short left field. It was one of the finest catches ever seen at Washington Park. In the tenth, Bob Ganley sent a hot shot toward right field, but Alperman ranged over to snare it and throw the batter out at first.

Brooklyn staged another threat in the bottom of the tenth. Lewis was walked to lead off, and Bergen bunted him to second. McIntire fouled out. Billy Maloney blooped one to right field, which Ritchey caught in sensational style to save the game for Pittsburg again.

In the top of the eleventh, Ritchey came to bat after the rain delay with two out. McIntire had him set up for a strikeout, but twice he just missed the plate. The Brooklyn fans howled their disapproval of the umpire's calls, but Ritchey still had a chance. He used it to send Pittsburg's first hit bouncing up the middle. Phelps also hit the ball hard, but Lewis was there to grab the line drive.

Wagner turned in yet another fielding gem in the bottom of the eleventh. With Lumley on first and one out, Jordan popped one in front of the big Dutchman. The disgusted Jordan started to walk toward the bench, and Wagner cannily let the ball bounce and started a double play.

Brooklyn got two hits in the twelfth but could not score. McCarthy got the first bingle with one out. But he was again caught off base and was put out sliding into second. Lewis then bunted safely. Bergen hit one up the middle, but Ritchey and Wagner turned it into a force out.

The Pirates finally broke through in the thirteenth. Ganley opened with a hit to center. Wagner followed a double to center that sent Ganley to third. Jim Nealon laced a clean hit to left,and Ganley trotted home. Wagner made a rare base-running mistake by holding up while the Brooklyn infield was making a double play. Then Hans tried to steal home only to be tagged out.

The luckless McIntire did his best in the bottom of the thirteenth, leading off with a clean hit to right. Maloney sacrificed him to second. With a chance to tie the game with a hit, Doc Casey chased a high pitch with the count full and struck out. Lumley then grounded out to Wagner to end the game.

So despite his truly great pitching feat of 10⅔ hitless innings,McIntire left the field as the losing pitcher. Pitching for Brooklyn, sometimes anything less than perfect was just not good enough.

Pittsburg	ab	r	h	bi	o	a	e
T. Leach, lf	5	0	0	0	1	0	0
G. Beaumont, cf	5	0	0	0	2	0	0
B. Ganley, rf	5	1	1	0	1	0	0
H. Wagner, ss	5	0	1	0	6	8	0
J. Nealon, 1b	4	0	1	1	17	2	0
T. Sheehan, 3b	5	0	0	0	1	4	0
C. Ritchey, 2b	4	0	1	0	5	7	0
E. Phelps, c	4	0	0	0	6	1	0
L. Leifield, p	4	0	0	0	0	4	0
	41	1	4	1	39	26	0

Brooklyn	ab	r	h	bi	o	a	e
B. Maloney, cf	5	0	0	0	1	0	0
D. Casey, 3b	5	0	1	0	1	2	0
H. Lumley, rf	5	0	1	0	2	0	0
T. Jordan, 1b	5	0	1	0	14	0	0
W. Alperman, 2b	5	0	2	0	2	3	1
J. McCarthy, lf	4	0	2	0	1	0	0
P. Lewis, ss	4	0	1	0	5	5	0
B. Bergen, c	4	0	0	0	13	1	0
H. McIntire, p	5	0	1	0	0	4	0
	42	0	9	0	39	15	1

Pittsburg	000 000 000 000 1 = 1
Brooklyn	000 000 000 000 0 = 0

	ip	h	r-er	bb	so
Leifield (W 12-6)	13	9	0-0	2	5
McIntire (L 8-13)	13	4	1-1	1	8

HBP: by Leifield (Casey)

Time—2:12
Attendance—3,000
Umpire: J. Johnstone

Game-Winning RBI: Nealon
LOB: Pittsburg 2, Brooklyn 9
BE: Pittsburg 1
DP: McIntire-Lewis-Jordan (Sheehan)
Wagner-Nealon (Jordan)
Alperman-Lewis-Jordan (Sheehan)
2B: Lumley, Wagner
SH: McCarthy, Bergen, Maloney
SB: Lewis, Casey
CS: McCarthy, Wagner
Picked Off: McCarthy

Brooklyn got a measure of revenge when it beat Pittsburg the next day, 2-1, with two runs in the bottom of the ninth.

The Superbas spent most of the rest of the season in sixth place but spurted at the end to nose out Ned Hanlon's Cincinnati Reds for fifth place in the final standings. Brooklyn's record was 66-86.

McIntire finished at 13-21.

1907 SATURDAY, APRIL 20TH, AT WASHINGTON PARK

Nap Rucker Loses Brooklyn Debut

Stupid Base Running Ruins the Dodgers
Phillies Get Only Three Hits But Win, 2-0

THIS NEW PITCHER OUGHT TO FIT RIGHT in in Brooklyn. George Napoleon "Nap" Rucker pitched his first home game for the Dodgers on this date. He twirled an impressive three-hitter and still lost, 2-0.

Today he showed the Washington Park fanatics fine speed, a good variety of curves, and a cool and collected demeanor on the mound. In fielding his position, he was credited with seven assists, a couple on difficult chances toward third base. At bat he made one hit and lined another ball hard. Only his base running was open to criticism.

Today's Results			
Philadelphia 2-BROOKLYN 0			
Chicago 5-Pittsburg 1 (8 innings)			
New York 13-Boston 2			
St. Louis 2-Cincinnati 1			
Standings	**W-L**	**Pct.**	**GB**
Chicago	4-1	.750	—
New York	5-2	.714	—
Philadelphia	4-2	.667	½
Cincinnati	3-3	.500	1½
St. Louis	3-4	.429	2
Boston	3-4	.429	2
Pittsburg	1-3	.250	2½
BROOKLYN	1-5	.167	3½

Rucker was not alone in making mistakes on the basepaths. In all, five Brooklyn runners were put out on the basepaths when they should not have been. This was the primary reason for the Superbas being shut out, although the Phillies' Johnny Lush pitched a strong game against them.

Rucker was recommended to president Ebbets by scout Larry Sutton. A left-hander out of Georgia, Nap had been pitching in the Sally League for two years, compiling a 27-9 record in 1906. In his first game with Brooklyn, last Monday in Boston, he allowed only four hits but made two throwing errors and lost, 3-2.

Today he allowed only three hits, walked three, and made no errors. But the Phillies put two of their hits behind one of the walks and in front of an error in the outfield to score two runs. That was enough to win.

The rookie hurler got off to a shaky start by walking the first batter he faced, veteran leadoff man Roy Thomas. Kid Gleason bunted to the pitcher, who had no play at second but got the out at first. Otto Knabe bounced one up the middle, and Rucker snared it. Thomas was run down between second and third, while Knabe reached the midway station. Up stepped the Phillies' slugger, Sherry Magee. The count went full, and Rucker snapped off a big curve that utterly fooled Magee for strike three. The crowd went wild, and Rucker became an instant favorite.

In the second inning, however, the youngster was found for two runs. After Kitty Bransfield fouled out, Ernie Courtney worked Rucker for a walk. Mickey Doolan smashed a double down the left field line, and Courtney came all the way home. Fred Jacklitsch followed with a hit to right, and Doolan scored when outfielder Harry Lumley juggled the ball. Rucker struck Lush out and got Thomas on a comebacker to the mound, but the damage was done.

The ex-Superbas started their base-running misadventures in the bottom of the second. Phil Lewis singled with one out, and Heinie Batch followed with a safe one to right. Lewis foolishly tried to go to third and was out by plenty on Knabe's fine throw to Courtney. John Butler walked to put two men on again. But Rucker fanned in the pinch.

Bransfield got the third and final Philadelphia hit leading off the fourth. It was a low liner to center that Billy Maloney got to with a fine effort but could not hold. Rucker eventually picked Bransfield off first, and the runner was tagged trying desperately to reach second.

After that, the Phils got only two men to first. Thomas walked again in the eighth, but he was left on first. In the ninth, Batch muffed Magee's drive, giving the batter second. Rucker threw Magee out at third after gloving Bransfield's grounder. And Bransfield was left on first when Courtney bounced out to Rucker.

Brooklyn's second big chance to score and its second big base-running blunder came in the fifth inning. Batch, first up, was given a base on balls. He took second on an infield out. Rucker cracked a clean hit to right, and Batch timidly did not try to score. Maloney lifted a high pop on the infield. First baseman Bransfield muffed the ball, forcing Rucker to run for second. As Bransfield threw to shortstop Doolan, Batch belatedly broke for home. Doolan relayed the ball to the catcher, and Batch was caught in a rundown. He was eventually tagged out. Rucker, who had reached third in the meantime, suddenly wandered off the base and was also tagged, completing a very strange double play. Rucker later explained that he thought he had been forced out on Bransfield's initial throw to shortstop. No one else seemed to think so.

The bad base running continued in the sixth. Doc Casey led off with a walk. Lumley sent him to second with a hit to center. When "Big City" Tim Jordan missed a bunt, Casey was neatly caught off second and tagged at third. Jordan and Alperman then hit ground outs.

The Superbas kept up the bad work in the seventh. Lewis hit a crisp single to right to start the inning. After Batch flied out, Butler singled to center, with Lewis stopping at second. Rucker then lined one to right, and the runners took off. But Knabe made a nice running catch of the ball. Butler was just barely able to get back to first ahead of Knabe's throw. But Lewis refused to leave third, and he was easily doubled off second, ignominiously ending another promising rally.

Lush set the Brooks down in order in the eighth, although Lumley's line drive sent Knabe back to the fence.

Jordan opened the ninth with a drive off the wall, which Knabe's fast fielding held to a single. Alperman and Lewis both went out on taps to the mound. Batch ended the game with a ground out to short.

The Superbas had lost another one, the final score being 2-0. But the day had not been a total loss for the Brooklyn fans. After all, it looked like the Dodgers had come up with a first-class pitcher in Nap Rucker.

Now if the team could just learn how to run the bases!

Philadelphia	ab	r	h	bi	o	a	e
R. Thomas, cf	2	0	0	0	1	0	0
K. Gleason, 2b	3	0	0	0	2	7	0
O. Knabe, rf	4	0	0	0	3	2	0
S. Magee, 1f	4	0	0	0	1	0	0
K. Bransfield, 1b	4	0	1	0	11	2	1
E. Courtney, 3b	3	1	0	0	3	1	0
M. Doolan, ss	3	1	1	1	1	5	0
F. Jacklitsch, c	3	0	1	0	5	3	0
J. Lush, p	3	0	0	0	0	4	0
	29	2	3	1	27	24	1

Brooklyn	ab	r	h	bi	o	a	e
B. Maloney, cf	4	0	0	0	1	0	0
D. Casey, 3b	3	0	0	0	2	3	0
H. Lumley, rf	3	0	1	0	0	0	1
T. Jordan, 1b	4	0	1	0	12	1	0
W. Alperman, 2b	3	0	0	0	1	2	0
P. Lewis, ss	4	0	2	0	2	3	0
H. Batch, 1f	3	0	1	0	2	0	1
J. Butler, c	1	0	1	0	7	1	0
N. Rucker, p	3	0	1	0	0	7	0
	28	0	7	0	27	17	2

Philadelphia	020 000 000	=	2
Brooklyn	000 000 000	=	0

	ip	h	r-er	bb	so
Lush (L 1-1)	9	7	0-0	4	4
Rucker (L 0-2)	9	3	2-1	3	2

Time—1:42
Attendance—6,000
Umpires: B. Klem & C. Rigler

Game-Winning RBI: Doolan
LOB: Philadelphia 4, Brooklyn 7
BE: Philadelphia 1, Brooklyn 1
DP: Bransfield-Doolan-Jacklitsch-Gleason-Lush-Courtney, Knabe-Bransfield-Doolan
2B: Doolan
SH: Gleason, Butler, Alperman
SB: Jacklitsch
CS: Bransfield, Casey

In his next start, on April 27th, Rucker was given a lead for the first time, but he failed to hold it and lost, 4-2. He finally got his first win for Brooklyn on May 11th, beating the champion Cubs, 1-0. He finished the year with a 15-13 record.

The Superbas got off to the worst start in the franchise's history by winning only one of their first seventeen decisions. But the team rose slowly after that and left the cellar on Memorial Day. By mid-July, Brooklyn had climbed to fifth. They finished there by beating Cincinnati out by 1½ games. Brooklyn's final record was 65-83.

1908 SATURDAY, SEPTEMBER 5TH, AT WASHINGTON PARK

Rucker Hurls No-Hitter

Fans 14 Doves While Walking None
Gives Dodgers 6-0 Victory After 4-3 Defeat

Today's Results			
Boston 4-BROOKLYN 3 (1st game)			
BROOKLYN 6-Boston 0 (2nd game)			
New York 5-Philadelphia 1			
Chicago 11-Pittsburg 0			
Cincinnati 6-St. Louis 5			
Standings	**W-L**	**Pct.**	**GB**
New York	75-45	.625	—
Pittsburg	75-48	.610	1½
Chicago	75-49	.605	2
Philadelphia	65-54	.546	9½
Cincinnati	59-63	.484	17
Boston	52-73	.416	15½
BROOKLYN	44-78	.361	32
St. Louis	43-78	.355	32½

THE GEORGIA CRACKER NAP RUCKER TOday reached the pinnacle of pitching by shutting the Boston Doves out on no runs, no hits, and no bases on balls. He also struck out 14 batters. Only three palpable errors spoiled his perfect record.

The victory came in the second game of a doubleheader at Washington Park. Boston won the first game, thanks to some loose play by the Superbas, who lost their seventh consecutive game. But Rucker snapped the losing streak in the second game and kept his team from falling into last place in the National League standings.

The Brooks made three errors in each game and accumulated just thirteen hits all day. The sixth-place Bostons totalled six errors and got eight hits, all the hits coming in the first game, of course.

The opener was decided by bad fielding, although the victorious Doves outplayed the Superbas at all points.

Boston earned a run in the first inning against Brooklyn pitcher Irvin "Kaiser" Wilhelm with a walk, a single, and two infield outs.

Brooklyn took the lead with two runs in the second. Both runners scored on pitcher Cecil Ferguson's wild throw home trying to break up an attempted steal.

Boston tied the game in the third, with George Browne scoring for a second time. He reached first on an infield hit. Johnny Bates grounded to the third baseman and was thrown out at first. No one was covering third, and Browne rounded second at full speed. Shortstop Phil Lewis ran to cover the bag, but he missed the throw from first baseman Tim Jordan, and Browne continued home.

Brooklyn regained the lead in the fifth on a base on balls, a sacrifice, and a run-scoring single by Al Burch.

The Dodgers gave the game away in the eighth, however. A hit by Bates and a pass to Ginger Beaumont opened the inning. A passed ball moved the runners up one base each. Bates was tagged out at home after a ground ball. But on the next grounder, Lewis threw wildly and allowed Beaumont to score. Bill Sweeney followed with a clean double to give Boston the winning run. The final score was 4-3.

The second game was all Rucker, although his teammates gave him good batting support with four runs in the second inning and two more in the eighth.

The first batter of the game, Browne, was given first base on a fumble by Lewis. But Rucker grabbed Bates's bunt in the air and fired to first to double Browne off base. Joe Kelley then fouled to the catcher.

Dan McGann opened the second for Boston with an easy fly to right. Bill Dahlen fanned, the first of 14 Doves to be retired on strikes. Sweeney flied to center.

Brooklyn had been retired in order in the first but roared through with four runs in the second. Jordan opened with a single to right. Whitey Alperman bunted safely. Lewis walked to load the bases. Tommy Sheehan was hit by a pitch from Patsy Flaherty to force the first run home. Bill Bergen bounced one to first, and Dan McGann threw home wildly, allowing two runs to score. One out later, Burch flied to shallow left and outfielder Bates threw wildly past second to allow another run.

Pumped up by the lead, Rucker mowed down the Doves. After George "Peaches" Graham bounced out to open the third, Rucker struck out five batters in a row.

McGann broke the strikeout string in the fifth with a bouncer to third, which Sheehan kicked. Rucker struck out two of the next three batters and got the other one on a pop to short.

Browne was the only strikeout victim in the sixth, as Jack Hannifan and Flaherty grounded to Alperman and Rucker, respectively.

Bates and McGann fanned the breeze in the seventh, with Kelley fouling to the catcher in between.

Brooklyn threw away a sure run in their half of the seventh when Bergen left third base too early tagging up on a long fly. He was declared out on an appeal.

Boston got its closest thing to a hit in the eighth. After Dahlen struck out to lead off, Sweeney lifted a fly to shallow right. Outfielder Harry Lumley misjudged the ball at first, then came charging in after it. He got both hands on the ball and then dropped it. There was a little hesitation on the part of the official scorer, but it was finally ruled an error. Umpire Jim Johnstone later agreed with that ruling. Rucker retired the side on a fly to center and another strikeout.

Brooklyn added two runs in the last of the eighth. Jordan began by knocking a ball clear over the right field fence for a home run. It was his ninth homer of the year, the best total in the league. Alperman followed with a hit and eventually scored on a double by Bergen.

Boston manager Joe Kelley sent three righthanded pinch-batters up in the ninth to try and end the southpaw's bid for a no-hit game. But it was to no avail. Claude Ritchey led off and grounded out, second to first. Frank Bowerman did the same. And Rucker ended the game with a flourish by striking out Harry Smith.

The exuberant crowd rushed onto the field and surrounded their hero. The mob of adoring fans followed Rucker to the clubhouse, cheering him all the way. With Brooklyn winning so seldom, a no-hit victory was an especial treat.

FIRST GAME

			r	h	e
Boston	101 000 020	=	4	8	2
Brooklyn	020 010 000	=	3	5	3

Game-Winning RBI: Sweeney

Batteries: C. Ferguson (W 9-7) & H. Smith
K. Wilhelm (L 13-18) & B. Bergen

SECOND GAME

Boston	ab	r	h	bi	o	a	e
G. Browne, rf	3	0	0	0	0	0	0
F. Bowerman, ph 9	1	0	0	0	-	-	-
J. Bates, 1f	3	0	0	0	3	1	1
H. Smith, ph9	1	0	0	0	-	-	-
J. Kelley, cf	3	0	0	0	0	0	0
D. McGann, 1b	3	0	0	0	14	0	1
B. Dahlen, ss	3	0	0	0	2	3	0
B. Sweeney, 3b	3	0	0	0	1	1	1
G. Graham, c	3	0	0	0	2	1	0
J. Hannifan, 2b	3	0	0	0	2	4	0
P. Flaherty, p	2	0	0	0	0	5	1
C. Ritchey, ph9	1	0	0	0	-	-	-
	29	0	0	0	24	15	4

Brooklyn	ab	r	h	bi	o	a	e
A. Burch, cf	4	0	1	0	2	0	0
H. Lumley, rf	4	0	1	0	1	0	1
J. Hummel, 1f	4	0	0	0	0	0	0
T. Jordan, 1b	3	2	3	1	7	0	0
W. Alperman, 2b	3	2	2	0	0	4	0
P. Lewis, ss	2	1	0	0	1	0	1
T. Sheehan, 3b	3	1	0	1	0	0	1
B. Bergen, c	4	0	1	1	15	1	0
N. Rucker, p	4	0	0	0	1	2	0
	31	6	8	3	27	7	3

Boston	000 000 000	=	0
Brooklyn	040 000 02x	=	6

	ip	h	r-er	bb	so
Flaherty (L 10-15)	8	8	6-3	2	2
Rucker (W 15-14)	9	0	0-0	0	14

HBP: by Flaherty (Sheehan)
Time—1:28 Attendance—6,000
Umpire: J. Johnstone

Game-Winning RBI: Sheehan
LOB: Boston 2, Brooklyn 6
BE: Boston 3, Brooklyn 3
DP: Rucker-Jordan
Dahlen-McGann (Alperman)
Bates-Graham-Sweeney
2B: Bergen
HR: Jordan
SH: Alperman, Lewis

Brooklyn lost the next three games it played by 1-0 scores and wound up losing nine games in a row. But the equally terrible play of St. Louis kept the Superbas out of last place. Brooklyn finished with a 53-101 record, four games ahead of the Cardinals.

1909 OPENING DAY, THURSDAY, APRIL 15TH, AT THE POLO GROUNDS, NEW YORK

No-Hit for 9, Brooklyn Wins Opener in 13

Ames Pitches Great Ball for Giants, But Loses
Wilhelm Overshadowed at First but Wins on 4-Hit Shutout

TODAY HARRY LUMLEY'S BROOKLYN Superbas opened the season by going hitless for the first nine innings. But the game went into extra innings, and Brooklyn wound up beating the New York Giants in thirteen, 3-0.

Today's Results

BROOKLYN 3-New York 0 (13 innings)
Chicago 10-St. Louis 4
Cincinnati 7-Pittsburg 2
Philadelphia at Boston, ppd.—rain

Standings	W-L	Pct.	GB
Chicago	2-0	1.000	—
BROOKLYN	1-0	1.000	½
Boston	1-0	1.000	½
Cincinnati	1-1	.500	1
Pittsburg	1-1	.500	1
New York	0-1	.000	1½
Philadelphia	0-1	.000	1½
St. Louis	0-2	.000	2

It was an auspicious way for Lumley to open his career as a manager. Especially since Harry started the winning rally with a ringing triple to deep left center field.

But the big hero of the day for the winners was Brooklyn pitcher Irvin "Kaiser" Wilhelm. Although overshadowed through nine innings by Leon "Red" Ames's no-hit pitching, the Superba righthander allowed only one hit in the first nine rounds himself. And he wound up giving only four hits in the game, as compared to seven off of Ames. Wilhelm, however, walked seven men, and Ames passed only two.

The game also featured scintillating fielding by both nines. Only two errors were made, both by the Giants. Brooklyn first baseman Tim Jordan saved his teammates from several errors by catching wild throws to first. New York shortstop Al Bridwell robbed the Dodgers of three or four hits with spectacular stops and throws. And a tremendous throw to the plate by Brooklyn center fielder Jimmy Sebring saved the game for Wilhelm in the eighth inning.

Since the opener had been scheduled for yesterday but postponed by rain, the usual opening-day ceremonies were curtailed somewhat. But a huge crowd of around 30,000 jammed the Polo Grounds to see the season finally get under way. Retired Tammany Hall "Boss" Richard Croker threw out the first ball from a box in the second deck.

Both pitching choices were surprises. Staff aces Nap Rucker and Christy Mathewson were held out of the game because of the cold weather. But they could hardly have been any better than their replacements. New York manager John McGraw was not present, since he was in the hospital for surgery on an infected hand.

Three great plays by Bridwell helped Ames retire the Superbas in order in the first two innings.

The Giants made a bid to score in their second, even though did not get a hit. With one out, Bill O'Hara walked and stole second. Art Devlin walked behind him. Bridwell then shot a hot smash up the middle, but shortstop John Hummel nabbed it and flipped to second for a force out. The Giants then tried a double steal, but Bridwell was tagged at second before O'Hara could cross the plate.

Brooklyn's first runner got on in the third, when Edgar Lennox walked. He was wiped out in a fast double play.

In the fifth, Jordan was given a life on a bad fumble by second baseman Art Fletcher. But Big City Tim was quickly cut down trying to steal second.

In the New York sixth, George "Admiral" Schlei worked Wilhelm for a leadoff walk. Ames struck out. Buck Herzog sent a hot shot toward the corner. Third baseman Lennox made a fine pickup, spun around, and threw to second just barely in time to force Schlei. The Giants argued the call, and their fans howled, but it didn't help. Herzog was caught stealing by a strong throw by catcher Bergen.

The double no-hitter was finally broken in the bottom of the eighth. After one out and two walks, Schlei knocked a clean single into center. Devlin tried to score from second on the hit, but Sebring uncorked a perfect peg to nip the runner at home. Even the New York partisans had to applaud the fine play.

Both sides went out in order in the ninth, Ames getting credit for an official no-hit game.

Alperman broke up Ames's hitless string with one out in the tenth when he crashed a double to deep left. He got to third on an infield out but was left when Sebring tapped to Ames.

New York wasted two walks in the bottom of the tenth.

Jordan doubled with one gone in the Brooklyn eleventh. Hummel's out moved Big City to third. Bergen rapped a sure hit up the middle, but Fletcher made an impossible play to throw him out at first.

Herzog singled for the Giants with one out. Fletcher fouled out. Red Murray hit a dangerous looper into center. But Sebring was once again on the job, making a fine shoestring catch.

Brooklyn wasted yet another double in the twelfth, this one a two-out drive by Whitey Alperman. New York went out in order.

With darkness setting in, Sebring opened the thirteenth by grounding out. Lumley then strode to the plate and laced a long drive to left center. The hit might have yelded a home run, but with only one out, Lumley stopped at third. It was decided to pass Jordan to get to Lennox. The rookie crossed up the strategy by singling over second to drive Lumley in with the first run of the game. Bergen hit safely to right, and Jordan scored when catcher Schlei failed to stop the throw from the outfield. A third run scored on an infield hit by Al Burch.

Wilhelm needed only three more outs for the victory. He got Bridwell and Schlei on flies to left. John "Chief" Meyers, batting for Ames, singled, and Herzog followed with another hit. But pinch-batter Harry "Moose" McCormick bounced back to the mound for the third out.

For New York, it was a bitter defeat. But it was some victory for Brooklyn. There's never been an opener like it.

Brooklyn	ab	r	h	bi	o	a	e
A. Burch, lf	6	0	1	1	5	0	0
W. Alperman, 2b	6	0	2	0	2	10	0
J. Hummel, ss	5	0	0	0	3	3	0
J. Sebring, cf	5	0	0	0	3	1	0
H. Lumley, rf	5	1	1	0	1	0	0
T. Jordan, 1b	4	1	1	0	19	0	0
E. Lennox, 3b	4	1	1	1	1	2	0
B. Bergen, c	5	0	1	0	5	2	0
K. Wilhelm, p	5	0	0	0	0	4	0
	45	3	7	2	39	22	0

New York	ab	r	h	bi	o	a	e
B. Herzog, lf	6	0	2	0	0	0	0
A. Fletcher, 2b	5	0	0	0	0	7	1
M. McCormick, ph13	1	0	0	0	-	-	-
R. Murray, rf	5	0	0	0	0	1	0
F. Tenney, 1b	5	0	0	0	24	1	0
B. O'Hara, cf	3	0	0	0	0	0	0
A. Devlin, 3b	2	0	0	0	0	0	0
A. Bridwell, ss	4	0	0	0	4	7	0
G. Schlei, c	4	0	1	0	10	0	1
R. Ames, p	4	0	0	0	1	9	0
C. Meyers, ph13	1	0	1	0	-	-	-
	40	0	4	0	39	26	2

Brooklyn	000	000	000	000	3	=3
New York	000	000	000	000	0	=0

	ip	h	r-er	bb	so
Wilhelm (W 1-0)	13	4	0-0	7	4
Ames (L 0-1)	13	7	3-1	2	10

WP: Ames
Umpires: J. Johnstone & S. Cusack

Game-Winning RBI: Lennox
LOB: Brooklyn 5, New York 8
BE: Brooklyn 1
DP: Fletcher-Bridwell-Tenney (Wilhelm)
2B: Alperman 2, Jordan
3B: Lumley
CS: Bridwell, Jordan, Herzog
Time—2:20 Attendance—30,000

Things went downhill for Wilhelm, Lumley, and the Superbas after the opening-day victory. Wilhelm won only two more games all season and finished 3-13. Lumley broke a finger in the very next game and was out for a month. Later on, other ailments kept him out of the lineup. The Superbas finished the season a weak sixth with a 55-98 record.

1910 WEDNESDAY, JUNE 15TH, AT WASHINGTON PARK

Cy Barger Pitches and Bats Dodgers to Victory

Hurls 14-Inning Gem and Drives in Winning Run
Carried Off the Field on the Shoulders of the Adoring Throng

THE LOWLY BROOKLYN DODGERS TODAY rose up and defeated the first-place Chicago Cubs behind the heroics of pitcher Eros Bolivar Barger. Better known as "Cy," Barger starred in all phases of the game except base running. As a pitcher, he scattered 11 hits over fourteen innings to limit the dangerous Cubs to just two runs. As a batter, Cy made four of his team's 12 hits, and two of his blows were run-scoring doubles. He fielded seven chances without an error. On the basebaths, however, he was thrown out trying to stretch one of his doubles into a triple.

Today's Results

BROOKLYN 3-Chicago 2 (14 innings)
New York 5-Pittsburg 1
Philadelphia 3-Cincinnati 3 (TIE)(16 inn.)
Boston 2-St. Louis 0

Standings	**W-L**	**Pct.**	**GB**
Chicago	30-16	.652	—
New York	29-19	.604	2
Cincinnati	24-20	.545	5
Pittsburg	22-22	.500	7
BROOKLYN	22-26	.458	9
St. Louis	22-26	.458	9
Philadelphia	18-25	.419	10½
Boston	18-31	.367	13½

After he won the game with his second double, Barger was surrounded by adoring Brooklyn fans. In a rare demonstration of affection, they carried him off the field on their shoulders. Club president Charles Ebbets also showed his appreciation by giving Barger the credit for a new suit at a downtown Brooklyn clothing store.

The hard-luck losing pitcher was Leonard "King" Cole, who previously had been undefeated in six decisions. He pitched another fine game today. But two errors by his catcher led to two for the three Brooklyn runs.

Chicago got off to a good start with a run in the first inning. Johnny Evers, leading off, worked Barger for a base on balls. He moved to second on Jimmy Sheckard's tap to the mound. Frank Schulte struck out. But Frank Chance came through with a hit past shortstop, and Evers raced home with the run.

Brooklyn got its first two runners on but then failed to score. Al Burch, first up, walked. He went to second on Jake Daubert's high-hop single. But catcher Jimmy Archer picked Burch off second, and the runner made an unsuccessful dash for third. Daubert took second on the play. Zack Wheat nearly beat out a hit to Cole, but umpire Gus Moran called him out. John Hummel left Daubert on third by grounding sharply to shortstop.

Burch atoned for his base-running mistake with an eye-popping catch in the second. Archer drove a long liner over Burch's head, but Al raced back and made a corking one-handed, leaping catch just in front of the fence.

Barger pitched his way out of a bases-loaded jam in the third. With one gone, Evers beat out a bunt. Sheckard singled him to second. Barger again struck slugger Schulte out with a fadeaway. But a passed ball moved the runners to second and third. Manager Bill Dahlen ordered a pass to Chance to load the bases. The strategy paid off when Harry Steinfeldt bounced into a force play at second.

Chicago was again turned back in the fourth. Solly Hofman opened with a double and went to third on Joe Tinker's sacrifice. Archer grounded one to second baseman Hummel, who threw Hofman out at the plate. Cole flied out.

The Superbas came in and tied the game in their half. Wheat hit safely to left and sprinted to second ahead of Sheckard's return throw. Hummel struck out and Edgar Lennox lined to deep left, Wheat remaining on second. Bill Davidson then came to the rescue with a hit to right to bring Zack home.

The Dodgers took the lead in the bottom of the fifth. Pryor McElveen opened the inning with a short pop behind the plate, which Archer muffed badly. Thusly reprieved, McElveen came up with a hit to left. Bill Bergen struck out trying to sacrifice. Then Barger, who had hit a respectable .247 at Rochester in 1909, pounded out a long hit to right center. McElveen rounded third base and fell flat on his face. Barger was rounding second at the time, and the Cubs threw to third to get him out. Luckily, they did not seem to notice McElveen's distress, and he was able to scramble across the plate while Steinfeldt was tagging Barger.

The lead did not last long. In the sixth, Steinfeldt led off with a hit to left. A wild pitch moved him to second, and Hofman's long fly out got him to third just ahead of Wheat's throw. Tinker's grounder up the middle bounced off second base for a hit, and Steinfeldt scampered home.

The score remained 2-2 for the next seven innings, although each side had opportunities to score. Chicago's best chance came in the seventh when Hofman tripled with just one out. But Barger rose to the occasion by getting Tinker to foul to first and fanning Archer on a sharp curve. Brooklyn got a man to third in the ninth and again in the tenth. In the ninth, a walk and a two-out single by Davidson put Hummel on the far corner. But McElveen bounced out. In the tenth, Tex Erwin got a pinch single, and Barger followed with a safe bunt. Burch bunted to force Barger, with Erwin moving to third. Daubert tapped to the pitcher, and Erwin had to hold up on the out at first. Wheat was walked intentionally to fill the sacks. Hummel hit a long fly to left that was captured near the wall in fine style by Sheckard.

Cole's speed and change-of-pace and Barger's curves and fadeaways kept the hitters off balance until the break finally came in the bottom of the fourteenth.

Cole passed McElveen to open the rally. Erwin bunted in front of the plate, and Archer tried for the force at second. His low throw skidded into center field, and Burch tried for third. Hofman threw Burch out, and Erwin took second on the play. Barger came to the plate and picked out a fat pitch. He pulled a long drive to right field that Schulte could not flag down. As the ball bounded toward the fence, Erwin got home easily. He delayed his arrival until Barger had gotten to second for a double. Then he touched the plate to win the game and set off the celebration.

Barger was barely off second when he found himself on the shoulders of the throng of spectators. At least for this one day, he was the King of Brooklyn.

Chicago	ab	r	h	bi	o	a	e
J. Evers, 2b	6	1	2	0	2	4	0
J. Sheckard, 1f	5	0	2	0	3	0	0
F. Schulte, rf	6	0	0	0	3	1	0
F. Chance, 1b	5	0	3	1	15	1	0
H. Steinfeldt, 3b	5	1	1	0	4	0	0
S. Hofman, cf	6	0	2	0	4	2	0
J. Tinker, ss	5	0	1	1	4	8	0
J. Archer, c	6	0	0	0	5	3	2
K. Cole, p	5	0	0	0	0	5	0
	49	2	11	2	40	24	2

Brooklyn	ab	r	h	bi	o	a	e
A. Burch, rf	5	0	0	0	6	1	0
J. Daubert, 1b	5	0	1	0	12	1	0
Z. Wheat, lf	5	1	1	0	7	0	0
J. Hummel, 2b	5	0	0	0	4	2	1
E. Lennox, 3b	6	0	1	0	0	0	1
B. Davidson, cf	4	0	3	1	2	0	0
P. McElveen, ss	5	1	1	0	2	3	0
B. Bergen, c	3	0	0	0	6	3	0
T. Erwin, ph10-c	3	1	1	0	2	0	0
C. Barger, p	6	0	4	2	1	6	0
	47	3	12	3	42	16	2

Chicago	100	001	000	000	00	=	2
Brooklyn	000	110	000	000	01	=	3

one out when winning run scored

	ip	h	r-er	bb	so
Cole (L 6-1)	13⅓	12	3-1	6	4
Barger (W 6-4)	14	11	2-2	3	7

WP: Barger
PB: Bergen
Time—2:40 Attendance—4,000
Umpires: J. Johnston & G. Moran

Game-Winning RBI: Barger
LOB: Chicago 11, Brooklyn 11
BE: Chicago 1, Brooklyn 1
DP: Evers-Chance-Tinker (Burch)
Hummel-McElveen
Burch-Daubert
2B: Hofman, Wheat, Barger 2
3B: Hofman
SH: Tinker, Sheckard, Davidson, Steinfeldt
SB: Davidson 2
CS: Burch, Sheckard

Barger finished the season with a 15-15 record, a .231 batting average and 7 runs-batted in.

Brooklyn struggled to avoid seventh place and wound up sixth in the final standings, 40 games behind the pennant-winning Cubs and ½ game ahead of the seventh-place Cardinals. Brooklyn's final record was 64-90.

1911 SATURDAY, JULY 8TH, AT WASHINGTON PARK

Fans Bombard Umpire

Caused Disturbance by Ordering Brooklyn Bench Cleared
Is Rescued by Police

NATIONAL LEAGUE PRESIDENT T.J. LYNCH sent his newest umpiring recruit, Robert Frary, down to Washington Park this weekend. In today's game, the new man's work enraged the fans and both teams. Hardly anyone in the park would have been willing to bet that he would make a long career of umpiring in the National League.

Today's Results

Pittsburg 3-Brooklyn 1
New York 5-Chicago 2
St. Louis 6-Philadelphia 2
Cincinnati 11-Boston 7

Standings	W-L	Pct.	GB
New York	45-29	.608	—
Chicago	43-28	.606	½
Philadelphia	44-30	.595	1
St. Louis	42-31	.575	2½
Pittsburg	41-31	.569	3
Cincinnati	31-40	.437	12½
BROOKLYN	27-45	.375	17
Boston	17-56	.233	27½

Then the situation got completely out of hand in the ninth inning, and not many in attendance would have been willing to wager that Frary would even get out of the ballpark unharmed. He became the target of hundreds of bottles and drinking mugs hurled from the stands. Luckily the Brooklyn fans were off in their aim and short in their range, and the police were able to quell the disturbance before the umpire was seriously hurt. After the game ended in defeat for the home team, the cops again had to be called to keep the mob away from Frary.

Bad work calling balls and strikes characterized Frary's work throughout the game, and both sides made numerous complaints. The two pitchers, Al "Lefty" Leifield of the visiting Pittsburgs and Brooklyn's Bill Schardt, appeared to be the chief beneficiaries, as neither was charged with a base on balls.

Pittsburg scored the first run of the game in the second inning on a home run by Hans Wagner. The big Dutchman hit a drive down the left field line, and the ball caromed around the corner and got past outfielder Zack Wheat.

The Superbas tied the game in the bottom of the fifth, but the feature of that inning was the umpiring. Light-hitting Bill Bergen surprised Leifield with a hot shot through the box for a single. Schardt hit into a force play, but Bergen prevented a double play by running into shortstop Wagner before he could throw. The Pirate tried to claim that Bergen had deliberately interfered and that Schardt should therefore be called out also. But umpire Bob Emslie, working the bases, would not allow the claim. After a foul out, Jake Daubert topped one to the right of the mound and got a hit when no one covered first base.

Now Frary got a chance to get into the act. The next batter, Wheat, sliced a hit down the left field line that looked like a double. Schardt came home from second, but Daubert was thrown out after overrunning third. After the dust had cleared, however, Frary announced that the ball was foul! The home fans howled, but Wheat had to bat again. Luckily, he came through with a safe hit to right to score Schardt again, and this time Daubert reached third safely. Wheat and Daubert then tried the old double steal. Wheat lit out for second on the pitch, and Daubrt broke for home when catcher Mike Simon threw down to second base. Second sacker Jack "Dots" Miller took the throw and immediately returned it home. Simon made the tag on Daubert before he really made the catch, and he juggled the ball. Although Simon admitted later that he had never even touched Daubert, ump Frary called the runner out. Brooklyn manager Bill Dahlen, who had just come off of a three day suspension, exploded off the bench to protest. The fans again screamed themselves hoarse, but Frary, of course, would not change his decision.

A relative calm set in until the ninth inning.

The score was still 1-1 when the Pirates came to bat. With one out, Wagner fouled off two pitches. Schardt tried to get the slugger to chase a couple of bad balls, and the count went even. The next pitch looked like a perfect strike to the Brooklyn patrons and players. Catcher Bergen had started to throw the ball around the infield when Frary called it ball three. When the next pitch was smacked through third base for a hit, the crowd became unruly. Wagner broke for second and was safe when second baseman Tony Smith dropped Bergen's good throw. Newt Hunter then singled to left, and Wagner scored the go-ahead run.

Now the stands erupted with shouts of "Thief," "Robber," and worse. Bottles began to land in the vicinity of home plate. But Captain N.J. Hayes and a small squad of police came onto the field, and the disturbance subsided.

The catcalling from the Brooklyn bench continued. Suddenly Frary whipped off his mask and ejected everyone sitting there. Even little mascot Frankie Deery was ordered to the clubhouse. The youngster was so proud of himself as he trooped off the field at the end of the file of banished players that he had a hard time maintaining the proper expression of outrage.

Frary was not watching the batboy, however, since he was now under full attack from the grandstand. Hundreds of bottles and glasses were heaved at him. He retreated far enough to avoid any direct hits, although one bouncing bottle bruised his face. Captain Hayes and his men finally had to go into the stands before the riot ended.

When quiet had been restored, a group of five Brooklyn pitchers came marching belligerently in from the bullpen to the abandoned bench, scowling at the umpire all the way. But Frary had lost his stomach for confrontation, and he said nothing.

When play resumed, Hunter stole second and scored on a double by Owen Wilson. Brooklyn went out in order in the bottom of the ninth, and Pittsburg won, 3-1.

Captain quickly escorted Frary to the dressing room with some fans in hot pursuit. Hayes then put up a show of protecting one door while Frary and Emslie slipped out another unnoticed and made their way back to their hotel.

No one said umpiring was easy. But by doing a bad job in front of the notorious Brooklyn fans, it could become downright hazardous to your health.

Pittsburg	ab	r	h	bi	o	a	e
M. Carey, lf	4	0	0	0	3	0	0
T. Leach, cf	4	0	0	0	4	0	0
B. Byrne, 3b	4	0	0	0	1	1	0
H. Wagner, ss	4	2	2	1	2	5	1
N. Hunter, 1b	4	1	2	1	9	0	0
J. Miller, 2b	4	0	1	0	2	3	1
O. Wilson, rf	4	0	2	1	1	0	0
M. Simon, c	4	0	0	0	5	1	0
L. Leifield, p	3	0	1	0	0	2	0
	35	3	8	3	27	12	2

Brooklyn	ab	r	h	bi	o	a	e
B. Davidson, cf	4	0	0	0	4	0	0
J. Daubert, 1b	4	0	2	0	7	0	0
Z. Wheat, lf	4	0	1	1	4	0	0
B. Tooley, ss	4	0	0	0	3	4	1
B. Coulson, rf	4	0	0	0	3	0	0
E. Zimmerman, 3b	4	0	1	0	1	3	0
T. Smith, 2b	4	0	1	0	3	1	1
B. Bergen, c	3	0	1	0	2	1	0
B. Schardt, p	3	1	0	0	0	0	1
	34	1	6	1	27	9	3

Pittsburg	010	000	002	=	3
Brooklyn	000	010	000	=	1

	ip	h	r-er	bb	so
Leifield (W 9-7)	9	6	1-1	0	2
Schardt (L 3-5)	9	8	3-1	0	2

Time—1:56
Attendance—6,000
Umpires: R. Frary & B. Emslie

Game-Winning RBI: Hunter
LOB: Pittsburg 5, Brooklyn 6
BE: Pittsburg 2, Brooklyn 2
DP: Tooley-Smith
Zimmerman-Smith-Daubert (Miller)
2B: Wilson
HR: Wagner
SB: Wilson, Miller, Hunter
CS: Daubert

Ump Frary was dropped by the league a week later.

The Dodgers remained in seventh place, slipping to 33½ games behind by the end of the season. Their final record was 64-86.

1912 TUESDAY, SEPTEMBER 17TH, AT WASHINGTON PARK

Stengel Makes 4 Hits in Debut

Wheat Also Hits Safely Four Times
Heavy Hitting Leads Superbas to 7-3 Victory

A BRASH YOUNG ROOKIE BROKE INTO THE Brooklyn lineup today with four hits, helping the Superbas to a 7-3 victory over the Pittsburg Pirates. Named Charles Dillon Stengel and hailing from Kansas City, the rookie was recently called up from Montgomery in the Southern League.

Today's Results

BROOKLYN 7-Pittsburg 3
Chicago 5-New York 3
Philadelphia 7-Cincinnati 1
Boston 5-St. Louis 4

Standings	W-L	Pct.	GB
New York	95-42	.693	—
Chicago	85-51	.625	9½
Pittsburg	83-54	.606	12
Cincinnati	70-69	.504	26
Philadelphia	64-72	.471	30½
St. Louis	57-82	.410	39
BROOKLYN	51-86	.372	44
Boston	44-93	.321	51

At the recommendation of scout Larry Sutton, Brooklyn had purchased Stengel's contract at the end of the 1911 season from Aurora in the Wisconsin-Illinois League. The youngster was optioned to Montgomery in the spring. But with the Dodgers going nowhere at the end of the season, manager Bill Dahlen decided that he wanted to look at new prospects. So Brooklyn exercised its option and called Stengel up.

If one game could be any indication, he came to stay. He smacked out four clean hits today, three of them off of the Pirates' top pitcher, Claude Hendrix. In his final trip to the plate, he walked. And he certainly was not shy on the basepaths, stealing twice and being thrown out another time. In the outfield he had no difficult chances.

Stengel certainly was not at all overawed by his first exposure to the big leagues. He went right up to the club president and introduced himself. Then he went to the clubhouse and quickly joined his new teammates in a recreational game of chance. After the baseball game started, he only made one mistake, missing a bunt sign in the first inning. But he singled instead, and the oversight was forgiven.

What young Stengel did not do to beat the Pirates, established players Zack Wheat and Nap Rucker did. Rucker's pitching held the visitors to three runs on eight hits. And Wheat, who like Stengel was from western Missouri, banged out four hits, including a double and a home run.

In the field, however, Wheat had a tough time in the first inning, when Pittsburg whizzed a couple of shots past him. The first was a leadoff double down the left field line by Bobby Byrne. Byrne scored on an infield out and a wild pitch. Hans Wagner knocked a two-bagger over Wheat's head, and Zack's fumble gave the Dutchman third. Jack Miller flied out to right to end the inning, however.

The Superbas wasted no time tying the game up. Herbie Moran led off the home half of the first by waiting out a base on balls. Stengel, ignoring the bunt, singled over second. George Cutshaw bunted and beat the throw to first to load the bases. After Jake Daubert fanned, Wheat smashed an infield hit to knock in a run. The bases were then left loaded.

Rucker scored in the second to put Brooklyn ahead. He singled with one out, and Moran again walked. Stengel smoked a bouncer off Wagner's shins for a hit. Rucker scored on the play, but Moran was thrown out trying for third. Stengel was soon caught stealing second.

Speedster Max Carey tied the game again in the Pittsburg third with a drive to center field bleachers for a home run.

And once again, Brooklyn took the lead with a run in its half, Daubert tripling and scoring on a double by Wheat.

A walk to Miller, a sacrifice, and a hit over second by Art Butler again brought Pittsburg even in the top of the fourth, 3-3.

Brooklyn got its fourth consecutive single run in the bottom of the inning. Otto Miller grounded one through the infield for a hit. Rucker bunted him to second. Moran got his third consecutive free pass. That brought up Charley Stengel. He picked on a spitball and shot it to center for a hit, bringing Miller home with what proved to be the winning run. Moran and Stengel pulled a double steal to move to third and second. But Cutshaw fouled out to end the inning.

Pittsburg tried a new pitcher, Jack Ferry, in the fifth. Daubert and Wheat liked the switch, since both of them hit home runs. Jake hit the hurler's second serve over the fence in right field, and Zack did exactly the same thing on the very next pitch. Stengel got a safe hit to left in the sixth against Ferry.

Pittsburg manager Fred Clarke used pitcher Babe Adams in the seventh, and Brooklyn scored a run off him. Wheat opened with a bad-hop single, and Enos Kirkpatrick knocked another safe one to right. Wheat came around on outs by Bobby Fisher and O. Miller.

Clarke tried rookie Sherrod Smith in the eighth. Like Rucker, Smith was born in Georgia and grew up throwing with his left hand. When it came time for the lefthanded Stengel to bat, Clarke challenged the rookie to cross over and swing from the right side. I guess Clarke was scared that he would no longer be the only batter ever to get five hits in his first major league game, a feat accomplished back in 1894. Stengel certainly was feeling bold, and he batted righthanded against Smith, although he had been strictly a lefthanded sticker in the bushes. He did not get a chance to show off his switch-hitting prowess, however, since Smith walked him. Not to be denied some glory, Stengel stole second. But he was left on base.

Rucker survived two hits in the ninth and nailed down the game for Brooklyn. The final score was 7-3.

And in the victory, young Charles Stengel from K.C., Mo., had shown that he might be around for a long time.

Pittsburg	ab	r	h	bi	o	a	e
B. Byrne, 3b	4	1	1	0	4	0	0
M. Carey, lf	4	1	1	1	2	0	0
M. Donlin, rf	4	0	0	0	1	1	0
H. Wagner, ss	4	0	1	0	0	4	0
J. Miller, 1b	3	1	0	0	9	1	0
O. Wilson, cf	3	0	1	0	0	0	0
A. Butler, 2b	4	0	2	1	3	1	0
M. Simon, c	3	0	2	0	3	2	0
O. Nicholson, pr7	0	0	0	0	-	-	-
B. Kelly, c7	0	0	0	0	0	1	0
E. Blackburn, c8	0	0	0	0	2	0	0
J. Viox, ph9	1	0	0	0	-	-	-
C. Hendrix, p	2	0	0	0	0	2	0
J. Ferry, p5	0	0	0	0	0	1	0
S. Gray, ph7	1	0	0	0	-	-	-
B. Adams, p7	0	0	0	0	0	0	0
S. Smith, p8	0	0	0	0	0	1	0
	33	3	8	2	24	14	0

Brooklyn	ab	r	h	bi	o	a	e
H. Moran, rf	2	1	0	0	1	0	0
C. Stengel, cf	4	0	4	2	1	0	0
G. Cutshaw, 2b	5	0	1	0	1	2	0
J. Daubert, 1b	5	2	2	1	13	0	0
Z. Wheat, lf	4	2	4	3	2	0	1
E. Kirkpatrick, 3b	3	0	1	0	2	5	0
B. Fisher, ss	3	0	0	0	0	1	0
O. Miller, c	3	1	1	1	7	2	0
N. Rucker, p	3	1	1	0	0	5	0
	32	7	14	7	27	15	1

Pittsburg	101 100 000	= 3
Brooklyn	111 120 10x	= 7

	ip	h	r-er	bb	so
Hendrix (L 21-9)	4	9	4-4	3	1
Ferry	2	3	2-2	1	0
Adams	1	2	1-1	0	0
Smith	1	0	0-0	1	2
Rucker (W 16-20)	9	8	3-2	1	6

WP: Rucker 2
Umpires: B. Klem & A. Orth

Game-Winning RBI: Stengel
LOB: Pittsburg 5, Brooklyn 9
BE: none
2B: Byrne, Wagner, Simon, Wheat, Butler
3B: Daubert
HR: Carey, Daubert, Wheat
SH: Wilson, Rucker, Fisher
SF: O. Miller
SB: Moran, Stengel 2
CS: Simon, Stengel, Wheat, Butler
Time—1:50

Stengel stayed in the lineup for the remainder of the season and had a .316 batting average for 17 games.

Brooklyn finished in seventh with a 58-95 record.

1913 SATURDAY, APRIL 5TH, AT EBBETS FIELD, BROOKLYN

Opening of Ebbets Field Draws 30,000

Beautiful New Plant Wins Approval of Fans
Dodgers Beat Yankees in Exhibition Game, 3-2

CHARLES HERCULES EBBETS, THE PRESIDENT OF THE BROOKLYN BASEBALL CLUB, opened his new ballpark to the public for the first time today, and almost 30,000 persons came to satisfy their curiosity. The $750,000 plant was the pride and joy of Squire Ebbets, and the press and fans agreed that it was among the finest ball yards in the country.

The specific occasion today was a pre-season exhibition game between the New York Yankees of the American League and the hometown Brooklyn Dodgers of the National League. The game, which was well-played and exciting, was won by Ebbets's boys, 3-2.

But before describing the game, a few words about the park. It was built in the Flatbush district of Brooklyn on the block bounded by Cedar Place, Sullivan Place, Bedford Avenue, and Montgomery Street. Ebbets had bought the block lot by lot over the last few years, and the plans for the park were unveiled in January, 1912. The layout was supervised by Mr. Ebbets himself, and it reflected his views of what should be in a modern baseball facility. There were separate entrances for the reserved and the non-reserved seats so that the higher-classed patrons would not have to mingle with the "groundlings" in the upper deck and down the foul lines. Long inclined ramps eliminated the need for staircases and speeded the flow of traffic before and after the games. A splendid rotunda under the stands behind home plate allowed customers to buy their tickets away from the elements. The grandstand, constructed with concrete and steel, extended from the far corner in right field around to beyond third base. A bleacher section was put up in the remaining territory along the left field foul line. The distance to the right field fence was measured at just over 300 feet, while the left field wall was over 410 feet from the plate.

Today's opening game was accompanied by a few embarrassing oversights, as might be expected. The outfield grass had not yet grown very much, and the outfielders had to slosh and slide through much mud. Access to the bleachers was delayed for a time while the key to the entrance was being located. And the final piece of embarrassment came after Mrs. Edward McKeever had led the march out to the center field flag pole only to discover that no one had brought the flag.

Mrs. McKeever's husband and his brother Stephen had been taken on by Ebbets as partners in the club to help finance the construction of the squire's dream park. Edward McKeever was made the president of the corporation which legally built and owned the park, so to his wife fell the honor of raising Old Glory for the first time. After the delay while the flag was retrieved from a storage room, Mrs. McKeever hoisted it up the staff, while the band played "The Star-Spangled Banner," and the crowd stood silently at attention.

The Brooklyn players, who had accompanied Mrs. McKeever out to center field, then marched back to the home dugout, and the crowd called for baseball. But there was one more little ceremony to be completed first. Mr. Ebbets's daughter Genevieve was allowed to throw out the first ball. Like a veteran she tossed one to umpire Bob Emslie, and then the players finally took their positions.

Nap Rucker, the Superbas' star southpaw, was given a great hand as he strode to the mound. Another cheer acknowledged the first pitch, which was a called strike. The Yankee leadoff batter, Bert Daniels, then fouled Miss Ebbets's ball into the upper deck. And he bounced a new one to Rucker and was thrown out at first base. The next man flied out, and Roy Hartzell was walked and caught stealing.

Over the course of the game, Brooklyn catcher Otto Miller threw out three Yankees stealing and picked another one off first base. New York catcher Ed Sweeney also had a good day, throwing out two would-be thieves.

The first Brooklyn batter, Charles "Casey" Stengel, smashed one to shortstop and was retired on a fine play by Claude Derrick. George Cutshaw and Benny Meyer followed with singles. After Zack Wheat flied out, Cutshaw was caught trying to pilfer third.

The two pitchers, Rucker and Ray Caldwell, showed that they were ready for the opening of the championship season by pitching scoreless ball until the fifth inning. In that round, however, the Superbas got a run on a lucky break. With two out, Stengel worked the count to 3-and-2 and then lined one to deep left center. Center fielder Harry Wolter went slogging after the ball. But just as he was about to cut it off, he slipped and kicked the ball to the fence. Stengel circled the bases with a home run, and the Brooklyn partisans cheered.

Jake Daubert hit a clean homer for the Dodgers in the sixth inning, a deep drive that scooted past Wolter and skipped into the deepest part of the park.

Rucker was only allowed to work five innings today by manager Bill Dahlen, and Frank Allen took his place in the sixth. Allen protected the 2-0 lead until the ninth.

Then New York rallied to tie the score. Hal Chase led off the last inning by drawing a base on balls. Manager Frank Chance, making his first appearance in Greater New York in a Yankee uniform, followed with a solid hit to center. Sweeney bunted, and Allen made a terrible throw past first base. The ball went into deepest right field, and two men scored before it was retrieved. This tied the game.

The Superbas then won the game in the bottom of the ninth. Wheat led off with a surprise bunt. Sweeney picked the ball up and threw late and wild past first base, allowing Zack to reach second. Daubert sacrificed Wheat to third. And J. Carlisle "Red" Smith singled him home with the winning tally.

Although there was a large contingent to Yankee rooters in the crowd, just about everyone was happy with the game. And they had nothing but praise for the new Ebbets Field.

New York (AL)	ab	r	h	bi	o	a	e
B. Daniels, rf	4	0	1	0	3	0	0
H. Wolter, cf	3	0	1	0	1	0	0
R. Hartzell, 3b	3	0	1	0	2	2	0
B. Cree, lf	4	0	0	0	1	0	0
H. Chase, 2b	3	0	1	0	1	0	0
E. Midkiff, pr9	0	1	0	0	-	-	-
B. Stumpf, 2b9	0	0	0	0	0	0	0
F. Chance, 1b	4	1	2	0	7	0	0
E. Sweeney, c	4	0	1	0	6	4	1
C. Derrick, ss	4	0	0	0	4	1	0
R. Caldwell, p	2	0	1	0	0	2	0
R. Fisher, p7	2	0	0	0	0	1	0
	33	2	8	0	25	10	1

Brooklyn (NL)	ab	r	h	bi	o	a	e
C. Stengel, cf	3	1	1	1	4	0	0
G. Cutshaw, 2b	4	0	1	0	1	3	2
B. Meyer, rf	3	0	1	0	0	0	0
Z. Wheat, lf	3	1	2	0	1	0	0
J. Daubert, 1b	3	1	1	1	11	0	0
R. Smith, 3b	4	0	2	1	1	2	0
B. Fisher, ss	3	0	0	0	5	1	0
O. Miller, c	3	0	0	0	4	5	0
N. Rucker, p	1	0	0	0	0	3	0
H. Moran, ph5	0	0	0	0	-	-	-
F. Allen, p6	1	0	0	0	0	1	1
	28	3	8	3	27	15	3

New York	000	000	002	=	2
Brooklyn	000	011	001	=	3

one out when inning run scored

	ip	h	r-er	bb	so
Caldwell	6	6	2-2	3	5
Fisher (L)	2⅓	2	1-0	1	2
Rucker	5	4	0-0	1	1
Allen (W)	4	4	2-0	2	3

Balk: Allen

Umpires: B. Emslie & T. Hurst

Game-Winning RBI: Smith
LOB: New York 7, Brooklyn 5
BE: New York 2, Brooklyn 0
2B: Smith
HR: Stengel, Daubert
SH: Daubert
CS: Hartzell, Cutshaw, Wheat, Chance, Derrick
Picked Off: Daniels, Moran
Time—2:04
Attendance—30,000

In the regular-season opening game on April 9th, only about 13,000 Brooklyn fans braved the cold to come to Ebbets Field. They saw Rucker and the Superbas lose to the Phillies, 1-0, because of an error by Benny Meyer.

For the season, the Superbas were only 29-47 with one tie in the new park. They were 36-37 on the road and finished in sixth place overall.

Chapter V Uncle Robbie Arrives

1914 July 4th
Daubert Knocked Unconscious Scoring Winning Run

1915 September 9th
Dodgers Win in One Scratch Hit

1916 October 3rd
Brooklyn Clinches the Pennant

1916 World Series Game #3
Dodgers Hold Off Red Sox, 4-3

1917 September 26th
Robins Slip to 7th

1918 August 7th
Zack & Mack Wheat Star

1919 May 15th
Lose 10-0 in 13th Inning

WILBERT ROBINSON FINALLY JOINED THE BROOKLYN CLUB IN NOVEMBER, 1913. BACK in 1899 and 1900, when many of his Baltimore Oriole teammates had been tranferred, Robinson and his friend John McGraw had refused to come to the City of Churches. Robinson had worked for a time in the family trade of butchery, but he had been a coach in New York under McGraw from 1911 through 1913. At the end of the 1913 campaign, however, he had had a falling out with his old crony and had left the Giants. He came to Brooklyn with a reputation as a good developer of pitchers, which he continued to be in Brooklyn. However, he was neither an inspiring leader nor a master tactician. In eighteen years in Brooklyn, he won only two pennants and only finished in the first division six times. He never showed much talent for getting his team to "play over its head."

In the autumn of 1913, Robinson took over leadership of the Superbas just in time to take the team on a barnstorming trip to Cuba. Over the next thirty-five years, the Brooklyn club would periodically go to that island for spring training.

In December, 1913, Ebbets engineered a deal to fill the team's biggest need, shortstop. Or so he thought. The purchase of Joe Tinker for $25,000 from Cincinnati was announced. But Tinker soon jumped to the outlaw Federal League, nixxing the transaction.

The Federal League caused other problems for the Dodgers, too. A rival team was placed in Brooklyn, in old Washington Park no less. This club was backed by bakery millionaires Robert B. and George S. Ward. The wags in the press dubbed the new team the "Tip Tops" after the brothers' famous brand of bread. The Wards made a big bid for Superba star Jake Daubert, and Ebbets countered by giving Daubert a five-year contract at the outlandish salary of $9,000 per year. The Dodgers did not lose any key players to the Feds in 1914, although they did in 1915. In 1915 Ebbets was also hurt by the transfer of another Federal League team to Newark, New Jersey, where the Dodgers owned the minor league team.

On the field in 1914, Robinson's squad did poorly at the outset. But there was some reason for optimism. Edward "Jeff" Pfeffer, who had been drafted from Grand Rapids the previous September, pitched great ball and wound up a 23-game winner. Unfortunately, his arrival as a top winner coincided with the sudden decline of Nap Rucker, who pitched in only 16 games. The entire outfield hit over .300, and (wonder of wonders) Brooklyn led the league in batting. Daubert won another batting title and fielded well. He showed his desire on the Fourth of July when he was

Wilbert Robinson

knocked unconscious in a collision at home plate but still scored the winning run.

The Superbas were in last place as late as September 8th. But they spurted at the end and finished fifth with a 75-79 record, their best since 1904.

In 1915, pitcher Ed Reulbach and outfielder Jack Dalton jumped to the Feds. Casey Stengel suffered a bout of typhoid fever over the winter and played below par all year. Zack Wheat's batting average dropped from .319 to .258. And shortstop Ollie O'Mara and third baseman Gus Getz were below average both offensively and defensively.

Somehow, the team managed to do quite well. The National League race was closely packed all year, and the Dodgers bounced from third place to eighth in two weeks in June. Then they leaped from last on June 30th to second by July 19th. Fine pitching fueled the takeoff. Pfeffer was still the ace of the staff, but veteran Jack Coombs (picked up from the Philadelphia A's) and rookies Wm. G. "Wheezer" Dell and Sherrod Smith did consistently well.

For the next two months, Brooklyn stayed on the heels of the league-leading Phillies. On September 9th, the Superbas won a game, 1-0, on only one very scratchy hit off Boston's Lefty Tyler but slipped to 3 games back when the Phils won a doubleheader. With the Dodger offense sputtering, Brooklyn dropped out of the race thereafter and finished third, 10 games behind.

During the 1915 season, Ebbets had acquired two pitchers and an infielder. They were southpaw Rube Marquard, righthanded spitballer Larry Cheney, and shortstop Ivy Olson. These three players contributed nicely in 1916. So did veteran third baseman Mike Mowrey, who was signed after the Federal League folded. And a young outfielder named Jimmy Johnston was acquired from the Pacific Coast League. The Brooklyn team had also acquired yet another nickname by this time. They were called the "Robins" by newspapermen in honor of their manager Wilbert Robinson. They were also still called the Dodgers and the Superbas, as well. Luckily, the name Bridegrooms had disappeared some years before.

By winning their first five meetings with the champion Phillies in 1916, the Robins moved into the league lead in early May. Except for a few brief lapses, they stayed on top all the way. Pfeffer and Cheney were the workhorses of the pitching crew, and Smith, Marquard, and Coombs also did well. Zack Wheat rebounded with a fine year at the plate, leading the league in slugging and total bases. Daubert hit over .300 again. When Jake suffered a hip injury in August, Ebbets traded a promising catcher (Lew McCarty) to the Giants for veteran first baseman Fred Merkle. Daubert returned to the lineup just as the Robins were losing the league lead to Boston on September 4th. But the next weekend, Brooklyn swept three games at Braves Field to move back into first place.

They held onto the lead until September 30th, when they lost a morning game to the Phillies to fall ½ game behind the Quakers. But Robbie's men bounced back in the afternoon game and beat the great Grover Cleveland Alexander, 6-1, to regain the league lead. Then they beat the fourth-place Giants in the next two games to clinch the pennant with two games left to play.

In the World Series, the defending-champion Boston Red Sox were a tougher proposition. In the opening game, Rube Marquard was knocked out early, and the Dodgers fell way behind. But they rallied to four runs in the ninth and had the bases loaded when they finally lost, 6-5. In the second game, Sherry Smith pitched brilliantly but lost a 14-inning duel to Boston's Babe Ruth, 2-1. In the third game, the Superbas got a 4-0 lead and just managed to hold on and win, 4-3. Marquard was hit hard in the fourth game and lost, 6-2. In the fifth and final game, a wide throw by Wheat and a botched double play by Olson doomed Pfeffer to a 4-1 defeat. The loss of the series was a disappointment, of course, but it was not unexpected.

What happened in 1917 was totally unexpected. The defending champs fell all the way to seventh place in the final standings. Although nothing had gone really wrong, nothing went right. Four of the big five on the pitching staff had poor years, Marquard being the one exception. Of the hitters, only Wheat came close to his 1916 average. With the team already struggling, Daubert went out of the lineup in late June with leg troubles. Three days after he got back, Wheat hurt his ankle and was on the bench for five weeks. Hi Myers missed a month with a shoulder injury. Chief Meyers and Mike Mowrey were now too old and had to be let go.

Through all this the Robins slid farther and farther back in the standings. On September 26th, they finally dropped to seventh when they lost to a bunch of Cub rookies, 1-0.

A major rebuilding seemed in order, so Ebbets traded Stengel and second baseman George Cutshaw to Pittsburgh for infielder Chuck Ward and pitchers Al Mamaux and Burleigh Grimes. The nation was involved in World War I, and Ward was drafted before he had a chance to report for the 1918 season. Mamaux stayed with the Robins just long enough to collect his first paycheck, then he quit for a draft-deferred job in a shipyard. But Grimes made the trade look good. Although he enlisted in the Navy during the season, he was not called to active duty until

Jake Daubert

after the end of the season, and he turned in a 19-9 record.

The military services also claimed pitchers Pfeffer, Leon Cadore, and Clarence Mitchell, among others. Zack Wheat stayed on his farm all spring, ostensibly to keep his agricultural deferment but really as a holdout for more money. When the Superbas lost their first nine games of the regular season, Ebbets was willing to reach a compromise with Wheat, who wanted a $5,800 salary. Without spring training, Zack started kind of slowly. But he got hot in July and ran up a long hitting streak. His brother Mack, who was also on the team at the time, hit a three-run home run on the day Zack's streak reached its peak of 26 games. Zack was stopped the next day, but he was able to hold on and win the league batting title. Mack finished the season with just those three runs-batted-in.

The loss of pitchers and the terrible start kept the Robins from rising above fifth place, where they finished. The season was ended on Labor Day by order of the War Department, and the club announced plans to turn Ebbets Field over to the military for use as a storage facility for the duration. Luckily the war ended in November.

Daubert's big contract, a relic of the Federal League "war," finally expired, and Ebbets, who had resented every paycheck Jake got, was able to trade him to Cincinnati for outfielder Tommy Griffith. Ray Schmandt was ticketed to take over at first base in 1919. But Ebbets bought old Ed Konetchy on opening day, and Schmandt was soon benched.

The Dodgers got off to a fine start (9-1) in 1919 and stayed near the top through most of May. Pfeffer was back from the naval reserve, and he won his first seven decisions. Grimes also started well, even though he pitched 20 innings in one game and only got a tie out of it. Al Mamaux had a shutout going for 12 innings one day in May, then he gave up ten runs in the 13th and lost, 10-0.

On May 28th, Pfeffer lost his first game of the year in 13 innings. In his next start, he pitched 18 innings and lost again. By this time the Robins were starting to slip. On their June road trip, things fell apart. Marquard broke his leg and was out for the season. Grimes came down with tonsilitis. And the team lost ten games in a row to fall to sixth place. Uncle Robbie could not get the men going again, and Brooklyn finished fifth.

Zack Wheat (right) shakes hands with brother Mack

Burleigh Grimes

1914 SATURDAY, JULY 4TH, AT THE SOUTH END GROUNDS, BOSTON

Daubert Knocked Unconscious Scoring Winning Run

Is Carried Off the Field but is not Seriously Injured
Superbas Win Two Games in Boston

Today's Results
BROOKLYN 7-Boston 5 (11 inn.)(morning)
BROOKLYN 4-Boston 3 (afternoon)
New York 5-Philadelphia 4 (morning)
New York 3-Philadelphia 0 (afternoon)
Chicago 1-Pittsburgh 0 (morning)
Chicago 4-Pittsburgh 2 (afternoon)
St. Louis 4-Cincinnati 3 (morning)
St. Louis 8-Cincinnati 1 (afternoon)

Standings	W-L	Pct.	GB
New York	40-24	.625	—
Chicago	39-32	.549	4½
St. Louis	37-35	.514	7
Cincinnati	34-36	.486	9
BROOKLYN	31-33	.484	9
Pittsburgh	31-34	.477	9½
Philadelphia	30-34	.469	10
Boston	26-40	.394	15

JAKE DAUBERT, LAST YEAR'S LEAGUE BATting champion and most valuable player, today capped a double Brooklyn victory with the ultimate sacrifice. He was knocked unconscious in a collision at home plate while scoring the winning in the second game of the holiday doubleheader in Boston.

The Dodgers had beatened the Braves in eleven innings in the morning game, 7-5.

In the afternoon game, the score was tied, 3-3, in the ninth inning when Daubert forced the runner ahead of him for the first out of the round. Jake then took off to steal second. Catcher Hank Gowdy's throw went past both the second baseman and the center fielder, and Daubert went careening around the basepaths. Throwing caution to the wind, he tried to come all the way home. The relay had him beaten by a fraction, so Jake had to try and separate Gowdy from the ball. He did so with a hard slide and was safe. But the force of his slide sent his head against Gowdy's shinguard, and the runner was knocked unconscious. Daubert's leg was also slightly injured, and he was carried from the field on a stretcher. But he had done his job, and his run won the game for Brooklyn.

The double victory jumped Wilbert Robinson's Brooklyns from seventh place to fifth in the National League standings. The last-place Bostons fell to 15 games behind the league-leading New York Giants.

Bad running cost Brooklyn in each of the first two innings of the morning game. But the Robins broke through for two runs in the third. Bill Fischer led off with a base on balls, and Elmer Brown reached safely when the Boston pitcher fumbled his bunt. A sacrifice moved the runners up. Daubert punched a hit to left, and both runners scored when the outfielder bobbled the ball.

Boston got a run in its third on two hits and a double play.

Bad fielding gave the Brooks another run in the sixth. Zack Wheat reached first when he swung at a wild pitch on the third strike. He tried to steal second and was safe only because Rabbit Maranville dropped the throw. An infield out advanced him to third. Then a two-out fumble by Maranville allowed him to score.

Wheat scored again in the eighth on his single and a double by George Cutshaw.

Pitcher Brown was in control until the ninth, when he weakened. He hit the leadoff batter, Charlie Deal, in the ribs with a pitch. Josh Devore followed with a single. A fumble on Gowdy's grounder loaded the bases. Pitcher Bill James was allowed to bat for himself, and he came through with a pop-fly single to right. Unfortunately for Boston, James also had to run for himself, and he got hung up between first and second and was tagged out.

It was decided to replace Brown with a fresher man, and Pat Ragan was sent in. Johnny Evers and Jim Murray singled runs home to tie the game. Luckily for Brooklyn, Murray was cut down trying to make second on his hit, and the inning was ended.

The Superbas batted James for three runs in the eleventh inning to win the game. J. Carlisle "Red" Smith tripled to the left field fence to drive home the first two.

Smith then scored on a single by Ragan.

Boston got a run on two hits in its half, but Brooklyn won, 7-5.

Two lefthanders, Nap Rucker and George Tyler, were the starting pitchers in the second game. Boston got to Rucker for three runs in the first two innings on two hits, a walk, and a throwing error. Nap was lifted for a pinch hitter in the fourth, and Ed Reulbach took over the pitching duites for the visitors. He shut the Braves out for the final six innings.

Meanwhile, Brooklyn rallied to win the game with single runs in the fourth, fifth, eighth, and ninth innings.

Cutshaw tripled in the fourth and scored on a wild pitch with two out.

In the fifth, Ollie O'Mara eventually scored after the two teams nearly brawled. A pitch that hit O'Mara in the neck caused the altercation. Both benches emptied, but no blows were struck. O'Mara came around to score on a bunt, a passed ball, and a single by Wheat.

A fumble by Maranville gave Wheat a life with one down in the eighth. Zack moved to second on an out and scored when Smith delivered another key hit.

Leading off the ninth, O'Mara got hit by another pitch and was forced out on Daubert's grounder. Jake then made his dash to the winning run and unconsciousness.

So Brooklyn had won both games and moved into fifth place. And with the great Daubert leading the way, they hoped to go higher.

MORNING GAME—Attendance 6,000

						r	h	e
Brooklyn	002	001	010	03	=	7	17	2
Boston	001	000	003	01	=	5	14	4

Game-Winning RBI: Smith

Batteries: E. Brown 8⅓ IP, P. Ragan (W 3-6) 2⅔ IP & B. Fischer.
B. James (L 7-6) & B. Whaling.

AFTERNOON GAME

Brooklyn	ab	r	h	bi	o	a	e
O. O'Mara, ss	3	1	0	0	1	6	1
J. Daubert, 1b	4	1	0	0	9	0	0
D. Egan, 1b9	0	0	0	0	2	0	0
J. Dalton, cf	4	0	0	0	1	0	0
Z. Wheat, lf	5	1	1	1	3	0	0
G. Cutshaw, 2b	3	1	2	0	6	3	0
C. Stengel, rf	2	0	0	0	1	0	0
R. Smith, 3b	4	0	2	1	1	2	0
L. McCarty, c	4	0	0	0	3	2	1
N. Rucker, p	1	0	0	0	0	1	0
J. Hummel, ph4	1	0	0	0	-	-	-
E. Reulbach, p4	1	0	0	0	0	0	0
	32	4	5	2	27	14	2

Boston	ab	r	h	bi	o	a	e
O. Dugey, lf	2	1	1	0	0	0	0
J. Connolly, ph6-lf	2	0	1	0	0	0	0
J. Evers, 2b	4	1	2	0	3	2	0
T. Cather, rf	3	0	0	1	0	0	0
R. Maranville, ss	4	0	0	1	3	6	3
B. Schmidt, 1b	4	0	0	0	10	1	1
W. Collins, pr9	0	0	0	0	-	-	-
C. Deal, 3b	4	0	1	0	0	2	0
G. Whitted, pr9	0	0	0	0	-	-	-
L. Mann, cf	0	1	0	0	2	0	0
J. Devore, ph5-cf	2	0	1	0	1	1	1
H. Gowdy, c	3	0	0	0	7	1	1
L. Tyler, p	3	0	0	0	1	4	0
	31	3	6	2	27	17	6

Brooklyn	000	110	011	=	4
Boston	210	000	000	=	3

	ip	h	r-er	bb	so
Rucker	3	2	3-2	2	1
Reulbach (W 5-12)	6	4	0-0	1	2
Tyler (L 5-9)	9	5	4-1	5	4

WP: Tyler
PB: Gowdy 2
HBP: by Tyler 2 (O'Mara 2)
Umpires: B. Byron & H. Johnson

Winning Run scored on a double error
LOB: Brooklyn 9, Boston 4
BE: Brooklyn 4, Boston 1
DP: Maranville-Evers-Schmidt (Wheat)
Tyler-Schmidt
Cutshaw-Egan (Devore)
3B: Cutshaw
SH: Daubert
SB: Cather, Devore, Evers, Daubert
CS: Cather, Wheat, Devore
Time—2:20 Attendance—10,500

Brooklyn could not get going in July and August, and the Superbas were in last place briefly in early September. Then they spurted up to a fifth-place finish with a final record of 75-79.

Daubert won his second consecutive batting title.

The Braves, meanwhile, pulled off their famous miracle and won the pennant by 10½

1915 THURSDAY, SEPTEMBER 9TH, AT EBBETS FIELD

Dodgers Win on One Scratch Hit

Pfeffer Allows Two Hits and Beats Tyler and Braves, 1-0
Tyler Misses No-Hitter on Controversial Offical Scoring

THE BROOKLYN ROBINS SQUEEZED PAST the Boston Braves today, 1-0, to regain second place in the topsy-turvy National League standings. The game was one of the best-pitched in history, with only three little hits being made. Boston was credited with two safeties, but only one was clean. That was a grounder that just trickled between the third baseman and the shortstop. The Braves' other hit was a pop fly near the mound that three Dodgers watched drop to the ground between them. Brooklyn's only hit was of the scratchiest variety imaginable. But it led to the game's only run.

Today's Results

BROOKLYN 1-Boston 0
Philadelphia 3-New York 0 (1st game)
Philadelphia 9-New York 4 (2nd game)
Cincinnati 4-St. Louis 3 (14 inn.)(1st)
Cincinnati 5-St. Louis 0 (6 inn.)(2nd)
no other game scheduled

Standings	W-L	Pct.	GB
Philadelphia	72-56	.562	—
BROOKLYN	71-61	.538	3
Boston	68-60	.531	4
St. Louis	65-69	.485	10
Chicago	61-66	.480	10½
Pittsburgh	63-70	.474	11½
Cincinnati	60-69	.4651	12½
New York	59-68	.4646	12½

The victory put Brooklyn back into second place ahead of Boston after the Braves' doubleheader sweep the day before had dropped the Superbas to third. That double defeat had obviously put a damper on the spirit of the Brooklyn fans. Only 4,500 saw today's game after nearly 20,000 had come to Wednesday's twinball.

Edward "Jeff" Pfeffer and George "Lefty" Tyler were the opposing hurlers. Both were magnificent. Pfeffer allowed the two hits and one base on balls. Tyler pitched a one-hitter and walked two. Each side made one error, which allowed one opponent to reach first base safely.

The first base runner of the game was the Braves' Johnny Evers. He walked with one out in the first inning. After Herbie Moran popped out, Evers tried to steal second and was gunned down by catcher Lew McCarty.

Sherry Magee was robbed of an extra-base hit in the top of the second on a great running catch by Casey Stengel in right field. Later that same inning, Gus Getz made a fine stop to rob Boston's Red Smith of a hit.

Brooklyn got its first runner in the second inning, and he scored the game's run. With one out, Hi Myers worked Tyler for a walk. Getz then bunted toward first. Big first baseman Butch Schmidt charged in on the ball and scooped it up. But just as he was straightening up to throw, he slipped and fell. He still had time to try for the out at second, but his throw hit Myers in the back, and both runners were safe. Schmidt wrenched his back on his tumble, and the game was delayed for a few minutes while he was being attended to.

Up in the press box, a controversy was raised when the official scorer ruled Getz's bunt a single. Many of the writers seemed to think that it was an error because if the throw had not hit Myers, a force out would probably have been made. But the ruling stuck, and it wound up costing Tyler a no-hitter.

When play resumed, Boston's poor fielding also resumed, and Brooklyn scored. With Al Nixon at the plate, Myers and Getz moved up on a double steal. Catcher Bert Whaling's throw to third was quite high, allowing Myers to slide in under Smith's quick tag. Smith thought he had gotten the runner nonetheless, and he argued long and loud with the umpire. The infield drew in close, hoping for a play at the plate. Nixon shot a hot one right to second baseman Evers, and Myers looked like a dead duck at home. But the infielder juggled the ball long enough to ruin his chances for an out at the plate. Although he recovered in time to nip the batter at first, Brooklyn had a 1-0 lead. McCarty left Getz on third by popping to shortstop.

Pfeffer and his fielders protected their minimal margin with great tenacity for the rest of the game. In the third inning, first baseman Jake Daubert made a neat pickup of Dick Egan's grounder for an unassisted putout. And Al Nixon, playing left field in place of the injured Zack Wheat, reached over the railing and into the stands to catch a foul fly to end the inning.

In the fourth, Herbie Moran got the only real hit of the day. With two out in the Boston half of the inning, he grounded one into left field for a single. Third baseman Getz might have had a chance at the ball, but he got a late jump, and the hit went past him. Moran was thrown out stealing.

Pfeffer had no trouble in the fifth and sixth, but Boston made its biggest threat in the seventh. Shortstop Ollie O'Mara fumbled Fred Snodgrass's easy grounder to start the inning. Evers bunted the runner to second. Moran then smacked a dangerous liner toward left. Here O'Mara redeemed himself by making a wonderful leaping catch and doubling Snodgrass off second. Boston went out in order in the eighth.

In the meantime, Tyler had been very effective against the Robins. He walked a man in the fourth, but catcher Whaling then caught the man stealing. Brooklyn's only other runner reached on a fumble by shortstop Egan in the seventh. He was left on first. After Tyler retired the Dodgers in the eighth, he got a great hand from the Brooklyn fans, who thought he had pitched a no-hitter. They did not know about the official scorer's ruling.

Boston made one last bid to tie the game in the ninth. Egan led off with an easy pop near the pitcher's mound. Pfeffer could have put it in his back pocket, but pitchers were not supposed to catch flies. So first baseman Daubert and third baseman Getz converged on the ball. They called each other off, then stood and watched the ball plop to the ground. The generous official scorer ruled this a hit also. Unperturbed, Pfeffer went back to work and retired the next three batters to end the game.

So it was Pfeffer who emerged victorious in this great pitching duel. And poor Lefty Tyler, who deserved a no-hitter, wound up losing both the no-hit bid and the game.

Boston	ab	r	h	bi	o	a	e
F. Snodgrass, cf	3	0	0	0	4	0	0
J. Connolly, ph9	1	0	0	0	-	-	-
J. Evers, 2b	1	0	0	0	2	4	0
H. Moran, rf	3	0	1	0	0	0	0
S. Magee, lf	3	0	0	0	2	0	0
B. Schmidt, 1b	3	0	0	0	10	1	0
R. Smith, 3b	3	0	0	0	0	1	0
D. Egan, ss	3	0	1	0	2	3	1
B. Whaling, c	2	0	0	0	3	1	0
P. Compton, ph9	1	0	0	0	-	-	-
L. Tyler, p	3	0	0	0	1	0	0
	26	0	2	0	24	10	1

Brooklyn	ab	r	h	bi	o	a	e
O. O'Mara, ss	3	0	0	0	5	3	1
J. Daubert, 1b	3	0	0	0	11	0	0
C. Stengel, rf	2	0	0	0	2	0	0
G. Cutshaw, 2b	3	0	0	0	2	0	0
H. Myers, cf	2	1	0	0	2	0	0
G. Getz, 3b	3	0	1	0	1	4	0
A. Nixon, lf	3	0	0	1	1	0	0
L. McCarty, c	3	0	0	0	3	2	0
J. Pfeffer, p	3	0	0	0	0	3	0
	25	1	1	1	27	12	1

Boston	000	000	000	=	0
Brooklyn	010	000	00x	=	1

	ip	h	r-er	bb	so
Tyler (L 9-8)	8	1	1-1	2	2
Pfeffer (W 16-10)	9	2	0-0	1	3

Time—1:34 Attendance—4,500
Umpires: B. Klem & B. Emslie

Game-Winning RBI: Nixon
LOB: Boston 1, Brooklyn 2
BE: Boston 1, Brooklyn 1
DP: O'Mara-Cutshaw
SH: Evers
SB: Myers, Getz
CS: Evers, Moran
Picked Off: Cutshaw

The Dodger pennant hopes faded quickly after this game. Brooklyn's offense sputtered, and the team was unable to win with any consistency. Meanwhile, the Phillies pulled away to take the pennant easily.

Brooklyn finished third, 10 games behind Philadelphia and 3 behind Boston. The Superbas had a final record of 80-72.

1916 TUESDAY, OCTOBER 3RD, AT EBBETS FIELD
Brooklyn Clinches the Pennant

Beat Giants, 9-6, While Phillies Lose Two to Boston
McGraw Accuses New York Players of Disobeying his Orders

Today's Results			
BROOKLYN 9-New York 6			
Boston 6-Philadelphia 3 (1st game)			
Boston 6-Philadelphia 1 (2nd game)			
no other games scheduled			
Standings	**W-L**	**Pct.**	**GB**
BROOKLYN	93-59	.612	—
Philadelphia	90-61	.596	2½
Boston	88-62	.587	4
New York	85-65	.567	7
Chicago	67-86	.438	26½
Pittsburgh	65-89	.422	29
Cincinnati	60-93	.392	33½
St. Louis	60-93	.392	33½

NEW YORK MANAGER JOHN McGRAW stirred up a tempest by accusing his own players of not obeying his orders in today's game in Brooklyn. But that could not alter the fact that the Dodgers won the game and clinched their first pennant since 1900.

Brooklyn had first moved into the lead on May 2nd and had held it the rest of the way except for two days in May and four days in September. Yet the Robins never got more than 5 games ahead and in September and October never had a margin greater than 2½ games. On September 30th they actually fell to second place between games and of a morning-afternoon doubleheader with the Phillies. But they won the second game and regained the top spot.

McGraw's Giants, meanwhile, were a distant fourth, 13½ games behind after splitting a doubleheader with Brooklyn on September 6th. The next day the Giants beat the Dodgers, 4-1, to launch the most incredible winning streak in major league history. They won 25 games in 22 days to close to within 5 games of the top. On September 30th, they won the first game of a doubleheader with Boston for 26 consecutive victories. But they lost the second game that day, 8-3, to end both their streak and their mathematical chances for the pennant.

After a day off, the Giants came to Brooklyn for a four-game series to end the season. The strain of their winning streak now snapped, they played listless ball and lost, 2-0. Meanwhile in Philadelphia, the Braves and the Phillies split a doubleheader, giving Brooklyn a 2-game lead with three to play. Philadelphia, the only remaining contender, had four games left.

So the Brooklyn players and fans were primed for the celebration in the next few days, while the New York players were suffering from a severe letdown. It showed today, although the Giants scored three runs in the top of the first inning. McGraw's men ran the bases poorly, fielded lackadaisically, and pitched indifferently. Wilbert Robinson's Dodgers, on the other hand, pounded the ball hard to overcome deficiencies in pitching and fielding. The sum total was a 9-6 Brooklyn victory.

Shortly after the game in Brooklyn ended, word arrived that the Phillies had lost both of their games today, and the Dodgers had therefore clinched the pennant. This set off a loud celebration in the home clubhouse and out on the streets of the borough.

There was one cloud on the horizon. Manager McGraw had left his team's bench in a huff in the fourth inning. After returning briefly in the fifth, he left again for good. After the game he told the press that his runners had ignored his signs and that pitcher Pol Perritt had allowed the Brooks to steal bases by using an exaggerated motion with men on base. He did not come right out and say that his team had thrown the game, but he was obviously disgusted with its conduct.

League president John K. Tener, who saw the game, said that no investigation would be made into the conduct of the New York players. He also extended his congratulations to the new champions.

Everyone present agreed that the game was a strange affair. Bad bounces, slipshod fielding and base running, and lackluster pitching all abounded. Brooklyn played nearly as poorly as New York.

The oddities started in the first inning. Robin pitcher Sherry Smith made two errors on the first two batters, putting men on first and third. A third Brooklyn error was made on a throw from the outfield after a single. One runner scored and the other two wound up on second and third. When the next batter bunted and was thrown out, the runner on third held up but the runner on second ran to third. Eventually the runner from third was run down and tagged out. The next batter, Art Fletcher, hit a long fly to center, which was misplayed into a home run. So the Giants led 3-0.

After Brooklyn scored in the bottom of the second, New York got a run in the third on two singles and a throwing error by the center fielder.

Then the Superbas turned the game around with four runs in the bottom of the third. Jimmy Johnston and Jake Daubert beat out infield hits to start. Hi Myers forced Daubert, but shortstop Fletcher missed a double play by throwing wide to first. The Giants went into a conference on the mound, and captain Charlie "Buck" Herzog and pitcher Rube Benton could be heard cursing at each other. The next batter, Zack Wheat, smashed one to the mound, and Johnston scored when Benton fumbled the ball. George Cutshaw smacked a clean bingle to right, knocking Myers in and Benton out. Perritt came on to pitch and was greeted by a run-scoring single by Mike Mowrey. Cutshaw scored on a ground out by Ivy Olson.

The Giants tied the game with a run in the fifth, but bad judgement on the bases by Perritt ran them out a possible big inning.

Brooklyn then won the game with single runs in each of the next four innings. In the fifth, a hit batsman, a two-base wild pitch, and a single to left by Olson produced the go-ahead run. A double by Casey Stengel and a single by Myers yielded a tally in the sixth. In the seventh, Cutshaw singled, stole second, and came home on a hit by Mowrey. A walk, a throwing error on a pickoff attempt, and a squeeze bunt plated the final Brooklyn tally in the eighth.

Jeff Pfeffer, who replaced Smith in the fourth, held New York off for six innings, yielding runs in the fifth and ninth. He finished the game was was credited with his 25th win of the season. The final score was 9-6.

McGraw may not have liked it, but the Superbas had won the pennant, and all of Brooklyn was happy.

New York	ab	r	h	bi	o	a	e
G. Burns, lf	5	2	2	0	0	0	0
B. Herzog, 2b	3	1	1	0	1	3	0
D. Robertson, rf	4	1	4	2	2	1	0
H. Zimmerman, 3b	4	0	0	0	1	3	0
A. Fletcher, ss	4	1	1	2	4	0	1
B. Kauff, cf	4	0	0	0	1	0	0
W. Holke, 1b	4	1	1	0	11	0	0
B. Rariden, c	3	0	0	1	4	3	0
R. Benton, p	1	0	0	0	0	1	0
P. Perritt, p3	2	0	1	0	0	2	0
G. Smith, p7	0	0	0	0	0	1	1
H. Lobert, ph9	1	0	1	0	-	-	-
	35	6	11	5	24	14	2

Brooklyn	ab	r	h	bi	o	a	e
J. Johnston, rf	3	1	1	0	0	1	0
C. Stengel, ph6-rf	1	2	1	0	0	0	0
J. Daubert, 1b	3	0	1	1	12	1	0
H. Myers, cf	5	1	1	1	3	1	1
Z. Wheat, lf	4	1	1	1	3	0	1
G. Cutshaw, 2b	4	2	2	1	1	3	0
M. Mowrey, 3b	3	2	3	2	1	4	0
I. Olson, ss	4	0	2	3	2	3	0
O. Miller, c	4	0	0	0	5	1	0
S. Smith, p	1	0	0	0	0	2	2
J. Pfeffer, p4	3	0	2	0	0	1	0
	35	9	14	9	27	17	4

New York	301	010	001	=	6
Brooklyn	014	011	11x	=	9

	ip	h	r-er	bb	so
Benton	2⅓	6	5-5	1	1
Perritt (L 18-11)	3⅔	8	3-3	0	3
G. Smith	2	0	1-0	1	0
S. Smith	3	5	4-3	0	1
Pfeffer (W 25-11)	6	6	2-2	1	3

HBP: by Perritt (Mowrey)
WP: Perritt, G. Smith
Time—1:49
Attendance—15,000

Game-Winning RBI: Olson
LOB: New York 4, Brooklyn 6
BE: New York 1, Brooklyn 1
DP: S. Smith-Daubert-Miller-Olson
Myers-Miller
Robertson-Rariden
2B: Mowrey, Pfeffer, Stengel
HR: Fletcher
SH: Herzog, Daubert
SB: Myers, Cutshaw, Holke 2
CS: Daubert, Robertson
Picked Off: Mowrey
Umpires: E. Quigley & C. Rigler

Brooklyn split the final two games to finish at 94-60

1916 TUESDAY, OCTOBER 10TH, AT EBBETS FIELD World Series—Game #3

Dodgers Hold Off Red Sox, 4-3

TODAY THE WORLD SERIES RETURNED TO BROOKLYN FOR THE FIRST TIME SINCE THE ill-starred day in 1890 when the local club made its last attempt to stage a world championship. This time, the club's management looked bad because it failed to sell all of the possible tickets to the game. But the home team celebrated the occasion by beating the Boston Red Sox, 4-3.

Brooklyn had lost the first two games of the series, which were played in Boston.

President Charles Ebbets was somewhat embarrassed by the numerous and noticeable blocks of empty seats in his park. It seems that the $5 box seats had more vacancies than the $3 reserved sections. And the $1 bleachers were pretty much full.

On the field, the big heroes for the Dodgers were pitchers Jack Coombs and Jeff Pfeffer, shortstop Ivy Olson, who scored one run and drove in two others, and first baseman Jake Daubert, who got three hits.

There was one big argument. In the sixth inning, plate umpire Hank O'Day reversed his decision on an attempted inside-the-park home run by Daubert. The lefthanded-hitting Daubert had lined a drive into the left field corner. Outfielder Duffy Lewis had to run a long way to get the ball, and the batter tried to come all the way home. He looked like a sure bet, although Lewis made an accurate throw to relay man Everett Scott. Scott relayed the ball home as Daubert neared the plate. Jake inexplicably slid way too soon, and he had no momentum when he was blocked off the plate by catcher Chester Thomas.

Because Daubert arrived well ahead of the ball, umpire O'Day called him safe. But catcher Thomas and third baseman Larry Gardner pointed out that Daubert (who was still spreadeagled on the ground) had never touched the plate. So O'Day reversed his call and declared Daubert out. The Brooklyn players came screaming out of the dugout to protest, but to no avail. Luckily the Dodgers won the game anyway.

After losing two close games in Boston, 6-5 and 2-1 in 14 innings, Brooklyn badly needed a victory today. Having lost twice with lefthanders, manager Wilbert Robinson chose veteran righty Jack Coombs to start in the box today. Jack had very little speed, but he was successful at bending his curves over the corners of the plate. He ran out of gas in the seventh inning, and big Jeff Pfeffer was called in. With a 4-3 lead, Pfeffer retired the eight batters he faced to save the game for Brooklyn.

Both sides had chances to score in the first inning but failed. The visitors got consecutive singles with two out, but right fielder Casey Stengel threw a man out trying to advance to third on the second hit. The home team loaded the bases with one out on a hit batsman, a bunt single, a sacrifice, and an intentional pass. But George Cutshaw hit into a force out at home. And with a full count and three runners running, Mike Mowrey was called out on a slow curve ball from pitcher Carl Mays.

In the third inning, hits by Daubert and Stengel put runners on first and second with one out. Zack Wheat lined out for the second out. Then Cutshaw broke out of his slump by slapping a hit down the right field line to drive Daubert home with the first run of the game. Stengel and Cutshaw got to third and second when the throw from the outfield was wide of the plate. But Boston shortstop Scott cut off a couple of runs by robbing Mowrey of a hit with a great stop and throw from far over behind the third baseman.

The Brooklyn shortstop, Olson, did not have as much action in the field, but he made up for that with his hitting. In the fourth, he tapped a perfect bunt for a single and took second on a wild throw by third baseman Larry Gardner. A sacrifice and a single by Coombs got him home. Two men had walked and two were out when Olson came to bat in the fifth. This time he slammed a triple to the front of the temporary box seats in far left field, driving the two runners in. Another fine stop and throw by Scott ended the inning.

Coombs had a 4-0 lead to work with, but he was tiring. He had held the Red Sox to four hits through the first five innings. And three of the runners had been thrown out on the bases, one at third by Stengel and two at second trying to steal by catcher Otto Miller. With one out in the sixth, Coombs issued his first walk. Harry Hooper followed with a triple to deep center, and Chick Shorten chipped a single up the middle to give Boston two runs.

In the seventh, Coombs got the first hitter, Lewis, to ground out to Daubert. But Larry Gardner crashed a liner over the right field wall for a home run. Coombs then gave up the ghost and motioned to the bench for a replacement.

Robinson had Pfeffer ready. The fastballer gave the fans a scare when the first man he faced, Scott, lined one to deepest center field. But Hi Myers ran the ball down and caught it near the fence. After that Pfeffer was invincible. He retired the final seven batters without a semblance of a hit to nail down the 4-3 victory for Brooklyn.

After the game, hundreds of fans and a local band paraded around the field in triumph. And the players were very happy in their dressing room. But the many empty seats must have dampened Charley Ebbets's spirits just a little bit.

Boston (AL)	ab	r	h	bi	o	a	e
H. Hooper, rf	4	1	2	1	1	0	0
H. Janvrin, 2b	4	0	0	0	1	0	0
C. Shorten, cf	4	0	3	1	0	0	0
D. Hoblitzell, 1b	4	0	1	0	12	2	0
D. Lewis, lf	4	0	0	0	1	1	0
L. Gardner, 3b	3	1	1	1	2	0	1
E. Scott, ss	3	0	0	0	1	7	0
C. Thomas, c	3	0	0	0	5	0	0
C. Mays, p	1	0	0	0	0	4	0
O. Henriksen, ph6	0	1	0	0	-	-	-
R. Foster, p6	1	0	0	0	1	2	0
	31	3	7	3	24	16	1

Brooklyn (NL)	ab	r	h	bi	o	a	e
H. Myers, cf	3	0	0	0	3	0	0
J. Daubert, 1b	4	1	3	0	7	0	0
C. Stengel, rf	3	0	1	0	2	1	0
Z. Wheat, lf	2	1	1	0	4	0	0
G. Cutshaw, 2b	4	0	1	1	4	0	0
M. Mowrey, 3b	3	1	0	0	2	1	0
I. Olson, ss	4	1	2	2	1	2	0
O. Miller, c	3	0	0	0	4	2	0
J. Coombs, p	3	0	1	1	0	2	0
J. Pfeffer, p7	1	0	1	0	0	1	0
	30	4	10	4	27	9	0

Boston	000	002	100	=	3
Brooklyn	001	120	00x	=	4

	ip	h	r-er	bb	so
Mays (L 0-1)	5	7	4-3	3	2
Foster	3	3	0-0	0	1
Coombs (W 1-0)	6⅓	7	3-3	1	1
Pfeffer	2⅔	0	0-0	0	3

HBP: by Mays (Myers)
WP: Foster

Game-Winning RBI: Cutshaw
LOB: Boston 2, Brooklyn 9
BE: none
3B: Olson, Hooper, Daubert
HR: Gardner
SH: Stengel, Myers, Miller
SB: Wheat
CS: Hooper, Shorten
Time—2:01
Attendance—21,087

Umpires: H. O'Day, T. Connolly, E. Quigley, & B. Dineen.

With Rube Marquard getting hit hard, the Superbas lost the fourth game, 6-2.

Boston then wrapped up the series in the fifth game by winning, 4-1. Pfeffer finally got to start a game for Brooklyn, and he took the loss. His defensive support was partly to blame.

1917 WEDNESDAY, SEPTEMBER 26TH, AT WEEGHAM PARK, CHICAGO

Robins Slip to 7th

Marquard Loses a Tough One, 1-0
Cub Rookies Beat Last Year's Champs

Today's Results			
Chicago 1-BROOKLYN 0			
St. Louis 2-New York 1 (12 inn.)			
Philadelphia 5-Pittsburgh 0			
Boston 1-Cincinnati 0 (1st game)			
Boston 3-Cincinnati 0 (2nd game)			

Standings	W-L	Pct.	GB
New York	94-53	.639	—
Philadelphia	84-61	.579	9
St. Louis	81-68	.544	14
Cincinnati	75-75	.500	20½
Chicago	74-78	.487	22½
Boston	67-77	.465	25½
BROOKLYN	65-77	.458	26½
Pittsburgh	49-100	.329	46

MY, HOW HAVE THE MIGHTY FALLEN! The Brooklyn Robins, champions of the National League in 1916, today fell to seventh place in the 1917 standings. With just eight days remaining in the season, the Superbas seemed like a good bet to finish seventh. No National League champion had ever fallen that far in one year before.

To make matters seem even worse, the Dodger lineup today had seven of the men who started last year's World Series, and they were beaten by a Chicago Cub team that had five starting players who were minor leaguers less than two weeks ago. Champions humiliated by bushers. No wonder Wilbert Robinson was in such a cross mood.

The defending champs started the season badly, losing 14 of the first 19 games. Then the team improved from terrible to merely mediocre. One hot streak around the end of July got Brooklyn's record over .500 (47-46). But the Robins were over .500 for only one day, then decline set in again. Losing most all of the close games, the Dodgers hovered just under .500 for most of August. Then they collapsed in September, having lost 17 of the first 23 games in the month.

No one man was responsible for the team's dreary showing this year. The two big hitters on the club, Zack Wheat and Jake Daubert, however, had fallen off the most, Daubert especially. Wheat was able to keep his average up but injuries limited his playing time and hit production. Overall, the offense had fallen from the second-best in the league in 1916 to the second-worst in 1917.

But a bigger reason for the champs' demise was the decline of the pitching. Only one member of the championship staff of 1916 had done as well in 1917. That was Rube Marquard, 13-6 last year and 17-12 so far this year. Jeff Pfeffer had fallen from 25-11 to 11-13. This year he was losing the close ones that he won last season. Without the addition of young Leon Cadore (12-12), the vaulted Brooklyn pitching might have fallen from the best in the league to the worst.

Marquard was the hard-luck loser today. He allowed just six hits and one run, while striking out nine batters in seven innings of pitching. But that one run beat him.

The Robins were shut out by rookie Harry Weaver, who was making his very first major league start. The veteran Brooklyn lineup managed just four hits against him. Weaver's catcher was 20-year-old Bob O'Farrell, just brought up from Peoria and playing in only his sixth major league game. The Robins didn't steal a single base. They didn't even try.

The Chicago run was scored by Turner Barber, playing in his fifth game with the Cubs after being purchased from Baltimore in the International League. Barber was batted home by Roy Leslie, who was with Waco of the Texas League before coming to Chicago. And the Cubs' shortstop, Charlie Pechous, was another recent acquisition from Peoria in the "Three-Eye" League.

Weaver held the Superbas hitless until the fifth inning, when Wheat singled cleanly to right to lead off. Dave Hickman bunted, and Weaver threw high and wild to second base, allowing both Dodgers to be safe. George Cutshaw sacrificed them to second and third. Ernie Krueger came to bat needing only a long fly ball or a hard grounder through the drawn-in infield. Weaver got him to pop to short left field, and

Wheat did not dare to try and score after the catch. Marquard sent a hard liner to center, but Barber went back to make the catch, and Brooklyn was turned back.

Robinson's men missed another chance to score in the next inning. With one gone, Daubert singled to center and Hi Myers beat out a bunt. But Casey Stengel could only come up with a feeble fly to the second baseman, and Wheat hit into a force out.

In the meantime, Chicago had threatened a few times, but Marquard was equal to each challenge.

Then the Cubs finally broke through in the sixth. Barber, the Baltimore speed boy, easily outlegged a slow roller past the mound for a leadoff single. Charlie Deal struck out. Then Fred Merkle singled up the middle. When center fielder Hickman did not hustle in for the ball, Barber boldly raced to third, arriving ahead of Hickman's poor throw. When Leslie singled to right center, Barber trotted home. Leslie and Merkle worked a double steal to put men on third and second. Marquard got out of this jam by getting a pop out, issuing an intentional walk to O'Farrell, and retiring Weaver on a fly to center.

Brooklyn got only one hit in the final three frames, and that was immediately lost due to faulty base running. Krueger hit safely to left center in the seventh, but quick fielding by Merkle cut him down trying to stretch the hit into a double. By this time, Uncle Wilbert was wearing a very gray expression.

The Robins went down to defeat, 1-0, at the hands of the rookie pitcher and his rookie teammates. Since Boston had already won the first game of its double-header, the champions of 1916 left the field in seventh place. It was quite a fall from glory for Wilbert Robinson and his men.

Brooklyn	ab	r	h	bi	o	a	e
I. Olson, ss	4	0	0	0	0	2	0
J. Daubert, 1b	2	0	1	0	3	0	0
H. Myers, 3b	4	0	1	0	1	2	0
C. Stengel, rf	4	0	0	0	0	0	0
Z. Wheat, lf	4	0	1	0	2	0	0
D. Hickman, cf	4	0	0	0	5	0	0
G. Cutshaw, 2b	2	0	0	0	2	0	1
E. Krueger, c	3	0	1	0	11	1	0
R. Marquard, p	2	0	0	0	0	0	0
F. O'Rourke, ph8	1	0	0	0	-	-	-
J. Coombs, p8	0	0	0	0	0	0	0
	30	0	4	0	24	5	1

Chicago	ab	r	h	bi	o	a	e
M. Flack, rf	4	0	1	0	1	0	0
P. Kilduff, 2b	4	0	0	0	2	5	0
T. Barber, cf	4	1	1	0	4	0	0
C. Deal, 3b	4	0	2	0	1	4	0
F. Merkle, lf	4	0	2	0	4	1	0
R. Leslie, 1b	4	0	1	1	13	1	0
C. Pechous, ss	2	0	0	0	2	1	0
B. O'Farrell, c	2	0	0	0	0	0	0
H. Weaver, p	3	0	0	0	0	4	1
	31	1	7	1	27	16	1

Brooklyn	000 000 000	=	0		
Chicago	000 001 00x	=	1		

	ip	h	r-er	bb	so
Marquard (L 17-12)	7	6	1-1	2	9
Coombs	1	1	0-0	0	1
Weaver (W 1-0)	9	4	0-0	2	0

Time—1:27
Umpires: E. Quigley & B. Byron

Game-Winning RBI: Leslie
LOB: Bkn 6, Chi 8
BE: Bkn 1, Chi 1
3B: Merkle
SH: Cutshaw
SB: Merkle, Leslie
CS: Deal
Attendance—605

Although the Robins won five of their last nine, they still finished seventh. By losing the final game of the season to Boston, 4-2, they finished 1 game behind the Braves.

Brooklyn's final record was 70-81. Home attendance fell a full 50%, from 447,000 to 221,000

1918 WEDNESDAY, AUGUST 7TH, AT EBBETS FIELD

Zack & Mack Wheat Star

Brothers Bat Brooklyn to 3-2 Triumph
Mack Hits Three-Run Homer, Zack Runs Hitting Streak to 26 Games

THE WHEAT BROTHERS, ZACK AND MACK, batted the Brooklyn Superbas to victory today against the league-leading Chicago Cubs, 3-2. Zachariah Davis Wheat, the elder of the boys, got one single in three at bats. The hit extended his batting streak to 26 consecutive games, the most in the major leagues this season. It also kept him in the top spot in the National League batting-average list. McKinley Davis Wheat, generally not as good a hitter as his older brother, poled his first major league home run and batted home his first three big league runs with the blow. The three runs were just enough to give Brooklyn pitcher Burleigh Grimes a 3-2 victory.

Today's Results			
BROOKLYN 3-Chicago 2			
Cincinnati 8-New York 3 (1st game)			
Cincinnati 4-New York 2 (2nd game)			
Pittsburgh 4-Philadelphia 2			
Boston 4-St. Louis 3 (11 innings)			
Standings	**W-L**	**Pct.**	**GB**
Chicago	65-34	.657	—
New York	59-42	.584	7
Pittsburgh	52-45	.536	12
Cincinnati	45-52	.464	19
BROOKLYN	44-53	.454	20
Philadelphia	44-53	.454	20
Boston	45-55	.450	20½
St. Louis	42-62	.404	25½

Pitcher Grimes, a throw-in in the Casey Stengel and George Cutshaw for Al Mamaux and Chuck Ward trade with Pittsburgh last winter, won his fifth straight decision and raised his record to 14-7. Last season with the Pirates, he had a miserable 3-16 log. So the trade looked good for Wilbert Robinson's forces even with Mamaux and Ward gone to work for the national war effort. Burleigh enlisted in the Navy some weeks ago, but he has yet to be called to active duty. The Navy's loss so far had been the Robins' gain.

All in all, the Brooklyn club lost at least its share of personnel to the military and to war industries. Thirteen of its players had already gone into uniform, including important pitchers like Jeff Pfeffer, and Leon Cadore.

Z. Wheat started the season by staying on his Missouri farm. Zack was doing the essential work of providing the United States and its allies with food to defeat the Kaiser with. He was also holding out for an increase in pay to $5,800.

Without the elder Wheat and with its pitching staff depleted, the Brooklyn team lost its first nine games of the season. Then owner Charles Ebbets gave in to Zack's demands. Z. Wheat made his debut on May 7th, but the Dodgers were in last place as late as July 19th. Through July 10th, Zack was hitting .275. On the 11th, he began his batting streak. In the 26 games including today's, he hit at a .444 pace to raise his average to .334. That was high enough to put him past Cincinnati's Heinie Groh and into the league lead. Zack was now trying to break his own club record of hitting in 29 consecutive games, which he did in 1916.

Brother Mack, who did not hold out, raised his average today to a more modest .260. A catcher, he threw out two men stealing, tagged one out at the plate, and participated in a rundown that retired another runner between third and home. And, of course, he hit the winning home run.

Mack's throw helped turn back Chicago without a run in the top of the first, even though the Cubs got three hits.

Fred Merkle opened the second with a single and was forced at second by Charlie Pick. Pick was then caught trying to steal second.

Zack got his daily bingle in the bottom of the second. It was a sharp one-bagger over second base.

Chicago scored the first run of the game in the top of the fourth. With one gone, Les Mann reached first on a boot by second baseman Mickey Doolan. He moved to second on an infield out, and Merkle singled him home.

Brooklyn got all of its runs in the bottom of the fourth. Z. Wheat led off with a hopper to second baseman Rollie Zeider, who kicked it. After Hi Myers had whiffed, Ollie O'Mara singled to right. A ground out by Doolan advanced the runners to second and third. Mack Wheat came up and pulled a liner past third base and into the distant left field corner. Z. Wheat and O'Mara scored easily, but Mack had to run the race of his life to make the circuit. He slid into the plate just a fraction ahead of the relay and earned his first big league home run. Brooklyn led 3-1.

Chicago scored another run in the fifth to reduce the lead to 3-2. The tally came on a double steal, Bob O'Farrell scoring thanks to a wild return throw to the plate by shortstop O'Mara. But with the tying run on third, Grimes struck out Max Flack to preserve the lead.

Using his spitball and fastball effectively, Grimes held the Cubs to just one hit in the final four innings. But that hit, which was a double that followed an error in the eighth, gave Chicago a great scoring opportunity with none out. Grimes retired Mann on a comebacker, as the runners had to hold their bases. Dode Paskert then bounced to second base, and Doolan threw Flack out at home. Merkle ended the inning by grounding into a force out at second.

A fine lunging catch by Z. Wheat robbed Pick of a hit in the ninth, and Chicago went out in order. Grimes had his fifth straight win, Zack Wheat had a 26-game hitting streak, and Mack Wheat had the first home run and runs-batted-in of his career.

After the game, club president Ebbets announced that after the season ended on Labor Day, Ebbets Field would be turned over to the war department for a storage facility, and Brooklyn would be out of baseball for the duration.

Chicago	ab	r	h	bi	o	a	e
M. Flack, rf	4	0	1	0	4	0	0
C. Hollocher, ss	4	0	1	0	1	3	0
L. Mann, lf	4	1	1	0	2	0	0
D. Paskert, cf	4	0	1	0	1	0	0
F. Merkle, 1b	4	0	2	1	8	1	0
C. Pick, 3b	2	0	0	0	0	3	0
R. Zeider, 2b	3	0	0	0	2	1	1
B. McCabe, ph9	1	0	0	0	-	-	-
B. O'Farrell, c	3	1	1	0	4	0	1
P. Douglas, p	1	0	0	0	0	1	0
T. Barber, ph5	1	0	0	0	-	-	-
N. Carter, p5	0	0	0	0	1	2	0
C. Deal, ph7	1	0	0	0	-	-	-
C. Hendrix, p7	0	0	0	0	1	1	0
	32	2	7	1	24	12	2

Brooklyn	ab	r	h	bi	o	a	e
J. Johnston, rf	4	0	1	0	2	0	0
I. Olson, ss	3	0	0	0	2	5	1
J. Daubert, 1b	4	0	0	0	12	1	0
Z. Wheat, lf	3	1	1	0	1	0	0
H. Myers, cf	3	0	0	0	1	1	0
O. O'Mara, 3b	3	1	1	0	2	2	0
M. Doolan, 2b	3	0	0	0	4	4	2
M. Wheat, c	3	1	1	3	3	4	0
B. Grimes, p	3	0	1	0	0	6	0
	29	3	5	3	27	23	3

Chicago	000 110 000	= 2
Brooklyn	000 300 00x	= 3

	ip	h	r-er	bb	so
Douglas (L 8-7)	4	4	3-0	1	3
Carter	2	1	0-0	0	0
Hendrix	2	0	0-0	0	0
Grimes (W 14-7)	9	7	2-0	2	2

HBP: by Grimes (O'Farrell)
WP: Douglas
Umpires: B. Klem & B. Emslie

Game-Winning RBI: M. Wheat
LOB: Chicago 6, Brooklyn 3
BE: Chicago 2, Brooklyn 1
DP: Olson-Daubert
Carter-Merkle
2B: Hollocher
HR: M. Wheat
SB: Johnston, Olson, O'Farrell, Barber, Pick
CS: Mann, Pick
Time—1:55

Zack Wheat was held hitless in three at bats on the following day by Hippo Vaughn and Nick Carter, ending his hitting streak at 26 games. But he continued to hit well and won the batting title with a .335 average.

Mack Wheat finished the season with just three 3 RBIs.

Burleigh Grimes won his next four starts before losing. He wound up the shortened season with an excellent 19-9 record.

The season ended on Labor Day because of the War Department's "Work or Fight" order. Brooklyn finished with a 57-69 record, good enough for fifth place.

1919 THURSDAY, MAY 15TH, AT EBBETS FIELD

Lose 10-0 in 13th Inning

Mamaux Blows Up after Pitching 12 Scoreless Innings
Eller Pitches Shutout for Reds

AFTER MATCHING GOOSE-EGGS WITH Cincinnati's Hod Eller for twelve innings today, Brooklyn's Al Mamaux went completely up in the air in the thirteenth inning and lost the game, 10-0. After he had held the Reds to just five hits in the first twelve rounds, Mamaux gave up eight safeties in the unlucky thirteenth, including seven in a row. Two errors on bunts and another on a stolen base did not help, nor did two bases on balls.

Today's Results

Cincinnati 10-BROOKLYN 0 (13 innings)
New York 6-Chicago 2
Pittsburgh 5-Philadelphia 0
St. Louis at Boston, ppd.-rain

Standings	W-L	Pct.	GB
BROOKLYN	11- 4	.733	—
New York	11- 4	.733	—
Cincinnati	12- 6	.667	½
Pittsburgh	8- 8	.500	3½
Chicago	9- 9	.500	3½
Philadelphia	5- 8	.385	5
St. Louis	4-13	.235	8
Boston	2-10	.167	7½

The suddenly terrible defeat ended what had been an exciting and well-played game. The result dropped the Dodgers into a tie for first place with the New York Giants. The Reds, who had lost the first two games of their four-game series in Brooklyn, moved back to within ½ game of the leaders.

Horace "Hod" Eller pitched his second great game in a row for Cincinnati. He had beaten St. Louis on a no-hitter in his last start. And today he allowed only two hits in the first nine innings. Curiously, in his no-hitter only five balls were hit to the outfield, whereas in the first nine innings today, Brooklyn hit only seven ground balls against him. Most of today's outfield flies were easy chances.

Eller was brilliantly supported by his fielders. Right fielder Earle "Greasy" Neale was the most outstanding gloveman, catching ten fly balls. One of his catches robbed Brooklyn of a triple in the tenth inning and saved the game for the Reds.

The luckless Mamaux battled gamely throughout the long fight, although he was not as impressive as Eller. Constantly in trouble because of poor control, Al turned back many Cincinnati threats.

His pitching was helped by some fine defense. One Red was thrown out at the plate trying to score from second on a single. Another was caught in a rundown between third and home after Mamaux gloved a bouncer back to the box. Mamaux also picked two men off base. And catcher Ernie Krueger threw out a man stealing.

Cincinnati came within an eyelash of scoring in the fifth. Larry Kopf led off by receiving Mamaux's fifth walk of the game. Ivey Wingo singled. After Mamaux deftly picked Kopf off second, Wingo moved up on Eller's infield out. Morrie Rath singled to center, but Hi Myers fielded the ball quickly and made a great throw home to cut Wingo down trying to score.

The Reds' other good chance came in the ninth. Heinie Groh walked for starters, and Sherry Magee bunted him along. A hit by Edd Roush moved him to third. Jake Daubert, the former Dodger, bounced one back up the middle, but Mamaux speared it and caught Groh in a rundown for the second out. Kopf grounded out to short to end the threat.

In the meantime, Brooklyn could do very little against Eller. Their early hits came in the fourth and fifth innings by Lee Magee and Lew Malone, respectively. Zack Wheat hit a long fly in the sixth, but it was caught against the fence by Neale.

The Superbas nearly broke up the game in the tenth, but Neale saved the day for the Reds. Myers was given a life on a fumble by Groh with none out. Ed Konetchy forced the runner trying to sacrifice. Malone then lined what looked like a double or triple down the right field line. But Neale raced over and made a spectacular, nose-first diving catch while stretched out at full length. Myers was well past second when the ball was caught, but he got back to first while Neale was rolling around in the mud.

Rain was falling steadily as the game went into the thirteenth inning. Rath, first up for the Reds, worked his fourth walk of the day. Neale bunted down the third base line, and Malone fumbled the difficult chance. Groh bunted back to the mound. Mamaux had time to get a force at third base, but he threw wildly over Malone's head. Left fielder Wheat backed the play up to keep Rath from scoring, but the bases were now loaded with no one out.

Chagrined at his own error, Mamaux laid a fat pitch in to Roush. Edd lambasted it to deep left center for a bases-clearing triple. S. Magee struck out, and Jake Daubert flied out, with Roush scoring after the catch.

With two out and none on, the rally started all over again. Kopf walked. He stole second and got to third when Krueger's throw went into center field. Wingo tripled him home. Eller singled to right for another run. Rath hit safely through the box. Neale pounded a two-run double to right. Groh blooped a hit to left center, bringing Neale around. Roush hit safely for the second time in the inning, and S. Magee singled Groh home. Finally Daubert popped out to second, ending the agony.

Most of the fans had lost count of the runs by the end, and when the scoreboard operator posted a "10" on the board, a huge groan rose from the grandstand.

The Robins went feebly in the bottom of the tenth, getting only a two-out single, and the game was over.

For twelve innings it had been such a close game. Then it ended with a very one-sided final score. Oh well, if you're going to lose them, you might as well lose them big.

Cincinnati	**ab**	**r**	**h**	**bi**	**o**	**a**	**e**
M. Rath, 2b	3	2	2	0	1	4	0
G. Neale, rf	6	2	2	2	10	0	0
H. Groh, 3b	6	2	2	1	2	1	1
E. Roush, cf	6	1	3	3	4	0	0
S. Magee, lf	5	0	1	1	8	0	0
J. Daubert, 1b	6	0	0	1	7	0	0
L. Kopf, ss	3	1	0	0	4	1	0
I. Wingo, c	6	1	2	1	3	1	0
H. Eller, p	6	1	1	1	0	2	0
	47	10	13	10	39	9	1

Brooklyn	**ab**	**r**	**h**	**bi**	**o**	**a**	**e**
I. Olson, ss	6	0	1	0	6	3	0
L. Magee, 2b	5	0	2	0	3	6	0
T. Griffith, rf	4	0	0	0	2	0	0
Z. Wheat, lf	5	0	1	0	2	1	0
H. Myers, cf	5	0	0	0	4	0	0
E. Konetchy, 1b	5	0	0	0	15	2	0
L. Malone, 3b	5	0	1	0	1	3	1
E. Krueger, c	5	0	0	0	6	2	1
A. Mamaux, p	3	0	0	0	0	7	1
D. Hickman, ph13	1	0	0	0	-	-	-
	44	0	5	0	39	24	3

Cincinnati	000 000 000 000 (10)	= 10
Brooklyn	000 000 000 000 0	= 0

	ip	**h**	**r-er**	**bb**	**so**
Eller (W 4-0)	13	5	0-0	1	3
Mamaux (L 0-1)	13	13	10-1	10	4

HBP: by Eller (L. Magee)
PB: Krueger
Time—2:25
Attendance—3,000

Game-Winning RBI: Roush
LOB: Cincinnati 11, Brooklyn 8
BE: Cincinnati 2, Brooklyn 1
2B: Malone, L. Magee, Neale
3B: Roush, Wingo
SH: Griffith, S. Magee, Neale, Daubert
SB: Rath, Groh, Myers, Kopf, Olson 2
CS: Rath
Picked Off: S. Magee, Kopf
Umpires: B. Klem & B. Emslie

Cincinnati won the final game of the series,1-0, with Dolf Luque beating Rube Marquard.

Brooklyn bounced back and won five of its next seven games. Then disaster struck. From May 27th through June 14th, the Robins won only 4 out of 18 games and fell all the way to sixth place. For the remainder of the season, they played about .500 ball and finished with a 69-71 record. That left them in fifth place, 27 games behind the pennant-winning Reds.

Chapter VI Ups and Downs in the Twenties

1920 May 1st
Robins and Braves Play 26-Inning Tie

1920 September 10th
Two Big Rallies Keep Dodgers in 1st Place

1920 World Series Game #3
Robins Take 2-1 Lead in Series

1921 May 2nd
Brooklyn Pulls Out 11th Consecutive Victory

1922 July 1st
Ruether Stars in 1-0 Victory

1923 May 7th
At Least Johnston Wanted to Win

1924 September 7th
Big Mob Sees Robins Lose Key Game

1925 September 13th
Dazzy Gets a No-Hitter

BROOKLYN STARTED THE 1920 SEASON WITH PRETTY MUCH THE SAME TEAM THAT HAD finished fifth in 1919. Chuck Ward was given the starting job at shortstop, with Ivy Olson moved to second base. The feature of the first five weeks of the season was extra innings. Seven of the team's first twenty-one games went into overtime. The champion extra-inning game of them all came in Boston on May 1st, when the Robins and Braves played 26 innings and wound up tied, 1-1. The next day, a Sunday, the Robins played 13 innings at home against the Phillies and lost, 4-3. Then they returned to Boston on Monday and lost a 19-inning, 2-1 decision. Luckily they were rained out Tuesday.

Through it all, Brooklyn kept its record above .500. In May, Ward went out with a charley horse, and Olson was shifted to short. Pete Kilduff, acquired from the Cubs in 1919, became the starting second baseman. With Jimmy Johnston at third and Ed Konetchy at first, this became the Dodgers' set infield. It was not considered top-flight, but it performed reasonably well. One Brooklyn newspaper dubbed the unit "The $100 Infield" in contrast to the famous "$100,000 Infield" of the Philadelphia Athletics a decade before.

Hi Myers and Zack Wheat were fixtures in center and left fields, respectively, while Tommy Griffith platooned with Bernie Neis in right. Otto Miller was the number one catcher, backed by Ernie Krueger and Harold "Rowdy" Elliot.

With a lineup that was stable, though not great, the team's fortunes were to be dictated by its pitching. There was a lot of competition for the spots in the starting rotation, and Wilbert Robinson juggled his hurlers well. The Superbas pushed into first place in early June behind some fine pitching by Edward "Jeff" Pfeffer, Al Mamaux, Burleigh Grimes, and Rube Marquard. But later in the month, slumps overtook the pitching and Zack Wheat's big bat, and the team dropped to fourth.

On June 30th, Wheat started hitting again, Clarence Mitchell pitched well in a rare start, and Grimes won the second game of a doubleheader in New York. The sweep started the Dodgers on a hot streak (20-3) that put them back into first place. For the next seven weeks, Brooklyn played at about a .500 pace and kept trading the lead with the defending-champion Cincinnati Reds.

The Robins started September with back-to-back shutout victories by Grimes and Leon Cadore to grab the lead. On Labor Day, Pfeffer and Grimes were beaten in Philadelphia, and Brooklyn fell back to second place. Good hitting won the next three games against the Phils, and Grimes opened a homestand against the Cardinals with a 4-2 victory. This last win put the Robins back into first. The next day, Brooklyn trailed St. Louis 5-3 going into the bottom of the ninth before tying the game. In the eleventh, the Cardinals scored three runs, but the Dodgers rallied for four in their half to win the game and retain the league lead.

The Robins were on their way. They won five more games in the next three days to run their winning streak to ten. And they whipped the slumping Reds two out of three. Brooklyn then cruised to the pennant by 7 games over the new runners-up, the Giants.

In the World Series against the Cleveland Indians, Uncle Robbie nominated veteran Rube Marquard to pitch the first game, although his record was only 10-7. Rube did not pitch too badly, but he lost 3-1. In the second game, Grimes (23-11) pitched a 3-0 shutout. Sherry Smith (11-9) won the third game on a three-hitter, 2-1, to give Brooklyn the series lead. But then the bubble burst. The best-of-nine series shifted to Cleveland for four games. In their home park, the Indians' pitching was invincible. The Superbas scored only two runs in four games and lost all four. They lost the series, 5 games to 2.

Over the winter, the club made only one major trade, sending Marquard to Cincinnati for another lefthanded pitcher, Walter "Dutch" Ruether. Dutch did not have a good year in 1921, although the deal turned out to be a good one for Brooklyn in the long run.

The Robins started the season by losing five of their first six. Then they won eleven in a row. The streak was accomplished despite poor hitting, with the pitching being strong and the batters coming through with timely rather than frequent hits.

But then the situation deteriorated. Minor injuries to Al Mamaux and Jeff Pfeffer put the pitching staff into disarray, and the hitting was not good enough to carry the team. With the Superbas in fifth place in June, Pfeffer was traded to St. Louis for pitcher Ferdinand Schupp and first baseman Hal Janvrin. Neither did much with Brooklyn. Ed Konetchy was sold to Philadelphia on July 4th, and Ray Schmandt was given the first base job. Mamaux never bounced back from tooth troubles, and Smith and Cadore were disappointments. The net result was a fifth-place finish.

For 1922, president Ebbets brought in three notable minor leaguers. Andy High came up and took over at third base. From New Orleans, Brooklyn purchased the battery of Hank DeBerry and Clarence "Dazzy" Vance. Vance was 31 years old at the time and had been plagued by arm trouble through the years. But now he was ready. In 1922 he won 18 and lost 12.

After a slow start, the Robins rose to a close third by the end of June. The big stars were Johnston, Wheat, and Myers, all of whom were hitting well, and Ruether, who ran his record to 14-3 with a 1-0 victory on July 1st. But an eight-game losing streak in early July dropped the Superbas to fifth place. Ruether did not win #15 until July 26th, by which time the Robins were in sixth. They finished there. Despite poor years for both Grimes and Cadore, the pitching was passable. And the outfield was productive. But the infield was poor. Olson and Johnston were both tried at shortstop, but neither could do the job there anymore. And Schmandt continued to disappoint at first base.

In February, 1923, Brooklyn solved its first base problem by trading Schmandt and Myers to St. Louis for Jacques "Jack" Fournier. The hitch in the deal came when Fournier held out for the first three weeks of the season. The Robins started out in the cellar. They pulled out of last with a hectic, 12-11 victory in Boston on May 7th, thanks to Jimmy Johnston's five hits. Jimmy hit over .315 for the third year in a row, but he was still not the answer at shortstop. Andy High and a rookie named Moe Berg were also found lacking at short. Olson, aged 37, was hardly even tried there.

Only steady pitching by Vance and Grimes kept the team afloat through the summer. But an ankle injury to Wheat on July 8th doomed the team to the second division. The Dodgers finished sixth again with exactly the same final record as 1922, 76-78.

Over the winter, Uncle Robbie thought his shortstop problems had finally been solved with the acquisition of Portland star John "Binky" Jones. But Jones held out through most of spring training and then failed to hit when he got into the lineup. Veteran third baseman Milt Stock was picked up from St. Louis, and High was moved to second, where he did well. Johnston was installed at short, again for want of anyone better. A problem in center field was solved in early June by trading Jones and Gene Bailey to Indianapolis for Eddie Brown. Brown could hit and run, but he could barely throw to third base, and home plate was well beyond his range. Still, he was the best Brooklyn could get. Finally on July 25th, 1924, the Robins bought a decent defensive shortstop, Johnny Mitchell, from Minneapolis. The lineup was finally set.

The pitching staff was still headed by Vance and Grimes, of course. Veteran spitballer Bill Doak was added in mid-June. After losing three of his first four decisions with Brooklyn, Doak won ten in a row. Vance ran up a winning streak that got to 15 games before ending on September 20th.

The Dodgers were running a distant third most of the summer. But late in August, they caught fire. Ending a western trip with two wins in St. Louis, they came home and swept three games from the league-leading Giants. Then they startled the baseball world by sweeping four doubleheaders on the road in four days. On September 5th, rookie pitcher Rube Ehrhardt won his fourth straight game, 4-0 over the Braves, to run the Brooklyn winning streak to 14 games and put the Robins just ½ game out of first place. On the 6th, Doak won the first game of a doubleheader, 1-0, while the Giants were losing in Philadelphia in ten innings. But the Dodgers' streak and their league lead did not last through the afternoon. In the second game in Boston, the Robins scored a run in the top of the tenth, but relief pitcher Art

Decatur made a key error in the bottom half, and the Braves scored twice to win, 5-4. The Giants won the nightcap of their twin bill, 16-14, to regain first place.

The big showdown was scheduled for the next day, September 7th in Brooklyn. Ebbets Field was sold out early, and some of the thousands turned away got in by crashing through a gate in the outfield fence. With the fans cramping the outfielders and lots of doubles flying into the overflow, Burleigh Grimes and New York's Jack Bentley battled through seven innings tied, 3-3. In the eighth, shortstop Mitchell kicked a grounder with the bases loaded, and the Giants went on to score five runs. The Robins rallied valiantly, putting the tying and winning runs on second and third in the ninth before losing 8-7.

Vance kept Brooklyn in the race by winning his 25th game of the year (and 13th straight) the next day at the Polo Grounds, 7-2. But the Giants managed to stay a step ahead for the rest of the way, and Brooklyn finished second, a scant 1½ games behind.

The club netted over a quarter of a million dollars for the season, and Ebbets rewarded his stars with big contracts. Vance, who finished 28-6, was given a three-year contract calling for a total of $50,000. He also won a $1,000 prize from the league for being voted the Most Valuable Player. Wheat, Fournier, and Grimes became $15,000-a-year men. And $25,000 was laid out to acquire minor league lefthanded pitcher Jess Petty. But 1925 turned out to be a year of tragedies.

First of all, Ebbets died on April 18th, just after the season had started. His logical successor, Ed McKeever, died just eleven days later. Ebbets' heirs, headed by Joe Gilleaudeau, would not agree to have brother Steve McKeever as president, and finally Wilbert Robinson was elected. A poorer choice could not have been made. The team was in second place in mid-June when Robinson decided that he could not be effective as both president and manager. So he appointed Zack Wheat as "assistant manager," intimating that Zack would have to do well to retain the reins.

Without any authority of his own and with a personality not suited for command, Wheat let the team slip out of contention in the next six weeks. When Robinson returned to the bench, things got no better. With Petty weakened by an attack of tonsilitis and Grimes suffering through a poor season, only Vance held the pitching staff together. On September 8th, the Dazzler pitched a one-hitter. In his next start, five days later, Vance came through with a no-hitter against the Phillies. But the team collapsed utterly after that, winning only 2 more games while losing 17. Brooklyn's final game was rained out, keeping the team from falling to a tie for last place. As it ended, the Robins finished tied for sixth. A finish in the cellar would have given them a chance to draft Hack Wilson from minor leagues, but not losing could even hurt the Brooklyn club sometimes.

Sherry Smith

Dutch Ruether

1920 SATURDAY, MAY 1ST, AT BRAVES FIELD, BOSTON

Robins and Braves Play 26-Inning Tie

Sensational Double Plays Enliven Middle Innings
Joe Oeschger and Leon Cadore Pitch the Distance

SHATTERING ALL KNOWN RECORDS, THE Boston Braves and Brooklyn Robins today played a 26-inning game. The contest was called because of darkness as a 1-1 tie. The biggest stars of the epic battle were the pitchers, Joe Oeschger for Boston and Leon Cadore for Brooklyn. Both hurlers pitched the entire 26 innings, which of course set another record. In all, eight of the nine Braves' starters played the whole game, as did seven of the Robins.

Today's Results			
BROOKLYN 1-Boston 1 (Tie)(26 inn.)			
Cincinnati 7-Pittsburgh 1			
Philadelphia 5-New York 2			
St. Louis 12-Chicago 4			
Standings	**W-L**	**Pct.**	**GB**
Cincinnati	9-3	.750	—
BROOKLYN	8-4	.667	1
Philadelphia	7-5	.583	2
Pittsburgh	6-6	.500	3
St. Louis	6-7	.462	3½
Boston	4-5	.444	3½
Chicago	4-9	.308	5½
New York	3-8	.273	5½

It was the second time this season that Cadore and Oeschger had been matched against one another. On April 20th in Brooklyn, Cadore had won out in an 11-inning duel, 1-0.

In the marathon today, Oeschger had slightly the better of it. He allowed only nine hits, as compared to fifteen off of Cadore. The Brooklyn righthander walked five, while the Boston righty passed four. Each man recorded seven strikeouts.

Cadore had his curveball working very well. He also threw a baffling change of pace, which continued to fool the hitters all afternoon. He got noticeably more effective as the game wore on. In the first nine innings he allowed eleven hits and one run. In the final seventeen rounds, he gave up no runs, only four hits, and three walked.

Oeschger relied mostly on his tremendous speed. He finished the game with nine hitless innings in a row. Even though he must have lost some of his velocity, the Brooklyn hitters were evidently also exhausted and were totally ineffective with the stick in the late going.

Only around 3,000 fans were on hand for the game. It was a chilly day, and it had rained much of the morning. But the showers ended a little after the game got underway, and the game went on uninterrupted, despite a persistent overcast.

The visiting Dodgers got their run first, in the top of the fifth. Ernie Krueger led off with a base on balls. Cadore hit a hot comebacker to Oeschger, who could have completed a double play if he had fielded the ball cleanly. But it bounced out of his glove, and he had to settle for the out at first, with Krueger advancing to second. Ivy Olson then lined a clean hit over the shortstop's head, and Krueger came all the way home.

Boston tied the game in the bottom of the sixth. With Les Mann out, Walton Cruise cracked a long triple over the center fielder's head. Under normal conditions, Cruise would have had an easy home run, since the fence was over 500 feet from the plate. But the wet grass kept the ball from rolling to the wall. Now it was Brooklyn's turn to miss a double-play opportunity. Walter Holke popped what looked like a sure hit into short left field. But Zack Wheat sprinted in and made a remarkable shoetop catch. Cruise was nearly home when the ball was caught, but third baseman Jimmy Johnston and shortstop Chuck Ward had gone out after the pop, and third base was uncovered. Wheat's momentum carried him toward the base, but Cruise got back to the sack just ahead of the hard-charging outfielder. Tony Boeckel then whacked a two-out single to center, and Cruise sauntered home. Rabbit Maranville followed with a long double to center. Boeckel tried to score on the hit, but very quick fielding by outfielder Wallace Hood and second baseman Ivy Olson nipped him at the plate on a close play. Catcher Krueger hurt his leg making the tag and had to leave the game the next inning.

With the score tied 1-1, Boston made a bid to win in the bottom of the ninth. Maranville led off with a hit to left. Lloyd Christenberry bunted for a sacrifice but got a hit, instead. Oeschger sacrificed the runners to second and third. Manager Wilbert Robinson ordered Ray Powell intentionally walked to set up a possible double play. The strategy paid off immediately, thanks to a fine play by Olson. Charley Pick, who finished the day 0-for-11, grounded to the second baseman, who was playing close to the baseline. Powell did his best to avoid a tag, but Olson forced him out of the basepath for an automatic out and threw to first in time to nip Pick and save the game.

An even more spectacular double play kept the Robins from scoring in the seventeenth inning. Wheat and Ed Konetchy singled around a sacrifice, and a fielder's choice loaded the bases with one out. Harold "Rowdy" Elliott then bounced back to the mound. Oeschger threw to catcher Hank Gowdy for a force at home, and Gowdy tried for a double play at first. But his throw was low and wide of first. First baseman Holke blocked it partially, but the ball rolled away a short distance. Konetchy raced around third and tried to score. Holke's throw to Gowdy was off line, but the catcher got it and made a sensational dive into Konetchy's spikes just in time to put the runner out and end the inning.

In the final innings, the pitchers were in complete command, as the batters were as tired as they were. After each three outs, each hurler was loudly cheered by the fans. The game clipped along quickly, and many of the fans stayed around until the end.

In the overcast, the umpires finally called the game after 26 innings. Cadore and Oeschger wanted to go one more inning to give them three full games worth, but arbiter Bill McCormick said "No." Twenty-six innings was glory enough for the pair, even though neither man got a win for all that pitching.

Brooklyn	ab	r	h	bi	o	a	e
I. Olson, 2b	10	0	1	1	5	8	1
B. Neis, rf	10	0	1	0	9	0	0
J. Johnston, 3b	10	0	2	0	3	1	0
Z. Wheat, lf	9	0	2	0	3	0	0
H. Myers, cf	2	0	1	0	2	0	0
W. Hood, pr4-cf	6	0	1	0	9	1	0
E. Konetchy, 1b	9	0	1	0	30	0	0
C. Ward, ss	10	0	0	0	5	3	1
E. Krueger, c	2	1	0	0	4	3	0
R. Elliott, c7	7	0	0	0	7	3	0
L. Cadore, p	10	0	0	0	1	12	0
	85	1	9	1	78	31	2

Boston	ab	r	h	bi	o	a	e
R. Powell, cf	7	0	1	0	8	0	0
C. Pick, 2b	11	0	0	0	6	10	2
L. Mann, lf	10	0	2	0	6	0	0
W. Cruise, rf	9	1	1	0	4	0	0
W. Holke, 1b	10	0	2	0	42	1	0
T. Boeckel, 3b	11	0	3	1	1	7	0
R. Maranville, ss	10	0	3	0	1	9	0
M. O'Neill, c	2	0	0	0	4	2	0
L. Christenberry, ph9	1	0	1	0	-	-	-
H. Gowdy, c10	6	0	1	0	6	1	0
J. Oeschger, p	9	0	1	0	0	11	0
	86	1	15	1	78	41	2

Brooklyn 000 010 000 000 000 000 000 000 00 = 1
Boston 000 001 000 000 000 000 000 000 00 = 1
game called on account of darkness

	ip	h	r-er	bb	so
Cadore	26	15	1-1	5	7
Oeschger	26	9	1-1	4	7

WP: Oeschger

Time—3:50
Attendance—3,000

Umpires: B. McCormick & G. Hart

LOB: Brooklyn 11, Boston 17
BE: Brooklyn 1, Boston 1
DP: Olson-Konetchy (Pick)
Oeschger-Gowdy-Holke-Gowdy
2B: Maranville, Oeschger
3B: Cruise
SH: Powell, O'Neill, Cruise, Oeschger, Holke, Hood
SB: Myers, Hood
CS: Boeckel
Picked Off: Neis, Hood, Mann

Putting Cadore into bed in their Boston hotel, the Robins made a quick return trip to Brooklyn for a Sunday game against the Phillies. It lasted 13 innings, and the Dodgers lost, 4-3.

Sunday night they returned to Boston and found Cadore still in the sack. On Monday, the Braves and Robins again went well into extra innings tied 1-1. But this time Boston scored in the 19th to win, 2-1. So the Robins played a total of 58 innings in three days and got one tie and two defeats for their efforts.

1920 FRIDAY, SEPTEMBER 10TH, AT EBBETS FIELD

Two Big Rallies Keep Dodgers in 1st Place

Score Two in 9th to Tie the Game
Overcome Cardinal Lead with 4 in 11th to Win, 9-8

Today's Results			
BROOKLYN 9-St. Louis 8 (11 inn.)			
Pittsburgh 8-Philadelphia 3			
Cincinnati at Boston, ppd.—rain			
no other game scheduled			
Standings	**W-L**	**Pct.**	**GB**
BROOKLYN	78-57	.578	—
Cincinnati	74-55	.574	1
New York	74-59	.556	3
Pittsburgh	69-62	.527	7
Chicago	67-67	.500	10½
St. Louis	62-71	.466	15
Boston	51-75	.405	22½
Philadelphia	52-81	.391	25

STAGING NOT ONE BUT TWO LAST-OUT rallies, the Brooklyn Dodgers today beat the St. Louis Cardinals, 9-8 in eleven innings, to stay in first place in the National League pennant race. With the second-place Cincinnati Reds being rained out, a defeat would have dropped Brooklyn percentage points behind. But the victory gave them a 1-game lead and upped their current winning streak to five games.

The Reds and the Robins exchanged the league lead no fewer than 16 times since early June, and neither club had yet been able to get more than 4 games out in front. Yesterday the Dodgers regained first place with a 4-2 triumph in the first game of a 17-game homestand.

Today they widened the lead with a doubly dramatic victory over St. Louis. Trailing 5-3 going into the bottom of the ninth, Wilbert Robinson's flock put two men on, then got two two-out singles to tie the score. The Cardinals scratched out three runs in the top of the eleventh inning, and once again it looked like curtains for the home team. But the Robins gamely fought back to score four runs in the bottom of the inning and win the game. After the winning run was across the plate, the Brooklyn fans let loose with a barrage of straw hats, and manager Robinson was surrounded by back-slapping admirers. It was the most dramatic victory of a dramatic pennant fight.

The Superbas started the game out very well, scoring three runs in the first inning against St. Louis pitcher Ferdinand Schupp. With two out and two on, Hi Myers tripled off the wall in right center. Then he scored on a passed ball.

Rogers Hornsby hit a home run over the right field wall in the second inning to start St. Louis on a comeback. Jack Fournier's three-run homer over the same barrier in the seventh put the Cardinals ahead, 5-3, and knocked starting pitcher Rube Marquard out of the game.

Schupp was working on a six-hitter going into the ninth inning, and some of the Flatbush faithful were beginning to give up hope. But Myers led off with a shot that handcuffed the third baseman for a hit. Ed Konetchy popped out. Schupp walked Pete Kilduff on four pitches, and Brooklyn had the tying runs on base. Otto Miller flied out, and now the Dodgers were down to their last out. Ray Schmandt was sent up to hit for the pitcher, and he delivered a single over second to score Myers and sent Kilduff to third. Ivy Olson became a hero by singling past short to bring Kilduff home and tie the game. Several dozen fans skimmed their summer straws onto the field in the excitement. After the field was cleared, Jimmy Johnston grounded out to end the rally.

Jeff Pfeffer pitched the tenth for Brooklyn, and he allowed only a harmless single.

Brooklyn got runners to first and third with two out in the bottom of the tenth, but Kilduff flied out.

In the top of the eleventh, Doc Lavan rolled a hit through the right side of the infield with one gone. Hits to deep short by Cliff Heathcote and Vern Clemons loaded the bases. Mike Knode went up to hit for Schupp, and he worked a walk to bring home one run. Schultz singled solidly to center, and two more men scored. Knode and Schultz moved to third and second, respectively, on the late throw to the plate. Down three runs, the Dodgers halted the rally right there with some nice fielding. Fournier grounded to Konetchy at first, who threw Knode out at home. With men on first and third, St. Louis tried a double steal. But catcher Miller skillfully faked a throw to second and picked Schultz off third.

Needing three runs to tie and four to win, the Robins faced a big task in the bottom of the inning. Wee Willie Sherdel was the new St. Louis pitcher, and Miller greeted the lefthander with a double down the left field line. Pfeffer, a good-hitting pitcher, popped a single just in front of the left fielder, Miller stopping at third. Bill McCabe went in to run for Pfeffer. Olson grounded to third baseman Milt Stock, who threw him out at first as Miller scored. As Olson crossed the base, he knocked the ball out of the first baseman's glove, allowing McCabe to go to third. St. Louis argued that Olson had interfered intentionally, and Brooklyn countered by arguing that Olson was safe because the ball had been dropped. After a short harangue, play was resumed with McCabe on third and one out. Johnston's long fly sent McCabe home, but it was also the second out.

Still needing at least one run, Bernie Neis kept the Brooklyn hopes alive by beating out a hit to deep short. Zack Wheat, a great man to have up in the clutch, rifled a hit to right. When the ball rolled through outfielder Schultz, Neis came all the way home and Wheat raced to third just ahead of the throw. Straw skimmers rained out of the grandstand as the fans screamed their approval.

Myers was next up, and he sent a grounder toward the hole in the left side of the infield. Shortstop Lavan was able to barehand the ball, but his throw to first was way late, and Wheat was home with the winning run. Frustrated first baseman Fournier heaved the ball clear over the right field wall. Meanwhile, the happy patrons surged onto the field and congratulated their heroes and the manager.

If the Robins could win games like this, they reasoned, the pennant would surely be theirs.

St. Louis	ab	r	h	bi	o	a	e
J. Schultz, rf	6	1	3	2	4	0	1
J. Fournier, 1b	6	1	1	3	10	0	1
M. Stock, 3b	5	0	1	0	0	2	0
R. Hornsby, 2b	5	1	2	1	5	5	0
A. McHenry, lf	5	0	0	0	2	0	0
D. Lavan, ss	5	1	2	0	2	2	0
C. Heathcote, cf	4	2	2	0	4	0	0
V. Clemons, c	5	0	1	1	5	0	0
P. Dillhoefer, pr11-c	0	1	0	0	0	0	0
F. Schupp, p	3	1	0	0	0	3	0
M. Knode, ph11	0	0	0	1	-	-	-
W. Sherdel, p11	0	0	0	0	0	0	0
	44	8	12	8	32	12	2

Brooklyn	ab	r	h	bi	o	a	e
I. Olson, ss	6	0	3	2	1	5	1
J. Johnston, 3b	5	1	1	1	2	2	0
B. Neis, rf	5	1	3	0	5	0	0
Z. Wheat, lf	5	2	1	0	3	0	0
H. Myers, cf	5	2	3	3	1	0	0
E. Konetchy, 1b	5	0	0	0	8	3	0
P. Kilduff, 2b	4	1	1	0	3	3	1
O. Miller, c	5	1	1	0	10	1	0
R. Marquard, p	2	0	0	0	0	1	0
E. Krueger, ph7	1	0	0	0	-	-	-
S. Smith, p8	0	0	0	0	0	1	0
R. Schmandt, ph9	1	0	1	1	-	-	-
J. Pfeffer, p10	1	0	1	0	0	0	0
B. McCabe, pr11	0	1	0	0	-	-	-
	45	9	15	7	33	16	2

St. Louis	010	000	400	03	=	8
Brooklyn	300	000	002	04	=	9

two out when winning run scored

	ip	h	r-er	bb	so
Schupp	10	10	5-4	3	4
Sherdel (L 8-9)	⅔	5	4-3	0	0
Marquard	7	6	5-5	2	6
Smith	2	1	0-0	0	1
Pfeffer (W 14-9)	2	5	3-3	1	2

PB: Clemons

Game-Winning RBI: Myers
LOB: St. Louis 6, Brooklyn 9
BE: St. Louis 2, Brooklyn 0
2B: Johnston, Miller
3B: Myers, Schultz, Heathcote
HR: Hornsby, Fournier
SH: Wheat
SF: Johnston
Picked Off: Heathcote, Lavan, Schultz
Time—2:22 Attendance—7,000
Umpires: B. Klem & B. Emslie

The Dodgers won five more in a row and had a 14-3 record for their homestand. The hot finish won the pennant easily. Brooklyn finished 7 games ahead of New York. Cincinnati slumped to third, 10 games behind.

The Robins' final record was 93-61, and the club drew 808,722 paying fans, a new franchise record.

1920 THURSDAY, OCTOBER 7TH, AT EBBETS FIELD
World Series—Game #3

Robins Take 2-1 Lead in Series

LED BY SHERRY SMITH AND THEIR "$100 INFIELD," THE BROOKLYN DODGERS WON THE third game of the 1920 World Series today, 2-1, over the Cleveland Indians. The victory gave the Superbas a 2-games-to-1 lead in the best-of-nine world championship. After the game, the oddsmakers put Brooklyn into the role of favorites for the first time.

As had been predicted, pitching was dominating the series. In the first game, each team made only five hits, and Cleveland won, 3-1, behind Stan Coveleskie. In the second, each side got seven safeties, and Burleigh Grimes won for Brooklyn, 3-0.

Today Cleveland started its third 20-game winner in a row, Ray Caldwell. He lasted just five batters and gave up two runs. Relievers Walter "Duster" Mails and George Uhle shut Brooklyn out the rest of the game. But Brooklyn lefthander Sherrod Smith made those two runs stand up. He pitched a stunning three-hitter and allowed just one run, that unearned.

Although Smith was the biggest star of the game, he was ably supported. The much-maligned Brooklyn infield performed brilliantly. This unit, which had been sarcastically dubbed "The $100 Infield" in contrast to the famous "$100,000 Infield" of the Philadelphia Athletics of the early 1910's, was supposedly weak defensively. But today it gobbled up sixteen ground balls, several of which were difficult chances, and turned two double plays. First baseman Ed Konetchy, second sacker Pete Kilduff, shortstop Ivy Olson, and third baseman Jimmy Johnston all did fine work.

'Twas a bright and sunny day devoid of the chilling wind of the previous two, and over 25,000 fans shoehorned their way into Ebbets Field for the game. With the home team ahead most of the time, the crowd was enthusiastic to an extreme. Cowbells and noisemakers supplemented the roaring human voices in the din. One enterprising patron brought an automobile horn, much to the chagrin of the people directly in front of him. Across Bedford Avenue, the housetops were all densely populated and were just as raucous with cheers for Uncle Robbie's warriors.

Smith had a little control trouble in the first inning but got out of it with only one walk issued and no runs scored.

Caldwell also had trouble finding the plate, and he was out of the game before he got the second Dodger out. His first three pitches were balls to Olson. After two strikes, he issued ball four, and Olson walked to first. Johnston dropped a pretty sacrifice down the third base line and was only retired by a fine play by catcher Steve O'Neill. Olson moved to second on the bunt. With the count full, Tommy Griffith bounced a bouncer to shortstop Joe Sewell. The ball hopped into his glove and hopped right back out again for an error, Olson sidling along to third. Caldwell tried to pitch outside to Wheat, and Zack smacked a ground ball through the left side. Olson skipped on home, and the crowd was up and cheering. Hi Myers hit a little pop in back of first base on the next pitch, and George Burns could only get the tip of his glove on it. It fell for a hit, and Griffith came in with the second run.

Cleveland player-manager Tris Speaker trotted in from center field and dismissed Caldwell from any further duty. Mails was brought in, and he quickly got the side out.

The Robins put their gloves to work in the second inning. Griffith made a great charging catch of a sinking line drive off the bat of Joe Wood. And Konetchy smothered a sharply hit grounder by Sewell and tossed to Smith for the out.

The trickiest play came in the third. O'Neill hit a bounder to Koney's right. Ed got a glove on it, but it bounced away. Kilduff, however, was backing up, and he got the ball and flipped it to Smith at first in time for the out. Two batters later, Pete Kilduff made a nice stop without any deflections.

Cleveland got its run in the fourth. Bill Wambsganss led off and hit a grounder toward left field. Olson went out onto the grass to nab it and threw him out. Speaker then poked a grounder past third base and down the left field line. Wheat hustled over, bent down, and missed the ball completely. Speaker circled the bases and scored standing up.

In the fifth, the Indians put two men on base for the only time. Smith struck Wood out to open, then he walked Sewell in four pitches. O'Neill bounced a single up the middle just past the lunging Olson. Mails followed with a sizzler to short. Olson dug the ball out of the dirt in fine style and threw to Kilduff for a force. Pete relayed low to first, but Koney went to his knees to come up with the ball and complete a big double play.

Smith set the Indians down in order in the sixth and seventh. In the eighth, a fine pickup by Koney turned Sewell's grounder into the first out. O'Neill hit a looper to left center for a hit. Pinch-hitter Les Nunamaker sent an easy hopper to third base, and Johnston, Kilduff, and Konetchy turned a double play.

Came the ninth, and the score was still 2-1. Joe Evans went out on an easy bouncer back to the mound. Wambsganss again hit toward left and was again robbed by a great stop and throw by Olson. Smith thought he had a third strike past Speaker and started to walk off the field. But the umpire called it a ball. No matter, Smith served up another pitch, and Speaker grounded out to short to end the game.

Smith and the Brooklyn infield had shown the world that they were pretty good at this game, despite their lackluster reputation.

Cleveland (AL)	ab	r	h	bi	o	a	e
J. Evans, lf	4	0	0	0	2	0	0
B. Wambsganss, 2b	3	0	0	0	2	2	0
T. Speaker, cf	4	1	1	0	2	0	0
G. Burns, 1b	3	0	0	0	12	0	0
L. Gardner, 3b	3	0	0	0	0	0	0
J. Wood, rf	3	0	0	0	1	0	0
J. Sewell, ss	2	0	0	0	2	3	1
S. O'Neill, c	3	0	2	0	2	2	0
C. Jamieson, pr8	0	0	0	0	-	-	-
G. Uhle, p8	0	0	0	0	0	1	0
R. Caldwell, p	0	0	0	0	0	0	0
D. Mails, p1	2	0	0	0	1	3	0
L. Nunamaker, ph8-c	1	0	0	0	0	0	0
	28	1	3	0	24	11	1

Brooklyn (NL)	ab	r	h	bi	o	a	e
I. Olson, ss	2	1	1	0	0	6	0
J. Johnston, 3b	3	0	0	0	0	4	0
T. Griffith, rf	1	1	0	0	2	0	0
B. Neis, ph3-rf	3	0	0	0	0	0	0
Z. Wheat, lf	4	0	3	1	1	0	1
H. Myers, cf	4	0	2	1	1	0	0
E. Konetchy, 1b	3	0	0	0	17	2	0
P. Kilduff, 2b	1	0	0	0	2	6	0
O. Miller, c	1	0	0	0	2	0	0
S. Smith, p	3	0	0	0	2	2	0
	25	2	6	2	27	20	1

Cleveland	000	100	000	=	1
Brooklyn	200	000	00x	=	2

	ip	h	r-er	bb	so
Caldwell (L 0-1)	⅓	2	2-1	1	0
Mails	6⅔	3	0-0	4	2
Uhle	1	1	0-0	0	0
Smith (W 1-0)	9	3	1-0	2	2

Time—1:47
Attendance—25,088
Umpires: H. O'Day, B. Dineen, B. Klem, & T. Connolly

Game-Winning RBI: Wheat
LOB: Cleveland 2, Brooklyn 7
BE: Cleveland 0, Brooklyn 1
DP: Mails-Burns
Olson-Kilduff-Konetchy (Mails)
Wambsganss-Sewell-Burns (Konetchy)
Johnston-Kilduff-Konetchy (Nunamaker)
2B: Speaker
SH: Johnston, Kilduff, Miller
CS: Olson

After the series moved to Cleveland, the Dodgers did not win a game.

In the fourth game, Leon Cadore and Al Mamaux were hit for four early runs, and Stan Coveleski pitched the Indians to a 5-1 victory.

In Game #5, Burleigh Grimes gave up a grand slam and a three-run homer and lost, 8-1, to Jim Bagby.

Former Dodger Mails bested Smith in a great pitching duel in the sixth game, 1-0.

Cleveland wrapped up the series, 5 games to 2, with Coveleski winning the seventh game, 3-0, over Grimes.

1921 MONDAY, MAY 2ND, AT EBBETS FIELD

Brooklyn Pulls Out 11th Consecutive Victory

Score Two in 9th to Beat Phillies, 4-3
Timely Hitting and a Little Luck Do the Trick

Today's Results			
BROOKLYN 4-Philadelphia 3			
Pittsburgh 4-Chicago 3			
New York 8-Boston 1			
no other game scheduled			
Standings	**W-L**	**Pct.**	**GB**
Pittsburgh	13- 3	.812	—
BROOKLYN	12- 5	.706	1½
New York	9- 6	.600	3½
Chicago	6- 7	.462	5½
Cincinnati	7-10	.412	7½
Boston	6-11	.353	7½
Philadelphia	5-10	.333	7½
St. Louis	3- 9	.250	8

WILBERT ROBINSON'S DEFENDING-champion Brooklyn Robins did it again today. They staged another come-from-behind victory to run their winning streak to eleven games. Today's triumph came when two runs in the bottom of the ninth inning defeated the Philadelphia Phillies, 4-3. It was the eighth time in the eleven victories that the Dodgers had trailed in the game but had come back to win. Seven of those rallies came in the seventh, eighth, or ninth innings.

The champs got off to a poor start in the first week of the season, winning one and losing five. Then they found the formula for success. Solid pitching kept them in the game, and the batting attack, which often looked meager, would come alive in the late going and pull victory from the jaws of defeat.

Ed Konetchy, who got the game-winning triple today, won the first game of the streak with a two-out, two-run single in the ninth inning to beat the Phils, 4-2.

A three-run triple in the eighth by Bernie Neis beat Boston, 4-2, the next day. Another eighth-inning rally, this one keyed by a double by Tommy Griffith, beat Boston again, 4-2. In the final game of the Braves' series, Brooklyn won an easy one, 12-6.

There followed a four-game sweep of the Giants at Ebbets Field. The scores were 4-1, 3-1, 5-4, and 2-1. The most dramatic triumph was in the third game, when the Robins rallied for two runs in the bottom of the ninth to win.

The Phillies came to town, and the Brooklyn magic continued through three games. In Saturday's opener, Tommy Griffith and Zack Wheat hit back-to-back home runs to win the game, 3-2, even though the Dodgers were outhit, nine to four. Yesterday Brooklyn was again outhit, seven to five, but Burleigh Grimes shut the Phils out and won, 3-0. Today Philadelphia's Wilbert "Bill" Hubbell limited the champs to five hits. But two were triples by Konetchy with men on base, and Brooklyn won again.

Although the Robins' team batting average ranked a lowly seventh out of eight in the league, the team was getting the hits when they counted.

Today the Dodgers made four errors to go with their five hits, but they got a few breaks and made the most of them. And the Brooklyn fielding was not all bad. Ace catcher Otto Miller threw out three men trying to steal second base and picked another off first.

Two of the would-be thieves were cut down in the top of the first after they had singled against pitcher Leon Cadore.

Cadore pitched around an error in the second.

The Robins bunched two hits behind a Philadelphia error to score two runs in the bottom of the second. Wheat reached first on a boot by the second baseman to open the inning. Konetchy got a triple when his hit was allowed to get past the outfielders, Wheat scoring. Hi Myers followed with a scratch hit off of first baseman Jack Miller's shins to bring Koney home.

The Phillies wasted a one-out double and a walk in the third when Johnny Rawlings fanned and O. Mitter picked Greasy Neale off first base after the third strike.

An error hurt Brooklyn in the fourth, when it gave the Phils their first run. Cy

Williams scored from second when Ivy Olson allowed a ground ball to go through his legs.

Outfielders Wheat and Neis collided under J. Miller's fly to lead off the fifth, and the ball fell safely. But the Dodgers' luck got them out of the jam. Frank Bruggy was retired when he tried to duck out of the way of an inside pitch, the ball popping off his bat to the catcher. After Hubbell flied out and Neale walked, Rawlings grounded a sure hit to left. But J. Miller, running hard to try and beat a possible play at the plate, ran right into the ball for an automatic out.

The Phillies finally got the lead in the sixth on a two-run home run by Russ Wrightstone. The drive bounced into the temporary bleachers in left field.

Relievers Johnny Miljus and Clarence Mitchell held the Phillies scoreless in the seventh, eighth, and ninth.

The Dodgers still had just two hits and were still trailing 3-2 going into the bottom of the ninth. Then they came to life and pulled out another victory. Johnston started things off by smacking a solid hit to center. Griffith sacrificed Johnston to second. Wheat nearly decapitated pitcher Hubbell with a slam up the middle, and Johnston scored the tying run. The stands were uproarious when Konetchy came to the plate. Koney sent the assemblage into ecstasy in short order. He lined a clean triple over the second baseman's head and into the gap in right center. Wheat ran home with the winning run, and Brooklyn had another come-from-behind triumph.

Konetchy was mobbed by his teammates, and manager Robinson took off his cap and danced a jig between first base and home plate. If his men could keep this sort of thing up all season, Uncle Robbie might have a wonderful second childhood.

Philadelphia	ab	r	h	bi	o	a	e
G. Neale, rf	2	0	0	0	0	0	0
J. Rawlings, 2b	4	0	3	0	0	4	1
C. Williams, cf	4	1	2	0	4	0	0
I. Meusel, lf	4	1	1	0	4	0	0
R. Wrightstone, 3b	4	1	1	2	2	2	1
R. Miller, ss	4	0	1	0	1	3	0
J. Miller, 1b	4	0	0	0	12	0	0
F. Bruggy, c	4	0	1	0	2	1	0
B. Hubbell, p	4	0	1	0	0	2	0
	34	3	10	2	25	12	2

Brooklyn	ab	r	h	bi	o	a	e
I. Olson, ss	4	0	0	0	6	1	1
J. Johnston, 3b	4	1	1	0	0	1	0
T. Griffith, rf	3	0	0	0	3	0	1
Z. Wheat, lf	4	2	1	1	0	0	0
E. Konetchy, 1b	4	1	2	2	7	1	0
H. Myers, 2b	3	0	1	1	1	2	1
B. Neis, cf	2	0	0	0	0	0	1
O. Miller, c	2	0	0	0	8	5	0
L. Cadore, p	2	0	0	0	0	0	0
J. Miljus, p7	0	0	0	0	0	1	0
C. Mitchell, p7	1	0	0	0	1	1	0
	29	4	5	4	*26	12	4

*J. Miller out, hit by batted ball

Philadelphia	000	102	000	=	3
Brooklyn	020	000	002	=	4

one out when winning run scored

	ip	h	r-er	bb	so
Hubbell (L 0-2)	8⅓	5	4-3	0	2
Cadore	6	7	3-2	2	3
Miljus	⅔	1	0-0	1	1
Mitchell (W 2-0)	2⅓	2	0-0	0	2

Time—1:43
Attendance—7,500
Umpires: B. Brennan & B. Emslie

Game-Winning RBI: Konetchy
LOB: Philadelphia 7, Brooklyn 3
BE: Philadelphia 3, Brooklyn 2
DP: O. Miller-Konetchy
Myers-Olson-Konetchy (R. Miller)
2B: Hubbell
3B: Konetchy 2
HR: Wrightstone
SH: Neis, O. Miller, Griffith
SB: Bruggy
CS: Rawlings, Williams, R. Miller
Picked Off: Neale

The tables were turned on the Dodgers in their next game; the Giants rallied in the eighth inning to beat Brooklyn 3-2.

Minor injuries to Al Mamaux and Jeff Pfeffer precipitated a pitching collapse in May, and the team fell below .500 by Memorial Day. Instead of chasing another pennant, the Robins spent most of the summer chasing the Boston Braves.

Brooklyn finished fifth with a 77-75 record.

1922 SATURDAY, JULY 1ST, AT BRAVES FIELD, BOSTON

Ruether Stars in 1-0 Victory

Dutch Hurls 6-Hitter and Doubles Home Winning Run
Raises His Record to 14-3

WITH THE SEASON LESS THAN HALF over, Brooklyn's Walter "Dutch" Ruether was pitching so well that there was speculation in Flatbush that he might win 30 games this season. Today he pitched perhaps his best game of the year to beat the Boston Braves in ten innings, 1-0. That upped the southpaw's win total to 14 games against just 3 defeats.

Today's Results			
BROOKLYN 1-Boston 0 (10 inn.)			
St. Louis 9-Pittsburgh 5 (1st game)			
Pittsburgh 9-St. Louis 8 (2nd game)			
Chicago 6-Cincinnati 5			
Philadelphia at New York, ppd.-rain			

Standings	W-L	Pct.	GB
New York	43-24	.642	—
St. Louis	38-30	.559	5½
BROOKLYN	38-32	.543	6½
Cincinnati	34-34	.500	9½
Pittsburgh	33-34	.493	10
Chicago	32-35	.478	11
Boston	26-40	.394	16½
Philadelphia	25-40	.385	17

And not only did Ruether pitch a shutout, he started a nifty double play that cut short a Boston threat in the ninth inning, and he drove home the only run of the game with a double in the top of the tenth. What more could one man do on a ballfield?

With newcomer Dazzy Vance and veteran Burleigh Grimes also doing good work on the mound for Brooklyn, hopes were also running high that the Robins could come back from last year's disappointment and recapture the National League pennant. Today's victory edged the third-place Dodgers to within 6½ games of the league-leading Giants.

The game today was one of the best-played this year. Boston righthander John "Mule" Watson matched zeroes with Ruether for nine innings. And both pitchers received great fielding support. Although the field was rather sloppy from overnight rains, not a single error was made. Ruether had the Braves hitting the ball on the ground all day, and his infield was superb behind him. They turned three double plays. Boston made no twin-killings, but shortstop Hod Ford was all over the field making brilliant plays to bail Watson out of trouble.

The two hurlers clipped through the first five innings almost before anyone noticed that the game was on. Each side got just two hits in that period of time, and none of the runners got as far as second base.

In the sixth inning, Brooklyn was robbed of a run by the acrobatic Mr. Ford. With Andy High on third base and two out, Zack Wheat slashed a vicious shot back at Watson. The pitcher just had enough time to throw his glove up and deflect the ball toward left field. Shortstop Ford had broken to his left, and he now had to adjust his course at the last moment. Somehow he snagged the ball with an amazing twist and was able to make an underhanded throw to first just in time to retire Wheat and save the run. The Boston fans loved it, and even the Brooklyn players later had to admit that it was a sensational play.

Boston got its first man past first base in its half of the sixth. Al Nixon was the one, as he singled with two out and stole second on a passed ball. Ruether got Walter Barbare to roll to shortstop for the third out.

Fine plays by Ford turned Brooklyn back in the seventh and eighth innings. In the seventh he alertly ran to third to take a throw and tag a man out trying to advance two bases on a hit past the third baseman. In the eighth, he turned a sure hit into a key force out with a great stop.

It was Brooklyn's turn to come up with a fielding gem in the bottom of the eighth. Larry Kopf was on first with a walk when Mickey O'Neill bunted a short pop up. Clarence Mitchell, playing first base, charged in and made a fine shoetop catch. Then he threw to first, where second baseman Jimmy Johnston was covering, to double Kopf off.

Ruether made a fine fielding play in the bottom of the ninth. Nixon opened with a single to center and was bunted to second by Barbare. Manager Wilbert Robinson ordered an intentional pass to Fred Nicholson. Hank Gowdy was sent up by Boston manager Fred Mitchell to pinch-hit. Gowdy cut a low grasser back to the mound. Ruether dug the ball out of the dirt nicely and whipped it to third to force Nixon. Third baseman High relayed the ball across the diamond to complete the double play and end the inning.

Even another miracle by Ford could not stop the Dodgers from scoring in the tenth, thanks to Ruether's double. Mitchell opened the round by drawing a walk. Olson smashed one past the third baseman. But Ford ranged over from shortstop, grabbed the ball with his outstretched bare hand, pivoted and shot the ball to second base for a force on Mitchell. Hank DeBerry shot a single to right, and Olson was thrown out trying for third. DeBerry went to second on the throw, but two were out. Ruether came to the rescue after having gone hitless in his three previous at bats. He went with an outside pitch and cracked a hit over third base and down the left field line. DeBerry scored without a play, and Ruether pulled up at second base with a double and a one-run lead. High sent a difficult chance Ford's way, and of course the shortstop made the play for the third out.

Ford tried his hand on offense in the bottom of the tenth, singling with one out. But the next batter, Kopf, slapped a grounder to second base, and Johnston started a double play to end the game.

It was a great triumph for Brooklyn and especially for Ruether, what with his first shutout of the year, his fine fielding, and his game-winning hit. And it was win #14, putting right on schedule to finish the season with 30.

Brooklyn	ab	r	h	bi	o	a	e
A. High, 3b	5	0	2	0	2	1	0
J. Johnston, 2b	3	0	1	0	3	4	0
T. Griffith, rf	4	0	0	0	2	0	0
Z. Wheat, lf	4	0	0	0	0	0	0
H. Myers, cf	4	0	0	0	1	0	0
C. Mitchell, 1b	3	0	0	0	14	2	0
I. Olson, ss	4	0	2	0	4	7	0
H. DeBerry, c	3	1	2	0	4	1	0
D. Ruether, p	4	0	1	1	0	2	0
	34	1	8	1	30	17	0

Boston	ab	r	h	bi	o	a	e
A. Nixon, cf-lf10	4	0	2	0	1	0	0
W. Barbare, 2b	3	0	0	0	3	1	0
F. Nicholson, lf-rf10	3	0	0	0	3	2	0
W. Cruise, rf	3	0	0	0	1	0	0
H. Gowdy, ph9	1	0	0	0	-	-	-
R. Powell, cf10	0	0	0	0	0	0	0
W. Holke, 1b	4	0	1	0	12	0	0
H. Ford, ss	4	0	2	0	5	7	0
L. Kopf, 3b	3	0	1	0	3	1	0
M. O'Neill, c	3	0	0	0	2	1	0
M. Watson, p	3	0	0	0	0	2	0
	31	0	6	0	30	14	0

Brooklyn	000 000 000 1	= 1
Boston	000 000 000 0	= 0

	ip	h	r-er	bb	so
Ruether (W 14-3)	10	6	0-0	2	4
Watson (L 4-6)	10	8	1-1	2	2

PB: DeBerry
Time—1:27
Umpires: L. Sentelle & B. McCormick

Game-Winning RBI: Ruether
LOB: Brooklyn 6, Boston 4
DP: Mitchell-Johnston
Ruether-High-Mitchell (Gowdy)
Johnston-Olson-Mitchell (Kopf)
2B: Ruether
SH: Johnston, Barbare
SB: Nixon
CS: Kopf, Johnston

Brooklyn won a doubleheader the following day but then lost eight in a row. After July 13th, the Robins never got above the .500 mark. They finished in sixth place with a 76-78 record.

Ruether slumped in the second half along with most of the rest of the team. He did not get his 15th win until July 26th, and his record for the season was 21-12.

1923 MONDAY, MAY 7TH, AT BRAVES FIELD, BOSTON
At Least Johnston Wanted to Win

Jimmy Starts Double Play in 9th and Scores Winning Run in 10th
Dodgers Win, 12-11, In Spite of Themselves

TO ALL THE WORLD IT LOOKED LIKE THE Brooklyn pitchers were trying to give the game away today. But the Robins' Jimmy Johnston would not let them. After the moundmen walked home four runs in the final two innings to allow Boston to tie the score, Johnston saved the day by catching a line drive in the ninth and starting a double play. Then in the tenth, he got his fifth hit of the game and scored the winning run with a crashing slide.

Today's Results

BROOKLYN 12-Boston 11 (10 innings)
Pittsburgh 11-St. Louis 4
New York 13-Philadelphia 8
no other game scheduled

Standings	W-L	Pct.	GB
New York	15- 5	.750	—
Pittsburgh	11- 9	.550	4
Chicago	10- 9	.526	4½
St. Louis	10-10	.500	5
Boston	9- 9	.500	5
Cincinnati	8-11	.421	6½
BROOKLYN	7-12	.368	7½
Philadelphia	6-11	.353	7½

Thanks to Johnston's exploits, the Superbas were able to avoid the embarrassment of losing an 8-0 lead, and they emerged with a 12-11 victory.

Luckily, the Dodgers were playing against last year's last-place finishers, the Boston Braves. The Beantowners showed as little apparent desire to win the game as the Brooklyn bullpen did. The Braves' infield made four errors. And their outfield, not to be outdone, matched that total for eight errors in all.

Two Boston errors, with two walks by starting pitcher Mule Watson and four Brooklyn hits, gave the visiting Robins six runs in the second inning. Joe Genewich relieved Watson before the inning was over.

Triples by Jack Fournier and Zack Wheat in the third and fifth innings, respectively, led to more runs, and Brooklyn led 8-0 until the bottom of the sixth.

Then Robinson's starting pitcher, Leo Dickerman, blew up. He allowed five hits and five runs. He may never have gotten out of the inning if center fielder Bernie Neis had not thrown out a man trying to take an extra base.

But it still seemed that Brooklyn would win easily, especially after the Superbas added a single run in the seventh and another pair in the eighth, making the score 11-5.

Al Mamaux pitched a perfect seventh inning for the Robins. But he allowed a hit and two walks to start the eighth.

Manager Wilbert Robinson was in no mood for such charity, and he sent Art Decatur in place of Mamaux. The new man failed miserably, walking the only two men he faced to force two runs home.

George Smith was rushed in after Decatur was yanked out. Smith walked a man home, too. But at least he was able to get three outs and end the inning.

There were still three runs left in the lead at the start of the Boston ninth. But Smith evidently wanted to make it close. He walked two men for starters. The exasperated Robinson called in Dazzy Vance to try and put an end to the free tickets.

But Vance did not have his stuff today, either. He was greeted by a single by Art Conlon good for one run. Larry Kopf followed with another hit for another run. Pinch-hitter Hank Gowdy forced a man at third base for the inning's first out. But there were still two outs to go, and the Braves were only one run behind by now. Frank Gibson beat out an infield roller to load the bases. Ray Powell then worked Vance for a walk, and the game was tied.

The sparse Boston crowd was rapturous with glee. Their Braves had come all the way back to tie, and their best hitter, Billy Southworth, was at bat with the bases loaded and one out. Southworth connected with good wood, but the liner went right to shortstop Johnston. Jimmy grabbed it and alertly flipped to third baseman Andy High to double Gowdy off base and end the rally.

Having thusly saved the Dodgers from defeat, Johnson set about to win the game for Brooklyn in the tenth. Batting with one out, Jimmy dribbled one down the third base line and beat it out. It was his fifth hit in six trips on the day. Tommy Griffith walked behind him. Wheat hit a grounder to shortstop, and Kopf obligingly booted it to load the bases with one gone. Fournier lifted a shallow fly to left. Throwing caution to the wind, Johnston broke for home after Felix caught the ball. The throw home was not strong, and Johnston slid into catcher Gibson just as the ball arrived. Umpire Bill Klem leaned in to get a good look at the play, and the force of the slide bowled both Gibson and Klem over. From the seat of his pants, Klem signaled that Johnston was safe with his third run of the game. And the Robins were back in the lead.

Vance allowed one hit but no walks and no runs in the bottom of the tenth, and Brooklyn won the game, 12-11. It wasn't a very impressive victory, but Robinson and his men would take it. After all, Jimmy Johnston would not allow them to give it away.

Brooklyn	ab	r	h	bi	o	a	e
I. Olson, 2b	4	2	0	0	4	3	1
J. Johnston, ss	6	3	5	1	2	6	0
T. Griffith, rf	5	0	2	3	1	0	0
Z. Wheat, lf	5	3	2	0	6	0	1
J. Fournier, 1b	4	2	1	1	10	2	0
B. Neis, cf	5	0	2	1	3	1	0
A. High, 3b	5	1	1	2	2	0	0
H. DeBerry, c	4	1	2	1	2	0	0
L. Dickerman, p	3	0	0	0	0	3	0
G. Bailey, ph7	1	0	0	0	-	-	-
A. Mamaux, p7	0	0	0	0	0	0	0
A. Decatur, p8	0	0	0	0	0	0	0
G. Smith, p8	1	0	0	0	0	0	0
D. Vance, p9	0	0	0	0	0	0	0
	43	12	15	9	30	15	2

Boston	ab	r	h	bi	o	a	e
R. Powell, cf	5	0	0	1	4	0	2
B. Southworth, rf	5	0	2	1	3	1	2
T. Boeckel, 3b	6	1	1	0	3	3	2
S. McInnis, 1b	4	2	1	0	10	1	0
B. Bagwell, lf	0	0	0	0	1	0	0
G. Felix, lf3	3	3	1	0	3	1	0
A. Conlon, 2b	4	2	1	1	2	5	0
B. Smith, pr9	0	0	0	0	-	-	-
H. Ford, 2b10	1	0	0	0	1	0	0
L. Kopf, ss	4	2	2	3	0	3	2
M. O'Neill, c	3	1	2	2	2	2	0
A. Nixon, pr8	0	0	0	0	-	-	-
J. Oeschger, p9	0	0	0	0	0	0	0
H. Gowdy, ph9	1	0	0	0	-	-	-
R. Marquard, p10	0	0	0	0	0	0	0
M. Watson, p	0	0	0	0	0	2	0
J. Genewich, p2	2	0	1	0	1	0	0
S. Henry, ph6	1	0	1	2	-	-	-
J. Cooney, p7	0	0	0	0	0	0	0
L. Benton, p7	0	0	0	0	0	0	0
F. Gibson, ph8-c	2	0	1	0	0	0	0
	41	11	13	10	30	18	8

Brooklyn	061	010	120	1	=	12
Boston	000	005	033	0	=	11

	ip	h	r-er	bb	so
Dickerman	6	8	5-0	1	0
Mamaux	*1	1	3-3	2	1
Decatur	†0	0	0-0	2	0
G. Smith	‡1	0	2-2	3	1
Vance (W 1-3)	2	4	1-1	1	0
Watson	1⅔	3	6-2	3	0
Genewich	4⅓	6	2-2	0	2
Cooney	⅓	2	1-0	1	0
Benton	1⅔	2	2-1	1	0
Oeschger	1	1	0-0	0	0
Marquard (L 2-3)	1	1	1-0	1	0

Game-Winning RBI: Fournier
LOB: Brooklyn 9, Boston 10
BE: Brooklyn 2, Boston 1
DP: Southworth-O'Neill-Boecker-O'Neill
Conlon-McInnis (Fournier)
Johnston-High
2B: Griffith, Felix, Neis
3B: Fournier, Wheat
SH: Neis, Fournier, McInnis

*faced three batters in eighth
†faced two batters in eighth
‡faced two batters in ninth
Time—2:27
Umpires: B. Klem & G. Hart

Brooklyn played good ball through the rest of May and rose as high as tied for second place in early June. But the pitching staff was erratic except for Burleigh Grimes and Dazzy Vance, preventing the Robins from making a pennant bid.

An ankle injury sidelined Zack Wheat for most of July and August, and the Dodgers slipped to sixth place.

They finished the year exactly where they had finished in 1922: in sixth with a 76-78 record.

1924 SUNDAY, SEPTEMBER 7TH, AT EBBETS FIELD

Big Mob Sees Robins Lose Key Game

Unruly Fans Break Down Gate and Overflow Outfield
New York Holds onto First Place with 8-7 Victory

Today's Results			
New York 8-BROOKLYN 7			
Cincinnati 4-Pittsburgh 1 (1st game)			
Cincinnati 4-Pittsburgh 3 (2nd game)			
Chicago 2-St. Louis 1 (1st game)			
St. Louis 15-Chicago 4 (2nd game)			
no other game scheduled			
Standings	**W-L**	**Pct.**	**GB**
New York	82-53	.607	—
BROOKLYN	82-56	.594	1½
Pittsburgh	78-54	.591	2½
Cincinnati	74-63	.540	9
Chicago	70-63	.526	11
St. Louis	56-80	.412	26½
Philadelphia	51-84	.378	31
Boston	48-88	.353	34½

HALF OF BROOKLYN, OR SO IT SEEMED, was determined to see today's battle for first place between the New York Giants and the Brooklyn Robins. Ebbets Field was sold out early, and the gates were closed two and a half hours before game time. Thousands of eager fans were turned away for lack of space.

Some of the disgruntled fans tried scaling the high fences to get into the grounds, and a few were injured falling. Another mob organized its efforts against a closed gate down along the left field line. Using a telephone pole and the weight of numbers, the gate was crashed open and thousands rushed into the park without paying. The number of gate-crashers was variously estimated from 6,000 to 15,000.

With this large number of extra spectators added to the 30,400 paying customers, the crowd overran much of the outfield. A totally inadequate number of policemen battled all day to keep the crowds back and give the outfielders room in which to play. Although the fans were generally well-behaved once they were inside the grounds, there was at least one instance of the crowd interfering with a New York fielder. The mass of humanity on the field necessitated a ground rule of two bases for a hit into the mob. In all, eleven doubles were awarded.

The game itself was a thriller. New York worked its way to a 2-0 lead. Then Brooklyn rallied for three runs in the fifth inning. The Giants came back to tie the game in the seventh and take a five-run lead in the eighth. The Dodgers rallied back in the eighth and ninth but came up a run short, losing 8-7.

The sudden fan interest in the Borough of Churches was caused by the 15-game winning streak that the local team had run up through the first game of a doubleheader in Boston yesterday. By losing the nightcap in that twinbill, Brooklyn had missed a chance to come home in first place.

It took a police escort to get umpire-in-chief Bill Klem and his crew onto the field, but the game got under way on time. Jack Bentley and Burleigh Grimes were the opposing pitchers.

Both sides squandered opportunities to score in the first two innings.

New York finally got a run in the top of the third. Frankie Frisch singled and came home on one-basers by Ross Youngs and Bill Terry. Hack Wilson followed with a drive to deep left center, which looked like extra bases. But Zack Wheat made a great one-handed catch, and it turned out to be a double play when Terry, who did not see the catch, passed Youngs on the basepaths.

The Giants added another run in the fourth on a double by Travis Jackson and two infield outs.

The Superbas came to life in the fifth with three runs. Andy High singled, and Johnny Mitchell doubled. Wheat scored them both with a double into the crowd in right. And Eddie Brown singled Wheat home.

A walk to Youngs and hits by George Kelly and Terry tied the game in the seventh, 3-3.

The only error of the game came in the eighth, and it helped New York to score five runs, which won the game. One-out singles by Bentley, Heinie Groh, and Frisch loaded the bases. With the infield drawn in close for a play at the plate, Youngs hit a grounder to shortstop Mitchell. Johnny fumbled it in his haste to make the throw home, and all hands were safe, with Bentley scoring the tie-breaking run. Grimes fanned Kelley for the second out. But Terry doubled into the crowd for two runs. After Wilson walked, Jackson singled for another pair, making the score 8-3.

Singles by Zack Taylor, Grimes, and Mitchell in the bottom of the eighth cut the New York lead to 8-4.

Jack Fournier opened the last of the ninth with a single up the middle. Brown lifted a fly to center, which Wilson was unable to get because of the encroachment of the crowd. The Giants wanted an out on interference, but umpire Klem would not allow it. Klem did, however, order the Brooklyn club to move the crowd back or risk a forfeit. After ten minutes of arguing by the contestants and pushing by the police, play resumed.

New York pilot John McGraw brought righthander Hugh McQuillan in to pitch at this juncture. Milt Stock greeted him with a hit that scored Fournier. Griffith flied out, and Brown counted after the catch. Taylor skied to left for the second out. Grimes, who was hitting over .300, singled for the second time in two innings. Andy High pulled a double into the standees in right field, and Stock scored.

It was now 8-7, and Brooklyn had the tying run on third and the winning run on second. Uncle Robbie decided to send Dutch Ruether up to hit for Mitchell. Every fan in the place was primed for a big hit and a hilarious victory celebration. In his seat near the dugout, baseball's commissioner, Kenesaw Mountain Landis, leaned forward on his cane in anticipation. McQuillan threw two curve balls, and Ruether missed them both. Would the pitcher now waste a fastball, or would he try for the strikeout? The next pitch was another curve. Ruether took a mighty swing and missed. Strike Three, and the game was over and lost.

The throng fell almost silent, although a few Giant fans could not contain their glee. It had been a wild game and a wild scene, but there was no joy in Flatbush afterwards. The hated Giants had held off the Robins' rush and and had won out, 8-7.

New York	ab	r	h	bi	o	a	e
H. Groh, 3b	6	1	1	0	0	2	0
F. Frisch, 2b	6	2	3	0	4	5	0
R. Youngs, rf	4	2	2	1	1	0	0
G. Kelly, lf	6	0	3	0	4	0	0
B. Terry, 1b	5	1	3	4	7	0	0
H. Wilson, cf	3	0	0	0	1	0	0
T. Jackson, ss	4	1	2	2	2	3	0
F. Snyder, c	4	0	0	0	8	0	0
J. Bentley, p	5	1	3	1	0	0	0
H. McQuillan, p9	0	0	0	0	0	0	0
	43	8	17	8	27	10	0

Brooklyn	ab	r	h	bi	o	a	e
A. High, 2b	4	1	2	1	1	4	0
J. Mitchell, ss	3	1	2	1	2	7	1
D. Ruether, ph9	1	0	0	0	-	-	-
Z. Wheat, lf	4	1	1	2	3	2	0
J. Fournier, 1b	5	1	2	0	10	0	0
E. Brown, cf	5	1	3	1	2	0	0
M. Stock, 3b	5	1	1	1	1	1	0
T. Griffith, rf	4	0	1	1	1	0	0
Z. Taylor, c	4	1	2	0	5	2	0
B. Grimes, p	5	0	2	0	2	1	0
	40	7	16	7	27	17	1

New York	001	100	150	=	8
Brooklyn	000	030	013	=	7

	ip	h	r-er	bb	so
Bentley (W 13-4)	*8	13	6-6	6	5
McQuillan	1	3	1-1	0	1
Grimes (L 20-12)	9	17	8-4	6	4

*faced two batters in ninth
Time—3:09
Attendance—30,400 paid; 37,000 total
Umpires: B. Klem, F. Wilson, & C. Moran

Game-Winning RBI: Youngs
LOB: New York 14, Brooklyn 13
BE: New York 1
DP: Wheat-Mitchell-Taylor-Grimes
Groh-Frisch-Terry (Mitchell)
2B: Kelly, Griffith, Fournier, Jackson, Mitchell, Wheat, Bentley, Brown 2, Terry, High
SF: Griffith
SB: Jackson
CS: Frisch

The next day Dazzy Vance won his 13th straight decision to beat the Giants 7-2 in New York.

The Robins kept within 1½ games of the Giants until the final Saturday, when New York finally clinched the pennant. Brooklyn finished 1½ games back with a 92-62 record.

1925 SUNDAY, SEPTEMBER 13TH, AT EBBETS FIELD

Dazzy Gets a No-Hitter

Had Pitched a One-Hitter in his Last Start
Wins 10-1 as Dodgers Split a Doubleheader

Today's Results

BROOKLYN 10-Philadelphia 1 (1st game)
Philadelphia 7-Brooklyn 3 (2nd game)
St. Louis 8-Pittsburgh 4 (1st game)
St. Louis 6-Pittsburgh 2 (2nd game)
Cincinnati 5-Chicago 2
no other game scheduled

Standings	W-L	Pct.	GB
Pittsburgh	84-54	.609	—
New York	78-60	.565	6
Cincinnati	75-63	.543	9
BROOKLYN	66-69	.489	16½
St. Louis	67-73	.479	18
Boston	64-77	.454	21½
Chicago	61-80	.433	24½
Philadelphia	59-78	.431	24½

IN FOUR YEARS WITH BROOKLYN, DAZZY Vance had already achieved a fair amount of fame. In 1924 he was 28-6 and was voted the league's Most Valuable Player. And in each of those years, he led the National League in strikeouts. This season he was sure to lead in strikeouts again, too.

But he had never pitched a no-hitter in fast company until he did it today against the Phillies. On June 17th, 1923, he had held the Cincinnati Reds hitless until Sammy Bohne singled with two out in the ninth inning. And just last Tuesday, Vance pitched another one-hitter, this time the hit coming in the second frame.

That hit on Tuesday was made by the Phils' Nelson "Chicken" Hawks. Hawks was the only batter to reach base against Vance, and he was quickly caught stealing. So Dazzy faced the minimum number of batters possible, 27, and won 1-0.

Today, pitching against Philadelphia again, he was just as brilliant. This time, however, he won easily, 10-1, and faced 29 hitters. He walked one man and lost his shutout due to a double error by left fielder Jimmy Johnston in the second inning.

By allowing only one hit in two consecutive complete games pitched, Vance tied a record achieved three times previously in the major leagues.

Of course Dazzy used his famous fastball to good effect today. But he also relied on his curves and slower stuff more than usual. And the Phillies were helpless against all of it. Vance struck out nine batters to raise his league-leading total to 213 for the season.

Heinie Sand, the first batter of the day, got the only walk off of Vance in the first inning. He moved to second on a passed ball. But the Dodger righthander struck out Freddy Leach and Fred "Cy" Williams and got George Harper on a grounder back to the box.

In the bottom of the first, the Robins routed old teammate Clarence Mitchell and scored four runs. Johnny Mitchell opened with a double, Milt Stock singled, and Jimmy Johnston tripled. The Phillies quickly changed pitchers, but Dick Cox greeted the new man (Art Decatur) with another double. Cox scored on two outs.

Leading 4-0, the Dodgers gave the Phillies a gift run in the second inning. Hawks, who had spoiled Vance's no-hitter last Tuesday, led off with a medium fly to left field. With regular outfielder Zack Wheat out of the lineup with stomach troubles, old Johnston was in the left garden. Jimmy had difficulty with the sun and ran around in circles trying to get an angle on the ball. He got under it just in time to make a blatant muff. Then Johnston confounded his error by throwing so wildly to the infield that Hawks was able to get all the way to third base. Johnston was charged with two errors on the play. Vance struck Clarence Huber out. But Barney Friberg scored Hawks with a deep fly out to center. Jimmy Wilson popped out.

The Dazzler retired Philadelphia in order in the last seven innings. The only difficult play in the middle innings came in the fifth. With two out, Wilson slashed a hard grounder to first. Charlie Hargreaves, normally a catcher but pressed into first baseman duty by Jack Fournier's stiff neck, fielded the smash nicely and flipped the ball to Vance in time for the out.

Brooklyn scored another four runs in the fourth inning. Cotton Tierney started the rally by walking. And Hank DeBerry, Mitchell, Stock, Johnston, and Cox all singled.

Three hits and a walk yielded a run against Walter "Huck" Betts in the sixth. And two hits and a sacrifice fly got Brooklyn its tenth run in the seventh.

With the crowd of 20,000 cheering every pitch, Vance pitched the ninth inning with a flourish, throwing eight straight strikes. Pinch-hitter Lew Fonseca fouled off the first two. He lifted a foul near first base on the third one. But Hargreaves muffed the pop, and the crowd groaned uncomfortably. Undaunted, Vance fooled Fonseca on the next pitch, an off-speed curve, for a called third strike. Wally Kimmick, another pinch-hitter, struck out on three pitches. Freddie Leach jumped on the first pitch and lined one to left. At first it looked as if it might fall in. But Johnston got a good jump on the ball and raced in to glove it near the foul line for the final out. It was the best fielding play of the game, and it certainly redeemed Jimmy for his double error earlier.

With the no-hitter officially on the books, Vance was given a great ovation by the Brooklyn fans, who covered the field with their straw hats.

In the second game, Hawks hit a grand slam, and Leach hit a two-run homer off of Burleigh Grimes, as Ray Pearce pitched the Phillies to a 7-3 victory.

But September 13, 1925, would always be remembered as the day Dazzy Vance got his no-hitter.

FIRST GAME

Philadelphia	**ab**	**r**	**h**	**bi**	**o**	**a**	**e**
H. Sand, ss	1	0	0	0	2	1	1
R. Wrightstone, ph6	1	0	0	0	-	-	-
L. Metz, ss6	0	0	0	0	1	1	0
W. Kimmick, ph9	1	0	0	0	-	-	-
F. Leach, cf	4	0	0	0	3	0	0
C. Williams, rf	3	0	0	0	2	0	0
G. Harper, lf	3	0	0	0	3	0	0
N. Hawks, 1b	3	1	0	0	3	0	0
C. Huber, 3b	3	0	0	0	1	2	0
B. Friberg, 2b	2	0	0	1	4	0	1
J. Wilson, c	2	0	0	0	0	0	0
L. Wendell, c5	1	0	0	0	5	2	0
C. Mitchell, p	0	0	0	0	0	0	0
A. Decatur, p1	1	0	0	0	0	0	0
H. Betts, p5	1	0	0	0	0	1	0
L. Fonseca, ph9	1	0	0	0	-	-	-
	27	1	0	1	24	7	2

Brooklyn	**ab**	**r**	**h**	**bi**	**o**	**a**	**e**
J. Mitchell, ss	5	2	3	0	1	2	0
M. Stock, 2b	4	3	2	3	1	2	0
J. Johnston, lf	4	2	3	3	3	0	2
D. Cox, rf	5	1	4	1	2	0	0
E. Brown, cf	4	0	0	0	3	0	0
C. Hargreaves, 1b	4	1	1	1	6	2	1
C. Tierney, 3b	3	0	1	0	0	0	0
H. DeBerry, c	3	1	1	1	9	0	0
D. Vance, p	4	0	0	0	2	1	0
	36	10	15	9	27	7	3

Philadelphia	010	000	000	=	1
Brooklyn	400	401	10x	=	10

	ip	**h**	**r-er**	**bb**	**so**
C. Mitchell (L 10-16)	*0	3	3-3	0	0
Decatur	4	7	5-5	2	0
Betts	4	5	2-2	1	4
Vance (W 22-8)	9	0	1-0	1	9

*faced three batters in first
PB: DeBerry, Wilson
Umps: C. Pfirman, F. Wilson, & H. O'Day

Game-Winning RBI: Stock
LOB: Philadelphia 1, Brooklyn 6
BE: Philadelphia 1, Brooklyn 1
DP: Huber-Sands
2B: J. Mitchell, Cox
SH: Friberg, DeBerry
SB: J. Mitchell, Stock, Johnston, Cox, Hargreaves
CS: Hargreaves, Tierney
Time—1:45
Attendance—20,000

SECOND GAME

					r	**h**	**e**
Philadelphia	004	300	000	=	7	13	0
Brooklyn	000	000	003	=	3	9	0

Game-Winning RBI: Hawks

Batteries: R. Pierce (W 4-4) & J. Wilson
B. Grimes (L 12-16) 3⅔ IP, L. Brown 4⅓ IP, B. Hubbell 1 IP, & Z. Taylor

The defeat in the second game of the doubleheader started Brooklyn on a 12-game losing streak. The streak was snapped by two wins in a row, then the Robins ended the season with five consecutive defeats. The late nosedive left Brooklyn tied for sixth and just ½ game ahead of the last-place Cubs. The Dodgers' final record was 68-85.

Vance was routed in the eighth inning of his next start and lost to the Cardinals, 9-5.

Chapter VII The Daffiness Boys

1926 August 15th
Three Dodgers on Third Base

1927 May 1st
Carey's Daring Dash Wins for Brooklyn

1928 June 12th
Uncle Robbie Shakes Up Lineup & Wins 13-1

1929 May 17th
Nail-Biter Ends Losing Streak

1930 September 15th
League-Leading Flock Wins 11th Straight

1931 April 15th
Alta Cohen's Strange Debut

WITH WILBERT ROBINSON ACTING AS BOTH PRESIDENT AND MANAGER, AND WITH THE stock in the club divided 50/50 into two opposing blocks, the Brooklyn club was unable to get anywhere in the latter part of the 1920's. But the team on the field got nowhere in a style unmatched in history. Led by the absent-minded Uncle Robbie, the team drifted occasionally into a brand of comedy baseball that earned it the nicknames "the Daffy Dodgers" and "the Daffiness Boys." The main characters in the act were Robinson and a loose-jointed slugger named Floyd Caves Herman, nicknamed Babe. These two were supported ably by other members of the cast, headed by the free-spirited Dazzy Vance. A reputation for the unusual followed the Dodgers long after Robinson, Herman, Vance, and company had departed.

Herman arrived on the scene as a hard-hitting, erratic-fielding first baseman in 1926. Through spring training the press corps was fascinated by his ability to drive in runs with his bat and let in runs with his glove. His base running did not become famous until the regular season started. It was on August 15, 1926, that Herman was a principal in the legendary incident in which three Dodgers wound up on third base at the same time. Over the years, Herman was given the blame for this and occasionally credited with tripling into a triple play. In fact, Vance was also at least as guilty of faulty base running on the play, and Herman actually only doubled into a double play. He also drove in the game-winning run with that hit.

Base running had been a problem for Brooklyn for years, but never was it more so than in 1926. The team was old, and in 1926 it picked up six new players who were all in their thirties. That was Robinson's idea of rebuilding. The prize "youngster" was 33-year-old shortstop Johnny Butler, for whom Robbie traded no fewer than six players to Minneapolis. When Butler arrived at spring camp, he immediately collapsed from stomach ulcers. Although he played regularly for two years for the Robins, Butler never turned out to be a top major leaguer.

The other disappointment in 1926 was pitching star Dazzy Vance. Bothered by a severe case of boils all spring, he did not win a game until June 4th and finished just 9-10. Burleigh Grimes was 12-13 and had a falling out with Robinson after the manager berated his base running. Silver-haired Jess Petty, a 31-year-old lefthander, turned out to be the ace of the staff. He won his first five starts but found himself 6-6 by June 5th because of poor hitting support. He finished 17-17.

The saddest base-running incident of the year took place on August 5th. Zack Wheat, in his 18th season with the team, hit a home run over the wall. But he pulled up so lame with charley horses in both legs that he had to sit down on second base and rest. For a full five minutes, he tried to get his legs ready for the final 180 feet.

Babe Herman

Uncle Robbie came out and talked to him and even announced that he would send in a pinch-runner to complete the home run. Wheat asked for more time, however, and finally limped home. It was Zack's final home run in Ebbets Field, as he was released after the season.

The Dodgers were in a position to contend for the pennant through most of July. But they slipped to sixth in August and stayed there.

Grimes was traded over the winter for a 32-year-old catcher named Butch Henline. Old Bill Doak was coaxed out of retirement to shore up the pitching, and he had an 11-8 record in 1927. Vance bounced back and had ten wins by mid-July. He finished 16-15. And a couple of lefthanders bought from the minors helped. They were slightly-built William Watson "Watty" Clark and huge "Jumbo" Jim Elliot.

While the pitching was good, the fielding was poor. Especially weak were first base (with Herman and newcomer Harvey Hendrick) and third base (with Bobby Barrett). But the biggest weakness was the offense. Only Hendrick (.310) hit over .275, and Brooklyn finished a distant last in runs scored.

The team started the 1927 season horrendously (2-12), rose to fifth place at the end of May, and then slipped to sixth by the end of July. After a couple of weeks in seventh, they finished sixth again.

In an effort to improve the offense of 1928, slugging Del Bissonette was called up from Buffalo, and veteran Rube Bressler was picked up on waivers. Since Bissonette could barely throw the ball across the infield, he was put on first base, with Herman moving to the outfield. Luckily Babe proved to be a better outfielder than he was a first sacker. Trying to strengthen the team at shortstop, Robinson signed old Dave Bancroft from Boston.

With the improved hitting and fine pitching by Vance, the Robins started the 1928 campaign well. They stayed within hailing distance of the league leaders through June. Petty was suspended in May for breaking training, but he came back strong and finished 15-15. Still, he was unhappy all year about losing over $1,000 in pay and fines.

The big troubles hit in July. On the 3rd, center fielder Al Tyson collided with infielder Harry Riconda, Tyson breaking his leg while the ball rolled away for a three-run homer. The Robins wound up losing that game in eleven innings. With Tyson out for the year and replacements Arnold "Jigger" Statz and Max Carey unable to help the offense much, the Robins slid to sixth place by August 2nd. There they finished.

In one big bright note, third baseman Wally Gilbert was called up from Atlanta in August and remained in the Brooklyn lineup of the next three years.

With Gilbert at third and Bissonette at first, those positions were set for 1929. And Jake Flowers seemed to have a lock on second base. To round out the infield, Robinson traded Riconda and the disgruntled Petty to Pittsburgh for star shortstop Glenn Wright. But Wright showed up at spring training with a dead throwing arm, the result of an off-season basketball injury. Bancroft again wound up playing the most at short for Brooklyn in 1929. Wright would help out later.

A nine-game losing streak in early May dropped the Dodgers into the cellar. The streak was snapped in a poorly-played, 14-13 struggle in Philadelphia on May 17th. Bissonette was out with sinus trouble, and Flowers, who had gotten off to a fine start, went down with appendicitis. A flu bug ravaged the team on its first western road trip. And the pitching was weak for the first time in years. Still, the Robins rose to fifth place in late June. Among the encouraging signs were a .328 performance (with 52 doubles) by rookie Johnny Frederick, a .381 season from Babe Herman, and 13 wins from curveballer Johnny Morrison (whom Robinson had resurrected from the minors in early June). But rather than break the pattern, the Robins lost a doubleheader on the final day of the season to nose into sixth place for the fifth year in a row.

Over the winter, a compromise of sorts was worked out in the front-office feud between Steve McKeever on the one hand and Wilbert Robinson and the Ebbets heirs on the other. Robinson was given a two-year contract as manager, but Frank B. York replaced him as president.

With both Wright and Flowers questionable for 1930, Brooklyn purchased the keystone combination of Neal Finn and Gordon Slade from the Mission club of San Francisco. Righthanded pitcher Ray Phelps was bought from Jacksonville, and catcher Al Lopez was recalled from Atlanta. Old righty Dolf Luque was picked up from Cincinnati in a trade. Lopez became the regular catcher and wound up his career many years later with more games caught than any other major leaguer. Phelps and Luque each won 14 games in 1930. Finn split the second base duties with Flowers. With Wright's arm fairly sound again, Slade rode the bench until May 24th, when he celebrated his big chance by hitting a home run in his first big league at bat.

After a poor start (2-7), the Robins rose rapidly, paced by solid pitching and Wright's sensational shortstopping. On Memorial Day, they moved into undisputed possession of first place, even though Del Bissonette was called out for passing Babe

Alta Cohen

Herman on the basepaths on an apparent home run.

Ankle troubles plagued Wright for the next few months, and Morrison jumped the team in June. Still, the Robins stayed ahead of the defending-champion Cubs for most of the next two and a half months. On August 8th, Herman went 4-for-4 with two home runs, and the Dodgers beat the Cardinals 11-5. That kept Brooklyn 3½ games ahead of Chicago and dropped fourth-place St. Louis to 12 games behind. But the Robins dropped the next four games in St. Louis and three out of four in Chicago. Robinson's Flock skidded all the way to fourth place by September 1st.

Then just as suddenly as the team had fallen out of the race, it vaulted back into it. Returning home, they ripped off eleven wins in a row, including three from the Cubs, to regain first place. Herman, Wright, and Bissonette all swung hot bats, and the pitching was brilliant.

But the red-hot Cardinals came to town and swept three games. The opener was a thrilling pitching duel between Vance and Bill Hallahan, which the Cards won in ten innings, 1-0. St. Louis again rallied late to take the second game, 5-3. And the Robins were edged in the finale, 4-3. The pennant bubble was finally burst. Four more losses in a row dropped Brooklyn to a fourth-place finish.

Still, 1930 had been an exciting and profitable year, with the club drawing over a million fans for the first time. Over the winter Ebbets Field's capacity was expanded with the extension of the double-decked grandstand around left field and into center.

In 1931, the Robins lost their first five games. The only feature in the early going was the unusual big-league debut of Alta Cohen. He hit in two different spots in the batting order after a mixup involving, naturally, Robinson and Herman. On May 22nd, Vance was knocked cold by a line drive to the skull. But he was ready for his next start.

The team slowly got its act together in May. Then it rose dramatically in June. On the Fourth of July, 42,500 fans overflowed the new capacity of Ebbets Field and saw the Dodgers shut the Giants out twice. Later in the month, Brooklyn edged into second place. Lefty O'Doul, acquired in a trade over the winter, began to tear the cover off the ball after a slow start. But Glenn Wright suffered a debilitating ankle injury and went out for a month. The Robins slipped to fourth, which was where they finished. The last month of the season saw Vance lose five games in a row. But a new man was brought up from Hartford, and he eventually took Dazzy's place as the king of the Brooklyn pitching staff. His name was Van Lingle Mungo.

After the season ended, Uncle Wilbert Robinson was let go after 18 years at the helm. And Babe Herman was traded just before the start of the next season. But try as they might, the Dodgers never really lost their "Daffiness" reputation until they moved to Los Angeles.

Al Lopez, Harvey Hendrick, and Wally Gilbert

1926 SUNDAY, AUGUST 15TH, EBBETS FIELD

Three Dodgers on Third Base

Weird Running Turns Herman's Double into a Double Play
Hit Drives in Winning Run as Dodgers Sweep Two from Braves

Today's Results			
BROOKLYN 4-Boston 1 (1st game)			
BROOKLYN 11-Boston 2 (8 inn.)(2nd game)			
St. Louis 7-Chicago 2			
Cincinnati 4-Philadelphia 2			
no other game scheduled			
Standings	**W-L**	**Pct.**	**GB**
Pittsburgh	61-45	.575	—
St. Louis	62-50	.554	2
Cincinnati	63-51	.553	2
Chicago	58-53	.523	5½
New York	57-53	.518	6
BROOKLYN	55-60	.478	10½
Boston	46-66	.411	18
Philadelphia	42-66	.389	20

THE SLUMPING BROOKLYN DODGERS ENlivened the dog days of August with one of the strangest pieces of team base running in major league history. Somehow, they wound up with three runners on third base at the same time and turned a bases-loaded double into a double play.

Still, the hit did drive in the winning run in the first game of a double-header against the Boston Braves. And the Robins also won the second game to complete a sweep for the day.

The victories were only the second and third for Brooklyn in the last fourteen games, a slump which dropped the team from fourth place to sixth.

Dazzy Vance was the winning pitcher in the the first game, gaining only his sixth win of the year. Babe Herman, Dick Cox, and Johnny Butler each contributed four hits in the two games. Both Herman and Vance figured prominently in the great base-running gaffe.

Here's how the Dodgers were able to get three men onto the same base at the same time. Trailing 1-0 against Boston righthander Johnny Wertz, Brooklyn opened its half of the seventh with a long single by Butler. Hank DeBerry doubled to the left field corner to knock in the tying run. Vance then dribbled a hit down the third base line. Wertz hit Chick Fewster with a pitch to load the bases with no one out.

Braves' manager Dave Bancroft relieved Wertz with veteran George Mogridge. The new man retired Merwin Jacobson on a pop to the mound. Hard-hitting rookie Floyd C. "Babe" Herman was the next batter. Mogridge was hoping for a double play to end the inning, and Herman was looking for a long hit to put Brooklyn into the lead. As it turned out, they both got what they were looking for, although both had to be a bit disappointed with the result.

Herman found a pitch to his liking and sent a very high fly to deep right field. DeBerry on third, making the proper play, stayed tagged up at the base, even though it looked like the ball might hit the fence. Vance at second also held up, although he probably should have gone half way to third. Fewster, who started on first, properly went nearly to second while the ball was still in flight. Herman, sure that the ball would hit the wall, tore away from the plate at top speed with his head down.

The drive did indeed bounce off the fence. DeBerry scored easily. Vance lumbered around third and headed home, with Fewster nearing third right behind him. But the 35-year-old pitcher had never won any sprinting contests, and halfway home he decided that he couldn't score. So he beat a retreat to third. At the same time, Fewster was arriving at the bag. Seeing Vance coming back, Chick started back for second. But before he could get more than a few steps off the base, Herman, who was oblivious to all the commotion, slid past him and into third. Poor Fewster was totally confused, and he decided to join the party as well. For a brief moment, Brooklyn had three runners on the base.

By this time, of course, the ball he had been relayed from the right fielder to the second baseman to the catcher. When catcher Oscar Siemer threw to third baseman Eddie Taylor, Fewster and Herman scattered. Vance was certain that he was the rightful occupant and had no intention of budging. Taylor tagged Vance and Herman, who had given up all hope of safety and was waiting docilely for his just desserts. In fact, Babe was already out for passing Fewster. Taylor even tagged third base coach Mickey O'Neill, whose garbled shouts had helped create this mess.

Fewster, however, was hightailing it for second. Taylor threw to second baseman Walter "Doc" Gautreau. Drawing out the comedy a little bit more, Fewster ran out of the baseline and into the outfield with Gautreau in pursuit. Finally this last tag was made. After a short discussion, the umpires confirmed that it was a double play, ending the inning. Almost lost in the confusion was the fact that DeBerry had scored the go-ahead run, and Brooklyn was up by a 2-1 score.

The Robins added two runs in the eighth inning without getting the ball out of the infield and won the game, 4-1. They totalled six stolen bases in the game, but one could not say that they ran the bases well.

It was agreed that the second game would not last past 6:00 p.m., since the Robins had to catch a train for St. Louis to start a road trip.

The contest was never in doubt. Brooklyn scored two runs in the first inning and five in the second. Dodger pitcher Jesse Barnes allowed only one hit in the first four innings. He slackened up a bit in the later going, but he still won handily, 11-3.

When the appointed hour arrived, eight innings had been played, and the game was called. The Robins took off immediately in a mad dash for New York's Pennsylvania Station and the train west, leaving their fans to ponder the wonders of baseball in Brooklyn.

After all, where else could you ever see three runners on third base.

FIRST GAME

Boston	ab	r	h	bi	o	a	e
D. Gautreau, 2b	3	0	0	0	3	3	0
J. Smith, cf	4	0	1	0	2	0	0
J. Welsh, rf	4	0	1	0	3	1	0
E. Moore, ss	4	1	2	0	1	2	1
E. Brown, lf	4	0	0	0	1	0	0
D. Burrus, 1b	4	0	1	1	8	1	0
E. Taylor, 3b	3	0	0	0	2	4	0
F. Wilson, ph9	1	0	0	0	-	-	-
O. Siemer, c	3	0	1	0	3	1	0
J. Wertz, p	3	0	1	0	0	3	0
G. Mogridge, p7	0	0	0	0	1	0	0
	33	1	7	1	24	15	1

Brooklyn	ab	r	h	bi	o	a	e
C. Fewster, 2b	3	0	2	0	2	2	0
M. Jacobson, cf	3	0	0	0	4	0	0
B. Herman, 1b	4	0	2	1	10	0	0
D. Cox, rf	3	0	2	0	6	0	0
G. Felix, lf	4	1	1	0	0	0	0
B. Marriott, 3b	3	0	1	0	0	4	0
J. Butler, ss	3	2	1	0	1	3	0
H. DeBerry, c	4	1	2	2	4	0	0
D. Vance, p	4	0	1	0	0	3	0
	31	4	12	3	27	12	0

Boston	000	001	000	=	1
Brooklyn	000	000	22x	=	4

	ip	h	r-er	bb	so
Wertz (L 6-7)	*6	9	2-2	1	1
Mogridge	2	3	2-0	1	1
Vance (W 6-8)	9	7	1-1	1	3

*faced four batters in seventh
HBP: by Wertz (Fewster)
Time—1:50 Attendance—15,000
Umpires: E. Quigley, C. Moran, B. Reardon

Game-Winning RBI: Herman
LOB: Boston 6, Brooklyn 8
BE: none
DP: Taylor-Burrus
Butler-Fewster-Herman
Welsh-Gautreau-Siemer-Taylor-Gautreau
2B: DeBerry, Herman
SH: Marriott, Jacobson
SB: Smith, Moore, Fewster, Cox 2, Marriott, Butler

SECOND GAME

					r	h	e
Boston	000	010	11	=	3	9	3
Brooklyn	251	001	02	=	11	16	2

Game-Winning RBI: Felix

game called by mutual agreement to allow Brooklyn to catch a train
Batteries: H. Goldsmith (L 5-7) 1⅔ ip, B. Hearn 6⅓ ip & T. Womack
J. Barnes (W 8-7) & M. O'Neill

The Robins finished sixth with a 71-82 record.

1927 SUNDAY, MAY 1ST, AT EBBETS FIELD

Carey's Daring Dash Wins for Brooklyn

Pinch-Runner Scores Winner in 9th on Short Fly
Robins' Rally Delights Over-Capacity Crowd

Today's Results			
BROOKLYN 4-New York 3			
St. Louis 12-Cincinnati 4			
Pittsburgh 7-Chicago 6			
no other game scheduled			
Standings	**W-L**	**Pct.**	**GB**
New York	11-5	.688	—
St. Louis	10-5	.667	½
Pittsburgh	9-6	.600	1½
Philadelphia	8-6	.571	2
Boston	8-9	.471	3½
Chicago	7-8	.467	3½
BROOKLYN	5-12	.294	6½
Cincinnati	5-12	.294	6½

ALTHOUGH THE ROBINS WERE OFF TO A terrible start this season, a huge crowd of Brooklyn fans stormed the gates today to see the first Sunday game against the New York Giants this season. Thanks to the daring efforts of pinch-runner Max Carey in the ninth inning, the fans were treated to a thrilling victory by the home team. Although the victory only lifted the Dodgers into a tie for seventh place, today's game was good enough to make diehard fans out of anyone who witnessed it.

The ever-popular Dazzy Vance got roughed up at the start of the game, but he pitched brilliantly for the balance of the contest. Still, the Robins trailed throughout the contest until they rallied for two runs in the ninth inning to win, 4-3. It was Carey who scored the winning tally with some great sprinting and sliding.

On a clear, comfortable afternoon, the fans came out in unexpectedly large numbers. All the seats were sold well before game time, and thousands were turned away from the ticket windows. Part of this mob milled around outside the park. Some disgruntled fans crashed through a gate in right center field. When a mounted policeman inside the grounds tried to plug the breech, he and his horse were bowled over by the rush of people. However, reinforcements soon arrived and held down the number of gate crashers.

When the Robins came onto the field for practice, they were warmly greeted by the Brooklyn partisans. The Giants received some ritual booing when they made their appearance.

Vance started off on the wrong foot by walking Al Tyson, the first batter of the afternoon. Freddie Lindstrom pounded a long triple over center fielder Jigger Statz's head for a run. Although Edd Roush grounded out, Rogers Hornsby singled Lindstrom home. As quick as that, Brooklyn was behind 2-0. The Dodgers did not gain the lead until the final play of the game.

Vance got a measure of revenge in the second inning when he induced Lindstrom to chase an outside curveball for a third strike with two on and two out.

The Robins got one run back in their half of the second, thanks to a Giant error. Babe Herman led off with an easy grounder to shortstop Edward "Doc" Farrell, who obligingly threw high past first base. Herman got second on the heave. He moved to third on a grounder to the right side by Gus Felix and scored on a long fly to left by Bobby Barrett.

Vance ran his team out of a possible run in the third. He led off the inning with a drive off the right field fence. But he only dared to try for a single. Then, when he was just a few feet off the bag, he was caught napping by a snap throw from catcher Sam Hamby. Jay Partridge got a hit later in the inning, but to no avail.

Vance's questionable fielding gave New York its third run in the fourth. Hamby led off with a walk, and he moved to second on an out. Tyson hit safely to center. Statz had a good chance to throw Hamby out at home, but Vance cut the throw off in the infield to allow the run.

Brooklyn got that run right back. Herman pushed a double down the third base line, and Felix outraced a dribbler to second. Herman scored while Farrell was turning a spectacular double play.

Vance retired the Giants in order in each of the last five innings. And New York pitcher Fred Fitzsimmons was also effective, although he kept arguing with umpire Hank O'Day.

Brooklyn still needed a run to tie in the bottom of the ninth. Herman lifted the hopes of the faithful with a solid single over shortstop on the first pitch from Fitzsimmons. Felix bunted, and Fitz made a fine play to force Herman at second. Barrett pulled a hit to left center, and Felix raced to third. Manager Wilbert Robinson sent the 37-year-old Carey to run for Barrett. He represented the winning run. A roar went up from the crowd when Johnny Butler got a clean hit to left to send Felix in with the tying run. And when outfielder Tyson fumbled the ball momentarily, Carey kept sprinting for third. He just slid in ahead of the tag, and the fans screamed their approval. New York manger John McGraw ordered an intentional pass to Hank DeBerry to load the bases and bring up the pitcher's spot in the batting order. Robinson sent Merwin Jacobson up to pinch-hit. The first pitch to him was very high, but Hamby saved it with a fine stop.

Jacobson eventually lifted a pop behind shortstop. Roush came in fast from center field and made the catch. Carey surprised everyone by breaking for home. Roush threw quickly but not very accurately. Hamby got the throw behind the plate on the third base side. Carey made a great slide, fading away toward the mound, eluding Hamby's tag, and scraping his toe across the plate. O'Day hesitated for a second, then he signaled that Carey was safe with the winning run.

The already boisterous crowd broke into hand-clapping, foot-stomping, shrieking pandemonium that lasted long after the players were gone from the field. Eventually the last individuals left the park. But they were sure to come back for some more.

New York	ab	r	h	bi	o	a	e
A. Tyson, lf	3	1	1	1	5	0	1
F. Lindstrom, 3b	3	1	1	1	0	2	0
E. Roush, cf	4	0	1	0	2	0	0
R. Hornsby, 2b	4	0	1	1	1	3	0
B. Terry, 1b	4	0	0	0	9	0	0
G. Harper, rf	3	0	0	0	3	0	0
D. Farrell, ss	4	0	1	0	4	3	1
S. Hamby, c	3	1	0	0	2	1	0
F. Fitzsimmons, p	4	0	0	0	0	1	0
	32	3	5	3	26	10	2

Brooklyn	ab	r	h	bi	o	a	e
J. Statz, cf	4	0	0	0	2	0	0
J. Partridge, 2b	4	0	1	0	1	1	0
H. Hendrick, rf	4	0	0	0	0	0	0
B. Herman, 1b	4	2	2	0	7	0	0
G. Felix, lf	4	1	1	0	3	0	1
B. Barrett, 3b	3	0	1	1	2	1	0
M. Carey, pr9	0	1	0	0	-	-	-
J. Butler, ss	4	0	3	1	4	2	0
H. DeBerry, c	3	0	1	0	7	1	0
C. Fewster, pr9	0	0	0	0	-	-	-
D. Vance, p	3	0	1	0	1	2	0
M. Jacobson, ph9	0	0	0	1	-	-	-
	33	4	10	3	27	7	1

New York	200 100 000	= 3
Brooklyn	010 100 002	= 4

two out when winning run scored

	ip	h	r-er	bb	so
Fitzsimmons (L 3-1)	8⅔	10	4-3	1	2
Vance (W 1-3)	9	5	3-3	5	7

Time—1:50
Attendance—30,000
Umpires: H. O'Day, B. McCormick, & C. Rigler

Game-Winning RBI: Jacobson
LOB: New York 7, Brooklyn 6
BE: New York 1, Brooklyn 1
DP: Farrell-Terry (Barrett)
2B: Butler 2, Herman
3B: Lindstrom
SH: Barrett, Jacobson
SB: Partridge
CS: Tyson. Picked off: Vance

Unfortunately, it takes more than good pinch-running to be a consistent winner. And the Dodgers in 1927 did not have enough else.

The team had excellent pitching with a lot of depth. But the Brooklyn offense and fielding ranked last in the league, and most of the good pitching efforts went for naught.

The Robins never got to the .500 mark and finished with a 65-88 record, good enough for sixth place.

1928 TUESDAY, JUNE 12TH, AT EBBETS FIELD

Uncle Robbie Shakes Up Lineup & Wins 13-1

Bissonette Leads Attack With Four Hits, Including Homer
Hendrick Steals Second, Third, and Home in 8th

Today's Results			
BROOKLYN 13-Chicago 1			
New York 10-Cincinnati 1			
St. Louis 9-Boston 6			
Pittsburgh 15-Philadelphia 4			
Standings	**W-L**	**Pct.**	**GB**
Cincinnati	35-22	.614	—
St. Louis	32-21	.604	1
New York	28-20	.583	2½
Chicago	30-24	.556	3½
BROOKLYN	27-24	.529	5
Pittsburgh	24-27	.471	8
Boston	18-30	.375	12½
Philadelphia	10-36	.217	19½

REMEDYING THE ROBINS' CHRONIC LACK of scoring punch had been the top priority of Brooklyn president and manager Wilbert Robinson since the end of last season. His success had been limited.

But today, our Uncle Wilbert reshuffled his lineup and was rewarded with a most satisfying 13-1 victory over the Chicago Cubs. Slumping Jigger Statz (center field) and Harry Riconda (second base) were benched today. Jay Partridge was shifted from third to second, and Harvey Hendrick, a good hitter and base runner but a poor fielder, was inserted at third. Al Tyson, a decent hitter, took Statz's place. Tyson got three hits and drove in four runs. And Hendrick got two hits in the game and stole his way around the bases in the ninth inning.

The other top hitting stars for Brooklyn today were Rube Bressler and Del Bissonette. Bressler got three singles, scored twice, and drove home two. Bissonette smacked a single, two doubles, and a home run for three runs scored and five batted in. And pitcher Jim Elliott not only twirled a seven-hitter, he also clubbed a home run.

Elliott and Cub starter Charley Root battled through the first five innings without allowing any runs. Root only gave up one hit in that time.

The early Brooklyn hit was made by Bissonette in the second inning. He hit a drive so hard off the right field wall that the ball bounced all the way back to the second baseman, who threw the batter out trying to stretch the hit into a double.

Fine catches by the two left fielders, Bressler and Riggs Stephenson, helped the pitchers.

The game was still tied at 0-0 going into the bottom of the sixth. Partridge, leading off for Brooklyn, got the rally started by dragging a bunt past the pitcher for a hit. Hendrick's sacrifice bunt moved him along. Root passed the dangerous Babe Herman. Bressler then clouted a single to center, and Partridge galloped home with the first run.

Bissonette was the next batter. A 28-year-old rookie, Del had been kept in the International League by the Dodgers for two years. Uncoiling out of his crouched batting stance, he blasted Root's first pitch far over the right field wall for a three-run home run. It was his twelfth of the young season, tying him for the league lead in that category. And by the game's end, Bissonette had 48 runs-batted-in, also tops in the National League. Last year with Buffalo, he had led the I.L. with 31 homers and 167 RBIs. He had also led the league in doubles, triples, hits, and runs scored and had batted .365.

Root was removed for a pinch-hitter in the seventh, and Hal Carlson was the new pitcher facing Brooklyn in the bottom of that inning. The Robins pounded him for nine runs in 1⅓ innings pitched.

In the seventh Hendrick, an American League reject whom Robinson had bought from New Orleans after the 1926 season, doubled to left center with one gone. Max Carey, who had replaced Herman as a defensive manuever, beat out an infield hit. Bressler, whom Robinson had picked up on waivers from Cincinnati, singled Hendrick home. Carey scored on a double by Bissonette, with Bressler stopping at third. Tyson, another Buffalo pickup, knocked Bressler and Bissonete home with a hit to center.

Chicago scored its run in the top of the eighth. Kiki Cuyler singled with two out and scored on a triple by Hack Wilson.

Miffed at being scored upon, Jumbo Jim Elliott took it out on Carlson in the bottom of the inning. He led off with a home run over the right field fence and onto Bedford Avenue.

After Partridge flied out, Hendrick singled to left to set up his record-tying base-stealing feat. With Carey at bat, Hendrick stole second without trouble. As Carey watched ball four break low, Hendrick swiped third. Hendrick and Carey, who had been third and second in the league in steals in 1927, went for a double steal at the first opportunity today. With Bressler at the plate, Carey broke for second. When catcher Gabby Hartnett threw down to second base, Hendrick broke for home and beat the return throw. As he got up from his slide, Harvey was given a wild ovation by the Brooklyn fans. He had become, after all, only the second Dodger player this century to steal three bases in one trip around the diamond.

But the Flock was not quite through yet. Bressler's infield hit got Carey to third with the help of an error. And Bissonette whacked another double for his fifth RBI of the day. After Ed Holley replaced Carlson on the mound, Tyson upped his RBI total to four with his second two-run single in as many innings. That made the score 13-1, which turned out to be the final out.

Uncle Robbie could not have been happier. New men Tyson, Bressler, and Bissonette had been acquired pretty cheaply, and their good returns on the modest investments made president Robinson look good. And manager Robinson's new lineup looked pretty productive all up and down. The Brooklyn fans were keeping their fingers crossed in hopes that the hitting would keep up over the long run.

Chicago	ab	r	h	bi	o	a	e
C. Beck, 3b	3	0	0	0	1	2	1
W. English, ss	4	0	1	0	1	0	0
K. Cuyler, rf	2	1	1	0	1	0	0
H. Wilson, cf	4	0	1	1	0	0	1
R. Stephenson, lf	4	0	0	0	6	0	0
C. Grimm, 1b	3	0	1	0	8	0	0
N. McMillan, 2b	4	0	2	0	1	4	0
G. Hartnett, c	4	0	1	0	6	0	1
C. Root, p	2	0	0	0	0	2	0
F. Maguire, ph7	1	0	0	0	-	-	-
H. Carlson, p7	0	0	0	0	0	1	0
E. Holley, p8	0	0	0	0	0	0	0
	31	1	7	1	24	9	3

Brooklyn	ab	r	h	bi	o	a	e
J. Partridge, 2b	5	1	1	0	1	4	0
H. Hendrick, 3b	4	2	2	0	2	1	0
B. Herman, rf	2	1	0	0	0	1	0
M. Carey, rf7	1	2	1	0	2	0	0
R. Bressler, lf	5	3	3	2	6	0	0
D. Bissonette, 1b	4	3	4	5	8	0	0
A. Tyson, cf	4	0	3	4	3	0	0
D. Bancroft, ss	5	0	0	0	2	1	0
B. Henline, c	5	0	1	0	3	1	0
J. Elliott, p	3	1	1	1	0	1	0
	38	13	16	12	27	9	0

Chicago	000 000 010	= 1
Brooklyn	000 004 45x	= 13

	ip	h	r-er	bb	so
Root (L 6-7)	6	6	4-4	4	5
Carlson	1⅓	9	9-8	1	0
Holley	⅔	1	0-0	0	0
Elliott (W 3-5)	9	7	1-1	4	3

Time—1:55
Umpires: L. Jorda, C. Rigler, & G. Hart

Game-Winning RBI: Bressler
LOB: Chicago 7, Brooklyn 7
BE: none
2B: English, Hendrick, Bissonette 2
3B: Wilson
HR: Bissonette, Elliott
SH: Hendrick
SB: Cuyler, Hendrick 3, Carey
Picked Off: English
CS: Culyer

Although the Brooklyn offense was improved relative to 1927, it still ranked only sixth in the league in 1928. Bissonette finished fourth in the circuit in home runs with 25 and had 106 RBIs and a .320 batting average. Hendrick stole only 15 bases for the year, but he batted .318. Herman led the team with a .340 average.

The Robins continued to have fine pitching, and by the end of June had edged their way into third place. But the hitting and fielding prevented any bid for the league lead, and the team slipped to sixth place by August 2nd.

They finished sixth, even though their record was above .500 (77-76).

1929 FRIDAY, MAY 17TH, AT BAKER BOWL, PHILADELPHIA
Nail-Biter Ends Losing Streak

Robins Win 14-13 after Nine Consecutive Losses
Phils Leave Bases Loaded in 9th

Today's Results			
BROOKLYN 14-Philadelphia 13			
Chicago 9-Cincinnati 3			
Pittsburgh 6-St. Louis 2			
New York 9-Boston 5 (10 innings)			
Standings	**W-L**	**Pct.**	**GB**
Chicago	16- 8	.667	—
St. Louis	16- 9	.640	½
Pittsburgh	12-10	.545	3
Boston	13-11	.542	3
Cincinnati	11-13	.458	5
Philadelphia	10-12	.455	5
New York	8-13	.381	6½
BROOKLYN	7-17	.292	9

ALL LOSING STREAKS MUST COME TO AN end. Even the Robins' current string somehow was stopped at nine games today. But it was through no fault of the Brooklyn players. They made five errors and issued nine free passes and still managed to win, 14-13, over the Philadelphia Phillies. In this laughable exhibition of baseball, neither side seemed to want to win. But the rules required that one side had to win, so it was Brooklyn that came away with the prize.

A total of ten pitchers worked in the game, and nearly all seemed eager to make it easy for the hitters.

The first artist to audition on the hill was Luther Roy of the home team. He faced four batters and gave up a home run, two doubles, and a single and left the game trailing 3-0.

Brooklyn's starter was Alex Ferguson. This was his first appearance for the Robins, and his new teammates made him feel welcome by making four errors behind him in the first inning. After giving up a double to open the second, he was sent to the showers. Ray Moss followed him to the clubhouse after a brief tenure on the mound of five batters, three on whom eventually scored. By the time N. Winfield "Win" Ballou got the side out, the Phillies led 6-3.

A couple of doubles off of Hal Elliott, along with a miscellaneous hit, walk, and error, tied the game for Brooklyn in the third.

Johnny Milligan was given a look by the Phillies in the fourth. He turned out to be the most comical of all of the day's pitchers, although Johnny Frederick and Wally Gilbert did not think he was that funny. They were both hit by pitches. After Babe Herman singled Frederick home, Milligan was given the gate. By the time his relief, Bob McGraw, got out of the inning, the score was 10-6 in favor of the visitors.

Herman blasted a two-run homer off McGraw in the fifth. And Harvey Hendrick hit a solo homer in the sixth. Brooklyn's final run came after a triple off Claude Willoughby in the ninth by Val Picinich.

The Phillies got four runs and six hits off of Ballou in the fifth, sixth, and seventh. They were held scoreless in the eighth.

Brooklyn entered the bottom of the ninth with a 14-10 lead. When the inning finally ended, the lead was down to one run, the bases were loaded, and nearly everyone on the Brooklyn team was quaking for fear of yet another defeat.

When the first Phillie batter, Fresco Thompson, flied out, some of the Robins on the bench dared to hope that the losing streak would finally end. But Ballou walked Lefty O'Doul, and Chuck Klein followed with a drive over the handy right field wall for a two-run home run. Ballou then walked Don Hurst and gave up a hit through the box by Pinky Whitney.

With the tying runs on base, distraught manager Wilbert Robinson ordered Watty Clark in to pitch. Clark added a little drama to the slapstick by giving Homer Peel a free pass to load the bases.

But then Brooklyn got a break. Barney Friberg hit a shot toward third baseman Gilbert. Wally could not stop it, and the ball caromed off his wrist as a runner scored. The ball went right to shortstop Dave Bancroft, but Whitney (who had been on second before the hit) thought it had gone through, and he rounded third. Bancroft threw the ball to Gilbert, and Whitney was tagged out. This gift put the Dodgers just one out away from victory.

But it would have been just too easy to get the next man out. So Clark issued another walk, and the bases were loaded one more time. On the bench Uncle Wilbert turned purple with anxiety. George Susce, a pinch-hitter, was the decisive batter. An out would give the Robins the long-sought-after victory. But a walk or a hit would at least send the game into extra innings.

As it turned out, Brooklyn got two outs, although the second one wasn't needed. Susce hit to third base. Gilbert grabbed the ball and stepped on the base for a force out, ending the game. But in typical Robin style, he had forgotten how many outs there were, and he threw across to first base trying for a double play. First baseman Hendrick was slightly taken aback by this development, but he managed to recover to make the catch and step on the base ahead of the batter. He got spiked while making this unnecessary putout.

Somehow, the Robins had finally won a game and snapped their losing streak.

Brooklyn	ab	r	h	bi	o	a	e
J. Frederick, cf	5	2	2	0	2	0	0
W. Gilbert, 3b	4	4	2	2	2	3	0
B. Herman, rf	5	3	4	3	2	0	1
R. Bressler, lf	5	1	1	2	2	0	1
H. Hendrick, 1b	4	2	2	3	9	1	2
B. Rhiel, 2b	4	1	0	1	2	4	0
V. Picinich, c	4	1	2	1	5	1	0
D. Bancroft, ss	4	0	2	2	2	3	1
A. Ferguson, p	1	0	1	0	1	0	0
R. Moss, p2	0	0	0	0	0	0	0
W. Ballou, p2	4	0	0	0	0	2	0
W. Clark, p9	0	0	0	0	0	0	0
	40	14	16	14	27	14	5

Philadelphia	ab	r	h	bi	o	a	e
F. Thompson, 2b	5	2	3	0	4	5	0
L. O'Doul, lf	4	4	4	3	1	0	0
C. Klein, rf	5	1	1	3	4	0	0
D. Hurst, 1b	4	1	0	0	8	1	0
P. Whitney, 3b	4	0	2	2	0	3	0
D. Sothern, cf	3	0	0	0	2	0	0
H. Peel, cf5	2	1	0	0	3	0	0
B. Friberg, ss	6	0	2	2	2	2	1
V. Davis, c	5	1	2	0	2	1	0
P. Collins, pr8	0	0	0	0	-	-	-
W. Lerian, c9	0	0	0	0	1	0	0
L. Roy, p	0	0	0	0	0	0	0
H. Elliott, p1	1	1	1	0	0	0	0
J. O'Rourke, ph3	1	0	0	0	-	-	-
J. Milligan, p4	0	0	0	0	0	0	0
B. McGraw, p4	1	1	1	0	0	1	1
J. Green, ph7	1	0	1	0	-	-	-
R. Benge, pr7	0	1	0	0	-	-	-
J. Holloway, p8	0	0	0	0	0	0	0
C. Williams, ph8	1	0	0	0	-	-	-
C. Willoughby, p9	0	0	0	0	0	1	0
G. Susce, ph9	1	0	0	0	-	-	-
	44	13	17	10	27	14	2

Brooklyn	303 421 001	= 14
Philadelphia	240 011 203	= 13

	ip	h	r-er	bb	so
Ferguson	*1	3	3-1	1	1
Moss	⅓	2	3-3	2	1
Ballou (W 1-1)	7	11	7-6	4	2
Clark	⅔	1	0-0	2	0
Roy	†0	4	3-3	0	0
Elliott	3	4	3-2	1	0
Milligan (L 0-1)	‡0	1	3-3	0	0
McGraw	4	6	4-4	0	1
Holloway	1	0	0-0	1	1
Willoughby	1	1	1-1	0	1

*faced one batter in second
†faced four batters in first
‡faced three batters in fourth

Game-Winning RBI: Herman
LOB: Brooklyn 5, Philadelphia 14
BE: Brooklyn 1, Philadelphia 3
DP: Whitney-Thompson-Hurst (Rhiel)
2B: Frederick, Herman 2, Gilbert, Davis, Thompson, Friberg, O'Doul
3B: Picinich 2
HR: Gilbert, Herman, Hendrick, Klein
SH: Picinich, Klein, Bancroft
CS: Hurst, Frederick

HBP: by Milligan 2 (Frederick, Gilbert)

Time—2:32

Umpires: B. Klem, L. Jorda & G. Magerkurth

The hapless Robins did not escape the cellar for good until June 13th. They spent all of July and August and most of September in fifth place, but they lost a doubleheader on the final day of the season to finish sixth for the fifth year in a row. Brooklyn's final record was 70-83.

1930 MONDAY, SEPTEMBER 15TH, AT EBBETS FIELD

League-Leading Flock Wins 11th Straight

Robins Rout Reds, 13-5, Despite Weird Base Running
Give 3 Runs in Top of First but Rally for 6 in Bottom

Today's Results			
BROOKLYN 13-Cincinnati 5			
Philadelphia 12-Chicago 11 (1st game)			
Chicago 6-Philadelphia 4 (2nd game)			
New York 6-Pittsburgh 1			
no other game scheduled			
Standings	**W-L**	**Pct.**	**GB**
BROOKLYN	84-60	.583	—
St. Louis	82-60	.577	1
Chicago	82-61	.573	1½
New York	78-65	.545	5½
Pittsburgh	74-68	.521	9
Boston	67-78	.462	17½
Cincinnati	55-85	.393	27
Philadelphia	49-94	.343	37½

TODAY THE BROOKLYN ROBINS WERE without three of their four best outfielders, had their starting pitcher knocked out of the box in the very first inning, and pulled off a couple of their fabled base-running shenanigans. Yet they won the game easily, 13-5, for their eleventh consecutive triumph, and they increased their league lead to 1 full game with just ten games left to play.

The club's pitching depth was shown today when relief pitcher Watty Clark worked 8⅔ and was charged with only two runs. And the Robins also hit the ball hard and fielded very well. Of the hitters, Babe Herman and Del Bissonette stood out, each making four hits in five at bats. The sum total of the team's work yielded another victory and edged the high-flying Flock one length closer to the pennant.

The Robins led the league for most of June and July and were ahead by 3½ games on August 8th. Then a tailspin (7 wins and 19 losses) dropped them all the way to fourth place, 6 games behind. But starting on September 6th, Brooklyn rebounded with a big winning streak, which today reached eleven games. With the red-hot St. Louis Cardinals due to open a three-game series here tomorrow, Brooklyn could use all the momentum it could get.

The streak was marred by some injuries, however. Starting outfielders Johnny Frederick and Rube Bressler were both laid up in recent games. And Frederick's replacement in center field, Eddie Brown, pulled a leg muscle yesterday. So substitutes Harvey Hendrick and Ike Boone joined regular Babe Herman in the garden for the Robins today. All three were reputedly deficient defensively, but they did the job today. Only one fly that might have been caught by better fielders fell safely for a hit. And the three sluggers pounded out seven hits and scored five runs.

Pennant fever brought out a big Monday crowd of around 15,000 to Ebbets Field. Many of the fans were not even in their seats by the time starting pitcher Ray Moss was heading for the showers. The first Cincinnati batter, Curt Walker, flied to short center field, where shortstop Glenn Wright made a nice catch. That was the only out Moss got. Bob Meusel, batting second, hit a home run into the left field bleachers. Joe Stripp doubled down the left field line, and Tony Cuccinello doubled over Boone's head in left. After Harry Heilmann hit a tremendous foul into the stands in left, manager Wilbert Robinson hustled Clark into the game.

Watty got Heilmann on a line-drive out. But Hod Ford singled Cuccinello home for Cincinnati's third run.

The Robins came in and roared past the Reds for a 6-3 lead. And they did it in spite of a terrible mistake on the basepaths. With one out, Wally Gilbert walked and Herman singled. Wright followed with a long fly to left center. Center fielder Meusel appeared to have a chance to make the catch, and Herman held up between first and second. Meusel misjudged the fly and allowed it to bounce into the bleachers for an apparent home run. But Wright, who had only been watching the ball, passed Herman on the bases and was automatically out. That turned a three-run homer into a two-run single and an out. Undeterred by this setback, the Robins kept hitting. Bissonette and Boone singled, and Neal Finn walked to load the bases.

Al Lopez blasted a 3-and-2 pitch to deep left field for a three-run double. That gave Brooklyn a 5-3 lead and sent pitcher Red Lucas to the clubhouse. Clark greeted reliever Larry Benton with a hit, which scored Lopez.

Clark's pitching held the Reds safe the rest of the way. Cincinnati got two runs in the seventh inning on a single by Cuccinello and a homer by Heilmann. But other than that, they were shut out.

Benton held the Robins scoreless in the second and third.

In the fourth, Brooklyn scored three times, despite another weird adventure on the bases. Clark, Hendrick, and Gilbert all singled to bring Clark home and put Hendrick on third. Herman lined a solid drive to right, but Hendrick held third until the right fielder picked the ball up on one bounce. Finally he started for home. He would have been an easy out at home, but the second baseman, who took the throw from the outfield, assumed that he had scored already and did not relay the ball home. An RBI single by Bissonette off relief pitcher Benny Frey brought Gilbert home.

Two walks and two hits added up to two more Brooklyn runs in the fifth and knocked Frey out of the game.

The last scoring of the day came in the eighth. Herman singled and stole second. Bissonette tripled Babe home and scored himself on Boone's infield out. That made the final count 13-5.

Although they were unable to field their best lineup, and their running was still mistake-prone, the Brooklyn Robins were holding up under the pressure of the pennant race very well so far. And they were heading into the critical series with the Cardinals riding the crest of an eleven-game winning streak.

Cincinnati	ab	r	h	bi	o	a	e
C. Walker, lf	1	0	0	0	0	0	0
E. Swanson, ph2-cf	3	0	0	0	0	0	0
B. Meusel, cf-lf2	4	1	2	1	1	0	0
J. Stripp, 1b	4	1	1	0	11	0	0
T. Cuccinello, 3b	3	2	2	1	1	0	0
H. Heilmann, rf	4	1	1	2	1	0	0
H. Ford, 2b	4	0	3	1	2	5	0
J. Gooch, c	4	0	0	0	6	1	0
L. Durocher, ss	4	0	0	0	2	4	0
R. Lucas, p	0	0	0	0	0	0	0
L. Benton, p1	1	0	0	0	0	3	0
B. Frey, p4	1	0	1	0	0	0	0
J. May, p5	1	0	1	0	0	0	0
C. Dressen, ph9	1	0	0	0	-	-	-
	35	5	11	5	24	13	0

Brooklyn	ab	r	h	bi	o	a	e
H. Hendrick, cf	4	2	2	0	4	0	0
W. Gilbert, 3b	3	3	1	1	0	2	0
B. Herman, rf	5	2	4	2	1	0	0
G. Wright, ss	4	0	2	3	2	8	0
D. Bissonette, 1b	5	2	4	2	13	0	0
I. Boone, lf	5	1	1	1	2	0	0
N. Finn, 2b	4	1	0	0	3	4	0
A. Lopez, c	3	1	1	3	1	0	0
V. Picinich, c6	1	0	0	0	1	0	0
R. Moss, p	0	0	0	0	0	0	0
W. Clark, p1	4	1	2	1	0	1	0
	38	13	17	13	27	15	0

Cincinnati	300	002	000	=	5
Brooklyn	600	320	02x	=	13

	ip	h	r-er	bb	so
Lucas (L 13-16)	⅔	5	6-6	2	0
Benton	*2⅓	6	3-3	0	1
Frey	1⅔	3	2-2	2	0
May	3⅓	3	2-2	0	3
Moss	⅓	3	3-3	0	0
Clark (W 13-12)	8⅔	8	2-2	1	0

*faced four batters in fourth

Time—2:00 Attendance—15,000

Umpires: C. Moran, B. Reardon, & M. Donohue

Game-Winning RBI: Lopez
LOB: Cincinnati 4, Brooklyn 6
DP: Wright-Finn-Bissonette (Gooch)
Clark-Wright-Bissonette (Swanson)
Wright-Finn-Bissonette (Heilmann)
2B: Stripp, Cuccinello, Lopez, Hendrick, Ford
3B: Bissonette
HR: Meusel, Heilmann
SH: Wright
SB: Herman
CS: Herman

Brooklyn's pennant dream was shattered within a week. On Tuesday, the Robins lost a heartbreaker to St. Louis, 1-0 in ten innings. The Cardinals won again on Wednesday with a late rally, 5-3. On Thursday, St. Louis completed the sweep with a 4-3 decision, as Brooklyn's late rally fell short.

Brooklyn lost four more games and was eliminated from the race before it won another game. The Robins finished in fourth place, 6 games behind the pennant-winning Cardinals, with an 86-68 record.

The exciting pennant bid put the club's attendance over the 1,000,000 mark for the first time ever.

1931 WEDNESDAY, APRIL 15TH, AT BRAVES FIELD, BOSTON

Alta Cohen's Strange Debut

Gets a Hit Batting Fourth and a Hit Batting Ninth
Robins Make Seven Errors and Lose to Braves, 9-3

ALBERT "ALTA" COHEN MADE HIS MAJOR league debut with Brooklyn today under rather unusual circumstances. Entering the game in the fifth inning as a defensive replacement for Ike Boone (or was it for Babe Herman?), he went to bat in the sixth inning in the number-four slot in the Brooklyn order and singled. In the seventh inning he batted ninth in the order and singled again. After making a couple of nice plays in the infield, Cohen finally sank to the level of his teammates and grounded into a double play in his final trip to the plate.

Today's Results			
Boston 9-BROOKLYN 3			
Chicago 6-Pittsburgh 5			
St. Louis 4-Cincinnati 0			
Philadelphia 10-New York 7			

Standings	W-L	Pct.	GB
Boston	2-0	1.000	—
St. Louis	2-0	1.000	—
Chicago	2-0	1.000	—
Philadelphia	1-1	.500	1
New York	1-1	.500	1
BROOKLYN	0-2	.000	2
Cincinnati	0-2	.000	2
Pittsburgh	0-2	.000	2

Brooklyn lost the game to Boston, 9-3, and except for the work of young Cohen, the game was a total fiasco for the Robins. They made seven errors of commission and a few of omission to hand the Braves an early eight-run lead.

Although it was only the second game of the regular season, manager Wilbert Robinson and outfielder Babe Herman were in mid-season form. Herman was charged with one error in right, but he also botched a couple of other plays. Robinson got so peeved at this that he got into a shouting match with Herman and preemptively told him he was out of the game. Old Uncle Wilbert forgot about the fact that the next right fielder, Ike Boone, was even worse with the glove than Herman. In desperation, Robbie sent rookie Cohen into the game, giving Alta his big chance. Cohen was with the team just for the ride, as he was scheduled to be delivered to the Hartford Eastern League team on Friday.

The game was scoreless and reasonably uneventful until the bottom of the third. Then the Braves blasted five hits off of Robin pitcher Hollis "Sloppy" Thurston good for four runs. One of the runners scored from second on a short single because Herman held the ball in the outfield.

Boston added four more runs in the fourth. Rabbit Maranville singled with one out. Red Worthington hit a long double to right center, and Maranville scored and Worthington took third when catcher Al Lopez could not handle Herman's throw. Two more singles followed.

Earl Mattingly came in to replace the shell-shocked Thurston. During the pitching change, Herman lost all his concentration in right. Earl Sheely, the Braves' next batter, hit a fly toward the right field line. Herman, however, broke in directly the opposite direction, and the ball fell untouched for an RBI single. Freddie Maguire lifted a pop to short right. This time Herman got under it, but he dropped it for an error. Wally Berger, who had been on third, lit out for home, while Sheely, who had stayed close to first, was forced to try for second. Sizing up the situation in an instant, Herman threw home too late, even though he probably could have rolled the ball to second for an easy force out. On the bench, Robinson was choking on his tobacco in exasperation.

After the next two batters mercifully grounded out to end the inning, Herman came into the dugout and got an earful of insults from the manager. Babe threw down his glove and told Uncle Wilbert that if he didn't like the outfielding, he could get another outfielder. In a huff, Robinson replied that he would send Boone out in Herman's place. In the meantime, Brooklyn had loaded the bases with none out, and pitcher Mattingly was due to hit. Robinson decided to use Boone as a pinch-hitter.

Ike went to the plate and helped kill the rally by hitting into a force out at home. A run scored on a sacrifice fly, but another out ended what might have been a big inning with only one run scored.

Disconsolate about missing this chance to get back into the game, Robbie forgot everything else. With the Braves about to come to bat, he suddenly noticed Herman still on the bench. Then he looked out to right and was surprised to see Boone out there with a glove. This was a mistake, Robinson decided, and he sent Herman back out. But the umpire had already announced a switch, and Herman was officially out of the game. Still, Robinson did not want Boone in right. Looking down the bench, he noticed little Alta Cohen, who happened to be an outfielder, and sent him to right.

When the Robins came to bat in the sixth, Herman's spot was due to lead off. Cohen thinking that he had replaced Babe, went to the plate and poked an opposite-field hit to left. The inning was over before anyone on the field seemed to realize that Cohen had replaced Boone, who had batted ninth, rather than Herman. So before the Brooklyn seventh, a conference was held in which the umpires decided that Cohen would bat in the number-nine position for the rest of the game. This gave Alta a chance to hit again in the seventh, and he singled again and this time scored a run.

In the bottom of the seventh, both Worthington and Clark tried to stretch singles to right into doubles. But Cohen threw them both out at second.

But the youngster finally came back to earth in the ninth when he grounded into a double play. One out later the game was over and the Robins had lost, Boston's Harry "Socks" Seibold having pitched the complete game. For Brooklyn, at least young Albert Cohen had done himself proud in his first big league game.

Brooklyn	ab	r	h	bi	o	a	e
J. Frederick, cf	5	0	1	1	0	0	0
W. Gilbert, 3b	4	0	1	2	2	0	2
B. Herman, rf	2	0	0	0	0	0	1
C. Moore, p5	0	0	0	0	0	1	0
J. Flowers, ph7	1	0	0	0	-	-	-
F. Heimach, p7	0	0	0	0	0	1	0
L. O'Doul, lf	4	0	0	0	1	0	0
G. Slade, ss	4	0	0	0	1	4	1
D. Bissonette, 1b	4	0	1	0	10	1	0
N. Finn, 2b	4	1	1	0	6	3	1
A. Lopez, c	1	0	0	0	3	1	2
E. Lombardi, c5	2	1	2	0	0	1	0
H. Thurston, p	1	0	0	0	0	1	0
E. Mattingly, p4	0	0	0	0	0	1	0
I. Boone, ph4-rf	1	0	0	0	-	-	-
A. Cohen, rf5	3	1	2	0	1	2	0
	36	3	8	3	24	16	7

Boston	ab	r	h	bi	o	a	e
C. Wilson, 3b	6	0	1	0	1	3	0
R. Maranville, ss	5	2	2	0	1	4	1
R. Worthington, rf	5	2	3	1	1	0	0
W. Berger, cf	4	2	3	1	3	0	0
E. Clark, lf	4	2	3	2	2	0	1
E. Sheely, 1b	5	1	3	2	11	0	0
F. Maguire, 2b	5	0	0	0	4	2	1
A. Spohrer, c	5	0	1	0	4	0	0
S. Seibold, p	5	0	1	1	0	4	0
	44	9	17	7	27	13	3

Brooklyn	000	010	200	=	3
Boston	004	401	00x	=	9

	ip	h	r-er	bb	so
Thurston (L 0-1)	3⅓	9	8-6	2	1
Mattingly	⅔	1	0-0	0	0
Moore	2	3	1-0	0	0
Heimach	2	4	0-0	0	0
Seibold (W 1-0)	9	8	3-2	1	2

Game-Winning RBI: Berger
LOB: Brooklyn 7, Boston 13
BE: Brooklyn 1, Boston 5
DP: Seibold-Maranville-Sheely (Cohen)
2B: Worthington, Clark
Time--2:03

Umpires: L. Jorda, D. Stark, &B. Klem

Cohen was kept with the team for three weeks, but he was not used again. Finally he was shipped to Hartford, where he spent the rest of the season. He played nine games for the Dodgers in 1932 before being shipped out again.

After the exciting season of 1930, the 1931 Robins got off to a terrible start. They did not escape the cellar until April 30th. Still, the team had some talent and rose to second place by mid-July. The Robins slipped to fourth place in the final standings, 21 games behind, with a 79-73 record.

Chapter VIII "Is Brooklyn Still in the League?"

1932 September 12th
Frederick Hits 6th Pinch Homer

1933 May 14th
Pinch Grand Slam by Hack Wilson

1934 September 30th
Brooklyn IS Still in the League!

1935 July 22nd
Dodgers Win a Wild One, 14-13

1936 April 16th
"Once a Dodger, Always a Dodger"

1937 August 31st
Dodgers Blow the Game, Grimes Blows a Fuse

WILBERT ROBINSON WAS DISMISSED AS MANAGER OF THE BROOKLYN ROBINS ON October 22, 1931. With "Uncle Robbie" gone, the nickname of the team reverted to "Dodgers," although the collective noun "the Flock," which had originated from "flock of robins," was used in reference to the team through the rest of the Brooklyn years.

Max Carey succeeded Robinson as manager. Max was a serious baseball man who fancied himself a good teacher and a sound fundamentalist. It seemed logical, therefore, that some of the older players like Dolf Luque and Rube Bressler be released. During spring training, Babe Herman was traded along with Wally Gilbert and a young catcher named Ernie Lombardi to Cincinnati for catcher Clyde Sukeforth and infielders Tony Cuccinello and Joe Stripp. With Glenn Wright able to play shortstop again, the infield looked solid. But during training, first baseman Del Bissonette suffered a crippling Achilles tendon injury that more or less ended his career. First base was held down in 1932 first by ancient George Kelly and later by Bud Clancy. Another new acquisition was Lewis "Hack" Wilson, an outfielder with power.

In the first couple of months of the season, the Dodgers couldn't seem to get over .500. Pitchers Hollis Thurston and Van Lingle Mungo showed flashes of brilliance, and Dazzy Vance came up with an occasional good game. But none of them could win consistently. The outfield had troubles, too. Johnny Frederick was in and out of the lineup with both hand and leg problems. But he did some great pinch-hitting. Wilson and Lefty O'Doul hit well, but they were getting old and didn't cover much ground. Finally, Danny Taylor was acquired from the Cubs to play center.

On July 23rd, Brooklyn fell to seventh place, 12 games out of first. Then suddenly the team got hot. Winning 24 out of 30, the Dodgers leaped to second place, just 1½ games behind the league-leading Cubs. O'Doul was leading the league in hitting, and Wilson was particularly devastating against Chicago pitching.

Then came a fateful series in the Windy City. On three successive days, the Cubs knocked out Mungo, Watty Clark, and Thurston and won by big scores. The Dodgers never threatened again and finished third. O'Doul won the batting title, Clark closed with a rush and won 20 games, and Frederick set a record with six pinch-hit home runs. The third-place finish was the club's best since 1924.

But the apparent improvement was illusionary. Wright, Wilson, and O'Doul were getting old, and Thurston and Clark also began to slip. Vance was traded away after eleven seasons in Brooklyn. In return, the Dodgers got pitcher Owen Carroll, who had one decent season with Brooklyn.

Casey Stengel

Other new pitching prospects for 1933 included Walter "Boom-Boom" Beck (picked up from Memphis) and Ray Benge (brought over from the Phillies). Along with Mungo and Carroll, they were the heart of the staff after Clark developed a sore arm. Watty was traded to the Giants along with the slumping O'Doul for first baseman Sam Leslie, who helped. Wilson was relegated to part-time duty, although he had one moment of glory when he hit a pinch grand slam to win a game in the ninth inning. Only Frederick and catcher Al Lopez hit over .300. Beck absorbed 20 defeats. After flirting with the cellar in late July, the Dodgers managed to finish a distant sixth. Despite the poor showing, Carey's contract was renewed in August.

Bob Quinn, a veteran of many years in baseball, was named general manager after the season. He promised some big changes, but nothing of note happened through most of the winter. One day, a sportswriter looking for some fuel for the "Hot Stove League" asked New York player-manager Bill Terry about the various clubs around the league. When the subject of the Dodgers came up, Terry alluded to Quinn's inactivity by asking, "Is Brooklyn still in the league?"

Quinn read this in his newspaper and nearly blew a gasket. He did not, however, arrange any big deals. Instead, he changed managers, even though Carey was under contract for 1934. The new pilot was one of Carey's coaches, Casey Stengel, the colorful old Superba.

Stengel inherited the same problems that had plagued Carey, especially at shortstop and in the outfield. In 1934, Linus "Lonny" Frey wound up playing the most at short, although his arm was inadequate for the position. Ralph "Buzz" Boyle, Johnny Frederick, Len Koenecke, and Danny Taylor did most of the outfielding. Koenecke was very streaky, and the rest were average at best.

Benge, Mungo, and young Emil "Dutch" Leonard pitched well, but overall the staff was among the worst in the league. Virtually the entire season was spent in sixth place, although the Dodgers slipped to seventh for a while in July. Attendance slipped to its lowest level since 1919.

But there was glory at the very end of the campaign. All year long, the Brooklyn fans had seethed with rage at Bill Terry's crack about still being in the league. When the pennant race came down to the final two games of the year, the Giants were tied for first and were scheduled to finish with two games against the Dodgers in the Polo Grounds. Fans from Brooklyn subwayed over to Manhattan in swarms and howled with glee as the Dodgers beat the Giants in both games to knock Terry out of the pennant.

Quinn again failed to make any major changes over the winter, and it was pretty much the same squad that took the field in 1935. The only major addition was fleet-footed outfielder Stan Bordagaray. He was known as "Frenchy" and sported the only mustache in the major leagues.

The pitching was still troublesome. Oldtimers George Earnshaw and Dazzy Vance were brought back in 1935 on the hope that they could regain their old stuff. Earnshaw had his moments, but Vance quit in August. On the other hand, Watty Clark, who had been reacquired late in 1934, bounced back with a 13-8 season. Mungo was 16-10, his best full-season percentage with Brooklyn, but his work was limited by a mid-season finger injury.

The Dodgers did very well in spring training and started the regular season with a 17-9 record. Then they slipped to a more representative level. With a week to go in the season, Brooklyn was flirting with seventh place. But the Dodgers won their last seven decisions and finished fifth for 1935.

Quinn quit as general manager after the season to take over the Boston Bees. He was replaced in Brooklyn by John Gorman, who had been traveling secretary. Quinn and Gorman quickly hatched a deal that brought pitchers Eddie Brandt and Fred Frankhouse and outfielder Randy Moore to Brooklyn in exchange for catcher Al Lopez and three other players. Sam Leslie was sold back to the Giants, and first baseman Buddy Hassett was purchased from the Yankee farm system. Brandt and Frankhouse were aging veterans, but they were still useful. Moore saw only limited duty. Hassett turned out to be pretty good.

Freddy Lindstrom, a 30-year-old twelve-year veteran, was picked up after the Cubs released him. As a young Giant, Lindstrom had once derided the ineptness of the Brooklyn franchise with the saying, "Once a Dodger, always a Dodger." Now he was a Dodger, and strange things began to happen to him. On the third day of the season, he collided with the shortstop and let a pop fly become a two-run double that beat Brooklyn, 7-6. This sort of thing drove Lindstrom to retire in mid-May.

This ragtag squad won only 24 of the first 77 games and fought the Phillies for last place. In the second half, the Dodgers had a respectable 43-34 record, but that only got them a seventh-place finish. Even though Stengel still had a year left on his contract, he was fired. Like Carey before him, Casey was paid for a full season not to manage.

The new manager was Burleigh Grimes, the terrible-tempered old pitcher. In

Van Lingle Mungo and Randy Moore

an attempt at rebuilding, several deals were made before the 1937 campaign began. In one, Brandt went to Pittsburgh for infielder Harry "Cookie" Lavagetto and a useless pitcher named Ralph Birkofer. Bordagaray and infielder Jimmy Jordan were exchanged for a highly-prized prospect named Tom Winsett, who turned out to be a big bust. And Lonny Frey, the young infielder, was dealt to the Cubs for an old infielder, Woody English, and a young pitcher, Roy Henshaw. Ancient Heinie Manush was signed after being released by the Red Sox. He had one good year left.

With this collection, Grimes did not have much hope for a dramatic improvement. The Dodgers were in sixth place on June 11th when they made one of the only good trades of the year. Pitcher Tom Baker, who had won 2 games for Brooklyn over two years, was swapped for knuckleballer Freddie Fitzsimmons, who had won 170 for the Giants. Fat Freddie was only 4-8 with Brooklyn in 1937, but he won a total of 47 games for the Dodgers before he was through. Baker won only one game for New York.

Van Lingle Mungo was still the ace of the pitching staff for the first half of the season. He had a 9-6 record and had been selected to the All-Star team when he went out to pitch on the Fourth of July. After no-hitting the Giants until the sixth inning, he pulled a muscle in his side. Trying to grit it out, he lost 6-5. He went off to the All-Star Game with instructions not to pitch unless he felt 100% healthy. He pitched two innings and aggravated his injury. Peeved at this, Grimes stubbornly sent Mungo out to pitch in his turn when the regular season resumed. Favoring his side, Van injured his arm. He never regained his fastball or his winning form, although he stayed with the Dodgers until 1941.

Grimes tried to harangue his team into a winning unit, but it was impossible. On August 31st, he even ran onto the field to remove Hassett from the game after the first baseman had made an error. And Burleigh also screamed constantly at the umpires, getting himself ejected from ten games over the course of the season.

Brooklyn was in last place briefly in August and lost 14 in a row in September but somehow managed to finish sixth. Grimes was not blamed for the poor work, however, and he returned to manage in 1938. That was the year that things began to turn around for Brooklyn.

Manager Burleigh Grimes addresses his men

1932 MONDAY, SEPTEMBER 12TH, AT EBBETS FIELD
Frederick Hits Sixth Pinch Homer

Ninth-Inning Clout with One On Beats Cubs, 4-3
Johnny Extends His Own Big League Record

JOHNNY FREDERICK CAME OFF THE bench today and hit another pinch home run. It was his sixth of the year, a baseball record by far, since the old record was thought to be either three or four. Today's blast was the best yet for Frederick because it was the first one that directly won the game for Brooklyn. It came with one out, one on, and the Dodgers one run behind in the bottom of the ninth. None of Johnny's other pinch homers had been as dramatic.

Today's Results			
BROOKLYN 4-Chicago 3			
Pittsburgh 4-Philadelphia 2			
no other games scheduled			
Standings	**W-L**	**Pct.**	**GB**
Chicago	83-57	.593	—
Pittsburgh	78-62	.557	5
BROOKLYN	74-68	.521	10
Philadelphia	71-70	.504	12½
Boston	71-72	.497	13½
St. Louis	65-75	.464	18
New York	64-75	.460	18½
Cincinnati	58-85	.406	26½

He first connected in the pinch on July 12th off of Bill Harris in Pittsburgh. That was a dramatic hit, since it tied the game in the ninth inning. But Brooklyn lost the game in twelve, 8-7.

Three days later, he hit another pinch homer, this time in Chicago. Lon Warneke was the pitcher, and Frederick's eighth-inning four-bagger came in an 8-3 Dodger loss.

On August 10th, the Cincinnati Reds were in Brooklyn for a doubleheader. With Frederick on the bench, the home team won the first game, 6-1. In the second game, Cincinnati was leading 7-3 going into the bottom of the eighth. But Johnny batted for pitcher Cy Moore and hit a three-run homer to help Brooklyn to an eventual 10-9 victory.

The Dodgers won three games in the next three days in New York and were scheduled to end the series with a doubleheader on Sunday, August 14th. In the first game, New York's Carl Hubbell was nursing a 1-0 lead in the top of the ninth. Brooklyn manager Max Carey sent Frederick up to hit for pitcher Van Lingle Mungo. Johnny picked on one of Hubbell's rare mistakes and hit it into the seats to tie the game. Ther Dodgers went on to win in the tenth, 2-1, to extend their winning streak to six games. The streak was ended in the nightcap, however, when the Giants won 8-4. Frederick pinch-hit in that game but only flied out.

Last Saturday, the Brooklyn fans were treated to another pinch-hit home run by Frederick, his fifth of the year. But the Flatbush rooters had little else to cheer about, as Pat Malone pitched the Cubs to an easy 9-2 victory.

Today, Bud Tinning was the starting pitcher for Chicago, although Frederick hit his home run off of reliever Burleigh Grimes. Carey had his top hurler, lefty Watty Clark, on the hill. Both starters pitched well, although Tinning was removed for a pinch-hitter in the eighth inning.

The Cubs rallied for two runs in the ninth to take a 3-2 lead. But Frederick's heroic smash brought victory back to the Brooklyn side.

Clark was uncharacteristically wild in the first inning, walking two men. But he also struck out two to avoid any damage. He walked another man in the second and gave up two hits in the third. But he pitched around these threats. Over the course of the game, Lefty walked six and fanned six.

The Dodgers got the first run of the game in the bottom of the third. Al Lopez opened with a hit to center. Clark deftly bunted him to second. Danny Taylor's single to left drove Lopez home.

D. Taylor also saved a run with a nice catch with a man on base in the top of the fourth.

Brooklyn's Lefty O'Doul, the league's leading hitter with a .370 average, opened the bottom of the fourth with a single. But Hack Wilson hit into a double play behind him. Tony Cuccinello and Glenn Wright followed with singles, but Bud Clancy grounded out to end the inning.

Chicago tied the game in the sixth on a triple by Charlie Grimm and a single by Gabby Hartnett.

But Brooklyn got the lead in the seventh on an unearned run. Clancy was given a life at first on a fumble by second baseman Billy Herman. He moved to third on a pair of infield outs and scored on an infield hit by Taylor.

Chicago came back in the ninth with two runs to take a 3-2 lead. Woody English started the rally with a one-out single to center. Kiki Cuyler looped a hit to right, but English was cut down at third by a strong throw from Hack Wilson. Cuyler took second on the play, so Carey ordered an intentional walk to Riggs Stephenson, putting the go-ahead run on base. The move backfired. Frank Demaree hit a hard shot to first base, which Clancy could not handle, and Cuyler scored while Stephenson raced to third. Grimm singled Stephenson home.

So the Dodgers were down by one going into the bottom of the ninth. Burleigh Grimes was on the hill for Chicago. He got Cuccinello to ground out to open the inning. Then Wright smashed a ringing double off the right field scoreboard.

Carey picked this as the time to play his ace, and Frederick was sent up to hit for Clancy. Grimes's first pitch was a ball. The next one was fouled into the dirt. Old Burleigh then tried to slip a fastball by the hitter. But Frederick jumped on it and hit it into the screen atop the scoreboard for a home run.

Wright trotted around the bases with the tying run, and Frederick followed him around with the run that won the game for Brooklyn. That's what made this one the best of Johnny's six pinch-hit homers this season.

Chicago	ab	r	h	bi	o	a	e
B. Herman, 2b	5	0	0	0	4	6	1
W. English, 3b	5	0	2	0	1	1	0
K. Cuyler, rf	4	1	3	0	2	0	0
R. Stephenson, lf	2	1	1	0	0	0	0
F. Demaree, cf	4	0	1	0	2	0	0
C. Grimm, 1b	5	1	2	1	9	4	0
G. Hartnett, c	4	0	2	1	0	1	0
B. Jurges, ss	3	0	0	0	4	5	0
R. Hemsley, ph8	1	0	0	0	-	-	-
M. Koenig, ss8	0	0	0	0	0	1	0
B. Tinning, p	3	0	0	0	3	0	0
Z. Taylor, ph8	1	0	0	0	-	-	-
B. Grimes, p8	0	0	0	0	0	0	0
	37	3	11	2	25	18	1

Brooklyn	ab	r	h	bi	o	a	e
D. Taylor, cf	4	0	3	2	4	0	0
N. Finn, 3b	4	0	0	0	3	5	0
L. O'Doul, lf	4	0	1	0	0	0	0
H. Wilson, rf	4	0	0	0	1	1	0
T. Cuccinello, 2b	4	0	2	0	1	5	0
G. Wright, ss	4	1	3	0	0	4	0
B. Clancy, 1b	3	1	0	0	13	0	1
J. Frederick, ph9	1	1	1	2	-	-	-
A. Lopez, c	2	1	1	0	5	1	0
W. Clark, p	2	0	0	0	0	0	0
	32	4	11	4	27	16	1

Chicago	000	001	002	=	3
Brooklyn	001	000	102	=	4

one out when winning run scored

	ip	h	r-er	bb	so
Tinning	7	9	2-1	0	0
Grimes (L 6-10)	1⅓	2	2-2	0	0
Clark (W 17-12)	9	11	3-3	6	6

Time—1:58 Attendance—5,000

Umpires: B. Klem, D. Stark & C. Pfirman

Game-Winning RBI: Frederick
LOB: Chicago 13, Brooklyn 5
BE: Chicago 0, Brooklyn 1
DP: Herman-Grimm (Finn)
Herman-Jurges-Grimm (Wilson)
2B: Wright 2, Hartnett
3B: D. Taylor, Grimm, English
HR: Frederick
SH: Clark, Lopez
SB: Cuyler, Stephenson
CS: D. Taylor

In the final two weeks of the season, Frederick was in the starting lineup, and he failed to hit another home run. Still, his record of six pinch homers had not been matched fifty years later.

With Clark winning three games to reach the 20-win plateau, the Dodgers won seven of their last twelve to finish at 81-73. That put them in third place, 9 games behind Chicago.

1933 SUNDAY, MAY 14TH, AT EBBETS FIELD

Pinch Grand Slam by Hack Wilson

Drive in 9th Wins Game for Dodgers, 8-6
Philly Hurler Liska Throws Only One Pitch

HACK WILSON, THE EX-SLUGGING CHAMPion of the Cubs turned Brooklyn bench-warmer, got a rare opportunity to win a game for the Dodgers today. And he made the most of it by crashing a pinch-hit grand slam home run in the bottom of the ninth inning to turn a two-run deficit into an 8-6 Brooklyn victory.

Just three years ago, in 1930, Wilson had set league records with 56 home runs and 190 runs-batted-in. But he fell from favor with Chicago's new manager, Rogers Hornsby, in 1931 and stopped slugging. Before the 1932 season, he was acquired by the Dodgers. Playing at half of his old salary of $33,000, he had a fine year with Brooklyn, hitting 23 homers and batting in 123 runs.

Today's Results

BROOKLYN 8-Philadelphia 6
New York 5-Pittsburgh 1
Cincinnati 5-Chicago 3 (1st game)
Cincinnati 1-Chicago 0 (2nd game)
St. Louis 4-Boston 0 (1st game)
Boston 8-St. Louis 4 (2nd game)

Standings	W-L	Pct.	GB
New York	15- 8	.652	—
Pittsburgh	15- 8	.652	—
Cincinnati	13-11	.542	2½
St. Louis	14-12	.538	2½
BROOKLYN	10-11	.476	4
Boston	12-16	.429	5½
Chicago	11-15	.423	5½
Philadelphia	8-17	.320	8

But this year, he lost his starting job in the outfield to Johnny Frederick and was relegated to pinch-hitting duty by manager Max Carey. Hack entered today's game with a .182 average and just 1 RBI on the season. But this afternoon, Carey was banished to the clubhouse, and Wilson came off the bench to blast a four-run four-bagger and bring back a little of his lost glory.

Before the Dodgers won out in the ninth, the lead had seesawed from Brooklyn to Philadelphia to Brooklyn and back again. But the game was still rather desultory, owing partly to the nagging drizzle. By the time the bottom of the ninth rolled around, the weather had become downright miserable. Luckily, Wilson's homer sent the remaining fans home before they got any wetter.

Aided by a wild throw by Philly pitcher Frank Pearce, Brooklyn got the lead with two runs in the first inning.

Walter "Boom-Boom" Beck was the Dodgers' starting pitcher, and he did okay until the third inning. Then he blew his cork at the umpire, lost his concentration, and was knocked out of the box by three singles, a hit batsman, and a walk, which yielded the Phillies three runs.

Joe Stripp hit a tremendous line drive into the lower left field stands in the bottom of the third for a home run to tie the game. And Brooklyn got another run in the sixth to go ahead, 4-3.

Philadelphia broke through against reliever Joe Shaute in the seventh and tied the game, 4-4.

Shaute twisted his ankle running the bases in the seventh, so Ray Benge was sent out to pitch in the top of the eighth. Four hits and some poor Dodger fielding gave the Phillies two runs and a 6-4 lead.

The Dodgers left the bases loaded in the eighth while failing to score. Carey was so upset that he was thrown out of the game for arguing a called third strike. Coach Casey Stengel assumed command for the final inning.

It was still 6-4 in favor of the visitors when the Dodgers came to bat in the bottom of the ninth. It was raining hard by now, and the game might have been called if this had not been the final inning. Most of the 12,000 fans had already headed for home or at least for cover under the overhangs around the park.

Danny Taylor started Brooklyn's winning rally with a single. Pitcher Phil Collins issued a base on balls to Lefty O'Doul. With the tying runs on base, Frederick stepped to the plate, and Wilson stood up in the dugout and picked out a bat. Collins was having trouble gripping the wet ball, and he walked Frederick to load the bases with none out.

This was the perfect spot to utilize Wilson's long-ball power. Philadelphia manager Burt Shotton was aware of that, of course, and he yanked Collins out of the game in favor of righthanded submarineballer Ad Liska, who was presumably harder to hit a home run off of. With Wilson swinging his clubs in the on-deck circle, Liska tried to get warmed up on the muddy mound. Finally, he was ready, and Hack stepped into the box. Figuring that Liska would be thinking that he would go to bat looking at a couple of balls trying for a walk, Hack decided to be ready to jump on the first pitch. Sure enough, Liska's first and only serve was right over the middle of the plate. Wilson stepped into it with all the force of his 5'6", 200-pound frame and connected solidly. The ball sailed high and deep to right field and landed in the screen atop of the fence for a grand slam home run and an 8-6 Brooklyn victory.

The Dodgers left town immediately after the game to start a road trip. As the train sped west, the happy-go-lucky Wilson was in an especially gregarious mood. He regaled his teammates and the press with tales of his past exploits on the diamond and off. Gee, it sure was nice to be in the limelight again, even if only for a brief while.

Philadelphia	ab	r	h	bi	o	a	e
C. Fullis, cf	4	1	1	0	6	0	0
D. Bartell, ss	4	1	1	1	0	2	0
C. Klein, rf	4	0	1	1	0	0	0
V. Davis, c	5	0	1	2	4	0	0
D. Hurst, 1b	4	1	2	0	7	0	0
A. Cohen, lf	4	1	1	0	4	0	0
P. Whitney, 3b	4	0	1	1	0	0	1
N. Finn, 2b	4	1	2	1	2	2	0
F. Pearce, p	2	1	1	0	1	2	0
A. Todd, ph7	1	0	0	0	-	-	-
R. Hansen, p7	0	0	0	0	0	0	1
P. Collins, p7	1	0	0	0	0	1	0
A. Liska, p9	0	0	0	0	0	0	0
	37	6	11	6	24	7	2

Brooklyn	ab	r	h	bi	o	a	e
J. Stripp, 3b	4	2	2	1	0	5	0
D. Taylor, cf	5	2	2	0	1	0	0
L. O'Doul, lf	2	1	0	1	2	0	1
J. Frederick, rf	4	1	0	1	2	0	0
J. Flowers, ss	3	1	0	0	3	1	0
H. Wilson, ph9	1	1	1	4	-	-	-
T. Cuccinello, 2b	4	0	2	0	1	3	0
D. Bissonette, 1b	4	0	1	1	13	0	0
C. Sukeforth, c	3	0	1	0	4	0	0
C. Outen, c7	1	0	0	0	1	0	0
W. Beck, p	1	0	0	0	0	0	0
J. Shaute, p3	2	0	1	0	0	2	0
J. Jordan, pr7	0	0	0	0	-	-	-
R. Benge, p8	0	0	0	0	0	0	0
J. Judge, ph8	0	0	0	0	-	-	-
O. Carroll, pr8	0	0	0	0	-	-	-
H. Thurston, p9	0	0	0	0	0	0	0
	34	8	10	8	27	11	1

Philadelphia	003	000	120	=	6
Brooklyn	201	001	004	=	8

none out when winning run scored

	ip	h	r-er	bb	so
Pearce	6	6	4-3	2	1
Hansen	*0	1	0-0	0	0
Collins (L 0-3)	†2	2	3-3	4	2
Liska	‡0	1	1-1	0	0
Beck	2⅓	4	3-3	2	0
Shaute	4⅔	3	1-1	0	1
Benge	1	4	2-2	0	1
Thurston (W 1-1)	1	0	0-0	0	1

Umpires: C. Pfirman & H. McCormick

Game-Winning RBI: Wilson
LOB: Philadelphia 7, Brooklyn 9
BE: Philadelphia 0, Brooklyn 2
DP: Stripp-Cuccinello-Bissonette (Whitney)
HR: Stripp, Wilson
SH: Stripp
SB: Bissonette

HBP: by Beck (Fullis)
*faced two batters in seventh
†faced three batters in ninth
‡faced one batter in ninth
Time—2:45
Attendance—12,000

Glorious moments were few and far between for Wilson and the Dodgers in 1933. Hack fell to just 9 home runs and 54 runs-batted-in in 1933.

The team hovered near the .500 mark through June. But then it nose-dived in the second half and finished with a 65-88 record. That left Brooklyn in sixth place, 26½ games behind the pennant winners. The poor showing cost manager Carey his job.

1934 SUNDAY, SEPTEMBER 30TH, AT THE POLO GROUNDS, NEW YORK

Brooklyn *IS* Still in the League!

Dodgers Eliminate Giants from Race with 8-5 Win
Brooklyn Fans Boo Terry and Giants

Today's Results			
BROOKLYN 8-New York 5 (10 innings)			
St. Louis 9-Cincinnati 0			
Chicago 8-Pittsburgh 2 (1st game)			
Chicago 7-Pittsburgh 5 (2nd game)			
Boston 4-Philadelphia 3 (10 inn.)(1st game)			
Boston 5-Philadelphia 4 (7 inn.)(2nd game)			
Standings	**W-L**	**Pct.**	**GB**
St. Louis	95-58	.621	—
New York	93-60	.608	2
Chicago	86-65	.570	8
Boston	78-73	.517	16
Pittsburgh	74-76	.493	19½
BROOKLYN	71-81	.467	23½
Philadelphia	56-93	.376	37
Cincinnati	52-99	.344	42

YES MR. TERRY, BROOKLYN *IS* STILL IN the league. The Dodgers may not have given their fans much to cheer about most of the summer. But they made up for it in style in the last two days of the season by knocking New York out fo the pennant race. It was sweet revenge against Bill Terry and his Giants.

Last winter, Terry had asked a sportswriter offhandedly, "Is Brooklyn still in the league?" The remark, made innocently enough, had rankled the Dodger organization and a boroughful of fans all season. While the Giants spent most of the summer in first place, the Dodgers floundered in sixth, and the Flatbush fans seethed.

Then, suddenly and unexpectedly, the Giants lost their big lead and fell into a tie with the Cardinals for first place with just two games left to play. And as fate would have it, those two games were against Casey Stengel's Dodgers.

Like wolves clustering for the kill, thousands of Dodger fans descended upon the Polo Grounds for Saturday's game, outscreaming if not outnumbering the home team's partisans.

With pitcher Van Lingle Mungo doing most of the damage, Stengel's warriors dealt Terry's men the body blow, winning 5-1. St. Louis won 6-1, and the Giants were out of first place for the first time since June 5th. Mungo not only limited New York to five hits and one run, he also scored the first Brooklyn run and drove in the second one. The defeat meant that the Giants' only hope was to win the pennant in a playoff.

Today the Brooklyn fans were primed for the final kill. Like howling hyenas ripping at a dying corpse, they mobbed the subways and turned the Giants' home park into a sea of vengeance and spite. The crowd of 44,055 was over twice as large as Saturday's, and most of the people seemed to have come from Brooklyn to glory in the demise of Terry and his Giants.

When the Dodgers rallied to win the game in extra innings, 8-5, the mob reacted as if Brooklyn had won the pennant. Stengel was encircled by the throng, and his uniform was almost torn off in admiration. And catcher Al Lopez was carried halfway to the clubhouse on the shoulders of some fans. And this was a sixth-place team that had just finished its last game of the season playing on the road!

Having played his ace (Mungo) on Saturday, Stengel led with his best remaining pitcher today, Ray Benge. But the Giants trumped him with a four-run outburst in the first inning.

Emil "Dutch" Leonard came in in relief and did a fine job. The young knuckleballer quickly retired the side in the first and held New York to two hits over the next six innings. One of those hits, however, was a home run by Freddie Fitzsimmons, the Giants' pitcher.

Brooklyn got one run in the second inning on a triple by Tony Cuccinello and a single by Danny Taylor.

While the Dodgers were rallying for thir second run in the fourth inning, a "2" was posted on the scoreboard for St. Louis in the first inning there. With the great Dizzy Dean pitching against the last-place Reds, New York's pennant chances were diminished substantially.

A wild throw by shortstop Blondy Ryan helped the Brooklyns to another tally in the sixth, making the score 5-3.

By the time the Dodgers rallied to tie the game in the eighth, St. Louis was leading 5-0. A single by Ralph "Buzz" Boyle and a double by Len Koenecke plated one run and knocked Fitzsimmons out of the game. Hal Schumacher relieved, and he allowed the tying run to score on a two-base wild pitch.

New York put two men on base in the bottom of the eighth, but Tom Zachary came on and ended the threat by getting pinch-hitter Harry Danning to bounce into a double play. Johnny Babich pitched a 1-2-3 ninth for the Dodgers.

Brooklyn won the game in the tenth. A single to right by Sam Leslie and a double past third base by Cuccinello put runners on second and third with none out. In desperation, player-manager Terry brought in Carl Hubbell to pitch. King Carl fanned Babich and intentionally walked Joe Stripp to load the bases. Al Lopez sent a possible double-play ball to Ryan, but the shortstop kicked it, and Brooklyn took the lead. A scoring fly by Glenn Chapman and a one-run single by Boyle made the count 8-5.

The Brooklyn partisans got one last chance to rub it in in the tenth. With one man already out, Bill Terry came to bat. He was greeted with a merciless chorus of boos and catcalls. And he grounded out weakly. After Mel Ott bounced out, it was all over for New York.

In the Giant clubhouse, Terry was his usual grim self. But next door in the visitors' dressing room, Stengel was even bubblier than usual. He could muster little but sarcastic sympathy for the Giants, while he praised his players and the Brooklyn fans. Despite a sixth-place finish, this would be a pleasant winter for the Flatbush Faithful.

Brooklyn	ab	r	h	bi	o	a	e
R. Boyle, rf	6	2	3	1	4	0	0
L. Frey, ss	5	0	1	1	3	5	1
L. Koenecke, cf	5	1	2	1	3	0	0
S. Leslie, 1b	5	1	2	1	12	2	0
J. McCarthy, pr10-1b	0	1	0	0	2	0	0
T. Cuccinello, 2b	4	2	3	0	1	4	0
D. Taylor, lf	3	0	1	1	0	0	0
J. Babich, p9	1	0	0	0	0	2	0
J. Stripp, 3b	4	1	0	0	0	2	0
A. Lopez, c	5	0	0	0	4	0	0
R. Benge, p	0	0	0	0	0	0	0
D. Leonard, p1	3	0	0	0	1	2	0
T. Zachary, p8	0	0	0	0	0	0	0
G. Chapman, pr9-lf	1	0	0	1	0	0	0
	42	8	12	6	30	17	1

New York	ab	r	h	bi	o	a	e
J. Moore, lf	5	1	1	0	1	0	0
H. Critz, 2b	5	1	1	0	1	5	0
B. Terry, 1b	4	0	1	1	11	1	0
M. Ott, rf	5	1	0	0	0	0	0
T. Jackson, 3b	4	0	0	0	0	3	0
G. Watkins, cf	3	1	1	0	4	0	0
G. Mancuso, c	2	0	1	1	4	0	0
L. O'Doul, ph8	0	0	0	0	-	-	-
H. Danning, ph8-c	1	0	0	0	3	0	0
B. Ryan, ss	4	0	1	2	5	4	2
F. Fitzsimmons, p	3	1	1	1	1	2	0
H. Schumacher, p8	1	0	0	0	0	2	0
C. Hubbell, p10	0	0	0	0	0	0	0
	37	5	7	5	30	17	2

Brooklyn	010	101	020	3	=	8
New York	400	100	000	0	=	5

	ip	h	r-er	bb	so
Benge	⅔	4	4-4	2	1
Leonard	6⅔	3	1-1	1	1
Zachary	⅔	0	0-0	0	0
Babich (W 7-11)	2	0	0-0	0	1
Fitzsimmons	7⅓	9	5-4	0	4
Schumacher (L 23-10)	*1⅔	2	2-1	4	1
Hubbell	1	1	1-0	1	2

*faced two batters in tenth

WP: Fitzsimmons, Schumacher

Game-Winning run scored on error

LOB: Brooklyn 9, New York 5

BE: Brooklyn 1, New York 1

DP: Critz-Ryan-Terry (Cuccinello)
Frey-Cuccinello-Leslie (Danning)

2B: Moore, Koenecke 2, Cuccinello

3B: Cuccinello

HR: Fitzsimmons

SB: Boyle

Time—2:37

Attendance—44,055

Umpires: D. Stark, G. Magerkurth, & C. Pfirman

1935 MONDAY, JULY 22ND, AT WRIGLEY FIELD, CHICAGO

Dodgers Win a Wild One 14-13

Frey's Single in 11th Finally Brings Home Winning Run
Phelps and Mungo Suffer Finger Injuries

Today's Results			
BROOKLYN 14-Chicago 13 (11 inn.)			
St. Louis 8-New York 5			
Pittsburgh 5-Philadelphia 4			
Boston 4-Cincinnati 2			
Standings	**W-L**	**Pct.**	**GB**
New York	53-29	.646	—
St. Louis	53-30	.639	½
Chicago	51-35	.593	4
Pittsburgh	47-41	.534	9
BROOKLYN	39-44	.470	14½
Cincinnati	39-48	.448	16½
Philadelphia	36-48	.429	18
Boston	22-65	.253	33½

ALTHOUGH IT MAY HAVE COST MORE than it was worth, the Brooklyn Dodgers beat the Chicago Cubs in an eleven-inning slugfest today, 14-13. The triumph was tempered by a broken thumb suffered by catcher Ernest "Babe" Phelps. His replacement, Al Lopez, suffered a finger injury yesterday but played the last part of today's game because there were no other catchers. Despite a painfully swollen finger, Lopez even hit a home run. Pitcher Van Lingle Mungo, who got the win with 3⅓ innings of relief pitching, also aggrevated an injured finger and would need rest and possibly surgery. And manager Casey Stengel used four pitchers in the game, leaving his staff rather depleted for the two doubleheaders scheduled for the next two days.

The Cubs used five pitchers, so their pitching was also set back for the upcoming twinbills. In all, 32 players saw action in today's game, and 19 of them got base hits. A grand total of 42 safe blows were struck, including six for the circuit. The two teams split the home runs evenly, although Chicago had the two most dramatic. Both in the bottom of the ninth and in the bottom of the tenth, the Cubs tied the game with four-baggers.

The Dodgers finally won out when Ralph "Buzz" Boyle, Len Koenecke, and Linus "Lonny" Frey put singles together in the eleventh inning, and the Cubs failed to answer the run.

The visitors scored a run in the first inning on two walks and a two-out single by Phelps.

The home team took the lead in the second on a two-run homer by Chuck Klein. The drive cleared the exit gate in right field and landed on the street, the first of four balls that bombarded the pedestrians this afternoon.

Chicago's lead was gone before the Cubs could retire a batter in the top of the third. Three singles and a double routed starting pitcher Fabian Kowalik and put Brooklyn ahead, 4-2. Young Hugh Casey relieved, and his first pitch was driven off the fence in center field by Sam Leslie for a triple and another run. The next pitch was lofted onto the street by Phelps, upping the score to 7-2.

A double by Billy Herman knocked in two runs in the Chicago third.

In the Cub fourth, pinch-hitter Gabby Hartnett knocked one man in and one man out. Batting with men on second and third and one down, he foul-tipped one that broke Phelps's thumb, forcing the hard-hitting catcher out of the game. Hartnett then bounced out to drive a run home.

The Dodgers' Danny Taylor hit a two-run homer off pitcher Tex Carleton in the fifth.

A one-base hit by Herman and a two-bagger by Ken O'Dea earned Chicago a run in the bottom.

A hit by Leslie and two misplayed bunts gave Brooklyn a run and a 10-6 lead in the sixth.

After having used a pinch-runner for his starting pitcher, George Earnshaw, Stengel sent Ray Benge to the mound in the seventh. He was pounded for four hits and three runs before being replaced by Emil "Dutch" Leonard.

Three singles, a key fumble, and a double steal added up to two runs in the Dodger half of the eighth.

Leonard was knocked around in the Cub half for three singles, two long flies, and a walk. With two runs in and the tying run on third, Stengel decided to use Mungo. Van had been bothered by an injured knuckle on the middle finger of his right hand since early in the month, but he had been announced as one of the starters in tomorrow's doubleheader. He got out of the jam left by Leonard by getting Stan Hack on a ground ball.

Chicago trailed 12-11 with two out and a 2-and-2 count on Augie Galan in the bottom of the ninth. One strike away from victory, Mungo got a pitch too high, and Galan knocked it into the right field seats to tie the game.

In the top of the tenth, Lopez hit a drive over the left field bleachers and onto Waveland Avenue to put Brooklyn ahead, 13-12.

But Phil Cavaretta quickly tied the game by sending the first pitch of the bottom of the inning onto Sheffield Avenue beyond the right field wall.

Boyle singled with one gone in the top of the eleventh and advanced to second on Koenecke's two-out safety. Frey, who had struck out three times in a row, then stroked a hit to left, and Boyle scored.

A walk and a single put Cubs on first and third with one out in the bottom of the eleventh. But Mungo got Galan on a short fly to left, and Herman hit into a game-ending force out.

It had been quite a struggle, and the Dodgers had won it, 14-13. Now they had to worry about who was left to pitch and catch in their upcoming games.

Brooklyn	ab	r	h	bi	o	a	e
L. Koenecke, cf	7	1	3	0	4	0	0
L. Frey, ss	6	2	3	2	5	2	0
J. Bucher, 3b	5	2	2	1	1	2	0
J. Stripp, 3b9	2	0	0	0	0	1	0
S. Leslie, 1b	5	1	3	1	13	4	0
B. Phelps, c	2	1	2	3	2	1	0
A. Lopez, c4	3	2	2	2	2	1	0
T. Cuccinello, 2b	2	0	0	0	0	3	1
J. Jordan, 2b4	3	2	1	0	4	8	0
D. Taylor, lf	5	1	2	4	1	0	0
R. Boyle, rf	4	1	2	0	0	0	0
G. Earnshaw, p	4	1	2	0	0	0	0
L. Munns, pr7	0	0	0	0	-	-	-
R. Benge, p7	0	0	0	0	0	0	0
D. Leonard, p7	0	0	0	0	0	0	0
V. Mungo, p8	2	0	0	0	1	0	1
	50	14	22	13	33	22	2

Chicago	ab	r	h	bi	o	a	e
A. Galan, lf	7	3	2	1	3	1	0
B. Herman, 2b	7	2	4	2	5	6	0
P. Cavaretta, 1b	6	3	2	1	9	1	1
K. O'Dea, c	4	1	1	1	7	1	0
F. Demaree, cf	6	1	3	3	1	1	0
C. Klein, rf	6	2	4	3	3	0	0
S. Hack, 3b	4	0	2	1	2	3	0
B. Jurges, ss	4	0	0	0	3	2	1
F. Kowalik, p	0	0	0	0	0	0	1
H. Casey, p3	1	1	1	0	0	1	0
G. Hartnett, ph4	1	0	0	1	-	-	-
T. Carleton, p5	2	0	0	0	0	2	0
T. Stainback, ph9	1	0	0	0	-	-	-
L. French, p10	0	0	0	0	0	0	0
C. Root, p11	0	0	0	0	0	0	0
W. Stephenson, ph11	1	0	1	0	-	-	-
	50	13	20	13	33	18	3

Brooklyn	106	021	020	11	=	14
Chicago	022	110	321	10	=	13

	ip	h	r-er	bb	so
Earnshaw	6	9	6-5	1	3
Benge	⅓	4	3-3	1	0
Leonard	1⅓	3	2-2	1	0
Mungo (W 12-7)	3⅓	4	2-2	1	0
Kowalik	*2	5	5-5	2	0
Casey	2	4	2-2	1	1
Carleton	5	8	5-4	2	5
French (L 8-6)	1⅔	5	2-2	0	0
Root	⅓	0	0-0	0	0

*faced four batters in third

WP: Kowalik

Game-Winning RBI: Frey
LOB: Brooklyn 10, Chicago 10
BE: Brooklyn 2, Chicago 2
DP: Bucher-Cuccinello-Leslie (Jurges)
Cavaretta-O'Dea
Frey-Jordan-Leslie (Stainback)
2B: Demaree, Frey 2, Herman, O'Dea
HR: Klein, Phelps, Taylor, Galan, Lopez, Cavaretta
SH: Jurges 2, Lopez, Jordan
2B: Lopez, Jordan
CS: Boyle, Klein
Time—3:24 Attendance—2,500
Umpires: Z. Sears, B. Reardon & E. Quigley

In the catching emergency, the Dodgers called old Zack Taylor away from his minor league managing job to fill in behind the plate.

The Brooklyn pitching got pounded for 30 runs in the next two days, and the Dodgers lost back-to-back doubleheaders.

With Mungo's effectiveness limited for much of the rest of the season, the Dodgers wound up in fifth with a 70-83 record.

1936 THURSDAY, APRIL 16TH, AT THE POLO GROUNDS, NEW YORK

"Once a Dodger, Always a Dodger"

Newcomer Lindstrom Drops a Fly, and Brooklyn Loses
Collision in 9th Allows Giants to Win, 7-6

Today's Results			
New York 7-BROOKLYN 6			
Philadelphia 7-Boston 5			
Chicago 5-St. Louis 3			
Cincinnati 7-Pittsburgh 4			
Standings	**W-L**	**Pct.**	**GB**
New York	3-0	1.000	—
Philadelphia	2-1	.667	1
Pittsburgh	2-1	.667	1
Chicago	2-1	.667	1
Cincinnati	1-2	.333	2
St. Louis	1-2	.333	2
Boston	1-2	.333	2
BROOKLYN	0-3	.000	3

SOME YEARS BACK, WHEN FREDDY LINDstrom was young and talented and a member of the powerful New York Giants, a newspaper reporter joined the New York traveling party after being switched from covering the Dodgers. When this reporter made a foolish mistake in a poker game to lose a hand, Lindstrom derided him with the immortal words, "Once a Dodger, always a Dodger."

Some years and uncounted fly balls later, Lindstrom found himself in a Dodger uniform. And sure enough, he was involved in feats of slapstick truly worthy of the Brooklyn team's hallowed heritage. Although only 30 years old, he had already played in twelve National League seasons when he found himself released by the Chicago Cubs last winter. In January, he unwittingly signed to play with Brooklyn. Well, it took only until the third game of the season for being a Dodger to catch up with Lindstrom. Freddy collided with the shortstop under a pop fly, and what should have been the final out of the game was transformed into a two-out, two-run double that gave the hated New York Giants a 7-6 victory over Brooklyn.

The hapless Dodgers, therefore, were swept in the season-opening, three-game series in New York. Poor Van Lingle Mungo, who already knew all about being a Dodger, was the losing pitcher in two of those three games. And he had pitched well both times. Yesterday he yielded one unearned run in the first inning and got ejected from the game in the second. Since the Dodgers never caught up with the Giants, Mungo was credited with the loss. Today, Van would have had 4⅓ innings of shutout relief if the fatal collision hadn't caused the last ball to be dropped.

It already looked like it would be a long and painful season for manager Casey Stengel and his Dodgers. On opening day, they couldn't hold a 5-2 lead and lost 8-5. Yesterday, they did not even get a base runner until the sixth inning. They lost, 5-3, but at least they got the best of the fight that enlivened the game. Big Van Mungo and little Dick Bartell were the principals in the scuffle. Mungo threw a pitch at Bartell's head, and Dick later bunted to the first baseman. Mungo covered first, deftly avoided Bartell's spikes, and tripped the runner. Then he proceeded to land a couple of punches on the little guy before the fight was broken up. Both men were ejected from the game.

Today, Mungo came to the park to find that he had been fined $25. Then he wound up pitching some great ball only to get another loss. With the season only three days old, Van owned an 0-2 record and was out a nice piece of change to boot. Such could be the joys of pitching for the Dodgers.

For the Giants, righthanded Dick Coffman got his second win of the season with seven innings of relief work.

Knuckleballer Freddie Fitzsimmons started for New York and was bashed for four runs on five hits and a walk in the first inning.

Dodger starter Ed Brandt gave up two runs in the second on three hits and a walk.

After the Dodgers upped their lead to 5-2 with a tally in the top of the fifth, the Giants scored three in the bottom to tie the game. Lefthander Brandt was routed, and Stengel called Mungo into the game. The fastballing righthander got the final out with two men on base. Then he proceeded to mow the Giants down in order in the next three innings.

Brooklyn regained the lead with a gift run in the seventh, thanks to an error by New York first baseman Sam Leslie.

So the Dodgers were ahead 6-5 going into the bottom of the ninth. Mungo quickly got the first two batters out and thought he had a third strike on the third one, Burgess Whitehead. After an argument with the umpire, Mungo walked Whitehead. Mel Ott cracked a crisp hit to center, and Whitehead sprinted to third.

Against Hank Leiber, Mungo again got to within one strike of victory. Trying to fight off the potential third strike, Leiber lifted a little pop fly in back of shortstop. With two out, Whitehead and Ott took off from their bases at top speed. Shortstop Jimmy Jordan turned his back to the infield and raced back, looking over his shoulder at the ball the whole time. Left fielder Lindstrom came charging in at full speed with his eyes also glued to the ball. The veteran outfielder got his glove on it about waist high. Half a step later, Jordan crashed into him. The ball was jarred loose and fell to the ground. Lindstrom picked himself up and scrambled after it. But his throw home was too late to keep Ott from sliding across the plate with the winning run for the Giants.

In the clubhouse afterwards, Lindstrom swore that that sort of thing had never happened to him before. But now he was a Dodger, and anything was possible. And, as he had said himself long ago, "Once a Dodger, always a Dodger."

Brooklyn	ab	r	h	bi	o	a	e
O. Eckhardt, rf	5	1	1	0	0	0	0
F. Bordagaray, rf9	0	0	0	0	0	0	0
J. Cooney, cf	4	1	2	0	2	0	0
L. Frey, 2b	3	1	1	0	2	4	0
F. Lindstrom, lf	5	1	3	1	1	0	0
J. Bucher, 3b	5	2	1	2	0	2	0
B. Hassett, 1b	4	0	2	0	16	0	0
J. Jordan, ss	4	0	2	2	1	5	0
R. Berres, c	4	0	1	1	4	0	0
E. Brandt, p	3	0	0	0	0	1	0
V. Mungo, p5	1	0	0	0	0	0	0
	38	6	13	6	26	12	0

New York	ab	r	h	bi	o	a	e
J. Moore, lf	5	0	0	0	2	0	0
B. Whitehead, 2b	4	2	1	0	4	7	0
M. Ott, rf	5	1	1	0	0	0	0
H. Leiber, cf	5	1	3	3	2	1	0
S. Leslie, 1b	4	2	2	1	13	1	1
T. Jackson, 3b	3	1	1	0	2	1	0
G. Mancuso, c	3	0	1	1	2	3	0
M. Koenig, ss	4	0	2	2	1	3	0
F. Fitzsimmons, p	0	0	0	0	0	0	0
A. Smith, p1	0	0	0	0	0	0	0
C. English, ph2	1	0	0	0	-	-	-
D. Coffman, p3	2	0	0	0	1	3	0
B. Terry, ph9	1	0	0	0	-	-	-
	37	7	11	7	27	19	1

Brooklyn	400	010	100	=	6
New York	020	030	002	=	7

two out when winning run scored

	ip	h	r-er	bb	so
Brandt	4⅔	9	5-5	2	2
Mungo (L 0-2)	4	2	2-2	1	2
Fitzsimmons	⅓	5	4-4	1	0
Smith	1⅔	2	0-0	0	1
Coffman (W 2-0)	7	6	2-1	1	3

WP: Brandt

Game-Winning RBI: Leiber
LOB: Brooklyn 8, New York 7
BE: Brooklyn 1
DP: Koenig-Whitehead-Leslie (Berres)
Leiber-Whitehead
2B: Leiber 2
SH: Frey
Time—2:23
Attendance—6,000
Umpires: L. Ballanfant, B. Reardon, & G. Barr

The thought of being a Dodger was obviously too much for Lindstrom, and he retired on May 18th.

Mungo pitched some fine ball only to wind up with an 18-19 record for the year.

The Dodgers flirted with the cellar much of the year and were last as late as August 6th. They finished a distant seventh with a 67-87 record, and Stengel was fired as manager.

1937 TUESDAY, AUGUST 31ST, AT EBBETS FIELD

Dodgers Blow the Game, Grimes Blows a Fuse

Manager Storms Out of Dugout to Yank Hassett after Error
Bad Base Running, Worse Fielding

Today's Results			
Chicago 4-BROOKLYN 2			
St. Louis 8-New York 1			
Philadelphia 3-Pittsburgh 0			
Boston 7-Cincinnati 2			

Standings	W-L	Pct.	GB
Chicago	73-47	.608	—
New York	71-47	.602	1
St. Louis	65-54	.538	7½
Pittsburgh	62-58	.517	11
Boston	58-62	.483	15
Philadelphia	51-68	.429	23½
BROOKLYN	48-69	.410	23½
Cincinnati	46-69	.400	24½

IT FINALLY GOT TO POOR OLD BURLEIGH Grimes today. The high-strung manager of the Brooklyn Dodgers saw his fumbling ballplayers giving a game away to the Chicago Cubs. The Bums made three errors, and they all contributed directly to Chicago runs. And the other run the Cubs scored came after an infield boot that was officially ruled a hit.

After Brooklyn first baseman Buddy Hassett had the cheek to talk back to his manager after making a critical error in the eighth inning, Grimes could stand it no longer. The tromped onto the field, upbraided Hassett in front of the crowd, and ordered him out of the game. Hassett didn't take kindly to this, and neither did the Brooklyn fans. And when the Cubs scored the winning runs moments later, no one was happy.

As if the fielding was not bad enough, Grimes's Kelly-green-clad warriors did some bad base running. Chicago catcher Gabby Hartnett caught three runners stealing, two of them with men on first and third and less than two out.

All this ruined a credible pitching performance by the Dodgers' Fred Frankhouse. The righthander allowed nine hits and two walks but pitched well in the pinch. Unfortunately, his infielders did their worst work with men on base.

Chicago got the first run in the third inning. Augie Galan worked a walk with two out. He stole second, and when catcher Babe Phelps's throw was wide and wild, he got up and scooted to third. Billy Herman drove him in with a single to right.

Brooklyn scored two tainted runs in the bottom half to grab the lead. Eddie Wilson led of by drawing a base on balls. Frankhouse bunted and got a single when no one covered first base. Johnny Cooney sacrificed the runners to second and third. With shortstop Billy Jurges slipping in behind Frankhouse for a pickoff throw, the pitcher pitched instead. Jim Bucher grounded a hit through the big hole, and both runners scored.

The Dodgers got men to first and third in the fourth with one out. But Woody English was caught stealing second while Blimp Phelps remained glued to third. Not only was the rally ruined, English's leg was injured, and he had to leave the game.

Chicago tied the score in the sixth, aided by a "drop kick" by Bucher. Frank Demaree led off with a grounder up the middle. Second baseman Bucher ranged over to his right and caught up with the ball, only to kick it into left field. By the time it was run down, Demaree was on second with a "double." He took third on a single by Hartnett and scored as Jurges was grounding into a double play.

In the seventh, poor running again squelched a Brooklyn rally. Red Brown led off with a single. Wilson bunted, pitcher Tex Carleton threw late to second, and shortstop Jurges confounded things further by throwing wildly past first, allowing Brown to take third. With the double steal in the works, Hartnett faked a throw to second and picked Brown off third. Frankhouse then fanned and Cooney bounced out.

The irascible Grimes was in no mood for further mistakes, but his players gave him some in the top of the eighth. Galan led off with a double off the screen in right. Herman bunted toward first base. Hassett came charging in and tried to scoop the ball up quickly to make a throw to third. But he fumbled the ball, and all hands were safe. Grimes yelled out at his fielder to "get two hands on the ball." Hassett took offense and told his manager that if he thought he could do better, he should come out and try. This was the kind of challange that could set "Old Boiley" to steaming. He rushed out of the dugout spewing abuse at his first baseman. He also motioned for center fielder Cooney to come in and take over for Hassett at first base. After a short but sharp exchange, Hassett stormed to the dugout.

There followed an embarrassing delay while the Dodgers tried to find a first baseman's mitt for Cooney. Chicago manager Charlie Grimm offered his, but Hassett certainly did not offer his. One was finally procured, and the game got under way again with men on first and third and none out.

Demaree drove Galan home with a long fly to left, putting the Cubs ahead. After another fly out, Jurges singled Herman to third. Phil Cavaretta grounded to short, where Brown booted the chance, allowing Herman to score.

With the score 4-2 against them, the Dodgers threatened in each of the last two innings but could not score. So the game was lost.

In the clubhouse afterwards, Grimes and Hassett refused to talk to the press about their set-to. But Burleigh was not reticent about giving his players a little piece of his mind about their performance on the field. They deserved some of it, and Grimes's temper needed some outlet. Luckily for all, the season only had another month left.

Chicago	ab	r	h	bi	o	a	e
S. Hack, 3b	5	0	1	0	0	4	0
A. Galan, lf	3	2	2	0	1	0	0
B. Herman, 2b	4	1	2	1	6	3	0
F. Demaree, rf	4	1	2	1	0	0	0
G. Hartnett, c	4	0	1	0	6	3	0
B. Jurges, ss	4	0	1	0	2	5	1
P. Cavaretta, 1b	4	0	0	0	11	1	0
J. Marty, cf	4	0	0	0	1	0	0
T. Carleton, p	4	0	0	0	0	0	0
	36	4	9	2	27	16	1

Brooklyn	ab	r	h	bi	o	a	e
J. Cooney, cf-1b8	4	0	0	0	4	0	0
J. Bucher, 2b	4	0	2	2	0	3	0
B. Hassett, 1b	3	0	0	0	8	1	1
T. Winsett, lf8	1	0	0	0	2	0	0
C. Lavagetto, 3b	3	0	0	0	1	1	0
B. Phelps, c	4	0	2	0	2	0	1
G. Brack, lf-cf8	4	0	1	0	4	0	0
W. English, ss	2	0	1	0	1	1	0
R. Brown, ss5	2	0	1	0	1	1	1
E. Wilson, rf	0	1	0	0	3	0	0
F. Frankhouse, p	3	1	1	0	1	4	0
J. Stripp, ph9	1	0	0	0	-	-	-
	31	2	8	2	27	11	3

Chicago	001 001 020	=	4
Brooklyn	002 000 000	=	2

	ip	h	r-er	bb	so
Carleton (W 12-5)	9	8	2-2	4	5
Frankhouse (L 9-8)	9	9	4-2	2	1

Time—1:59 Attendance—2,275
Umpires: L. Goetz, B. Reardon, & B. Pinelli

Game-Winning RBI: Demaree
LOB: Chicago 8, Brooklyn 8
BE: Chicago 2, Brooklyn 0
DP: Brown-Hassett (Jurges)
2B: Phelps, Demaree, Galan
3B: Galan
SH: Cooney, Wilson, Herman
SB: Galan
CS: Brack, English, Brown

Hassett was back in the lineup the next day. Brooklyn won 13 of its next 19 games. Then the Dodgers lost 16 of their final 17, including 14 in a row. Somehow they managed to finish in sixth place. Their final record was 62-91.

Chapter IX Larry and Leo

1938 June 15th
No-Hitter in First Brooklyn Night Game

1939 June 1st
Triple Play & Steal of Home Win for Dodgers

1940 April 30
Flock's Record 9-0 After No-Hitter

1941 September 25th
Bums Clinch Pennant

1941 World Series—Game#4
Mickey Owen Misses the Third Strike

1942 August 4th
Wartime Curfew Robs Dodgers of a Win

BETWEEN THE END OF THE 1937 SEASON AND THE START OF THE 1938 CAMPAIGN, TWO men joined the Brooklyn club who were destined to lead it out of the wilderness. The first to arrive was Leo Ernest Durocher, a slick-fielding shortstop for whom Brooklyn traded four players on October 4, 1937. Leo did some shortstopping for the Dodgers, but his greatest fame came as their manager. The second arrival was that of Leland Stanford MacPhail, better known as Larry. MacPhail was a dynamic, volcanic baseball executive who had introduced night baseball to the major leagues in 1935 when he was general manager of the Cincinnati Reds.

The Brooklyn club was deeply in debt to the Brooklyn Trust Company, and the bank pushed for changes. MacPhail, who was the man chosen to make the changes, was hired as executive vice-president in January, 1938, and became president when Stephen McKeever died in March. Larry convinced the bank to loan more money for improvements in Ebbets Field, including lights for night games, and for acquiring players. The first big player purchased was Dolph Camilli, a power-hitting first baseman.

The addition of Durocher and Camilli gave the Dodgers a respectable infield in 1938. But their outfield was poor. And at catcher, Ernest "Blimp" Phelps could do the job, but he did not always want to play, and his back-ups were barely passable.

But it was the pitching staff that caused manager Burleigh Grimes the most heartache. The squad had no southpaws when it broke camp, and the righties might have done better using their left arms. When Grimes was asked by a reporter early in the year where he thought the Dodgers would finish, he quite honestly said seventh place.

The Dodgers spent almost the entire first half in seventh. But on June 15th, MacPhail pulled out all the stops and attracted a huge crowd to the first night game in Brooklyn. The fans were treated to an array of pre-game activity. But the big show was put on by Cincinnati pitcher Johnny Vander Meer, who pitched his second consecutive no-hitter.

Three days later, MacPhail hired Babe Ruth as a coach. Babe helped draw customers for a while, but he clashed with Grimes and Durocher and was gone after the season ended. Largely because of night games, the club's attendance jumped to 663,000 for the year, even though the team was only 30-41 at home. On the road, the Dodgers played .500 ball, but they finished seventh, just as Grimes had predicted. By the end of the campaign, Burleigh was as good as gone.

Durocher was named to succeed him. Over the winter, MacPhail picked up a couple of pitchers who had failed in previous major league trails. Their names were Hugh Casey and Whitlow Wyatt. On July 24th, 1939, they picked up an American

Larry MacPhail and Leo Durocher

League reject on waivers to bolster the Brooklyn outfield. This man's name was Fred "Dixie" Walker. A minor league prospect named Pete Reiser was sent back down after spring training over Durocher's objections. Leo had been stubborn enough about it to get himself fired by MacPhail. But Larry would fire Leo many times over the next four years and always forget about it the next day.

MacPhail's big innovation for the year was to institute radio coverage. Red Barber was the announcer, and he outlasted both MacPhail and Durocher on the Brooklyn scene.

When the season started, the Dodgers looked about the same as before. The outfield was terrible and the pitching lacked depth. The hallmark of the season was long games. The Dodgers played one 19-inning tie and another 23-inning draw. In the first night game of the year, the Dodgers pulled off a triple play in the 12th inning and won the game in the 14th on a steal of home. The radio listeners did not hear the end, however, because the radio station allocated a set amount of time for the broadcast and switched to other programming whether the game was over or not. This heart-rending practice continued through the cardiac season of 1941.

The Dodgers were all but glued to the .500 mark through July and into August, and sixth place was a distinct possibility. But Durocher's crew surprised the baseball world by winning 30 of its last 45 games to squeeze into third place.Durocher's barbed tongue goaded Luke Hamlin into a 20-win season, and Casey turned out to be a workhorse. Wyatt won his first eight decisions before being sidelined with a sore heel and a twisted knee. Camilli hit 26 home runs. Attendance was up to 955,000, with radio helping at attract a much wider following to the ballpark.

For 1940, MacPhail continued to pick up players waived by other big league clubs. But he also bought a young shortstop whom he thought would provide some back-up for the aging Durocher. His name was Harold Reese, but everyone called him Pee Wee. After he arrived, Leo did not have to play much at short.

The team clicked immediately, winning its first nine games in the regular season. The ninth victory was a no-hit shutout by Tex Carleton, whom MacPhail had purchased conditionally from the minor league Milwaukee club. The defending-champion Cincinnati Reds battled the Dodgers for the lead through the first half of the season. A big blow to Brooklyn's hopes came on June 1st, when Reese was hit on the head by a pitch. On the 13th, MacPhail made a trade that brought Joe Medwick and Curt Davis over from the Cardinals. But just five days later, Medwick was beaned by former teammate Bob Bowman and knocked unconscious. Joe returned to the lineup after only a short time out, but he did not hit with his old authority.

The Dodgers fell from the lead on July 7th and were 5 games out by August 15th. On that day, Brooklyn's chances went down the tubes after Reese broke a couple of bones in his heel. The Dodgers finished second, 12 games behind. The outstanding individual performance was turned in by Freddie Fitzsimmons, who had a 16-2 record as a pitcher.

The Reds were on the verge of clinching the pennant when they beat the Dodgers in the last meeting between the two clubs on September 16th in Brooklyn. A questionable call by umpire George Magerkurth in the tenth inning hurt, and one irate fan took it out on the arbiter with his fists after the game ended.

To put the Dodgers over the top, MacPhail made two key trades over the winter, acquiring catcher Mickey Owen from St. Louis and hard-working pitcher Kirby Higbe from Philadelphia. Three weeks into the season, Brooklyn picked up veteran second baseman Billy Herman.

The 1941 race quickly developed into a two-team affair involving the Dodgers and the Cardinals. Brooklyn ran off two nine-game winning streaks in the first two months but could not pull away. The lead switched hands no fewer than 17 times over the course of the summer.

Pete Reiser spent his first full season with the Dodgers, and he did sensationally, winning the batting title. Camilli had a big year with the bat, too, leading the league in home runs and runs-batted-in and winning the Most Valuable Player Award. Wyatt and Higbe were the leading pitchers in the league with 22 wins each.

The final showdown came in St. Louis with just over two weeks left in the season. The Dodgers came to town with a 1-game lead, and the teams split two thrillers in the first two games of the three-game series. In the final game, Wyatt and Mort Cooper engaged in a classic pitchers' duel. Brooklyn was held hitless until the eighth inning, when Walker and Herman doubled back-to-back for a run. Wyatt had the margin he needed and won 1-0. That gave the Dodgers a 2-game lead. They held on to win by 2½.

In the World Series against the New York Yankees, Durocher pulled a surprise by starting Curt Davis in the first game. He pitched well but lost 3-2. Wyatt evened

The First Night Game at Ebbets Field

the series with a 3-2 victory in the second game. Fitzsimmons pitched seven shutout innings in the third game, but a line drive cracked his kneecap and knocked him out of the game. Casey came in and gave up two runs to lose, 2-1.

The fourth game was the crusher. Higbe was knocked out in the fourth inning, but the Dodgers rallied from three runs down to take a 4-3 lead. With two out in the ninth, Casey struck out Tommy Henrich, but catcher Mickey Owen missed the third strike. The Yankees took this reprieve and pounded out four runs to win, 7-4. The series was as good as lost right there, although it was not officially over until the Yankees won the next day, 3-1.

In 1942, the Dodgers added veteran infielder Arky Vaughan to their attack. Johnny Allen and Larry French, both of whom had been acquired during the 1941 season, pitched very well. The Dodgers were loaded with veteran talent and by May 16th had a bigger lead (4½ games) that they had had at any time in 1941. By May 19th, the lead was 7 games.

Reiser was well on his way to another batting title with a .356 average when he crashed into the concrete wall in St. Louis chasing a fly ball on July 19th. He was out of the lineup only six days, but he slumped badly over the last two months.

By August 4th, the lead had ballooned to 10 full games. It might have been 10½, except that wartime "dimout" regulations nullified a big Dodger rally that night. A week later, MacPhail came into the Brooklyn clubhouse and warned the players that they might not win the pennant. Some of the men thought Larry was joking. Others, like Dixie Walker, took offense. But MacPhail's ill-chosen prophesy came true.

From that date on, St. Louis won 43 and lost only 8. Brooklyn did not exactly collapse, winning 30 and losing 17, but they did lose the pennant by 2 games. The Cardinals won both games of the key series in Brooklyn on September 11th and 12th to tie the race. The next day, the Dodgers lost a doubleheader to the Reds to fall behind. Brooklyn rebounded and won 10 of the last 12, but St. Louis won 11 of 12 to cop the flag.

Even before the race was over, MacPhail quit to join the army. Brooklyn's loss was the war effort's gain. When Branch Rickey was hired to take MacPhail's place, the Dodgers were assured of a bright future.

Dolph Camilli, Pee Wee Reese, Arky Vaughan, Billy Herman, & Lew Riggs

1938 WEDNESDAY NIGHT, JUNE 15TH, AT EBBETS FIELD

No-Hitter in First Brooklyn Night Game

Vander Meer Hurls Second Gem in a Row
He Upstages the Inauguration of Night Baseball at Ebbets Field

Today's Results			
Cincinnati 6-BROOKLYN 0			
Pittsburgh 2-New York 0			
Boston 2-Chicago 0			
St. Louis 9-Philadelphia 7			
Standings	**W-L**	**Pct.**	**GB**
New York	32-18	.640	—
Chicago	31-21	.596	2
Cincinnati	26-22	.542	5
Pittsburgh	25-22	.532	5½
Boston	23-22	.511	6½
St. Louis	22-26	.458	9
BROOKLYN	21-29	.420	11
Philadelphia	12-32	.273	17

CARNIVAL MASTER LARRY MACPHAIL staged the first nocturnal production in his new Big Top in Brooklyn tonight, and his show was stolen right in the center ring by Cincinnati's Johnny Vander Meer.

MacPhail had arranged for all sorts of sideshows for the customers this evening, but he could never have planned a more memorable event. For the price of admission,a capacity crowd of 38,748 at Ebbets Field got to see more than just an ordinary ballgame in the first night game ever played here. They got to see Vander Meer pitch his second consecutive no-hitter, a feat never before accomplished in the history of the major leagues. Vander Meer stopped the Dodgers tonight, 6-0, after pitching another no-hit shutout against the Boston Bees last Saturday in Cincinnati, 3-0.

Night ball, which became well-established in the minor leagues in 1930, was first introduced to the majors by MacPhail when he was general manager at Cincinnati in 1935. Larry moved on to Brooklyn this winter, and he brought night baseball with him.

If tonight's crowd could be taken as any indication, night games would be a definite success in Brookyn. Although some 25,000 general admission and 3,000 bleacher tickets did not go on sale until 5 o'clock, the stands were packed well before game time, and the fire department ordered the gates closed at 8:36 p.m. Standing room was hard to come by, and some 20,000 people were turned away. Babe Ruth and Babe Herman were both among the interested spectators, and they each got a big hand from the throng.

Ringmaster MacPhail had provided a multitude of amusements for the fans. Bands marched on the field and blared in the stands. Olympic track star Jesse Owens gave a broad jump demonstration and ran a couple of races against Dodger players. With the skies finally growing dim, a rocket was shot into the air, and the bands struck up "The Star-Spangled Banner." The lights were turned on at 8:37, and the crowd roared. The seven light towers contained 615 floodlights that generated 92,000,000 candlepower of illumination onto the field. The system had cost the club around $110,000 to build, with the money being advanced by the Brooklyn Trust Company. The lighting was proclaimed the best in the land.

The game finally got under way at 9:23, with Max Butcher on the mound for the Dodgers. He lasted until the third inning, when the Reds scored four times to knock him out. The first three runs came home on a three-run homer by Frank McCormick.

Cincinnati later added two runs against relievers Tot Pressnell, Luke Hamlin, and Vito Tamulis.

But the big story was not the Cincinnati offense, it was the pitching of Vander Meer. By the end of the fourth inning, the Cincinnati writers in the press box were discussing the possibility of another no-hitter. The lefthanded fireballer was known to be particularly effective at night. And tonight he had the added incentive of pitching in front of at least 500 of his family and friends from his home town of Midland Park, New Jersey.

In the fifth inning, Vander Meer did a nice job of grabbing Dolph Camilli's grounder to prevent a single up the middle. In the sixth, third baseman Lew Riggs had to charge hard on Buddy Hassett's slow roller to nip the batter at first base.

Although the Dodgers were not hitting the ball hard, Vander Meer had some trouble with his control, especially in the late innings. He walked men in the second, third, and sixth. Then in the seventh, he walked two men with one out. But he got the next two outs easily enough.

In the eighth, he struck out two men and got the other one to fly out.

By the bottom of the ninth, everyone in the house was rooting for the youngster. Hassett led off with a high bouncer down the first base line. Vander Meer hustled to the ball and made the tag for the out. "Blimp" Phelps was walked on five pitches. Vander Meer lost Cookie Lavagetto on a full count. The first pitch to Camilli was a strike, but the next four were balls, and this walk loaded the bases. Manager Bill McKechnie came out to the mound and told his pitcher to just pour it in there, since the batters "are more afraid to swing at it then you are to throw it."

After a ball and a strike, Ernie Koy grounded to third baseman Riggs, who threw home for a force out. With one out to go, Leo Durocher was the batter. With a 1-and-2 count, Durocher hit a long foul to right. On 2-and-2, he lifted a shallow fly beyond second base. Fleet center fielder Harry Craft raced in and caught it, and the no-hitter was complete.

The Reds rushed out to surround their pitcher and hustle him through the crowd and off the field. The fans then turned their attention to Vander Meer's parents, cheering them in place of their son. Johnny Vander Meer had upstaged the historic inaugural night baseball game in Brooklyn with an even more historic second consecutive no-hitter.

Cincinnati	ab	r	h	bi	o	a	e
L. Frey, 2b	5	0	1	0	2	2	0
W. Berger, lf	5	1	3	1	1	0	0
I. Goodman, rf	3	2	1	0	3	0	0
F. McCormick, 1b	5	1	1	3	9	1	0
E. Lombardi, c	3	1	0	0	9	0	0
H. Craft, cf	5	0	3	1	1	0	0
L. Riggs, 3b	4	0	1	1	0	3	0
B. Myers, ss	4	0	0	0	0	1	0
J. Vander Meer, p	4	1	1	0	2	4	0
	38	6	11	6	27	11	0

Brooklyn	ab	r	h	bi	o	a	e
K. Cuyler, rf	2	0	0	0	1	0	0
P. Coscarart, 2b	2	0	0	0	1	2	0
G. Brack, ph6	1	0	0	0	-	-	-
J. Hudson, 2b7	1	0	0	0	1	0	0
B. Hassett, lf	4	0	0	0	3	0	0
B. Phelps, c	3	0	0	0	9	0	0
G. Rosen, pr9	0	0	0	0	-	-	-
C. Lavagetto, 3b	2	0	0	0	0	2	2
D. Camilli, 1b	1	0	0	0	7	0	0
E. Koy, cf	4	0	0	0	4	0	0
L. Durocher, ss	4	0	0	0	1	2	0
M. Butcher, p	0	0	0	0	0	1	0
T. Pressnell, p3	2	0	0	0	0	0	0
L. Hamlin, p6	0	0	0	0	0	1	0
W. English, ph8	1	0	0	0	-	-	-
V. Tamulis, p9	0	0	0	0	0	0	0
	27	0	0	0	27	8	2

Cincinnati	004 000 110	=	6
Brooklyn	000 000 000	=	0

	ip	h	r-er	bb	so
Vander Meer (W 7-2)	9	0	0-0	8	7
Butcher (L 4-3)	2⅔	5	4-4	3	1
Pressnell	3⅔	4	1-1	0	3
Hamlin	1⅔	2	1-0	1	3
Tamulis	1	0	0-0	0	1

Umpires: B. Stewart, D. Stark, & G. Barr

Game-Winning RBI; McCormick
LOB: Cincinnati 9, Brooklyn 8
BE: Cincinnati 1
2B: Berger
3B: Berger
HR: McCormick
SB: Goodman
Time—2:22
Attendance—38,748

In his next start, Vander Meer gave up four hits and won 14-1.

The Dodgers got as high as fifth place later in the year but finished seventh. Still, their 69-80 record was an improvement over 1937. And MacPhail's various programs boosted attendance to over 650,000.

1939 THURSDAY NIGHT, JUNE 1ST, AT EBBETS FIELD

Triple Play & Steal of Home Win for Dodgers

Rare Plays in Extra Innings Beat Cubs, 3-2
Crowd Gets Out of Control Before Game Starts

Today's Results			
BROOKLYN 3-Chicago 2 (14 inn.)			
Cincinnati 9-Boston 4 (13 inn.)			
St. Louis 1-New York 0			
Pittsburgh 5-Philadelphia 2			

Standings	W-L	Pct.	GB
Cincinnati	26-13	.667	—
St. Louis	23-14	.622	2
Pittsburgh	20-18	.526	5½
Chicago	20-19	.513	6
BROOKLYN	18-18	.500	6½
New York	17-22	.436	9
Boston	15-22	.405	10
Philadelphia	12-25	.324	13

TWO RARE PLAYS, A TRIPLE PLAY IN THE twelfth inning and a steal of home in the fourteenth, gave the Brooklyn Dodgers a 3-2 victory over the Chicago Cubs in the first night game of the season here. It all added up to a very exciting night for the 32,574 fans at Ebbets field.

There was excitement even before the game started. Brooklyn president Larry MacPhail had arranged a program of pre-game entertainment for those fans who got to the park early. Since most of the early arrivals had stood in line to get unreserved seats, the upper deck and rear sections of the lower deck were filled first. When the precision drill team of the 14th Regiment of the New York National Guard began marching around the field, many of the fans with 55¢ tickets moved into the $1.10 seats, which had been sold in advance. Soon the 200 special policemen on duty were completely unable to stop the migration. When the fans with reserved tickets showed up and tried to claim their seats, they were often unsuccessful. Fights broke out in many sections before the game, and some continued after play had started. A call was sent to the city police, who helped quiet things down somewhat. And MacPhail helped with an announcement that anyone with a $1.10 ticket who had lost his or her seat would get a refund.

On the field, the starting pitchers controlled the early going. Through the first six innings, Claude Passeau of the visiting Cubs allowed only two hits, while the Dodgers' Van Mungo gave up just three.

Brooklyn finally got onto the scoreboard in the bottom of the seventh. With one out, Dolph Camilli walked. Ernest "Blimp" Phelps grounded into a force out, but shortstop Billy Jurges's poor throw to first prevented a double play. Player-manager Leo Durocher then lined a two-out infield hit off of Passeau's leg. Johnny Hudson followed by pounding a triple high off the right field scoreboard for two runs.

The Cubs scored two in the ninth to tie the game, and it took four Dodger pitchers to get them out in the inning. Mungo issued a base on balls to leadoff batter Jimmy Gleeson. Augie Galan doubled off the screen atop the right field wall, Gleeson stopping at third. Durocher took Mungo out of the game.

Luke Hamlin was the first relief pitcher. Carl Reynolds teed off on his delivery for a high fly to deep left center. Since it looked like the ball might be caught, the runners held up. When the ball hit the fence for a double, only Gleeson was able to score. Rip Russell's long fly out to center got Galan home with the tying run. A walk to Dick Bartell signaled the end for Hamlin.

Ira Hutchinson came in. Bob Garbark bounced one over the new pitcher's head, but a great play by shortstop Durocher retired the batter at first. A walk to Charley Root loaded the bases. Vito Tamulis was called in as the fourth Dodger pitcher. He finally got the third out when Stan Hack bounced into a force play at second base.

Root, who had taken over the pitching duties for Chicago in the eighth, pitched six hitless innings through the thirteenth.

Tamulis, however, had to pitch around trouble. In the eleventh, he escaped a jam by fanning Root with runners on second and third and two out.

In the twelfth, he was saved by the triple play. Hack led off the round with a bunt single. Billy Herman laid down a bunt, and Tamulis threw to second too late to force Hack. With two on and none out, Gleeson also bunted. This one was popped into the air toward third base. Third sacker Cookie Lavagetto, thinking fast, let the ball drop to the ground, picked it up, and threw to first. First baseman Camilli tagged Herman for one out and stepped on the base for the second out. Meanwhile, Hack had broken for third. Camilli threw back to Lavagetto, and Hack was hung up. Cookie ran him toward second and flipped to Durocher, who made the tag to complete the triple killing.

Tamulis, who had pitched 11 innings of shutout ball in a 19-inning tie in Chicago on May 17th, pitched around a double and a walk in the thirteenth. He set the Cubs down in order in the top of the fourteenth.

It was now about half past midnight, and much of the crowd had gone home.

With one out in the bottom of the fourteenth, Gene Moore got the first hit off of Root. It was a drive off the screen in right, and Moore legged it into a triple. Chicago's strategy was obvious. The next two batters were walked intentionally to set up a force at home.

Durocher was the next batter for Brooklyn. After the first pitch went by for a ball, Durocher called for his favorite play, the suicide squeeze. Root threw a curveball low and away. Leo missed the bunt, but catcher Garbark dropped the ball. He quickly picked it up, but Moore slid across the plate ahead of the tag for the winning run. It was officially scored a stolen base.

Garbark and the other Cubs surrounded umpire George Barr arguing that Durocher had interfered with the tag and the runner should be sent back to third.

But by this time, the fans had overrun the field. Those who had stuck it out had gotten to witness two rare plays and an exciting Dodger victory.

Chicago	ab	r	h	bi	o	a	e
S. Hack, 3b	5	0	2	0	3	1	0
B. Herman, 2b	6	0	1	0	0	4	0
J. Gleeson, rf	5	1	0	0	3	0	0
A. Galan, lf	6	1	1	0	2	0	0
C. Reynolds, cf	6	0	3	1	6	0	0
R. Russell, 1b	4	0	0	1	10	1	0
D. Bartell, ss	3	0	1	0	2	3	0
G. Mancuso, c	2	0	1	0	8	0	0
G. Hartnett, ph8	0	0	0	0	-	-	-
G. Lillard, pr8	0	0	0	0	-	-	-
B. Garbark, c8	3	0	0	0	5	0	0
C. Passeau, p	2	0	0	0	1	0	0
H. Leiber, ph8	1	0	0	0	-	-	-
C. Root, p8	2	0	0	0	0	0	0
	45	2	9	2	40	9	0

Brooklyn	ab	r	h	bi	o	a	e
G. Rosen, cf	6	0	0	0	5	0	0
C. Lavagetto, 3b	6	0	1	0	3	6	0
G. Moore, rf	5	1	1	0	1	0	0
D. Camilli, 1b	4	0	0	0	7	1	0
B. Phelps, c	5	1	0	0	13	2	0
L. Durocher, ss	5	1	1	0	2	2	0
J. Hudson, 2b	5	0	1	2	10	3	0
T. Stainback, lf	4	0	0	0	1	0	0
V. Mungo, p	3	0	1	0	0	0	0
L. Hamlin, p9	0	0	0	0	0	0	0
I. Hutchinson, p9	0	0	0	0	0	0	0
V. Tamulis, p9	2	0	0	0	0	0	0
	45	3	5	2	42	14	0

Chicago	000 000 002 000 00	= 2
Brooklyn	000 000 200 000 01	= 3

one out when winning run scored

	ip	h	r-er	bb	so
Passeau	7	4	2-2	2	7
Root (L 0-1)	6⅓	1	1-1	3	5
Mungo	*8	4	2-2	5	7
Hamlin	⅓	1	0-0	1	0
Hutchinson	⅓	0	0-0	1	0
Tamulis (W 2-2)	5⅓	4	0-0	1	4

*faced two batters in ninth

Game-Winning run scored on stolen base
LOB: Chicago 12, Brooklyn 7
TP: Lavagetto-Camilli-Lavagetto-Durocher
2B: Herman, Hack, Galan, Reynolds 2
3B: Hudson, Moore
SH: Russell 2, Herman
SB: Moore
CS: Mancuso, Hack
Time—3:38
Attendance—32,574
Umpires: G. Barr, C. Moran, & Z. Sears

Durocher's Dodgers continued to play exciting baseball throughout the summer, though for a while it seemed to be getting them nowhere. Brooklyn was in sixth place as late as August 11th and below .500 as late as August 18th. Then the team got hot and finished the season with an 84-69 record, which was good enough for third place.

1940 TUESDAY, APRIL 30TH, AT CROSLEY FIELD, CINCINNATI

Flock's Record 9-0 After No-Hitter

Carleton Holds Reds Hitless
Coscarart's Homer Powers Brooklyn to 3-0 Victory

AFTER BLITZING THROUGH THE FIRST eight battles of the campaign unchecked, Leo Durocher's Brooklyn storm troopers today triumphantly assaulted the bastion of the defending-champion Reds of Cincinnati. Not only were the Reds defeated, Dodger pitcher J. Otto "Tex" Carleton came through the engagement untouched by even one safe hit.

Today's Results			
BROOKLYN 3-Cincinnati 0			
Chicago 8-Boston 7 (10 inn.)			
Philadelphia 6-Pittsburgh 2			
New York at St. Louis, ppd.—rain			

Standings	W-L	Pct.	GB
BROOKLYN	9-0	1.000	—
Cincinnati	6-3	.667	3
Chicago	7-7	.500	4½
New York	4-4	.500	4½
St. Louis	4-6	.400	5½
Pittsburgh	4-6	.400	5½
Philadelphia	3-5	.375	5½
Boston	1-7	.125	7½

The resultant no-hitter gave the undefeated Dodgers a 9-0 record in the young season. Even though it was still only April, pennant fever was reaching epidemic proportions back in Brooklyn. Work in factories and offices in the borough ground to a halt this afternoon as fans huddled around radios to hear the details of the final innings and to root Tex on to his gem.

The Dodgers made only five hits themselves. But one of them was a home run by Pete Coscarart with two men on base. It provided the Flock with its runs in a 3-0 victory.

Brooklyn also committed three errors, but Carleton was able to pitch around them. None of the misplays could possibly have been scored a hit. But on a few other occasions, the Reds hit the ball hard only to have the Brooklyn outfielders catch the flies. Careleton walked two hitters and faced only three men over the minimum possible number.

Billy Werber walked to lead off the Cincinnati first. He was left on second base as the next three hitters went out on the infield.

Two errors put a runner on second for the Reds in the second inning. With one out, Harry Craft's grounder was fumbled by rookie shortstop Pee Wee Reese. Mike McCormick lifted a pop into short right center. Second baseman Coscarart made a fine catch and then tried to double Craft off first. The throw was wild high, and Craft was able to reach second. But Carleton got Eddie Joost to ground out to third.

Werber walked again in the third, this time with one out. Lonny Frey flied out to Dixie Walker in deep right center. Werber was then thrown out stealing by catcher Herman Franks.

With one out in the fourth, Frank McCormick grounded to third baseman Cookie Lavagetto and was given second base when the low throw skipped past the first baseman. Ernie Lombardi followed with a tremendous drive onto the roof of the laundry beyond the left field fence. Luckily the ball was about 20 feet foul. Lombardi then flied out. Craft hit a hard liner to left, but Joe Vosmik was there to make the catch.

Through the first four innings, the Dodgers had made three hits off of Reds' starter Jim Turner but had been unable to get anyone past second base. Franks led off the fourth with a walk. Reese popped out. Carleton was also given a free pass. Walker hit a grounder to second baseman Frey, who tagged Carleton and threw to first. Walker just beat the play to prevent an inning-ending double play. On the next pitch, Coscarart lined his homer over the left field wall, and Brooklyn had a 3-0 lead.

Carleton had little trouble holding onto it the rest of the way. Cutting the corners beautifully with his fastball and curve, he set the Reds down in order in the last five innings. Frey made a bid for extra bases in the sixth with a long drive to right. But Roy Cullenbine made a one-handed, over-the-shoulder catch. In the seventh, F.

McCormick sent Vosmik back to the wall for another long fly.

By the last two innings, everyone was rooting for Tex to get his no-hitter. The Cincinnati fans were cheering his every pitch, and the masses back in Brooklyn nervously leaned toward their radios to better hear all the details. The announcer went out of his way to keep from mentioning directly that Carleton had not allowed any hits, but he beat around the bush enough to let everyone know what was happening. Likewise, it was taboo in the bars around the borough to mention the word "no-hitter," since that would undoubtedly jinx old Tex.

Carleton had never pitched a no-hitter in the major leagues. He had come up in 1932 with the Cardinals, and had been released by the Cubs after injuring his elbow in 1938. He had spent the 1939 season with Milwaukee in the American Association. Brooklyn had given him a trial this spring, and he had made the squad. Now he was about to make history.

Werber led off the ninth by grounding out easily to third base. Carleton started Frey off with a curve for a strike. After missing with the next two pitches, Tex got another curve over to even the count. A fastball came in high, and the count was full. Frey lofted the next pitch deep to right. But the ball stayed in the park, and Cullenbine caught it near the fence. Ival Goodman was the only man left. The first pitch to him was a ball. The next one was hit on a line to right center. The drive was sinking and for a moment it looked like a hit. But Walker had a good jump and raced in to make the catch about knee high.

The no-hit game was complete. Carleton threw his glove into the air and was surrounded by teammates before it came down. Nine in a row and getting better each time! Back in Brooklyn, the happy fans were ready to order their World Series tickets right away.

Brooklyn	ab	r	h	bi	o	a	e
D. Walker, cf	4	1	0	0	4	0	0
P. Coscarart, 2b	4	1	2	3	1	3	1
J. Vosmik, lf	4	0	1	0	2	0	0
C. Lavagetto, 3b	4	0	2	0	1	4	1
D. Camilli, 1b	4	0	0	0	9	0	0
R. Cullenbine, rf	3	0	0	0	3	0	0
H. Franks, c	3	1	0	0	6	1	0
P. Reese, ss	4	0	0	0	1	2	1
T. Carleton, p	2	0	0	0	0	0	0
	32	3	5	3	27	10	3

Cincinnati	ab	r	h	bi	o	a	e
B. Werber, 3b	2	0	0	0	1	1	0
L. Frey, 2b	4	0	0	0	2	2	0
I. Goodman, rf	4	0	0	0	2	0	0
F. McCormick, 1b	3	0	0	0	10	1	0
E. Lombardi, c	3	0	0	0	5	0	0
H. Craft, cf	3	0	0	0	3	0	0
M. McCormick, lf	3	0	0	0	1	0	0
E. Joost, ss	3	0	0	0	2	2	0
J. Turner, p	2	0	0	0	1	2	0
W. Berger, ph8	1	0	0	0	-	-	-
W. Moore, p9	0	0	0	0	0	0	0
	28	0	0	0	27	8	0

Brooklyn	000 030 000	=	3
Cincinnati	000 000 000	=	0

	ip	h	r-er	bb	so
Carleton (W 2-0)	9	0	0-0	2	4
Turner (L 0-1)	8	4	3-3	2	2
Moore	1	1	0-0	1	1

Umpires: B. Stewart, G. Magerkurth, & G. Barr

Game-Winning RBI: Coscarart
LOB: Brooklyn 5, Cincinnati 3
BE: Cincinnati 2
2B: Vosmik
HR: Coscarart
CS: Werber
Time—1:47 Attendance—10,544

The Dodgers' winning streak ended the next day when the Reds scored eight runs in the fourth inning and won, 9-2.

Cincinnati caught Brooklyn by May 11th, but the Dodgers battled the Reds for the lead well into July. Cincinnati proved just too powerful, however, and the Dodgers finished second, 12 games behind. Still, their second-place finish and 88-65 record were the club's best since 1924.

Carleton finished the year with a 6-6 mark.

1941 THURSDAY, SEPTEMBER 25TH, AT BRAVES FIELD, BOSTON

Bums Clinch Pennant

Beat Braves, 6-0, as Cardinals Lose to Pirates
Brooklyn Celebrates its 1st Pennant in 21 Years

Today's Results			
BROOKLYN 6-Boston 0			
Pittsburgh 3-St. Louis 1			
Cincinnati 6-Chicago 0			
New York 3-Philadelphia 2			
Standings	**W-L**	**Pct.**	**GB**
BROOKLYN	99-53	.651	—
St. Louis	96-55	.636	2½
Cincinnati	86-65	.570	12½
Pittsburgh	80-71	.530	18½
New York	73-78	.483	25½
Chicago	69-83	.454	30
Boston	61-91	.401	38
Philadelphia	42-110	.276	57

THEY'RE IN! THE BROOKLYN DODGERS, Leo Durocher's Beloved Bums finally were in for sure. The pennant that had been striven for for so long was finally clinched beyond all mathematical doubt today, setting off wild celebrations all over the Borough of Churches.

The Dodgers clinched when pitching star Whitlow Wyatt shut the Boston Braves out, 6-0, while the second-place St. Louis Cardinals were losing in Pittsburgh, 3-1. The Dodgers' lead was thereby increased to 2½ games with each team having only two games left to play. St. Louis had one game cancelled a week and a half ago. One of the greatest races in history was finally decided, and Brooklyn had come out on top.

Ever since the Dodgers finished April with a 9-game winning streak and passed the Cardinals in early May, the lead had alternated back and forth from Brooklyn to St. Louis. The Cardinals regained the lead on May 19th. In June the teams traded places four times. The Dodgers got back on top on the Fourth of July and built up the biggest lead of the year (4 games) on July 15th. But the Red Birds were back in front by the 24th and had their biggest lead (3 games) by the 30th. Brooklyn caught up by August 6th, and the lead changed hands six times that month. On September 4th, the Dodgers finally took over first place for good.

When the Dodgers visited St. Louis for three games starting on the 11th, their lead was just 1 game. The critical series opened on Friday night with Freddie Fitzsimmons pitching for Brooklyn against Ernie White. The game went into extgra innings before Dixie Walker won it in the eleventh, 6-4, with a two-run single. St. Louis edged the Bums and Curt Davis, 4-3, in the second game.

The deciding game of the series, played on Sunday, September 13th, was a classic pitchers' duel between Wyatt and Mort Cooper. The Dodger righthander overpowered the St. Louis hitters, striking out nine. Cooper held Brooklyn hitless through seven innings, but Walker and Billy Herman put doubles back to back in the eighth, and the Dodgers won the game 1-0.

The Dodgers won 7 of their next 10, but the Cardinals won 8 of 11 over the same period, and the Brooklyn lead was only 1½ games when the Dodgers arrived in Boston for yesterday's game. Kirby Higbe was trailing 2-1 when he was removed for a pinch-hitter in the seventh inning. But the Dodgers rallied to win the game on a three-run double by Walker, and Higbe was given credit for his 22nd win of the season, 4-2. Although the Cardinals won in Pittsburgh yesterday, Brooklyn had a chance to clinch the pennant today.

The boys did their part in Boston, starting right off with a run in the top of the first. Walker led off with a single to left center. Pete Reiser walked with one out. An infield out moved the runners along. Joe Medwick topped an infield hit down the third base line, and Walker scored the game's first run.

Mickey Owen singled, stole second, and scored on a hit by Walker and a misplayed rundown in the second inning. In the third, a hit by Reiser followed by two errors by the second baseman made it 3-0. And the telegraphic bulletins announced that the Pirates had scored a run to lead the Cardinals, 1-0.

In Brooklyn, everyone was congregating to hear the news. Traffic ground to a halt in the Borough Hall crossroads as a large crowd gathered to watch *The Brooklyn Citizen* bulletin board. Radios blared on every corner in downtown Brooklyn.

Elbie Fletcher hit a two-run homer for the Pirates in the sixth inning. And Pete Reiser hit a two-run homer for the Dodgers in the seventh. Now it was looking like the pennant for sure.

Wyatt, the veteran fastballer, had a four-hit shutout and a 6-0 lead going into the bottom of the ninth. And the final score from Pittsburgh had just come in: Pirates 3-Cardinals 1. Gene Moore of the Braves grounded out on the first pitch. Buddy Hassett popped out to short left for the second out. Paul Waner delayed the celebration for a moment with a hit to left center. The count went to 2-and-2 on Max West. The next pitch was grounded to third. Cookie Lavagetto picked it up and threw across to first baseman Dolph Camilli, and the Dodgers had won the pennant!

The players pounded each other and poured champagne everywhere in the visitors' clubhouse. The liquor continued to flow freely on the train back to New York. Cookie Lavagetto started snipping everyone's neckties as the celebration rolled through Connecticut.

In Brooklyn, the saloons did a brisk business well into the morning hours. Ten thousand Dodgers fans congregated at Grand Central Station in Manhattan to await the return of the conquering heroes. Club president Larry MacPhail made arrangements to join the team at the 125th Street Station, but through a mixup he was left standing on the platform as the train roared on past.

The Dodgers arrived at Grand Central at 10:25, and the fans had packed the place, waving banners and tooting horns. The disheveled players had to run a gauntlet of handshakes, backslaps, and kisses before getting to their cabs and off toward home and a well-deserved rest.

After 21 years, the National League pennant had come back to Brooklyn.

Brooklyn	ab	r	h	bi	o	a	e
D. Walker, lf	5	1	3	0	3	0	0
B. Herman, 2b	4	0	0	0	2	2	0
P. Coscarart, ph9-2b	1	0	0	0	0	1	0
P. Reiser, cf	3	1	2	3	2	0	0
D. Camilli, 1b	4	1	0	0	10	0	0
J. Medwick, lf	4	0	1	1	1	0	0
C. Lavagetto, 3b	2	1	0	0	1	4	0
P. Reese, ss	3	0	1	0	2	3	0
M. Owen, c	4	1	1	0	5	1	0
W. Wyatt, p	4	1	1	0	1	0	0
	34	6	9	4	27	11	0

Boston	ab	r	h	bi	o	a	e
S. Sisti, 3b	3	0	0	0	1	4	0
J. Dudra, ph8-3b	1	0	0	0	0	0	0
J. Cooney, cf	1	0	0	0	0	0	0
G. Moore, cf2	3	0	0	0	0	0	0
B. Hassett, 1b	4	0	0	0	8	2	0
P. Waner, rf	3	0	1	0	1	0	0
M. West, lf	4	0	2	0	3	0	0
E. Miller, ss	3	0	0	0	4	4	1
S. Roberge, 2b	0	0	0	0	1	0	0
B. Rowell, ph2-2b	3	0	2	0	2	3	3
R. Berres, c	2	0	0	0	5	2	0
F. Demaree, ph8	1	0	0	0	-	-	-
A. Johnson, p9	0	0	0	0	0	1	0
T. Earley, p	2	0	0	0	1	3	0
P. Masi, ph8-c	1	0	0	0	1	0	0
	31	0	5	0	27	19	4

Brooklyn	111	000	210	=	6
Boston	000	000	000	=	0

	ip	h	r-er	bb	so
Wyatt (W 22-10)	9	5	0-0	1	5
Earley (L 6-8)	8	8	6-3	5	5
Johnson	1	1	0-0	1	1

Time—2:08
Attendance—10,098
Umpires: B. Reardon, L. Goetz, & B. Stewart

Game-Winning RBI: Medwick
LOB: Brooklyn 7, Boston 5
BE: Brooklyn 2
DP: Hassett-Miller-Hassett (Walker)
Herman-Reese-Camilli (Berres)
Miller-Roberge-Hassett (Owen)
Johnson-Miller-Hassett (Coscarart)
2B: West
HR: Reiser
SB: Owen
CS: Lavagetto

The Dodgers split their final games and finished 100-54.

1941 SUNDAY, OCTOBER 5TH, AT EBBETS FIELD
World Series—Game #4

Mickey Owen Misses the Third Strike

THE DODGERS WERE LEADING THE NEW YORK YANKEES THIS AFTERNOON IN EBBETS Field, 4-3, when Hugh Casey struck Tommy Henrich out to end the game. Only the strikeout did not end the game. Mickey Owen, the catcher, dropped the third strike, and Henrich ran safely to first base. So the third strike wasn't an out, and the third out wasn't made. And the Dodgers didn't win the ballgame.

The Yankees, curse their luck, won the game after a strikeout with two out in the ninth. They didn't lose to the Dodgers, because the last out wasn't made, 'cause Mickey Owen missed the third strike. They scored four runs after the third out wasn't made. So those damned Yankees won the game, 7-4. And all because Mickey Owen missed that third strike.

'Cause Owen missed the third strike, the Dodgers weren't tied in the series. The Dodgers were behind, 3 games to 1, instead. Because of that missed third strike, Brooklyn's chances went from fair to slim, from good to very bad.

And poor Mickey Owen, the Dodgers' live-wire catcher, became one of the all-time goats of the World Series by missing that third strike. Something of a hero in the series up to that point, his reputation would forever be stained by that one pitch. After the game finally was over, the Dodger management asserted its complete confidence in Owen. And well they should have. A fine receiver, Mickey had made only three errors and two passed balls in 128 games in the regular season. He had saved many a wild pitch and many a run by blocking pitches in the dirt. And his take-charge style of defense had been a cornerstone of the team's success.

In the series, Mickey had given the Yankees fits. In the first game, he pounded a triple to drive in a run and tie the score, although the Yanks won out, 3-2. In the second game, Owen drove home the tying run with a single and made a slashing slide to try and break up a double play. The Dodgers won that game, 3-2. In the third game, Owen went hitless, but he handled Freddie Fitzsimmon's knuckleball well and even picked a runner off first base with a snap throw. Brooklyn lost 2-1.

Today he scored the first run in a Dodger comeback, threw out a man stealing, and generally directed the Brooklyn defense. Then he missed the third strike, and all was quickly lost thereafter.

Up until the unexpected finish, the game was a high-caliber struggle between two very good teams. The Yankees knocked 22-game winner Kirby Higbe out of the game and built up a 3-0 lead by the middle of the fourth inning. But the Beloved Bums bounced right back with two runs in the bottom of the fourth and two more in the fifth to grab a 4-3 lead, which lasted until the fatal ninth.

The first New York run came in the first inning. Red Rolfe singled with one out, and Joe DiMaggio walked with two gone. Charlie "King Kong" Keller rammed a single through the right side, and Rolfe scored.

The Yankees scored two more runs in the fourth to rout Higbe. Keller, a World Series hero all the way, blasted a double off the right field screen. Bill Dickey walked, and Joe Gordon dropped a single into left to load the bases. After a force out at home and a strikeout, Johnny Sturm lined a single to center to plate two runs.

Two Dodgers were out in the last to the fourth when pitcher Atley Donald walked Owen and Pete Coscarart. Manager Leo Durocher sent Jimmy Wasdell up to pinch-hit. He fouled one off the right field wall, then sliced a two-run double into the left field corner, cutting the Dodger deficit to 3-2.

In the top of the fifth, the Yanks loaded the bases against Johnny Allen, but Hugh Casey came in and got the last out.

In the bottom, Dixie Walker led off with a double to left. Pete Reiser hit the next pitch over the scoreboard for a two-run homer, sending the fans into ecstasy. The Dodgers were now ahead 4-3.

It was still 4-3 in the ninth inning, and old Ebbets Field was rocking with delight. Casey retired the first two Yankees and had a 3-and-2 count on Henrich. Casey snapped off a breaking ball on the inside. It broke very sharply and was out of the strike zone, but Henrich was fooled and swung for strike three. But Owen tried to one-hand the ball across his body, and the pitch glanced off the side of his mitt. It rolled nearly to the corner of the dugout, and Mickey had no chance of throwing Henrich out at first base.

So the game was not over. The last out was not yet made. The policemen who had rushed onto the field after Henrich had swung now had to pile back into the stands. Some of the New York players who had already started down the ramp toward the clubhouse returned to the dugout. Casey was still on the mound, looking confused and angry.

Joe DiMaggio came up and cracked a solid single to left. A terrible feeling that the Dodgers might lose the game occurred to thousands of fans at once. Charlie Keller missed on two big swings, and Casey was once again just one strike away from victory. But Keller, the cursed King Kong, clouted a high drive off the screen in right field. The ball took an unusual bounce off of a support strut, and caromed over Walker's head. Henrich and DiMaggio both scored, and the Yankees went ahead. Bill Dickey walked on a full count, and Joe Gordon doubled over the left fielder's head for two more runs. Johnny Murphy finally made the third out by grounding to short.

Trailing 7-4, the Dodgers went out in order in the bottom of the ninth, and they had suddenly lost the game that they had already won. All because Mickey Owen missed the third strike on the last out in the ninth inning.

New York (AL)	ab	r	h	bi	o	a	e
J. Sturm, 1b	5	0	2	2	9	1	0
R. Rolfe, 3b	5	1	2	0	0	2	0
T. Henrich, rf	4	1	0	0	3	0	0
J. DiMaggio, cf	4	1	2	0	2	0	0
C. Keller, lf	5	1	4	3	1	0	0
B. Dickey, c	2	2	0	0	7	0	0
J. Gordon, 2b	5	1	2	2	2	3	0
P. Rizzuto, ss	4	0	0	0	2	3	0
A. Donald, p	2	0	0	0	0	1	0
M. Breuer, p5	1	0	0	0	0	1	0
G. Selkirk, ph8	1	0	0	0	-	-	-
J. Murphy, p8	1	0	0	0	1	0	0
	39	7	12	7	27	11	0

Brooklyn (NL)	ab	r	h	bi	o	a	e
P. Reese, ss	5	0	0	0	2	4	0
D. Walker, rf	5	1	2	0	5	0	0
P. Reiser, cf	5	1	2	2	1	0	0
D. Camilli, 1b	4	0	2	0	10	1	0
L. Riggs, 3b	3	0	0	0	0	2	0
J. Medwick, lf	2	0	0	0	1	0	0
J. Allen, p5	0	0	0	0	0	0	0
H. Casey, p5	2	0	1	0	0	3	0
M. Owen, c	2	1	0	0	2	1	1
P. Coscarart, 2b	3	1	0	0	4	2	0
K. Higbe, p	1	0	1	0	0	1	0
L. French, p4	0	0	0	0	0	0	0
J. Wasdell, ph4-lf	3	0	1	2	2	0	0
	35	4	9	4	27	14	1

New York	100 200 004	= 7
Brooklyn	000 220 000	= 4

	ip	h	r-er	bb	so
Donald	*4	6	4-4	3	2
Breuer	3	3	0-0	1	2
Murphy (W 1-0)	2	0	0-0	0	1
Higbe	3⅔	6	3-3	2	1
French	⅓	0	0-0	0	0
Allen	⅔	1	0-0	1	0
Casey (L 0-2)	4⅓	5	4-0	2	1

*faced two batters in fifth

Game-Winning RBI: Keller
LOB: New York 11, Brooklyn 8
BE: New York 1 (on missed 3rd strike)
DP: Gordon-Rizzuto-Sturm (Reiser)
2B: Camilli, Keller 2, Wasdell, Walker, Gordon
HR: Reiser
CS: Rizzuto
HBP: by Allen (Henrich)
Time—2:54 Attendance—33,813
Umpires: L. Goetz, B. McGowan, B. Pinelli, & B. Grieve

The next day, Ernie Bonham held the Dodgers to just four hits, and New York beat Whit Wyatt, 3-1, to wrap up the series. Wyatt tried to stir his teammates up by low-bridging Joe DiMaggio a couple of times and starting a bench-clearing altercation. But it did not help.

1942 TUESDAY EVENING, AUGUST 4TH, AT THE POLO GROUNDS, NEW YORK
Wartime Curfew Robs Dodgers of a Win

4-Run Tenth Inning Nullified by Dimout
But Brooklyn Extends Lead to 10 Games Anyway

Today's Results

BROOKLYN 1-New York 1 (tie)(9 inn.)
Cincinnati 4-St. Louis 3
Pittsburgh 2-Chciago 1 (11 inn.)
Philadelphia 4-Boston 2

Standings	W-L	Pct.	GB
BROOKLYN	73-30	.709	—
St. Louis	62-39	.614	10
Cincinnati	55-47	.539	17½
New York	54-50	.519	19½
Pittsburgh	46-53	.465	25
Chicago	48-53	.453	26½
Boston	43-64	.402	32
Philadelphia	30-70	.300	41½

PEE WEE REESE WAS ROBBED OF A GRAND slam, and the Brooklyn Dodgers were denied a victory this evening because the game could not be completed because of wartime dimout regulations. Yesterday's game had also been called before it was completed, but in it the Dodgers were leading, 7-4, in the ninth and were credited with an eight-inning victory. Tonight the game was tied, 1-1, through nine innings. In the top of the tenth, Brooklyn scored four runs, but the curfew hour arrived before the inning could be completed, and the game reverted officially to a 1-1, nine-inning tie.

Although another twilight game was on tap for Wednesday evening at Ebbets Field, the club owners indicated that they were going to abandon such games in the near future.

The Dodgers were playing today without star outfielder Pete Reiser, who took himself out of the lineup because of dizziness. The problem had been with him since he crashed into the wall in St. Louis on July 19th.

But even without Reiser and with the loss of an apparent victory, the Brooklyn lead over second-place St. Louis was extended to 10 games when the Cardinals lost an afternoon game in Cincinnati, 4-3. This was the largest lead any Brooklyn team had ever had in any pennant race yet.

But tonight's result was far from satisfying. The New York fans booed vociferously when the umpires called the game, despite the fact that the curfew saved the Giants from defeat.

The game entered the tenth inning with only 12 minutes left before the announced stopping time of 9:10 p.m. (one hour after sunset). All of the brightest lights in the city were to be extinguished at that time as a defense precaution.

At the top of the tenth, the Dodgers rallied for four runs and had only one out when the time limit was reached. Billy Herman opened the doomed frame with a single to center. Mickey Owen followed with a bunt, and both runners were safe when shortstop Dick Bartell dropped a throw. Frenchy Bordagaray was sent in to run for Herman at second, and Arky Vaughan was sent up to bat for pitcher Kirby Higbe. Vaughan drew a base on balls. The Giants, stalling for time, argued the call on the last pitch. When play resumed, the bases were loaded and Reese was at bat. Pee Wee cracked a long drive to straightaway center that flew way over the center fielder's head and rolled to the clubhouse steps. Reese circled the bases and just barely beat the relay to the plate for an inside-the-park grand slam home run.

Manager Mel Ott removed starting pitcher Bill McGee and brought Ace Adams in to pitch. Adams walked Augie Galan and got Dixie Walker on a fly out to center. Then, with the count at 2-and-1 on Joe Medwick, the witching hour arrived, and umpire Lou Jorda called the game. Since the Giants had not gotten their at bats in the tenth inning, the game went back to the ninth inning and a tie. Poor Pee Wee Reese lost his homer, and the Dodgers lost their big lead.

In those first nine innings, the game was dominated by the pitchers, McGee and Higbe. "Fidder Bill" was more consistent than "Koiby Higlebee," but both men were effective in the clutch.

In the first three innings, the Giants put men on in each round and failed to score.

In the first, Bartell opened with a single, but Billy Werber hit into a double play. Babe Young led off the New York second with another hit, and Buster Maynard walked with one out. Higbe then fanned Harry Danning and got Mickey Witek to hit into a force out. A hit by McGee, a pass to Ott, and a hit batsman loaded the bases with two out in the third. But Willard Maynard bounced out, first baseman to the pitcher covering.

The Dodgers got a man to third in their half of the third, but Reese popped out to leave him stranded.

Two singles opened the Brooklyn fourth, but once again the runners were left on base.

The Flatbush Flock finally broke the tie in the fifth. Herman walked for openers, but he was forced out by Owen. Higbe bunted the new runner to second, and Reese drove him home with a single to left. Galan followed with an infield hit, but Walker popped out to end the rally.

The Giants tied the game in the sixth on Ott's single, Young's double, and Marshall's long fly out. But a fine fielding play by Higbe cut off a second run. With men on first and third, Danning tried to squeeze Young home. But the Dodger pitcher pounced on the ball and flipped it to catcher Owen just in time to nip the sliding runner. Witek was then walked to load the bases. But Higbe struck McGee out, and the score remained tied.

Neither side got a man past second base in the seventh, eighth, and ninth. And the runners in the ill-fated top of the tenth were not counted.

The appended box score includes only the official statistics and not any of the tenth-inning action that was nullified by the dimout. Chalk Pee Wee Reese's grand slam and a possible Dodger victory up as casualties of the war.

Brooklyn	ab	r	h	bi	o	a	e
P. Reese, ss	4	0	1	1	1	3	0
A. Galan, cf	4	0	2	0	0	0	0
D. Walker, rf	4	0	1	0	3	0	0
J. Medwick, lf	4	0	0	0	2	0	0
D. Camilli, 1b	4	0	0	0	7	2	0
L. Riggs, 3b	4	0	0	0	1	4	0
B. Herman, 2b	2	0	1	0	6	4	0
M. Owen, c	3	1	1	0	6	0	0
K. Higbe, p	2	0	0	0	1	1	0
	31	1	6	1	27	14	0

New York	ab	r	h	bi	o	a	e
D. Bartell, ss	5	0	2	0	3	1	0
B. Werber, 3b	5	0	1	0	3	1	0
M. Ott, rf	3	1	1	0	2	0	0
B. Young, 1b	3	0	3	0	7	2	0
W. Marshall, lf	3	0	0	1	0	0	0
B. Maynard, cf	2	0	0	0	3	0	0
H. Danning, c	3	0	0	0	5	1	0
M. Witek, 2b	3	0	0	0	3	2	0
B. McGee, p	4	0	1	0	1	1	0
	31	1	8	1	27	8	0

Brooklyn 000 010 000 = 1
New York 000 001 000 = 1
game called on account of wartime dimout regulations

	ip	h	r-er	bb	so
Higbe	9	8	1-1	5	4
McGee	9	6	1-1	1	4

HBP: by Higbe (Young)
Time—2:25
Attendance—14,693 paid
15,562 total
Umpires: L. Jorda, G. Barr, & G. Magerkurth

LOB: Brooklyn 5, New York 10
DP: Riggs-Herman-Camilli (Werber)
Reese-Herman-Camilli (Werber)
Danning-Bartell, Riggs-Camilli
2B: Owen, Young
SH: Higbe, Marshall

The Giants and Dodgers played a twilight game the next evening in Brooklyn, with the Dodgers winning 4-0. But the evening games were soon abandoned.

Over the next six weeks, Brooklyn played at a modest 21-16 pace, while St. Louis won 32 and lost only 7 to tie for first place. In the final two weeks of the season, the Dodgers were 10-4, but the Cardinals were 12-2 and won the pennant by 2 games.

Brooklyn's final record of 104-50 was not good enough.

Chapter X Rickey Builds a Winner

1943 July 10th
Dodgers Almost Go On Strike, Then Win 23-6

1944 July 16th
Bums Snap 15⅝ Game Losing Streak

1945 July 8th
Babe Herman Returns with a Hit

1946 September 14th
Leo Plays a Hunch & Branca Stars

1946 Playoff—Game #2
Dodgers Lose Pennant as Desperate Rally Fails

EVEN BEFORE LARRY MACPHAIL HAD QUIT THE DODGERS IN SEPTEMBER, 1942, THERE had been rumors that he would be replaced by Branch Rickey. As vice-president and general manager of the St. Louis Cardinals, Rickey had gained a reputation as a great judge of playing talent and as an innovative administrator. It was he who was credited with developing the system of farm teams that had made the Cardinals perennial contenders in the National League and incidently helped the St. Louis club turn a good profit. Rickey was available to Brooklyn because his contract with St. Louis was about to expire, and Cardinal owner Sam Breadon was dissatisfied with Rickey's percentage-of-the-profits arrangement.

Rickey took over a Brooklyn team that had posted 204 victories in the previous two seasons but which had many problems lurking just beyond the horizon. The player personnel on the parent team was getting pretty old, and the farm system was not strong. These problems were complicated by the demands of World War II on America's manpower. Pee Wee Reese, Hugh Casey, and Pete Reiser were all in the military service by the time spring training started in 1943.

Since the nation's transportation system was already taxed to the limit, especially in the South, major league teams all trained near home in the next three springs. The Dodgers were billeted just up the Hudson River at Bear Mountain Lodge, and they held most of their workouts indoors in the cavernous U.S. Military Academy Field House at West Point.

In putting a team onto the field for the season, Rickey's instincts told him to clear out the older players and emphasize youth. But in a short-term decision, the Dodgers relied on veterans early in the season. In the Brooklyn starting lineup on opening day, only two players were under 30 years of age.

The older players had Brooklyn in first place from the first game until June 5th, when the Cardinals passed them. But after the Bums lost three games to St. Louis on July 3rd and 4th to drop 4 games behind, Rickey started the housecleaning in earnest. Johnny Allen (who had been suspended for a month for attacking an umpire), Dolph Camilli, Fred Fitzsimmons, and Bobo Newsom were all traded away in July.

The departure of Newsom was surrounded by controversy. Bobo was the team's top pitcher (9-4) but had repeatedly clashed with manager Leo Durocher. Claiming that Newsom was undermining his authority, Durocher suspended the pitcher on July 9th. After reading about this in the newspaper, infielder Arky Vaughan got so indignant that he turned in his uniform the next day. The wildcat strike threatened to spread to the whole team, but at the last minute Durocher was able to convince the men to go out and play. The Dodgers took the field and clobbered the unsuspecting Pittsburgh Pirates 23-6. Newsom was traded four days later, but no action was taken against Vaughan.

Ebbets Field

The transition to youth was not without its difficulties. The Dodgers suffered through a 10-game losing streak as July turned to August, dropping from second place to fourth. But old Whitlow Wyatt won ten games in a row in the late going, and rookies Luis Olmo and Rex Barney did well. The Dodgers wound up in third place at the finish.

By the opening of the 1944 season, veterans Kirby Higbe and Billy Herman were in the service, and Arky Vaughan had decided to stay on his farm in California. The Dodger infield was terribly inexperienced, and the pitching was weak. The one positive note was the acquisition of second baseman Eddie Stanky from the Cubs on June 8th.

Somehow, the Dodgers found themselves in fourth place, 3 games above .500, when they left Brooklyn for a western road trip starting on June 28th. It turned out to be the worst trip in the history of the franchise. The Bums dropped the first 13 games and were trailing in the 14th one, 9-7, when the contest was suspended by a curfew after eight inning. After a five-day break for the All-Star Game, the Dodgers lost two more games in Boston to run the losing streak to 15 8/9 games (when the suspended game was completed and lost, the streak officially became 16 games long, a club record). In the second game of a doubleheader on July 16th, the Brooks finally won, 8-4.

Much of August was spent in the cellar, but Brooklyn wound up 1½ ahead of Philadelphia to finish seventh. The redeeming factors in the season were Augie Galan's leadoff hitting, and Dixie Walker's .357 average, which won the batting title.

In late 1944, Rickey, attorney Walter O'Malley, and Andrew Schmitz bought a

Spring Training on Skis—Bear Mountain Lodge, New York

financial stake in the team. This was the beginning of what developed into a controlling interest for O'Malley.

On the field, 1945 was a big improvement over 1944. Stanky established himself as second baseman and leadoff batter and had a great season. Never much of a hitter he developed a crouching, fidgetting style that drove the pitchers crazy and earned him the league lead in walks and runs scored. Walker had another great year, leading the league in runs-batted-in.

First base, third base, and catcher were all problems, but the outfield of Walker, Goody Rosen, and Olmo was solid. An 11-game winning streak in early May and a 15-of-16 run in late June vaulted Brooklyn into first place. On July 1st, the Bums actually led by 4½ games.

After a nearly disastrous plane trip to Cherry Point, N.C., for an exhibition game, the Dodgers' pennant hopes dive-bombed in the first half of July. The team won only 4 of the first 15 games in the month and fell to third. But the fans were mollified somewhat by the signing of old Brooklyn hero Babe Herman. In his first at bat, on July 8th, Babe singled sharply and then tripped rounding first base, much to the delight of the Flatbush Faithful.

The Dodgers could not mount another drive to the top and finished the 1945 campaign in third.

With the war over, Rickey had big plans for the future. His policy during the war had been to sign as many prospects as possible in the hope that they would come back from the service older and more mature. This turned out to be excellent judgement, and the Dodgers were loaded with young talent in training camp in 1946. But Rickey's most innovative move was the signing of blacks ("Negroes" in the parlance of the time), who had been barred from Organized Baseball for more than a half century. The first man signed was a carefully-chosen and very talented infielder named Jack Roosevelt Robinson. On October 23, 1945, he was given a contract with a minor-league Montreal Royals.

Robinson, whose best position was second base, had an outstanding season in the International League in 1946, winning the batting title and the Most Valuable Player award and adjusting to (and being adjusted to by) Organized Baseball.

Meanwhile back in Brooklyn, the Dodgers already had two second basemen, Eddie Stanky and Billy Herman. Herman was still a better hitter, but his once-great fielding was a thing of the past. He was traded to Boston in June, much to the dismay of many Brooklyn backers.

Despite raids by the Mexican League (which took Mickey Owen and Luis Olmo) and a heavy reliance on rookies, the Dodgers led the league most of the season. Their pitching was suprisingly good, although Durocher had to adjust his starting rotation constantly. Lefthanders Joe Hatten and Vic Lombardi and righties Hal Gregg, Hank Behrman, and Kirby Higbe all did good work. Hugh Casey headed the bullpen. In late June, catcher Bruce Edwards was acquired from Mobile, and he turned out to be the answer behind the plate.

Brooklyn held the lead over pre-season favorite St. Louis most of the way through August. On July 2nd, the margin had bulged to 7½ games. At the All-Star break, Dixie Walker was leading the league in batting (.368) and RBIs (68), and Pete Reiser was hitting .330 with five steals of home. But St. Louis swept four from Brooklyn in mid-July, and the race was very tight the rest of the way. The Cardinals nosed ahead on August 28th and stayed there until September 27th, when they fell back into a tie. Two days later, the season ended with the Dodgers and Cardinals still tied, making necessary the first playoff in big league history.

The playoff was best-of-three with the first game in St. Louis. Durocher started little-used Ralph Branca against St. Louis ace Howie Pollet. Branca did not pitch all that badly, but Brooklyn could not break through against Pollet and the St. Louis defense and lost, 4-2.

After a day of travel, the series resumed in Brooklyn. The Dodgers scratched a run in the first inning against Murray Dickson. But then they were shut down while St. Louis built up an 8-1 lead. The Dodgers put a little excitement into the game with a rally in the ninth. But with the tying run at the plate and one out, two batters struck out. St. Louis won the game, 8-4, and with it the pennant.

So the Dodgers had come up just short. It was disappointing to lose out. But the Brooklyn fans had plenty of hope for the future, and their cry of "Wait until next year" was filled with anticipation.

Joe Medwick, Leo Durocher, & Curt Davis

1943 SATURDAY, JULY 10TH, AT EBBETS FIELD

Dodgers Almost Go On Strike, Then Win 23-6

Players Upset over Newsom's Suspension
But They Take It Out on Pittsburgh, Scoring 10 Runs Twice

Today's Results

BROOKLYN 23-Pittsburgh 6
St. Louis 6-Boston 0
Cincinnati 6-Philadelphia 2
Chicago 10-New York 4 (1st game)
New York 9-Chicago 2 (2nd game)

Standings	W-L	Pct.	GB
St. Louis	46-24	.657	—
BROOKLYN	46-33	.582	4½
Pittsburgh	37-34	.521	9½
Cincinnati	37-37	.500	11
Philadelphia	34-40	.459	14
Boston	32-38	.457	14
Chicago	32-42	.432	16
New York	29-45	.392	19

ON ONE OF THE MOST EVENTFUL DAYS IN the long and eventful history of the Brooklyn club, the Dodger players nearly staged a wildcat strike in support of their teammate Bobo Newsom. At the last minute (almost literally), the strike was averted, and the Dodgers fielded a team that proceeded to massacre the Pittsburgh Pirates 23-6. The Bums scored ten runs in the first inning and another ten in the fourth, becoming only the third team in history to score in double figures twice in the same game.

Newsom's troubles with manager Leo Durocher were brewing for some time. Leo felt that Bobo was not obeying orders and was undermining his authority with the other players. Then on Friday, Newsom berated young catcher Bobby Bragan for a passed ball that cost the Dodgers a run. To some, the pitch looked like a spitball, and it seemed that Newsom had crossed Bragan up. After the game, Durocher and Newsom had a heated argument, and Durocher wound up suspending the big pitcher.

Unfortunately, the altercation was overheard by a newspaper reporter, who wrote up the lurid details, including the spitball allegation.

When the players and staff were preparing for today's game, the usually cool-headed Arky Vaughan was in an uproar over the newspaper article and the suspension of his friend Newsom. He finally stormed into the manager's office and threw his uniform at the unsuspecting Durocher. After a short argument, Vaughan went to shower and change into his street clothes.

The rest of the clubhouse was now gathering to hear the controversy, and it seemed that the players were solidly behind Vaughan and Newsom. Durocher admitted that he had tried to get Newsom suspended for the remainder of the season, but club president Branch Rickey had set the term at three days. And Newsom conceded about his pitch to Bragan, "a pitcher's hand gets wet from perspiration."

Dixie Walker, the acknowledged leader among the players, also offered to turn in his uniform. That would have meant a strike for sure.

At about this point,the clubhouse attendant announced that the umpires had already taken the field, and game time was only a few minutes away. It was Kitchen Fat Day, and 4,512 women had brought a pound of more of household fats to aid the war effort and earn free admission to the game. In addition, 930 uniformed servicemen were on hand, as were 441 blood donors, not to mention 8,748 paying customers. The public mood was definitely against strikes in wartime.

Now Durocher had to act fast to avoid a forfeit. By emphasizing that he had no beef with Vaughan and intended to take no disciplinary action against him, the rest of the players were convinced to take the field.

When the game began, the poor Pirates didn't know what hit them. The Dodgers took out their frustrations on the Pittsburgh pitchers, starting with ten runs in the bottom of the first inning. After leadoff man Alban Glossop (substituting for Vaughan) flied out, Paul Waner singled, Walker doubled, and Augie Galan walked. Billy Herman cleared the bases with a three-run double to right center. A walk and an infield hit routed starting pitcher Johnny Podgajny, and Harry Shuman went to the mound. Red Barkley greeted him with a two-run single to left. Curt Davis flied to right for the second out. But Shuman never got the third out. A single, an error, and a three-run triple by Galan raised the score to 10-0 before big Johnny Gee came in to retire the side.

The Bums got two more runs in the third inning when Herman drove Waner and Galan home with a single. Herman finished the day with 7 RBIs and a league-leading season total of 58.

Pittsburgh got four runs back in the fourth inning. Gee drove in the last two with a triple.

But the base running must have taken a lot out of the Pirate hurler. He gave up four walks and five hits in the bottom of the fourth before being removed. Glossop hit a two-run homer off of Bill Brandt to give the Dodgers another ten-run innings and a 22-4 lead.

The Brooks settled down after that. They got one more run in the fifth inning when pinch-runner Max Macon stole home. After the fifth, Durocher took the regulars out of the lineup and gave some of the other fellows a chance to play. Davis stayed on the mound for the complete game. He allowed only two more runs and won, 23-6.

Even Vaughan reappeared in uniform, although Durocher did not put him into the game. Arky had been sitting in the stands with Newsom when the game had started. But president Rickey had gone down and had a long talk with Arky, convincing him to return to the bench before the end of the game.

Although the controversy between the players and the manager was not as yet resolved, another meeting was scheduled for Sunday morning, and Durocher's job appeared to be in jeopardy, the players had not let it affect their performance on the field. Too bad for the Pirates.

Pittsburgh	ab	r	h	bi	o	a	e
F. Gustine, ss	3	0	1	0	1	0	0
H. Geary, ss5	2	0	0	0	0	0	0
J. Barrett, rf	5	0	1	0	4	0	0
J. Russell, lf-1b5	4	0	0	0	6	0	0
B. Elliott, 3b	5	1	2	0	1	3	1
E. Fletcher, 1b	2	1	0	0	4	0	0
T. O'Brien, lf5	2	0	0	0	0	0	0
V. DiMaggio, cf	2	1	1	0	3	0	0
J. Wyrostek, cf5	1	1	0	0	1	0	0
A. Lopez, c	1	1	0	0	1	1	0
B. Baker, c5	2	0	2	1	1	0	0
P. Coscarart, 2b	4	1	2	2	2	3	0
J. Podgajny, p	0	0	0	0	0	0	0
H. Shuman, p1	0	0	0	0	0	0	0
J. Gee, p1	1	0	1	2	0	0	0
B. Brandt, p4	2	0	0	0	0	0	0
	36	6	10	5	24	7	1

Brooklyn	ab	r	h	bi	o	a	e
A. Glossop, 3b-2b6	6	3	3	2	2	1	0
P. Waner, rf	4	4	3	1	0	0	1
F. Bordagaray, rf6	1	0	0	0	1	0	0
D. Walker, lf	4	3	2	1	2	0	0
J. Medwick, lf6	1	0	0	0	1	0	0
A. Galan, cf	3	3	2	4	3	0	0
J. Cooney, cf6	1	0	0	0	2	0	0
B. Herman, 2b	4	2	3	7	0	1	0
D. Moore, 3b6	1	0	0	0	0	1	0
D. Camilli, lb	3	2	1	1	7	0	0
M. Macon, pr5-1b	1	1	0	0	4	0	0
B. Bragan, c	4	2	2	0	3	0	1
R. Barkley, ss	5	3	3	4	2	2	0
C. Davis, p	5	0	1	1	0	3	0
	43	23	20	21	27	8	2

Pittsburgh	0 00	4 00	020	=	6
Brooklyn	(10)02	(10)10	00x	=	23

	ip	h	r-er	bb	so
Podgajny (L 0-4)	⅓	4	6-5	2	0
Shuman	⅓	3	4-0	2	0
Gee	2⅔	10	11-11	4	1
Brandt	4⅔	3	2-2	3	1
Davis (W 5-5)	9	10	6-3	4	2

Time—2:10
Attendance— 8,748 paid
14,631 total

Game-Winning RBI: Herman
LOB: Pittsburgh 8, Brooklyn 8
BE: Pittsburgh 0, Brooklyn 1
DP: Elliott-Coscarart-Fletcher (Glossop)
2B: Walker, Herman, Galan, Coscarart, Barkley, Barrett, Glossop
3B: Galan, Gee
HR: Glossop
SH: Gee, Davis
SB: Barkley, Macon
Umpires: L. Ballanfant, B. Reardon, & L. Goetz

Newsom was traded to the St. Louis Browns within a week. No disciplinary action was taken against Vaughan. Despite the speculation in the press, Durocher kept his job.

A ten-game losing streak at the end of July and beginning of August dropped the Dodgers to fourth place. Brooklyn bounced back and finished third with an 81-72 record.

1944 SUNDAY, JULY 16TH, AT BRAVES FIELD, BOSTON

Bums Snap 15 8/9 Game Losing Streak

Lose First Game 8-4, Then Win Second 8-5
Seven Unearned Runs Give Brooks First Win Since June 25th

Today's Results			
Boston 8-BROOKLYN 4 (1st game)			
BROOKLYN 8-Boston 5 (2nd game)			
St. Louis 4-Cincinnati 2 (1st game)			
Cincinnati 3-St. Louis 2 (2nd game)			
Chicago 1-Pittsburgh 0 (1st game)			
Pittsburgh 1-Chicago 0 (2nd game)			
Philadelphia 6-New York 2 (1st game)			
New York 6-Philadelphia 3 (suspended) (8 innings)(2nd game)			

Standings	W-L	Pct.	GB
St. Louis	54-23	.701	—
Pittsburgh	41-33	.554	11½
Cincinnati	44-36	.550	11½
New York	39-41	.488	16½
Philadelphia	34-43	.442	20
Chicago	32-42	.432	20½
BROOKLYN	34-45	.430	21
Boston	42-47	.405	23

THE BROOKLYN DODGERS EXTENDED their losing streak to 15 8/9 games by losing the first game of today's doubleheader against the Boston Braves. The streak brought the Brooks to within 1 game of last place. But the Braves subbornly refused to yield the cellar, and Brooklyn was given the second game of the day, 8-5, to halt their downward plunge.

In the first game, the visiting Dodgers blew a key play in the first innings, and the Braves went on to score five runs in what turned out to be an 8-4 victory. In the nightcap, three Boston errors in the second inning gave Brooklyn seven unearned runs and an 8-5 triumph.

The victory was the first in 16 decisions for the Bums since they last won a game on June 25th. Besides the 15 straight losses, Brooklyn also was eight-ninths of the way to defeat in Pittsburgh on July 9th (trailing 9-7 with one inning left to play) when the game was suspended by the Sunday curfew law. The Dodgers were in a virutal tie for third place when they left home on June 26th for a 17-game road trip.

The sportswriters traveling with the team took perverse delight in the Bums' troubles, but manager Durocher looked like a couple of years had been taken off his life expectancy.

Righthander Hal Gregg, who had last won a game on Memorial Day, was Durocher's pitching selection in the opener. Boston leadoff man Connie Ryan solved Gregg for a two-bagger to right field. Max Macon sent him to third with a bloop hit to right center. Tommy Holmes popped out.

Then came the play that ruined Gregg. Butch Nieman hit sharply to first baseman Howie Schultz. Schultz elected to throw home to head off Ryan. But catcher Mickey Owen tried to make the tag before he caught the throw, and the ball went right between his legs. Not only did Ryan score, Macon also galloped home.

You could almost see the smoke coming out of Gregg's ears as he was forced to deliver an intentional walk to Chuck Workman. He walked Phil Masi unintentionally to load the bases. Putting one over for Damon Phillips, Gregg was rocked for a two-run single. He took his frustrations out on Warren Huston, who was hit by a pitch. After Jim Tobin was retired, Ryan came up for the second time and drove in the fifth run with a hit to left center.

Homers by Augie Galan and Dixie Walker cut the Boston lead to 5-3 by the middle of the eighth inning. But the Braves put the game away in the bottom of the eighth with three runs off pitcher Les Webber.

After two were out in the ninth, Bobby Bragan, Paul Waner, Luis Olmo, and Goody Rosen singled in succession for Brooklyn. With one run in and the bases loaded, Galan came up representing the tying run. He popped out to second base, and the Dodgers had lost another one.

In today's second game, it was the Braves' turn to give one away. Al Javery was the starting pitcher for Boston. He lasted just 1⅔ innings and was charged with 7 runs, all unearned. His own error was largely to blame.

The big Dodger rally came in the second inning. Dixie Walker led off with a clean hit to center. A bingle by Frenchy Bordagary put Walker on second. Owen tried to bunt the runners along but missed the pitch, and Walker was stranded halfway between second and third. Catcher Clyde Kluttz threw behind the runner, and Walker stole third, Bordagaray moving to second when third baseman Huston dropped the throw from second. Owen fanned, and Schultz was intentionally walked. Bragan popped out. Curt Davis hit an easy tap to the left of the mound. Javery got the ball and had an obvious out at first. But he threw home instead. His toss was too hard, and it handcuffed Kluttz, allowing Walker to score the game's first run. Olmo's wind-blown pop dropped untouched near the mound for a two-run "single." Javery walked the next two men, forcing the fourth run home. Walker, batting again, shot a smash off the first baseman's shins, and two more runs came in on the error. Javery was finally removed from the game. His successor, Red Barrett, allowed a run-scoring single by Bordagary to make the score 7-0.

Ab Wright hit a three-run pinch home run in the third for Boston. And Macon homered in the sixth.

Each side got a run in the ninth. But Boston never got the tying run to the plate, and Davis finished the game for his fifth win of the year.

More importantly, the Dodgers had won for the first time in 17 tries. Sure, they got a little help, but they were ready to take a victory under any circumstances.

FIRST GAME

			r	h	e
Brooklyn	000 002 011	=	4	11	2
Boston	500 000 03x	=	8	8	2

Game-Winning RBI: Nieman

Batteries: H. Gregg (L 6-10) 4 IP, R. Branca 2 IP, L. Webber 2 IP & M. Owen.
J. Tobin (W 10-10) & P. Masi

SECOND GAME

Brooklyn	ab	r	h	bi	o	a	e
L. Olmo, 2b	5	1	2	3	1	6	0
G. Rosen, cf	3	1	0	0	1	0	0
A. Galan, lf	3	1	0	1	3	0	0
D. Walker, rf	4	1	2	0	3	0	0
F. Bordagaray, 3b	4	1	2	1	2	2	0
M. Owen, c	4	0	0	0	2	0	0
H. Schultz, 1b	3	1	0	0	12	1	0
B. Bragan, c	4	1	1	0	2	3	1
C. Davis, p	3	1	0	0	1	1	0
	33	8	7	5	27	13	1

Boston	ab	r	h	bi	o	a	e
C. Ryan, 2b	4	0	0	0	6	5	0
M. Macon, 1b	4	1	1	1	10	1	1
T. Holmes, cf	4	0	0	0	4	0	0
B. Nieman, lf	4	0	1	0	1	0	0
C. Workman, rf	3	1	1	0	2	0	0
C. Kluttz, c	4	0	1	0	4	1	0
P. Capri, pr9	0	0	0	0	-	-	-
D. Phillips, ss	4	1	0	1	0	4	0
W. Huston, 3b	3	1	2	0	0	2	1
B. Etchison, ph9	1	0	0	0	-	-	-
A. Javery, p	0	0	0	0	0	1	1
R. Barrett, p2	0	0	0	0	0	0	0
A. Wright, ph3	1	1	1	3	-	-	-
I. Hutchinson, p4	1	0	0	0	0	0	0
C. Ross, ph7	1	0	0	0	-	-	-
S. Klopp, p8	0	0	0	0	0	1	0
P. Masi, ph9	1	0	0	0	-	-	-
	35	5	7	5	27	15	3

Brooklyn	070 000 001	=	8
Boston	003 001 001	=	5

	ip	h	r-er	bb	so
Davis (W 5-6)	9	7	5-4	1	2
Javery (L 3-13)	1⅔	3	7-0	3	1
Barrett	1⅓	1	0-0	0	1
Hutchinson	4	1	0-0	0	0
Klopp	2	2	1-1	0	1

Umpires: G. Magerkurth, B. Stewart, & T. Dunn

Game-Winning run scored on throwing error
LOB: Brooklyn 2, Boston 4
BE: Brooklyn 2, Boston 1
DP: Huston-Ryan-Macon (Bordagaray)
2B: Nieman, Workman
HR: Wright, Macon
SH: Davis
SB: Walker
Time—1:36 Attend.—10,002 pd.; 11,269 total

On August 21st, the Dodgers played the final inning of their suspended game of July 9th and lost. That officially made their losing streak of June 28th through July 16th sixteen games long, the longest in the history of the franchise.

Brooklyn flirted with last place through the remainder of the season but managed to finish seventh with a 63-91 record.

1945 SUNDAY, JULY 8TH, AT EBBETS FIELD

Babe Herman Returns with a Hit

But Dodgers Lose Two to St. Louis and Drop to 2nd Place
Babe Singles in First At Bat, Dixie Walker Hits Grand Slam

Today's Results			
St. Louis 6-BROOKLYN 4 (1st game)			
St. Louis 6-BROOKLYN 4 (2nd game)			
Chicago 12-Philadelphia 6 (1st game)			
Chicago 9-Philadelphia 2 (2nd game)			
Cincinnati 5-New York 2 (1st game)			
New York 5-Cincinnati 2 (2nd game)			
Pittsburgh 10-Boston 8 (1st game)			
Boston 13-Pittsburgh 1 (2nd game)			
Standings	**W-L**	**Pct.**	**GB**
Chicago	42-28	.600	—
BROOKLYN	43-31	.581	1
St. Louis	42-31	.575	1½
New York	41-36	.532	4½
Pittsburgh	37-36	.507	6½
Boston	36-36	.500	7
Cincinnati	33-37	.471	9
Philadelphia	20-59	.253	21½

THE SURPRISING BROOKLYN DODGERS finally fell out of the top perch in the National League nest after a three-week stay. Today they lost both games of a doubleheader to the St. Louis Cardinals and fell 1 game behind the new leaders, the Chicago Cubs.

But the day was not a total loss for the 36,053 Brooklyn fans who packed little Ebbets Field. Two of the borough's greatest baseball heroes delivered hits in high style, much to the delight of the crowd. "The People's Cherce," Frederick E. Walker (better known as "Dixie") hit a grand slam in the second game. And an old-timer named Floyd C. Herman (better known as "Babe") delivered a single in his first at bat as a Dodger since 1931. Then flashing the style that made him famous so many years ago, Babe fell flat on his face rounding first base. The fans went crazy in appreciation.

Unfortunately, only Walker (with 7) and Herman (with 1) were able to drive in runs for the home team. Helped by three Brooklyn errors, the Cardinals were able to win both games by the same score, 6-4.

The Dodgers, pre-season picks for last place, had vaulted into first on June 17th in the midst of a hot streak in which they won 15 out of 16 decisions. They had built up a lead of 4½ games by July 1st. Then came a hair-raising adventure trying to fly home from an exhibition game in Cherry Point, North Carolina, on July 2nd. After false starts, terrible storms, and defective navy transport planes, the Bums got home and lost six out of eight including today. After the double defeat by the Cardinals, the feeling was that the Dodger bubble had burst beyond repair.

Bad fielding by the Brooklyn pitchers hurt in each game today, starting in the second inning of the opener. After Whitey Kurowski had tripled and scored on a fly, Vic Lombardi made a terrible throw past first base on a bunt. A walk, a two-run triple by George Fallon, and another run-scoring fly ball gave St. Louis four runs in the inning.

A crazy bounce in the outfield and an error by Eddie Stanky gave the Cards single runs in the sixth and seventh innings.

The Dodgers got two runs in their half of the sixth on a single by Goody Rosen, a double by Augie Galan, and a two-run single by Walker.

Luis Olmo smacked a one-out triple in the home half of the seventh. Durocher decided this was the time to see if Herman could still hit. Babe hadn't been in the big leagues since 1937, but he had averaged over .300 in each of six seasons in the Pacific Coast League since 1939. As he strode to the platter, the Flatbush Faithful gave him a tremendous ovation. Herman broke his bat fouling off the first pitch. After getting some new lumber, he cracked the next serve on a line to right field as the crowd roared. Olmo scored on the hit. Babe tore around first, tripped over the bag, and fell face down. He had to hustle back on his hands and knees to keep from being picked off, and the fans could not contain their glee about the return of the fabled Babe of old. Durocher sent in a pinch-runner, and Herman received another big hand as he trotted off.

After an error, Walker drove the runner home with another single, cutting the St. Louis lead to 6-4.

But pitcher Red Barrett settled down and retired the Brooks in order in the last two innings to win the game for the Cardinals.

The Dodgers grabbed a 4-1 lead in the first inning on the second game on three singles and Walker's grand slam. Dixie's drive cleared the right field wall and landed on Bedford Avenue.

But Ken Burkhart shut the Dodgers out the rest of the way, and the Cardinals came back to win the game.

A walk, a double, two long flies, and two singles around a stolen base tied the game in the fourth inning and knocked pitcher Hal Gregg out.

After the Dodgers wasted a couple of scoring chances, St. Louis was given the lead in the eithth. Relief pitcher Clyde King made the key error. With Ken O'Dea on first with a hit, Emil Verban dropped a two-strike bunt toward third. King picked it up and made an ill-advised throw to first. The ball sailed past the first baseman and went all the way into the corner, allowing O'Dea to come all the way home and Verban to reach third. Fallon's long fly scored Verban to make the score 6-4.

The Dodgers couldn't score again, and St. Louis won. Herman popped out in the ninth inning in another pinch-hitting role.

The Dodgers had fallen to second place, but at least Walker and Herman had given the fans something to cheer about.

FIRST GAME

St. Louis	ab	r	h	bi	o	a	e
R. Schoendienst, lf	4	0	1	1	2	0	0
J. Hopp, rf	4	0	1	0	1	0	0
B. Adams, cf	4	0	0	0	5	0	0
W. Kurowski, 3b	4	2	2	1	0	0	0
R. Sanders, 1b	4	0	0	1	8	2	0
D. Rice, c	4	1	0	0	5	0	0
E. Verban, 2b	3	2	0	0	1	4	1
G. Fallon, ss	4	1	2	2	3	2	1
R. Barrett, p	2	0	1	1	2	1	0
	33	6	7	6	27	9	2

Brooklyn	ab	r	h	bi	o	a	e
E. Stanky, 2b	3	0	0	0	4	2	1
B. Herman, ph7	1	0	1	1	-	-	-
M. Sandlock, pr7-2b	1	1	0	0	0	0	0
G. Rosen, cf	5	1	1	0	6	0	0
A. Galan, lf-1b8	3	1	1	0	4	0	0
D. Walker, rf	4	0	2	3	1	0	0
F. Bordagaray, 3b	4	0	0	0	2	4	0
E. Basinski, ss	4	0	0	0	1	3	0
H. Schultz, 1b	3	0	1	0	6	0	0
A. Herring, p8	0	0	0	0	0	1	0
M. Aderholt, ph8	1	0	0	0	-	-	-
C. Buker, p9	0	0	0	0	0	0	0
S. Andrews, c	2	0	0	0	0	1	0
J. Peacock, c7	2	0	0	0	3	0	0
V. Lombardi, p	2	0	1	0	0	1	1
L. Olmo, ph7-lf	2	1	1	0	0	0	0
	37	4	8	4	27	12	2

St. Louis	040	001	100	= 6
Brooklyn	000	002	200	= 4

	ip	h	r-er	bb	so
Barrett (W 10-6)	9	8	4-3	1	4
Lombardi (L 5-6)	7	7	6-3	1	0
Herring	1	0	0-0	0	0
Buker	1	0	0-0	0	1

Attendance—32,001 paid; 36,053 total
Umpires: J. Conlan, D. Boggess, & B. Pinelli

Game-Winning RBI: Sanders
LOB: St. Louis 2, Brooklyn 7
BE: St. Louis 2, Brooklyn 2
DP: Bordagaray-Stanky-Schultz (Adams)
2B: Galan
3B: Kurowski, Fallon, Olmo
HR: Kurowski
SH: Barrett
CS: Hopp
Time--1:45

SECOND GAME

					r	h	e
St. Louis	100	300	020	=	6	12	2
Brooklyn	400	000	000	=	4	9	1

Game-Winning run scored on error by King

Batteries: K. Burkhart (W 9-4) & K. O'Dea
H. Gregg 3⅔ IP, C. King (L 4-2) 5⅓ IP & J. Peacock

The Dodgers were unable to keep pace with the Cubs and Cardinals over the second half of the season and finished third, 11 games behind pennant-winning Chicago. Brooklyn's final record was 87-67.

1946 SATURDAY, SEPTEMBER 14TH, AT EBBETS FIELD

Leo Plays a Hunch & Branca Stars

Youngster Shuts Out Cardinals on 3 Hits
Dodgers Close to Within ½ Game of St. Louis

Today's Results			
BROOKLYN 5-St. Louis 0			
Philadelphia 6-Chicago 3			
Boston 9-Pittsburgh 3			
Cincinnati 4-New York 0			
Standings	**W-L**	**Pct.**	**GB**
St. Louis	88-53	.624	—
BROOKLYN	86-52	.623	½
Chicago	74-63	.540	12
Boston	72-67	.518	15
Cincinnati	60-77	.438	26
Philadelphia	62-80	.437	26½
Pittsburgh	58-80	.420	28½
New York	57-85	.401	31½

LEO DUROCHER HAD A LITTLE SCHEME cooked up for the crucial final game against St. Louis on Brooklyn's 1946 schedule. He decided he could get his team a slight advantage if he sent 20-year-old righthander Ralph Branca to the mound at the start of the game and then switched to lefty Vic Lombardi after the Cardinals had submitted a lineup loaded with lefthanded hitters.

Branca was supposed to pitch to only one batter before the switch was to be made. But Durocher had a hunch that Ralph had the stuff to win today, and he left his "decoy" out on the mound the whole game. Branca responded by striking out nine batters and shutting the first-place Cardinals out on just three hits. He also chipped in a pair of base hits and runs scored for the Dodgers.

As a result, Brooklyn won 5-0 to move to within ½ game of the leaders. The Dodgers still had 16 games left to play, while the Redbirds' slate showed 13 games left. This was the last scheduled game between the two clubs, and it drew a capacity crowd to Ebbets Field. The attendance today pushed the club's season total over 1,500,000 for a new National League record.

Needing badly to win, Durocher took a long gamble with young Branca. Ralph had not lasted past the sixth inning in any of his six previous starts this season. Lombardi, on the other hand, was tied for the team lead in complete games with 12, including a 1-0 victory over Boston in his last outing. It was Leo's intention all along to use Lombardi today, but he had Branca warm up before the game.

After exchanging lineup cards with St. Louis manager Eddie Dyer, Durocher had Lombardi start to get ready in the bullpen. But by the rules, Branca had to pitch to one batter before he could be removed. So the youngster faced leadoff man Red Schoendienst and got him to pop out. Then he feigned shoulder troubles and looked expectantly into the dugout for the call to leave the game.

But by this time, Leo's mind was racing along another track. Branca had looked good warming up, and he had disposed of the first hitter so quickly that Lombardi might not be entirely ready yet. So Durocher stayed in the dugout, and Branca stayed in the game. The next hitter, Harry Walker, was one of the lefties that Leo wanted to get out of the game. But Harry obligingly jumped on Branca's first pitch and fouled out. Stan Musial then bounced out, and Branca had completed the inning on just five pitches.

Durocher was impressed enough to send the big righty back out in the second inning. Lombardi remained at ready in the bullpen. The first St. Louis batter, Enos Slaughter, lined out deep to center, which was a bad sign. But the next two hitters fanned, and Leo's mind was made up: Branca would stay.

The Dodgers got a run in the bottom of the second on a two-out homer to left field by veteran Cookie Lavagetto.

Branca started a Dodger rally in the bottom of the third with a sharp single off the second baseman's glove. After Eddie Stanky lined out, Pee Wee Reese popped a hit into short left field. One out later, Dixie Walker hit a liner into the gap in right center, doubling Branca and Reese home.

After St. Louis starter Harry Brecheen was removed for a pinch-hitter, Branca started another rally in the fifth with a solid single to right off of Ted Wilks. He came around to score on a bloop single by Stanky, a fumbled bunt, and an infield out.

The fastballing Dodger had little trouble with the Cardinal hitters, lefthanded and righthanded. He walked the leadoff man in the third, but he was left on second base. In the fourth, Walker opened with a hit but was thrown out stealing. With two out in the fifth, Joe Garagiola singled and Marty Marion walked. But then Branca struck out pinch-hitter Walter Sessi on three pitches. The Cards went out in order in the sixth, and seventh. And in the eighth it was three up and three down all on called third strikes!

The Dodgers were given a run in the bottom of the eighth when shortstop Marion fumbled a double-play ball and Freddy Schmidt walked Bruce Edwards with the bases loaded.

Musial solved Branca for a two-out single in the ninth. But Slaughter lofted to first baseman Ed Stevens for the final out. Branca had won only his second game of the year, and it was his first shutout of the season. It couldn't have come at a better time, since it kept the Dodgers right in the thick of the pennant race by giving them the final series with the Cardinals, two games to one.

Leo's cute little trick hadn't worked out quite as had been planned, but no one in Brooklyn was complaining. If his schemes would always "backfire" this well, the Dodgers would never lose the pennant!

St. Louis	ab	r	h	bi	o	a	e
R. Schoendienst, 2b	4	0	0	0	2	0	0
H. Walker, cf	4	0	1	0	5	0	0
S. Musial, 1b	4	0	1	0	6	0	0
E. Slaughter, rf	4	0	0	0	2	0	0
W. Kurowski, 3b	3	0	0	0	0	1	0
D. Sisler, lf	3	0	0	0	2	0	0
J. Garagiola, c	2	0	1	0	4	2	0
M. Marion, ss	2	0	0	0	3	4	1
H. Brecheen, p	1	0	0	0	0	0	0
W. Sessi, ph5	1	0	0	0	-	-	-
T. Wilks, p5	0	0	0	0	0	2	1
N. Jones, ph8	1	0	0	0	-	-	-
F. Schmidt, p8	0	0	0	0	0	0	0
R. Barrett, p8	0	0	0	0	0	0	0
	29	0	3	0	24	9	2

Brooklyn	ab	r	h	bi	o	a	e
E. Stanky, 2b	4	0	1	0	1	2	0
P. Reese, ss	2	1	1	0	1	2	0
J. Medwick, lf	2	0	0	0	0	0	0
A. Galan, ph5-lf	1	0	0	0	1	0	0
D. Walker, rf	4	1	1	3	0	0	0
C. Furillo, cf	4	0	1	0	5	0	0
C. Lavagetto, 3b	4	1	1	1	1	0	0
B. Edwards, c	3	0	1	1	9	1	0
H. Schultz, 1b	3	0	0	0	7	1	0
E. Stevens, ph8-1b	1	0	0	0	1	0	0
R. Branca, p	4	2	2	0	1	1	0
	32	5	8	5	27	7	0

St. Louis	000	000	000	=	0
Brooklyn	012	010	01x	=	5

	ip	h	r-er	bb	so
Brecheen (L 13-14)	4	5	3-3	1	2
Wilks	3	2	1-0	0	2
Schmidt	⅓	1	1-0	2	0
Barrett	⅔	0	0-0	0	1
Branca (W 2-0)	9	3	0-0	2	9

Time—2:18

Umpires: W. Henline, L. Ballanfant, A. Barlick, & B. Pinelli

Game-Winning RBI: Lavagetto
LOB: St. Louis 4, Brooklyn 7
BE: Brooklyn 2
DP: Edwards-Reese
2B: D. Walker
HR: Lavagetto
SH: Reese
CS: Reese, H. Walker
Attendance—32,960 paid
33,480 total

Branca pitched another shutout in his next start against Pittsburgh.

The Dodgers won 9 of their next 14 and tied the Cardinals (who were 7-4) on the final Friday of the season. Both contenders won on Saturday and lost on Sunday to finish the schedule in a tie.

1946 THURSDAY, OCTOBER 4TH, AT EBBETS FIELD
Playoff—Game #2

Dodgers Lose Pennant as Desperate Rally Fails

Today's Results			
St. Louis 8-BROOKLYN 4 (St. Louis wins best-of-three playoff, 2 games to 0)			
Standings	**W-L**	**Pct.**	**GB**
St. Louis	98-58	.628	—
BROOKLYN	96-60	.615	2
Chicago	82-71	.536	14½
Boston	81-72	.529	15½
Philadelphia	69-85	.448	28
Cincinnati	67-87	.435	30
Pittsburgh	63-91	.409	34
New York	61-93	.396	36

GENERAL LEO DEROCHER HURLED 18 OF Commander-in-Chief Branch Rickey's troops into the final battle of the campaign today to no avail. The long-range bombardment by the opposing St. Louis Cardinals defeated Durocher's Dodgers, 8-4, to end one of the most closely contested pennant races in history. Brooklyn had battled the highly-rated St. Louis forces throughout the year, and the two teams had finished their schedules exactly tied. So an unprecedented best-of-three playoff was arranged. In this final confrontation, St. Louis finally won a decisive victory, taking the first two games played.

Despite the ultimate defeat, Generals Rickey and Durocher had cause to be proud of their men. The Cardinals had been overwhelming favorites all season. They had a set lineup and good pitching depth. By comparison, the Dodgers had no regular at first or third base, had shuffled outfielders frequently, and did not come up with a suitable catcher until mid-June. And the Brooklyn pitching staff had no "ace" of the caliber of St. Louis's Howie Pollet. Yet the Flatbush Flock came within a hair's breadth of grabbing the pennant.

The playoff opener in St. Louis on Tuesday was won by the home team, 4-2. Pollet's pitching, superior fielding, and a few seeing-eye base hits at critical moments gave the Cardinals the victory.

Today's game in Brooklyn was more of a rout. The Dodgers scored the first run. But then it was all St. Louis until the ninth. Trailing 8-1 going into the bottom of the last, the Dodgers suddenly came to life. They routed starting pitcher Murry Dickson and scored three runs. With one out, the tying run came to the plate with the bases loaded. The Brooklyn fans were suddenly roaring with anticipation, and pitcher Harry Brecheen seemed shaky. But Brecheen steadied and struck out the final two batters to finish off the pesky Dodgers once and for all.

Brooklyn opened the scoring in the bottom of the first with a two-out rally. Galan started it with an infield tap past the mound for a hit. Dixie Walker drew a base on balls. And Ed Stevens ripped an RBI single up the middle.

The Dodger lead did not last. St. Louis scored twice in the second inning to take command. With one out, Erv Dusak poled a long drive to left center. Dick Whitman tried desperately for a catch, but the ball glanced off his glove and hit the wall for a triple. Marty Marion flied out deep, and Dusak scored easily. Clyde Kluttz bounced a single to center. And Dickson pounded a triple over center fielder Carl Furillo's head to drive in the go-ahead run.

In the fifth, the Cards finally drove Dodger starter Joe Hatten out of the game. With two gone, Stan Musial cracked a double off the right field wall. Durocher ordered the lefthanded Hatten to walk righthanded Whitey Kurowski to get to lefthanded batter Enos Slaughter. Slaughter, however, was the league leader in runs-batted-in. And he added two to his total with a triple into the gap in right center. Hatten got ahead of Dusak, 0-and-2, then laid one down the middle, and it was lined to center for a hit and a run. Hank Behrman then replaced Hatten on the hill.

St. Louis got a run in the seventh on two walks and two bunts.

In the eighth, Kirby Higbe gave up two singles, one double, and two bases on balls to net St. Louis its final two runs.

By the time the bottom of the ninth rolled around, many of the 31,875 fans had left. But those who stayed got one more chance to cheer for their Bums.

Galan led off the inning with a double off the right field barrier. It was the first Dodger hit since the first inning. Walker flied out. Stevens pounded a triple to right center, and Galan scored. Furillo's single drove Stevens home. A wild pitch sent Furillo to second. Pee Wee Reese walked.

Cardinal manager Eddie Dyer rushed Brecheen in to pitch. The little lefthander was greeted by a single to left by Edwards. The hit sent Furillo home, although Reese stopped at second when the throw went to third. Cookie Lavagetto drew a walk pinch-hitting to load the bases. That brought the tying run to the plate.

But Brecheen was now warmed up and was equal to the challange. Although the fans were screaming for a home run to tie the game, pesky Eddie Stanky went up trying to wheedle a walk. Eventually, he struck out instead. Down to the last out, Durocher sent Howie Schultz, a righthander with power, to the plate. Howie had hit for the circuit in St. Louis on Tuesday. With the stands imploring him, Howie took some big cuts but hit nothing and struck out.

So it was finally over. The young Dodgers had lost out at the very end. But they would be back, and the Cardinals and the rest of the league had better watch out.

St. Louis	ab	r	h	bi	o	a	e
R. Schoendienst, 2b	5	1	1	0	1	5	0
T. Moore, cf	5	1	2	0	2	0	0
S. Musial, 1b	4	1	1	0	14	1	0
W. Kurowski, 3b	2	2	1	2	1	1	0
E. Slaughter, rf	3	1	1	2	0	0	0
E. Dusak, lf	3	1	2	1	1	0	0
H. Walker, ph8-lf	1	0	0	0	0	0	0
M. Marion, ss	3	0	1	2	4	3	0
C. Kluttz, c	5	1	2	0	3	2	0
M. Dickson, p	5	0	2	1	1	5	0
H. Brecheen, p9	0	0	0	0	0	0	0
	36	8	13	8	27	17	0

Brooklyn	ab	r	h	bi	o	a	e
E. Stanky, 2b	5	0	0	0	3	4	0
D. Whitman, lf	4	0	0	0	2	0	0
H. Schultz, ph9	1	0	0	0	-	-	-
A. Galan, 3b	4	2	2	0	0	4	0
D. Walker, rf	3	0	0	0	1	0	0
E. Stevens, 1b	4	1	2	2	11	0	0
C. Furillo, cf	4	1	1	1	4	0	0
P. Reese, ss	2	0	0	0	2	3	0
B. Edwards, c	2	0	1	1	3	1	0
J. Hatten, p	1	0	0	0	0	1	0
H. Behrman, p5	0	0	0	0	0	0	0
G. Hermanski, ph5	1	0	0	0	-	-	-
V. Lombardi, p6	0	0	0	0	0	1	0
K. Higbe, p7	0	0	0	0	1	0	0
R. Melton, p8	0	0	0	0	0	0	0
J. Medwick, ph8	1	0	0	0	-	-	-
H. Taylor, p9	0	0	0	0	0	0	0
C. Lavagetto, ph9	0	0	0	0	0	0	0
	32	4	6	4	27	14	0

St. Louis	020 030 120	=	8
Brooklyn	100 000 003	=	4

	ip	h	r-er	bb	so
Dickson (W 15-6)	8⅓	5	4-4	5	3
Brecheen	⅔	1	0-0	1	2
Hatten (L 14-11)	4⅔	7	5-5	3	0
Behrman	⅓	1	0-0	0	0
Lombardi	1⅓	1	1-1	2	0
Higbe	1	3	2-2	2	1
Melton	⅔	0	0-0	0	0
Taylor	1	1	0-0	0	1

WP: Dickson

Game-Winning RBI: Dickson
LOB: St. Louis 11, Brooklyn 7
DP: Dickson-Marion-Musial (Stanky)
Stanky-Reese-Stevens (Schoendienst)
2B: Musial, Moore, Galan
3B: Dusak, Dickson, Slaughter, Stevens
SH: Schoendienst, Dusak, Marion

Time—2:44
Attendance—31,437 paid
31,875 total
Umpires: B. Pinelli, L. Goetz,
D. Boggess, & B. Reardon

Chapter XI The Incredible Era Begins

1947 July 31st
Win 13th Straight, Lead League by 10

1947 World Series Game No. 4
Spoil No-Hitter in 9th and Beat Yanks

1948 July 4th
Campanella's First N.L. Home Runs

1949 October 2nd
Win Pennant in Extra Innings on Last Day

1949 World Series Game No. 2
Roe Stops Yankees 1-0

1950 August 31st
Hodges Hits 4 Home Runs

1950 October 1st
Tenth-Inning Homer Ends Pennant Hopes

1951 September 30th
Robinson's Heroics Force a Playoff

1951 Playoff Game No. 3
Thomson's Homer Kills Dodgers

THE YOUNG DODGERS WHO HAD CHALLENGED THE POWERFUL CARDINALS FOR THE pennant in 1946 were not the only big newsmakers in the Brooklyn organization that season. Down in the minor leagues, the club had a handful of black players under contract, the first in Organized Baseball in over 50 years. The pioneer was Jackie Robinson, who starred with the Montreal Royals in the International League in 1946. Robinson was ready for the National League in 1947. Other Negro prospects included catcher Roy Campanella and pitcher Don Newcombe.

Robinson was promoted to the Brooklyn roster on April 9, 1947, near the end of spring training. A second baseman by trade, he was assigned to the Dodgers' trouble spot at first base. On opening day, April 15, 1947, he became the first balck man ever to play in an official National League game.

On the same day that Robinson was promoted to the parent club, Commissioner Albert B. "Happy" Chandler suspended Dodger manager Leo Durocher for one season "for conduct detrimental to baseball." The charges revolved around some of Durocher's friends, particularly George Raft, an actor who was alleged to have contacts with known gamblers.

The team opened the season with coach Clyde Sukeforth as interim manager. After two games, Burt Shotton took over. Shotton was an old associate of Branch Rickey's dating back to 1913, when Rickey had become manager of the St. Louis Browns, and Shotton was the center fielder and leadoff hitter. In contrast to the tempestuous Durocher, Shotton was soft-spoken and likeable. He soon gained the respect of the players.

With Robinson and third baseman John "Spider" Jorgensen solidifying the infield, the Dodgers were in the thick of the pennant race from the beginning. After a slow start himself, Robinson began to contribute on the field and gain the acceptance of his teammates. And the open hostility of players on the other teams to the young Negro helped unify the Dodgers into a winning team.

On July 6th, Ralph Branca won his 12th game of the season, and the Dodgers went back into first place to stay. Brooklyn ended the month with a 13-game winning

Carl Furillo, Jackie Robinson, Roy Campanella, Pee Wee Reese, Duke Snider, Preacher Roe, & Gil Hodges

streak, which upped its league lead to a full 10 games.

St. Louis made a bid in early August and pulled to within 3 games of the Dodgers. But Brooklyn won 28 of its final 44 to take the pennant by 5 lengths. Branca finished with a 21-12 record, and Joe Hatten pitched in with a 17-8 log. Hugh Casey was 10-4 with many other games saved coming out of the bullpen. The offense was well balanced. Robinson led the team in runs with 125 and led the league in stolen bases with 29. He hit .297 as a rookie. Dixie Walker had one last good year, hitting .306 and leading the team with 94 runs-batted-in.

The 1947 World Series against the Yankees was a classic. After New York won the first two games, the Dodgers came back to win two thrillers, 9-8 and 3-2. In that second victory, Brooklyn had no hits and was trailing 2-1 with two out in the bottom of the ninth. But Cookie Lavagetto came through with a pinch double to break up the no-hitter and drive home two runs to win the game. New York won the fifth game, 2-1. But the Dodgers bounced back to take the sixth, 8-6, with a great catch by Al Gionfriddo saving the bacon. Brooklyn took the early lead in the seventh game, but the Yankees prevailed, 5-2, leaving the Brooklyn fans to "wait until next year."

Leo Durocher was back as manager the next spring.

In 1948, Rickey put his hopes heavily on younger players, trading away established heroes Dixie Walker and Eddie Stanky. Stanky was dealt to the Braves for cash and two useless players. Walker and pitchers Hal Gregg and Vic Lombardi were traded to Pittsburgh for young infielders Billy Cox and Gene Mauch and 30-year-old pitcher Elwin "Preacher" Roe. Perhaps the best prospect in the farm system was catcher Roy Campanella. Rickey wanted him to break the color barrier in the American Association, so he was sent to St. Paul.

Although these moves paid solid dividends in the long term, the roster machinations may have cost Brooklyn the pennant in 1948. The strengthened Boston and Pittsburgh teams beat the Dodgers more than any other teams that year, and the Braves won the championship. The Dodgers developed problems at catcher and third base when Bruce Edwards and Spider Jorgensen both hurt their arms in May. In the latter part of the month, the Dodgers lost eight in a row, four of them to the Braves and Pirates.

On July 2nd, the Bums slipped to last place. That same day, Campanella rejoined the club, and two days later he hit his first two home runs in the National League

Jackie Robinson and Branch Rickey

to help the Dodgers rally to win a wild one from the Giants, 13-12.

The day after the All-Star break, the incredible news came that Durocher had been released by Brooklyn and signed to manage the New York Giants. This move shocked fans in both boroughs, but it turned out to help both clubs. Burt Shottom was brought back to pilot the Dodgers, who leaped into the pennant race.

On August 29th, the hard-charging Brooks reached first place. On the 30th, they won a doubleheader for a 1½-game lead. On September 3rd, however, Durocher's Giants came to Ebbets Field and won a doubleheader to knock the Dodgers back out of the lead. Three days later the Flock lost a pair to the first-place Braves to fall 4 games behind. Brooklyn had to settle for third place, 7½ games behind Boston, 1 behind St. Louis, and 1 ahead of surprising Pittsburgh.

In 1949, Brooklyn was a serious contender all the way. Don Newcombe was brought up from Montreal in May, and he pitched a shutout and drove in two runs in his first starting assigment. Ralph Branca won ten of his first eleven decisions. Young Edwin "Duke" Snider became a fixture in center field, with Carl Furillo moving permanently to right.

Through most on June and July, the Dodgers led the league. But they were never able to get farther than 3½ games ahead of the second-place Cardinals. St. Louis went ahead on August 20th and stayed on top for the next five weeks. But Brooklyn never fell more than 2½ behind.

With less than a week to play, the Dodgers were still 1½ back. But they grabbed the lead with three days to go and clinched the flag on the final day with a tension-packed, ten-inning, 9-7 victory in Philadelphia.

Jackie Robinson won the batting title with a .342 mark and was named the league's Most Valuable Player.

In the World Series, Newcombe lost a heartbreaker to the Yankees in the opener, 1-0. Preacher Roe came back to pitch the Dodgers to a 1-0 win of their own in the second game. But New York won the next three, 4-3, 6-4, and 10-6, to take the series in five games.

The Dodgers started the 1950 campaign well enough. They held the league lead as late as June 29th. But beginning the next day, they lost three in a row in Philadelphia, and the Phillies took over first place. Although Newcombe and Roe did very well, the rest of the Dodger pitching was erratic. But at least there was nothing wrong with the Dodger hitting. Three different players had three-homer games during the season, and on August 31st, Gil Hodges hit four home runs in one game.

With less than two weeks left in the season, the Dodgers fell all the way to 9 games out. Then in the next eleven days they won 12 and lost 3. Over the same period, the Phillies were only 3-8.

The Phils came to Brooklyn for the final two games of the season leading by only 2 lengths. On Saturday, Erv Palica pitched Brooklyn to a 7-3 victory. Incredibly, the Bums still had a chance to win the pennant. They needed another victory on the final day to send the race into a playoff. Don Newcombe battled Robin Roberts to a 1-1 tie in the ninth inning. In the Dodger half of the ninth, the potential winning run was thrown out at the plate. Then the Dodgers lost the game 4-1 on a home run by Dick Sisler in the top of the tenth.

After the end of the 1950 season, Walter O'Malley replaced Rickey as club president, and manager Burt Shotton was replaced by Chuck Dressen.

In 1951, Roe and Newcombe were backed by good pitching by Carl Erskine, Clyde King, and Ralph Branca. And the hitting continued to be devastating. The Dodgers took over first place in mid-May and were 8½ games ahead of the pack by the All-Star Game. When they split a doubleheader on August 11th, the Brooks led by 13 full games.

Then the second-place Giants ran off a 16-game winning streak to slice the margin to 5 games. But with ten games to play, Brooklyn still led by 4½. Then the Dodgers lost six of nine and found themselves in a tie with the Giants on the last day of the schedule.

For the third straight year, the Dodger pennant hopes came down to the final game on the slate. Once again the game was against the Phillies. And for the third incredible season in a row, the game went into extra innings. In the bottom of the 12th, Jackie Robinson saved the game and the Dodger pennant hopes with a great diving catch. In the 14th, Jackie won the game with a home run.

Since the Giants had also won on the final day, a playoff was necessary. In the first game, Branca gave up home runs to Bobby Thomson and Monte Irvin and lost, 3-1. In the second game, Robinson drove in the first three runs of the game, and Clem Labine shut the Giants out, 10-0. In the decisive third game, the Dodgers broke a 1-1 tie with three runs in the eighth. But the Giants rallied against starter Don Newcombe in the ninth. With the tying runs on base, Branca was brought in to face Thomson. His second pitch was hit into the stands for the most famous home run in history, and the Dodgers lost, lost the game, lost the playoff, and lost the pennant.

Cookie Lavagetto breaking up Bill Beven's no-hitter in the 1947 World Series

1947 THURSDAY, JULY 31ST, AT SPORTSMAN'S PARK, ST. LOUIS

Win 13th Straight, Lead League by 10

Dodgers Top Cardinals Again, 2-1
Reese Hits Triple in 9th to Win Game

Today's Results			
BROOKLYN 2-St. Louis 1			
Cincinnati 8-New York 7			
Philadelphia 3-Chicago 0			
Boston at Philadelphia, ppd.—rain			
Standings	**W-L**	**Pct.**	**GB**
BROOKLYN	63-36	.636	—
New York	49-42	.538	10
St. Louis	51-44	.537	10
Boston	50-45	.526	11
Cincinnati	47-52	.475	16
Chicago	44-52	.458	17½
Pittsburgh	40-56	.417	21½
Philadelphia	40-57	.412	22

THE HARD-CHARGING BROOKLYN DODgers continued to make a shambles out of the National League pennant race today by winning their 13th consecutive decision. The 2-1 victory over the St. Louis Cardinals, combined with the New York Giants' defeat at the hands of the Cincinnati Reds, extended Brooklyn's lead in the race to 10 full games. When the streak started, the Dodgers led by only 2½.

Here is a review of the streak day-by-day:

July 20 The Dodgers thought they had pulled out a 3-2 victory with three runs in the bottom of the ninth. But later the league office upheld a protest by the Cardinals, and the game officially became a 3-3 tie.

July 21 Brooklyn beat Cincinnati twice, 7-4 and 4-3, winning the second game in the bottom of the ninth.

July 22 Ralph Branca had an easy time winning his 16th game of the year, and the Bums crushed the Reds in Cincinnati, 12-1.

July 23 An eighth-inning rally beat Cincy, 5-2. Hank Behrman got the win with relief help from Hugh Casey.

July 24 Vic Lombardi cruised to a six-hit, 6-1 victory over the Reds.

July 25 Harry Taylor pitched the Dodgers to a 4-1 win in Pittsburgh.

July 26 Two runs in the ninth beat the Pirates, 6-4. Casey got the win.

July 27 A doubleheader sweep in Pittsburgh, 8-4 and 11-4. Behrman and Hal Gregg were the winning pitchers.

July 28 The Brooks scored four in the ninth to break a 0-0 tie. Joe Hatten shut the Cubs out on three hits.

July 29 Taylor drove in three runs, scored the fourth, and pitched a three-hitter to beat St. Louis, 4-0.

July 30 The Dodgers blew a 10-0 lead, but they won out in the tenth inning on a hit by Pee Wee Reese, 11-10. Clyde King got credit for the win.

For today's game, manager Burt Shotton nominated Lombardi to pitch. St. Louis skipper Eddie Dyer chose Howie Pollet. Both lefthanders did very well, and the pitching duel was not decided until the final out was made.

The Dodger defense, which had been excellent of late, had some trouble today. In the first inning, second baseman Eddie Stanky, center fielder Carl Furillo, and right fielder Dixie Walker called each other off of a pop fly, allowing it to drop for a gift double. In the second, Stanky fumbled a smash off the bat of Enos Slaughter for only the second error of the winning streak. Shortstop Reese made another error with a wild throw in the seventh. But Lombardi pitched around each of these mistakes.

Stanky scored the first run of the game in the third inning. With one out, Eddie at first faked a bunt, which brought third baseman Whitey Kurowski charging in toward the plate. Stanky made an exaggerated reaction to Kurowski's maneuver, as if to indicate that he wouldn't try to bunt again. But on the very next pitch, Stanky dragged one down the line. Caught flat-footed, Kurowski could not throw the batter out. Stanky went to second as Jackie Robinson bounced out. Pete Reiser then rifled a single to right center, and Stanky came all the way home. Furillo followed with a hit that sent Reiser to third. Walker flied out to left to end the inning.

Double plays held the Dodgers down in the first, fourth, fifth, and seventh innings.

St. Louis tied the game in the sixth. Erv Dusak led off with a base on balls. Stan Musial sacrificed him to second. First baseman Robinson made a fine stop to retire Kurowski, with Dusak moving to third on the play. Slaughter sent a solid ground single up the middle to plate the run.

The tie was broken in the top of the ninth. Bruce Edwards lined a single over second with one out. Pollet tried to jam Reese on the fists, but Pee Wee swung "inside out" and shot the ball down into the right field corner. By the time the ball was returned to the infield, Edwards was home, Reese had a triple, and the Dodgers were ahead, 2-1.

Joe Medwick started a last-ditch rally for the Cardinals in the bottom of the ninth with a double off the screen in right field. Chuck Diering went in to run for Medwick. Marty Marion sacrificed Diering to third. Terry Moore, who was out of the lineup because of a sore knee, was sent up to pinch-hit. He smacked one down the third base line. Spider Jorgensen dug it out of the dirt near the bag, and Diering was caught off base. Jorgensen tagged the runner and threw to first. The throw was low, and Robinson could not pick it up cleanly. Moore crossed the bag and turned toward second. Robinson alertly tagged him out, and the Dodgers started running off the field. But umpire Dusty Boggess ruled that Moore had not tried for second base and was therefore not liable to be put out. A big argument erupted, as half the Dodger team surrounded Boggess. When play finally resumed, Del Rice ended the game with a long, lazy fly out to Walker in right.

Brooklyn had another victory and another game added to its lead. Sure, the Cardinals had overcome a 10-game deficit in 1942. But the Dodgers were still in a pretty comfortable position, and no one was complaining.

Brooklyn	ab	r	h	bi	o	a	e
E. Stanky, 2b	3	1	2	0	4	5	1
J. Robinson, 1b	4	0	0	0	11	3	0
P. Reiser, lf	4	0	2	1	2	0	0
C. Furillo, cf	4	0	1	0	2	0	0
D. Walker, rf	4	0	0	0	3	0	0
B. Edwards, c	4	1	2	0	1	0	0
P. Reese, ss	4	0	3	1	1	1	1
S. Jorgensen, 3b	4	0	0	0	1	1	0
V. Lombardi, p	3	0	0	0	2	4	0
	34	2	10	2	27	14	2

St. Louis	ab	r	h	bi	o	a	e
R. Schoendienst, 2b	4	0	0	0	2	5	0
E. Dusak, cf	3	1	2	0	4	0	0
S. Musial, 1b	3	0	0	0	12	0	1
W. Kurowski, 3b	4	0	1	0	0	2	0
E. Slaughter, lf	4	0	1	1	1	0	0
J. Medwick, rf	4	0	1	0	1	0	0
C. Diering, pr9	0	0	0	0	-	-	-
M. Marion, ss	3	0	1	0	7	6	0
D. Wilber, c	3	0	0	0	0	0	0
T. Moore, ph9	1	0	0	0	-	-	-
J. Cross, pr9	0	0	0	0	-	-	-
H. Pollet, p	3	0	1	0	0	2	0
D. Rice, ph9	1	0	0	0	-	-	-
	33	1	7	1	27	15	1

Brooklyn	001	000	001	=	2
St. Louis	000	001	000	=	1

	ip	h	r-er	bb	so
Lombardi (W 6-8)	9	7	1-1	1	1
Pollet (L 6-9)	9	10	2-2	3	0

Time—2:20
Attendance—21,873
Umpires: L. Jorda, D. Boggess, & G. Barr

Game-Winning RBI: Reese
LOB: Brooklyn 8, St. Louis 8
BE: Brooklyn 1, St. Louis 1
DP: Marion-Schoendienst-Musial (Robinson)
Schoendienst-Marion-Musial (Lombardi)
Marion-Musial
Kurowski-Marion-Sch'd'nst (Lombardi)
2B: Reiser, Dusak, Medwick
3B: Reese
SH: Musial, Marion

The Dodgers' streak was broken the next day in Chicago, starting Brooklyn on a cold spell that saw the team lose 8 games out of its next 11. At the same time, St. Louis won 11 of 13 to pull within 3 games of the league leaders.

But that was as close as the Cardinals got. By the end of August, the Dodgers' lead was back up to 7½ games. They won the pennant by a final margin of 5 games, with a record of 94-60.

1947 FRIDAY, OCTOBER 3RD, AT EBBETS FIELD
World Series—Game #4

Spoil No-Hitter in 9th and Beat Yanks

WITH ONE OF THE MOST DRAMATIC HITS IN WORLD SERIES HISTORY, THE BROOKLYN Dodgers turned an imminent no-hit defeat into an incredible 3-2 victory over the New York Yankees. Cookie Lavagetto, a pinch-hitter, delivered the hit, a two-out, two-run double off the right field wall, to ruin Bill Beven's bid to become the first hurler to pitch a no-hitter in the World Series.

The stunning victory enabled Brooklyn to even the series at two games apiece. After the Yanks had won the first two games in Yankee Stadium, 5-3 and 10-3, the Dodgers rebounded with two in a row in Ebbets Field, 9-8 and 3-2. Hugh Casey was credited with both wins, today making only one pitch to earn it.

Floyd "Bill" Bevens, the hard-luck loser, had a no-hitter for 136 pitches. But his 137th serve made him a loser. He set a World Series record by walking ten batters,and all three Dodger runs came as a result of bases on balls. His pitching was backed by some spectacular fielding.

Both managers, Burt Shotton of Brooklyn and Bucky Harris of New York, employed some questionable strategy. Shotton had the runner representing the tying run try to steal second base in the ninth inning. He made it thanks to a poor throw. Harris then decided to walk the next hitter intentionally, putting the winning run on base. That man scored, so the second-guessers convicted Harris of poor judgement and acquitted Shotton.

Shotton made the first big mistake of the day by sending sore-armed righthander Harry Taylor to the mound as his starter. Taylor faced four batters and retired none of them. Two singles, an infield error, and a walk gave the Yankees a run.

Hal Gregg was rushed into the game, and he got out of the bases-loaded jam with a pop out and a double play.

The Yankees pounded out a run against Gregg in the fourth inning on a triple by Billy Johnson and a double by Johnny Lindell.

Through the first four innings, Bevens walked four men and made a wild pitch.

But good fielding saved him. After Eddie Stanky had led off the first inning with a walk, second baseman George Stirnweiss ranged far to his right to rob Pee Wee Reese of a hit. In the third, Stanky was on second after a pass and a wild pitch. But Lindell defused the situation with a tremendous one-handed, diving, rolling catch of Jackie Robinson's fly down the left field line. In the fourth, Joe DiMaggio raced to deep center and made an over-the-shoulder catch of Gene Hermanski's long drive.

Brooklyn finally capitalized on Bevens's wildness in the fifth, when the Dodgers got a run without a hit. Spider Jorgensen and Gregg walked to open the inning. Stanky sacrificed the runners along. And Reese's infield out sent Jorgensen home.

Hermanski was robbed again in the eighth, this time by a high-leaping catch at the fence by right fielder Tommy Henrich.

In the ninth, the Yankees loaded the bases with one out against Hank Behrman. Hugh Casey was brought in in relief. His first pitch resulted in a double play.

Bruce Edwards led off the bottom of the ninth with a long drive to left. The crowd leaped to its feet, but Lindell caught the ball at the fence. Carl Furillo raised the hopes again with a walk. Al Gionfriddo was sent in as a pinch-runner. Jorgensen fouled out to first.

Bevens was now only one out away from a no-hit victory. Pete Reiser, who had injured his ankle in the third game, was sent up to pinch-hit. Bevens fell behind on the count, 2-and-1. On the next pitch (which was a ball), Giofriddo surprised everyone by breaking for second. He did not get a great jump, but catcher Yogi Berra's throw was high and off the base, allowing the runner to dive in safely with a steal. Harris now ordered an intentional fourth ball to Reiser. Eddie Miksis was sent in to run for Reiser at first.

With Eddie Stanky due to bat, Shotton decided at the last moment to send Lavagetto to the plate. Bevens' first pitch to the hitter was a swinging strike over the outside of the plate. The next pitch was in about the same place. Lavagetto was ready for it this time. Going with the pitch, Cookie sent a high fly toward the right field fence. Henrich did not get a good jump on the ball and had no chance to make the catch. The ball hit about ten feet up the barrier and caromed away from Henrich. Both Gionfriddo and Miksis were able to score ahead of the return, and Brooklyn suddenly had the winning runs across the plate.

For a moment the crowd was quiet. But it quickly realized that not only had Lavagetto's hit broken up the no-hitter, it had also won the game for the home team. Suddenly the whole ballpark was in bedlam. Gionfriddo and Miksis were mauling each other at home plate, while the rest of the Dodgers were pounding Lavagetto on the back at second base. The happy fans joined in and nearly tore Cookie's uniform off as he struggled to the clubhouse.

And poor Bill Bevens stood in the middle of it all thinking about what might have been.

New York (AL)	ab	r	h	bi	o	a	e
G. Stirnweiss, 2b	4	1	2	0	2	1	0
T. Henrich, rf	5	0	1	0	2	0	0
Y. Berra, c	4	0	0	0	6	1	1
J. DiMaggio, cf	2	0	0	1	2	0	0
G. McQuinn, 1b	4	0	1	0	7	0	0
B. Johnson, 3b	4	1	1	0	3	2	0
J. Lindell, lf	3	0	2	1	3	0	0
P. Rizzuto, ss	4	0	1	0	1	2	0
B. Bevens, p	3	0	0	0	0	1	0
	33	2	8	2	26	7	1

Brooklyn (NL)	ab	r	h	bi	o	a	e
E. Stanky, 2b	1	0	0	0	2	3	0
C. Lavagetto, ph9	1	0	1	2	-	-	-
P. Reese, ss	4	0	0	1	3	5	1
J. Robinson, 1b	4	0	0	0	11	1	0
D. Walker, rf	2	0	0	0	0	1	0
G. Hermanski, lf	4	0	0	0	2	0	0
B. Edwards, c	4	0	0	0	7	1	1
C. Furillo, cf	3	0	0	0	2	0	0
A. Gionfriddo, pr9	0	1	0	0	-	-	-
S. Jorgensen, 3b	2	1	0	0	0	1	1
H. Taylor, p	0	0	0	0	0	0	0
H. Gregg, p1	1	0	0	0	0	1	0
A. Vaughan, ph7	0	0	0	0	-	-	-
H. Behrman, p8	0	0	0	0	0	1	0
H. Casey, p9	0	0	0	0	0	1	0
P. Reiser, ph9	0	0	0	0	-	-	-
E. Miksis, pr9	0	1	0	0	-	-	-
	26	3	1	3	27	15	3

New York	100 100 000	= 2
Brooklyn	000 010 002	= 3

two out when winning run scored

	ip	h	r-er	bb	so
Bevens (L 0-1)	8⅔	1	3-2	10	5
Taylor	*0	2	1-0	1	0
Gregg	7	4	1-1	3	5
Behrman	1⅓	2	0-0	0	0
Casey (W 2-0)	⅔	0	0-0	0	0

*faced four batters in first

WP: Bevens

Game-Winning RBI: Lavagetto
LOB: New York 9, Brooklyn 8
BE: New York 2, Brooklyn 0
DP: Reese-Stanky-Robinson (Johnson)
Gregg-Reese-Robinson (Henrich)
Casey-Edwards-Robinson (Henrich)
2B: Lindell, Lavagetto
3B: Johnson
SH: Stanky, Bevens
SB: Rizzuto, Reese, Gionfriddo
Time—2:20 Attendance—33,443

Umpires: L. Goetz, B. McGowan, B. Pinelli, E. Rommel, J. Boyer, & G. Magerkurth

Lavagetto struck out the next day with the tying run on second and two out in the ninth, and the Yankees won, 2-1.

In Game #6, the Dodgers won a hitfest, 8-6. A great catch by Gionfriddo robbed DiMaggio of a possible home run to save the victory.

In the decisive seventh game, Brooklyn got two runs in the top of the second. But New York came back with one in their half and two more in the fourth to take the lead. With Joe Page pitching five innings of shutout relief, the Yankees won by a 5-2 final score.

1948 SUNDAY, JULY 4TH, AT EBBETS FIELD

Campanella's First N.L. Home Runs

Lead Dodgers to Comeback Victory

Reiser's Pinch Single Caps 4-Run 9th, Giants Beaten 13-12

Today's Results			
BROOKLYN 13-New York 12			
Philadelphia 7-Boston 2 (1st game)			
Philadelphia 5-Boston 2 (2nd game)			
Pittsburgh 5-Chicago 1 (1st game)			
Pittsburgh 6-Chicago 2 (2nd game)			
Cincinnati 8-St. Louis 6 (1st game)			
St. Louis 8-Cincinnati 1 (2nd game)			
Standings	**W-L**	**Pct.**	**GB**
Boston	40-29	.580	—
Pittsburgh	36-30	.545	2½
St. Louis	36-31	.537	3
Philadelphia	36-35	.507	5
New York	33-33	.500	5½
BROOKLYN	29-35	.453	8½
Cincinnati	31-38	.449	9
Chicago	29-39	.426	10½

ROY CAMPANELLA BEGAN HIS PROFESsional baseball career in 1937, when he was just 15 years old. As veteran of the Negro National League and various winter leagues, the slugging catcher had hit home runs all over the United States, Canada, Mexico, and the Caribbean. From Minneapolis to Maracaibo, St. Louis to Santo Domingo, Campy had hit them out. But it was not until today that he finally hit his first home runs in the major leagues.

When he finally got his chance, he did it right, pounding two balls to the upper deck in Ebbets Field to lead the Brooklyn Dodgers to a double-comeback victory over the New York Giants. The first homer tied the game in the fourth inning, 3-3. The second came in the ninth inning to start the Dodgers to a four-run rally that won the game, 13-12. Both shots came with a teammate on base.

Pete Reiser capped the winning rally with a no-out, two-run pinch single.

Campanella had been with the Dodgers this spring until May 15th, when he was sent down to St. Paul. But Brooklyn catcher Bruce Edwards developed arm trouble, and manager Leo Durocher finally convinced general manager Branch Rickey to call Campy back up. Roy arrived on July 2nd, and today was his third game as the Dodgers' starting catcher.

Today's slugfest was great entertainment for the 28,770 fans, most of whom had forked over the newly-increased 10¢ subway fare to get to the park.

Harry Taylor was the starting pitcher for Brooklyn. He allowed only two hits. But he walked seven and was charged with three runs before being removed in the top of the fourth.

The Dodgers got their first run in the third inning when Pee Wee Reese broke off third base and caused Giant starter Ray Poat to balk. They tied the game in the last of the fourth on Campanella's first home run, a two-run shot off the facade of the upper deck in left field.

New York regained the lead with two runs in the fifth and three in the sixth, aided by errors by George Shuba and Pee Wee Reese.

But the Dodgers rallied back. In the seventh, they scored three runs with some great base running.. With two out, Reese and Jackie Robinson singled. Gene Hermanski doubled Reese home, with Robinson stopping at third. Robby then stole home against relief pitcher Andy Hansen. Catcher Walker Cooper, seeing that he had no chance to tag the black speedster at home, threw to third to try and catch Hermanski. But third baseman Sid Gordon was asleep on the play, and the throw sailed into left field, allowing Hermanski to come all the way home behind Robinson.

Brooklyn took the lead with three more runs in the eighth on three singles, a pinch double by Arky Vaughan, and two bases-loaded walks.

In the top of the ninth, Ralph Branca was sent to the mound to try and protect the Dodgers' new-found lead. The first batter he faced, Willard Marshall, tied the game with a home run over the clock in right field. The next man fanned. But an error by Eddie Miksis gave Jack Conway a life. Bobby Thomson's pop fly fell safe in the outfield for a hit. And Bill Rigney's poke reached the lower left field stands for a three-run homer. Suddenly the Giants led 12-9. Branca was derricked, and Erv Palica came in to retire the side.

Giant manager Mel Ott nominated Monte Kennedy to pitch the bottom of the ninth. Gil Hodges led off with a line single to left. Campanella followed with a prodigious home run into the upper deck in left center.

With the New York lead down to one run, Sheldon Jones was hustled into the fray. Dick Whitman got an infield hit on a wide throw by the shortstop. Reese walked. And Robinson beat out a bunt single to load the bases.

With the winning runs in scoring position, Durocher sent Reiser up to bat for the pitcher. Pete was hobbled by a sprained ankle, but he could still swing the bat. After fouling off several pitches that did not appeal to him, he smacked one on a line to right. The ball fell safely, and Whitman and Reese scored the winning runs.

The Dodgers had come back to win by the unlikely score of 13-12. Not only had they won, they had found themselves a major league catcher and power hitter in Roy Campanella.

New York	ab	r	h	bi	o	a	e
B. Rigney, 2b	4	1	1	3	2	2	0
W. Lockman, cf	3	2	1	0	5	0	0
L. Layton, lf	6	0	1	2	3	0	0
J. Mize, 1b	4	2	1	0	6	0	0
W. Cooper, c	4	1	1	0	7	0	0
W. Marshall, rf	4	2	2	4	0	0	0
S. Gordon, 3b	3	1	0	1	1	2	1
J. Lohrke, 3b9	0	0	0	0	0	0	0
J. Conway, ss	5	1	2	1	0	2	0
R. Poat, p	3	1	0	0	0	0	0
A. Hansen, p7	0	0	0	0	0	0	0
L. Jansen, p7	0	0	0	0	0	0	0
D. Koslo, p8	0	0	0	0	0	0	0
A. Konikowski, p8	0	0	0	0	0	1	0
B. Thomson, ph9	1	1	1	0	-	-	-
M. Kennedy, p9	0	0	0	0	0	0	0
S. Jones, p9	0	0	0	0	0	0	0
	37	12	10	11	24	7	1

Brooklyn	ab	r	h	bi	o	a	e
P. Reese, ss	5	4	3	1	3	2	1
J. Robinson, 2b	5	1	3	0	2	1	0
G. Hermanski, rf	4	1	2	1	3	0	0
B. Cox, ph8	0	0	0	1	-	-	-
R. Branca, p9	0	0	0	0	0	0	0
E. Palica, p9	0	0	0	0	0	0	0
P. Reiser, ph9	1	0	1	2	-	-	-
G. Shuba, lf	4	0	1	1	3	0	1
B. Edwards, 3b	4	0	1	0	0	1	0
E. Miksis, 3b9	0	0	0	0	0	0	1
C. Furillo, cf	5	1	2	0	1	0	0
G. Hodges, 1b	5	2	2	0	4	2	0
R. Campanella, c	5	2	3	4	10	1	0
H. Taylor, p	1	0	0	0	1	1	0
P. Minner, p4	1	0	0	0	0	0	0
W. Ramsdell, p5	0	0	0	0	0	1	0
M. Rackley, ph7	1	0	0	0	-	-	-
H. Behrman, p8	0	0	0	0	0	0	0
A. Vaughan, ph8	1	1	1	0	-	-	-
D. Whitman, rf9	1	1	1	0	0	0	0
	43	13	20	10	27	9	3

New York	002	123	004	=	12
Brooklyn	001	200	334	=	13

none out when winning run scored

	ip	h	r-er	bb	so
Poat	6⅔	10	6-6	0	3
Hansen	*0	1	0-0	1	0
Jansen	⅔	4	3-3	0	0
Koslo	†0	0	0-0	2	0
Konikowski	⅔	0	0-0	0	1
Kennedy	‡0	2	2-2	0	0
Jones (L 2-5)	§0	3	2-2	1	0
Taylor	3⅔	2	3-3	7	3
Minner	1	3	2-1	1	1
Ramsdell	2⅓	1	3-0	4	2
Behrman	1	0	0-0	0	1
Branca	⅓	3	4-3	0	1
Palica (W 3-4)	⅔	1	0-0	0	1

Game-Winning RBI: Reiser
LOB: New York 10, Brooklyn 11
BE: New York 2, Brooklyn 0
DP: Reese-Robinson-Hodges (Layton)
2B: Reese, Edwards, Hermanski, Vaughan
3B: Hermanski, Layton, Conway, Marshall
HR: Campanella 2, Marshall, Rigney
SH: Robinson
SB: Robinson, Hermanski, Gordon
CS: Lockman

*faced two batters in seventh
†faced two batters in eighth
‡faced two batters in ninth
§faced four batters in ninth
Time—3:30
Attendance—28,770
Umpires: S. Robb, A. Gore, & B. Pinelli

Brooklyn ran this little winning streak to six games and by the All-Star Game was in fifth place.

Then Leo Durocher was released to become the manager of the hated Giants, with Burt Shotton returning to the Dodger helm.

The Dodgers climbed all the way to the top by August 29th. But they faltered in September and finished third. Their final record was 84-70.

1949 SUNDAY, OCTOBER 2ND, AT SHIBE PARK, PHILADELPHIA

Win Pennant in Extra Innings on Last Day

Dodgers Blow 5-0 Lead before Winning in 10, 9-7
Finish the Season 1 Game Ahead of St. Louis

Today's Results			
BROOKLYN 9-Philadelphia 7 (10 inn.)			
St. Louis 13-Chicago 5			
Boston 2-New York 1			
Pittsburgh 4-Cincinnati 2 (1st game)			
Cincinnati 6-Pittsburgh 5 (2nd game)			
Standings	**W-L**	**Pct.**	**GB**
BROOKLYN	97-57	.630	—
St. Louis	96-58	.623	1
Philadelphia	81-73	.526	16
Boston	75-79	.487	22
New York	73-81	.474	24
Pittsburgh	71-83	.461	26
Cincinnati	62-92	.403	35
Chicago	61-93	.396	36

DESPITE SOME HARROWING MOMENTS IN Philadelphia this weekend, the Brooklyn Dodgers brought the National League pennant safely home to the Borough of Churches. By winning the final game of the season, the Bums clinched the flag and avoided a playoff with the St. Louis Cardinals. This was the third time in eight years that the Cardinals and Dodgers had gone down to the last day of the season with the championship still in doubt. After losing out in 1942 and 1946, Brooklyn came away with the pennant this time.

St. Louis had held a 1½-game lead last Tuesday morning, and its chances looked a lot better than Brooklyn's. But the Cardinals then lost four games in a row, while the Dodgers won a pair in Boston and lost one in Philadelphia. That gave Brooklyn a 1-game lead going into today's final game for each team. The Dodgers could clinch the flag with a victory or a St. Louis defeat, while the Cardinals' only hope was to win while the Dodgers lost and to then win a playoff.

Brooklyn manager Burt Shotton sent rookie Don Newcombe, his top winner at 17-8, to the mound to try and nail down the clincher. Russ Meyer, also 17-8, was the Phillies' starter.

After two scoreless innings, the Dodgers routed Meyer in the third and grabbed a 5-0 lead. With one out, Spider Jorgensen singled sharply to center field. He advanced to second on a wild pitch and to third on an infield out. Jackie Robinson, who wrapped up the league batting title today, bounced a hit over the third baseman to send Jorgensen home. Robinson stole second (he also led the league in steals) and went to third on another wild pitch. Meyer walked Gene Hermanski. Carl Furillo beat out a hit to deep short, and Robinson scored. A solid hit to left by Gil Hodges plated Hermanski and sent Meyer to the showers. Robin Roberts came in to pitch, and he walked Roy Campanella intentionally to get to pitcher Newcombe. Big Don fouled up the strategy by sizzling a two-run single down the left field line, upping the score to 5-0.

But the Phillies got right back into the game with four runs in the bottom of the fourth. A single by Del Ennis, a walk to Bill Nicholson, and a home run by Willie Jones plated three runs. A single by Mike Goliat and a pinch double by Stan Hollmig knocked Newcombe out of the game. Richie Ashburn drove Goliat in with a sacrifice fly off of reliever Rex Barney.

Brooklyn got its lead back up to three with two runs in the top of the fifth. Furillo and Hodges singled, and Campanella drove them both in with a double into the left field corner.

The Phils got one run back in the bottom on a walk and a double by Nicholson.

Philadelphia finally caught up in the sixth, knotting the count at 7-7 with a pair of runs. With one out, Johnny Blatnik got a pinch single to right and took second when Furillo misplayed the ball. With two out, Granny Hamner slapped a hit up the middle for a run. Dick Sisler also singled. That was all for Barney, and 24-year-old Jack Banta was called in to pitch. The first batter he faced, Ennis, bounced a hit through the left side of the infield to score Hamner with the tying run.

Ken Heintzelman, the Phillies' ace lefthander, came in to pitch in the seventh. He and Banta matched zeroes for three innings. Although the Dodger righthander tore the fingernail away from the flesh of the middle finger of his pitching hand, his fastball was very effective. He pitched hitless ball in the seventh, eighth, and ninth, walking only one.

The Dodgers finally broke the tie and won the game in the tenth. Pee Wee Rese opened with a looping hit to left. Eddie Miksis bunted him to second. Duke Snider was next up. The big Californian had had trouble with lefthanders early in the year. But now he stepped into the first pitch from Heintzelman and rifled a hit up the middle. Reese rounded third and slid home with the pennant-winning run. Snider took second on the throw home. Robinson was walked intentionally. Luis Olmo then spanked a shot through the third baseman, and Snider galloped home with an insurance run.

Leading 9-7, Banta allowed a one-out single to Goliat in the bottom of the tenth. Coach Clyde Sukeforth went to the mound to talk to the youngster but left him in the game. Banta quickly struck out Ed Sanicki and got Ashburn on a fly to short left field. The Dodgers had won the pennant, and their fans in the park made the stands rock with cheering.

But the big demonstration took place in Pennsylvania Station, New York. About 25,000 Dodger enthusiasts were on hand to greet the returning heroes tonight. Small clutches of fans raced from one platform to another trying to jockey for the best position for greeting the arriving train. When the team finally arrived, the players were surrounded by the adoring mob and led on a parade of sorts through the station. Music was provided by the Brooklyn "Sym-phony Band," and all the players were cheered. The biggest crowd followed Jackie Robinson, whose tremendous individual play was the highlight of a thrilling season.

Brooklyn	ab	r	h	bi	o	a	e
P. Reese, ss	5	1	1	0	0	1	0
S. Jorgensen, 3b	3	1	1	0	2	2	0
B. Edwards, ph7	1	0	0	0	-	-	-
E. Miksis, 3b7	0	0	0	0	1	2	0
D. Snider, cf	4	1	1	1	2	0	0
J. Robinson, 2b	3	1	1	1	1	2	0
G. Hermanski, lf	3	1	0	0	0	0	0
L. Olmo, ph8-lf	2	0	1	1	2	0	0
C. Furillo, rf	6	2	4	1	4	0	1
G. Hodges, 1b	4	2	2	1	10	1	0
R. Campanella, c	3	0	1	2	7	0	0
D. Newcombe, p	2	0	1	2	1	0	0
R. Barney, p4	1	0	0	0	0	0	0
J. Banta, p6	1	0	0	0	0	1	0
	38	9	13	9	30	9	1

Philadelphia	ab	r	h	bi	o	a	e
R. Ashburn, cf	6	0	2	1	4	0	0
G. Hamner, ss	5	1	1	1	4	5	0
D. Sisler, 1b	4	0	1	0	11	2	1
D. Ennis, lf	4	2	2	1	0	0	0
A. Seminick, c	5	0	0	0	1	1	1
B. Nicholson, rf	4	1	1	1	2	0	0
W. Jones, 3b	5	1	1	3	1	4	0
M. Goliat, 2b	5	1	2	0	6	0	0
R. Meyer, p	0	0	0	0	1	0	0
R. Roberts, p3	0	0	0	0	0	0	0
B. Blattner, ph3	0	0	0	0	-	-	-
J. Thompson, p4	0	0	0	0	0	0	0
S. Hollmig, ph4	1	0	1	0	-	-	-
C. Simmons, p5	0	0	0	0	0	0	0
J. Konstanty, p5	0	0	0	0	0	0	0
J. Blatnik, ph6	1	1	1	0	-	-	-
K. Heintzelman, p7	1	0	0	0	0	2	0
K. Trinkle, p10	0	0	0	0	0	0	0
E. Sanicki, ph10	1	0	0	0	-	-	-
	42	7	12	7	30	14	2

Brooklyn	005	020	000	2	= 9
Philadelphia	000	412	000	0	= 7

	ip	h	r-er	bb	so
Newcombe	3⅓	6	4-4	2	2
Barney	2⅓	4	3-3	1	1
Banta (W 10-6)	4⅓	2	0-0	1	3
Meyer	2⅔	5	5-5	3	0
Roberts	⅓	1	0-0	1	0
Thompson	1	0	0-0	1	0
Simmons	*0	2	2-2	0	0
Konstanty	2	1	0-0	1	1
Heintzelman (L 17-10)	3⅓	4	2-2	4	0
Trinkle	⅔	0	0-0	0	0

Game-Winning RBI: Snider
LOB: Brooklyn 12, Philadelphia 9
BE: none
DP: Hamner-Sisler (Furillo)
2B: Hollmig, Campanella, Nicholson
HR: Jones
SH: Banta, Robinson, Miksis
SB: Robinson 2
CS: Robinson
WP: Meyer 2
Time—3:17 Attendance—36,765
Umpires: L. Goetz, B. Reardon, A. Barlick, & L. Jorda
*faced two batters in fifth

1949 THURSDAY, OCTOBER 6TH, AT YANKEE STADIUM, NEW YORK
World Series—Game #2

Roe Stops Yankees, 1-0

IN THE SECOND GAME OF THE 1949 WORLD SERIES, ELWIN "PREACHER" ROE PITCHED the masterpiece of his career to shut out the powerful New York Yankees, 1-0. The skinny lefthander from Ash Flat, Arkansas, allowed six hits and walked no one. His Dodger teammates manufactured one run in the second inning against Yankee pitcher Vic Raschi, and that was enough to win the game.

Although both contesting teams were noted for good hitting, thus far the series had been entirely dominated by pitching. In the first game it was the Yankees who won by a 1-0 score. Allie Reynolds pitched the shutout for New York, and Brooklyn's Don Newcombe finally went down to defeat when Tommy Henrich hit a home run in the bottom of the ninth.

Roe was in control all the way today. Mopping his brow and hitching his pants up before every pitch, his rhythm was flawless. He had some trouble controlling his slow curves, but his slider and sinker were effective. And occasionally he was able to sneak a fastball past the hitters. New York got only one runner as far as third base. And only once did the Yankees put two men on at the same time. The Preacher's biggest difficulties came on balls hit back to him. His right index finger was injured by a line drive, and he dropped a bunt for an error.

The Dodgers had more than one runner only in the second inning, when they plated their run. Jackie Robinson led off the inning with a double to left. Gene Hermanski lifted a foul near the seats down the right field line. Second baseman Jerry Coleman made a nice catch near the railing, and Robinson broke for third. Coleman slipped slightly while pivoting around, and Jackie slid into third safely. Marv Rackley hit a slow roller toward third, and Robinson had to hold up while the batter was being thrown out. Gil Hodges came through with a solid single to left, and Robinson trotted home. Hodges took second when the ball was bobbled in the outfield. Roy Campanella was intentionally walked, and Roe struck out.

The only other runner to reach base in the first three innings was New York's Phil Rizzuto, who did it twice. He singled in the first inning and was left on first base. In the third, he reached base with two out on a fumble by shortstop Pee Wee Reese. Rizzuto stole second this time. But Henrich grounded out to end the inning.

Brooklyn was robbed of another run in the top of the fourth by a great fielding play. With one out, Hermanski dropped a clean hit into short center field. As Joe DiMaggio closed in on the ball, it took a crazy bounce past him, and Hermanski made it all the way to third with a fluke triple. Rackley then hit a slow roller past the pitcher's mound. Coleman charged the ball hard, scooped it up and threw home in one motion, and barely nipped Hermanski sliding in. The runner argued the call by the umpire, but he was out.

New York also had a man thrown out on the bases in the fourth. Hank Bauer led off with a bloop hit to center. The ball died in the outfield grass, but Duke Snider hustled in and made a nice throw to second to retire Bauer trying to stretch the hit into a double.

Two batters later, Johnny Lindell sizzled one back through the box. Roe knocked it down with his glove hand and threw the batter out. But the impact caused quite a bruise, and the trainer had to drill a hole in the fingernail of Roe's forefinger to drain the blood out. Preacher stayed in the game.

In the fifth Coleman doubled with one out and went to third on a ground out. But Raschi could not bring him home, grounding out to third, instead.

The Dodgers' Spider Jorgensen got to third in the sixth inning. He led off with a pop-fly double along the left field line. After a fly out, he advanced to third on an infield out by Robinson. But he was left when Hermanski bounced out to the first baseman.

A fast double play turned the Dodgers back in the seventh after Luis Olmo had led off with a hit.

In the New York seventh, Billy Johnson singled with two out. He stole second, thanks to late coverage by shortstop Reese. Then Coleman ended the inning with an easy grounder to second baseman Robinson.

The Yankees made their most serious threat in the eighth, aided by Roe's error. Pinch-hitter Johnny Mize slapped a hit to right to lead off. George Stirnweiss went in as a pinch-runner. Bobby Brown, another pinch-swinger, was called out on strikes when Roe slipped a sinker past him. Rizzuto then bunted down the third base line. Roe picked the ball up and dropped it, and all hands were safe. The pitcher was upset with himself, but Captain Reese came in from shortstop and calmed him down. Tommy Henrich was the next batter. The count went full before Henrich popped a slider to left field for an easy out. Bauer bounced to Jorgensen, who threw to second for an inning-ending force out.

Snider got a hit off of reliever Joe Page in the top of the ninth, but no run resulted.

In the bottom of the ninth, DiMaggio led off with an infield hit toward third. Lindell went up trying to bunt, but the fouled off two pitches. Roe then struck him out on an inside breaking ball. Johnson popped out to second. And Coleman ended the game with a routine fly to right.

The Bronx Bombers had been halted, and the Dodgers were even in the series. And Ash Flat, Arkansas, was as happy about it as Brooklyn, New York, was.

Brooklyn (NL)	ab	r	h	bi	o	a	e
P. Reese, ss	4	0	0	0	1	3	1
S. Jorgensen, 3b	4	0	1	0	1	4	0
D. Snider, cf	4	0	1	0	3	1	0
J. Robinson, 2b	3	1	1	0	3	1	0
G. Hermanski, rf	3	0	1	0	2	0	0
C. Furillo, ph9	1	0	0	0	-	-	-
M. McCormick, rf9	0	0	0	0	1	0	0
M. Rackley, lf	2	0	0	0	0	0	0
L. Olmo, lf4	2	0	1	0	2	0	0
G. Hodges, 1b	3	0	1	1	9	1	0
R. Campanella, c	2	0	1	0	4	0	0
P. Roe, p	3	0	0	0	1	1	1
	31	1	7	1	27	11	2

New York (AL)	ab	r	h	bi	o	a	e
P. Rizzuto, ss	3	0	1	0	0	6	0
T. Henrich, 1b	4	0	0	0	11	1	0
H. Bauer, rf	4	0	1	0	1	0	0
J. DiMaggio, cf	4	0	1	0	1	0	0
J. Lindell, lf	4	0	0	0	2	1	1
B. Johnson, 3b	4	0	1	0	0	2	0
J. Coleman, 2b	4	0	1	0	6	3	0
C. Silvera, c	2	0	0	0	6	0	0
J. Mize, ph8	1	0	1	0	-	-	-
G. Stirnweiss, pr9	0	0	0	0	-	-	-
G. Niarhos, c9	0	0	0	0	0	0	0
V. Raschi, p	2	0	0	0	0	0	0
B. Brown, ph8	1	0	0	0	-	-	-
J. Page, p9	0	0	0	0	0	0	0
	33	0	6	0	27	13	1

Brooklyn	010 000 000	=	1
New York	000 000 000	=	0

	ip	h	r-er	bb	so
Roe (W 1-0)	9	6	0-0	0	3
Raschi (L 0-1)	8	6	1-1	1	4
Page	1	1	0-0	0	0

Game-Winning RBI: Hodges
LOB: Brooklyn 5, New York 7
BE: Brooklyn 0, New York 2
DP: Rizzuto-Coleman-Henrich (Hodges)
2B: Robinson, Coleman, Jorgensen
3B: Hermanski
SH: Rizzuto, Robinson
SB: Rizzuto, Johnson

Time—2:30 Attendance—70,053
Umpires: B. Reardon, A. Passarella, L. Jorda, C. Hubbard, E. Hurley, & G. Barr

This was Brooklyn's only victory in the series.

The Yankees won the third game, 4-3, breaking a 1-1 tie with three runs in the top of the ninth and surviving two Dodger homers in the bottom half.

Newcombe was routed in the fourth inning of Game #4, allowing three runs in the innings. A three-run triple by Brown off of Joe Hatten in the fifth gave New York a 6-0 lead. The Dodgers scored four runs in the sixth inning against Eddie Lopat. But Allie Reynolds came in and saved the game for New York, 6-4.

The Yankees raced out to a 10-1 lead in the fifth game and held on to win 10-6, winning the series, 4 games to 1.

1950 THURSDAY NIGHT, AUGUST 31ST, AT EBBETS FIELD

Hodges Hits 4 Home Runs

Ties All-Time Record for One Game
Drives in 9 Runs as Dodgers Rout Braves 19-3

Today's Results			
BROOKLYN 19-Boston 3			
New York 2-Pittsburgh 1			
no other games scheduled			
Standings	**W-L**	**Pct.**	**GB**
Philadelphia	78-47	.624	—
BROOKLYN	69-50	.580	6
Boston	68-54	.557	8½
New York	65-57	.533	11½
St. Louis	65-57	.533	11½
Chicago	54-70	.435	23½
Cincinnati	49-73	.402	27½
Pittsburgh	42-82	.339	35½

THE DODGERS' INDIANA STRONG BOY, Gil Hodges, today joined the very small circle of baseball players to ever hit four home runs in one game in the major leagues. Hodges's slugging feat came at the expense of four different Boston Brave pitchers. The first three homers went into the lower left field stands in Ebbets Field, while the fourth sailed into the upper deck. All landed within twenty yards of the foul line.

The homers were not consecutive, as an infield out and an infield hit were interspersed. Luckily, Gil's teammates batted around enough to give him six trips to the plate. Each of the four homers came with teammate Carl Furillo on base, and on one Jackie Robinson was also on. Hodges's 9 RBIs and five runs scored (both team records) led the Dodgers to an easy 19-3 victory.

Twice earlier this season, a Dodger player had hit three homers in a game. Duke Snider did it on Memorial Day, and Roy Campanella did it on August 26th. When Hodges was asked tonight if he thought he would hit four home runs, he scoffed, "I didn't think I'd even hit three, and when I did, I didn't figure to come up a sixth time." His wife, a Brooklyn girl, was a lot more excited about the feat than her soft-spoken husband was.

All this came about because of four rainouts in the Braves' previous trips to Brooklyn. With all those games to make up, tonight's contest was inserted into what had been an off-day in the schedule.

Southpaw Warren Spahn was Boston's starting pitcher, with young Carl Erskine on the mound for Brooklyn.

Sid Gordon got the Braves a lead, albeit a brief one, with a solo homer in the top of the second.

Hodges started his cannonading in the bottom of the second to put the Dodgers into the lead. His first home run came with one out and Furillo on first. Spahn got a fastball too high, and Gil drilled it a couple of rows into the seats in left. The Dodgers added a third run before the inning was over.

Spahn obviously did not have his good stuff, and he was removed after Robinson and Furillo opened the third with hits. Norman Roy, a righthander, was brought in to pitch. The first batter he faced was Hodges. Mr. Roy hung a curve, and Mr. Hodges's fly ball just did clear the fence and land in the stands. Two more hits routed Roy, and lefthander Mickey Haefner came in. An infield out and throwing error and a two-run homer by Snider brought the Dodger total for the inning to seven runs, making the score 10-1.

Haefner got Hodges to ground out to the third baseman in the fourth inning.

Bob Hall, a righty, was on the hill when Hodges came up in the sixth inning. Furillo, naturally, was on first, and no one was out. Hall served up a nice fastball, and Hodges hit homer #3 into the lower left field seats four or five rows back. The Dodgers added four singles and a force out for two more runs. Hall was felled by a line drive that hit him in the shoulder, and lefthander Johnny Antonelli took his place.

Hodges got a chance to hit a fourth home run with one out in the seventh. But he didn't get under the ball and sent a wicked liner to third base instead. Bob Elliott knocked it down, but it went for a hit.

It looked like Hodges had missed his chance for the record. But the Dodgers continued to bat around, and six men followed Gil to the plate before the inning was finally over, assuring Hodges of an at bat in the eighth.

Boston got two runs in the top of the eighth, but Brooklyn still led by 17-3 going into the bottom of inning.

Bobby Morgan led off by walking. Furillo forced him at second and was safe at first when second baseman Roy Hartsfield threw wildly trying for a double play. As Hodges strode to the plate, the stands buzzed with anticipation. Would he hit another homer? Pitcher Antonelli unwittingly obliged with a curve ball that didn't break much. Hodges swung and lifted it high into Section 33 in the upper grandstand in left field. As he rounded the bases, he got a standing ovation from the Flatbush fans. Not bad for the son of a Princeton, Indiana, coal miner!

The four homers brought Gil's season total to 23, tying the career high he had set in 1949. It also put him second on the team, one behind Snider, who had hit #24 in the third inning. The five total home runs gave the team a total of 153 for the season, breaking the club record set a year before.

Lost in all the slugging was a fine pitching effort by Erskine. Carl got his second win and first complete game since being called up from Montreal at the beginning of the month. He also had an outstanding day at the plate, going 4-for-5 and reaching first on a hit by pitch.

Although it seemed a little late for this season, the development of youngsters like Hodges, Snider, Campanella, and Erskine promised to keep the Dodgers in contention for the National League pennant for years to come.

Boston	ab	r	h	bi	o	a	e
R. Hartsfield, 2b	5	0	1	0	4	1	3
S. Jethroe, cf	5	0	0	0	1	0	0
E. Torgeson, 1b	4	1	1	0	7	0	0
B. Elliott, 3b	3	0	1	0	1	4	0
W. Cooper, c	3	0	0	0	3	0	0
D. Crandall, c6	1	1	0	0	2	0	1
S. Gordon, lf	4	1	3	2	4	0	0
W. Marshall, rf	4	0	2	1	1	0	0
B. Kerr, ss	3	0	0	0	1	4	0
W. Spahn, p	1	0	0	0	0	0	0
N. Roy, p3	0	0	0	0	0	1	0
M. Haefner, p3	0	0	0	0	0	0	0
P. Reiser, ph5	1	0	0	0	-	-	-
B. Hall, p5	0	0	0	0	0	1	0
J. Antonelli, p6	1	0	0	0	0	0	0
T. Holmes, ph9	1	0	0	0	-	-	-
	36	3	8	3	24	11	4

Brooklyn	ab	r	h	bi	o	a	e
T. Brown, lf	4	0	1	2	2	0	0
P. Reese, ss	5	1	2	3	2	3	1
D. Snider, cf	5	1	1	3	4	0	0
J. Robinson, 2b	5	1	1	0	2	1	0
B. Morgan, 3b8	0	0	0	0	0	1	0
C. Furillo, rf	5	4	2	0	0	0	0
G. Hodges, 1b	6	5	5	9	6	1	0
R. Campanella, c	4	2	2	0	5	0	0
B. Edwards, c7	1	1	1	0	2	0	0
B. Cox, 3b-2b8	5	3	2	0	2	3	0
C. Erskine, p	5	1	4	0	2	0	0
	45	19	21	17	27	9	1

Boston	010 000 020	= 3
Brooklyn	037 004 32x	= 19

	ip	h	r-er	bb	so
Spahn (L 16-15)	*2	7	5-5	1	2
Roy	⅓	3	3-3	0	0
Haefner	1⅔	1	2-2	1	0
Hall	1⅔	6	4-4	3	1
Antonelli	2⅓	4	5-4	2	2
Erskine (W 2-3)	9	8	3-3	3	6

*faced two batters in third

Game-Winning RBI: Hodges
LOB: Boston 9, Brooklyn 11
BE: Boston 1, Brooklyn 1
2B: Reese, Marshall 2, Edwards
HR: Gordon, Hodges 4, Snider
SH: Cox
HBP: by Antonelli (Erskine)
Time—3:03
Attendance—14,226
Umpires: J. Conlan, A. Gore, & B. Stewart

Hodges hit nine home runs in September to finish the season with 32. That gave him the team lead by one over both Snider and Campanella.

1950 OCTOBER 1ST, AT EBBETS FIELD

Tenth-Inning Homer Ends Pennant Hopes

Phillies Win a Thriller, 4-1, to Grab Flag
Potential Winning Run for Dodgers Thrown Out at Home in 9th

Today's Results			
Philadelphia 4-BROOKLYN 1 (10 innings)			
New York 5-Boston 1			
Chicago 3-St. Louis 2 (11 innings)			
Cincinnati 3-Pittsburgh 2 (1st game)			
Pittsburgh 3-Cincinnati 1 (2nd game)			
Standings	**W-L**	**Pct.**	**GB**
Philadelphia	91-63	.591	—
BROOKLYN	89-65	.578	2
New York	86-68	.558	5
Boston	83-71	.539	8
St. Louis	78-75	.510	12½
Cincinnati	66-87	.431	24½
Chicago	64-89	.418	26½
Pittsburgh	57-96	.373	33½

THE NEWS FROM THE VARIOUS BATTLE fronts today was decidely mixed. Way out in Korea, the United Nations' counterattack surged across the 38th Parallel and took the war into the North Koreans' home territory. But on the home front, the news was disastrous for Brooklyn. The Dodgers' last-ditch counteroffensive (which had carried the Bums from a nearly hopeless position back to the very brink of victory) was finally halted, as the invading Philadelphia Phillies successfully defended their position as National League leaders.

Just thirteen days ago, the Dodgers were as good as dead, trailing the Phillies by 9 games. But the Flock valiantly battled against its seemingly-inevitable elimination in the pennant race. They won 12 of the next 15 games. Meanwhile, Philadelphia hit the skids and lost 8 of 11. So when the Phils came into Brooklyn for the final two games of the season, the Dodgers still had a chance to force a playoff by winning both contests.

On Saturday, the Dodgers got a two-run homer and a three-run homer off of the Phillies' ace relief pitcher, Jim Konstanty, and won 7-3.

So the campaign came down to the final game today. Brooklyn needed a victory to tie the race. And with Philadelphia in full retreat, the Phils could hardly be counted upon to win the playoff.

The sudden excitement brought out the Brooklyn fans in big numbers. Long lines had formed outside the Ebbets Field ticket windows by 7:00 a.m. Scalpers had a field day on the perimeter of the field of battle. The Fire Department ordered the gates closed an hour before game time, and 35,000 paying customers were already inside.

The struggling Phillies and the surging Dodgers sent their best moundsmen to compete for the victory. Robin Roberts of Philadelphia was making his fourth start in nine days in a desperate effort to halt his team's retreat. Brooklyn's Don Newcombe was working for the fourth time in nine days, including two short relief stints.

With the big crowd at the park watching and millions more along the Eastern Seaboard tuning in on radio and television, the two pitchers battled brilliantly. Neither side could score through the first five innings, and few balls were even hit hard.

Then each side scored a run in the sixth.

For the Phillies, Eddie Waitkus and Richie Ashburn both hit sharp grounders to the right side. But first baseman Gil Hodges made fine pickups on both balls and threw to Newcombe covering first to get the batters out. Dick Sisler followed with another grounder toward the hole, and this one got past the diving Hodges for a hit. Del Ennis hit a little pop to short center field. Second baseman Jackie Robinson went back for it but slowed down at the last moment, apparently thinking that center fielder Duke Snider would make the catch. But Duke had been playing deep, and the ball fell safely, Sisler scooting to third. Willie Jones then hit sharply past shortstop, and Sisler score.

The Dodgers tied the count on the flukiest of home runs. With two out, Pee

Wee Reese lifted a high fly down the right field line. The ball hit the screen atop the fence. But instead of bouncing off the screen, the ball hugged the wire and came to rest on the ledge at the top of the wall, allowing Reese to circle the bases for a homer.

Neither side could score in the seventh or eighth.

In the top of the ninth, Cal Abrams averted trouble by making a spectacular leaping, twisting catch at the fence to rob Granny Hamner of an extra-base hit.

In the bottom of the ninth, the Dodgers missed a golden opportunity to win the game. Abrams led off with a walk on a full count. Reese fouled off a couple of bunts, then lined a hit to left, Abrams stopping at second. Snider was the next hitter, and the Phillies' defense crept in expecting a bunt. But Duke swung at the first pitch and lined a hit to center. Coach Milt Stock waved Abrams around third and on to home. But center fielder Richie Ashburn, who had been playing shallow, picked the ball up on one bounce and threw a perfect strike to the plate. Abrams was out by 15 feet, and the crowd groaned in unison.

Still, the Dodgers had men on second and third and only one out. Phillie manager Eddie Sawyer wisely ordered an intentional walk to Robinson, loading the bases. Needing only a long fly to win the game, Carl Furillo jumped on Roberts' first pitch. But he only lifted and easy pop to the first baseman. Hodges then sent a long fly to right, which was caught easily for the third out.

The crowd was still moaning about its disappointment when Roberts led off the top of the tenth with a single up the middle. Waitkus blooped a hit to center, and Roberts went to second. Ashburn tried to sacrifice, but Newcombe made a fine play to get a force out at third. The crowd cheered Newk's effort. With a count of 1-and-2 on Sisler, Newcombe threw an outside fastball. Sisler went to the opposite field with it and lammed a drive to deep left. Abrams backed up to the wall then watched helplessly as the ball sailed into the second row of seats for a three-run home run.

The Phillies erupted from the dugout and mobbed Sisler at the plate after he rounded the bases. Roberts quickly disposed of the Dodgers in order in the bottom of the tenth, and Philadelphia had finally nailed down the pennant. In the clubhouse after the game, the victorious Whiz Kids whooped it up gleefully.

But outside in the stands, on the streets and inside the taverns, a pall hung over Brooklyn. After a few more tears, and maybe a few more beers, the heartbroken fans silently shuffled home. Oh well, wait until next year!

Philadelphia	ab	r	h	bi	o	a	e
E. Waitkus, 1b	5	1	1	0	18	0	0
R. Ashburn, cf	5	1	0	0	2	1	0
D. Sisler, lf	5	2	4	3	0	0	0
J. Mayo, lf10	0	0	0	0	1	0	0
D. Ennis, rf	5	0	2	0	2	0	0
W. Jones, 3b	5	0	1	1	0	3	0
G. Hamner, ss	4	0	0	0	1	2	0
A. Seminick, c	3	0	1	0	2	1	0
P. Caballero, pr9	0	0	0	0	-	-	-
S. Lopata, c9	0	0	0	0	2	0	0
M. Goliat, 2b	4	0	1	0	1	3	0
R. Roberts, p	2	0	1	0	1	6	0
	38	4	11	4	30	16	0

Brooklyn	ab	r	h	bi	o	a	e
C. Abrams, lf	2	0	0	0	2	0	0
P. Reese, ss	4	1	3	1	3	3	0
D. Snider, cf	4	0	1	0	3	0	0
J. Robinson, 2b	3	0	0	0	4	3	0
C. Furillo, rf	4	0	0	0	3	0	0
G. Hodges, 1b	4	0	0	0	9	3	0
R. Campanella, c	4	0	1	0	2	4	0
B. Cox, 3b	3	0	0	0	1	2	0
J. Russell, ph10	1	0	0	0	-	-	-
D. Newcombe, p	3	0	0	0	3	2	0
T. Brown, ph10	1	0	0	0	-	-	-
	33	1	5	1	30	17	0

Philadelphia	000 001 000 3	=	4
Brooklyn	000 001 000 0	=	1

	ip	h	r-er	bb	so
Roberts (W 20-11)	10	5	1-1	3	2
Newcombe (L 19-11)	10	11	4-4	2	3

Time—2:33
Attendance—35,073
Umpires: L. Goetz, F. Dascoli, L. Jorda, & A. Donatelli

Game-Winning RBI: Sisler
LOB: Phila 7, Bkn 5
DP: Reese-Robinson-Hodges (Jones) Roberts-Waitkus
2B: Reese
HR: Reese, Sisler
SH: Roberts
CS: Caballero

Over the winter, Walter O'Malley replaced Branch Rickey as club president, and Charley Dressen succeeded Burt Shotton as manager.

1951 SUNDAY, SEPTEMBER 30TH, AT SHIBE PARK, PHILADELPHIA

Robinson's Heroics Force a Playoff

Jackie's Catch in 12th Saves the Game, Homer in 14th Wins It
Dodgers and Giants End Regular Season Tied

Today's Results			
BROOKLYN 9-Philadelphia 8 (14 innings)			
New York 3-Boston 2			
Chicago 7-St. Louis 6 (1st game)			
St. Louis 3-Chicago 0 (6 innings) (2nd)			
Pittsburgh 8-Cincinnati 4 (11 innings)			
Standings	**W-L**	**Pct.**	**GB**
BROOKLYN	96-58	.623	—
New York	96-58	.623	—
St. Louis	81-73	.526	15
Boston	76-78	.494	20
Philadelphia	73-81	.474	23
Cincinnati	68-86	.442	28
Pittsburgh	64-90	.416	32
Chicago	62-92	.403	34

As he had done so many times before, Jack Roosevelt Robinson turned in a nearly miraculous performance today to win a game for the Brooklyn Dodgers. But he never led the team to a bigger victory than today's, and he never performed his feats more dramatically. With a Dodger loss meaning elimination from the pennant race, Jackie contributed a key triple as the Bums rallied to overcome a 6-1 deficit to tie the tenacious Philadelphia Phillies. Then, with the winning run all but across the plate in the bottom of the twelfth inning, Robinson made a superhuman catch of a line drive to turn what looked like the game-winning hit for the Phillies into an inning-ending out. Finally, in the fourteenth inning, Robinson blasted a long home run to provide Brooklyn with the winning run in a 9-8 victory.

All this took place with the Dodgers and New York Giants tied for first place on the final day of the National League schedule. New York won its game in Boston, so the pennant would be decided by a best-of-three playoff starting tomorrow at Ebbets Field.

Brooklyn had held sole possession of first place from May 12th until New York caught them last Friday, September 28th. On the night of August 11th, the Dodgers had enjoyed a 13-game lead. New York played great ball down the stretch, but Brooklyn still held a 4½-game lead as late as September 20th. Then the Dodgers lost six out of eight, while the Giants won five of five, and the race was tied by Friday night. Brooklyn's Don Newcombe and New York's Sal Maglie each pitched shutouts on Saturday to keep the contenders even. So the season came down to the last day in a dead heat.

The sputtering Bums started today's game off badly. Preacher Roe (22-3) was pitching with just two days of rest, and he was knocked out of the box in thesecond inning. Former Dodger Tommy Brown started the rout with a home run. Before the inning was over, four runs were in.

Pee Wee Reese tripled home a run for Brooklyn in the top of the third.

But Philly pitcher Bubba Church drove in two runs with a single in the bottom of the inning to make the score 6-1.

Roy Campanella tripled and scored on an error in the fourth for Brooklyn.

The Dodgers pulled to within one run, 6-5, with a three-run rally in the fifth. Singles by Carl Furillo and Reese preceded a triple by Robinson. And Andy Pafko drove Jackie home with a hit off reliever Karl Drews.

But the Phils came right back with two runs off Brooklyn relievers Clyde King and Clem Labine to up the count to 8-5.

Drews held the lead for Philadelphia until the eighth, when the Dodgers finally tied the score. Gil Hodges got a one-out infield hit. Billy Cox rammed a single down the right field line. Rube Walker went up to pinch-hit. He knocked an 0-and-2 fastball all the way to the fence in left center for a two-run double. Don Thompson went in as a pinch-runner, and Robin Roberts replaced Drews on the mound. Furillo greeted the Phillies' ace with a hit to left, and Thompson scored the tying run.

Don Newcombe went in to pitch for Brooklyn in the bottom of the eighth.

Roberts and Newcombe labored through five scoreless innings. Since the Giants had already won, the tension here increased with every pitch.

In the twelfth, the Phillies seemed sure to score. Newcombe walked Roberts to start, then he threw late to second trying for a force on a bunt. After a force out at second base, Willie Jones was walked to load the bases. With a full count, Newcombe fanned Del Ennis for the second out. Eddie Waitkus then hit a low line drive that was ticketed for center field. Here Robinson made his miraculous catch. With only time enough for one step, Jackie dove far to his right. He caught the ball inches from the earth to save the game and save the pennant. As he bulldozed into the ground, his elbow was jammed into his stomach, knocking the wind out of him. Still clutching the precious ball, Robinson lay on the ground for a few minutes, only semi-conscious. But he finally got up and stayed in the game.

Newcombe walked two batters in the thirteenth inning and removed himself from the game. Bud Podbielan came in and got the last out.

Robinson came to bat in the top of the fourteenth with two out. With a count of 1-and-1, Jackie got hold of a fastball and drove it into the upper deck in left field for a home run.

Richie Ashburn opened the bottom of the fourteenth with a hit. But Podbielan got the next three batters out, and the game was over.

The Dodgers were still alive in the pennant race, and now they had it within their power to beat the Giants themselves. Now just how many more miracles could they get out of Jackie Robinson?

Brooklyn	ab	r	h	bi	o	a	e
C. Furillo, rf	7	1	2	1	2	0	0
P. Reese, ss	6	0	3	1	3	3	0
D. Snider, cf	7	1	3	1	3	0	0
J. Robinson, 2b	6	2	2	2	6	5	0
R. Campanella, c	7	1	2	0	8	0	0
A. Pafko, lf	7	0	1	2	7	2	0
G. Hodges, 1b	5	1	2	0	10	5	0
B. Cox, 3b	6	1	1	0	2	3	0
P. Roe, p	0	0	0	0	0	0	0
R. Branca, p2	0	1	0	0	0	0	0
J. Russell, ph4	1	0	0	0	-	-	-
C. King, p4	0	0	0	0	0	0	0
C. Labine, p5	0	0	0	0	0	0	0
W. Belardi, ph6	1	0	0	0	-	-	-
C. Erskine, p6	0	0	0	0	0	0	0
R. Walker, ph8	1	0	1	2	-	-	-
D. Thompson, pr8	0	1	0	0	-	-	-
D. Newcombe, p8	2	0	0	0	1	0	0
B. Podbielan, p13	0	0	0	0	0	0	0
	56	9	17	9	42	18	0

Philadelphia	ab	r	h	bi	o	a	e
E. Pellagrini, 2b	6	1	2	2	5	6	0
R. Ashburn, cf	8	0	4	2	2	0	0
W. Jones, 3b	4	0	1	0	3	3	1
D. Ennis, lf	8	0	1	0	6	1	0
T. Brown, 1b	2	1	1	1	3	1	0
E. Waitkus, 1b3	6	0	0	0	10	1	0
M. Clark, rf	1	0	0	0	1	0	0
B. Nicholson, ph3-rf	6	2	2	0	2	0	0
G. Hamner, ss	5	3	2	1	2	6	0
A. Seminick, c	2	1	0	0	7	1	0
B. Church, p	2	0	1	2	1	0	0
K. Drews, p5	2	0	1	0	0	1	0
R. Roberts, p8	1	0	0	0	0	1	0
	53	8	15	8	42	21	1

Brooklyn	001 130 030 000 01	= 9
Philadelphia	042 020 000 000 00	= 8

	ip	h	r-er	bb	so
Roe	1⅔	5	4-4	1	1
Branca	1⅓	2	2-2	2	1
King	*1	3	2-2	0	0
Labine	1	1	0-0	1	2
Erskine	2	2	0-0	0	0
Newcombe	5⅔	1	0-0	6	3
Podbielan (W 2-2)	1⅓	1	0-0	0	0
Church	4⅓	6	5-5	3	3
Drews	3	5	3-3	0	2
Roberts (L 21-15)	6⅔	6	1-1	0	1

*faced two batters in fifth

Umpires: L. Jorda, A. Gore, L. Warneke, & L. Goetz

Game-Winning RBI: Robinson
LOB: Brooklyn 9, Philadelphia 18
BE: Brooklyn 1
DP: Hamner-Pellagrini-Brown (Robinson)
Ennis-Pellagrini-Waitkus
Seminick-Hamner-Pellagrini (Cox)
2B: Jones, Hamner, Pellagrini, Snider, Walker, Campanella
3B: Reese, Campanella, Robinson, Hamner
HR: Brown, Robinson
SH: Jones 2, Robinson, Pellagrini
HBP: by King (Jones)
by Newcombe (Pellagrini)
WP: Branca
Time—4:30 Attendance—31,755

1951 WEDNESDAY, OCTOBER 3RD, AT THE POLO GROUNDS, NEW YORK

Playoff—Game #3

Thomson's Homer Kills Dodgers

Today's Results			
New York 5-BROOKLYN 4 (New York wins best-of-three playoff, 2 games to 1)			
Standings	**W-L**	**Pct.**	**GB**
New York	98-59	.624	—
BROOKLYN	97-60	.618	1
St. Louis	81-73	.526	15½
Boston	76-78	.494	20½
Philadelphia	73-81	.474	23½
Cincinnati	68-86	.442	28½
Pittsburgh	64-90	.416	32½
Chicago	62-92	.403	34½

OH WOE IS US! A HOME RUN IN THE BOTtom of the ninth by New York's Bobby Thomson turned an impending Dodger victory and pennant into a shattering defeat this afternoon.

And Dodger fans thought that losing the pennant last year on a last-inning homer was bad! This year it happened again, and it was ten thousand times worse. Last season it was the Dodgers who were making a late bid to snatch the pennant away. They had nothing to lose. This year they had everything to lose, but they found themselves three runs to the good with only three outs to go. Then they lost it all, lost the game, lost the playoff, lost the pennant that had once seemed so sure.

Today's decisive playoff game was tied 1-1 after seven innings.

Now the Dodgers would either do or die. They did, and right away, too, with three runs in the top of the eighth. Then they made quick work of the Giants in the bottom of the eighth.

The bottom of the ninth, and the pennant that had been slipping out of Brooklyn's grasp for the last seven weeks was just three little outs away.

Then the Dodgers died. Don Newcombe couldn't get the Giants out. So Ralph Branca was brought in, brought in to face Bobby Thomson. Thomson, who had homered against Branca on Monday. Thomson, representing the winning run.

The game-winning run. The Pennant-Winning run.

On the second pitch, a home run flew over the left field wall, carrying the 1951 National League pennant with it.

The Dodgers had never been behind in the game until the last instant. But in the very end, all was lost. And never was a loss so heartfelt.

Having been as far as 13 games behind, the Giants finally caught the Dodgers on last Friday. But Brooklyn had survived by winning Saturday and Sunday.

The playoff started Monday. It was decided, ominously enough, by a home run by Thomson off of Branca. The two-run swat came in the fourth inning and put the Giants ahead 2-1. Jim Hearn pitched a five-hitter, and New York won, 3-1.

Tuesday, the Dodgers had to win just to survive again. And just like on Sunday, Jackie Robinson rose to the occasion. He started things off with a two-run homer in the first inning. A sixth-inning RBI single made it 3-0. By the end of the game, it was 10-0, as Clem Labine pitched the shutout.

Now it was Wednesday, and this game was for all the marbles. The winner would be champion. Both teams had their ace pitchers ready, Don Newcombe for Brooklyn and Sal Maglie for New York.

Just like in the pennant race, Brooklyn jumped into the early lead. Maglie had a shaky start, and the Dodgers got a run in the top of the first. After getting Carl Furillo on a called third strike, Sal the Barber walked Pee Wee Reese and Duke Snider. Jackie Robinson came through with a sharp single to left to put the Dodgers ahead.

Newcombe held onto the 1-0 lead until the bottom of the seventh. Then Monte Irvin led off with a double to left. Whitey Lockman bunted, and Newcombe's throw to third was too late. Thomson's long fly to center field drove in the tying run. Rookie

Willie Mays grounded into a double play to end the inning.

The Dodgers stormed right back into the lead in the eighth. With one gone, Reese lined a single just over the second baseman's glove. Snider bounced a hit to right, and Pee Wee ran to third. Maglie threw a curve in the dirt, allowing Reese to score and Snider to advance all the way to third. Robinson was then given an intentional pass. Andy Pafko bounced one to third, and Thomson missed a back-handed try. The ball went into the corner for a run-scoring single. After the second out, Billy Cox grounded a single under Thomson's glove for another run, making it 4-1.

Newcombe got the Giants out in order in the bottom of the eighth, and the Brooklyn fans in the stands started throwing confetti.

The whole park was mighty quiet when New York came up in the last of the ninth. Alvin Dark grounded a hit that first baseman Gil Hodges could not quite reach. Don Mueller whizzed a liner past Hodges, who had been holding the runner on first, and Dark raced to third. Irvin checked the tide momentarily by fouling out. Then Lockman lined a double to left. Dark scored, and Mueller slid into third, breaking his ankle in the process.

During the delay to carry Mueller off the field, Dodger manager Charley Dressen went to the mound to change pitchers. With Branca and Carl Erskine in the bullpen, Dressen fatefully chose Branca.

Thomson was the batter. Branca's first pitch was a called strike. The second one was a little inside and up. Thomson stepped in the bucket and lined it into the lower left field seats for THE home run.

As Thomson pranced around the bases, Robinson watched grimly and made sure he touched each bag. Then Jackie folded his glove into his pocket and joined his teammates on the long, painful walk to the center field clubhouse.

The Dodgers were too stunned to speak, and mercifully no one asked them to. Ralph Branca lay on the floor and cried. Oh, woe was he. Oh, woe was all of Brooklyn on this dark day.

Brooklyn	ab	r	h	bi	o	a	e
C. Furillo, rf	5	0	0	0	0	0	0
P. Reese, ss	4	2	1	0	2	5	0
D. Snider, cf	3	1	2	0	1	0	0
J. Robinson, 2b	2	1	1	1	3	2	0
A. Pafko, lf	4	0	1	1	4	1	0
G. Hodges, 1b	4	0	0	0	11	1	0
B. Cox, 3b	4	0	2	1	1	3	0
R. Walker, c	4	0	1	0	2	0	0
D. Newcombe, p	4	0	0	0	1	1	0
R. Branca, p9	0	0	0	0	0	0	0
	34	4	8	3	25	13	0

New York	ab	r	h	bi	o	a	e
E. Stanky, 2b	4	0	0	0	0	4	0
A. Dark, ss	4	1	1	0	2	2	0
D. Mueller, rf	4	0	1	0	0	0	0
C. Hartung, pr9	0	1	0	0	-	-	-
M. Irvin, lf	4	1	1	0	1	0	0
W. Lockman, 1b	3	1	2	1	11	1	0
B. Thomson, 3b	4	1	3	4	4	1	0
W. Mays, cf	3	0	0	0	1	0	0
W. Westrum, c	0	0	0	0	7	1	0
B. Rigney, ph8	1	0	0	0	-	-	-
R. Noble, c9	0	0	0	0	0	0	0
S. Maglie, p	2	0	0	0	1	2	0
H. Thompson, ph8	1	0	0	0	-	-	-
L. Jansen, p9	0	0	0	0	0	0	0
	30	5	8	5	27	11	0

Brooklyn	100	000	030	=	4
New York	000	000	104	=	5

one out when winning run scored

	ip	h	r-er	bb	so
Newcombe	8⅓	7	4-4	2	2
Branca (L 13-12)	*0	1	1-1	0	0
Maglie	8	8	4-4	4	6
Jansen (W 23-11)	1	0	0-0	0	0

*faced one batter in ninth
WP: Maglie

Game-Winning RBI: Thomson
LOB: Brooklyn 7, New York 3
DP: Cox-Robinson-Hodges (Stanky)
Reese-Robinson-Hodges (Mays)
2B: Thomson, Irvin, Lockman
HR: Thomson
SH: Lockman
CS: Snider
Time—2:28 Attendance—34,320
Umpires: L. Jorda, J. Conlan,
B. Stewart, & L. Goetz

Chapter XII Triumph and Twilight

1952 September 8th
Dodgers Whip Giants, 10-2, amidst Beanballs

1952 World Series Game No. 5
Bums Top Bombers in Classic Struggle, 6-5

1953 September 6th
Furillo & Durocher Brawl

1953 World Series Game No. 3
Erskine Fans 14 Yankees

1954 August 8th
Score 12 Runs With Two Out

1955 May 10th
Newcombe's One-Hitter Gives Brooklyn a 22-2 Record

1955 World Series Game No. 7
"Next Year" Finally Arrives!

1956 September 30th
Duke & Newk Lead Dodgers to Pennant

1956 World Series Game No. 6
Stay Alive with 1-0 Victory

1957 September 24th
The Last Game at Ebbets Field

AFTER THE PLAYOFF DEBACLE IN 1951, THE DODGER FRONT OFFICE SURPRISED MANY observers by rehiring Charley Dressen as manager. With Don Newcombe gone into the military service, the club's major need was additional pitching. The Dodgers filled the need with youngsters. Joe Black, a Negro League product, was called up from Montreal, and he starred (15-4) mostly in relief. Billy Loes returned from the service and became a regular starter (13-8). Ben Wade, a Cubs' reject, was resurrected, and he also won a job in the rotation and had an 11-9 record. Carl Erskine continued to improve and finished 14-6. Preacher Roe was 11-2, but his work was limited by arm trouble.

Brooklyn broke from the starting gate fast in 1952, and the race was nip and tuck with the Giants through May. On June 1st, Black saved a 3-2 victory for Wade, and the Dodgers regained the league lead for good. By August 25th, the Brooklyn lead was 10½ games.

But then the Giants and the ghosts of the 1951 collapse started to catch up to the Dodgers. By losing 9 of 12, including a doubleheader in New York on September 6th, Brooklyn saw its lead cut to 4 games. Preacher Roe righted the ship on September 7th with a three-hitter against the Giants, and four Dodger home runs off of Sal Maglie won the game, 4-1. The next day Black pitched 7⅔ innings of shutout relief, and Brooklyn won one game 10-2. The Giants salvaged a split of the doubleheader, but the Dodgers emerged from the big confrontation with a 5-game lead.

The Giants inched to within 3 games of the top with two weeks to play but then faltered down the stretch, and the Dodgers won the pennant by 4½ games.

In the World Series, the Dodgers were matched against the New York Yankees. In only his third start of the year, Black won the first game, 4-2, as Pee Wee Reese, Jackie Robinson, and Duke Snider hit home runs. New York's Vic Raschi stopped the Bums in the second game, 7-1, with a three-hitter. Roe, Reese, and Robinson paced a 5-3 Dodger triumph in the third game. Allie Reynolds evened the series for the Yanks by pitching a four-hit shutout in the fourth game to beat black, 2-0. The Dodgers took a 3-games-to-2 lead in the series with a dramatic eleven-inning, 6-5 victory in the fifth game. Carl Erskine survived a five-run fifth and went the distance.

But the Dodgers lost the last two games in Ebbets Field to lose the series. Loes lost a tough one in the sixth game, 3-2. And Black and Roe were beaten in the seventh game, 4-2, as the Dodgers blew a bases-loaded chance in the seventh inning.

Brooklyn fielded an even stronger team in 1953. The key addition was Jim "Junior" Gilliam. Like Campanella and Black before him, Gilliam had played for the Baltimore Elite Giants of the Negro National League before signing with the Dodger organization. A switch-hitter, gifted base runner, and versatile fielder, Junior ousted Jackie Robinson from the second base job, with Robinson becoming a sort of roving left fielder/third baseman.

The Dodgers celebrate winning the 1956 pennant
(above) Don Bessent, Don Newcombe, Sandy Amoros, & Duke Snider
(below) Walt Alston, Walter O'Malley, & Pee Wee Reese

Leo Durocher & Carl Furillo (circled) just after their fight on September 6, 1953

The Dodgers' starting lineup was at its very peak. The team hit 208 home runs, and six different players scored over 100 runs. Campy had his best season, pounding 41 homers with 142 RBIs and a .312 average. Carl Furillo won the batting title, despite missing the final three weeks after his hand was broken in a melee with Leo Durocher and the Giants.

Joe Black slumped badly in 1953, but journeyman Jim Hughes picked up a lot of the slack in the bullpen, and Russ Meyer, acquired from the Phillies, did a fine job as a starter. Erskine had his best year, winning 20 games.

The Dodgers trailed the Milwaukee Braves through most of June. But an impressive three-game sweep in Milwaukee on the last weekend of the month vaulted the Brooks into first place to stay. From the All-Star Game through Labor Day, the Dodgers played incredible baseball, winning 46 and losing only 11. That included a 13-game winning streak in mid-August. The Dodgers clinched the pennant on September 12th. Brooklyn finished with the best record in the history of the franchise, 105-49, and a 13-game margin over the second-place Braves.

But the World Series was another disappointment. Playing a very strong Yankee team, the Dodger dropped the first two games, 9-5 and 4-2. Erskine struck out 14 Yanks in the third game and won, 3-2. Loes won the fourth game with relief help from Clem Labine, 7-3, to even the series. But the Bronx Bombers battered four Dodger pitchers in the fifth game to win 11-7. In the sixth game, the Dodgers rallied to tie the score in the top of the ninth, but the Yankees scored in the bottom to win, 4-3, and wrap up the series.

After winning two pennants in a row, manager Dressen demanded a three-year contract. President Walter O'Malley balked, and Dressen quit. Walter Alston, a virtual unknown in Brooklyn who had been managing Dodger farm teams for ten years, was hired in his stead. Alston wound up getting 23 one-year contracts from the O'Malleys.

His first season with the team, 1954, was not a success. Campanella suffered nagging hand injuries and his average slipped all the way to .207. The pitching, always the weak link, could not overcome the drop in offensive production. The Dodgers were neck and neck with the Giants through June and got as close as ½ game behind New York in mid-August. But Brooklyn could not mount a good stretch drive and finished second, 5 games behind.

In 1955, however, the Dodgers won the pennant with the greatest of ease. Campanella bounced back to win the MVP award for the third time. Snider had his best season. Newcombe, who had returned from the service in 1954, was back in top form. Brooklyn won its first ten games of the regular season and had a 22-2 record and a 9½-game lead by May 10th. Newcombe had an 18-1 record through July 31st and finished 20-5 with a .359 batting average. The Dodgers had a 17-game lead when they clinched the pennant on September 8th.

The first two games of the World Series, however, were lost to the Yankees, 6-5 and 4-2. The classic shifted to Ebbets Field, and young lefthander Johnny Podres got the Dodgers back into the running with an 8-3 victory. Homers by Campanella, Snider, and Gil Hodges were enough to win the fourth game, 8-5. Sandy Amoros hit a two-run shot in the fifth game, and Snider hit two solo homers to power the Dodgers to their third win in a row, 5-3. Young Karl Spooner was given the start in Game #6, and he was bombed for five runs in the first inning to allow the Yankees to win 5-1 and even the series. In the decisive seventh game, Podres pitched a beauty. Aided by two RBIs by Hodges and a great catch in left field by Amoros, Podres pitched Brooklyn to a 2-0 victory and its first (and last) World Series championship. It was the borough's greatest moment.

Tiny old Ebbets Field was decrepit and becoming unsafe, and some move was needed. In 1956, O'Malley shifted seven home games to Roosevelt Stadium in Jersey City, New Jersey. He kept pushing for a stadium at Flatbush and Atlantic Avenues, while the city offered a site in Flushing Meadows, Queens. O'Malley also entertained offers from other cities, notably Los Angeles.

The Dodger team spent most of 1956 trailing the league-leading Milwaukee Braves. Although Snider and Gilliam were having outstanding seasons, the rest of the old guard was slipping. Campanella was again way down in the lower .200s in batting average. But despite the loss of Podres to the military draft, the Brooklyn pitching was excellent. Sal Maglie, the one-time villain with the Giants, was acquired by Brooklyn and pitched great ball. Youngsters Roger Craig, Don Drysdale, and Ed Roebuck all made good contributions. And Newcombe had a super season.

Brooklyn was still trailing with two days left in the season. But the Dodgers won a doubleheader on the final Saturday and leaped into the league lead when the Braves lost in St. Louis. Brooklyn clinched the pennant with an 8-6 victory over Pittsburgh on Sunday and finished with a 1-game margin when Milwaukee also won. Newcombe got the win the last game to finish 27-7, and Snider hit two homers to wind up with 43.

In the World Series, again against the Yankees, Brooklyn reversed the 1955 pattern by winning the first two games. Maglie took the opener 6-3. In the second game, New York got an early 6-0 lead, by the Dodgers rallied to win 13-8. The series shifted to Yankee Stadium, and New York won three in a row, 5-3, 6-2, and 2-0, Don Larsen pitching a perfect game in the last one. Faced with elimination, Clem Labine got a rare start and saved the Dodgers with a thrilling 1-0 victory in ten innings in the sixth game. But in the seventh game, Newcombe was pounded for two two-run home runs by Yogi Berra, and the Dodgers lost decisively, 9-0.

In 1957, the Dodgers played eight games in Jersey City, and the negotiations with Los Angeles became very serious. By the time the season ended, it was obvious that the team would move west. Talks with New York City officials had gone nowhere, and Los Angeles afforded opportunities which would have been impossible to ignore. On the field, the Brooklyn Dodgers stayed in contention until August, when Milwaukee pulled away from the field. Brooklyn finished third, 11 games behind. When the Dodgers closed out their home schedule on September 24th with a 2-0 victory over Pittsburgh, everyone knew it would be their final game in Brooklyn. The official announcement of the move to Los Angeles was made on October 8th.

Brooklyn was without a professional baseball team for the first time since the club that became the Dodgers was founded in 1883. There were a lot of hard feelings in the New York area about the move. But O'Malley and the Los Angeles Dodgers would lead baseball to unimagined new heights in the coming years.

1952 MONDAY, SEPTEMBER 8TH, AT THE POLO GROUNDS, NEW YORK

Dodgers Whip Giants, 10-2, Amidst Beanballs

Joe Black Flattens New York in Opener
Giants Win Second Game, 3-2, to Remain 5 Games Behind

RELIEF STAR JOE BLACK STRODE OUT OF the Dodger bullpen today throwing high and hard, and he whipped the New York Giants in the first game of a day-night doubleheader, 10-2. The victory gave Brooklyn two victories in the five-game final showdown with the hard-charging Giants. The series concluded with New York winning the final game, but the Bums remained 5 games in front of the Giants in the standings.

Today's Results			
BROOKLYN 10-New York 2 (day game)			
New York 3-BROOKLYN 2 (night game)			
no other games scheduled			
Standings	**W-L**	**Pct.**	**GB**
BROOKLYN	86-49	.637	—
New York	81-54	.600	5
St. Louis	79-57	.581	7½
Philadelphia	74-62	.544	12½
Chicago	67-71	.486	20½
Cincinnati	60-76	.441	26½
Boston	59-76	.437	27
Pittsburgh	39-100	.281	44

Less than two weeks before, Brooklyn had built up a 10½-game lead. But then the Dodgers slumped, and on Saturday, the Dodgers made four errors in one game and lost a doubleheader in the dreaded Polo Grounds.

With the Giants only 4 games behind and the ghost of the dreadful loss of last year's big lead haunting them, the Dodgers came to the park on Sunday in shaky condition. But Preacher Roe pitched a magnificent three-hitter and beat New York, 4-1. All four Dodger runs came on home runs off of Sal Maglie.

And the Dodgers won this afternoon's game in convincing fashion, 10-2, with Black pitching seven scoreless innings in relief.

But as important as the actual victory was for Brooklyn, the manner in which the Dodgers and Black handled the Giants was equally significant. A hard slide by Hodges knocked the Giant second baseman out of the game. And Black low-bridged several hitters and had the rest intimidated. The New York pitchers hit three Dodger batters with pitches, but the Bums kept coming up to the plate swinging. Even though the Dodgers let the night game get away, it looked as if there would be no blowing of the pennant this year.

The Dodgers took it right to the foe early today and kept pouring it on. In the first inning, Billy Cox homered, Pee Wee Reese tripled, and Duke Snider doubled as the Dodgers scored five runs.

The Giants got two runs on a homer by Monte Irvin in the first, and they knocked starting pitcher Ken Lehman out of the game with one out in the second.

Dodger manager Chuck Dressen was taking no chances, and he called Black in with the bases loaded and the score 5-2. Joe got pinch-hitter George Wilson on an infield pop, and Al Dark lined out to left field to end the inning.

The long-standing bad blood between the two teams surfaced by the fifth inning. Yesterday, Hodges had disabled Davey Williams with a crunching slide at second base. Today, Gil was hit by a pitch in the top of the fifth. When the next batter hit a double-play ball, Hodges again went into second base hard. This time he spiked second baseman Bill Rigney badly enough to put Rig out of action.

Black went to the mound and let the Giants know who was boss. When Wilson came to bat in the bottom of the fifth, Black nearly removed the poor batter's head from his shoulders with a high inside fastball. Wilson ducked out of the way so fast that the ball sailed between his cap and his skull.

New York pitcher Monte Kennedy decked both Hodges and Black in the seventh. Larry Jansen of the Giants plunked Pafko with a pitch in the eighth. Finally, the umpires warned the pitchers and the managers about stiff penalties for any further beanballs. In the ninth inning, Jansen hit Cox with a pitch and earned an automatic ejection from the game.

In between "purpose pitches," the Dodgers managed to score some five runs. Carl Furillo and Duke Snider hit home runs.

While shaving between games, New York manager Leo Durocher had to concede that "they kicked our butts" in the first game. He was referring not only to the Dodgers' hitting but to their aggresive play.

In the night game, great relief pitching by Maglie and Don Mueller's two-out double in the ninth won the game for the Giants, 3-2.

DAY GAME

Brooklyn	ab	r	h	bi	o	a	e
B. Cox, 3b	5	1	1	1	2	0	0
P. Reese, ss	5	2	2	0	0	2	1
J. Robinson, 2b	6	1	2	2	5	3	0
R. Campanella, c	5	1	3	0	6	0	0
A. Pafko, lf	3	1	1	0	1	0	0
G. Hodges, 1b	2	1	0	0	7	1	0
C. Furillo, rf	5	1	1	2	2	0	0
D. Snider, cf	4	2	2	4	3	0	0
K. Lehman, p	1	0	0	0	0	0	0
J. Black, p2	4	0	0	0	1	1	0
	40	10	12	9	27	7	1

New York	ab	r	h	bi	o	a	e
D. Mueller, rf	1	0	0	0	0	0	0
B. Elliott, ph2	0	0	0	0	-	-	-
G. Wilson, ph2-rf	4	0	1	0	0	0	0
A. Dark, ss	5	1	2	0	0	4	1
W. Lockman, 1b	4	0	1	0	13	0	0
M. Irvin, lf	4	1	2	2	0	0	0
B. Thomson, 3b	4	0	1	0	3	0	0
H. Thompson, 3b	3	0	0	0	2	3	0
B. Rigney, 2b	2	0	1	0	2	2	0
B. Hofman, 2b5	1	0	1	0	1	2	0
W. Westrum, c	4	0	0	0	6	1	1
M. Lanier, p	0	0	0	0	0	0	0
H. Wilhelm, p1	2	0	0	0	0	0	1
M. Kennedy, p7	0	0	0	0	0	0	0
D. Rhodes, ph7	1	0	0	0	-	-	-
L. Jansen, p8	0	0	0	0	0	0	0
D. Koslo, p9	0	0	0	0	0	0	0
C. Hartung, ph9	1	0	0	0	-	-	-
	36	2	9	2	27	12	3

Brooklyn	500 001 211	=	10
New York	200 000 000	=	2

	ip	h	r-er	bb	so
Lehman	1⅓	3	2-2	1	0
Black (W 13-3)	7⅔	6	0-0	2	6
Lanier (L 7-12)	*0	4	4-4	0	0
Wilhelm	6	4	2-1	3	6
Kennedy	1	1	2-2	1	1
Jansen	1⅔	2	2-1	1	0
Koslo	⅓	1	0-0	0	0

HBP: by Wilhelm (Hodges)
by Jansen 2 (Pafko, Cox)
PB: Westrum

Game-Winning RBI: Cox
LOB: Bkn 11, NY 10
BE: Bkn 2, NY 1
DP: Black-Robinson-Hodges (Thomson)
Dark-Rigney-Lockman (Furillo)
2B: Snider, Dark, Lockman, Campanella
3B: Reese
HR: Cox, Irvin, Furillo, Snider
SB: Reese

Time—3:12
Attendance—21,266
Umpires: L. Ballanfant, J. Conlan, B. Stewart, & A. Barlick

NIGHT GAME—Attendance-35,420

			r	h	e	
Brooklyn	000 001 100	=	2	7	0	Game-Winning RBI: Mueller
New York	000 002 001	=	3	9	0	two out when winning run scored

Batteries: B. Loes (L 13-7) & R. Campanella
A. Corwin 6 IP, S. Maglie (W 15-6) 3 IP & S. Yvars

By winning five of their next six, the Giants closed to within 3 games of the Dodgers. But New York then won only two of its next seven games, and the Dodgers put the pennant away with a modest four-game winning streak. They clinched the flag on Tuesday, September 23rd, and finished 4½ games ahead. Brooklyn's final record was 96-57.

1952 SUNDAY, OCTOBER 5TH, AT YANKEE STADIUM, NEW YORK
World Series—Game #5

Bums Top Bombers in Classic Struggle, 6-5

OH, WHAT A GAME TO WIN! THE DODGERS DID IT IN SPECTACULAR FASHION TODAY and beat those Yankees. Not only did they win a thriller, 6-5 in eleven innings, the victory put the Brooklyns just one win away from the world championship with two games to play.

Every Dodger was a hero on this bright and beautiful day in the Bronx. Billy Cox not only exercised his magic glove and made a big play, he also scored the tying and winning runs. George Shuba cut off a triple with a fine catch in left. Andy Pafko made an astounding catch to save two runs in the second inning. And Carl Furillo saved the game in the bottom of the eleventh by robbing Johnny Mize of a home run.

But the biggest heroes had to be the Dodgers' pitcher and their leading hitter. Carl Erskine went the distance and pitched brilliantly, retiring the Bronx Bombers in order in nine of the eleven innings. Duke Snider made a leaping catch in center field and pounded three very big hits. The first was a prodigious home run with a man on in the fourth. The second was a solid single with two out in the seventh to drive home the tying run. And the final blow was a ringing double off the wall in the eleventh inning to knock in the winning tally.

Erskine had been knocked out of the second game of the series in the sixth inning and was working today with only two days rest. He effectively mixed his fastball, slider, change of pace, and overhand curveball, with the latter being especially sharp.

The Yankees were held to just one infield hit in the first four innings. One hit they didn't get was a home run by Gene Woodling in the second inning. Woodling hit a drive toward the seats in right field, but Andy Pafko made a perfectly-timed, twisting leap to catch the ball while bending over the low fence. A fan a few rows back yelled to him, "Hey, I wanted that ball!" "Lady, I wanted it more than you ever did," Pafko shot back.

New York skipper Casey Stengel gambled with veteran Ewell Blackwell as his starting pitcher today. The sidearming righthander had been waived out of the National League this summer with a 3-12 record and a 5.38 ERA.

Brooklyn scored against him in the second inning on a walk, a bad-hop single, a steal of third, and a hit by Pafko. But a squeeze play failed, and the Dodgers left the bases loaded.

In the fifth, Blackwell was routed as the Brooks scored three more runs. A walk to Gil Hodges and a late throw to second on a bunt set up the rally. A sacrifice bunt and a run-scoring fly plated the first run. Snider's 420-foot blast into the bleachers in right center brought home the last two.

Then, quicker than you could say "Jackie Robinson" (or "Carl Erskine"), the Yankees scored five runs in the bottom of the fifth to take the lead. A base on balls and two ground-ball singles by Billy Martin and Irv Noren scored the first run. An infield force out scored another run, and Phil Rizzuto's single put the tying runs on base. Now the bullpen started to work. Mickey Mantle fouled out, and the situation improved. But Johnny Mize hit a 1-and-2 pitch well into the seats for a three-run home run, and New York went ahead 5-4. Snider made a great catch to rob Yogi Berra and end the inning.

Just as suddenly as he had been in trouble, Erskine settled down again. Over the next six innings, the Yankees went out in order.

Another National League veteran, Johnny Sain, was sent in to replace Blackwell in the sixth. The Dodgers tied the score against him in the seventh. With one down, Cox scratched an infield hit toward third. Pee Wee Reese sacrificed him to second. Snider then cracked a clean hit to center, and Cox beat Mantle's desperate throw to the plate.

Neither side could score in the next three rounds.

But in the eleventh, Cox and Snider repeated their act. With one out, Billy hit a hard grounder to third, and Gil McDougald was unable to glove the hit cleanly. Reese then shot a single to center and Cox raced around to third. Duke stroked a liner over the right fielder's head that caromed off the wall for a double. Cox scored easily, and Reese held third. An intentional pass and a neat double play kept the Dodgers from scoring more.

In the bottom of the eleventh, Mantle made the first out on an easy tap to the mound.

Johnny Mize was next. The count went to 2-and-2, with Mize arguing with the umpire over both called strikes. On the next pitch, he decided he had better swing. Connecting solidly, he sent a long fly to right. Outfielder Furillo, who had gone to right in the fifth inning, ran back to the fence. Seeing he would have to jump, Furillo pushed off the wall with his right hand, leaped, and caught the ball in his outstretched left hand, right in the center of the glove, to rob Mize of another homer.

The final batter was Berra. Erskine got two strikes and then broke off a big curve. It dropped into the strike zone, and the Dodgers had won the game.

The eleated players celebrated the emotional victory in the clubhouse. One more and they could break out the champagne!

Brooklyn (NL)	**ab**	**r**	**h**	**bi**	**o**	**a**	**e**
B. Cox, 3b	5	2	3	0	2	2	0
P. Reese, ss	5	0	1	1	1	1	0
D. Snider, cf	5	1	3	4	4	0	0
J. Robinson, 2b	2	1	0	0	2	1	0
G. Shuba, lf	2	0	1	0	4	0	0
C. Furillo, rf5	4	0	1	0	3	0	0
R. Campanella, c	5	0	0	0	6	1	0
A. Pafko, rf-lf5	4	0	1	1	3	0	0
T. Holmes, lf9	1	0	0	0	2	0	0
G. Hodges, 1b	3	1	0	0	6	0	0
C. Erskine, p	4	1	0	0	0	1	0
	40	6	10	6	33	6	0

New York (AL)	**ab**	**r**	**h**	**bi**	**o**	**a**	**e**
G. McDougald, 3b	4	1	0	1	0	2	0
P. Rizzuto, ss	5	1	1	0	1	4	1
M. Mantle, cf	5	0	1	0	1	0	0
J. Mize, 1b	5	1	1	3	9	1	0
Y. Berra, c	4	0	0	0	10	1	0
G. Woodling, lf	4	0	0	0	5	0	0
H. Bauer, rf	3	1	0	0	1	0	0
B. Martin, 2b	4	1	1	0	6	3	0
E. Blackwell, p	1	0	0	0	0	1	0
I. Noren, ph5	1	0	1	1	-	-	-
J. Sain, p6	2	0	0	0	0	2	0
	38	5	5	5	33	14	1

Brooklyn	010 030 010 01	=	6
New York	000 050 000 00	=	5

	ip	**h**	**r-er**	**bb**	**so**
Erskine (W 1-1)	11	5	5-5	3	6
Blackwell	5	4	4-4	3	4
Sain (L 0-1)	6	6	2-2	3	3

HBP: by Sain (Snider)
Time—3:00 Attendance—70,536

Game-Winning RBI: Snider
LOB: Brooklyn 11, New York 3
BE: Brooklyn 1
DP: Martin-Rizzuto-Mize (Snider)
McDougald-Berra-Mize (Furillo)
2B: Furillo, Snider
HR: Snider, Mize
SH: Erskine, Cox, Reese
SB: Robinson

Umpires: B. Pinelli, A. Passarella, L. Goetz, B. McKinley, D. Boggess, & J. Honochick

The Dodgers did not get Win #4.

In the sixth game, Snider hit two home runs, but Berra and Mantle hit one apiece. The difference was a balk by Dodger pitcher Billy Loes followed by a bouncer off Loes's knees. They gave New York a run, and the Yankees won, 3-2.

In Game #7, each side scored single runs in the fourth and fifth. In the sixth Mantle homered, and in the seventh he singled across another run. The Dodgers could not answer, and they lost the game, 4-2, and with it the series.

1953 SUNDAY, SEPTEMBER 6TH, AT THE POLO GROUNDS, NEW YORK

Furillo & Durocher Brawl

Dodger Outfielder's Hand is Broken in Scuffle
Brooklyn Beats New York, 6-3, Behind Roe

Today's Results			
BROOKLYN 6-New York 3			
Milwaukee 3-St. Louis 1 (1st game)			
St. Louis 3-Milwaukee 3 (Tie-8 innings) (2nd)			
Philadelphia 7-Pittsburgh 2			
Chicago 7-Cincinnati 6 (1st game)			
Chicago 7-Cincinnati 2 (2nd game)			
Standings	**W-L**	**Pct.**	**GB**
BROOKLYN	94-42	.691	—
Milwaukee	83-53	.610	11
Philadelphia	75-60	.556	18½
St. Louis	73-61	.545	20
New York	64-72	.471	30
Cincinnati	59-77	.434	35
Chicago	53-82	.393	40½
Pittsburgh	42-96	.304	53

"I'LL KILL HIM, I'LL KILL HIM," CARL Furillo muttered to himself in the Dodger clubhouse today. To newspapermen he vowed, "I'm gonna get him the first time I see him." He was referring, of course, to Giant manager Leo Durocher, whom Furillo blamed for several beanings and brushbacks in the past few years.

Today Furillo was hit on the wrist by a pitch from Giant righhander Ruben Gomez. Furillo yelled at him and made a few steps toward the mound. But teammates intervened, and Carl trotted down to first base. In Furillo's mind, Gomez was not the real culprit but was only acting on orders from his manager.

While Billy Cox was at bat, Furillo started motioning toward the Giant bench, pointing to Durocher and yelling. Suddenly the runner charged toward the dugout with fire in his eyes. Durocher came out to meet him, and Furillo clamped a furious headlock on the balding New York manager's skull. They wrestled to the ground, and Durocher was turning purple by the time that Furillo was pulled off of him.

In the melee a few swings were taken by each side. But the only casualty was Furillo, whose hand had been stepped on. His shoulder was also bruised, apparently by a punch from behind. Both he and Durocher were ejected from the game. As Furillo approached the steps leading to the clubhouse in center field, he was assaulted by missiles from the bleacher fans. One man swiped at him with an umbrella and grazed his cap. It took two cops to quiet the crowd and afford safe passage up the stairs for the Dodger outfielder, team doctor, and trainer.

Furillo was taken to a Brooklyn hospital for x-rays. The examination revealed a fracture of the fifth metacarpal bone of the left hand. The injury would keep Carl out of the lineup for some weeks. Since he was fighting for the National League batting crown, this setback added to his rage. He was back in the clubhouse by the end of the game and was still seething.

He seemed less concerned about his injury than he was about being unable to land a solid punch on Durocher's chin before being pulled away. He claimed that he had looked into the New York dugout and had seen Durocher talking and pointing toward him at first base. When Leo had given him the sign to "come here" with his index finger, Furillo had charged. Durocher later denied having made any gestures toward Furillo and had come out of the dugout only when he was aware that Carl was after him.

Ever since Furillo was hospitalized by a beanball by New York's Sheldon Jones on June 28, 1950, he had been convinced that Durocher ordered the Giant hurlers to throw at him. In that year he was hit by pitches three times after getting extra base hits against New York. Earlier this year, the Giants' Sal Maglie decked Furillo with a high inside fastball, and Carl got up and threw his bat at the pitcher. So today's incident was not an isolated thing.

Although the Giants had been out of the pennant race for months, their pitchers hadn't let up on the Dodgers in the war of beanballs. Just last Friday, the teams traded "purpose pitches" and drag bunts until the umpires had called out the managers to warn them to stop.

Today's big ruckus came just after the Dodgers had taken the lead in the second inning.

In the bottom of the first, Alvin Dark had put the Giants on the board with a solo home run. It was a "Chinese" shot that hit the ramp protruding from the upper deck in right field near the line.

In the top of the second, Jackie Robinson singled to lead off. Roy Campanella then knocked a fly ball into the upper deck in left for a two-run homer. It was Campy's 38th home run of the season. Gil Hodges was retired before Furillo was hit by the pitch, and all the trouble started.

Brooklyn pitcher Preacher Roe matched zeroes with New York's Gomez for the next three innings. Then each side scored two runs in the sixth. The Dodgers counted on a single up the middle by Duke Snider followed by a two-run homer into the upper tier in left by Robinson. The Giants got the runs back when Dark reached base on a boot by Pee Wee Reese and Bobby Thomson hit a homer. This pop just nicked the scoreboard in left field as it was descending.

Other than a pair of singles and those two cheap home runs, Roe held the New Yorkers at bay. He walked three and struck out four. After Thomson's one-out homer in the sixth, Preach retired the last eleven men to face him. He got the win to raise his record to 11-2.

Gomez also pitched well. But those two two-run shots ruined him.

The Dodgers added two unearned runs in the eighth inning to pad their final margin of victory. A walk to Snider, a hit by Robinson, and an out put runners on second and third. Catcher Wes Westrum tried to pick Snider off third but threw wildly past the base. Snider scored easily, and Robinson made it home with a long leap. Westrum thought he had tagged Jackie in time, and another long argument ensued.

The final score was 6-3, and the pennant-bound Dodgers maintained an 11-game lead over the second-place Milwaukee Braves. But the victory knocked Carl Furillo out of the lineup for a while.

Brooklyn	ab	r	h	bi	o	a	e
J. Gilliam, 2b	4	0	0	0	0	4	0
P. Reese, ss	4	0	1	0	4	3	1
D. Snider, cf	3	2	1	0	2	0	0
J. Robinson, lf	4	3	3	2	3	0	0
R. Campanella, c	4	1	1	2	5	0	0
G. Hodges, 1b	4	0	0	0	11	0	0
C. Furillo, rf	0	0	0	0	0	0	0
D. Thompson, pr2-rf	3	0	1	0	1	0	0
B. Cox, 3b	4	0	1	0	1	1	0
P. Roe, p	4	0	0	0	0	5	0
	34	6	8	4	27	13	1

New York	ab	r	h	bi	o	a	e
W. Lockman, 1b	4	0	0	0	10	2	0
A. Dark, ss	4	2	2	1	1	4	0
B. Hofman, 2b	4	0	0	0	3	2	0
B. Thomson, cf	3	1	1	2	2	0	0
D. Mueller, rf	4	0	0	0	1	0	0
D. Spencer, 3b	2	0	0	0	1	2	0
D. Rhodes, lf	3	0	1	0	1	0	0
W. Westrum, c	3	0	0	0	7	0	1
R. Gomez, p	3	0	0	0	1	1	0
	30	3	4	3	27	11	1

Brooklyn	020	002	020	= 6
New York	100	002	000	= 3

	ip	h	r-er	bb	so
Roe (W 11-2)	9	4	3-2	3	4
Gomez (L 13-8)	9	8	6-4	1	6

HBP: by Gomez (Furillo)
Time—2:26 Attendance—25,321
Umpires: D. Boggess, B. Engeln, B. Stewart, & B. Pinelli

Game-Winning RBI: Campanella
LOB: Brooklyn 3, New York 3
BE: Brooklyn 0, New York 1
DP: Dark-Hofman-Lockman (Cox)
Roe-Reese-Hodges (Gomez)
Roe-Reese-Hodges (Hofman)
2B: Reese
HR: Dark, Campanella, Robinson, Thomson

The hand injury kept Furillo out of the lineup for the remainder of the regular season. Still, he wound up winning the batting title with a .344 average.

The Dodgers clinched the pennant on the following Saturday, September 12th, with a 5-2 victory in Milwaukee. Brooklyn finished with an impressive 105-49 record and a 13-game margin over the second-place Braves.

1953 FRIDAY, OCTOBER 2ND, AT EBBETS FIELD
World Series—Game #3

Erskine Fans 14 Yankees

CARL ERSKINE, THE LITTLE BIG MAN OF THE DODGER PITCHING STAFF, TODAY PUT Brooklyn back into the 1953 World Series by striking out 14 New York Yankees and winning 3-2. The strikeouts broke the existing record for a World Series game. But more importantly, the hard-fought victory was Brooklyn's first after defeats in the first two games of the classic.

Not that "Oisk" was the only hero in Flatbush this afternoon. Jackie Robinson helped the Dodgers to their first two runs with his bat and his legs. Roy Campanella hit a majestic home run in the eighth to bring home the winning run. And Billy Cox cut off a Yankee run with a tremendous play at third base and pushed a savvy squeeze bunt to bring home a Dodger run.

The weather was ideal in Brooklyn as the series shifted after two games in the Bronx. This was a "must" game for the Dodgers, as a defeat would put them behind 3 games to 0. So Charley Dressen was forced to come back with the ace of his staff (Erskine) on only one day of rest. Not that Carl was tired. On Wednesday, he had been knocked out of the game after facing only eight batters.

Today, it was a different story for him. Using mostly fastballs early and shifting to more overhand curves later (with a few sliders and change-ups thrown in), Erskine handcuffed the Yankees. With New York's Vic Raschi also pitching a strong game, neither team could score more than one run in any inning, and the lead seesawed back and forth.

Both pitchers got through the first four innings without much trouble. Erskine struck out seven batters in that time while walking two and hitting one with a pitch. Raschi was found for two singles and two walks, but he was backed up by a double play and a "caught stealing."

Even though they never got the ball out of the infield, the Yankees got their first three hits of the game in the fifth inning and scored a run. Billy Martin beat out a hit to deep short. On a hit-and-run play, Phil Rizzuto bounced one up the middle. Second baseman Jim Gilliam tried to field the hopper and get to the base at the same time, but the ball rolled free for a hit. Raschi sacrificed the runners to second and third. Gil McDougald then smashed one down the third base line. It looked like a sure double, but Cox made a headlong dive and knocked the ball down. One run scored on the hit, but Cox's stop prevented a second tally. Erskine escaped further trouble by getting Joe Collins on a called third strike and Hank Bauer on an easy ground ball.

The Yankee lead lasted only until Robinson got a chance to prance around the bases in the bottom of the inning. Jackie drilled a drive off the screen in right field and got a double with the help of a fadeaway slide. As he danced off second base, pitcher Raschi committed a balk trying to fake him back to second, and Robinson gleefully trotted to third. Acting on his own, Cox laid down a "safety squeeze" bunt. The ball was perfectly placed, rolling past the pitcher, and Robinson easily beat the second baseman's throw home.

A nice catch by Carl Furillo on a ball Duke Snider lost in the sun saved a run in the sixth.

The Bums took the lead in the bottom of the sixth. Snider opened with a single to right, and Hodges walked. For the first time all year, manager Dressen ordered Campanella to bunt. Inexperienced at this, Campy popped out. Furillo struck out. But Robinson came to the rescue by punching a single through the left side to drive Snider home.

In the eighth, Erskine gave up a run even though he struck out both Collins and Mickey Mantle for the fourth time in the game. In between the whiffs, Bauer singled and Yogi Berra was hit by a pitch. With two down, Gene Woodling stroked a hit over shortstop, and Bauer steamed home from second to tie the score.

In the Dodger half, Campanella came up with one out. The rotund catcher was playing despite a badly bruised hand and had looked very weak at the plate. Raschi tried to get him to chase a high fastball but didn't get the pitch quite high enough. The ball came across about shoulder height, and the big slugger got a hold of it. The ball arched well over the fence in left field and landed in the lower deck for a home run. That gave the Dodgers a 3-2 lead.

Erskine went to the mound in the top of the ninth needing two strikeouts to break the old World Series record set in 1929 by Howard Ehmke. Erskine did not know about that, but he did know that he needed three more outs to win the game.

The first Yankee batter in the ninth, Don Bollwig, struck out on three pitches. The second batter, Johnny Mize, fanned awkwardly on a slow curve, giving Erskine the new record. Irv Noren worked Erskine for a walk, putting the tying run on base. But an overmatched Collins could only hit a feeble tap to the mound, and Erskine threw him out to end the game and nail down the victory.

Carl was the new World Series strikeout champ.

And the Dodgers weren't dead yet!

New York (AL)	ab	r	h	bi	o	a	e
G. McDougald, 3b	4	0	1	1	2	3	0
I. Noren, ph9	0	0	0	0	-	-	-
J. Collins, 1b	5	0	0	0	8	0	0
H. Bauer, rf	4	1	1	0	1	0	0
Y. Berra, c	1	0	1	0	4	1	0
M. Mantle, cf	4	0	0	0	2	0	0
G. Woodling, lf	4	0	1	1	0	0	0
B. Martin, 2b	3	1	1	0	3	4	0
P. Rizzuto, ss	3	0	1	0	3	3	0
D. Bollwig, ph9	1	0	0	0	-	-	-
V. Raschi, p	2	0	0	0	1	1	0
J. Mize, ph9	1	0	0	0	-	-	-
	32	2	6	2	24	12	0

Brooklyn (NL)	ab	r	h	bi	o	a	e
J. Gilliam, 2b	4	0	1	0	1	2	0
P. Reese, ss	4	0	1	0	1	4	0
D. Snider, cf	3	1	1	0	0	0	0
G. Hodges, 1b	2	0	1	0	8	1	0
R. Campanella, c	4	1	1	1	14	0	0
C. Furillo, rf	4	0	0	0	1	0	0
J. Robinson, lf	4	1	3	1	1	0	0
D. Thompson, lf9	0	0	0	0	0	0	0
B. Cox, 3b	3	0	0	1	0	1	0
C. Erskine, p	3	0	1	0	1	2	0
	31	3	9	3	27	10	0

New York	000 010 010	= 2
Brooklyn	000 011 01x	= 3

	ip	h	r-er	bb	so
Raschi (L 0-1)	8	9	3-3	3	4
Erskine (W 1-0)	9	6	2-2	3	14

WP: Erskine Balk: Raschi
HBP: by Erskine 2 (Berra 2)

Game-Winning RBI: Campanella
LOB: New York 9, Brooklyn 8
DP: Rizzuto-Martin-Collins (Furillo)
2B: Robinson
HR: Campanella
SH: Raschi, Cox
CS: Gilliam
Time—3:00 Attendance—35,270

Umpires: E. Hurley, A. Gore, B. Grieve, B. Stewart, H. Soar, & F. Dascoli

The Dodgers evened the series by winning the next game, 7-3. Snider hit two doubles and a homer, and Gilliam hit three doubles.

In Game #5, young Johnny Podres of the Dodgers was routed in the third inning by control troubles and an error. Russ Meyer relieved and was greeted by a grand slam home run by Mantle. New York won easily, 11-7.

The Yankees wrapped up the series by taking the sixth game, 4-3. The Dodgers managed to tie the game on a two-run homer in the ninth by Furillo. But the Yanks won out on Martin's game-winning single in the bottom of the ninth.

Shortly after the series ended, manager Dressen quit over the matter of a multi-year contract. Montreal manager Walter Alston was hired in his stead.

1954 SUNDAY, AUGUST 8TH, AT EBBETS FIELD
Score 12 Runs With Two Out

Intentional Walk with the Bases Empty Sets Up Big Rally
Brooklyn Buries Cincinnati with 13 in 8th to Win, 20-7

Today's Results			
BROOKLYN 20-Cincinnati 7			
Milwaukee 5-New York 2			
Philadelphia 8-Chicago 4 (1st game)			
Philadelphia 8-Chicago 3 (2nd game)			
Pittsburgh 12-St. Louis 4 (1st game)			
Pittsburgh 5-St. Louis 3 (2nd game)			
Standings	**W-L**	**Pct.**	**GB**
New York	69-41	.627	—
BROOKLYN	66-44	.600	3
Milwaukee	60-47	.561	7½
Philadelphia	54-52	.509	13
St. Louis	52-57	.477	16½
Cincinnati	52-58	.473	17
Chicago	44-65	.404	24½
Pittsburgh	39-72	.351	30½

WOULD YOU WALK A .198 HITTER WITH two out and none on and your team trailing 8-5 in the bottom of the eighth? How about if the count was already 3-and-0, and the pitcher was due to bat next?

Well, that's exactly what Cincinnati manager Birdie Tebbetts did today; he ordered an intentional fourth ball to the Dodgers' Roy Campanella (who had a .198 average at the moment) with one run already in, two out, and no one on base in the eighth inning. Before the third out was made, Brooklyn had sent 15 more men to the plate, and 12 more runs had scored.

The defending-champion Dodgers had had troubles this year. Their pitching had been downright poor, and their vaunted offense had been less productive than last year. The biggest decline in production had been from Campanella, who was tortured by hand injuries. Demoted to the number-eight slot in the lineup, Campy entered today's game with only 40 runs-batted-in. Last season he had a total of 142.

Up until the big blowout in the home half of the eighth, today's game at Ebbets Field was well-contested. Through five innings, the score was tied, 3-3. Brooklyn's third run came of a home run by Campanella off of Cincinnati starting pitcher Fred Baczewski. It was Campy's 17th homer of the season.

The Dodgers took the lead with four runs off of reliever Karl Drews in the sixth. Jackie Robinson walked and came around on singles by Gil Hodges and Carl Furillo. Junior Gilliam followed with a three-run homer.

The Reds got single runs in the seventh and eighth innings to knock starter Carl Erskine out of the game. Clem Labine came in and got the final two outs in the eighth on a double play.

With the score 7-5 in favor of the home team, Howie Judson went in to pitch for the visitors in the bottom of the eighth. Hodges led off with a tremendous drive off the exit gate in right center for a triple. Furillo's long fly brought Hodges home. Gilliam bounced to second for out #2. Judson then threw three straight balls to Campanella. Not wanting to risk another home run, Tebbetts ordered an intentional fourth ball.

The strategy cost Cincinnati twelve runs. Judson could not locate the plate against either Labine or Don Hoak, and two more walks loaded the bases. Pee Wee Reese hit a sharp grounder to third for what should have been the third out. But the ball went through third baseman Chuck Harmon's grasp for an error. Two runs scored on the misplay, and the other runners wound up at second and third.

Jackie Collum was sent in to relieve the unfortunate Judson. He immediately walked Duke Snider on four pitches to load the bases again. With a full count and the runners automatically going with the pitch, Robinson cracked a long single to right. The throw came in to second base, and all three runners scored on the hit. Sandy Amoros went in to run for Robinson. Hodges, batting for the second time, lined a ground-rule double to right, Amoros having to stop at third. Furillo singled to left center to score two runs.

By now the score was 15-5, and the Reds had lost the game beyond all reasonable doubt. So Tebbetts left Collum in to try to get the last out. But he continued to fail. Gilliam was hit by a pitch, Campanella hit an RBI single, and Labine walked again to load the bases.

This was too much for Tebbetts, and he sent his best reliever, Frank Smith, directly from the bench into the game in an effort to finally end the rally. With only his eight warmup pitches on the mound, Smith was unprepared. He went to 3-and-2 on the first man he faced, Hoak, before the batter hit a grand slam over the left field fence. Reese walked, and Snider singled to right. A pass to Amoros loaded the bases for the fourth time in the inning.

So yet another pitching change was made. Art Fowler became the fourth Cincinnati hurler in the inning. Hodges laid into one of his pitches and drove it to deepest center field. It looked like it might be another grand slammer, but Gus Bell went back to the wall and made a leaping catch. That finally made it three outs. Just 12 runs after the second out.

Labine gave up three hits and two meaningless runs in the ninth inning, and the Dodgers won by a final score of 20-7. Combined with the Giants' defeat at the hands of Milwaukee today, Brooklyn moved to within 3 games of first place.

But they could not count on getting very many more intentional walks to their .198 hitters with no one on base.

Cincinnati	ab	r	h	bi	o	a	e
B. Adams, 2b	4	1	1	1	4	2	0
N. Escalara, cf-lf7	4	2	2	0	2	0	0
L. Merriman, lf	3	0	1	0	0	0	0
G. Bell, ph7-cf	2	1	1	0	2	0	0
T. Kluszewski, 1b	4	2	3	2	6	0	0
W. Post, rf	3	0	2	1	3	0	0
C. Harmon, 3b	4	0	1	3	1	3	1
R. McMillan, ss	3	0	0	0	2	3	0
B. Borkowski, ph8	1	0	0	0	-	-	-
R. Bridges, ss8	0	0	0	0	0	0	0
H. Landrith, c	3	1	1	0	4	1	0
F. Baczewski, p	2	0	0	0	0	0	0
K. Drews, p5	0	0	0	0	0	0	0
E. Bailey, ph7	1	0	0	0	-	-	-
H. Perkowski, p7	0	0	0	0	0	0	0
J. Greengrass, ph8	1	0	0	0	-	-	-
H. Judson, p8	0	0	0	0	0	0	0
J. Collum, p8	0	0	0	0	0	0	0
F. Smith, p8	0	0	0	0	0	0	0
A. Fowler, p8	0	0	0	0	0	0	0
	35	7	12	7	27	9	1

Brooklyn	ab	r	h	bi	o	a	e
D. Hoak, 3b	4	3	2	4	1	0	0
P. Reese, ss	5	1	2	1	2	5	0
D. Snider, cf	4	1	1	0	0	0	1
J. Robinson, lf	4	1	1	3	3	0	0
S. Amoros, pr8-lf	0	1	0	0	1	0	0
G. Hodges, 1b	6	4	4	0	10	1	0
C. Furillo, rf	4	2	3	4	2	0	0
J. Gilliam, 2b	4	2	1	3	1	4	0
R. Campanella, c	3	3	2	2	6	0	0
C. Erskine, p	3	0	0	0	1	1	0
C. Labine, p8	0	2	0	0	0	1	0
	37	20	16	17	24	12	1

Cincinnati	102 000 1 1 2	= 7
Brooklyn	100 204 0(13)x	= 20

	ip	h	r-er	bb	so
Baczewski	4	5	3-3	3	1
Drews (L 3-3)	2	4	4-4	1	2
Perkowski	1	0	0-0	0	0
Judson	⅔	1	5-1	3	0
Collum	*0	4	7-7	2	0
Smith	†0	2	1-1	2	0
Fowler	⅓	0	0-0	0	0
Erskine (W 14-10)	7⅓	9	5-5	4	5
Labine	1⅔	3	2-2	0	0

*faced seven batters in eighth
†faced four batters in eighth
WP: Erskine

Game-Winning RBI: Furillo
LOB: Cincinnati 8, Brooklyn 6
BE: Cincinnati 1, Brooklyn 1
DP: Harmon-Kluszewski (Robinson)
Adams-McMillan-Kluszewski (Gilliam)
Gilliam-Reese-Hodges (McMillan)
Reese-Gilliam-Hodges (Greengrass)
2B: Reese, Kluszewski, Hodges
3B: Escalara, Hodges
HR: Campanella, Gilliam, Hoak
SF: Adams, Harmon, Furillo, Post
CS: Hoak
HBP: by Collum (Gilliam)
Time—2:58 Attendance—10,884
Umpires: T. Gorman, A. Donatelli, J. Conlan, & A. Gore

On the following weekend, the Dodgers swept three games from the Giants to close to within ½ game of the lead. But New York rebounded with a seven-game winning streak, and Brooklyn never did catch the leaders.

While the Dodgers' hitting continued to be good over the next month, the pitching was woefully inconsistent. As a result, Brooklyn had to settle for a second-place finish. Its final record of 92-62 left it 5 games behind New York.

1955 THURSDAY, MAY 10TH, AT WRIGLEY FIELD, CHICAGO

Newcombe's One-Hitter Gives Brooklyn a 22-2 Record

Don Wins First Start After his Suspension, 3-0
Dodgers Lead League by 9½ Games Already

Today's Results			
BROOKLYN 3-Chicago 0			
New York 8-Cincinnati 4			
Pittsburgh 9-Milwaukee 6			
St. Louis 5-Philadelphia 3 (10 innings)			

Standings	W-L	Pct.	GB
BROOKLYN	22- 2	.917	—
New York	12-11	.522	9½
Milwaukee	12-12	.500	10
Chicago	12-14	.462	11
Pittsburgh	11-13	.458	11
St. Louis	9-12	.429	11½
Cincinnati	9-15	.375	13
Philadelphia	8-16	.333	14

SOMETIMES IT HELPS TO GET THINGS SETtled right away. In less than a month, the Brooklyn Dodgers had shown the rest of the National League that they had far and away the best team. Manager Walter Alston had demonstrated to his veteran squad that he was the boss on the team. And Don Newcombe today disspelled any doubts about the soundness of his pitching arm.

Newk had gotten three starts in the first two weeks of the season and had failed to complete any of them. In the third one he left after only four innings because of a stiff shoulder. Alston decided to rest Newcombe for a couple of days, then asked him to pitch some batting practice. The big pitcher refused, and he continued to sit on the bench. Last Thursday, pitching coach Joe Becker told Newcombe that he would get to start two games for the Dodgers in their upcoming road trip and that he should pitch some batting practice that morning. Newk balked at the order. And Alston calmy informed him that if he wouldn't pitch batting practice, he was suspended.

Vice-President Emil "Buzzie" Bavasi backed the manager all the way, and Newcombe's walkout lasted only one day. His loss of pay was thought to be around $100, based on an estimated salary of $17,500. The big righthander was back on the team in Philadelphia by Friday, and he pitched two perfect innings in relief to get credit for a win.

This was not the first time that Alston had had disagreements with his players this spring. Other complaints were made by Jackie Robinson, Roy Campanella, and Russ Meyer. But Alston came out of each controversy with his authority better established.

And what friction there may have been, it certainly did not hurt the team's performance on the field. The Dodgers roared out of the starting gate by winning their first ten regular-season games. After the Giants edged them in two out of three, the Brooks started up again and ran off another streak that today reached eleven wins in a row. That brought the season record to an incredible 22 victories and only 2 defeats. No other team in major league history ever did that well in the first 24 games of any season.

Although May 11th seemed awfully early for such things, many experts felt that the Dodgers would win the pennant in a walk. The team was already 9½ games ahead of second place.

And today Newcombe showed he was physically and emotionally sound by giving Brooklyn its best pitching performance of the year, beating the Chicago Cubs, 3-0. Newk allowed only one hit, walked none, and faced the minimum possible number of batters, 27. It was his first complete game of the season, and it lowered his ERA to 3.41. He also collected two hits in four at bats to keep his batting average at .500.

Newcombe threw 96 pitches, including 64 fastballs, 34 curves, and 1 lonely change of pace. He fell behind on the count to just three hitters, and he came back to strike each of them out. He fanned six in all.

Through the first three innings, the Cubs went out in order and only hit one ball to the outfield.

Gene Baker got the Cubs' hit with one out in the fourth. It was a solid liner that buzzed past Newcombe's ear on its way to center field. After Eddie Miksis struck out, Baker tried to steal second and was thrown out by catcher Campanella.

It was "three up and three down" for the Cubs in each of the last five innings.

In the meantime, Warren Hacker was pitching a fairly good game against the Dodgers. Through five innings he had a three-hit shutout.

Brooklyn finally got a run in the sixth. With one down, Duke Snider lined Hacker's second pitch into a stiff breeze. But the ball was hit hard enough to clear the fence in right field for a home run. It was Duke's ninth of the season, the best in the league, and it gave him 30 RBIs, which also topped the list.

Brooklyn added single runs in the seventh and ninth innings. In the seventh, Don Hoak walked with one out, and Newcombe singled him to third. Jim Gilliam drove Hoak home with a sacrifice fly to right. In the ninth, Gilliam singled with two gone, and Pee Wee Reese doubled into the gap in right center to bring him around.

When pinch-hitter Frankie Baumholtz flied out to short left to end the game, the Brooklyn pennant machine had notched its 22nd victory. There seemed to be no other team in the league that could hope to overcome them the rest of the way. And with any questions about internal difficulties apparently solved already, the only question left seemed to be how early the pennant clinching would come.

Brooklyn	ab	r	h	bi	o	a	e
J. Gilliam, 2b	4	1	1	1	1	3	0
P. Reese, ss	5	0	2	1	0	3	0
D. Snider, cf	4	1	1	1	0	0	0
R. Campanella, c	4	0	1	0	7	1	0
S. Amoros, rf-lf8	4	0	2	0	3	0	0
G. Hodges, 1b	4	0	0	0	12	1	0
J. Robinson, lf	3	0	0	0	2	0	0
C. Furillo, rf8	0	0	0	0	0	0	0
D. Hoak, 3b	3	1	0	0	1	2	0
D. Newcombe, p	4	0	2	0	1	1	0
	35	3	9	3	27	11	0

Chicago	ab	r	h	bi	o	a	e
J. Bolger, cf	2	0	0	0	1	0	0
L. Merriman, ph7-cf	1	0	0	0	0	0	0
G. Baker, 2b	3	0	1	0	4	3	0
E. Miksis, rf	3	0	0	0	3	0	0
R. Jackson, 3b	3	0	0	0	0	2	0
B. Speake, lf-1b3	3	0	0	0	7	1	1
E. Banks, ss	3	0	0	0	3	4	0
D. Fondy, 1b	0	0	0	0	1	0	0
J. King, lf3	3	0	0	0	5	1	0
H. Chiti, c	3	0	0	0	3	0	0
W. Hacker, p	2	0	0	0	0	1	0
F. Baumholtz, ph9	1	0	0	0	-	-	-
	27	0	1	0	27	12	1

Brooklyn	000 001 101	=	3
Chicago	000 000 000	=	0

	ip	h	r-er	bb	so
Newcombe (W 4-0)	9	1	0-0	0	6
Hacker (L 1-2)	9	9	3-3	2	2

Time—1:55 Attendance—6,686

Umpires: H. Dixon, J. Conlan, A. Gore, & A. Donatelli

Game-Winning RBI: Snider
LOB: Brooklyn 8, Chicago 0
BE: Brooklyn 1
2B: Amoros, Reese
HR: Snider
SF: Gilliam
CS: Baker

The Dodgers slumped slightly after this, losing six out of nine. But their lead never got to less than 5½ games. By June 11th, the margin was over 10 games, and it never fell under that number again. Brooklyn clinched the pennant on September 8th, having built up a 17-game lead by that time. The Dodgers finished 13½ games ahead with a 98-55 record.

Newcombe was 18-1 by the end of July. He suffered three consecutive defeats in August, all in tight games, then developed shoulder trouble. He finished the season 20-5.

1955 TUESDAY, OCTOBER 4TH, AT YANKEE STADIUM, NEW YORK World Series—Game #7

"Next Year" Finally Arrives!

LET THE YANKEES WAIT UNTIL NEXT YEAR. THIS YEAR WAS "NEXT YEAR" FOR THE long-suffering Brooklyn Dodger fans around the world. The ultimate triumph that many felt in their heart of hearts might never come to their beloved Dodgers, winning the World Series, became a reality for Brooklyn today.

Young Johnny Podres pitched the Dodgers to victory in the seventh and decisive game of the series, shutting out the hated Yankees, 2-0. The Bums were outhit, 8 to 5, but Podres was tough in the clutch, and he was saved by a great catch by Sandy Amoros in the sixth inning.

Gil Hodges drove in both of Brooklyn's runs.

When the Dodgers lost the first two games of the series, 6-5 and 4-2, everyone wrote them off again this year. After all, no team had ever before come back to win a best-of-seven World Series after losing the first two games. But Brooklyn bounced back by winning three straight at Ebbets Field, 8-3, 8-5, and 5-3. Podres got the first of those victories with his first complete game since June 14th.

Then the Yankees tied the series by taking Game #6, 5-1, and the pessimists were sure that the Dodgers would blow the last game.

The starting pitchers today were both lefthanders, Tommy Byrne pitching for New York. He did well, but the Dodgers scratched two runs off of him. Against Podres, the Yankees had base runners in six of the nine innings, but the 23-year-old out of the iron mining village of Witherbee, N.Y., turned them back every time. Although he had a little trouble controlling his curveball, Johnny had plenty of speed and an effective change-up.

The Yankees mounted the first scoring threat in the third. With two out, Podres walked Phil Rizzuto on four pitches. Billy Martin followed with a bloop hit to right, Rizzuto stopping at second. The count went to 3-and-2, and batter Gil McDougald bounced a slow one toward third base. It looked like an infield hit until Rizzuto, who was sliding into third, was struck by the ball for an automatic out.

Duke Snider struck out to open the fourth. Roy Campanella hit a robust double into the left field corner. Carl Furillo grounded to short, and Campy went to third on the play. Byrne jammed Hodges with a fastball, but Gil got enough of it to muscle a hit to left to bring Campanella home with a run.

The Dodgers nearly gave the run back to New York in the bottom of the inning. Yogi Berra led off with a high pop to short left center. Snider and left fielder Jim Gilliam converged, but at the last second they both pulled up short, and the ball fell safely for a cheap double. Podres got out of the jam with three quick outs.

Pee Wee Reese led off the Brooklyn sixth with a ground-ball single past shortstop. Snider dropped a nice bunt down the first base line. Byrne got to the ball quickly and threw to first. First baseman Bill Skowron was not yet back to the base, and he whirled to tag Snider after taking the throw. But the runner's shoulder knocked the ball out of the glove, and all hands were safe. Campanella sacrificed the men to second and third. An intentional walk filled the bases. Bob Grim replaced Byrne on the mound. Hodges hit him for a long sacrifice fly to right center, Reese scoring after the catch. Another walk loaded the bases, but George Shuba, pinch-hitting for second baseman Don Zimmer, grounded out.

In the bottom of the sixth, manager Walter Alston had to shift his defense. Gilliam came in to play second, and Amoros went out to left. Podres walked Martin leading off, and McDougald beat out a bunt. With men on first and second and no outs, the dangerous Berra came to the plate. Normally a pull-hitting lefthanded batter, Yogi lifted a drive toward the left field corner. Amoros sprinted over from left center toward the foul line. Just as it seemed that the ball would land fair, the lefthanded Amoros caught the ball in his outstretched right hand. McDougald was nearly to third when the catch was made, and he was doubled off first by a relay from Amoros to Reese to Hodges. A ground out ended the inning, and the wind was out of the Yankee sails.

Using his fastball more and more as the shadows lengthened, Podres moved toward victory. He allowed a two-out single by Elston Howard in the seventh but got pinch-hitter Mickey Mantle to pop weakly to short.

In the eighth, Rizzuto led off with a solid hit to left. Martin also hit the ball hard, but his liner was caught in far right. McDougald sent Rizzuto to third with a bouncing hit to left. Rearing back, Podres got Berra to hit an easy fly to short right. Then he blew a high, hard one past Hank Bauer for a third strike.

Came the ninth inning, and Brooklyn was only three outs from Nirvana. With a count of 2-and-2, Skowron bounced to Podres for the first out. Bob Cerv hit the fourth pitch to left field, where Amoros caught it easily. Podres got a couple of strikes on Howard. A couple of fastballs were fouled off. Then came a change of pace, which was grounded weakly toward short. Reese charged the ball and threw to first. Hodges stretched to get the low throw, and the last out was made.

Podres was mobbed near the mound, and everyone was later doused with beer and champagne in the clubhouse.

Over in Brooklyn, the offices and bars were soon in pandemonium. The streets filled with celebrants. Car horns honked endlessly; policemen cried for joy. People danced with perfect strangers on the street corners. After all those years, all those tears, and all those fears, the impossible had finally happened. No more Next Year, Brooklyn was now home of the Champions of the World.

Brooklyn (NL)	ab	r	h	bi	o	a	e
J. Gilliam, lf-2b6	4	0	1	0	2	0	0
P. Reese, ss	4	1	1	0	2	6	0
D. Snider, cf	3	0	0	0	2	0	0
R. Campanella, c	3	1	1	0	5	0	0
C. Furillo, rf	3	0	0	0	3	0	0
G. Hodges, 1b	2	0	1	2	10	0	0
D. Hoak, 3b	3	0	1	0	1	1	0
D. Zimmer, 2b	2	0	0	0	0	2	0
G. Shuba, ph6	1	0	0	0	-	-	-
S. Amoros, lf6	0	0	0	0	2	1	0
J. Podres, p	4	0	0	0	0	1	0
	29	2	5	2	27	11	0

New York (AL)	ab	r	h	bi	o	a	e
P. Rizzuto, ss	3	0	1	0	1	3	0
B. Martin, 2b	3	0	1	0	1	6	0
G. McDougald, 3b	4	0	3	0	1	1	0
Y. Berra, c	4	0	1	0	4	1	0
H. Bauer, rf	4	0	0	0	1	0	0
B. Skowron, 1b	4	0	1	0	11	1	1
B. Cerv, cf	4	0	0	0	5	0	0
E. Howard, lf	4	0	1	0	2	0	0
T. Byrne, p	2	0	0	0	0	2	0
B. Grim, p6	0	0	0	0	1	0	0
M. Mantle, ph7	1	0	0	0	-	-	-
B. Turley, p8	0	0	0	0	0	0	0
	33	0	8	0	27	14	1

Brooklyn	000 101 000	= 2
New York	000 000 000	= 0

	ip	h	r-er	bb	so
Podres (W 2-0)	9	8	0-0	2	4
Byrne (L 1-1)	5⅓	3	2-1	3	2
Grim	1⅔	1	0-0	1	1
Turley	2	1	0-0	1	1

WP: Grim

Game-Winning RBI: Hodges
LOB: Brooklyn 8, New York 8
BE: Brooklyn 1
DP: Amoros-Reese-Hodges
2B: Skowron, Campanella, Berra
SH: Snider, Campanella
SF: Hodges
CS: Gilliam
Time—2:44 Attendance—62,465

Umpires: J. Honochick, F. Dascoli, B. Summers, L. Ballanfant, R. Flaherty, & A. Donatelli

1956 SUNDAY, SEPTEMBER 30TH, AT EBBETS FIELD

Duke & Newk Lead Dodgers to Pennant

Clinch Flag with 8-6 Victory over Pittsburgh
Snider Hits 2 Homers for 4 Runs, Newcombe Wins #27

Today's Results

BROOKLYN 8-Pittsburgh 6
Milwaukee 4-St. Louis 2
Cincinnati 4-Chicago 2
New York 8-Philadelphia 3 (1st game)
Philadelphia 5-New York 2 (2nd game)

Standings	W-L	Pct.	GB
BROOKLYN	93-61	.604	—
Milwaukee	92-62	.597	1
Cincinnati	91-63	.591	2
St. Louis	76-78	.494	17
Philadelphia	71-83	.461	22
New York	67-87	.435	26
Pittsburgh	66-88	.429	27
Chicago	60-94	.390	33

THOUGH THEY DIDN'T EXACTLY DO IT the easy way, the Brooklyn Dodgers won the 1956 National League pennant. Today's 8-6 victory over Pittsburgh on the final day of the season gave Brooklyn the championship by the slim margin of 1 game over Milwaukee and 2 games over Cincinnati.

Just two days before, the Braves had held a 1-game lead. But they lost on Friday and Saturday in St. Louis. The Dodgers were rained out on Friday, then won a doubleheader yesterday, 6-2 and 3-1, to take the lead in the race. Today both Brooklyn and Milwaukee were victorious, but the Dodgers came away with the pennant.

Appropriately, the biggest heroes in Brooklyn today were the team's top pitcher, Don Newcombe, and its top slugger, Duke Snider. Big Newk was not in top form, allowing six runs and eleven hits before being relieved by Don Bessent in the eighth inning. But he had kept his team ahead all the way and got credit for his 27th win of the season. The Duke gave Brooklyn the lead with a three-run homer in the first inning and blasted a solo shot in the fifth. The homers gave him 43 for the season. He also made a spectacular catch in the seventh inning to rob Pittsburgh of at least one run.

With the stakes so high and the Dodger lead diminishing in the late going, the 31,983 fans at Ebbets Field were nearly hysterical by the end of the game. But when victory finally came, the place went wild with joy.

The Dodgers started the game off on the right foot. They knocked Pirate starter Vernon Law out of the box with three runs in the first inning. Jim Gilliam led off with a base on balls. Pee Wee Reese followed with a pretty hit-and-run single to send Gilliam to third. Snider jumped on the first pitch and sent it into the seats in center field for a three-run homer.

Pittsburgh, however, was not about to roll over and play dead. The Pirates came back with two runs in the third inning. Jack Shepard got the rally started with a scratch single off Newcombe's glove. Dick Cole walked. Newk wild-pitched the runners along, and Roberto Clemente singled them home.

Batting against Bob Purkey in the bottom of the third, Jackie Robinson golfed a home run into the upper deck in left to give Brooklyn a 4-2 lead.

Newcombe and Snider made it 6-2 against Ron Kline in the fifth. Don led off with an opposite-field double to left and scored on two outs. Duke then sent a blast over the wall and onto Bedford Avenue for a home run.

Sandy Amoros opened the sixth with a homer over the right field wall and onto the street, and the Dodgers had a comfortable 7-2 lead.

But the Pirates came charging back. In the seventh, Dick Groat doubled off the scoreboard in right. He held up as Bill Mazeroski beat out a hit up the middle. A bunt single loaded the bases. Newcombe got the next two batters on a pop-up and a strikeout. But Bill Virdon split the gap in right center for a three-run double. Bob Skinner sent a drive to the wall in center, but Snider made a great leaping catch at the barrier to rob him of at least a double.

In the eighth, Lee Walls homered with one out to cut the lead to 7-6. Dodger manager Walter Alston finally removed Newcombe and brought in Bessent. Groat singled, and an error by Robinson put men on first and second. Shepard flied to Snider in deep center. And Bessent fanned Dale Long.

Amoros gave Brooklyn a little insurance with a leadoff home run in the bottom of the eighth, his second of the game. He got an enthusiastic greeting from his teammates when he reached the dugout. The Dodgers got three more hits in the inning but had a man thrown out at home on some poor baserunning.

Clemente opened the ninth inning with a clean single to right. Virdon came up representing the tying run. He hit the ball hard, but it went right to second baseman Gilliam, who started a double play. The stands were now rocking with anticipation. Bessent then struck out pinch-hitter Hank Foiles on a fastball, and the game was over.

The Dodgers had done it; Brooklyn had won another pennant! The players on the field were quickly surrounded by adoring fans. Torn-up newspapers and programs rained down onto the field in an imitation of ticker tape. Fans who had been watching on television ran onto the streets to wave at passers-by.

The Dodger dressing room was a cacaphony of delirious screaming. Champagne and beer was squirted around in great quantities. It was even wilder than the celebration after winning last year's World Series. For the first time in history, the makeshift "Brooklyn Sym-phony Band" was admitted to the clubhouse, and they tooted away madly. Perhaps the happiest man in the room was owner Walter O'Malley. He summed up the tension and the ecstasy best by telling the players, "I can't take any more of this, but give me more, it's wonderful."

Pittsburgh	ab	r	h	bi	o	a	e
R. Clemente, rf	5	0	2	2	1	1	0
B. Virdon, cf	5	0	2	3	1	0	0
B. Skinner, 1b	4	0	0	0	8	0	0
B. Friend, p7	0	0	0	0	0	0	0
H. Foiles, ph9	1	0	0	0	-	-	-
F. Thomas, 3b	4	0	1	0	0	0	0
L. Walls, lf	4	1	2	1	5	0	0
D. Groat, ss	4	1	2	0	2	3	0
E. O'Brien, pr8-ss	0	0	0	0	0	0	0
B. Mazeroski, 2b	3	1	1	0	2	6	0
G. Freese, ph8-2b	1	0	0	0	0	0	0
J. Shepard, c	4	2	3	0	3	0	0
V. Law, p	0	0	0	0	0	0	0
R. Face, p1	0	0	0	0	0	1	0
D. Cole, ph3	0	1	0	0	-	-	-
B. Purkey, p3	0	0	0	0	0	0	0
J. Powers, ph5	1	0	0	0	-	-	-
R. Kline, p5	0	0	0	0	0	0	0
D. Long, ph7-1b	2	0	0	0	2	0	0
	38	6	13	6	24	11	0

Brooklyn	ab	r	h	bi	o	a	e
J. Gilliam, 2b	4	1	0	0	6	2	0
P. Reese, ss	3	1	2	1	6	8	0
D. Snider, cf	4	2	2	4	3	0	0
J. Robinson, 3b	4	1	1	1	0	1	1
S. Amoros, lf	4	2	2	2	1	0	0
G. Hodges, 1b	4	0	2	0	6	0	0
C. Furillo, rf	4	0	0	0	1	0	0
R. Campanella, c	3	0	1	0	4	0	0
D. Newcombe, p	3	1	1	0	0	3	0
D. Bessent, p8	1	0	1	0	0	0	0
	34	8	12	8	27	14	1

Pittsburgh	002	000	310	= 6
Brooklyn	301	021	01x	= 8

	ip	h	r-er	bb	so
Law (L 8-16)	⅔	3	3-3	1	0
Face	1⅓	0	0-0	0	0
Purkey	2	1	1-1	0	0
Kline	2	3	3-3	1	2
Friend	2	5	1-1	0	0
Newcombe (W 27-7)	7⅓	11	6-6	1	2
Bessent	1⅔	2	0-0	0	2

WP: Newcombe

Umpires: B. Jackowski, V. Delmore, J. Conlan, & S. Landes

Game-Winning RBI: Snider
LOB: Pittsburgh 6, Brooklyn 5
BE: Pittsburgh 1
DP: Newcombe-Reese-Hodges (Virdon)
Robinson-Reese-Hodges (Powers)
Gilliam-Reese-Hodges (Virdon)
2B: Newcombe, Groat, Virdon
3B: Walls
HR: Snider 2, Robinson, Amoros 2, Walls
SF: Reese
Time—2:30
Attendance—31,983

1956 TUESDAY, OCTOBER 9TH, AT EBBETS FIELD World Series—Game #6

Stay Alive with 1-0 Victory

CLEM LABINE DOES NOT PITCH MANY SHUTOUTS, BUT HE SURE PICKS GOOD TIMES FOR them. Normally the Dodgers' top relief pitcher, today he started the sixth game of the World Series for Brooklyn and pitched his first shutout in five years to beat the New York Yankees, 1-0, in a ten-inning thriller. His last previous shutout had come in the 1951 playoff against the New York Giants.

This season he had started only three games and completed just one. But that one came on the final Saturday of the regular season, and the 3-1 triumph put Brooklyn into the league lead.

It had to be a shutout if the slumping Dodgers were going to win today. Facing fireballer Bob Turley, the Dodgers managed just four hits and did not score until extra innings.

The Brooks had pounded out 21 hits in winning the first two games of the series, 6-3 and 13-8. But in the next two games they got only 14 hits and lost 5-3 and 6-2. In the fifth game yesterday, they got no hits as the Yankees' Don Larsen pitched a perfect game against them and won, 2-0.

Today's game was a classic pitching confrontation. Labine pitted his curveball and sinker against Turley's blazing speed. Clem threw 121 pitches, Bob needed 143. Labine yielded seven hits and two walks, while Turley gave up four hits and eight bases on balls.

Turley was a surprise choice by Yankee manager Casey Stengel. He had been erratic despite obviously great potential. With New York ahead 3 games to 2, Stengel could afford to gamble on Bullet Bob. Pitching without a windup, just like Larsen had done on Monday, the righthander turned in a superb performance, even though he lost.

Dodger skipper Walter Alston did not have the luxury of a one-game lead, but he still confounded some observers by starting Labine. The Brooklyn righty was in trouble on numerous occasions but always survived.

The game started with a leadoff single by Hank Bauer in the New York first inning. The second batter, Joe Collins, grounded into a double play.

A great play by second baseman Billy Martin on a slow roller retired the Dodger leadoff batter in the bottom of the first. With two down, Duke Snider stroked a hit to left. But Jackie Robinson lined to shortstop to end the inning.

Yogi Berra opened the second with a hit. But a fine play by Jim Gilliam forced him at second base, and the next two hitters were easy.

Bauer got his second hit of the game with two gone in the third. Collins beat out a hit up the middle. Triple-Crown winner Mickey Mantle came to the plate with two men on, but Labine got him to ground to first base on the first pitch.

The Dodgers got a gift hit in their half but immediately wasted it. With one gone, Gilliam lifted a routine fly to short left field. Outfielder Enos Slaughter came in on the ball, but lost it in the sun. It dropped safely, but he made a quick recovery and throw to nip Gilliam trying for second.

A two-out single by Martin was the only hit in the fourth inning.

No one reached base in the fifth.

New York hit the ball hard in the sixth but came up empty. Collins opened with a long fly to center, which Snider ran under and caught. Mantle grounded sharply up the middle, but Gilliam flagged the ball down and threw him out. Berra knocked a double to right center. Slaughter walked, but Labine came through in the pinch to get Martin to foul out.

Heads-up play by Martin prevented trouble for Turley in the bottom of the sixth. With two out and Gilliam on first after a walk, Robinson lifted a pop fly between short and third. Both infielders on that side had trouble with the sun, but Martin raced over from second and made the catch.

After a quick seventh, both sides made noises in the eighth. For the Yanks, Collins hit a line drive off the scoreboard for a one-out double. Labine walked Mantle intentionally. Then he broke off a beautiful curve on the inside to Berra, and Yogi popped out to short center. Slaughter grounded out to Gilliam to end the Yankee threat. Labine led off the Dodger half with a fly down the left field line, which Slaughter allowed to bounce into the stands for a ground-rule double. Turley fanned Gilliam and got Pee Wee Reese on an easy fly. After intentionally passing Snider, Turley induced Robinson to pop to third.

Neither side got a hit in the ninth. And Labine disposed of the Yankees in order in the top of the tenth.

With one out in the bottom of the tenth, Gilliam walked on four pitches. Reese sacrificed successfully, Gilliam advancing to second. Again Stengel ordered an intentional pass to Snider to get to Robinson. Robinson had been having trouble all day with Turley's sidearm fastball. With the count at 2-and-1, he got another one of them about thigh high. This time Jackie lined it deep to left. Outfielder Slaughter took his first step inwards, then realized his mistake too late. The ball sailed over his desperate leap and crashed against the fence. Gilliam scored easily as the ball rattled around the outfield, and the Dodgers had won.

The ecstatic Labine raced onto the field and kissed Robinson. Then he kissed Reese. And he kissed just about everybody he could find. He had won a mighty big game, perhaps as big as the one in the '51 playoff, to keep the Dodgers alive.

That Clem Labine sure pitched his shutouts at good times.

New York (AL)	ab	r	h	bi	o	a	e
H. Bauer, rf	5	0	2	0	2	0	0
J. Collins, 1b	5	0	2	0	4	1	0
M. Mantle, cf	3	0	0	0	2	0	0
Y. Berra, c	4	0	2	0	12	0	0
E. Slaughter, lf	3	0	0	0	1	1	0
B. Martin, 2b	4	0	1	0	3	1	0
G. McDougald, ss	4	0	0	0	3	0	0
A. Carey, 3b	4	0	0	0	2	0	0
B. Turley, p	4	0	0	0	0	2	0
	36	0	7	0	29	5	0

Brooklyn (NL)	ab	r	h	bi	o	a	e
J. Gilliam, 2b	3	1	1	0	0	7	0
P. Reese, ss	4	0	0	0	2	3	0
D. Snider, cf	2	0	1	0	4	0	0
J. Robinson, 3b	4	0	1	1	1	1	0
G. Hodges, 1b	2	0	0	0	14	0	0
S. Amoros, lf	3	0	0	0	2	0	0
C. Furillo, rf	4	0	0	0	2	0	0
R. Campanella, c	4	0	0	0	5	0	0
C. Labine, p	4	0	1	0	0	3	0
	30	1	4	1	30	14	0

New York	000 000 000 0	=	0
Brooklyn	000 000 000 1	=	1

two out when winning run scored

	ip	h	r-er	bb	so
Turley (L 0-1)	9⅔	4	1-1	8	11
Labine (W 1-0)	10	7	0-0	2	5

Umpires: H. Soar, D. Boggess, L. Napp, B. Pinelli, E. Runge, & T. Gorman

Game-Winning RBI: Robinson
LOB: New York 8, Brooklyn 10
DP: Gilliam-Reese-Hodges (Collins)
2B: Berra, Collins, Labine
SH: Reese
Time—2:37
Attendance—33,224

In the seventh and decisive game, the Dodgers again failed to hit. Young Johnny Kucks shut them out on three safeties. Yogi Berra hit two two-run home runs against Brooklyn starter Don Newcombe, and Bill Skowron later hit a grand slam off of Roger Craig. The Yankees won with ease, 9-0, to take the series.

Robinson's hit in the sixth game was his last. In December he was traded to the Giants, but he decided to retire rather than play for New York.

1957 TUESDAY NIGHT, SEPTEMBER 24TH, AT EBBETS FIELD

The Last Game at Ebbets Field

Only 6,702 on Hand to Bid Farewell
Dodgers Beat Pirates, 2-0, on Shutout by McDevitt

Today's Results

BROOKLYN 2-Pittsburgh 0
Milwaukee 6-St. Louis 1
Cincinnati 4-Chicago 3 (1st game)
Cincinnati 11-Chicago 9 (2nd game)
Philadelphia 5-New York 0

Standings	W-L	Pct.	GB
Milwaukee	93-57	.620	—
St. Louis	86-64	.573	7
BROOKLYN	83-68	.550	10½
Cincinnati	79-71	.527	14
Philadelphia	75-76	.497	18½
New York	69-83	.454	25
Pittsburgh	60-92	.395	34
Chicago	58-92	.387	35

BEFORE AN INTIMATE GATHERING OF family and friends at venerable old Ebbets Field, the Dodgers played their last home game in Brooklyn tonight. Although the Brooklyn franchise was not officially dead quite yet, all signs pointed to a move to Los Angeles, California, next year, with an official announcement expected shortly after the close of the season.

Negotiations between club owner Walter O'Malley and the City of New York over a new home for the Dodgers proved fruitless. The city was ready to offer a site in Flushing Meadows, in the Borough of Queens. O'Malley wanted to keep the team in Brooklyn itself, and saw little difference between a move to Queens or a move to Jersey City or Los Angeles.

The citizenry of Brooklyn tried desperately to keep their beloved Bums from moving with a "Let's Keep the Dodgers in Brooklyn" campaign, complete with television spots and a catchy jingle. But the fact remained that attendance was on the decline.

Ebbets Field had been a baseball showcase when it was opened in 1913. The storied stadium had seen three Dodgers on third base and a fan leap out of the stands to attack umpire George Magerkurth, witnessed Jackie Robinson's big league debut and the heartbreak of Dick Sisler's home run, been the stage for Wilbert Robinson and Dazzy Vance, for Leo Durocher and Whitlow Wyatt. Babe Herman, Gil Hodges, Roy Campanella, Otto Miller, Don Newcombe, Van Lingle Mungo, Duke and Oisk and Skoonj, all of them had worn the Brooklyn uniform here. Casey Stengel hit the first home run here as a 23-year-old rookie. Nap Rucker was the first man on the pitcher's mound.

But now Ebbets Field was inadequate for modern baseball. A seating capacity of under 32,000 limited the big gates. And a decline in the neighborhood kept thousands away every night game. There was practically no place to park your car, and it was at least three blocks to the nearest subway station.

So the time had come to move the Dodgers out of Ebbets Field. The team played fifteen "home games" over the last two seasons at Roosevelt Stadium in Jersey City, N.J. Initially crowds were good there, but even they fell off at the end of this season. As attempts to find a good site for a new park in Brooklyn failed, the club negotiated a fine package with eager Los Angeles officials. And the southern California metropolis was teeming with sports fans.

Although there had been no official announcement, everyone seemed sure that tonight would be the Dodgers' last game in Brooklyn. Borough President John Cashmore was on hand for the sad occasion, as was the team's unofficial mascot, circus clown Emmett Kelly. Public address announcer Tex Richards was on the job, but he did not come up with any of his famous malapropisms on this occasion. President O'Malley was conspicuous by his absence.

Suprisingly, the crowd was quite small. Only 6,702 paid to see the last game. Extra police were assigned to discourage souvenir taking, of which there was also surprisingly little.

Organist Gladys Gooding was at the center of the emotions tonight. She played nostalgic and sad, tunes like "So Long, It's Been Good to Know You," "Don't Ask Me Why I'm Leaving," "What Can I Say, Dear, After I Say I'm Sorry," and "Thanks for the Memories." "California Here I Come" drew scattered boos.

The fans mourned mostly in silence. They applauded each of the old heroes, and one man called to captain Reese, "Pee Wee, I'll write to ya." But there was little levity and less joy.

The Brooklyn lineup reflected a team in transition. Youngsters Gino Cimoli and Jim Gentile started along with veterans Gil Hodges and Roy Campanella. Journeyman Elmer Valo drove in the first run, and rookie Danny McDevitt pitched a 2-0 shutout for Brooklyn.

The young lefthander was the star of the game. He pitched a five-hitter, walked one, and struck out nine. All five Pirate hits were scratches that went off the gloves of Brooklyn infielders.

Another rookie, Benny Daniels, pitched for Pittsburgh. It was his first big league game.

Daniels walked Jim Gilliam to open the bottom of the first. Then he threw wildly past first base on a pickoff play, and Gilliam went to second. Valo doubled him home with a drive off the right field wall.

Brooklyn added its final run in the third on a hit by Cimoli, a fielder's choice, and a bloop single by Hodges.

Gil was the last batter for the home team in the eighth inning. After he struck out, Gooding played "Say It Ain't So."

After the final out in the ninth, someone put the old "Follow the Dodgers" song on the P.A. system. But it did not stay on long. Gooding cut in with "Auld Lang Syne." A few dozen fans lingered around the Dodger dugout. Some cried "Don't go, please don't go." Others just cried. In the press box there were also tears.

An incredible phenomenon, Brooklyn Baseball at Ebbets Field, had come to the end of its natural life. Now it was gone forever.

Pittsburgh	ab	r	h	bi	o	a	e
G. Baker, 3b	4	0	0	0	0	0	0
R. Mejias, rf	4	0	0	0	0	0	0
D. Groat, ss	3	0	1	0	2	3	0
B. Skinner, lf	4	0	1	0	2	1	0
D. Fondy, 1b	4	0	0	0	13	0	0
B. Mazeroski, 2b	3	0	1	0	0	5	0
R. Clemente, rf	3	0	1	0	0	0	0
H. Peterson, c	3	0	1	0	5	0	0
B. Daniels, p	2	0	0	0	1	4	1
G. Freese, ph8	1	0	0	0	-	-	-
R. Face, p8	0	0	0	0	1	0	0
	31	0	5	0	24	13	1

Brooklyn	ab	r	h	bi	o	a	e
J. Gilliam, 2b	3	1	0	0	3	4	0
G. Cimoli, cf	4	1	1	0	0	0	0
E. Valo, rf	4	0	1	1	2	0	0
G. Hodges, 3b-1b5	4	0	1	1	5	1	0
S. Amoros, lf	3	0	0	0	0	0	0
J. Gentile, 1b	2	0	0	0	4	0	0
P. Reese, 3b5	1	0	0	0	0	1	1
R. Campanella, c	2	0	0	0	2	0	0
J. Pignatano, c5	1	0	0	0	7	0	0
D. Zimmer, ss	2	0	2	0	4	5	0
D. McDevitt, p	1	0	0	0	0	1	0
	27	2	5	2	27	12	1

Pittsburgh	000 000 000	=	0
Brooklyn	101 000 00x	=	2

	ip	h	r-er	bb	so
Daniels (L 0-1)	7	5	2-1	3	2
Face	1	0	0-0	0	2
McDevitt (W 7-4)	9	5	0-0	1	9

Time—2:03 Attendance—6,702

Umpires: A. Donatelli, V. Delmore, V. Smith, J. Conlan, & E. Sudol

Game-Winning RBI: Valo
LOB: Pittsburgh 5, Brooklyn 5
BE: Pittsburgh 1, Brooklyn 0
DP: Hodges-Gilliam-Gentile (Peterson)
Mazeroski-Groat-Fondy (Gentile)
Zimmer-Hodges (Clemente)
2B: Valo, Clemente, Zimmer
SH: McDevitt

The Dodgers finished the season by losing two out of three in Philadelphia. They wound up with an 84-70 record, 11 games out.

On October 8th it was officially announced that the team would indeed move to Los Angeles. The Brooklyn Dodgers were no more.

Chapter XIII The Golden State

1958 April 18th
Big League Baseball Comes to Los Angeles

1959 September 19th
Dodgers Win Two to Catch Giants

1959 Playoff Game No. 2
Dodger Comeback Wins Pennant

1959 World Series Game No. 6
Los Angeles Wins the World Series

1960 April 12th
Essegian's Pinch Homer Wins Opening Game

1961 August 16th
Dodgers Shut Out Twice, Drop from 1st

ALTHOUGH CLUB PRESIDENT WALTER F. O'MALLEY HAD A COMMITMENT FROM THE Los Angeles city fathers to make a large block of property in Chavez Ravine available to the Dodgers for purchase and construction of a modern ballpark, some other park had to be used while the new stadium was being built. The Dodgers had purchased old Wrigley Field, home of the Pacific Coast League L.A. Angels, when they had purchased the territory from the Cubs. But that minor league structure was deemed inadequate. Memorial Coliseum was chosen, instead. This huge oval had been built for football and track and field. To fit a baseball field into it required an extremely close left field fence, 251 feet down the line. A 42-foot-high screen was put up to keep down the number of cheap home runs. As if to compensate for the proximity of the left field seats, the original baseball configuration placed the fence in straightaway right field at 440 feet from the plate.

Thus the temporary park was ideal for righthanded fly-ball hitters like Gil Hodges and Roy Campanella but a graveyard for lefthanded power hitters like Duke Snider. Campanella tragically got no chance to play in the Coliseum, however. He was paralyzed in an automobile accident near his Long Island home in January, 1958.

The players who did get to play in the Coliseum were critical of the background, especially in day games with big crowds, and of the screen. But it turned out that the oval was not as much of a home run haven as Wrigley Field. And the capacity of the Coliseum was over 90,000, compared to just 20,000 in the old PCL yard. Opening day in Los Angeles in 1958 brought out a crowd of 78,672 for a National League record that still stands. The game also featured three home runs to left field and some strange base running by the visiting San Francisco Giants.

The Dodgers set a new club attendance record in their first season in California, but on the field the team fell flat on its collective faces. The loss of Campanella hurt the most. But Snider, frustrated by the distant right field fence, fell from 40 homers to just 15, although his batting average went up to .312. Hodges contributed only 22 homers and was benched for a while in mid-season. Pee Wee Reese got into only 59 games and retired after the end of the year. Don Newcombe lost all 6 of his decisions before being traded away. And Carl Erskine was only 4-4. Clearly the old guard from Brooklyn was worn out.

The Dodgers fell to last place on May 12th and stayed there until July 20th. They finished seventh, the club's worst showing since 1944.

Meanwhile, the Chavez Ravine deal was held up by lawsuits and a special voters' referendum. In the Coliseum, the right field fence was brought in somewhat for 1959. And the Dodgers picked up a lefthanded hitter with a knack for hitting the

Los Angeles Memorial Coliseum on Opening Day, 1958

ball to left field, Wally Moon.

The season started out better than 1958, with the team staying above .500 after the first week. But it wasn't until June, when Los Angeles called up 26-year-old rookie shortstop Maury Wills, that the team became a serious pennant contender. Two pitchers called up from the minors, starter Roger Craig and reliever Larry Sherry, also made big contributions in the second half. The Dodgers poked their heads into first place for one day in late July, then they spent most of August fighting the Milwaukee Braves for second place while hanging on the heels of the league-leading San Francisco Giants.

On the last night of August, over 80,000 people (60,194 officially paid) saw left-handed fastballer Sandy Koufax strike out 18 Giants. Moon's three-run homer to left field in the ninth won the game and cut the San Francisco lead to just 1 game. With the Braves just 2½ games behind, it would be a tight race through September.

The key series came on the weekend of September 19th and 20th in San Francisco. The Dodgers came to town tied to the Braves for second, 2 games behind the Giants. Paced by the all-around play of Wills, the Dodgers swept three games and leaped into the lead with a week to go. They fell behind the Braves on Tuesday, tied the race on Wednesday, moved ahead by a game on Friday, and dropped back into a tie on Saturday. On the final Sunday, both Milwaukee and Los Angeles won, and they ended the schedule in a dead heat.

The best-of-three playoff opened in Milwaukee on Monday. The Dodgers took the opening game, 3-2, behind 7⅔ innings of scoreless relief pitching by young Larry Sherry. Johnny Roseboro's sixth-inning home run provided the winning tally. On Tuesday, the teams played in Los Angeles. The Braves had a 5-2 lead going into the bottom of the ninth. But the Dodgers put together five singles to tie the game. They won it in the 12th, 6-5, to take the pennant.

Although they entered the World Series as slight underdogs, the Dodgers were confident of beating the Chicago White Sox. After being routed 11-0 in the opening game of the series, Los Angeles bounced back to win three in a row. They failed to wrap up the series at home in Game #5, losing 1-0. But they trounced the Sox in Game #6 in Chicago, 9-3, to win the championship. Sherry was the big hero of the series, winning two games in relief and saving two others. So the Dodgers, who had tried for 70 years before bringing the world championship to Brooklyn, won it for Los Angeles in just their second year there.

The 1960 season started on a high note. In the opening game, Chuck Essegian hit a pinch home run in the eleventh inning to win the game for Los Angeles. But soon the Dodgers were bogged down in the second division. Two rookies, Tommy Davis and Frank Howard, became key hitters in an otherwise faltering offense. And Norm Larker turned out to be a competitor for the batting title. In July, the Dodgers won 19 and lost only 7 to leap to within 4 games of first place. But the streak did not last. Erratic batting nullified good pitching efforts, and the Dodgers were a .500 club in both August and September. They finished fourth, 13 games out of first. The team did, however, set a new National League attendance record for the season.

More delays at Chavez Ravine kept the Dodgers in the Coliseum in 1961. The team was in the pennant race almost from the start. The surprising Cincinnati Reds, however, got as far as 6 games ahead in mid-July. Then the Dodger hitting got hot, and Los Angeles grabbed the lead by winning 12 and losing only 1 to close July. When the Reds came to L.A. in mid-August, they trailed by 2 games in the standings and 5 in the loss column.

Then the Dodgers collapsed. They scored two runs in the first inning of the opening game of the Reds' series, then lost 5-2. On the next night, over 75,000 fans saw the Dodgers get shut out twice on only six hits. The double defeat dropped Los Angeles from the league lead. The Dodgers went on the road and lost six more in a row to run their losing streak to ten games.

Gil Hodges is mobbed just after scoring the pennant-winning run in the 1959 playoff

They halted the collapse with two victories in Cincinnati. On August 27th, they had a chance to regain the lead in a doubleheader against the Reds. But the Dodgers were swept instead, blowing a 5-1 lead in the first game and losing 6-5, then getting pounded in the nightcap 8-3. Although they got as close as 1 game out in early September, they never did catch the Reds again. Los Angeles finished 4 games behind. The biggest reason offered for the failure to win the pennant was poor work by the bullpen.

Dodger Stadium
O'Malley's Mecca in Chavez Ravine

1958 FRIDAY, APRIL 18TH, AT MEMORIAL COLISEUM, LOS ANGELES

Big League Baseball Comes to Los Angeles

Record Crowd of 78,672 Sees Dodgers Win Home Opener
Weird Base Running Costs Giants the Game

Major league baseball made its debut in Los Angeles today before a crowd of 78,672. The new hometown Dodgers (formerly of Brooklyn) won the first game here, 6-5, over the Giants (just moved from New York to San Francisco). The attendance was the largest ever to attend a National League game.

Today's Results
LOS ANGELES 6-San Francisco 5
Chicago 11-St. Louis 6
Milwaukee 4-Philadelphia 2
Cincinnati 4-Pittsburgh 1

Standings	W-L	Pct.	GB
Chicago	3-0	1.000	—
Milwaukee	2-1	.667	1
LOS ANGELES	2-2	.500	1½
San Francisco	2-2	.500	1½
Cincinnati	1-1	.500	1½
Philadelphia	1-1	.500	1½
Pittsburgh	1-2	.333	2
St. Louis	0-3	.000	3

The Giants and Dodgers had opened the regular season with three games in San Francisco, with the Giants winning two of the games.

Before today's opener in the southland, the Dodgers were honored in ceremonies at City Hall and cheered along the parade route to Memorial Coliseum.

There were long lines at the ticket windows when the ballplayers arrived, but there were plenty of seats available. The coliseum's capacity for baseball was set at over 90,000. The horseshoe-shaped arena was designed for football games and track meets and had first opened on October 6, 1923. It was most famous as the site of the 1932 Olympic Games.

Now it gained new fame as the largest stadium with the shortest left field line in the major leagues. Because of its shape, the park had to have one of the foul lines very short. Left field was decided upon, and the fence lay only 251 feet from home plate. To cut down on the number of home runs, a screen was constructed atop the fence. It had a height of 42 feet at the line and sloped down gradually toward left center field, where the fence was 8 feet tall. A chain-link fence was put across the wide open spaces in right field. It was as distant as the left field fence was close, ranging all the way out to 440 feet from the plate in straightaway right. In center field, the home run distance was 425 feet.

The Dodgers were hoping to have their own stadium in Chavez Ravine completed in a year or two, but they would play in the Coliseum until then.

The short left field porch proved very attractive to the hitters in batting practice, with about 30 fly balls going into the seats. But in the game, only three homers were hit. With the big crowd filling the stands to the top all they way around to center field, both the hitters and the fielders complained about the background.

The game began, appropriately enough, with a hit off the screen by San Francisco's Jim Davenport. Willie Kirkland followed with a routine single. After Willie Mays fouled out, Daryl Spencer hit a short pop in front of the mound. Pitcher Carl Erskine lost the ball in the sun, but the batter was called out on the infield fly rule. Kirkland, however, ran for second when he saw the ball drop. Erskine picked the ball up and threw it to second baseman Charlie Neal, who tagged both Davenport and Kirkland. Kirkland was declared out, completing an unusual double play.

The Giants got the first run of the game in the third inning. Davenport singled, and Kirkland doubled. An intentional walk loaded the bases, and an unintentional pass forced the run home.

The Dodgers got two runs in their half of the third on a walk and two line drives to center that were misjudged by Mays.

Hank Sauer hit the first Coliseum home run in the fourth for the Giants. It went over the end of the screen in left center and might have been a homer in half a dozen parks.

The Dodgers regained the lead with a three-run fifth against Giant starter Al Worthington. With one out, Neal walked, and Dick Gray singled. Gino Cimoli got a hit to right, and outfielder Kirkland threw home to try and head Neal off. The throw arrived just ahead of the runner, but Neal kicked it out of catcher Bob Schmidt's glove and scored. As the ball rolled away, Gray also came in to score, and Cimoli got to third. Gino scored on a wild pitch by reliever Mike McCormick.

Schmidt tripled and scored for the Giants in the sixth.

Gray hit a home run for the home team in the seventh.

Sauer hit a "Chinese" homer over the screen in the eighth, cutting the Dodger lead to 6-4.

Davenport opened the ninth with a line drive off the cables above the top of the screen. The ball bounced back into play, and Davenport only got a double. Clem Labine came in to replace Erskine on the mound. Kirkland hit a tremendous drive to right center, just beyond Cimoli's reach, and the ball bounded to the fence. Davenport went part way toward third, then turned and looked around to see if the ball would be caught. When it fell safely, Davenport headed home. But he missed third base, and the Dodgers and the umpire saw it. Although Kirkland got a triple on the hit, Davenport was declared out on an appeal at third, nullifying his run. That cost San Francisco the game. Mays drove Kirkland home with an infield hit, making the score 6-5. But Spencer and Orlando Cepeda flied out to end the game.

It had been a strange contest played in a strange ballpark. Still, the first major league game ever played in Los Angeles was a definite success.

San Francisco	ab	r	h	bi	o	a	e
J. Davenport, 3b	5	1	3	0	1	0	0
W. Kirkland, rf	5	1	3	0	4	0	0
W. Mays, cf	4	0	2	0	5	0	1
D. Spencer, ss-2b6	4	0	0	1	1	2	0
O. Cepeda, 1b	5	0	0	0	5	1	0
H. Sauer, lf	4	2	2	2	0	0	0
B. Schmidt, c	3	1	2	0	5	0	1
D. O'Connell, 2b	2	0	0	0	1	0	0
J. King, ph6	0	0	0	0	-	-	-
R. Gomez, pr6	0	0	0	0	-	-	-
E. Bressoud, ss6	0	0	0	0	0	0	0
W. Lockman, ph8	0	0	0	0	-	-	-
A. Rodgers, ss8	0	0	0	0	0	0	0
A. Worthington, p	2	0	0	0	1	2	0
M. McCormick, p5	0	0	0	0	0	1	0
B. Speake, ph6	1	0	0	0	-	-	-
J. Antonelli, p6	0	0	0	0	1	0	0
R. Jablonski, ph8	1	0	0	0	-	-	-
M. Grissom, p8	0	0	0	0	0	0	0
	36	5	12	3	24	6	2

Los Angeles	ab	r	h	bi	o	a	e
J. Gilliam, lf	3	1	0	0	2	0	0
P. Reese, ss	4	0	1	0	0	0	1
D. Snider, rf	5	1	2	1	1	0	0
C. Furillo, rf9	0	0	0	0	0	0	0
G. Hodges, 1b	4	0	0	0	7	1	0
C. Neal, 2b	3	1	2	1	5	2	0
D. Gray, 3b	3	2	2	1	1	5	1
G. Cimoli, cf	3	1	1	1	2	1	0
J. Roseboro, c	1	0	0	0	4	0	0
R. Jackson, ph5	1	0	0	0	-	-	-
J. Pignatano, c6	1	0	0	0	4	0	0
C. Erskine, p	4	0	0	0	1	1	0
C. Labine, p9	0	0	0	0	0	0	0
	32	6	8	4	27	10	2

San Francisco	001	101	011	=	5
Los Angeles	002	030	10x	=	6

	ip	h	r-er	bb	so
Worthington (L 0-1)	4⅓	7	5-3	5	4
McCormick	⅔	0	0-0	0	0
Antonelli	2	1	1-1	2	0
Grissom	1	0	0-0	0	1
Erskine (W 1-0)	*8	10	4-4	4	7
Labine	1	2	1-1	0	0

*faced one batter in ninth

WP: McCormick, Erskine

Umpires: T. Venzon, J. Conlan, F. Secory, & H. Dixon

Game-Winning RBI: Cimoli
LOB: SF 9, LA 9
BE: San Francisco 1, Los Angeles 0
DP: Erskine-Neal
Gray-Neal-Hodges (Worthington)
2B: Kirkland, Davenport
3B: Schmidt, Kirkland
HR: Sauer 2, Gray
SH: Lockman
SB: Neal
Time—3:06
Attendance—78,672

The opening day crowd was the largest of the year, and the Dodgers drew 1,845,556 at home, exceeding their highest total ever in Brooklyn.

On the field, however, the team was hardly a success. It spent over half the season in last place and finished in seventh. Its final record was 71-83.

The largest crowd in baseball history, 93,103, came to the Coliseum on the night of May 7, 1959, to seen an exhibition game against the New York Yankees as a benefit for Roy Campanella.

1959 SATURDAY, SEPTEMBER 19TH, AT SEALS STADIUM, SAN FRANCISCO

Dodgers Win Two to Catch Giants

Are Tied for First after 4-1 & 5-3 Victories
Wills & Craig Star in Day Game, 5-Run Rally Wins Night Game

AFTER TRAILING THE LEAGUE-LEADERS virtually all season, the Los Angeles Dodgers today grabbed a share of the top rung of the pennant ladder with just one week left on the schedule. The victories over the first-place San Francisco Giants moved the Dodgers from tied for second place with the Braves and 2 games behind the leaders to a tie for first with San Francisco. Milwaukee won a single game today to close to within ½ game of the top. The two games here, one played in the afternoon and the other at night, were won by the Dodgers by scores of 4-1 and 5-3, respectively.

Today's Results

LOS ANGELES 4-San Francisco 1 (day)
LOS ANGELES 5-San Francisco 3 (night)
Milwaukee 9-Philadelphia 3
Pittsburgh 4-Cincinnati 3 (12 inn.)
St. Louis 2-Chicago 1

Standings	W-L	Pct.	GB
LOS ANGELES	82-66	.554	—
San Francisco	82-66	.554	—
Milwaukee	81-66	.551	½
Pittsburgh	76-72	.514	6
Cincinnati	72-77	.483	10½
Chicago	70-77	.476	11½
St. Louis	67-80	.456	14½
Philadelphia	61-87	.412	21

Los Angeles had been in first place only one day since May 12th. And the team had been as far as 5½ games behind. But generally the Dodgers ran a close third.

After having finished seventh in 1958, Los Angeles was not rated as a possible contender in the pre-season polls in 1959. But the team played very good and exciting baseball. Although no one player had had an outstanding year, manager Walt Alston had made excellent use of his full roster, and each man had contributed something.

Today, Maury Wills and Roger Craig starred in the first game. Both of them had been called up from Spokane in June. Criag hurled a complete game this afternoon, allowing just one run and six hits. Wills got three straight singles, one in each inning in which Los Angeles scored.

The Dodgers got the first two runs of the day in the second inning against 19-game winner Johnny Antonelli. Don Demeter started the rally with a two-out single. Wills followed with another hit to left. Joe Pignatano singled to right, sending Demeter home and Wills to third. The rookie speedster then ran home when catcher Hobie Landrith made a wild throw to the mound after catching a pitch. That's an error you don't see very often.

Wills drove in the third run in the fourth inning. Carl Furillo scored it on a double, a bunt, and Wills's sharp single to left.

Maury got his third hit in the sixth with one out. On a hit-and-run play, Pignatano singled to right, and Wills motored to third. Craig laid down a squeeze bunt, and Wills scored as the ball was bobbled.

In the meantime, Craig had the Giant batters baffled with his curves and occasional fastballs. Through the first eight innings, he allowed no runs and five scattered hits.

San Francisco finally pushed a run across the plate in the ninth. Daryl Spencer opened with a walk, and Leon Wagner doubled him to third with one out. Jackie Brandt's ground out brought Spencer home. Then Ed Bressoud fanned to end the game.

With a couple of hours to kill before the night game, several Dodgers got involved in card games in the visitors' clubhouse. The atmosphere was surprisingly relaxed for this late in the pennant race.

When the second game got under way, it looked as if Dodgers starting pitcher Don Drysdale would walk himself right out of the game. In the first inning, he walked the first three batters he faced. But then the big righthander struck out the next three, all on swinging third strikes.

Another base on balls coupled with his own throwing error cost Drysdale a run in the second. Landrith was passed to open the frame. After Jim Davenport struck out, Mike McCormick bunted toward the mound. Drysdale tried for the force at second, but his throw was wide for an error, and both runners were safe. Bressoud struck out, but Willie McCovey drove Landrith home with a looping single to center.

The score remained 1-0 until the seventh inning, when a Giant misplay helped the Dodgers to five big runs. Demeter singled with one out, and Wills followed suit. Pignatano walked on a 3-2 pitch to load the bases. Chuck Essegian, pinch-hitting for Drysdale, hit a double-play ball to third baseman Davenport. His throw to second was a little low. In his haste to turn an inning-ending twin-killing, second baseman Spencer dropped the toss. One run scored on the error, and the bases remained filled. Jim Gilliam then drilled a double to left center, sending two men home and putting Los Angeles ahead, 3-1. Jack Sanford relieved McCormick, and Charlie Neal greeted him with a two-run single to center. That upped the score to 5-1.

Larry Sherry pitched the seventh inning for the Dodgers but was knocked out in the eighth. Two walks and two singles plated two runs before Danny McDevitt was called in. He halted the Giant rally by fanning McCovey with the count full. Chuck Churn pitched the ninth inning for the Dodgers, allowing one walk and no hits or runs. That nailed down the victory, 5-3.

Suddenly the Los Angeles "No-Stars" were tied for first place with just six games left to play!

DAY GAME attendance 22,823

			r	h	e	
Los Angeles	020 101 000	=	4	9	0	Game-Winning RBI: Pignatano
San Francisco	000 000 001	=	1	6	3	

Batteries: R. Craig (W 9-5) & J. Pignatano.
J. Antonelli (L 19-10) 3⅓IP, S. Miller 3⅔IP, A. Worthington 2IP & H. Landrith

NIGHT GAME

Los Angeles	ab	r	h	bi	o	a	e
J. Gilliam, 3b	4	1	2	2	0	0	0
C. Neal, 2b	5	0	1	2	1	1	0
W. Moon, lf	4	0	0	0	0	0	0
G. Hodges, 1b	5	0	0	0	5	0	0
C. Furillo, rf	3	0	0	0	1	0	0
R. Fairly, ph8-rf	1	0	0	0	0	0	0
D. Demeter, cf	3	1	2	0	4	0	0
M. Wills, ss	4	1	1	0	2	3	0
J. Pignatano, c	3	1	1	0	14	0	0
D. Drysdale, p	2	0	1	0	0	2	1
C. Essegian, ph7	1	0	0	1	-	-	-
B. Lillis, pr7	0	1	0	0	-	-	-
L. Sherry, p7	0	0	0	0	0	0	0
D. McDevitt, p8	0	0	0	0	0	0	0
D. Snider, ph9	1	0	0	0	-	-	-
C. Churn, p9	0	0	0	0	0	0	0
	36	5	8	5	27	6	1

San Francisco	ab	r	h	bi	o	a	e
E. Bressoud, ss	3	0	0	0	0	2	0
J. Brandt, ph8	1	0	1	1	-	-	-
S. Miller, p9	0	0	0	0	0	0	0
W. McCovey, 1b	3	0	1	1	7	1	0
W. Mays, cf	4	0	2	0	3	0	0
O. Cepeda, lf	5	0	0	0	0	0	0
W. Kirkland, rf	3	1	1	0	2	0	0
D. Spencer, 2b	4	1	0	0	2	4	1
H. Landrith, c	3	1	0	0	11	0	0
J. Davenport, 3b	3	0	0	0	0	0	0
L. Wagner, ph8	1	0	1	1	-	-	-
J. Pagan, pr8-ss	0	0	0	0	0	0	0
M. McCormick, p	3	0	0	0	0	1	0
J. Sanford, p7	0	0	0	0	1	0	0
D. Rhodes, ph8	1	0	0	0	-	-	-
D. O'Connell, 3b9	0	0	0	0	1	0	0
	34	3	6	3	27	8	1

Los Angeles	000 000 500	=	5
San Francisco	010 000 020	=	3

	ip	h	r-er	bb	so
Drysdale (W 17-13)	6	3	1-0	5	8
Sherry	1⅔	3	2-2	2	3
McDevitt	⅓	0	0-0	0	1
Churn	1	0	0-0	1	1
McCormick (L 12-15)	6⅓	6	5-4	2	7
Sanford	1⅔	1	0-0	0	2
Miller	1	1	0-0	1	1

Game-Winning RBI: Gilliam
LOB: LA 8, SF 12
BE: LA 1, SF 1

2B: Demeter
SB: Gilliam

HBP: by Sanford (Demeter)
Time—3:04 Attendance—22,737
Umpires: A. Barlick, D. Boggess, F. Dascoli, & J. Conlan

The Dodgers completed the sweep of the series by winning the last game, 8-2. The Braves also won on Sunday and won again on Monday while the Dodgers were idle, tying Los Angeles for first.

When the season ended the following Sunday, the Dodgers and Braves were still tied, necessitating a best-of-three-game playoff to determine the pennant winner.

1959 TUESDAY, SEPTEMBER 29TH, AT MEMORIAL COLISEUM
Playoff—Game #2

Dodger Comeback Wins Pennant

Today's Results			
LOS ANGELES 6-Milwaukee 5 (12 inn.) (Los Angeles wins best-of-three playoff, 2 games to 0)			
Standings	**W-L**	**Pct.**	**GB**
LOS ANGELES	88-68	.564	—
Milwaukee	86-70	.551	2
San Francisco	83-71	.539	4
Pittsburgh	78-76	.506	8
Cincinnati	74-80	.481	13
Chicago	74-80	.481	13
St. Louis	71-83	.461	16
Philadelphia	64-90	.416	23

RALLYING FROM FAR BEHIND, THE LOS Angeles Dodgers overtook the Milwaukee Braves in today's playoff game and won, 6-5, in twelve innings. The victory gave the Dodgers the National League pennant. Los Angeles won the playoff best-of-three playoff in two straight games after the Dodgers and Braves had ended the season with identical records.

The playoff opened in Milwaukee on Monday. The Dodgers scored a run in the first inning. But the Braves scored twice in the second and knocked Los Angeles starting pitcher Danny McDevitt out of the game. Larry Sherry relieved and shut the Braves out for the final seven innings. The Dodgers tied the game in the third and won it in the sixth on a home run by Johnny Roseboro.

The teams flew to Los Angeles last night.

Star righthanders Lew Burdette (21-15) and Don Drysdale (17-13) both started today's game with three days of rest. The crowd at the Coliseum was only 36,528, although the weather was in the southland was perfect.

The Braves jumped on Drysdale for two quick runs in the top of the first. Eddie Mathews walked with one out, and Hank Aaron hit one off the left field screen. Mathews made third on the hit, which Aaron stretched into a double with a fancy slide. Frank Torre grounded a sharp hit to left, and both runners scored.

Charlie Neal got the Dodgers a run in the bottom of the first. He tripled just beyond the center fielder and scored on Wally Moon's single.

Milwaukee scored a run in the second on singles by Johnny Logan and Burdette and a throwing error by center fielder Duke Snider.

In the Los Angeles fourth, Neal homered to make the score 3-2.

But Mathews hooked a drive around the right field foul pole in the top of the fifth to put Milwaukee two runs ahead again.

The Braves got another run in the eighth on a triple by Del Crandall and a sacrifice fly Felix Mantilla.

After Neal's home run, the Dodgers did very little against the fidgety Burdette. About their most solid hit was not even made with a bat. It was a football-style block by Norm Larker trying to break up a double play. Milwaukee turned the twin-killing, but shortstop Logan was knocked out of the game.

The game went into the bottom of the ninth with the hometown Dodgers trailing 5-2. Los Angeles then rallied to tie the game. Moon and Snider started things with two grounders through the box that just barely eluded Burdette and went into center field for singles. Gil Hodges looped a hit over third base, loading the bases and knocking Burdette out of the game. Don McMahon was the new pitcher. Larker picked on his third pitch and sliced it off the screen for a two-run single. With the tying run now on third and lefthanded hitter Roseboro due up, Milwaukee manager Fred Haney brought in southpaw Warren Spahn to pitch. Alston countered by sending righthanded Carl Furillo up to pinch-hit. The veteran outfielder lofted a long fly to right, and Hodges scored after the catch to tie the game, 5-5. A single by Maury Wills knocked Spahn out of the contest. But the rally finally ended when

Aaron made a great catch in right to rob Jim Gilliam of a pennant-winning hit.

Stan Williams pitched for the Dodgers in extra innings. His fastball was very effective, but he was a little wild. He loaded the bases on walks in the eleventh. But he got out of the jam when Joe Adcock hit into a force out to end the inning.

The Dodgers also loaded the bases in their half of the eleventh. But Bob Rush relieved Joey Jay, and he retired Neal on a grounder to third base.

Williams set the Braves down in order in the top of the twelfth.

Moon and Williams popped out to start the Dodger half of the twelfth. But Rush walked Hodges with two out. Joe Pignatano grounded a sharp single to left, and suddenly the Dodgers were threatening again. Furillo was next up. With one ball and two strikes, he slapped a grounder over second base. Shortstop Felix Mantilla cut behind the bag and made a nice pickup. His momentum made a force out at second impossible, so he tried for the out at first. But his off-balance throw was in the dirt. As Furillo slid into the bag, the ball took a high hop over the first baseman's glove. Hodges, who had stopped after reaching third, saw the ball get away and ran home. He scored the winning run without a play.

The Dodgers had risen from seventh place in 1958 to champions in 1959! They had a team without outstanding pitching or hitting. But they had outstanding spirit and teamwork, and that made them champs. Now on to the World Series!

Milwaukee	ab	r	h	bi	o	a	e
B. Bruton, cf	6	0	0	0	4	0	0
E. Mathews, 3b	4	2	2	1	2	2	0
H. Aaron, rf	4	1	2	0	3	0	0
F. Torre, 1b	3	0	1	2	10	2	0
L. Maye, lf	2	0	0	0	2	0	0
A. Pafko, ph5-lf	1	0	0	0	0	0	0
E. Slaughter, ph7	1	0	0	0	-	-	-
J. DeMerit, lf7	0	0	0	0	1	0	0
A. Spangler, ph11-lf	0	0	0	0	3	0	0
J. Logan, ss	3	1	2	0	2	5	0
R. Schoendienst, 2b7	1	0	0	0	0	0	0
M. Vernon, ph9	1	0	0	0	-	-	-
C. Cottier, 2b9	0	0	0	0	0	0	0
J. Adcock, ph11	1	0	0	0	-	-	-
B. Avila, 2b11	0	0	0	0	1	0	0
D. Crandall, c	6	1	1	0	6	1	0
F. Mantilla, 2b-ss7	5	0	1	1	1	1	2
L. Burdette, p	4	0	1	0	0	2	0
D. McMahon, p9	0	0	0	0	0	0	0
W. Spahn, p9	0	0	0	0	0	0	0
J. Jay, p9	1	0	0	0	0	0	0
B. Rush, p11	1	0	0	0	0	0	0
	44	5	10	4	35	13	2

Los Angeles	ab	r	h	bi	o	a	e
J. Gilliam, 3b	5	0	1	0	4	3	0
C. Neal, 2b	6	2	2	1	3	2	1
W. Moon, rf-lf10	6	1	3	1	3	1	0
D. Snider, cf	4	0	1	0	1	0	1
B. Lillis, pr9	0	1	0	0	-	-	-
S. Williams, p10	2	0	0	0	0	0	0
G. Hodges, 1b	5	2	2	0	11	0	0
N. Larker, lf	4	0	2	2	2	0	0
J. Pignatano, pr9-c	1	0	1	0	3	0	0
J. Roseboro, c	3	0	0	0	5	1	0
C. Furillo, ph9-rf	2	0	2	1	0	0	0
M. Wills, ss	5	0	1	0	2	5	0
D. Drysdale, p	1	0	0	0	1	1	0
J. Podres, p5	1	0	0	0	0	0	0
C. Churn, p7	0	0	0	0	0	1	0
D. Demeter, ph8	1	0	0	0	-	-	-
S. Koufax, p9	0	0	0	0	0	0	0
C. Labine, p9	0	0	0	0	0	0	0
C. Essegian, ph9	0	0	0	0	-	-	-
R. Fairly, ph9-cf	2	0	0	0	1	0	0
	48	6	15	5	36	14	2

Milwaukee	210	010	010	000 =	5
Los Angeles	100	100	003	001 =	6

two out when winning run scored

	ip	h	r-er	bb	so
Burdette	*8	10	5-5	0	4
McMahon	†0	1	0-0	0	0
Spahn	⅓	1	0-0	0	0
Jay	2⅓	1	0-0	1	1
Rush (L 5-6)	1	2	1-0	1	0
Drysdale	4⅓	6	4-3	2	3
Podres	2⅓	3	0-0	1	1
Churn	1⅓	1	1-1	0	0
Koufax	⅔	0	0-0	3	1
Labine	⅓	0	0-0	0	1
Williams (5-5)	3	0	0-0	3	3

*faced three batters in ninth
†faced one batter in ninth

Game-Winning Run scored on throwing error
LOB: Milwaukee 13, Los Angeles 11
BE: Milwaukee 1, Los Angeles 1
DP: Wills-Neal-Hodges (Maye)
Torre-Logan-Torre (Roseboro)
2B: Aaron
3B: Neal, Crandall
HR: Neal, Mathews
SF: Mantilla, Furillo
CS: Moon
HBP: by Jay (Pignatano)

WP: Podres
PB: Pignatano

Time—4:06 Attendance—36,528
Umpires: A. Barlick, D. Boggess, A. Donatelli, J. Conlan, B. Jackowski, & T. Gorman

1959 THURSDAY, OCTOBER 8TH, AT COMISKEY PARK, CHICAGO World Series—Game #6

Los Angeles Wins the World Series

THE LOS ANGELES DODGERS, WHO HAD FINISHED THE 1958 SEASON WAY DOWN IN seventh place, today wound up the 1959 campaign at the very pinnacle of the baseball world by winning the World Series. After the Milwaukee Braves and San Francisco Giants were nosed out for the National League pennant, the American League champion Chicago White Sox were a piece of cake, going down to defeat in six games. Today's final score was 9-3.

The series had opened in Chicago with the Dodgers getting crushed, 11-0. But the Los Angeles squad bounced back to win the next three games. The first victory for the N. L. champs was a come-from-behind, 4-3 affair in which Charlie Neal hit two home runs and Larry Sherry saved the win for Johnny Podres. In Game #3, Los Angeles broke a scoreless tie in the seventh inning with a two-run pinch single by Carl Furillo. Sherry again saved the game, this time in relief of Don Drysdale. The Dodgers won their third straight the next day, 5-4. Gil Hodges got the game-winning homer in the eighth inning, and Sherry was credited with the victory after two scoreless innings of relief pitching. The Dodgers had hoped to wrap up the series at home in Game #5, but the White Sox held them off and won, 1-0.

So the series moved back to Chicago for a sixth and possibly a seventh game. Today's capacity crowd of better than 47,000 brought the total attendance for the series to 420,784, easily an all-time World Series record. The three games that were played in the Los Angeles Coliseum each drew over 92,000 fans.

Facing elimination today, Chicago manager Al Lopez chose to start ace pitcher Early Wynn on only two days of rest. Wynn had pitched seven innings of the shutout in the first game and had been bombed in the fourth game, yielding four runs in less than three innings of work.

Walt Alston of the Dodgers nominated a well-rested Podres, who had not pitched since the second game.

Wynn appeared to be laboring in the first inning, giving up a hit and a walk. Another batter hit a long fly that was caught, and the Dodgers failed to score. Wynn also pitched around a base on balls in the second.

The Dodgers finally got some runs onto the board in the third. Wynn disposed of the first two batters before walking Wally Moon. The 1-and-1 pitch to Duke Snider was not quite outside enough, and the Duke blasted it over the fence in left center field for a two-run home run.

Despite Wynn's troubles, Lopez let the hurler hit for himself in the bottom of the third. He struck out.

In the fourth, Los Angeles knocked Wynn out of the box and put the game out of reach with six runs. Norm Larker opened with a hit up the middle and was replaced by pinch-runner Don Demeter. Johnny Roseboro sacrificed. Maury Wills slapped a hit through the box, scoring Demeter from second. Podres showed his hitting ability by doubling over the center fielder's head to drive Wills home.

Wynn was finally yanked at this point, and Dick Donovan came in to pitch. He walked the first man he faced, Jim Gilliam. Neal then cracked a two-run double off the wall in right center. Moon chased Donovan to the showers with a home run into the lower right center field stands. Turk Lown came in and got the final two outs of the inning.

Podres went to the mound in the bottom of the fourth with an 8-0 lead. After retiring the leadoff batter on a foul pop, he hit Jim Landis in the batting helmet with a pitch. Podres seemed to lose his concentration at this juncture. He walked Sherm Lollar. Then he served up a "gopher ball" to Ted Kluszewski. Big Klu deposited it into the upper deck in right field for a three-run home run. Alston went to the mound to talk to his lefthander yet left him in. But Podres walked Al Smith on five pitches.

Now Alston decided to make a move. He called in relief ace Sherry. Larry had been brilliant coming out of the bullpen since being called up from St. Paul in July. Including his fine work in the first game of the playoff against Milwaukee, his earned-run-average as a reliever was 0.74 for the season. And in his three previous World Series appearances, he had held the White Sox to just one run and four hits in seven innings.

The Chicago fans took heart when Bubba Phillips looped Sherry's first pitch into left center for a single, sending Smith to third. But Sherry struck Billy Goodman out. Earl Torgeson walked to load the bases. Then Luis Aparicio ended the rally by popping to short.

That was the Sox' last hurrah. Sherry scattered three hits over the final five innings and walked no one else.

Gerry Staley and Billy Pierce shut the Dodgers out through the eighth. But Pierce aggrevated a hip injury, and Ray Moore was sent out to pitch the ninth. Alston sent pinch-hitter Chuck Essegian up to lead off. Essegian, who had gone to the same high school (Fairfax) as Sherry had, lined the first pitch into the left field stands for his second pinch homer of the series. That made the score 9-3.

In the bottom of the ninth, the White Sox went out, one-two-three, and the victory and the World Series were complete.

The Dodgers had climbed all the way from the depths of seventh place in 1958 to the very top in 1959.

Los Angeles (NL)	ab	r	h	bi	o	a	e
J. Gilliam, 3b	4	1	0	0	0	2	0
C. Neal, 2b	5	1	3	2	4	4	0
W. Moon, lf	4	2	1	2	3	0	0
D. Snider, cf-rf4	3	1	1	2	2	0	0
C. Essegian, ph9	1	1	1	1	-	-	-
R. Fairly, rf9	0	0	0	0	0	0	0
G. Hodges, 1b	5	0	1	0	10	0	0
N. Larker, rf	1	0	1	0	0	0	0
D. Demeter, pr4-cf	3	1	1	0	4	0	0
J. Roseboro, c	4	0	0	0	2	0	0
M. Wills, ss	4	1	1	1	2	3	0
J. Podres, p	2	1	1	1	0	1	0
L. Sherry, p4	2	0	2	0	0	2	0
	38	9	13	9	27	12	0

Chicago (AL)	ab	r	h	bi	o	a	e
L. Aparicio, ss	5	0	1	0	1	2	1
N. Fox, 2b	4	0	1	0	2	2	0
J. Landis, cf	3	1	1	0	2	0	0
S. Lollar, c	3	1	0	0	5	2	0
T. Kluszewski, 1b	4	1	2	3	10	0	0
A. Smith, lf	2	0	0	0	2	0	0
B. Phillips, 3b-rf5	4	0	1	0	3	1	0
J. McAnany, rf	1	0	0	0	1	0	0
B. Goodman, ph4-3b	3	0	0	0	0	1	0
E. Wynn, p	1	0	0	0	0	1	0
D. Donovan, p4	0	0	0	0	0	0	0
T. Lown, p4	0	0	0	0	0	0	0
E. Torgeson, ph4	0	0	0	0	-	-	-
G. Staley, p5	0	0	0	0	1	0	0
J. Romano, ph7	1	0	0	0	-	-	-
B. Pierce, p8	0	0	0	0	0	0	0
R. Moore, p9	0	0	0	0	0	0	0
N. Cash, ph9	1	0	0	0	-	-	-
	32	3	6	3	27	9	1

Los Angeles	002	600	001	=	9
Chicago	000	300	000	=	3

	ip	h	r-er	bb	so
Podres	3⅓	2	3-3	3	1
Sherry (W 2-0)	5⅔	4	0-0	1	1
Wynn (L 1-1)	3⅓	5	5-5	3	2
Donovan	*0	2	3-3	1	0
Lown	⅔	1	0-0	0	0
Staley	3	2	0-0	0	0
Pierce	1	2	0-0	0	1
Moore	1	1	1-1	0	1

*faced three batters in fourth
HBP: by Podres (Landis)

Game-Winning RBI: Snider
LOB: LA 7, Chi 7
BE: none
DP: Podres-Neal-Hodges (Phillips)
2B: Podres, Neal, Fox, Kluszewski
HR: Snider, Moon, Kluszewski, Essegian
SH: Roseboro
CS: Demeter

Time—2:33 Attendance—47,653

Umpires: F. Dascoli, E. Hurley, F. Secory, B. Summers, J. Rice, & H. Dixon

1960 TUESDAY NIGHT, APRIL 12TH, AT MEMORIAL COLISEUM

Essegian's Pinch Homer Wins Opening Game

Eleventh-Inning Clout Beats Cubs, 3-2, Before 67,550
Drysdale Goes the Distance and Fans 14

CHUCK ESSEGIAN WAS NOT EVEN LISTED in the program. And the manager put him into the game only after the two previous batters had made outs. After all, why waste one of your good players on a two-out, none-on situation.

Essegian had hit two pinch-hit home runs in the 1959 World Series, but the Dodgers had tried to capitalize on his long-ball propensities by arranging to trade him for a pitcher. Publicist Red Patterson had been so convinced that Essegian would be gone that he had ordered the programs printed without him on the roster. But the right deal had not turned up, so Essegian was on the Los Angeles bench tonight.

Today's Results

LOS ANGELES 3-Chicago 2 (11 inn.)
San Francisco 3-St. Louis 1
Milwaukee 4-Pittsburgh 3
Cincinnati 9-Philadelphia 4

Standings	W-L	Pct.	GB
LOS ANGELES	1-0	1.000	—
San Francisco	1-0	1.000	—
Milwaukee	1-0	1.000	—
Cincinnati	1-0	1.000	—
Philadelphia	0-1	.000	1
Pittsburgh	0-1	.000	1
St. Louis	0-1	.000	1
Chicago	0-1	.000	1

When his chance finally came, the former Stanford footballer responded with a game-winning pinch homer in the eleventh inning. The blow, which was struck well after midnight, sent what was left of a huge Los Angeles crowd home happy, as it won the opening game of the season for the Dodgers.

Starting pitcher Don Drysdale, who had fanned fourteen opposing batters in eleven innings, was half way up the ramp to the clubhouse when Essegian connected. The Dodger righthander, who had thought that his fine effort had gone for naught, came running to the dugout when he heard the cheering and was one of the first of many teammates to mob Essegian after he had crossed the plate.

The opening-night crowd numbered over 70,000 total, including 67,550 paid. Among the many dignitaries on hand were Governor Edmund G. "Pat" Brown and Mayor Norris Poulson. The first ball was thrown out by National League president Warren Giles.

Then the Dodgers and visiting Chicago Cubs provided the fans with quite a show. Bob Anderson and Drysdale both pitched fine games, although Anderson was removed for a pinch-hitter after eight innings. Don Elston replaced him on the mound and was the losing pitcher. In all, the three hurlers struck out 26 batters while allowing only 14 hits. Drysdale was found for 7 safeties, but none came after the fifth inning.

Aside from Essegian and Drysdale, the hero for the Dodgers was Wally Moon, who drove in the first two Los Angeles runs with a double in the fifth. For Chicago, the hitting hero was Don Zimmer, whom the Dodgers had traded away just four days before. Zim hit a home run in his first at bat as a Cub, and the Los Angeles fans gave him a big hand as he rounded the bases.

Batting in the top of the third with a 2-and-2 count, Zimmer found a fastball to his liking and parked it over the left field screen with plenty of distance to spare. One out later, Anderson singled off third baseman Jim Gilliam's shoulder. Richie Ashburn's poke down the left field line sent Anderson to third. Tony Taylor doubled the Cub hurler home, while Ashburn held up at third. Drysdale then cannily pitched around dangerous Ernie Banks, and struck Frank Thomas out.

Los Angeles had base runners in each of the first three innings but did not score. In the third, Charlie Neal got on base the hard way, getting hit on the wrist by a pitched ball. The injury was painful enough to put Neal out of the game, but x-rays showed that no bones were broken.

The Cubs made their last bid to score in the fifth. Anderson and Ashburn again singled. T. Taylor hit into a force play trying to sacrifice. After Will again went out, Drysdale again walked Banks to get to Thomas. Thomas hit the ball this time, but third baseman Bob Lillis snared the grounder and just barely beat Taylor to the base for an inning-ending force out.

The Dodgers came in and scored two runs in their half of the fifth. Maury Wills walked to start. He stole second as Drysdale was striking out. Gilliam also walked. Bob Lillis hit into a fielder's choice, Wills being tagged out. Then Moon doubled off the screen in left, scoring Gilliam and Lillis and tying the game.

Drysdale's one-out triple in the seventh did not result in a run.

The score was still 2-2 going into the eleventh. After Thomas had opened the Cub half with his fourth strikeout of the night, George Altman and the ever-popular Mr. Zimmer walked. Drysdale was tiring, but he struck Del Rice out on three pitches. Elston hit a smash that bounced away from Lillis. But it went right to shortstop Wills, whose fast work got the out at first.

In the bottom of the eleventh, the first two Dodgers went out. If anyone had been on base, manager Walt Alston had planned to send Sandy Amoros up to try and drive them home. But with the bases empty, Alston chose a hitter with more home run power, Essegian. Elston's first pitch to the pinch-hitter was a ball. Then he got a breaking ball up high, and Essegian drove it far over the screen for the game-winning home run. Suddenly the man who was not even on the scorecard became the hero of the hour.

Chicago	ab	r	h	bi	o	a	e
R. Ashburn, cf	5	0	3	0	2	0	0
T. Taylor, 2b	5	0	1	1	2	4	0
B. Will, rf	5	0	0	0	0	0	0
E. Banks, ss	3	0	0	0	2	3	0
F. Thomas, lf	5	0	0	0	1	0	0
G. Altman, 1b	4	0	0	0	11	1	0
D. Zimmer, 3b	4	1	1	1	1	3	0
C. Neeman, c	3	0	0	0	9	1	0
S. Taylor, ph9	1	0	0	0	-	-	-
D.Rice, c9	1	0	0	0	3	0	0
B. Anderson, p	3	1	2	0	1	1	0
I. Noren, ph9	1	0	0	0	-	-	-
D. Elston, p9	1	0	0	0	0	1	0
	41	2	7	2	32	14	0

Los Angeles	ab	r	h	bi	o	a	e
J. Gilliam, 3b-2b4	3	1	0	0	2	0	0
C. Neal, 2b	1	0	0	0	0	0	0
B. Lillis, pr3-3b	1	1	0	0	4	0	0
N. Larker, ph7-1b	0	0	0	0	3	1	0
W. Moon, lf	5	0	2	2	1	0	0
D. Snider, rf	4	0	0	0	1	0	0
G. Hodges, 1b-3b8	5	0	0	0	3	1	1
J. Roseboro, c	5	0	2	0	14	0	0
D. Demeter, cf	5	0	0	0	2	0	0
M. Wills, ss	4	0	1	0	2	2	1
D. Drysdale, p	4	0	1	0	1	4	0
C. Essegian, ph11	1	1	1	1	-	-	-
	38	3	7	3	33	8	2

Chicago	002 000 000 00	=	2
Los Angeles	000 020 000 01	=	3

two out when winning run scored

	ip	h	r-er	bb	so
Anderson	8	5	2-2	5	9
Elston (L 0-1)	2⅔	2	1-1	1	3
Drysdale (W 1-0)	11	7	2-2	4	14

HBP: by Anderson (Neal)
WP: Drysdale
Umpires: A. Barlick, B. Jackowski, S. Landes, & C. Pelekoudas

Game-Winning RBI: Essegian
LOB: Chicago 10, Los Angeles 10
BE: Chicago 2
DP: Drysdale-Wills-Hodges (T. Taylor)
Banks-T. Taylor-Altman (Wills)
2B: Roseboro, T. Taylor, Moon, Wills
3B: Drysdale
HR: Zimmer, Essegian
SB: Wills
Time—3:17 Attendance—67,550

Essegian stayed with the club all season but only hit .215 with 3 homers.

Drysdale led the league in strikeouts, but his record was just 15-14, thanks in part to poor offensive support.

The team as a whole struggled through the first half of the season. The Dodgers got hot in July and got to within 4 games of first place. But the offense sputtered badly in the last two months, and the team never threatened the leaders seriously.

Los Angeles finished in fourth place, 13 games behind, with a final record of 82-72.

1961 WEDNESDAY NIGHT, AUGUST 16TH, AT MEMORIAL COLISEUM

Dodgers Shut Out Twice, Drop from 1st

Lose 6-0 & 8-0 Before 75,000 Fans
Reds Grab League Lead behind Pitching of Purkey & O'Toole

WHAT GOES UP MUST COME DOWN. THE Los Angeles Dodgers had jumped from 6 games behind to 2½ games ahead in a recent four-week stretch by winning 19 out of 22 games. But starting Monday night, they turned around and lost four games in a row to fall 1 game behind. To make matters worse, they managed just two runs in those four defeats. Tonight they capped the slump with exactly ZERO runs in a doubleheader against the Cincinnati Reds, who moved into first place with their double victory.

Today's Results
Cincinnati 6-LOS ANGELES 0 (1st game)
Cincinnati 8-LOS ANGELES 0 (2nd game)
San Francisco 4-St. Louis 3
Milwaukee 2-Pittsburgh 1
Chicago 9-Philadelphia 5

Standings	W-L	Pct.	GB
Cincinnati	73-46	.613	—
LOS ANGELES	69-44	.611	1
San Francisco	62-50	.554	7½
Milwaukee	60-51	.541	9
St. Louis	57-57	.500	13½
Pittsburgh	54-56	.491	14½
Chicago	47-65	.420	22½
Philadelphia	30-83	.265	40

Tonight's debacle was witnessed by a total of 75,364 people at the Los Angeles Memorial Coliseum, 72,140 of them being paid admissions. It was the largest paying crowd for a doubleheader and for a night game in National League history.

The throng had little to cheer about. The visiting Reds got four runs in the top of the first inning of the first game, and the home team never had a chance. In the nightcap, the Reds waited until the fourth inning to break a scoreless tie. They didn't get their second run until the seventh inning. But the Dodgers only got two hits in the entire game, so the Cincinnati lead was never seriously threatened. The final scores were 6-0 and 8-0, respectively. Bob Purkey pitched a four-hit shutout in the opener, and Jim O'Toole spun a two-hitter in the closer. Frank Robinson hit a two-run homer for the victors in the twilight contest, and Gene Freese hit two round-trippers good for four runs in the nightcap. Darrell Johnson also homered in the second game.

St. Louis's Ernie Broglio had snapped a six-game Dodger winning streak on Monday night with a 5-0 shutout.

Then the second-place Reds came to town for three games in two nights. On Tuesday, the Dodgers got two runs in the first inning. But Cincinnati came back with five runs off Sandy Koufax to win, 5-2. The Reds' Joey Jay recovered from his shaky start and went the distance.

With his club just 1 game ahead of Cincinnati, Los Angeles manager Walter Alston took a chance and used Larry Sherry as the starting pitcher in the first game. Sherry had not started a game since April 28, 1960. It quickly became evident that he was not used to starting.

The first batter of the night, Eddie Kasko singled. Don Blasingame followed with a triple to deep center, driving Kasko home. Vada Pinson sent Blasingame across with a single to right. Sherry hit the next batter, Robinson, in the back with a pitch. Pinson moved to third after Gordy Coleman's long fly was caught. Robinson then stole second, and Pinson trotted home when the throw was wild. Robinson scored the fourth run of the inning on an infield out and a wild pitch.

With the big lead, Purkey had an easy night. His wide variety of pitches and speeds completely baffled the Dodger hitters. The closest thing Los Angeles got to a scoring threat was a pair on two-out singles in the second inning. Daryl Spencer ended that "rally" by popping out.

The Reds knocked Sherry out of the box in the third inning. Pinson led off with a double. Sherry sent Robinson sprawling into the dirt with an inside pitch. The slugger cooly got up and hit the very next pitch over the screen in left field for a two-run homer. By the time the night was over, Robinson had raised his season total against the Dodgers to 24 RBIs in 17 games.

There was no further scoring in the opening game, and the Reds were quite content with a 6-0 victory.

In the nightcap, O'Toole went for the sweep matched against the Dodgers' Johnny Podres.

Podres held the Reds at bay until the fourth round. Then Freese golfed a low curveball over the screen in left for a home run. Johnson cleared the screen with a fly in the seventh, upping the Cincinnati lead to 2-0.

Although the game was still theoretically within the Dodgers' reach at this point, O'Toole's speed was virtually unhittable, and Los Angeles never mounted any threats.

In the eighth, Cincinnati broke the game open with three runs. Freese once again was the instrument of destruction, knocking a three-run homer over the screen. It was the Cincinnati third baseman's eighth home run versus the Dodgers this season, seven of them coming in the Coliseum.

Four singles, two wild pitches, and a walk gave the Reds three runs against reliever Dick Farrell in the ninth, making the score 8-0.

Not many of the 75,000 fans were still around to see the final three Dodgers outs in the bottom of the ninth. It was just too disheartening to watch the one-time league leaders fall ineptly to second place.

FIRST GAME

			r	h	e	
Cincinnati	402 000 000	=	6	7	0	Game-Winning RBI: D. Blasingame
Los Angeles	000 000 000	=	0	4	2	

Batteries: B. Purkey (W 14-7) & J. Edwards.
L. Sherry (L 4-3) 2 IP, R. Perranoski 4 IP, S. Williams 2 IP, J. Golden 1 IP & J. Roseboro.

SECOND GAME

Cincinnati	ab	r	h	bi	o	a	e
E. Chacon, 2b	4	1	1	0	5	1	0
E. Kasko, ss	5	2	2	0	1	2	0
G. Bell, rf	4	0	0	0	3	0	0
V. Pinson, cf8	1	1	1	1	0	0	0
F. Robinson, cf-rf8	3	1	2	2	1	0	0
G. Freese, 3b	4	2	2	4	0	3	0
W. Post, lf	5	0	2	0	2	0	0
G. Coleman, 1b	3	0	0	0	7	0	0
D. Johnson, c	4	1	1	1	8	0	0
J. O'Toole, p	4	0	1	0	0	1	0
	37	8	12	8	27	7	0

Los Angeles	ab	r	h	bi	o	a	e
M. Wills, ss	4	0	0	0	2	3	0
J. Gilliam, lf	1	0	0	0	1	0	0
T. Davis, cf	4	0	1	0	2	0	0
F. Howard, rf	4	0	0	0	3	0	0
G. Hodges, 1b	2	0	0	0	9	0	0
D. Spencer, 3b	3	0	0	0	2	3	0
C. Neal, 2b	3	0	1	0	1	2	0
N. Sherry, c	3	0	0	0	7	0	0
J. Podres, p	1	0	0	0	0	0	0
R. Perranoski, p8	0	0	0	0	0	1	0
B. Aspromonte, ph8	1	0	0	0	-	-	-
D. Farrell, p9	0	0	0	0	0	0	0
	26	0	2	0	27	9	0

Cincinnati	000 100 133	=	8
Los Angeles	000 000 000	=	0

	ip	h	r-er	bb	so
O'Toole (W 12-9)	9	2	0-0	4	7
Podres (L 15-4)	7⅓	8	5-5	4	7
Perranoski	⅔	0	0-0	0	0
Farrell	1	4	3-3	1	0

WP: Farrell 2
Time—2:21
Umpires: K. Burkhart, M.Steiner, C. Pelekoudas, & J. Conlan

Game-Winning RBI: Freese
LOB: Cincinnati 7, Los Angeles 4
DP: Wills-Neal-Hodges (Johnson)
Kasko-Coleman
Perranoski-Wills-Hodges (Coleman)
Freese-Chacon-Coleman (Davis)
2B: Post, Kasko
HR: Freese 2, Johnson
SH: Podres
Attendance—72,140 paid, 75,364 total

The Dodgers went on the road and lost three games in a row in both San Francisco and St. Louis, running their losing streak to ten games. Then they went to Cincinnati and snapped the string with two victories. But with a chance to regain first place, they dropped a doubleheader to the Reds on August 27th, 6-5 & 8-3.

Los Angeles never did catch Cincinnati, finishing 4 games behind with a record of 89-65.

Chapter XIV Flying Feet + Golden Arms = Glorious Years

1962 September 15th
Lead by 4 Games after Triple Steal

1962 Playoff Game No. 3
Giants "Walk Away" with the Pennant

1963 September 18th
Dodgers Sweep Big Series from Cardinals

1963 World Series Game No. 4
Dodgers Sweep Yankees!

1964 June 28th
Lose 1-0 & Fall to 9th Place

1965 September 9th
Koufax Hurls Perfect Game

1965 October 2nd
Win on 2 Hits to Clinch Flag

1965 World Series Game No. 7
Sandy's 3-Hitter Nails Down the Series

1966 October 2nd
Koufax Wins Last Game to Save Pennant

1966 World Series Game No. 4
Dodgers Shut Out in World Series

THE NEW DODGER STADIUM IN CHAVEZ RAVINE WAS FINALLY READY FOR BASEBALL IN 1962. The park was the personal project of Walter O'Malley, and it was an immediate success. The only major league park built by the club itself since 1923, it was the envy of professional sports. It offered no fewer than seven front rows, no obstructed views, and acres of parking, all owned by the club. Although its capacity was about 40,000 less than the Coliseum, the Dodgers shattered the season attendance record in Dodger Stadium in that first season and broke their own mark there three times in the next twenty years. In their new park, the Los Angeles Dodgers led baseball to revenue and salary levels undreamed of in the pre-expansion era.

The Cincinnati Reds spoiled the party by winning the opening game in the new park, 6-3, on April 10, 1962. But the Dodgers got off to a good start in the pennant race. A thirteen-game winning streak in late May pushed them into a tie for first with the San Francisco Giants. From that time on, it was a two-team fight for the flag.

On the last game before the All-Star break, Don Drysdale made a rare relief appearance to save a shutout for Sandy Koufax and beat the Giants, 2-0. The victory put Los Angeles in front by ½ game. At that point, Drysdale had a 15-4 record, and Koufax was 13-4 with a no-hitter and an 18-strikeout game to his credit. Tommy Davis was leading the league in batting average and RBIs, and Maury Wills was electrifying the baseball world with his base stealing.

Koufax was sidelined with a circulatory problem in his left hand on July 17th. But Drysdale, Davis, Wills, and the rest kept up the pace. Meanwhile, the Giants kept in dogged pursuit. San Francisco could never quite catch Los Angeles but never feel more than 4 games behind, either.

When the Dodgers went east for their final road trip of the year, their lead was just ½ game. They won the first three games of the trip, the last one on a dramatic triple

Maury Wills steals third base in the final 1962 playoff game

steal in Chicago. The Giants, meanwhile, went on a losing streak to fall 4 games back.

Then the Dodgers collapsed and eventually blew the pennant. They lost five of the final seven games on the trip. But thanks to poor play by the Giants, the margin was still a comfortable 3 games when the Dodgers came home for the final six games on the schedule. Los Angeles could win only one of those six, however. San Francisco won four of six, and the teams ended the schedule in a tie.

The Dodgers suffered their third straight shutout defeat in the first game of the playoff, 8-0. They were behind 5-0 in the second game before erupting for seven runs in the bottom of the sixth inning. The Giants came back to tie the game, but Los Angeles pushed across a run in the ninth to win it, 8-7, and tie the playoff. In the decisive third game, the Dodgers gave away two runs early, then rallied to take a 4-2 lead into the ninth inning. But two hits, two walks, and a sacrifice fly tied the game for the Giants. An intentional walk loaded the bases, and an unintentional one forced the go-ahead run home. The Dodgers added an error for good measure to give San Francisco the game, 6-4, and throw away the pennant.

The disastrous collapse overshadowed excellent years for Davis (.346 with 153 RBIs), Wills (130 runs and 104 stolen bases), and Drysdale (25-9).

In 1963, the Dodgers set out to wipe out the stigma of 1962. With Koufax healthy all season, Ron Perranoski pitching exceptionally well in relief, Davis winning another batting title, and Wills again leading the league in steals, the Dodgers had an excellent team. They took over first place for good on July 2nd, when Drysdale shut St. Louis out, 1-0.

It looked like an easy pennant until the Cardinals got hot in early September and won 19 out of 20. When the Dodgers came to St. Louis for a three-game series starting on September 16th, their lead had been reduced to just 1 game. In the opening game of the series, the Dodgers broke a 1-1 tie in the ninth inning and won, 3-1. In the second game, Koufax hurled his eleventh shutout of the season to win, 4-0. The Dodgers completed the sweep by overcoming a 5-1 deficit in the final game to win in 13 innings, 6-5. They clinched the pennant six days later.

In the World Series, Los Angeles faced the mighty New York Yankees. Koufax set the tone of the series by striking out 15 batters in the first game and winning, 5-2. Johnny Podres stopped New York in the second game, 4-1, with last-inning help from Perranoski. Drysdale was brilliant in the third game, winning 1-0 on a three-hitter. And Koufax came back to complete the unexpected sweep with a tightly-pitched, 2-1 victory. The Dodgers were world champions.

For the defending champs, 1964 was a year to forget. After winning their opening game, the Dodgers dropped the next seven. Podres was out almost all season with a bad elbow. Koufax missed the final eight weeks with an arthritic condition in his elbow. Davis and Johnny Roseboro were also injured. As the team dropped hopelessly out of the race in late June manager Walter Alston lashed out at his players for lack of pride and hustle. Still, the Dodgers finished tied for sixth with a sub-.500 record.

With Koufax still bothered by elbow trouble in spring training in 1965, the Dodgers were not looked upon as pennant contenders. But despite nagging arthritis, Sandy never missed a start. And Drysdale had a fine season. Claude Osteen, acquired in a trade for Frank Howard, pitched steadily as a starter. And Perranoski teamed with righthander Bob Miller to give the team excellent relief pitching.

Tommy Davis broke his ankle on May 1st, but veteran minor leaguer Lou Johnson was acquired, and he amazed everyone with his excellent play. The Dodgers finished last in the league in home runs, but the offense made up for it with speed and savvy.

Los Angeles led the league for most of the summer. But when September rolled around, three teams were right on their heels. The Giants reeled off 14 straight victories to push the Dodgers 4½ games behind by September 15th.

Sandy Koufax, minutes after completing his perfect game

On the 16th, Los Angeles launched a streak of its own. By September 30th, the Dodgers had won 13 in a row and were back ahead by 2 games with three left to play. Great pitching was the key in the streak, with seven of the games being won on shutouts. The string was stopped on October 1st, but the next day the Dodgers clinched the pennant. It was a typical Dodger victory: they were held to just two hits but managed three runs, and Koufax pitched a four-hitter to win, 3-1.

The Minnesota Twins grabbed the first two games of the World Series. But the Dodgers came back and won three in a row. The Twins won the sixth game to even the series. But Koufax pitched a shutout in the seventh, 2-0, to give the Dodgers the championship.

Spring training in 1966 saw Koufax and Drysdale stage a joint holdout for higher pay. They signed less than two weeks before opening day. Sandy had another fine season (27-9), but Don slipped from 23-12 in 1965 to 13-16 in 1966. Osteen was 17-14, and rookie Don Sutton added a 12-12 mark to manager Alston's four-man rotation. Phil Regan, plucked from the minor leagues, was the new ace of the bullpen with an incredible 14-1 record and 21 saves.

Despite great pitching, Los Angeles trailed by as many as 7 games in the early going. But they managed to climb into contention and stay close to the front-running Pirates and Giants through August. Then Los Angeles leaped into first place with a four-game shutout sweep of the Houston Astros on September 9th, 10th, and 11th. Neither Pittsburgh nor San Francisco could mount a big charge in the late stages, but he Dodgers had some trouble putting the pennant away. Needing just one victory in the final three-game series in Philadelphia, Los Angeles dropped the first two. So Koufax had to pitch the final game on just two days of rest. He was able to hold on and win, 6-3, to clinch the flag.

The World Series against the upstart Baltimore Orioles turned out to be a fiasco. In the opening game, Drysdale was routed by four runs in the first two innings. Los Angeles scored single runs in the second and third innings. But they didn't score again, not for the rest of the game, not for the rest of the series. They were shut out in each of the last three games, and Baltimore took the series in four straight.

Lou Johnson connecting for a home run in the seventh game of the 1965 World Series

1962 SATURDAY, SEPTEMBER 15TH, AT WRIGLEY FIELD, CHICAGO

Lead by 4 Games after Triple Steal

Steal on Wild Pitch in 9th Yield Two Runs
Dodgers Beat Cubs, 6-4, in Sloppy Game

Today's Results			
LOS ANGELES 6-Chicago 4			
Pittsburgh 5-San Francisco 4			
Cincinnati 9-New York 6			
Philadelphia 5-St. Louis 4			
Milwaukee 9-Houston 8			

Standings	W-L	Pct.	GB
LOS ANGELES	98-51	.658	—
San Francisco	94-55	.631	4
Cincinnati	93-58	.616	6
Pittsburgh	86-62	.581	11½
St. Louis	77-71	.520	20½
Milwaukee	77-73	.513	21½
Philadelphia	74-76	.493	24½
Houston	56-90	.384	40½
Chicago	52-96	.351	45½
New York	36-111	.245	61

THE LEAGUE-LEADING LOS ANGELES Dodgers today employed their favorite offensive tactic, the stolen base, to defeat the Chicago Cubs, 6-4. After setting up their first two runs with steals, the Dodgers broke a 4-4 tie in the ninth inning with a triple steal. The pitch got away from the catcher, and two runners scored on the play to give the visitors their final margin of victory.

The game was also characterized by errors and bases on balls. The Cub pitchers walked eleven hitters, and the Chicago fielders made three miscues. The Dodgers handed the Cubs five free passes and made four officially credited errors.

When the dust of the battle had finally settled, Los Angeles had won its seventh straight decision, and Chicago's losing streak was extended to nine games. In Pittsburgh, second-place San Francisco lost its fourth in a row. As a result, the Dodger lead, which had been just ½ game on Tuesday night, went up to 4 full games. With only thirteen games left on the schedule, Los Angeles's magic number was reduced to 10.

With the pennant looking secure, the big question remaining for Dodger fans was whether Maury Wills could break Ty Cobb's all-time single-season stolen base record of 96. Today Wills stole number 92, and he had seven games left to beat Cobb's record without "an asterisk."

While Wills had been the center of all the publicity about stolen bases, the rest of the Dodger squad was also stealing to a degree not seen in the National League since the 1920's. Today the team upped its total for the year to 178 steals, already the highest total in the major leagues since 1924. Even without Wills's 92 steals, the Dodgers would be leading the league by a wide margin.

Today they pilfered five bases, with Wills getting only one of them. Three, of course, came on the triple steal. Tommy Davis was the man on the front end of the rare play. And he also stole the other base. The Cubs failed to steal any, but they had the only runner caught trying to steal, rookie Lou Brock.

T. Davis's steal in the fourth inning set up the first run of the game. Tommy singled with one out and swiped second. He moved to third on an infield out and scored on a wild throw home by second baseman Ken Hubbs.

The Dodger defense collapsed in the bottom of the fourth, handing the Cubs four runs. Chicago made only two hits, but the Los Angeles fielders missed three throws to help the runs score. Pitcher Don Drysdale got out of more trouble by starting a very unusual double play. With men on first and second, Cal Koonce bunted. Drysdale pounced on the ball and fired to third for a force out. Third baseman T. Davis relayed to first base, where second baseman Jim Gilliam was covering, in time for a DP.

Another strange double play helped Drysdale out in the sixth. With George Altman and Ron Santo on base, Andre Rodgers got the hit-and-run sign. He lined one to right field, which Frank Howard caught. The right fielder threw the ball into the center of the diamond, where Drysdale caught it and relayed it to second to double Altman off.

Howard also threw Altman out at the plate in the eighth when the runner tried to score from second on a single by Rodgers.

The Dodgers, on the other hand, were doing some fine running. Wills opened the fifth with a hit. With the Chicago fans urging him to "Go, Go, Go," Maury stole second easily. After an infield out and two walks, he scored on a sacrifice fly.

Los Angeles finally tied the score against reliever Don Cardwell in the eighth inning. Duke Snider was hit on the foot by a pitch, and Johnny Roseboro walked. Wally Moon was sent up to pinch-hit for Drysdale, and he delivered a two-run double down the right field line. It took two more relievers, but Chicago got out of the inning with the score still 4-4.

Glen Hobbie was the Chicago pitcher in the ninth. An error by Rodgers gave T. Davis a life leading off. Ron Fairly's hit put men on first and second. Howard hit into a double play, with Davis going to third. With Davis trying to steal home, a pitch hit Tim Harkness, nullifying the run but putting a man on first. Roseboro walked on four pitches, filling the sacks. Andy Carey was sent up to hit for pitcher Ron Perranoski. Davis again took a walking lead off third and sprinted for home as Hobbie was in his windup. The hurried pitch sailed high. Catcher Dick Bertell tried desperately for a quick catch and tag, but he missed the ball as Davis slid home. Before Bertell could chase it down, Harkness had also scored.

Ed Roebuck pitched around one last Dodger error in the bottom of the ninth to end the game. So Los Angeles had stolen another game and had moved another big step closer to the pennant.

Los Angeles	ab	r	h	bi	o	a	e
M. Wills, ss	3	1	1	0	3	1	1
J. Gilliam, 2b-3b8-2b9	2	0	0	0	2	1	0
W. Davis, cf	5	0	1	0	2	0	0
T. Davis, 3b-lf8	4	2	1	0	1	2	0
R. Fairly, 1b	4	0	1	1	8	2	0
F. Howard, rf	4	0	0	0	1	2	0
D. Snider, lf	3	0	1	0	1	0	0
L. Burright, pr8-2b	0	1	0	0	0	0	0
T. Harkness, ph9	0	1	0	0	-	-	-
E. Roebuck, p9	0	0	0	0	0	0	0
J. Roseboro, c	1	1	0	0	8	2	1
D. Drysdale, p	2	0	0	0	0	4	0
W. Moon, ph8	1	0	1	2	-	-	-
R. Perranoski, p8	0	0	0	0	1	0	1
A. Carey, ph9-3b	1	0	0	0	0	0	1
	30	6	6	3	27	14	4

Chicago	ab	r	h	bi	o	a	e
L. Brock, cf	4	0	1	0	1	0	0
K. Hubbs, 2b	4	1	2	0	5	7	1
B. Williams, lf	4	1	0	0	2	0	1
E. Banks, 1b	4	1	0	0	14	1	0
G. Altman, rf	1	1	1	0	1	0	0
B. Ott, rf9	0	0	0	0	0	0	0
R. Santo, 3b	3	0	1	0	0	1	0
A. Rodgers, ss	3	0	1	0	1	7	1
D. Bertell, c	4	0	1	2	3	1	0
A. Lary, pr9	0	0	0	0	-	-	-
C. Koonce, p	2	0	0	0	0	1	0
D. Cardwell, p7	1	0	0	0	0	0	0
M. Steevens, p8	0	0	0	0	0	0	0
G. Hobbie, p8	0	0	0	0	0	0	0
D. Landrum, ph9	1	0	0	0	-	-	-
	31	4	7	2	27	18	3

Los Angeles	000	110	022	=	6
Chicago	000	400	000	=	4

	ip	h	r-er	bb	so
Drysdale	7	6	4-0	4	4
Perranoski (W 6-4)	1	1	0-0	1	1
Roebuck	1	0	0-0	0	1
Koonce	*6	4	2-1	8	2
Cardwell	1⅓	1	2-2	1	0
Steevens	†0	0	0-0	1	0
Hobbie (L 5-14)	1⅔	1	2-0	1	1

*faced two batters in seventh
†faced one batter in eighth
WP: Hobbie PB: Bertell
HBP: by Cardwell (Snider),
by Hobbie (Harkenss)
Umpires: F. Walsh, J. Conlan, C. Pelekoudas, & K. Burkhart

Game-Winning Run scored on steal of home
LOB: Los Angeles 12, Chicago 7
BE: Los Angeles 2, Chicago 3
DP: Rodgers-Hubbs-Banks (T. Davis)
Drysdale-T. Davis-Gilliam (Koonce)
Howard-Drysdale-Gilliam
Rodgers-Hubbs-Banks (Howard)
2B: Hubbs, Moon
SH: Hubbs, Drysdale, Santo
SF: Fairly
SB: T. Davis 2, Wills, Harkness, Roseboro
CS: Brock
Picked Off: Altman
Time—3:34
Attendance—16,238 paid
22,507 total

The Dodger offense suddenly fell apart, and the team won only three on the remaining thirteen scheduled games. Although San Francisco could win only seven of its final thirteen, that was just enough to finish tied with Los Angeles. Both clubs had 101-61 records, forcing a best-of-three-game playoff.

Wills stole bases #96 & #97 in game #156 to officially break Ty Cobb's single-season record.

1962 WEDNESDAY, OCTOBER 3RD, AT DODGER STADIUM
Playoff—Game #3

Giants "Walk Away" with the Pennant

Today's Results			
San Francisco 6-LOS ANGELES 4 (San Francisco wins best-of-three playoff, 2 games to 1)			
Standings	**W-L**	**Pct.**	**GB**
San Francisco	103-62	.624	—
LOS ANGELES	102-63	.618	1
Cincinnati	98-64	.604	3½
Pittsburgh	93-68	.578	8
Milwaukee	86-76	.531	15½
St. Louis	84-78	.519	17½
Philadelphia	81-80	.503	20
Houston	64-96	.400	36½
Chicago	59-103	.364	42½
New York	40-120	.250	60½

IT WASN'T "THE MIRACLE AT COOGAN'S Bluff" it was more like "The Suicide in Chavez Ravine." But the parallels were unmistakeable. Eleven years ago to the day, the Dodgers (then of Brooklyn) had lost what seemed like a comfortable ninth-inning lead when the Giants (then of New York) scored four runs to win the game, the playoff, and the pennant.

This year the two clubs, although transported to California in the interim, followed the same script almost exactly. In 1951, Brooklyn had had a 4-game lead with nine games to play only to finish tied with New York. This season, Los Angeles had also led by 4 with nine left and wound up tied with San Francisco. There was no Bobby Thomson-type home run today, so the Dodger pitchers gave the Giants the next best thing: four bases on balls in the last inning. The last one forced the go-ahead run across the plate. An error then made the final score 6-4.

In the first game of this year's playoff, the Giants romped to an easy 8-0 victory. Willie Mays hit two home runs, and Billy Pierce stopped the Dodgers on three hits.

When the Dodgers were shut out for the first five innings of the second game, their consecutive-scoreless-innings streak reached 35. They also trailed in the game, 5-0. Then they broke out with seven runs in the sixth inning. The Giants rallied to tie the game. But Maury Wills's speed got the Dodgers a run in the ninth to win, 8-7.

So, after 164 games for each team, it came down to today's contest; winner take all. The crowd at Dodger Stadium was a little less than capacity, but it brought the Dodgers' season attendance to 2,755,184, a major league record. The nation's television audiences were torn between two historic events: the splashdown ending Walter Schirra's six-orbit flight in space and the decisive playoff game.

It's a good thing the Dodgers weren't directing operations at Cape Canaveral. They threw away two runs in the third inning to give the Giants the early lead. Jose Pagan led off with a single. Juan Marichal laid down a bunt. Pitcher Johnny Podres threw the ball wildly into center field, and Pagan reached third. Harvey Kuenn singled a run home. Chuck Hiller squared around to bunt and missed a pitch. Marichal, trying to get a good jump off second, was hung up between the bases. But catcher Johnny Roseboro's throw to second skipped into the outfield, and Marichal reached third safely. Hiller flied out to left, and Duke Snider's quick return throw held Marichal at third. But Kuenn was hung up between first and second until second baseman Jim Gilliam's throw in the rundown hit him in the back. As the ball rolled away, Marichal scored.

The Dodgers got their first run in the bottom of the fourth. Snider opened with a double to the right field fence. Tommy Davis singled sharply to left, Snider stopping at third. After a fly out, Frank Howard grounded to third. The Giants tried for a double play, but Howard beat the relay to first, and Snider's run counted.

The Dodgers grabbed the lead in the sixth. Snider singled to open this rally, too. And T. Davis followed with a two-run homer into the pavilion seats in left field.

Wills got Los Angeles an insurance run in his own patented fashion. He singled with one out and stole second on the next pitch. After a fly out, Maury stole third and scored when the catcher's throw went into left field.

With the Giants trailing 4-2 in the ninth, Matty Alou was sent up to pinch-hit. He smacked a single to right center. Kuenn forced M. Alou at second. Willie McCovey, also pinch-hitting, was walked on four pitches by Ed Roebuck, a portent of things to come. Ernie Bowman ran for McCovey. Felipe Alou worked the count to 3-and-2 and walked.

The bases were loaded and Willie Mays was up. He slashed a liner back through the box. Roebuck got a glove on it, but the ball rolled away for a hit and a run. The bases were still full with one out.

Dodger manager Walter Alston decided to change pitchers, and he brought in Stan Williams. The first pitch to Orlando Cepeda was a strike. The next one was lined to right field. Outfielder Ron Fairly made the catch, but the tying run scored and F. Alou moved from second to third. Williams then delivered a pitch in the dirt. Roseboro did a fine job to block the ball and prevent Alou from scoring, but Mays moved down to second. So it was decided to give batter Ed Bailey an intentional pass to load the bases again. Williams followed by walking Jim Davenport on five pitches to force home a run and put San Francisco ahead, 5-4.

Ron Perranoski replaced Williams and got Pagan to ground to second base. But Larry Burright booted the ball, and another run scored. Bob Nieman finally ended the inning by striking out.

San Francisco skipper Alvin Dark chose Pierce to pitch the bottom of the ninth. He disposed of Wills, Gilliam, and Lee Walls in order to end the game and the Dodgers' season.

The despondent Dodgers retreated into the clubhouse and locked the door. They wrestled with their emotions and with the ghosts of Bobby Thomson and Ralph Branca for nearly an hour before finally mustering the courage to meet with the press.

San Francisco	ab	r	h	bi	o	a	e
H. Kuenn, lf	5	1	2	1	2	0	0
C. Hiller, 2b	3	0	1	0	4	1	0
W. McCovey, ph9	0	0	0	0	-	-	-
E. Bowman, pr9-2b	0	1	0	0	0	0	0
F. Alou, rf	4	1	1	0	4	0	0
W. Mays, cf	3	1	1	1	3	0	0
O. Cepeda, 1b	4	0	1	1	8	0	0
E. Bailey, c	4	0	2	0	3	0	1
J. Davenport, 3b	4	0	1	1	2	4	0
J. Pagan, ss	5	1	2	0	1	1	1
J. Marichal, p	2	1	1	0	0	0	1
D. Larsen, p8	0	0	0	0	0	1	0
M. Alou, ph9	1	0	1	0	-	-	-
B. Nieman, ph9	1	0	0	0	-	-	-
B. Pierce, p9	0	0	0	0	0	0	0
	36	6	13	4	27	7	3

Los Angeles	ab	r	h	bi	o	a	e
M. Wills, ss	5	1	4	0	3	6	0
J. Gilliam, 2b-3b7	5	0	0	0	3	1	1
D. Snider, lf	3	2	2	0	2	1	0
L. Burright, 2b7	1	0	0	0	4	2	1
L. Walls, ph9	1	0	0	0	-	-	-
T. Davis, 3b-lf7	3	1	2	2	1	1	0
W. Moon, 1b	3	0	0	0	7	0	0
R. Fairly, 1b8-rf9	0	0	0	0	2	0	0
F. Howard, rf	4	0	0	1	0	0	0
T. Harkness, 1b9	0	0	0	0	0	0	0
J. Roseboro, c	3	0	0	0	3	1	1
W. Davis, cf	3	0	0	0	2	0	0
J. Podres, p	2	0	0	0	0	2	1
E. Roebuck, p6	2	0	0	0	0	0	0
S. Williams, p9	0	0	0	0	0	0	0
R. Perranoski, p9	0	0	0	0	0	0	0
	35	4	8	3	27	14	4

San Francisco	002	000	004	=	6
Los Angeles	000	102	100	=	4

	ip	h	r-er	bb	so
Marichal	*7	8	4-3	1	2
Larsen (W 5-4)	1	0	0-0	2	1
Pierce	1	0	0-0	0	0
Podres	†5	9	2-1	1	0
Roebuck (L 10-2)	3⅓	4	4-3	3	0
Williams	⅓	0	0-0	2	0
Perranoski	⅓	0	0-0	0	1

*faced one batter in eighth
†faced three batters in sixth
WP: Williams

Game-Winning RBI: Davenport
LOB: San Francisco 12, Los Angeles 8
BE: San Francisco 1, Los Angeles 1
DP: Gilliam-Wills-Moon (Cepeda)
Wills-Moon (Marichal)
Wills-Burright-Fairly (Davenport)
2B: Snider, Hiller
HR: T. Davis
SH: Hiller, Marichal, Fairly
SF: Cepeda
SB: Wills 3, T. Davis
Time—3:00 Attendance—45,693
Umpires: D. Boggess, A. Donatelli, J. Conlan, & A. Barlick

1963 WEDNESDAY NIGHT, SEPTEMBER 18TH, AT BUSCH STADIUM, ST. LOUIS

Dodgers Sweep Big Series from Cardinals

Come from Four Runs Behind to Win in 13 Innings, 6-5
Ron Perranoski and Dick Nen Are Heroes for Los Angeles

SHOWING THEMSELVES TO BE EQUAL TO the challange, the Los Angeles Dodgers came to St. Louis this week and swept a three-game series from the hard-charging Cardinals. St. Louis had won 19 of its last 20 games to cut the Dodgers lead to just 1 game before the series began. Then Los Angeles all but ended St. Louis's pennant hopes by stopping the Cardinal drive cold.

In the opening game of the set, the Dodgers scored twice in the ninth inning to break a 1-1 tie and win, 3-1. In the second game, Sandy Koufax bested Curt Simmons and pitched the Dodgers to a 4-0 victory.

Tonight, the Cardinals had a great shot at salvaging the final game of the series. But first they lost a 5-1 lead, then they failed to break a 5-5 tie after getting a leadoff triple in the tenth inning. Finally, the Dodgers scored an unearned run in the thirteenth inning and won, 6-5.

Today's Results

LOS ANGELES 6-St. Louis 5 (13 innings)
Milwaukee 6-San Francisco 4
Philadelphia 5-New York 1
Houston 8-Cincinnati 4
Chicago 2-Pittsburgh 1

Standings	W-L	Pct.	GB
LOS ANGELES	94-59	.614	—
St. Louis	91-64	.587	4
San Francisco	83-70	.542	11
Philadelphia	81-72	.529	13
Milwaukee	81-73	.526	13½
Cincinnati	81-74	.523	14
Chicago	77-77	.500	17½
Pittsburgh	72-81	.471	22
Houston	59-94	.386	35
New York	49-104	.320	45

The biggest heroes for the winners were Dick Nen and Ron Perranoski. Nen, playing in his first major league game, hit a home run in the ninth inning to tie the score. Perranoski pitched six shutout innings to get the win.

The Dodgers scored the first run of the night in the second inning. Willie Davis started the rally with a single, his tenth hit in thirteen at bats. He came around on hits by Johnny Roseboro and Ken McMullen.

But the Los Angeles lead did not last long. With two out in the bottom of the second, Curt Flood singled, and Charlie James homered.

St. Louis added three runs in the bottom of the third. With one out, Dick Groat singled to left. Stan Musial walked. Los Angeles manager Walter Alston decided to remove starting pitcher Pete Richert, and Bob Miller was called in to pitch. Miller got Ken Boyer to force Musial at second. Then Bill White singled Groat home. And Flood knocked Boyer and White in with a double down the left field line.

Big Bob Gibson, pitching for St. Louis, was in total control in the middle innings. He had a string of eleven straight batters retired after pinch-hitter Nen lined out to start the eighth.

But then Los Angeles started to shoot balls through the infield, and Gibson was routed. Maury Wills grounded a hit to left. Jim Gilliam's bouncer took a high hop over the second baseman for a single. Wally Moon walked to load the bases. Tommy Davis cracked a hit through the left side, and Wills and Gilliam scored.

That was all for Gibson. Bobby Shantz was brought in in relief. He unfurled a wild pitch, then walked Frank Howard. Willie Davis delivered a sacrifice fly to make the score 5-4. Shantz was shelved in favor of righthander Ron Taylor, who got the last out.

With Los Angeles still trailing by a run, Nen came to bat with one out in the ninth. Just the day before, his minor league team, the Spokane Indians, had been eliminated in the Pacific Coast League playoff in Oklahoma City. Since it was cheaper to ship Nen to St. Louis then it was to fly him to Spokane, he had been called up to the parent club. Now in only his second major league at bat, he picked out a fastball from Taylor and drove it onto the roof in right field for a home run, tying the game.

In the bottom of the tenth, the Cardinals looked like a lead-pipe cinch to win the game. Groat led off by smacking a fastball into the gap in right center for a triple. Alston went to the mound to confer with his pitcher, Perranoski. It was decided to pitch to lefthanded hitting Gary Kolb. Southpaw Perranoski broke a couple of curves over the outside corner and struck Kolb out. Boyer and White were intentionally walked to load the bases. Pitching tough, Perranoski got Flood to bounce a low curve to shortstop Wills, who threw home for a force. Rookie Mike Shannon grounded to third for the final out, and the Dodgers were still in the game.

In the thirteenth, W. Davis started the winning rally with an opposite-field single to left. Perranoski struck out trying to bunt. Dick Tracewski grounded one up the middle. Second baseman Julian Javier made a fine stop, stumbling just as he nabbed the ball. With no chance at second, he whirled and threw to first. But his heave was wild and went into the dugout, putting runners on second and third. Nen was intentionally walked. Wills then hit a chopper over the mound. Javier got to it, but his only play was at first, and Davis scored the go-ahead run.

Perranoski worked a one-two-three bottom of the thirteenth and nailed down his sixteenth win of the season. His six innings tonight was his longest stint of the season.

Dick Nen, unknown just 24 hours before, was looking forward to a hero's welcome when the team got to Los Angeles.

And the rest of the Dodgers were looking forward to World Series money.

Los Angeles	ab	r	h	bi	o	a	e
M. Wills, ss	7	1	1	1	3	11	0
J. Gilliam, 2b-3b9	7	1	1	0	3	3	0
W. Moon, rf	4	1	0	0	1	0	0
T. Davis, lf	5	0	1	2	2	0	0
R. Fairly, 1b	3	0	0	0	6	0	0
F. Howard, ph8	0	0	0	0	-	-	-
R. Gleason, pr8	0	0	0	0	-	-	-
D. Camilli, c8	2	0	0	0	4	0	0
W. Davis, cf	5	2	2	1	1	0	0
J. Roseboro, c	3	0	2	0	8	2	0
B. Skowron, ph8	1	0	0	0	-	-	-
R. Perranoski, p8	2	0	1	0	0	0	0
K. McMullen, 3b	4	0	1	1	1	1	0
D. Tracewski, 2b9	2	0	1	0	2	0	0
P. Richert, p	0	0	0	0	0	0	0
B. Miller, p3	1	0	0	0	0	0	0
D. Nen, ph8-1b	3	1	1	1	8	0	0
	49	6	11	6	39	17	0

St. Louis	ab	r	h	bi	o	a	e
J. Javier, 2b	6	0	1	0	2	7	1
D. Groat, ss	6	1	2	0	2	2	0
S. Musial, lf	3	0	2	0	1	0	0
G. Kolb, pr7-lf	1	0	0	0	0	0	0
C. Withrow, ph12	1	0	0	0	-	-	-
D. Clemens, lf13	0	0	0	0	0	0	0
K. Boyer, 3b	5	1	0	0	0	6	1
B. White, 1b	4	1	2	1	16	2	0
C. Flood, cf	5	1	2	2	2	0	0
C. James, rf	3	1	1	2	1	0	0
M. Shannon, rf9	2	0	0	0	0	0	0
T. McCarver, c	6	0	1	0	11	0	1
B. Gibson, p	3	0	0	0	3	0	0
B. Shantz, p8	0	0	0	0	0	0	0
R. Taylor, p8	0	0	0	0	0	0	0
G. Altman, ph9	1	0	0	0	-	-	-
L. Burdette, p10	1	0	0	0	1	0	0
J. Buchek, ph13	1	0	0	0	-	-	-
	48	5	11	5	39	17	3

Los Angeles	010 000 031 000 1 = 6
St. Louis	023 000 000 000 0 = 5

	ip	h	r-er	bb	so
Richert	2⅓	4	4-4	1	2
Miller	4⅔	4	1-1	2	6
Perranoski (W 16-3)	6	3	0-0	2	3
Gibson	7⅓	7	4-4	1	9
Shantz	⅓	0	0-0	1	0
Taylor	1⅓	1	1-1	0	0
Burdette (L 9-12)	4	3	1-0	3	1

WP: Miller 2, Shantz

Game-Winning RBI: Wills
LOB: Los Angeles 11, St. Louis 10
BE: Los Angeles 2
DP: Groat-Javier-White (T. Davis)
2B: Flood, Roseboro
3B: Groat
HR: James, Nen
SF: W. Davis
SH: Richert, Flood
SB: T. Davis
CS: Kolb
Time—3:44 Attendance—25,975

Umpires: T. Gorman, A. Forman, S. Landes, & E. Sudol

The Cardinals lost their next three games also, while the Dodgers won two out of three to clinch the pennant.

1963 SUNDAY, OCTOBER 6TH, AT DODGER STADIUM
World Series—Game #4

Dodgers Sweep Yankees!

THE LOS ANGELES DODGERS TODAY WRAPPED UP THE WORLD SERIES WITH A 2-1 victory over the New York Yankees. That completed a four-game sweep against the defending-champions, who were trying for their third consecutive World Series triumph.

The story of the sweep could be summed up quickly: Dodger pitching. The Yankees managed just four runs in the four games. And Los Angeles never trailed in any of the games. Only in today's game were the Yanks even tied after the second inning. This was not to say that New York was totally outplayed. Their pitching and fielding were both impressive. But the Dodgers were able to capitalize on the few opportunities that the Yankees presented them, while the Bronx Bombers were totally handcuffed by the Los Angeles moundmen.

Sandy Koufax, 25-5 in the National League for the year, set the tone of the series in the first inning of the first game when he struck out the side. The Dodgers took the lead in the second on an RBI single by former Yankee Bill Skowron and a three-run homer by Johnny Roseboro. Koufax wound up the game with a series record of 15 strikeouts and with a 5-2 victory.

In the first inning of the second game, a misstep in the outfield and a botched pickoff play gave the first two Dodger batters bases. Willie Davis drove them both home with a double. That was all the offensive support Johnny Podres needed. With reliever Ron Perranoski getting the last two outs, Podres and the Dodgers won easily, 4-1.

In the third game, a walk and a wild pitch put Jim Gilliam on second base with two out in the first inning. Tommy Davis drove him in with a twisting grounder that glanced off the mound and off the second baseman's shins for a hit. That was the only run the Dodgers could muster against Yankee pitcher Jim Bouton. But Dodger starter Don Drysdale made that solitary tally stand up. He hurled an absolutely brilliant three-hit shutout and won 1-0.

Game #4 today was a rematch of the pitchers in the opening game, Koufax and Whitey Ford. The Dodger lefthander was not as overpowering as he had been in the first game, while the Yankee southpaw was much more effective this time. Los Angeles managed just two hits, yet still won the game. One of the hits was a mammoth home run by Frank Howard. The other Dodger run was scored on a three-base error and a sacrifice fly. Koufax scattered six hits and walked none. The only New York run came on a home run by Mickey Mantle.

The Dodgers only put four men on base, and two of them were soon taken off in double plays.

The first double play came in the bottom of the first inning. Maury Wills had opened with a walk but was doubled off first after catcher Elston Howard caught Jim Gilliam's bunt on the fly.

F. Howard got the first hit of the game in the second inning, lining a single to right center with one out. Skowron promptly bounced into a double play.

The Yankees did not get a man on base until the fourth. Then Bobby Richardson got a gift double when his short pop fly was lost in the sun by Willie Davis. Richardson was left on second.

E. Howard opened the New York fifth with a single but got no farther than first.

F. Howard put the first run on the board in the bottom of the fifth. Batting with one out, Frank went up to the plate guessing that Ford would start him off with a slow curve. He got his pitch, and the Dodger muscleman fished it off the outside corner around the knees and sent it soaring into the upper deck near the left field line. It was the first official home run ever hit into the upper deck in Dodger Stadium.

The Yankees matched that run with a homer of their own in the top of the seventh. Koufax got a fastball out over the plate a little too much, and Mantle knocked it into the seats beyond the left center field fence.

Leading off the bottom of the seventh, Gilliam chopped one toward third base. Clete Boyer leaped high and speared the ball. His throw to first was in plenty of time, but it caromed off first baseman Joe Pepitone's wrist and chest and rolled down into the right field corner. By the time the ball was returned, Gilliam was safely on third base. Pepitone later said that he had lost the ball in the background of sunswept shirts.

Willie Davis followed with a liner to deep right center for a sacrifice fly, and the Dodgers went ahead, 2-1.

Koufax was found for a pinch single in the eighth. But the next batter, Tony Kubek, grounded into a double play.

Richardson opened the ninth with a hit to right center. Koufax got two strikes on Tom Tresh and came in with a high curve ball. The pitch barely caught the top of the strike zone for strike three. Mantle swung and missed at two inside fastballs. Then Koufax dropped a slow curve over the plate. The surprised Mantle could only watch it for another strikeout. E. Howard grounded toward left field, but shortstop Wills made a fine pickup and threw to second. Second baseman Dick Tracewski fumbled the throw, and both runners were safe. Hector Lopez was next up. He hit a check-swing dribbler past the mound. Wills charged, scooped, and threw to first for the final out.

The series was over, and Koufax was mobbed by his happy teammates. Champagne flowed freely in the Dodger clubhouse. The old kings were dead, pitched into oblivion by the newly-crowned champions of the world, the Los Angeles Dodgers.

New York (AL)	ab	r	h	bi	o	a	e
T. Kubek, ss	4	0	0	0	0	2	0
B. Richardson, 2b	4	0	2	0	1	4	0
T. Tresh, lf	4	0	0	0	1	0	0
M. Mantle, cf	4	1	1	1	4	0	0
E. Howard, c	4	0	2	0	6	1	0
H. Lopez, rf	4	0	0	0	1	0	0
J. Pepitone, 1b	3	0	0	0	8	3	1
C. Boyer, 3b	3	0	0	0	0	2	0
W. Ford, p	2	0	0	0	2	0	0
P. Linz, ph8	1	0	1	0	-	-	-
H. Reniff, p8	0	0	0	0	1	0	0
	33	1	6	1	24	12	1

Los Angeles (NL)	ab	r	h	bi	o	a	e
M. Wills, ss	2	0	0	0	0	5	0
J. Gilliam, 3b	3	1	0	0	0	0	0
W. Davis, cf	2	0	0	1	2	0	0
T. Davis, lf	3	0	0	0	0	0	0
F. Howard, rf	3	1	2	1	2	0	0
R. Fairly, rf8	0	0	0	0	0	0	0
B. Skowron, 1b	3	0	0	0	9	1	0
J. Roseboro, c	3	0	0	0	11	0	0
D. Tracewski, 2b	3	0	0	0	2	1	1
S. Koufax, p	2	0	0	0	1	2	0
	24	2	2	2	27	9	1

New York	000	000	100	= 1
Los Angeles	000	010	10x	= 2

	ip	h	r-er	bb	so
Ford (L 0-2)	7	2	2-1	1	4
Reniff	1	0	0-0	0	0
Koufax (W 2-0)	9	6	1-1	0	8

Time—1:50
Attendance—55,912

Game-Winning RBI: W. Davis
LOB: New York 5, Los Angeles 0
BE: New York 1, Los Angeles 1
DP: E. Howard-Pepitone
Kubek-Richardson-Pepitone (Skowron)
Tracewski-Skowron (Kubek)
2B: Richardson
HR: F. Howard, Mantle
SF: W. Davis

Umpires: S. Crawford, J. Paparella, T. Gorman, L. Napp, J. Rice, & T. Venzon

1964 SUNDAY, JUNE 28TH, AT CANDLESTICK PARK, SAN FRANCISCO

Lose 1-0 & Fall to 9th Place

Dodgers Put 13 Men on Base But Fail to Score
Alston Appeals to Players' Pride and Pocketbooks

WITH HIS DEFENDING-CHAMPION DODgers slipping farther down in the standings, manager Walter Alston today called a closed-door meeting in which he appealed to his players to show their pride and concentrate on their jobs. If they did not, it was implied, they would be subjected to fines.

But the meeting did not stop the team from going out and losing today's game to the San Francisco Giants, 1-0. The defeat dropped Los Angeles to ninth place in the ten-team National League race. By winning, the Giants moved past the Phillies and into first place. And the game completed a four-game sweep of the series by San Francisco.

The Dodgers had had some injuries this season, but their biggest problem was lack of good fundamentals (like moving the runners over) and timely hitting. Today they demonstrated their troubles graphically by putting 13 men on base and failing to score even one run.

Today's Results

San Francisco 1-LOS ANGELES 0
Philadelphia 5-St. Louis 0 (1st game)
St. Louis 8-Philadelphia 2 (2nd game)
Cincinnati 6-Pittsburgh 2 (1st game)
Cincinnati 6-Pittsburgh 5 (2nd game)
Chicago 10-Houston 2 (1st game)
Houston 4-Chicago 1 (10 innings) (2nd game)
Milwaukee 7-New York 6 (1st game)
Milwaukee 9-New York 0 (2nd game)

Standings	W-L	Pct.	GB
San Francisco	44-27	.620	—
Philadelphia	42-26	.618	½
Pittsburgh	38-31	.551	5
Cincinnati	37-33	.529	6½
Chicago	34-33	.507	8
St. Louis	36-36	.500	8½
Milwaukee	34-37	.479	10
Houston	34-39	.466	11
LOS ANGELES	33-38	.465	11
New York	21-53	.284	24½

At least today's game featured an excellent fundamental defensive play by Dodger catcher Johnny Roseboro. One of the best in the business, Roseboro today made an unassisted putout on a runner trying to steal second. And that runner was none other than Willie Mays, also one of the best in the game. The play occurred with two out in the third inning. With a court of 2-and-2 on the batter and Mays on first, Roseboro called for a pitchout. Mays was running on the pitch and would have been out at second by plenty. So he stopped halfway between the bases and tried to draw a throw. Playing it by the book, Roseboro ran straight at Mays, hoping to force him to make a move. Mays tried to decoy a throw with a variety of head and shoulder fakes, but Roseboro kept the ball and kept closing in on him. Finally, Willie dodged back toward first. Johnny was close enough to cut him off. At the last moment, Mays tried to reverse field and head for second, but before he could get away, Roseboro lunged and made a barehanded tag.

But that was about the only good thing that happened for the Dodgers all day.

Don Drysdale, trying to become the first 11-game winner in the majors, was the hard-luck loser. He pitched into and out of several jams before the Giants finally pushed a run across the plate in the eighth inning.

Ron Herbel got the win for San Francisco, although Billy O'Dell relieved him in the ninth and pitched out of a bases-loaded, none-out jam.

The Dodgers had runners in every inning except the sixth but grounded into three double plays.

Their first serious scoring threat came in the fifth. Frank Howard cracked a long double to left center to open. Roseboro sliced a liner down the right field line. Harvey Kuenn made a great sliding catch on the ball, robbing Roseboro of a hit, though Howard was able to advance to third. Nate Oliver grounded out, with Howard having to hold. Drysdale hit the ball 400 feet, but he hit it to straightaway center field, where it was caught.

In the seventh, the visitors loaded the bases on a hit by Ron Fairly, an error by

Orlando Cepeda, and a walk to Jim Gilliam. With Drysdale at bat and two out, the Dodgers claimed that Herbel separated his hands while on the pitching rubber, thereby balking a run home. But the umpires did not agree. After a heated argument, Drysdale lined out to right.

Another error by Cepeda and a hit by Darrell Griffith put two Dodgers on in the eighth. But Tommy Davis grounded into a double play.

The Giants, who had had several scoring chances earlier, finally broke the tie in the eighth. Kuenn led off with a sharp single. After a pop out, Mays bounced a hit under the glove of shortstop Maury Wills. Kuenn went to third on the hit, and Mays cruised to second when the Dodgers left that base uncovered. An intentional walk loaded the bases. Cepeda lined one to the warning track in right field. Howard made a fine catch, but pinch-runner Jesus Alou scored from third with ease.

Then came the ultimate frustration. The first three Dodgers reached base safely in the ninth, but they were left on. Fairly started of with his third hit of the day. Howard also singled. San Francisco manager Alvin Dark removed Herbel in favor of lefty O'Dell. Roseboro bunted and beat it out for a hit, loading the bases.

A fly ball or a difficult grounder would tie the game. But Gilliam popped a foul to the catcher near the first base dugout, and the runners had to hold. Pinch-hitter Lee Walls struck out on three pitches, the last one being a fastball up around the eyes. Maury Wills was the last hope. He looked at a strike and a ball. He tried to pull the next pitch through the infield. But third baseman Jim Ray Hart came up with the grounder and threw Wills out, ending the game.

Although Alston would not comment after the game, this was just the sort of play that had inspired him to threaten the Dodgers with fines. Los Angeles would need some sort of shock to shake the team out of the doldrums.

Los Angeles	ab	r	h	bi	o	a	e
M. Wills, ss	5	0	0	0	1	1	0
W. Parker, cf	3	0	0	0	3	0	0
D. Griffith, 3b	4	0	2	0	0	2	0
T. Davis, lf	4	0	0	0	1	0	0
R. Fairly, 1b	4	0	3	0	9	0	0
F. Howard, rf	4	0	2	0	2	0	0
D. Tracewski, pr9	0	0	0	0	-	-	-
J. Roseboro, c	4	0	1	0	8	1	0
N. Oliver, 2b	2	0	1	0	0	3	0
J. Gilliam, ph7-2b	1	0	0	0	0	0	0
D. Drysdale, p	3	0	0	0	0	2	0
L. Walls, ph9	1	0	0	0	-	-	-
	35	0	9	0	24	9	0

San Francisco	ab	r	h	bi	o	a	e
H. Kuenn, rf	4	0	2	0	2	0	0
J. Alou, pr8-rf	0	1	0	0	0	0	0
C. Hiller, 2b	4	0	0	0	2	5	0
W. Mays, cf	3	0	2	0	4	0	0
D. Snider, lf	3	0	0	0	1	0	0
O. Cepeda, 1b	3	0	0	1	9	0	2
T. Haller, c	3	0	0	0	7	0	0
J. Hart, 3b	2	0	2	0	1	4	0
J. Pagan, ss	3	0	1	0	1	2	0
R. Herbel, p	3	0	0	0	0	1	0
B. O'Dell, p9	0	0	0	0	0	0	0
	28	1	7	1	27	12	2

Los Angeles	000 000 000	=	0
San Francisco	000 000 01x	=	1

	ip	h	r-er	bb	so
Drysdale (L 10-7)	8	7	1-1	4	5
Herbel (W 6-3)	*8	8	0-0	2	4
O'Dell	1	1	0-0	0	1

*faced two batters in ninth
PB: Roseboro
Time—2:42
Attendance—41,133

Game-Winning RBI: Cepeda
LOB: Los Angeles 10, San Francisco 8
BE: Los Angeles 2
DP: Pagan-Hiller-Cepeda (Howard)
Drysdale-Roseboro-Fairly (Herbel)
Hiller-Pagan-Cepeda (Davis)
Hart-Hiller-Cepeda (Davis)
2B: Howard, Hart
SF: Cepeda
SB: Parker
CS: Mays

Umpires: B. Williams, V. Smith, T. Gorman, & C. Pelekoudas

The Dodgers continued their mediocre play through the remainder of the season. They never rose higher than 2 games above .500 and were never in the first division. They finished tied for sixth with an 80-82 final record.

Drysdale finished with an 18-16 mark, despite four 1-0 losses.

1965 THURSDAY NIGHT, SEPTEMBER 9TH, AT DODGER STADIUM

Koufax Hurls Perfect Game

Dodgers Get Just One Hit off Cubs' Hendley
Score on a Walk, a Bunt, a Steal, & an Error to Win 1-0

THINGS HAD NOT BEEN GOING VERY well for Sandy Koufax recently. He had won his 21st game of the season back on August 14th. But he had failed five times to win #22 since then. He hadn't pitched all that badly, giving up as many as four runs only once. But with the lightweight Dodger offense, giving up three runs could be fatal.

Today's Results

LOS ANGELES 1-Chicago 0
San Francisco 4-Houston 0
Cincinnati 3-New York 2
Philadelphia at Milwaukee, ppd.—rain
no other game scheduled

Standings	W-L	Pct.	GB
San Francisco	79-59	.572	—
LOS ANGELES	80-61	.567	½
Cincinnati	80-61	.567	½
Milwaukee	77-62	.554	2½
Pittsburgh	77-66	.538	4½
Philadelphia	71-68	.511	8½
St. Louis	70-71	.496	10½
Chicago	65-77	.458	16
Houston	60-81	.426	20½
New York	45-98	.315	36½

Tonight the Dodgers backed Koufax with the magnificent total of just one hit and one unearned run. But that was enough for Mr. Koufax. Sandy set down the visiting Chicago Cubs in order for nine straight innings. He pitched a no-hitter, better than that, a perfect game. It was only the fourth complete nine-inning perfect game in National League history. And Koufax became the first pitcher in major league history to pitch four no-hitters.

The Golden Arm was at its very best tonight. He threw 113 pitches, mixing his fastball and curve. Only two balls were hit hard against him, and one of those was foul. Only once did Koufax give a batter three balls. And he struck out fourteen batters, including the final six men he faced.

His pitching opponent, Bob Hendley, also hurled a great game. He gave up just one hit, an opposite-field blooper that fell in, and he walked only one. But the only error of the game followed the walk, and the Dodgers got a run to beat Hendley, 1-0.

Warming up before the game, Koufax did not have exceptional stuff. His fastball wasn't quite right, so he used mostly curves in the early going. Obviously, his curve was pretty effective.

His first pitch in the game bounced in front of the plate. Then leadoff man Dick Young popped out in his first major league at bat. Glenn Beckert came up and ripped a shot down the left field line, which hooked just foul. As it turned out, that was the closest the Cubs came to a hit all night. Beckert eventually struck out. Billy Williams was called out on strikes.

Ron Santo fouled to catcher Jeff Torborg to open the second. Ernie Banks fanned. Byron Browne, also making his major league debut, cracked a solid line drive to center, where Willie Davis was in position to catch it.

Chris Krug flied to Davis in the third. Don Kessinger flied to Ron Fairly in right. And Hendley looked at a called third strike.

In the fourth, Young fouled out to first. Beckert flied to right. And Williams was again called out on strikes.

Santo flied out to left to open the fifth. Banks struck out swinging. Brown grounded out, short to first.

For the Dodgers in the bottom of the fifth, Lou Johnson led off with a walk to become the first base runner of the game. Fairly sacrificed Johnson to second. The runner then took off trying to steal third. Catcher Krug's throw sailed into left field, and Johnson got up and scored the game's only run. Jim Lefebvre fanned, and Wes Parker grounded out.

Krug led off the sixth with a grounder to short, not a difficult chance. But Maury

Wills's throw was in the dirt, and it took a nice pickup by first baseman Parker to record the putout. Kessinger went out, third to first. And Hendley struck out again, this time swinging.

When the Dodgers went out in order in the bottom of the sixth, the fans not only started thinking about a perfect game, they started thinking about a double no-hitter.

Koufax had good command of his fastball by this time. And he had great rhythm. He baffled poor Mr. Young for a strikeout to open the seventh. Beckert flied out to right. Koufax started Williams off with two curves. They both missed low. Then a fastball was high. The court was 3-and-0, and the perfect game was in jeopardy. Going with smoke, Sandy blew two strikes past the hitter. On the next hummer, Williams lofted a routine fly to left, which was caught. That was the last fair ball the Cubs hit.

With two out in the Dodger seventh, Johnson was fooled on an off-speed pitch by Hendley. But he blooped it off the end of the bat, and it landed fair along the right field line for a double. Oh well, so much for the double no-hitter.

Now the fans could concentrate on the perfect game. A called third strike to Santo leading off the eighth brought much of the crowd to their feet. From here on in, every strike was cheered. Banks fanned for the third time. Browne also fanned.

Three outs to go. Ninth inning. Krug was overmatched and went down swinging. Joey Amalfitano, pinch-hitting, struck out on three pitches. One out to go. Harvey Kuenn, tobacco-chewing veteran and former batting champion, was the pinch-hitter. Now they were on their feet even in the dugout. Missing the corners a couple of times, Koufax got behind on the count, 2-and-1. The next pitch was a little low, but Kuenn fished for it and missed, strike two. Then another fastball, this one over the plate. A swing and a miss!

Before he could take more than a couple of steps off the mount, Koufax was surrounded by adoring teammates. He had done it: no-hitter #4 and a perfect game!

Chicago	ab	r	h	bi	o	a	e
D. Young, cf	3	0	0	0	5	0	0
G. Beckert, 2b	3	0	0	0	1	1	0
B. Williams, rf	3	0	0	0	0	0	0
R. Santo, 3b	3	0	0	0	1	2	0
E. Banks, 1b	3	0	0	0	13	0	0
B. Browne, lf	3	0	0	0	1	0	0
C. Krug, c	3	0	0	0	3	0	1
D. Kessinger, ss	2	0	0	0	0	2	0
J. Amalfitano, ph9	1	0	0	0	-	-	-
B. Hendley, p	2	0	0	0	0	5	0
H. Kuenn, ph9	1	0	0	0	-	-	-
	27	0	0	0	24	10	1

Los Angeles	ab	r	h	bi	o	a	e
M. Wills, ss	3	0	0	0	0	2	0
J. Gilliam, 3b	3	0	0	0	0	1	0
W. Davis, cf	3	0	0	0	2	0	0
L. Johnson, lf	2	1	1	0	2	0	0
R. Fairly, rf	2	0	0	0	3	0	0
J. Lefebvre, 2b	3	0	0	0	1	0	0
D. Tracewski, 2b9	0	0	0	0	0	0	0
W. Parker, 1b	3	0	0	0	4	0	0
J. Torborg, c	3	0	0	0	15	0	0
S. Koufax, p	2	0	0	0	0	0	0
	24	1	1	0	27	3	0

Chicago	000 000 000	=	0
Los Angeles	000 010 00x	=	1

	ip	h	r-er	bb	so
Hendley (L 2-3)	8	1	1-0	1	3
Koufax (W 22-7)	9	0	0-0	0	14

Game-Winning Run scored on throwing error
LOB: Chicago 0, Los Angeles 1
BE: none
2B: Johnson
SH: Fairly
SB: Johnson

Time—1:43
Attendance—29,139
Umpires: E. Vargo, C. Pelekoudas, B. Jackowski, & P. Pryor

Los Angeles lost three of its next five games to fall 4½ games behind San Francisco. But then the Dodgers ripped off 13 straight victories to regain first place.

In Chicago on September 14th, Hendley and the Cubs beat Koufax, 2-1.

1965 SATURDAY, OCTOBER 2ND, AT DODGER STADIUM

Win on 2 Hits to Clinch Flag

Walks & Errors Give Dodgers 3-1 Victory over Braves
Koufax Wins #26 on Four-Hitter

Today's Results			
LOS ANGELES 3-Milwaukee 1			
San Francisco 3-Cincinnati 2			
Pittsburgh 3-Chicago 0			
Philadelphia 6-New York 0 (1st game)			
New York 0-Philadelphia 0 (tie) (18 innings) (2nd game)			
St. Louis 6-Houston 3			
Standings	**W-L**	**Pct.**	**GB**
LOS ANGELES	96-65	.596	—
San Francisco	94-67	.584	2
Pittsburgh	89-72	.553	7
Cincinnati	89-72	.554	7
Milwaukee	86-75	.534	10
Philadelphia	83-76	.522	12
St. Louis	79-81	.494	16½
Chicago	72-89	.447	24
Houston	65-96	.404	31
New York	50-110	.313	45½

COMPLETING ONE OF THE HOTTEST stretch runs in history, the Los Angeles Dodgers today clinched the pennant that no one gave them much of a chance to win. By winning today, the Dodgers copped their 14th victory in 15 games. Just over two weeks before, Los Angeles had trailed San Francisco by 4½ games. Then the Dodgers won 13 in a row to grab a 2-game lead. Yesterday the Dodgers lost to snap the streak, but the Giants also lost, leaving Los Angeles 2 games in front with only two to play. The Dodgers won today to clinch the flag.

The Dodgers, who had been predicted to finish fourth, won the pennant on speed and pitching. Their hitting was anemic, especially after their leading batter (Tommy Davis) broke his ankle severely on May 1st. Lou Johnson, a 32-year-old minor league journeyman, took over for T. Davis in left field and carried the offense for the first few weeks he was with the club. Then Ron Rairly got hot. As the summer wore on, practically every man on the squad was a hero at one time or another.

During the 13-game winning streak, the Dodger pitching was absolutely incredible. Seven of the victories were shutouts, and in three others the opposition was held to just one run.

Today's victory was quintessential Dodgers. The heroes were the rookie second baseman, the third baseman who had begun the season as a coach, Johnson the major league reject, and the pitcher with an arthritic elbow. The rookie, Jim Lefebvre, got the only two hits the team made in the game. The ex-coach, Jim Gilliam, scored the first run on a walk, a stolen base and throwing error, and a wild pitch. Johnson set up the Dodgers' "big inning" (two runs on one hit and three walks) with some heady base running. And the arthritic pitcher, Sandy Koufax, held the powerful Milwaukee Braves to one run. The final score was 3-1.

Needing to win just one of the final two games, Dodger manager Walter Alston had decided to use Koufax today after two days of rest and was planning on doing the same with Don Drysdale tomorrow if the pennant had still been undecided. Today's victory meant that Drysdale would be well-rested for the opening game of the World Series on Wednesday.

Dandy Sandy scored his 26th win of the season against 8 defeats. His 14 strikeouts today raised his record-shattering total to 382. And it was his 27th complete game of the campaign, tops in the majors. Not bad for a southpaw whose future was in doubt during spring training because of arthritis and sinovitis in the left elbow.

Gilliam got the Dodgers a run in the first inning without the aid of a hit. He walked with one out. As Willie Davis was striking out, Gilliam stole second and continued to third on catcher Gene Oliver's wild throw. Braves' pitcher Tony Cloninger then wild-pitched Gilliam home.

Koufax set the Braves down in order in the first two innings and pitched around an infield hit and an error in the third. But Oliver led off the Milwaukee fourth with a line drive over the low fence in left field for a home run to tie the game.

The game remained tied until the bottom of the fifth. Then Johnson walked to start things for Los Angeles. Lefebvre lofted a foul pop near first base, which Joe Torre lost in the sun and allowed to drop. Reprieved, Lefebvre grounded sharply toward third. The ball eluded Mike de la Hoz and went into left field for a single, Johnson racing to third. Wes Parker hit a routine grounder to first base. Torre fielded it and threw home to head Johnson off. The runner was caught in a rundown. Catcher Oliver faked a toss to third before throwing to de la Hoz. The third baseman tagged Johnson on the back as the runner was diving into the base. Umpire Tony Venzon called him safe, much to the disbelief of the Braves.

Obviously upset, pitcher Cloninger walked Johnny Roseboro on five pitches to force Johnson home with the tie-breaking run. Cloninger also threw three straight balls to Koufax before being relieved. Ken Johnson came in and completed to pass, forcing home yet another run. The bases were still loaded with none out, but the Dodgers could not drive any more runs home.

Koufax, however, was able to protect the two-run lead. He yielded a walk in the seventh and a single in the eighth but retired the side each time. In the ninth, he started to tire noticeably, but a fine throw by catcher Roseboro bailed him out. De la Hoz led off with a solid single. Mack Jones struck out on a pitch in the dirt, and Roseboro gunned pinch-runner Ty Cline down trying to steal second. Still one out shy of victory, Koufax walked Woody Woodward. But he had just enough left to get Denis Menke to fly out to left.

The celebration started in the middle of the field and soon moved to the clubhouse. The Dodgers' scratching, clawing, Katey-bar-the-door style had won yet another game. And this one had clinched the pennant. And these athletes were as proud as any group you could wish to find.

Milwaukee	ab	r	h	bi	o	a	e
F. Alou, lf	2	0	0	0	1	0	0
F. Thomas, lf4	1	0	0	0	2	0	0
H. Aaron, rf	4	0	0	0	1	0	0
G. Oliver, c	4	1	2	1	9	0	1
J. Torre, 1b	4	0	0	0	7	1	0
M. de la Hoz, 3b	4	0	1	0	1	2	0
T. Cline, pr9	0	0	0	0	-	-	-
M. Jones, cf	3	0	0	0	1	0	0
W. Woodward, ss-2b7	3	0	1	0	0	1	0
S. Alomar, 2b	2	0	0	0	0	2	0
D. Menke, ph7-ss	1	0	0	0	0	0	0
T. Cloninger, p	1	0	0	0	1	1	0
K. Johnson, p5	0	0	0	0	1	0	0
F. Bolling, ph7	1	0	0	0	-	-	-
C. Olivo, p7	0	0	0	0	0	0	0
	30	1	4	1	24	7	1

Los Angeles	ab	r	h	bi	o	a	e
M. Wills, ss	4	0	0	0	3	4	0
J. Gilliam, 3b	3	1	0	0	2	0	1
J. Kennedy, 3b8	0	0	0	0	0	0	0
W. Davis, cf	4	0	0	0	1	0	0
R. Fairly, rf	4	0	0	0	0	0	0
L. Johnson, lf	3	1	0	0	1	0	0
J. Lefebvre, 2b	3	1	2	0	0	0	0
W. Parker, 1b	3	0	0	0	7	0	0
J. Roseboro, c	1	0	0	1	13	1	0
S. Koufax, p	2	0	0	1	0	3	0
	27	3	2	2	27	8	1

Milwaukee	000 100 000	= 1
Los Angeles	100 020 00x	= 3

	ip	h	r-er	bb	so
Cloninger (L 24-11)	*4	1	3-2	4	3
K. Johnson	2	1	0-0	0	1
Olivo	2	0	0-0	1	3
Koufax (W 26-8)	9	4	1-1	4	13

*faced five batters in fifth

WP: Cloninger, Olivo

Umpires: T. Forman, D. Harvey, S. Crawford, & T. Venzon

Game-Winning RBI: Roseboro
LOB: Milwaukee 7, Los Angeles 5
BE: Milwaukee 1, Los Angeles 0
DP: Roseboro-Wills
HR: Oliver
SH: Cloninger
SB: Gilliam
CS: Cline
Time—2:42
Attendance—41,574

The Dodgers won the final game of the season, 3-0, with six pitchers combining for the shutout.

1965 AT METROPOLITAN STADIUM, BLOOMINGTON, MINNESOTA
World Series—Game #7 THURSDAY, OCTOBER 14TH

Sandy's 3-Hitter Nails Down the Series

LOS ANGELES DODGER MANAGER WALTER ALSTON HAD A PROBLEM TO SOLVE LAST night, the kind of problem every manager wishes for. He had to pick a starting pitcher for the seventh game of the World Series. And he had to choose between Don Drysdale (23-12 on the season and 1-1 in the series) and Sandy Koufax (26-8 & 1-1). Drysdale had three days of rest, while Koufax only had two. But Koufax had shown he could pitch well on short rest in the pennant clincher against Milwaukee.

Alston announced this morning that he had decided to go with Koufax. There was sound logic behind the choice. For one thing, he could always bring Drysdale in early if Koufax faltered. That might get the rival Minnesota Twins to replace some of their righthanded hitters with lefties. Then if Alston had to go with his relief ace, southpaw Ron Perranoski, Minnesota would be short of pinch-hitters. Furthermore, with lefthander Jim Kaat starting for the Twins and Drysdale being the top right-handed pinch-hitter for Los Angeles, Alston could send Don up to hit for Sandy if the situation called for it and leave him in the game to pitch.

Koufax did not have his good curve today, and Drysdale was warming up before the first inning was over. But Koufax's fastball was explosive enough to give him a three-hit shutout, which Drysdale could sit back and enjoy watching.

The Dodgers managed just two runs off of Kaat and four relievers, but that was plenty. The first run came on a home run by Lou Johnson, an old American League reject whom the Dodgers had resurrected from the minors in May. On defense, the Dodgers backed Koufax very well. Jim Gilliam saved one or more runs with a great play in the fifth inning, killing the Twins' biggest threat. So the Dodgers won 2-0 to capture their third world championship in seven years.

Minnesota had surprised the baseball world by beating Drysdale and Koufax in the first two games of the classic, 8-2 and 5-1, respectively. But the Dodgers had bounced back to win the next three games, 4-0, 7-2, and 7-0 on complete games by Claude Osteen, Drysdale, and Koufax, respectively. The Twins won Game #6, 5-1, to set up the decisive seventh game today.

The tension of the game was felt all over the park. The Twins did very little in the way of threatening to score, and the Minnesota fans were extremely quiet most of the afternoon.

The Dodgers were robbed of a run in the top of the first by a tumbling catch in right field by Tony Oliva.

Koufax had trouble with his control in the bottom of the first. He walked Oliva and Harmon Killebrew with two out. Drysdale hurriedly started to warm up. But Koufax broke a curveball over for a third strike on Earl Battey to retire the side. It was about the only good curve Sandy threw all afternoon.

The Dodgers failed to capitalize on a chance in the third. Johnny Roseboro led off with a double into the right field corner. Kaat walked Koufax. The runners moved up on Maury Wills's ground out. Gilliam lined out to right. Respecting Oliva's arm, Roseboro held third, even though the throw home bounced past the catcher. Kaat backed the play up and saved a run. Willie Davis then fouled out.

A rare ruling by the umpires held the Twins back in their third. Zoilo Versalles singled with one out and apparently stole second. But umpire Ed Hurley sent him back to first and called batter Joe Nossek out for interfering with the catcher's throw. Oliva struck out to end the inning.

Leading off the Los Angeles fourth, Johnson hit a waist-high fastball deep down the left field line. The ball was twisting, but it struck the foul pole for a home run. The happy Johnson clapped his hands as he rounded the bases, while the Minnesota fans looked on in stony silence. Ron Fairly ripped a hanging curve into the right field corner for a double. Wes Parker bounced a hit over the first baseman's head, driving Fairly home and knocking Kaat out of the game. Al Worthington came in to pitch, and he checked the Dodgers through the fifth.

Johnny Klippstein, Jim Merritt, and Jim Perry held Los Angeles scoreless the rest of the way.

Minnesota made its bid in the fifth inning. With one out, Frank Quilici lined a double off the left field screen. Rich Rollins worked Koufax for a walk. On a 1-and-2 pitch, Versalles pulled a shot down the third base line. Gilliam was playing toward the bag. He went to his knees, made a backhand grab, and scrambled to third base for a force out. It was the play of the series for Los Angeles, and it turned a potential two-run double into an out. Nossek followed by hitting into a force out to end the inning.

Having pretty much scrapped his curve, Koufax got into his groove with the fastball. He retired the Twins in order in the sixth, seventh, and eighth. With one out in the ninth, Killebrew gave Minnesota a ray of hope by lining a low fastball into left for a hit. Turning up the heat, Koufax fanned Battey and Bob Allison to close out the game.

The Dodgers were world champions! The team with the joke offense, an American League reject batting cleanup, and four switch-hitting infielders had won it all. With a lot of teamwork and a couple of pitchers like Koufax and Drysdale, it's amazing what obstacles could be overcome and what heights could be reached.

Los Angeles (NL)	ab	r	h	bi	o	a	e
M. Wills, ss	4	0	0	0	2	4	0
J. Gilliam, 3b	5	0	2	0	2	1	0
J. Kennedy, 3b9	0	0	0	0	0	1	0
W. Davis, cf	2	0	0	0	1	0	0
L. Johnson, lf	4	1	1	1	3	0	0
R. Fairly, rf	4	1	1	0	0	0	0
W. Parker, 1b	4	0	2	1	6	0	0
D. Tracewski, 2b	4	0	0	0	1	0	0
J. Roseboro, c	2	0	1	0	12	0	0
S. Koufax, p	3	0	0	0	0	1	0
	32	2	7	2	27	7	0

Minnesota (AL)	ab	r	h	bi	o	a	e
Z. Versalles, ss	4	0	1	0	0	2	0
J. Nossek, cf	4	0	0	0	0	0	0
T. Oliva, rf	3	0	0	0	4	0	1
H. Killebrew, 3b	3	0	1	0	2	2	0
E. Battey, c	4	0	0	0	8	1	0
B. Allison, lf	4	0	0	0	1	0	0
D. Mincher, 1b	3	0	0	0	10	0	0
F. Quilici, 2b	3	0	1	0	1	3	0
J. Kaat, p	1	0	0	0	0	1	0
A. Worthington, p4	0	0	0	0	1	1	0
R. Rollins, ph5	0	0	0	0	-	-	-
J. Klippstein, p6	0	0	0	0	0	0	0
J. Merritt, p7	0	0	0	0	0	0	0
S. Valdespino, ph8	1	0	0	0	-	-	-
J. Perry, p9	0	0	0	0	0	0	0
	30	0	3	0	27	10	1

Los Angeles	000 200 000	= 2
Minnesota	000 000 000	= 0

	ip	h	r-er	bb	so
Koufax (W 2-1)	9	3	0-0	3	10
Kaat (L 1-2)	*3	5	2-2	1	2
Worthington	2	0	0-0	1	0
Klippstein	1⅔	2	0-0	1	2
Merritt	1⅓	0	0-0	0	1
Perry	1	0	0-0	1	1

*faced three batters in fourth

Game-Winning RBI: Johnson
LOB: Los Angeles 9, Minnesota 6
BE: none
2B: Roseboro, Fairly, Quilici
3B: Parker
HR: Johnson
SH: Davis
CS: Wills
HBP: by Klippstein (Davis)
Time—2:27
Attendance—50,596

Umpires: E. Hurley, T. Venzon, R. Flaherty, E. Sudol, B. Stewart, & E. Vargo

1966 SUNDAY, OCTOBER 2ND, AT CONNIE MACK STADIUM, PHILADELPHIA

Koufax Wins Last Game to Save Pennant

Pitches Clincher in Final Game of Season
Dodgers Win Nightcap, 6-3, after Blowing Opener, 4-3

Today's Results			
Philadelphia 4-LOS ANGELES 3 (1st game)			
LOS ANGELES 6-Philadelphia 3 (2nd game)			
San Francisco 7-Pittsburgh 3 (11 innings)			
Atlanta 4-Cincinnati 2			
St. Louis 2-Chicago 0			
Houston 6-New York 1 (1st game)			
Houston 8-New York 2 (2nd game)			
Standings	**W-L**	**Pct.**	**GB**
LOS ANGELES	95-67	.586	—
San Francisco	93-68	.578	1½
Pittsburgh	92-70	.568	3
Philadelphia	87-75	.537	8
Atlanta	85-77	.525	10
St. Louis	83-79	.512	12
Cincinnati	76-84	.475	18
Houston	72-90	.444	23
New York	66-95	.410	28½
Chicago	59-103	.364	36

DESPITE THE DETERMINED OPPOSITION of the Philadelphia Phillies, the Los Angeles Dodgers were able to clinch the pennant today and avoid a possible playoff with the San Francisco Giants. Needing just one victory in today's season-ending doubleheader, the Dodgers blew a lead in the eighth inning of the first game and lost, 4-3. So pitching star Sandy Koufax was called upon to hurl the second game. Although he had only two days of rest, Koufax shut the Phillies out for eight innings and held on to win, 6-3, to nail down the flag.

The Los Angeles team came to Philadelphia for the final three games of the season leading Pittsburgh by 2 games and San Francisco by 3½. The Pirates and Giants were scheduled for three games in Pittsburgh. If the Giants had won three games, and the Dodgers had lost three, San Francisco would have had to win a make-up game in Cincinnati on Monday to force a playoff.

On Friday night, the fourth-place Phillies rose up and beat the Dodgers, 5-3. The game in Pittsburgh was rained out.

On Saturday the rains came to Philadelphia, causing a postponement. In Pittsburgh, the Giants won a doubleheader to eliminate the Pirates and clinch a tie for the Dodgers.

Don Drysdale was sent to the mound to try for the clincher in today's first game. Big D had pitched shutouts in his last two starts. But he did not have his best stuff today and lasted only two-plus innings. The Phillies got two runs in the first off of him on a home run by Johnny Briggs, a walk, and two singles. A line drive that was caught and turned into a double play prevented more scoring.

Relievers Ron Perranoski and Bob Miller kept the score at 2-0 until the Dodgers leaped into the lead in the sixth on a three-run homer by Ron Fairly.

Miller was still on the mound in the bottom of the eighth. He made one of three misplays that handed the Phillies two runs and the game. Richie Allen's leadoff grounder took a bad hop and eluded second baseman Jim Lefebvre. Bill White bunted, and Miller threw the ball into center field trying for a force at second. Phil Regan replaced Miller and intentionally walked Dick Groat to load the bases. Cookie Rojas hit a grounder to Dick Schofield at third. Schofield threw wide to the plate, and Allen was safe with the tying run. Clay Dalrymple blooped a hit to center, and the Phillies had the lead.

Chris Short shut the Dodgers out in the ninth, and the Phillies won.

With the Giants and Pirates tied in the ninth inning, manager Walter Alston had no choice but to use Koufax in the second game. Playing it tough all the way, Phillie pilot Gene Mauch chose 19-game winner Jim Bunning.

Hits by Jackie Brandt and Groat around a sacrifice put Phillies on first and third with one out in the first inning. But Koufax struck Allen out and got Harvey Kuenn on a grounder to third.

The Dodgers broke through with three runs in the third. Wes Parker walked and stole second. Two outs later, Schofield (who had been acquired from the Yankees on September 10th) singled up the middle to bring Parker home. Willie Davis followed by hitting the next pitch over the right field wall for a two-run home run.

Los Angeles added another tally in the fourth. Lefebvre opened with a double to right center. Lou Johnson beat out a bunt single. Johnny Roseboro delivered the run with a sacrifice fly to center.

A double by Fairly and two errors gave the visitors another run in the eighth.

A walk to Maury Wills and hits by Schofield and Fairly made the score 6-0 in the top of the ninth.

In the meantime, Koufax had been shutting the Phils out on four hits. His only real problem was not the hitters but his own back. He had hurt it somehow in the fifth inning. But trainer Bill Buhler had worked on him between innings with some hot linament, and Koufax stayed in the game.

In the bottom of the ninth, the Golden Arm almost ran out of juice. Allen led off and reached first when Lefebvre fumbled his smash. Kuenn singled. Tony Taylor knocked Allen home with a hit to center. White then drove home two runs with a double off the scoreboard in right. Suddenly the score was 6-3, and still no one was out.

But Koufax reached back and struck Bob Uecker out. Bobby Wine grounded sharply to shortstop, but Wills made the play to first for the out. And Brandt fanned on a fastball to end the game.

The Dodgers, who had agonized through the weekend, finally let loose. Their clubhouse was the scene of one of the wildest celebrations in memory. Pinch-hitter Wes Covington led the way by dousing everyone with champagne and shaving cream. It hadn't been easy, but the Dodgers had won the pennant again.

FIRST GAME

			r	h	e	
Los Angeles	000 003 000	=	3	5	3	Game-Winning RBI: Dalrymple
Philadelphia	200 000 02x	=	4	8	0	

Batteries: D. Drysdale 2 IP, R. Perranoski 2 IP, B. Miller (L 4-2) 3 IP, P. Regan, & J. Roseboro
L. Jackson 6⅔ IP, D. Knowles ⅓ IP, C. Short (W 20-10) 2 IP & C. Dalrymple

SECOND GAME

Los Angeles	ab	r	h	bi	o	a	e
M. Wills, ss	4	1	0	0	1	5	1
D. Schofield, 3b	5	1	2	1	1	2	0
W. Davis, cf	5	1	1	2	1	0	0
R. Fairly, rf	5	1	3	1	3	0	0
J. Lefebvre, 2b	3	1	1	0	3	1	1
L. Johnson, lf	4	0	2	0	1	0	0
J. Roseboro, c	3	0	0	1	9	1	0
W. Parker, 1b	1	1	0	0	8	0	0
S. Koufax, p	4	0	0	0	0	1	0
	34	6	9	5	27	10	2

Philadelphia	ab	r	h	bi	o	a	e
J. Brandt, cf	5	0	1	0	4	0	0
C. Rojas, rf	3	0	0	0	0	1	0
D. Groat, ss	4	0	1	0	2	5	0
R. Allen, 3b	4	1	0	0	1	0	1
H. Kuenn, lf	4	1	1	0	2	0	0
T. Taylor, 2b	4	1	2	1	2	2	1
B. White, 1b	4	0	2	2	8	0	0
B. Uecker, c	4	0	0	0	8	0	1
J. Bunning, p	1	0	0	0	0	1	0
G. Sutherland, ph5	1	0	0	0	-	-	-
R. Wise, p6	0	0	0	0	0	0	0
J. Briggs, ph8	0	0	0	0	-	-	-
D. Knowles, p9	0	0	0	0	0	0	0
B. Wine, ph9	1	0	0	0	-	-	-
	35	3	7	3	27	9	3

Los Angeles	003 100 011	=	6
Philadelphia	000 000 003	=	3

	ip	h	r-er	bb	so
Koufax (W 27-9)	9	7	3-2	1	10
Bunning (L 19-14)	5	5	4-4	2	4
Wise	3	2	1-0	1	2
Knowles	1	2	1-1	1	1

Game-Winning RBI: Schofield
LOB: Los Angeles 7, Philadelphia 7
BE: Los Angeles 2, Philadelphia 2
DP: Groat-White
2B: Lefebvre, White 2, Fairly
HR: Davis
SF: Roseboro
SH: Rojas, Lefebvre
SB: Parker, Johnson 2

Time—2:34 Attendance—23,215
Umpires: D. Harvey, H. Wendelstedt, S. Crawford, & E. Vargo

1966 SUNDAY, OCTOBER 9TH, AT MEMORIAL STADIUM, BALTIMORE World Series—Game #4

Dodgers Shut Out in World Series

IF THE DEFENDING WORLD CHAMPION LOS ANGELES DODGERS HAD A PROBLEM THIS season, everyone conceded, it was a weak offense. But they made up for it with great pitching. The American League champion Baltimore Orioles, on the other hand, had great fielding and a high-powered offense. But their pitching was young and unreliable. Since the accepted maxim stated that, "In a short series, pitching will win," the oddsmakers made the Dodgers 8-5 favorites in this year's World Series.

How wrong the forecasters turned out to be! Although the Dodger staff pitched credibly in the series, the Oriole hurlers shut the opposition down better than any team had ever done in the World Series before. The hapless Los Angeles batters had a team average of just .142 and scored only two runs in four games. They were shut out in the final three games and 33 innings as Baltimore swept in four straight.

The series started with the Orioles grabbing the lead in the top of the first inning of the first game on back-to-back homers by Frank Robinson and Brooks Robinson. Dodger starter Don Drysdale yielded another run in the top of the second. Jim Lefebvre hit a homer for Los Angeles in the bottom of the second. And control troubles drove Oriole starter Dave McNally out of the box in the bottom of the third. Moe Drabowsky relieved and forced a run home with the fourth walk of the inning before retiring the side. After the Orioles upped their lead to 5-2 in the top of the fourth, Drabowsky came back and struck out the side in both the fourth and fifth. He finished with 11 strikeouts in 6⅔ innings of one-hit relief. The Dodgers got only three hits total and lost, 5-2.

That poor showing turned out to be the Dodgers' best in the series. Twenty-year-old Jim Palmer stopped them on four hits in the second game, 6-0. It was Palmer's first complete-game shutout in the major leagues. The Dodgers made six errors, including three by Willie Davis in one inning. Sandy Koufax was the losing pitcher.

In the third game, 21-year-old Wally Bunker took the hill for Baltimore. He allowed six hits, the most the Dodgers got in any game. His pitching opponent, Claude Osteen, allowed only three. But one of the Oriole hits was a tremendous home run by Paul Blair. That was the only run of the game, and the Orioles won, 1-0.

So today's game gave Baltimore a chance to complete a sweep of the series. The pitchers were McNally and Drysdale. Both of them had been ineffective in the first game but were brilliant today. Each man gave up only four hits, and McNally walked two, while Drysdale passed only one. Big Don completed the game in only 78 pitches. But one of those was blasted deep into the seats by Frank Robinson for the game's only run. The Orioles wound up with their second consecutive 1-0 victory, their third straight shutout, and a four-game sweep of the world championship.

Neither side got a man to first in the first inning.

In the second, Lefebvre worked McNally for a walk with one out. He was forced at second, and Johnny Roseboro flied out. For Baltimore, two men got on, one on a hit and one on a walk. But Dave Johnson bounced into a double play.

Both sides went out in order in the third.

In the fourth, Lou Johnson singled for Los Angeles with one gone. Tommy Davis quickly ended the inning by grounding into a twin-killing.

With one down in the bottom of the fourth, Drysdale got a fastball a little too high to F. Robinson. The American League Triple Crown winner knocked it well over the left field fence for a home run. One out later, Boog Powell hit a drive just over the wall in straightaway center. But Willie Davis made a tremendous leaping catch to bring the ball back into the park and rob Powell of a homer.

Trailing 1-0, Los Angeles got a leadoff single from Lefebvre in the fifth. Wes Parker then grounded one toward the hole in the left side. But third baseman Brooks Robinson ranged far to his left, speared the ball, and started a double play. Roseboro looked at a called third strike.

John Kennedy led off the Dodger sixth with a hit on a hanging curve. With a full count on Drysdale, Kennedy broke for second. Drysdale fanned on the pitch, and Kennedy was thrown out at second for the third Baltimore double play in as many innings.

McNally got through the seventh and eighth in order. But the first batter in the eighth, Lefebvre, nearly tied the game with a long drive to center field. Blair, who had just gone into the game as a defensive replacement, however, made a leaping catch at the fence to save a possible home run.

The Dodgers made their biggest threat in the ninth. Dick Stuart was called out on strikes to open. Al Ferrara lined a pinch single to center. Maury Wills went up trying to knock the ball out of the park but walked, instead. W. Davis then cracked a hard liner to right, but F. Robinson was positioned perfectly and made the catch. Pitching coach Harry Brecheen went to the mound to talk to McNally, advising him to throw curveballs to Lou Johnson, the next hitter. Lou swung and missed the first two breaking pitches. Then he lofted a soft fly to center for the final out.

The Dodgers were dead, done in by 33 innings without a run. Their reign as champions was over with barely a whimper.

Los Angeles (NL)	ab	r	h	bi	o	a	e
M. Wills, ss	3	0	0	0	2	3	0
W. Davis, cf	4	0	0	0	1	0	0
L. Johnson, rf	4	0	1	0	4	0	0
T. Davis, lf	3	0	0	0	2	0	0
J. Lefebvre, 2b	2	0	1	0	1	1	0
W. Parker, 1b	3	0	0	0	7	0	0
J. Roseboro, c	3	0	0	0	7	1	0
J. Kennedy, 3b	2	0	1	0	0	1	0
D. Stuart, ph9	1	0	0	0	-	-	-
D. Drysdale, p	2	0	0	0	0	2	0
A. Ferrara, ph9	1	0	1	0	-	-	-
N. Oliver, pr9	0	0	0	0	-	-	-
	28	0	4	0	24	8	0

Baltimore (AL)	ab	r	h	bi	o	a	e
L. Aparicio, ss	3	0	1	0	0	3	0
R. Snyder, cf-lf8	3	0	0	0	0	0	0
F. Robinson, rf	3	1	1	1	3	0	0
B. Robinson, 3b	3	0	1	0	0	3	0
B. Powell, 1b	3	0	1	0	7	0	0
C. Blefary, lf	2	0	0	0	1	0	0
P. Blair, cf8	0	0	0	0	2	0	0
D. Johnson, 2b	3	0	0	0	7	3	0
A. Etchebarren, c	3	0	0	0	7	1	0
D. McNally, p	3	0	0	0	0	0	0
	26	1	4	1	27	10	0

Los Angeles	000	000	000	=	0
Baltimore	000	100	00x	=	1

	ip	h	r-er	bb	so
Drysdale (L 0-2)	8	4	1-1	1	5
McNally (W 1-0)	9	4	0-0	2	4

Time—1:45
Attendance—54,458

Game-Winning RBI: F. Robinson
LOB: Los Angeles 3, Baltimore 2
DP: Lefebvre-Wills-Parker (D. Johnson)
Aparicio-D. Johnson-Powell (T. Davis)
B. Robinson-D. Johnson-Powell (Parker)
Etchebarren-D. Johnson
HR: F. Robinson
CS: Kennedy, Aparicio

Umpires: J. Rice, M. Steiner, C. Drummond, B. Jackowski, N. Chylak, & C. Pelekoudas

Chapter XV The Wilderness Years

1967 September 15th
1-0 Wins for Singer and Drysdale

1968 June 4th
Six Shutouts in a Row for Drysdale

1969 September 3rd
Willie Davis's Hitting Streak Up to 31 Games

1970 July 22nd
Grand Slam by Pinch-Hitter Haller

1971 September 14th
Manny Mota's Biggest Pinch Hit

1972 September 30th
Osteen Bats His Way to Win #19

AFTER THE 1966 WORLD SERIES, THE DODGERS WENT ON A TOUR OF JAPAN. EVEN before the excursion started, there were rumors of discontent among the players. Halfway through the trip, the rumors were confirmed when captain Maury Wills "jumped ship" and came back to the United States. Wills was soon traded to Pittsburgh for shortstop Gene Michael and third baseman Bob Bailey.

The Dodgers were also weakened by a couple of retirements. Jim Gilliam, who had retired each of the previous two winters only to be called back to active service during the following seasons, retired for good this time. And superstar pitcher Sandy Koufax also called it quits. Although he had won 101 games in the previous four seasons (including World Series), Sandy's arthritic elbow forced him to retire at age 30.

Everyone knew that the changes had seriously weakened the team. In one pre-season poll of 255 sportswriters, the defending champions were picked to finish seventh in the ten-team league in 1967. As it turned out, they did worse than that. Los Angeles ran eighth from June 17th to the end of the season.

Veteran reliever Bob Miller was given the honor of starting on opening day. He lasted four innings and lost. Claude Osteen, Don Sutton, and Don Drysdale lost the next three games, and Los Angeles never did get as high as .500. Lou Johnson, one of the heroes of the 1965 & '66 championships, broke his ankle sliding into home plate on April 27th and was out of the lineup until June 11th. Newly-acquired Ron Hunt played well at second base for the first half of the season, but accumulated injuries slowed him down to a crawl in the second half. Gene Michael and Dick Schofield tried in vain to fill Wills's shoes at shortstop, hitting a combined .209. The Dodgers' offense, which had been weak enough the previous seasons, fell to ninth in the league in runs and tenth in batting average and homers in 1967. The fielding was not much better.

And the pitching even slumped, although that was partly due to poor support. Osteen was the top winner at 17-17. Drysdale duplicated his 1966 record of 13-16, although he lowered his ERA from 3.42 to 2.74. In his 16 defeats, the Dodgers scored a total of only 15 runs! Don Sutton was a disappointing 11-15. One bright note was the emergence of rookie righthander Bill Singer, who was 12-8. The Dodgers won only one doubleheader all season, and to do it Drysdale and Singer both had to pitch 1-0 shutouts.

The poor showing on the field caused attendance at Dodger Stadium to plummet from 2,617,026 to 1,664,362 in 1967.

For 1968, general manager Emil "Buzzie" Bavasi committed the team to a major house-cleaning. The biggest trade in the winter sent Bob Miller, relief star Ron

Don Drysdale working on his sixth consecutive shutout, June 4, 1968

Perranoski, and catcher Johnny Roseboro to Minnesota for shortstop Zoilo Versalles and pitcher Jim "Mudcat" Grant. Lou Johnson went to the Cubs for infielder Paul Popovich. Ron Hunt was traded to the Giants for catcher Tom Haller. Popovich and Haller played good ball for Los Angeles, but Versalles and Grant were disappointing.

The season was only in its second game when the left-fielder jinx struck for the third time in four years. Al Ferrara, who had been given Johnson's job, shattered his ankle trying for a shoestring catch and was out virtually all season. Jim Lefebvre was hit on the wrist by a pitch in late April and missed 51 games.

Still, the spectacular pitching of Don Drysdale provided something to cheer about in the early going. Starting with 1-0 victories over the Cubs and Astros, he ran up a streak of six consecutive shutouts from May 14th through June 4th, shattering the ancient major league record. On June 8th, he broke the consecutive-scoreless-innings-pitched record before finally being scored upon. The victory that day put the Dodgers into second place. By the time June ended, St. Louis's Bob Gibson had a streak of five shutouts himself and was scheduled to pitch against Drysdale in Los Angeles on July 1st. Before a packed house, the Dodgers scored a run in the first inning on two hits and a wild pitch to preserve Drysdale's hold on the record. But St. Louis won that game and swept the four-game series to drop Los Angeles to sixth place, 11 games behind.

July turned out to be a disastrous month. The Dodgers won only 7 games while losing 20. Late in the month, Drysdale hurt his shoulder making a diving tag at third base. Although he stuck around for another year, the injury more or less ended Big D's career.

On August 18th, the Dodgers fell to last place. But a ray of hope for the future burst through in September. Sparked by the play of rookie Bill Sudakis and the emergence of Willie Crawford, Los Angeles was 18-9 in the final month to move up to a tie for seventh in the final standings. However, it was too late to keep home attendance from falling to its lowest level since the club moved to Los Angeles.

In 1969, the National League expanded to 12 clubs and split into two six-team divisions. The biggest loss for the Dodgers was the move of general manager Buzzie Bavasi to the new San Diego Padres to become president of that club.

The young Dodger team, dubbed the "Mod Squad," quickly established itself as a contender in the West Division race. Infield rookie Ted Sizemore, newcomer Andy Kosco, and veteran Wes Parker paced the team in the early going. Maury Wills and Manny Mota were acquired in a June trade with the new Montreal Expos, and they both helped greatly.

Parker underwent an emergency appendectomy in late July, and Willie Davis was hospitalized three times during the year after being hit by pitched balls. But the team stayed in the thick of a very exciting pennant race. Davis got hot in August and ran up a 31-game hitting streak, the longest in Dodger history. The Dodgers were only ½ game out of first place as late as September 18th. Then they collapsed, losing eight in a row, and finished fourth, 8 games out. Still, that was a tremendous improvement over 1968.

In March, 1970, Peter O'Malley succeeded his father as club president. Walter remained board chairman until his death on August 9, 1979.

In 1970, the team had a great record in spring training. But they were beaten in their first five regular-season encounters with the powerful Cincinnati Reds and never got within striking distance of "The Big Red Machine." Hepatitis sidelined pitchers Pete Mikkelsen and Bill Singer in the early weeks. Singer, a 20-game winner in 1969, came back to pitch a no-hitter on July 20th. Less than four weeks later, however, he suffered a broken finger and was through for the season. Ted Sizemore was bothered by recurring leg troubles, but he managed to hit .306.

The infield was never set, with manager Walt Alston juggling Sizemore, Bill Grabarkewitz, Jim Lefebvre, Bill Sudakis, and rookie Steve Garvey between third, second, and short. And the pitching was not deep enough to sustain a long winning streak that would have been needed to catch Cincinnati. But the hitting was surprisingly strong. Wes Parker had a super season, and Willie Davis and Manny Mota both hit over .300. First-year man Grabarkewitz also swung a hot stick. Still, the Dodgers were only a distant second to the Reds most of the year and finished 14½ games behind.

Over the winter of 1970-71, player personnel chief Al Campanis made three notable trades. The biggest one sent Ted Sizemore to St. Louis for slugger Richie Allen. Pitchers Alan Foster and Ray Lamb went to Cleveland for catcher Duke Sims. And outfielder Andy Kosco was shipped to Milwaukee for lefthanded pitcher Al Downing.

Although favored to win the division, Los Angeles got off to a slow start and trailed the high-flying Giants by 11 games on May 26, 1971. But Downing and Claude Osteen were pitching well, and there were still plenty of good rookies coming out of the farm system to fuel a rise in the standings. By winning games in San Francisco on July 5th and 6th, the Dodgers cut their deficit to just 3½ games. But then they lost four in a row to the Cubs and two out of three to the Giants in Los Angeles to fall to 6 games back by the All-Star Game. By August 1st, they were 9 games behind, and they still trailed by 8 on Labor Day weekend.

Then veterans Allen, Sims, and Wills helped the Dodgers rip off eight straight victories, starting with three at home against the Giants and finishing with a pair of nerve-tinglers in San Francisco. The streak suddenly put Los Angeles only 1 game behind. But then the pendulum swung back again. The lowly Padres came to L.A. and took a pair, followed by two more losses to the Braves. The Dodgers never did quite catch the Giants, although they were only 1 game behind for the final five days of the race. The second-place finish was a disappointment, but the close race pushed attendance over the 2,000,000 mark.

Campanis swung a couple more deals over the winter. In the most significant one, Allen was sent to the White Sox with pitcher Tommy John coming in return. Frank Robinson was acquired from Baltimore in a big trade.

The Dodgers started the 1972 season with an 11-4 record in April. Don Sutton finally blossomed into a star, winning all four starts in the first month. Good hitting and pitching kept the Dodgers in first place as late as June 8th.

But then inadequacies in the infield defense hit hard. At shortstop, Maury Wills could no longer hit well enough to stay in the lineup. Outfielder Bill Russell, who had been with the team since 1969, was put at short. Although he showed some brilliance, he was erratic in the field. At second base, Grabarkewitz hurt his shoulder, and Lefebvre did not hit. Lee Lacy was brought up from the minors and did very well until injured in September by a hard slide. Young Davey Lopes, another converted outfielder, finished the season as the Los Angeles second baseman. Third base was a disaster, with the combined fielding average there being an embarrassing .900. Steve Garvey played only 85 games at third yet led the league in errors with 28. Finally, Ron Cey was called up in September, and he looked good in a brief trial at third.

Catching was also a problem, and the offense tailed off. But strong pitching kept the team in the first division. Sutton finished 19-9, John was 11-5, and Jim Brewer starred in relief. Claude Osteen became a 20-game winner by hurling five complete-game victories in the final four weeks. He also batted .273 with 11 RBIs. Only Bill Singer (6-16) was a big disappointment.

Singer, Robinson, Grabarkewitz, and others were traded down the freeway to the Angels in November for pitcher Andy Messersmith and third baseman Ken McMullen. Maury Wills was released. Jim Lefebvre went to play in Japan. And Wes Parker retired (although he later also played in Japan). The Dodgers were committed to youth, and it was now a matter of finding the proper combination, especially in the infield.

Tom Haller after hitting his pinch grand slam, July 22, 1970

1967 FRIDAY NIGHT, SEPTEMBER 15TH, AT CONNIE MACK STADIUM, PHILADELPHIA

1-0 Wins for Singer and Drysdale

Wind Aids Both Gems
Phillies Claim They Saw Spitballs

AIDED BY THE BLUSTERING ELEMENTS and allegedly by foreign substances, the Los Angeles Dodgers tonight parleyed two runs into two victories over the Philadelphia Phillies, 1-0 and 1-0. Dodger righthanders Bill Singer and Don Drysdale pitched the shutouts.

Today's Results			
LOS ANGELES 1-Philadelphia 0 (1st game)			
LOS ANGELES 1-Philadelphia 0 (2nd game)			
St. Louis 4-Cincinnati 0			
San Francisco 6-Pittsburgh 3			
Chicago 7-Atlanta 1			
no other game scheduled			
Standings	**W-L**	**Pct.**	**GB**
St. Louis	92-56	.622	—
San Francisco	81-66	.551	10½
Cincinnati	80-68	.541	12
Chicago	80-70	.533	13
Philadelphia	75-71	.514	16
Atlanta	74-73	.503	17½
Pittsburgh	73-75	.493	19
LOS ANGELES	68-79	.463	23½
Houston	59-88	.401	32½
New York	55-91	.377	36

The wind was howling through old Connie Mack Stadium because of a hurricane passing along the Eastern Seaboard. And the losing Phillies claimed they could see precipitation flying off the pitches thrown to the plate by both Singer and Drysdale. A couple of the balls that the Phils hit well were kept in the park by the wind whipping in from left field. And one of the two Dodger runs came on a wind-aided home run over the right field fence.

That homer by Johnny Roseboro provided Singer with his only run. But these days, Dodger pitchers had better be prepared to win with only one run because the team's offense was so weak. With Maury Wills and Tommy Davis traded away, the meager attack of 1965 and 1966 had dwindled down to next to nothing. And with pitching ace Sandy Koufax retired, the team as a whole had declined from champions to eighth place.

Rookie fireballer Singer partially filled the huge void created by Koufax's retirement. In tonight's first game, Singer looked as good as Sandy could have. He allowed only five hits, walked none and struck out nine. Only one Phillie got past first base.

The only scoring threat of the game for the hometown Phillies came in the second inning. Tony Gonzalez led off with a double off the scoreboard in right center. Johnny Briggs followed with a hard grounder toward the hole in the right side. But first baseman Wes Parker made a fine diving stop and flipped to Singer for the out at first. Had the ball gone through, Gonzalez might have scored, but as it was, he had to stop at third. Bill White fouled off an attempted suicide squeeze bunt and then fanned on a fastball. Clay Dalrymple struck out on three pitches, the last one a called strike.

After that, Philadelphia got four singles, and all four men were left on first base. The only moment of anxiety for the Dodgers came when Gonzalez hit a long liner to deep left. But the wind kept the ball from hitting the wall, and Len Gabrielson made the catch.

The Dodgers did very little hitting themselves. They made just four hits off Philly started Jim Bunning in eight innings and two off reliever Dick Ellsworth in the ninth. But one of the hits off Bunning was a home run. Roseboro hit it in the fourth inning. It was a high drive, and without the wind it might not have carried over the barrier.

Singer made that solitary run stand up and he won 1-0.

After the second game, Phillie manager Gene Mauch complained to the press that Singer was throwing spitballs, something the rookie had never been accused of before.

Don Drysdale, who pitched the second game, had often been accused of "loading them up," and tonight was no different. After the Phillies were shut out on six singles,

Mauch also accused Big D of using an illegal pitch. Gonzalez, who was 0-for-2 with a walk and another long fly that was held up by the wind, said that Drysdale threw him spitters on every pitch. Drysdale and Roseboro claimed that they had fed Gonzalez changeups and sliders. Roseboro added wryly that, "I wouldn't know the difference between a spitter and a sinker." And Drysdale was straight-faced when he mentioned that "the wind was playing tricks with the ball."

The Phillies put hits back-to-back twice in the second game, but Drysdale pitched out of each jam. In the fifth inning, Briggs led off with a single and stopped at second on White's one-bagger. Drysdale got Dalrymple to strike out and Bobby Wine to bounce into a double play. In the eighth, Dalrymple and Wine singled with one out. But Drysdale neatly picked Dalrymple off second and got Chris Short on a soft liner to second baseman Luis Alcaraz.

The Dodgers did not score until the top of the ninth. Lou Johnson, leading off, lifted a hump-backed liner over the second baseman for a hit. Al Ferrara sacrificed Johnson to second. Wes Parker stroked a clean single to left center, and Johnson scored without drawing a throw. Bob Bailey hit into a double play to end the inning.

Drysdale set the Phillies down in order in the bottom of the ninth, and the rare 1-0, 1-0 doubleheader sweep was complete. One run was not going to win too many ballgames, and the Dodgers' position in the standings showed it. But tonight Singer and Drysdale, with the assistance of a strong breeze and perhaps some "foreign substances," were both able to win with the absolute minimum of support.

FIRST GAME

			r	h	e
Los Angeles	000 100 000	=	1	6	0
Philadelphia	000 000 000	=	0	5	0

Game-Winning RBI: Roseboro

Batteries: B. Singer (W 12-6) & J. Roseboro
J. Bunning (L 16-13) 8 IP, D. Ellsworth ⅔ IP, D. Farrell ⅓ IP & C. Dalrymple

SECOND GAME

Los Angeles	ab	r	h	bi	o	a	e
W. Davis, cf	4	0	0	0	1	0	0
N. Oliver, ss	4	0	0	0	1	2	0
L. Johnson, lf	4	1	2	0	3	0	0
A. Ferrara, rf	3	0	1	0	2	0	0
R. Fairly, rf9	0	0	0	0	0	0	0
W. Parker, 1b	4	0	1	1	9	0	0
B. Bailey, 3b	4	0	0	0	0	1	0
L. Alcaraz, 2b	3	0	2	0	4	2	0
J. Torborg, c	2	0	1	0	6	0	0
D. Drysdale, p	2	0	0	0	1	5	0
	30	1	7	1	27	10	0

Philadelphia	ab	r	h	bi	o	a	e
C. Rojas, 2b	4	0	0	0	4	3	0
T. Taylor, 3b	4	0	0	0	0	2	0
J. Callison, rf	4	0	1	0	0	0	0
T. Gonzalez, lf	2	0	0	0	2	0	0
J. Briggs, cf	3	0	1	0	3	0	0
B. White, 1b	3	0	1	0	10	0	0
C. Dalrymple, c	3	0	1	0	7	1	0
B. Wine, ss	3	0	2	0	1	2	0
C. Short, p	3	0	0	0	0	3	0
	29	0	6	0	27	11	0

Los Angeles	000 000 001	=	1
Philadelphia	000 000 000	=	0

	ip	h	r-er	bb	so
Drysdale (W 11-15)	9	6	0-0	1	5
Short (L 7-11)	9	7	1-1	1	6

Time—2:03
Attendance—12,018
Umpires: S. Landes, A. Barlick, M. Steiner, & A. Donatelli

Game-Winning RBI: Parker
LOB: Los Angeles 5, Philadelphia 3
DP: Oliver-Alcaraz-Parker (Rojas)
Oliver-Parker (Wine)
Drysdale-Parker
White unassisted
Taylor-Rojas-White (Bailey)
2B: Johnson
SH: Torborg, Ferrara
SB: Alcaraz
Picked Off: Dalrymple

Los Angeles lost ten of its final fifteen games to finish at 73-89. That was enough to keep the Dodgers in eighth place.

1968 TUESDAY NIGHT, JUNE 4TH, AT DODGER STADIUM

Six Shutouts in a Row for Drysdale

Stops Pirates, 5-0, for Record
54 Consecutive Scoreless Innings and Still Counting

DON DRYSDALE ALREADY HAD 196 career pitching victories to his credit. His remarkable 25-9 record in 1962 won him the Cy Young Award as the most valuable pitcher in the major leagues. He had pitched an artistically brilliant World Series game in 1963, shutting out the Yankees, 1-0. And he had pitched very well in six All-Star Games.

Unfortunately for Don's public image, he was only the number-two pitcher on the Dodger staff during the stretch of years recently when Sandy Koufax dominated the National League and the national media.

But today Big Don reached a pinnacle of pitching achievement that Sandy Koufax had never reached. Nor Bob Gibson, nor Walter Johnson, nor Cy Young. Nor any of the thousands of men who ever pitched in the major leagues. Today Drysdale pitched his sixth consecutive complete-game shutout!

Today's Results

LOS ANGELES 5-Pittsburgh 0
St. Louis 3-Houston 2
Cincinnati 3-Atlanta 1
Philadelphia 5-San Francisco 1
New York 5-Chicago 0

Standings	W-L	Pct.	GB
St. Louis	29-21	.580	—
Atlanta	27-23	.540	2
Philadelphia	24-21	.533	2½
San Francisco	27-24	.529	2½
Chicago	25-24	.510	3½
LOS ANGELES	27-26	.509	3½
Cincinnati	24-24	.500	4
New York	21-27	.438	7
Houston	21-28	.429	7½
Pittsburgh	19-26	.422	7½

Only once previously had a pitcher even hurled five shutouts in succession. And that happened way back in 1904. The man who did it was Guy "Doc" White, a talented but long-forgotten lefthander with the Chicago White Sox.

Here's how Drysdale tied White's record:

Shutout #1: May 14th at Dodger Stadium. He stopped the Chicago Cubs on two hits, walking three, to win 1-0. Singles by Wes Parker and Willie Davis around an infield out gave the Dodgers their run against Ferguson Jenkins.

Shutout #2: May 18th at Los Angeles. A 1-0 victory over Dave Giusti and the Astros. Drysdale pitched a five-hitter and walked two. Parker again scored the only run, this time on an error.

Shutout #3: May 22nd at St. Louis. Big D beat the champion Cardinals, 2-0. He allowed five hits again and walked none. Bob Gibson held the Dodgers to just one hit in eight innings, but that hit, a third-inning double by Parker, drove in a run. Los Angeles added a run on two hits against reliever Joe Hoerner in the ninth.

Shutout #4: May 26th at Houston. A 5-0 six-hitter in the Astrodome. Houston threatened to score in the ninth as Drysdale tired. Two singles, a double play, a walk, and a hit batsman loaded the bases with two out. But Dave Adlesh grounded out to end the game.

Shutout #5: May 31st versus the Giants in L.A. Drysdale won 3-0 on a seven-hit, two-walk performance. Again his streak almost ended in the ninth inning. Two bases on balls around a single filled the bases with none out. Drysdale threw an inside breaking ball that did not break enough to the next batter, Dick Dietz. It rode in on the hitter, and Dietz threw his arm up and got hit on the elbow. The batter took two steps toward first base, but plate umpire Harry Wendelstedt ruled that he had not tried to avoid the pitch, and Dietz had to bat again. After a big argument, Dietz hit a shallow fly to left. Hal Lanier bounced to first, and Parker threw home for a force out. Jack Hiatt then ended the game by popping out.

That game gave Drysdale the National League record for consecutive shutouts and tied him with White for the major league mark.

Like many ballplayers on a hot streak, the big righthander followed the exact same ritual today that he had maintained throughout the streak. He got up about noon and took it easy around the house. Then he and his wife Ginger and daughter Kelly went to their restaurant. They sat at the same table and ate the same food as always. Shortly thereafter, Don headed to Dodger Stadium.

A crowd of 35,000 came to cheer him on tonight.

The opposition was the Pittsburgh Pirates, against whom Drysdale had not pitched a complete game in over three years. And he was mighty nervous tonight.

But the side-wheeling rightly quickly found his groove and pitched brilliantly. The Pirate batters complained that he was throwing a spitball, but the umpires did not agree.

Drysdale got excellent fielding support, especially from second baseman Paul Popovich. Popovich made fine plays to rob Maury Wills and Roberto Clemente of hits in their first at bats of the game.

The Dodgers gave him a three-run lead to work with with a rally in the fourth. A walk, three singles, and a throwing error brought the runs around.

The Pirates did not get their first hit until the fifth, when Donn Clendenon led off with a single. The next batter bounced into a double play.

Pittsburgh only got one runner past first base. That was Gary Kolb, who hit a pinch double with one out in the sixth. Matty Alou's ground out advance Kolb to third. Wills hit a dangerous chopper past the mound, but Popovich charged the ball and shoveled it to first just in time to nip the batter and preserve the shutout.

That was all Drysdale needed. He retired the Pirates in order until Wills singled with two gone in the ninth. Willie Stargell then hit an easy grounder to Popovich for the final out.

Drysdale finished with a three-hitter and had walked no one. And he had set a new record: six straight shutouts. In all the years that major league baseball had been played, no one had ever done that before.

Pittsburgh	ab	r	h	bi	o	a	e
M. Alou, cf	4	0	0	0	2	0	0
M. Wills, 3b	4	0	1	0	0	1	0
W. Stargell, 1b-lf2	4	0	0	0	2	0	0
R. Clemente, rf	3	0	0	0	2	0	0
M. Mota, lf	0	0	0	0	0	0	0
D. Clendenon, 1b2	2	0	1	0	5	1	0
B. Mazeroski, 2b	3	0	0	0	1	3	0
J. May, c	3	0	0	0	8	2	0
G. Alley, ss	3	0	0	0	3	2	0
J. Bunning, p	1	0	0	0	0	0	1
G. Kolb, ph6	1	0	1	0	-	-	-
J. Pizarro, p6	0	0	0	0	1	0	1
M. Jimenez, ph9	1	0	0	0	-	-	-
	29	0	3	0	24	9	2

Los Angeles	ab	r	h	bi	o	a	e
W. Parker, 1b	3	2	2	1	17	0	0
W. Davis, cf	4	1	1	0	1	0	0
L. Gabrielson, lf	3	1	1	0	0	0	0
J. Fairey, lf7	0	0	0	0	0	0	0
T. Haller, c	4	0	2	0	7	1	0
K. Boyer, 3b	2	0	1	1	0	7	0
R. Fairly, rf	4	0	0	0	0	0	0
P. Popovich, 2b	3	0	0	0	2	6	0
Z. Versalles, ss	3	1	0	0	0	3	0
D. Drysdale, p	3	0	1	0	0	3	0
	29	5	8	2	27	20	0

Pittsburgh	000 000 000	= 0
Los Angeles	000 301 10x	= 5

	ip	h	r-er	bb	so
Bunning (L 3-6)	5	5	3-2	2	5
Pizarro	3	3	2-1	4	3
Drysdale (W 7-3)	9	3	0-0	0	8

HBP: by Drysdale (Mota)
Time—2:20
Attendance—30,422 paid
35,148 total

Game-Winning Run scored on an error by Bunning
LOB: Pittsburgh 3, Los Angeles 6
BE: Los Angeles 1
DP: Mazeroski-Alley-Stargell (Gabrielson)
Wills-Mazeroski-Clendenon (Boyer)
Boyer-Popovich-Parker (Mazeroski)
2B: Kolb
3B: Haller
HR: Parker
CS: Boyer, Popovich

Umpires: H. Wendelstedt, B. Jackowski, F. Secory, & K. Burkhart

In his next start, on June 8th against the Phillies, Drysdale pitched $4\frac{2}{3}$ shutout innings before Howie Bedell's sacrifice fly ended his streak. That gave Big D $58\frac{2}{3}$ consecutive scoreless innings pitched, breaking Walter Johnson's old mark of 56. He finished the season with a 14-12 record, a 2.15 ERA, and 8 shutouts.

The Dodgers finished tied for seventh with a 76-86 record.

1969 WEDNESDAY NIGHT, SEPTEMBER 3RD, AT DODGER STADIUM

Willie Davis's Hitting Streak Up to 31 Games

After Going 0-for-4, He Gets a Hit on 5th Try
His Blow Beats Mets, 5-4, as Dodgers Remain 1 Game Out of 1st

Today's Results

LOS ANGELES 5-New York 4
San Francisco 2-Montreal 1
Cincinnati 2-Chicago 0
Atlanta 8-Pittsburgh 1
Philadelphia 9-San Diego 1
other clubs not scheduled

Standings	W-L	Pct.	GB
San Francisco	76-59	.563	—
LOS ANGELES	74-59	.556	1
Cincinnati	73-59	.553	1½
Atlanta	74-63	.540	3
Houston	70-64	.522	5½
San Diego	40-95	.296	36

IT CERTAINLY LOOKED LIKE WILLIE Davis's consecutive-game hitting streak would end at 30 tonight when he rolled out in the bottom of the seventh. That made Willie 0-for-4 for the game, and it seemed unlikely that he would get another at bat. The Dodgers were leading 4-0 at the time, so they would probably only bat in one more inning, and Davis was the eighth man scheduled to hit in the bottom of the eighth.

But the visiting New York Mets helped out by tying the game in the top of the eighth. And when the Dodgers had to bat in the bottom of the ninth, Davis was the third hitter due up. But when Maury Wills singled and was sacrificed to second, many people thought that the strategy would dictated that Davis would be walked intentionally, and his streak would end nonetheless. But New York manager Gil Hodges decided to let his pitcher pitch to Davis with first base open, and Willie not only got his hit for the day, he won the game for the Dodgers with it.

The dramatic victory kept Los Angeles in second place in the National League West Division pennant race, 1 game behind San Francisco and ½ game ahead of Cincinnati. The Mets remained 4 games behind the Cubs in the East Division.

While the Mets and Dodgers were splitting the first two games of their three-game series, Davis tied and broke Zack Wheat's 1916 club record of hitting safely in 29 consecutive games. Including tonight's game, Davis batted .435 during the streak to raise his season average from .260 to .315.

In tonight's series finale, both managers started their top lefthanded pitchers, Jerry Koosman (12-9) for New York, and Claude Osteen (18-11) for Los Angeles.

In the bottom of the first inning, Koosman got Davis to ground weakly to the first baseman.

The Dodgers scored a run in the second inning, thanks to an error and a wild pitch. Andy Kosco reached base on a one-out fumble by third baseman Ed Charles. He scored on a hit by Bill Sudakis, an infield out, and the wild pitch.

Los Angeles added another run on another wild pitch in the third. Wills beat out a bunt with one out and stole second. He took third on Manny Mota's grounder to the right side and came home on wild pitch #2 from Koosman. Davis, who was at the plate at the time, eventually fanned.

The Dodgers put another "1" on the board in the fourth on singles by Wes Parker and Kosco and a double by Ted Sizemore.

Davis batted again in the fifth. With Mota on first, Willie tapped to the second baseman for a force out.

Los Angeles got its fourth run in the sixth on consecutive singles with one out by Sudakis, Sizemore, and Jeff Torborg and a sacrifice fly by Osteen.

Koosman was replaced by righthander Cal Koonce in the seventh. Against Koonce, Davis tried to bunt his way on unsuccessfully.

Through seven innings, Osteen had a 4-0 lead and a string of 26 consecutive scoreless innings pitched. He had pulled a groin muscle in his previous start, and it kept him from throwing his breaking ball tonight. In the eighth, the Mets finally zeroed in on his fastball and tied the game abruptly. Bobby Pfeil, batting for Koonce, singled with one out, and Tommy Agee followed with a two-run homer over the right field wall. Bud Harrelson singled and was forced out by Cleon Jones. Donn Clendenon then unloaded on another high fastball for another two-run homer. That tied the score, 4-4.

Young Nolan Ryan shut the Dodgers out in the eighth, despite two walks.

And Pete Mikkelson, pitching for the Dodgers, blanked New York in the top of the ninth.

Lefthander Jack DiLauro was the Mets' pitcher in the bottom of the ninth. Wills, the first batter to face him, pulled a grounder through the left side for a hit. Mota sacrificed successfully. With the winning run on second, first base open, and one out, many reporters and fans assumed that Davis would be walked to set up a force out. The crowd started booing this strategy when they saw catcher Duffy Dyer looking into the visitors' dugout for instructions. But manager Hodges gave no orders for a walk, hoping instead that the lefthanded DiLauro could retire the lefthanded Davis.

Willie had struck out on a curveball from lefthander Tug McGraw in a similar situation in the ninth inning last night. So he went to the plate tonight looking for a curve. DiLauro obliged with a sidearm slant on the first pitch, and Davis lined it past the left fielder for a hit. Wills scored easily from second, and Davis was credited with a double.

After he touched second, Willie was mobbed by his happy teammates and given a hero's escort to the clubhouse. His hitting streak was still intact, and the Dodgers were still very much in the pennant race. Osteen joked with reporters that, "Of course, I just threw those two home runs so Willie could get up again." As it turned out, most everybody was glad he did.

New York	ab	r	h	bi	o	a	e
T. Agee, cf	4	1	2	2	0	1	0
B. Harrelson, ss	4	0	1	0	2	4	0
C. Jones, lf	4	1	0	0	2	0	0
D. Clendenon, 1b	4	1	2	2	11	0	0
R. Swoboda, rf	3	0	0	0	2	0	0
E. Charles, 3b	3	0	0	0	1	3	1
K. Boswell, ph9-2b	1	0	0	0	1	0	0
D. Dyer, c	4	0	2	0	5	1	1
A. Weis, 2b-3b9	3	0	0	0	1	4	0
J. Koosman, p	2	0	0	0	0	0	0
C. Koonce, p7	0	0	0	0	0	1	0
B. Pfeil, ph8	1	1	1	0	-	-	-
N. Ryan, p8	0	0	0	0	0	0	
A. Shamsky, ph9	1	0	0	0	-	-	-
J. DiLauro, p9	0	0	0	0	0	1	0
	34	4	8	4	25	15	1

Los Angeles	ab	r	h	bi	o	a	e
M. Wills, ss	5	2	2	0	1	9	0
M. Mota, lf	4	0	1	0	0	0	0
W. Davis, cf	5	0	1	1	3	0	0
W. Parker, 1b	4	1	2	0	15	0	0
A. Kosco, rf	4	1	1	0	1	0	0
B. Sudakis, 3b	3	1	2	0	0	2	1
T. Sizemore, 2b	4	0	2	1	5	3	0
J. Torborg, c	2	0	1	0	2	0	0
T. Haller, ph8-c	0	0	0	0	0	0	0
C. Osteen, p	2	0	0	1	0	4	0
W. Crawford, ph8	1	0	0	0	-	-	-
P. Mikkelsen, ph9	0	0	0	0	0	1	0
	34	5	12	3	27	19	1

New York	000 000 040	= 4
Los Angeles	011 101 001	= 5

one out when winning run scored

	ip	h	r-er	bb	so
Koosman	6	9	4-3	1	4
Koonce	1	1	0-0	0	0
Ryan	1	0	0-0	2	2
DiLauro (L 1-4)	⅓	2	1-1	0	0
Osteen	8	7	4-4	1	2
Mikkelsen (W 7-3)	1	1	0-0	0	0

WP: Koosman 2

Umpires: B. Williams, N. Colosi, T. Gorman, & S. Landes

Game-Winning RBI: Davis
LOB: New York 5, Los Angeles 9
BE: New York 1, Los Angeles 1
DP: Weis-Harrelson-Clendenon (Osteen)
Wills-Sizemore-Parker (Dyer)
2B: Sizemore, Parker, Davis
HR: Agee, Clendenon
SH: Weis, Mota
SF: Osteen
SB: Wills, Sudakis
Time—2:27
Attendance—26,625

Davis's hitting streak was stopped the next night in San Diego by Dick Kelley and Gary Ross. He finished the season with a .311 batting average.

The Dodgers were in the thick of the West Division race until they went on an eight-game losing streak starting on September 19th. Los Angeles finished fourth, 8 games behind, with an 85-77 record.

1970 WEDNESDAY NIGHT, JULY 22ND, AT DODGER STADIUM

Grand Slam by Pinch-Hitter Haller

Is Key Blow in 8-Run Rally in 7th
Expos Beaten 12-10

Today's Results			
LOS ANGELES 12-Montreal 10			
Chicago 10-Cincinnati 2			
Pittsburgh 5-Atlanta 3			
Philadelphia 5-San Francisco 2			
Houston 13-St. Louis 9			
San Diego 5-New York 4 (10 innings)			
Standings	**W-L**	**Pct.**	**GB**
Cincinnati	67-29	.698	—
LOS ANGELES	55-39	.585	11
Atlanta	46-48	.489	20
San Francisco	44-48	.478	21
Houston	42-53	.442	24½
San Diego	39-59	.398	29

WITH TOM HALLER GETTING THE BIGGEST hit, the Los Angeles Dodgers staged a stirring comeback to beat the Montreal Expos tonight by the score of 12-10. Montreal led 10-4 going into the bottom of the seventh, but Los Angeles scored eight runs in that round, all after two were out. It was Haller, pinch-hitting, who put the home team into the lead with a grand slam home run. The next batter, Von Joshua, also homered for an insurance run. And relief pitcher Jim Brewer held onto the lead for the final two innings.

The Dodgers, although in second place by a comfortable margin, came into the game in a slump and were trailing the first-place Cincinnati Reds by 12 games. With the Dodgers' pennant hopes apparently slipping farther and farther away, another defeat today would have hurt badly. The big rally tonight was inspiring, but there was still an awfully long way to go to catch the leaders.

For the Expos, a second-year expansion club, the loss was hard to take. Not only did they blow a big lead, the decisive home runs came off of their top relief pitcher, Claude Raymond. As a result, Montreal wasted some fine hitting. Bob Bailey had five runs-batted-in for them, and Adolpho Phillips scored four times.

Phillips got Montreal started in the first inning with a one-out single. Rusty Staub singled him to third, and he scored on a force out on Bailey's grounder. A wild throw by rookie third baseman Steve Garvey kept the inning going. Then Coco Laboy singled Bailey home to give the Expos a 2-0 lead.

The home team got a run back in the second on two-out hits by Bill Russell and Jeff Torborg.

Bailey unloaded a two-run homer in the third for Montreal.

The Dodgers matched those two runs in their half of the third. Maury Wills led off with a walk. Ted Sizemore singled him to second. Willie Davis hit safely to right, and Wills prepared to stop at third. But Davis had kept running, and before the confused Expos knew what to do with the ball, Wills had scored and the other runners were perched on second and third. Sizemore scored on a ground out by Jim Lefebvre.

The Dodgers tied the game at 4-4 in the fourth with a run. Torborg singled and came around on an infield out and a double by Wills. Bill Stoneman replaced Montreal starter Dan McGinn at this point.

The Expos regained the lead on a two-run single by John Bateman in the fifth, routing starter Claude Osteen. Reliever Jose Pena retired the side with the bases loaded.

Pena was eventually credited with the victory, but he was ineffective in the next two innings, yielding four runs. Bailey's double in the sixth brought home two men who had walked. And Ron Fairly poled a two-run homer in the seventh following a hit batsman.

With the score 10-4, pinch-hitter Joshua opened the bottom of the seventh by flying out. Wills and Sizemore singled. Davis lined to left for the second out. Parker walked to load the bases. And Lefebvre got a two-run single on a full-count pitch. Garvey drove in a third run with a hit to right.

With the lead down to 10-7, Montreal manager Gene Mauch decided it was time for Raymond. Claude entered the game looking for his 20th save of the year. He got his sixth loss, instead. Dodger manager Walt Alston sent lefthanded Willie Crawford to hit. He worked the count full, then watched a pitch that just missed the strike zone for ball four, loading the bases.

Haller, another lefthanded sticker, was sent up to bat for Torborg. With the bases now loaded, Raymond did not want to walk another man. So his first pitch to Haller was a slider over the middle of the plate. Unfortunately for the Expos, it was much higher than planned. It came across at the letters, and Haller slammed it over the fence for a grand slam. The blow suddenly propelled the Dodgers into the lead, 11-10.

Raymond was so upset that he hung another fat pitch to Joshua, who hit a drive over the right field fence for his first major league home run.

With a lead of his own to protect, Alston brought his best relief pitcher, Brewer, into the game. The lefty survived a double by Staub in the eighth and retired the Expos in order in the ninth. He got credit for his 13th save of the season, and the Dodgers got the victory, 12-10.

Grand slams being pretty rare things, and pinch-hit grand slams coming only about half a dozen times a year in the big leagues, Tom Haller's feat tonight was something to remember. And the fact that it won the game for Los Angeles gave it special significance. After the game, Haller said that he hoped it might inspire the Dodgers to a long winning streak that would put them into a position to threaten the Reds' big lead. After all, something dramatic was needed to make the race exciting.

Montreal	ab	r	h	bi	o	a	e
G. Sutherland, 2b	4	2	1	0	1	1	0
A. Phillips, cf	2	4	2	0	1	0	0
J. Gosger, cf7	1	0	0	0	0	0	0
R. Staub, rf	4	0	2	0	3	0	0
B. Bailey, lf	4	2	2	5	0	0	0
J. Fairey, lf6	1	0	0	0	1	0	0
J. Bateman, c	5	0	1	2	7	0	0
C. Laboy, 3b	4	1	2	1	1	2	0
R. Fairly, 1b	4	1	1	2	9	0	0
B. Wine, ss	5	0	0	0	1	2	0
D. McGinn, p	2	0	0	0	0	2	0
B. Stoneman, p4	2	0	1	0	0	1	0
C. Raymond, p7	0	0	0	0	0	0	0
J. Strohmayer, p8	0	0	0	0	0	0	0
	38	10	12	10	24	8	0

Los Angeles	ab	r	h	bi	o	a	e
M. Wills, ss	4	2	2	1	1	2	0
T. Sizemore, lf-2b9	5	2	2	0	1	0	0
W. Davis, cf	5	0	3	1	2	0	0
W. Parker, 1b	3	1	0	0	14	0	0
J. Lefebvre, 2b-3b9	5	1	1	3	3	7	0
S. Garvey, 3b	4	1	1	1	0	7	1
M. Mota, lf9	0	0	0	0	0	0	0
B. Russell, rf	3	1	1	0	1	0	0
W. Crawford, ph7-rf	0	1	0	0	0	0	0
J. Torborg, c	3	1	2	1	3	0	0
T. Haller, ph7-c	1	1	1	4	2	0	0
C. Osteen, p	2	0	0	0	0	0	0
J. Pena, p5	0	0	0	0	0	0	0
V. Joshua, ph7	2	1	1	1	-	-	-
J. Brewer, p8	0	0	0	0	0	0	0
	37	12	14	12	27	16	1

Montreal	202	022	200	=	10
Los Angeles	012	100	80x	=	12

	ip	h	r-er	bb	so
McGinn	3⅔	7	4-4	1	3
Stoneman	3	5	5-5	1	1
Raymond (L 3-6)	⅓	2	3-3	1	0
Strohmayer	1	0	0-0	1	2
Osteen	4⅔	8	6-5	1	3
Pena (W 4-2)	2⅓	3	4-4	3	0
Brewer (sv #13)	2	1	0-0	0	2

HBP: by Pena (Laboy)

Game-Winning RBI: Haller
LOB: Montreal 7, Los Angeles 5
BE: Montreal 1
DP: Sutherland-Fairly (Parker)
Lefebvre-Wills-Parker (Sutherland)
2B: Russell, Wills, Laboy, Bailey, Staub
HR: Bailey, Fairly, Haller, Joshua
SH: Staub
Time—2:53 Attendance—15,930
Umpirers: B. Williams, N. Colosi,
E. Sudol, & M. Steiner

Haller later won another game with a pinch-homer, this one with two men on in the tenth inning. He finished the year with ten round-trippers in all.

The Dodgers were never able to get closer than 10 games behind the Reds the rest of the season, and they wound up 14½ games in back. They barely edged San Francisco for second place. Los Angeles had a final record of 87-74.

1971

TUESDAY NIGHT, SEPTEMBER 14TH, AT CANDLESTICK PARK, SAN FRANCISCO

Manny Mota's Biggest Pinch Hit

Three-Run Double in 9th Beats Giants, 6-5
Dodgers Cut San Francisco's Lead to Just 1 Game

Today's Results			
LOS ANGELES 6-San Francisco 5			
Atlanta 5-Cincinnati 2			
San Diego 5-Houston 2			
Standings	**W-L**	**Pct.**	**GB**
San Francisco	83-65	.561	—
LOS ANGELES	82-66	.554	1
Atlanta	75-74	.503	8½
Houston	73-75	.493	10
Cincinnati	72-78	.480	12
San Diego	55-93	.372	28

MANNY MOTA DESCRIBED IT AS "THE biggest hit of my life." He further explained that that was "because we wanted to win so badly." Indeed, this was the second-place Dodgers' last direct confrontation with the first-place Giants, and the victory moved them to just 1 game behind with 14 games left on the schedule. And it kept the momentum definitely on the Dodgers' side. Los Angeles upped its winning streak to eight games, while San Francisco lost its ninth game in ten tries. The Giant lead was 8½ games just ten days before this. As the Dodgers celebrated after the game, they said they were quite confident that they would win the division title now.

The high-flying Dodgers had won the opener of this two-game series 5-4 amidst beanballing and brawling. Dodger pitcher Bill Singer hit two Giants with pitches. Giant starter Juan Marichal hit Bill Buckner on the elbow with a fastball. Buckner reacted by stalking to the mound brandishing his bat. No blows were struck, but four players were ejected from the game. Buckner was fined $500 by the league and was lucky to escape a suspension.

So the atmosphere tonight was highly charged. The weather was exceptionally warm for usually-frigid Candlestick Park, and the fans sweated and scuffled throughout the long contest. As the fortunes of the home team swayed back and forth, the decibel level in the park ranged from ear-splitting noise to pin-drop silence. After the game was finally decided, the victorious Dodgers' clubhouse was madcap, while the home clubhouse was like a morgue.

The starting pitchers were Al Downing (18-8) for Los Angeles and Gaylord Perry (14-11) for San Francisco. Each was found for a run in the second inning. The Dodger run was scored by Richie Allen on a bad-hop single, another one-bagger by Willie Crawford, and Wes Parker's infield out. Bobby Bonds tied the game right up with a line drive homer over the left field fence.

Los Angeles scored twice in the fourth to take a 3-1 lead. First baseman Dave Kingman opened the door by booting Buckner's grounder to start the inning. Willie Davis forced Buckner, but the Giant infield failed to turn the double play. Allen fouled out. Then Crawford drilled a double to left to score Davis. Parker's single to center plated Crawford.

Perry pitched out of a bases-laoded jam in the sixth and held the Dodgers scoreless in the seventh after a leadoff triple by Duke Sims.

Despite constant threats by the Giants, Downing protected the lead until the seventh.

The San Francisco crowd was beginning to change from moody to rowdy as the first two Giants were retired in the seventh. Fistfights were raging in the unfinished section of seats in right field.

Then the home team electrified the atmosphere with a four-run rally to take the lead. Rookie Chris Speier started the comeback with a home run to left. When Tito Fuentes doubled, Dodger manager Walter Alston removed Downing and brought in Joe Moeller in relief. The new hurler walked Willie Mays and allowed a long three-run homer to left by Bonds. The crowd erupted with joy as Bonds pranced around the bases with his hands triumphantly raised over his head.

Ace fireman Jerry Johnson still had the 5-3 lead going into the ninth. Sims gave the Dodgers hope with a leadoff single. He gave way for a pinch-runner. Bill Sudakis, pinch-hitting, looped one off the end of the bat and over the straining second baseman for another hit. Maury Wills beat out a bunt to load the bases.

Giant manager Charlie Fox made a pitching change, calling in southpaw John Cumberland. Alston responded by sending the righthanded Mota to bat in place of the lefthanded Buckner. The first pitch was a high slider, and Mota ripped it down the left field line and into the corner for a three-run double, putting Los Angeles ahead, 6-5.

After an infield hit by Davis, Don McMahon replaced Cumberland and retired the Dodgers without further scoring.

Alston selected 48-year-old knuckleballer Hoyt Wilhelm to try and save the game in the bottom of the ninth. He struck out Fran Healy leading off, although catcher Tom Haller dropped the third strike and had to throw to first for the out. Speier grounded out to short. Willie McCovey walked, and a passed ball sent the pinch-runner to second. But the flutterballer fanned 40-year-old Willie Mays with a sharply breaking pitch, and the game was over. The disappointed crowd sighed audibly, and the jubilant Dodgers charged to the mound to congratulate Wilhelm and each other.

In the clubhouse, the winners held a celebration, spraying each other with beer. Wills doused Mota with a brew and promised, "In a couple of weeks we'll make that champagne." Although the Dodgers were still in second place, they all expected to finish in first.

Los Angeles	ab	r	h	bi	o	a	e
M. Wills, ss	5	1	1	0	0	6	0
B. Buckner, rf	4	0	0	0	3	0	0
M. Mota, ph9-lf	1	0	1	3	0	0	0
W. Davis, cf	5	1	1	0	2	0	0
R. Allen, 3b	5	1	2	0	1	2	0
W. Crawford, lf	3	1	2	1	2	0	0
H. Wilhelm, p9	0	0	0	0	0	0	0
W. Parker, 1b	3	0	2	2	14	1	0
J. Lefebvre, 2b	4	0	0	0	2	2	0
D. Sims, c	4	0	2	0	1	0	0
B. Grabarkewitz, pr9	0	1	0	0	-	-	-
T. Haller, c9	0	0	0	0	1	1	0
A. Downing, p	3	0	0	0	1	0	0
J. Moeller, p7	0	0	0	0	0	0	0
B. Sudakis, ph9	1	0	1	0	-	-	-
B. Russell, pr9-rf	0	1	0	0	0	0	0
	38	6	12	6	27	12	0

San Francisco	ab	r	h	bi	o	a	e
C. Speier, ss	5	1	1	1	2	2	0
T. Fuentes, 2b	4	1	1	0	2	4	0
W. McCovey, ph9	0	0	0	0	-	-	-
J. Rosario, pr9	0	0	0	0	-	-	-
W. Mays, cf	3	1	0	0	0	0	0
B. Bonds, rf	4	2	2	4	0	0	0
D. Kingman, 1b	4	0	1	0	9	1	1
A. Gallagher, 3b	3	0	1	0	3	0	0
K. Henderson, lf	4	0	0	0	2	0	0
D. Dietz, c	3	0	1	0	7	0	0
J. Cumberland, p9	0	0	0	0	0	0	0
D. McMahon, p9	0	0	0	0	0	0	0
G. Perry, p	1	0	0	0	1	2	0
J. Hart, ph7	1	0	0	0	-	-	-
J. Johnson, p8	0	0	0	0	0	0	0
R. Gibson, c9	0	0	0	0	1	0	0
F. Healy, ph9	1	0	0	0	-	-	-
	33	5	7	5	27	9	1

Los Angeles	010	200	003	=	6
San Francisco	010	000	400	=	5

	ip	h	r-er	bb	so
Downing	6⅔	6	3-3	3	1
Moeller (W 2-3)	1⅓	1	2-2	1	0
Wilhelm (sv #3)	1	0	0-0	1	2
Perry	7	6	3-1	2	6
Johnson (L 12-7)	*1	4	3-3	1	1
Cumberland	†0	2	0-0	0	0
McMahon	1	0	0-0	0	1

*faced three batters in ninth
†faced two batters in ninth
WP: Moeller PB: Haller

Game-Winning RBI: Mota
LOB: Los Angeles 8, San Francisco 7
BE: Los Angeles 1
DP: Speier-Fuentes-Kingman (Lefebvre) Gallagher unassisted
2B: Crawford, Kingman, Fuentes, Mota
3B: Sims
HR: Bonds, Speier
SH: Perry
SB: Allen
Time—3:01
Attendance—31,907
Umpires: S. Landes, M. Steiner, S. Davidson, & S. Crawford

The Dodgers returned home only to lose the first four games of the homestand. Although they won seven of the remaining ten games, they never did catch San Francisco.

Los Angeles wound up 1 game behind with an 89-73 record.

1972 SATURDAY, SEPTEMBER 30TH, AT RIVERFRONT STADIUM, CINCINNATI

Osteen Bats His Way to Win #19

Drives In Tying Run in 8th & Winning Runs in 10th
Keeps Hopes of 20-Win Season Alive with 4-2 Win Over Reds

Today's Results			
LOS ANGELES 4-Cincinnati 2 (10 innings)			
Houston 6-San Diego 5 (12 innings)			
San Francisco 3-Atlanta 1			
Standings	**W-L**	**Pct.**	**GB**
Cincinnati	92-59	.609	—
Houston	84-66	.560	7½
LOS ANGELES	83-69	.546	9½
Atlanta	70-81	.464	22
San Francisco	66-86	.434	26½
San Diego	57-93	.380	34½

LOS ANGELES DODGER LEFTHANDER Claude Osteen kept his hopes for a 20-win season alive by beating the powerful Cincinnati Reds today in ten innings, 4-2. Claude pitched a fine game, going the distance and allowing just six hits. But almost more important was his hitting. He got two of the Dodgers' eight hits and drove in three of their four runs. His first hit drove in a run in the eighth inning to tie the score. And his second hit drove in two runs in the tenth inning to provide the final margin of victory.

The victory was his fourth in his last five starts this month. And manager Walter Alston indicated after the game that Osteen would get a chance to win #20 in the final game of the season Wednesday in Atlanta. Osteen's 2-for-4 batting performance raised his season average to a quite-respectable .286. And the three RBIs raised his season total to 11. Although he entered the 1972 season with just a .181 lifetime average, his hitting this year had been good enough to cause Alston to use him as a pinch-hitter on a couple of occasions.

The victory also kept the Dodgers' slim hopes of finishing second alive. In order to do that, however, Los Angeles would have to win its final three games, while Houston would have to lose its last three contests. Cincinnati clinched first place over a week before this.

Osteen handled all the Reds except Pete Rose well. Claude walked four and struck out eight. Rose, however, got three of the six Cincinnati hits, giving him 195 for the season. That bolstered his hope of reaching 200, even though this spring's players' strike wiped out eight scheduled games at the start of the season.

Wayne Simpson pitched one of his better games of the year for the Reds. He allowed just two runs on five hits before being removed for a pinch-hitter in the bottom of the eighth inning. Pedro Borbon pitched the ninth and tenth innings and was charged with the loss.

Both teams played errorless ball in the field.

Davey Lopes got things started off right for Los Angeles in the first inning by leading off with a double to left field. A wild pitch by Simpson moved Lopes to third, and Bill Buckner's ground out to second base brought him home.

Through the next six innings, only two Dodgers reached base safely. Ron Cey singled in the second inning and was quickly wiped out in a double play. And Tom Paciorek doubled in the fourth and was left on base.

Osteen zipped through the Cincinnati lineup in order in the first three innings.

But in the fourth, the Reds opened with three straight hits and took a 2-1 lead. Rose led off with a double to left field. Joe Morgan clouted and opposite-field triple to left, driving Rose home. Bobby Tolan laid down a pretty bunt single, and Morgan scampered home. Osteen then walked Johnny Bench, and it seemed doubtful that Claude would survive through the inning. But he hitched up his belt and retired the dangerous Tony Perez on a pop to first base. Hal McRae went out on a tap to the mound, as the runners advanced to second and third. Then Osteen got a third strike past Denis Menke to end the inning.

When the game got to the eighth inning and his team was still trailing by 2-1, Osteen had to take matters into his own hands. Willie Crawford singled to right to lead off. By the time Osteen was due up, Crawford was on second with two out.

Normal strategy would have called for a pinch-hitter. But Alston had already scrapped his five-man pitching rotation in order to give Osteen a chance at 20 wins, so he allowed the lefty to bat for himself. Claude made the decision pay off by stroking an opposite-field single to left, sending Crawford all the way home to tie the game, 3-2.

The Reds mounted mild threats in the eighth and ninth innings but failed to score.

Borbon got the Dodgers out in order in the top of the ninth.

Cey led off the Dodger tenth with a single to left. Maury Wills was sent in as a pinch-runner. Crawford popped out to third, and Steve Yeager skied to short, leaving Wills still on first with two out. Bill Russell barely beat out a hit on the infield, and Wills moved to second.

Osteen was again allowed to bat. His reputation as a slugger apparently preceded him, because Borbon started him off with three straight breaking balls. Definitely a fastball hitter, Claude let all three curves go by. Finally Borbon served up a fast one. Osteen stepped into it and drove it well over left fielder Rose's head and to the fence. Wills and Russell scored, and Osteen pulled up at second with a double, his fifth of the season. He was left there when Lopes popped out, but he had given himself and the Dodgers a 4-2 lead.

The irrepressible Mr. Rose got his third hit of the game with one out in the bottom of the tenth. But the next two men went out, and Osteen's 19th victory was on the books.

Although Claude had won 20 games once before, in 1969, he said that this season had probably been his most consistent as a pitcher. And it was also his best and most consistent as a batter. Without his own hitting today, his chances for another 20-win season would be nil.

Los Angeles	ab	r	h	bi	o	a	e
D. Lopes, 2b	5	1	1	0	1	4	0
B. Buckner, rf	4	0	0	1	3	0	0
W. Davis, cf	4	0	0	0	4	0	0
T. Paciorek, 1b	4	0	1	0	12	1	0
R. Cey, 3b	4	0	2	0	0	2	0
M. Wills, pr10-3b	0	1	0	0	0	0	0
W. Crawford, lf	4	1	1	0	1	0	0
J. Ferguson, c	2	0	0	0	6	0	0
M. Mota, ph8	1	0	0	0	-	-	-
S. Yeager, c8	1	0	0	0	2	0	0
B. Russell, ss	4	1	1	0	1	3	0
C. Osteen, p	4	0	2	3	0	2	0
	37	4	8	4	30	12	0

Cincinnati	ab	r	h	bi	o	a	e
P. Rose, lf	5	1	3	0	3	0	0
J. Morgan, 2b	5	1	2	1	2	5	0
B. Tolan, cf	5	0	1	1	5	0	0
J. Bench, c	2	0	0	0	2	0	0
T. Perez, 1b	3	0	0	0	8	0	0
G. Foster, pr9	0	0	0	0	-	-	-
J. Hague, 1b9	0	0	0	0	2	0	0
H. McRae, rf	3	0	0	0	2	0	0
C. Geronimo, rf8	0	0	0	0	0	0	0
D. Menke, 3b	3	0	0	0	0	2	0
D. Concepcion, ss	4	0	0	0	5	1	0
W. Simpson, p	2	0	0	0	1	0	0
J. Javier, ph8	1	0	0	0	-	-	-
P. Borbon, p9	0	0	0	0	0	1	0
T. Uhlaender, ph10	1	0	0	0	-	-	-
	34	2	6	2	30	9	0

Los Angeles	100 000 010 2	= 4
Cincinnati	000 200 000 0	= 2

	ip	h	r-er	bb	so
Osteen (W 19-11)	10	6	2-2	4	8
Simpson	8	5	2-2	0	2
Borbon (L 8-3)	2	3	2-2	0	0

WP: Simpson

Game-Winning RBI: Osteen
LOB: Los Angeles 3, Cincinnati 7
DP: Menke-Morgan-Perez (Ferguson)
2B: Lopes, Paciorek, Rose 2, Osteen
3B: Morgan
SH: Geronimo
CS: Morgan
Time—2:26 Attendance—20,080

Umpires: D. Stello, S. Davidson, S. Landes, & A. Donatelli

Osteen beat the Braves on the final day of the season to get his 20th win.
The Dodgers finished the year in third place, 10½ games out of first, with an 85-70 record.

Chapter XVI Alston Finds That New Infield

1973 September 3rd
Blow 8-1 Lead, Lose League Lead, Too

1974 September 15th
Wynn's Grand Slam Finishes Reds

1974 League Championship Series Game No. 4
Crush Pirates 12-1 for Title

1974 World Series Game No. 2
Pick Off A's to Even Series

1975 April 17th
Win 4th Straight Thriller from Reds

1976 May 5th
Dodgers Win Chicago Windfest, 14-12

WALTER ALSTON STARTED HIS TWENTIETH SEASON WITH THE DODGERS IN 1973. HE had the not unpleasant task of trying to shape a truckload of talented youngsters into a winning lineup. Of the eight infielders on the 25-man roster opening day, only one (Ken McMullen) was over 26 years old. Lee Lacy (23) started the season at second base, but Davey Lopes (26) soon ousted him from the starting lineup. McMullen started at third, but he soon went out with back problems, giving Ron Cey (25) a chance. Bill Buckner (23) was established at first base, and Bill Russell (24) was set at short. At catcher, Joe Ferguson (26) was the starter with Steve Yeager (24) as the primary backup. In the outfield, Willie Davis (32) and Willie Crawford (26) were set in center and right, while Manny Mota (35) platooned with Van Joshua (24) in left.

After losing six of their first seven games, the Dodgers played great ball. They were .500 by the end of April and went 19-8 in May. In the last half of June, they won 14 of 16 to jump from 1½ games behind to 7½ ahead. Everyone was hitting like crazy, with Cey and Ferguson leading the team in RBIs. Steve Garvey slugged his way into the lineup as the calendar was turning to July, with Buckner shifting to left field.

The pitching was also the best in the league. Claude Osteen led the staff with 10 victories by the end of June, while Don Sutton had 9, and Tommy John had 8.

By July 17th, Los Angeles led by 8½ games.

The defending champion Reds got hot in July (24-7) to vault into second place. They continued to play well in August and had closed to within 4 games of Los Angeles by the 30th.

Meanwhile, the Dodgers had begun to falter. The hitting slumped badly in August, especially Cey. Lopes was bothered by back spasms and a jammed thumb. Sutton went out for two weeks with a stiff shoulder. On August 30th, Willie Davis strained his knee sliding. The next day, Lee May hit a home run in the ninth inning off Jim Brewer to start the Dodgers on a 9-game losing streak. The worst day of the streak was September 3rd, when the Dodgers could not hold an 8-1 lead and lost to the Giants, 11-8, on another ninth-inning homer off of Brewer. On the next day, Los Angeles got just one hit and lost 3-1 to fall to second place behind the streaking Reds.

The losing streak was snapped on September 9th against the Padres. But then the Dodgers lost a pair in Cincinnati. Los Angeles turned around and won 11 of its final 15, but it was too late. The Reds won the division by 3½ games.

The late-season collapse obscured the fact that the Dodgers had arrived as a unit. The infield of Garvey at first, Lopes at second, Russell at short, and Cey at third

The Dodger infield of Ron Cey, Bill Russell, Davey Lopes, & Steve Garvey

played its first full game together on July 3rd, 1973. It would not play its last until the 1981 World Series. And Buckner had shown that he could do the job in the outfield in the last half of 1973.

The puzzle was completed with two trades in December. Willie Davis was dealt to Montreal for the leading relief pitcher in the league, Mike Marshall. And Claude Osteen was sent to Houston for center fielder Jimmy Wynn.

With Marshall and Wynn making big contributions, the Dodgers got off to a fast start in 1974, grabbing the division lead on April 14th. By June 7th, their cushion over the second-place Reds was up to 8 games. At that point, Marshall had worked in 35 of the team's 56 games. Wynn and Garvey were running one-two in the league in home runs and two-one in RBIs. Tommy John was 9-1, Doug Rau was 5-1, and Andy Messersmith was 6-1. Coming out of the bullpen ahead of the ubiquitous Marshall, knuckleballer Charlie Hough was 5-1. Joe Ferguson had done most of the catching, but Steve Yeager had started 24 games, and Los Angeles had won them all!

By July 10th, the lead had grown to 10½ games. Wynn and Garvey were joined by Ron Cey in the top five in RBIs, and Wynn was leading the league in runs scored. Marshall, who had pitched in 13 consecutive games in one recent stretch, was 11-4 with 13 saves.

But there were some signs of difficulties. Foremost was the slump of Don Sutton. After bagging his sixth win on May 14th, he went 14 starts without winning number seven. He finally got it on July 25th. By that time, John (13-3) had snapped a ligament in his elbow and was through for the year. Luckily, Sutton had a great second half.

Ghosts of 1973 began to emerge from the closet when the Dodgers lost six in a row in mid-August and saw the lead drop to 2½ games. The fall was halted on August 19th, when Marshall pitched six shutout innings and scored from second base on an infield out in the twelfth inning to beat the Cubs.

The Reds stayed close the rest of the way. The Dodgers won two out of three in Cincinnati in early September. But the Reds won the first two games of the return series in Los Angeles to pull within 1½ games. In the series finale, however, Sutton

Steve Garvey greeted by Jimmy Wynn after a home run in the 1974 playoffs

pitched a six-hitter, and Wynn and Garvey hit big home runs. The crisis past, the Dodgers won the flag by 4 games.

The new champions had plenty of heroes. Sutton won 14 of his last 17 starts and finished with a 19-9 mark. Messersmith posted a 20-6 record and a 2.59 earned-run average. Marshall set all sorts of records, including 106 games pitched, a remarkable feat. He pitched 208 innings (all in relief), won 15 games, lost 12, saved 21. He was voted the Cy Young Award. Wynn clouted 32 homers and drove in 108 runs. Buckner led the team with a .314 average. And Steve Garvey emerged as a top star. He hit .312 and drove in 111 runs and was voted the league's Most Valuable Player.

In the league championship playoffs against the Pittsburgh Pirates, Sutton was the star. He won the first and fourth games, 3-0 and 12-1. Messersmith and Marshall won the second game, 5-2. The only Dodger defeat came in the third game, when Doug Rau was bombed and the Pirates won, 7-0.

The National League champs did not do so well in the World Series. The Dodgers won only the second game, 3-2. The Oakland A's won three games by 3-2 scores and one game 5-2.

The 1975 race started off in exciting fashion. In the first three games of the season, the Reds came from behind to beat the Dodgers. But in a series a few days later, Los Angeles retaliated by sweeping four from Cincinnati. By mid-May, the Dodgers had built up a 5½-game lead, despite injuries to Russell, Buckner, Yeager, and Marshall. Burt Hooton had been acquired from the Cubs, and Don Sutton was off to a 7-1 start.

But it was too good to last. By early June, the hitting had fallen way off, and Wynn was unable to throw well from the outfield. Although most of the injured returned, Los Angeles could not keep up with white-hot Cincinnati. The Reds won 41 of 50 from May 20th to the All-Star break to open up a huge 12½-game lead. Ferguson was lost on July 1st when he broke his arm in a fight. Sutton's pace slowed down. And Marshall reinjured his rib cage in late August and was out for the season.

There was a danger of falling to third place in late July. But Hooton won his last 12 decisions, and Hough, Garvey, Lopes, and Cey all had good years. Los

Angeles finished second, a whopping 20 games behind Cincinnati. The pitching was the best in the league, but the run production dropped 19% compared to 1974.

Attendance fell only 5½%, despite the fact that the club increased ticket prices for the first time since the move to Los Angeles in 1958. At 2,539,349, the Dodgers still led the majors in attendance.

The big trade before the 1976 season sent Wynn and three others to Atlanta for Johnny "Dusty" Baker and a pinch-hitter. Andy Messersmith, who had played out his option in 1975 as a test case, was ruled a free agent, ushering in the era of "free agency" in professional baseball. Tommy John, who hadn't pitched in a year and a half, was given Messersmith's spot in the rotation.

Ominously, the Los Angeles home opener was rained out, the first home rain-out since the Dodgers had moved west. Taking a cue from the weather, the team lost its first five games. But a hot streak of 23-4 in late April and early May jumped Los Angeles into first place. The spurt proved to be illusionary. By June 1st, the powerful Big Red Machine had rolled past the Dodger Blue Juggernaut. Later in the month, Marshall was traded to the Braves, and Reggie Smith was acquired from the Cardinals.

Unfortunately, Smith did not help the offense that much. As the season went along, the hitting got weaker. But the pitching got stronger, especially Sutton. At the midpoint in the schedule, he was 7-8 with a 4.65 ERA. At the end of the year, his numbers were 21-10 and 3.06. Doug Rau went from 6-6 and 3.17 to 16-12 and 2.57.

The Dodgers never made a run at the Reds, falling as far as 13½ games behind on August 9th.

With a week to go in the season, the club made news by announcing the retirement of Walter Alston. After 23 years of triumphs and occasional wanderings into the nether regions, the quiet man from Darrtown, Ohio, finally called it quits. He was succeeded by coach Tommy Lasorda, a "rah-rah" type who claimed that his veins ran with Dodger Blue blood.

Joe Ferguson crosses the plate after homering in the 1974 World Series

1973 MONDAY EVENING, SEPTEMBER 3RD, AT CANDLESTICK PARK, SAN FRANCISCO

Blow 8-1 Lead, Lose League Lead, Too

Bonds's Grand Slam Caps Giants' 11-8 Comeback Victory
Fourth Straight Loss Drops Dodgers into Tie with Reds

Today's Results			
San Francisco 11-LOS ANGELES 8			
Cincinnati 4-Houston 3			
Atlanta 7-San Diego 3			
Standings	**W-L**	**Pct.**	**GB**
LOS ANGELES	83-55	.601	—
Cincinnati	83-55	.601	—
San Francisco	77-59	.566	5
Houston	71-69	.507	13
Atlanta	66-73	.475	17½
San Diego	48-88	.353	34

EVERY LOSS IS TOUGH. BUT THIS ONE WAS a crusher. The Los Angeles Dodgers blew an 8-1 lead and lost their fourth consecutive game to fall into a tie for first place. The Dodgers had once led by 8½ games. Today they lost to the San Francisco Giants by a final score of 11-8, with the winning runs coming on a ninth-inning grand slam home run by Bobby Bonds. Meanwhile in Houston, the Cincinnati Reds won their fifth straight game, 4-3, to finally catch Los Angeles in the standings.

The Dodgers had been suffering from a team-wide batting slump. But today they piled up eleven hits and eight runs in the first five innings to lead, 8-1. Then everything went wrong. The Giants rallied for six runs in the seventh inning, and the final two scored as Dodger second baseman Davey Lopes held the ball in the infield. Then in the fatal ninth, the Dodgers twice threw late trying for force plays on bunts before Bonds hit his home run.

Jim Brewer was the victim of the blast, and it was the third time in four appearances that Brewer had given up a homer in the ninth. After tonight's heartbreaker, Brewer was sent to Los Angeles for treatment for back spasms.

Brewer was not the only Dodger with physical problems. Pitchers Don Sutton (stiff shoulder) and Andy Messersmith (pulled hamstring) and center fielder Willie Davis (twisted knee) had all been laid up in the past ten days. Davis tried to play today but quit in the fourth inning.

And the team as a whole had not been hitting for a month and a half. On July 17th, the Dodgers sported a .277 team batting average and had built up an 8½-game lead. Since that date, the team had hit under .230, and the lead had vanished.

Manager Walter Alston benched slumping third baseman Ron Cey today, hoping that veteran Ken McMullen could provide some hits. McMullen went 0-for-5. Still, eight runs matched the team's biggest output since July 15th.

Bill Buckner got the attack started with a two-run home run in the third inning. Willie Crawford added another homer in the fourth.

The Giants got a home run from Willie McCovey in the bottom of the fourth.

The Dodgers routed Giant starter Tom Bradley in the fifth and scored five runs. A throwing error by shortstop Chris Speier opened the inning. Buckner singled for a run. Von Joshua followed with another one-bagger, and San Francisco manager Charlie Fox removed Bradley in favor of Don Carrithers. Joe Ferguson singled to load the bases. Crawford then unloaded them with a long triple to center field. Carrithers hit the next batter, Steve Garvey, with a pitch. Both benches emptied, but no punches were thrown. Jim Willoughby relieved Carrithers. Crawford was thrown out trying to score on an infield grounder, but Garvey eventually scored on an infield out by Tommy John.

Dodger starter John sailed through six innings with a three-hitter and an 8-1 lead. Then the roof caved in. Gary Matthews and McCovey singled to open the seventh. Speier bounced a ground-rule double over the fence in center, and one run scored. John struck out Chris Arnold and Dave Kingman. But Dave Rader looped a two-run single to center. And Steve Ontiveros followed with a pinch single.

That was all for John, and Pete Richert was brought in. Bonds greeted him with another ground-rule double, making the score 8-5 and putting runners on second and third. Tito Fuentes hit a twisting grounder up the middle. Lopes fielded the ball behind the base. Although he might have had a play at first, he held onto the ball, and Fuentes reached safely as Ontiveros scored from third. Bonds, who had rounded third and slowed down but had never stopped, poured on the juice and headed home. Lopes made a wide throw to the plate, and Bonds was safe. The Dodger lead was now down to one run, 8-7, and the San Francisco fans loved it.

It was still 8-7 going into the bottom of the ninth. Then the Giants hit one ball farther than the pitcher's mound and scored four runs to win. Gary Thomasson led off with a walk. Rader laid down a sacrifice bunt, and Richert threw to second too late to force Thomasson. The next batter, Mike Sadek, bunted toward third. McMullen charged the ball and tried for a force at second. Again the throw was late, and now the bases were loaded.

Manager Walt Alston brought Brewer into the game to face Bonds. His third pitch was a hanging breaking ball, and Bonds smacked it high and deep to left center. Left fielder Buckner did not even move for the ball, and it sailed far over the fence for a dramatic game-winning grand slam home run. The jubilant Giants mobbed Bonds at home plate, while the shell-shocked Dodgers sullenly retreated to the clubhouse.

The pennant that had seemed so secure in July was now very much in doubt.

Los Angeles	ab	r	h	bi	o	a	e
D. Lopes, 2b	5	1	0	0	1	1	0
B. Buckner, lf	5	2	3	3	3	0	0
W. Davis, cf	2	0	1	0	1	0	0
V. Joshua, cf4	3	1	1	0	0	0	0
J. Ferguson, c	5	1	1	0	9	1	0
W. Crawford, rf	5	1	2	4	1	0	0
S. Garvey, 1b	4	1	3	0	8	0	0
K. McMullen, 3b	5	0	0	0	0	6	0
B. Russell, ss	4	0	1	0	1	2	0
T. John, p	3	1	1	1	0	0	0
P. Richert, p7	0	0	0	0	0	0	0
J. Brewer, p9	0	0	0	0	0	0	0
	41	8	13	8	24	10	0

San Francisco	ab	r	h	bi	o	a	e
B. Bonds, rf-cf8	5	2	2	5	4	0	0
T. Fuentes, 2b	4	0	2	2	5	3	0
G. Matthews, lf	4	1	1	0	0	0	0
W. McCovey, 1b	4	2	2	1	8	0	0
C. Speier, ss	4	1	1	1	1	5	1
D. Kingman, 3b	4	0	0	0	3	5	1
J. Howarth, cf	2	0	0	0	3	0	0
C. Arnold, ph7	1	0	0	0	-	-	-
G. Thomasson, rf8	0	1	0	0	1	0	0
D. Rader, c	3	2	2	2	2	0	0
T. Bradley, p	0	0	0	0	0	0	0
D. Carrithers, p5	0	0	0	0	0	0	0
J. Willoughby, p5	0	0	0	0	0	0	0
B. Miller, ph6	1	0	0	0	-	-	-
R. Moffitt, p7	0	0	0	0	0	0	0
S. Ontiveros, ph7	1	1	1	0	-	-	-
D. McMahon, p8	0	0	0	0	0	0	0
M. Sadek, ph9	0	1	0	0	-	-	-
	33	11	11	11	27	13	2

Los Angeles	002 150 000	= 8
San Francisco	000 100 604	= 11

none out when winning run scored

	ip	h	r-er	bb	so
John	6⅔	8	6-6	0	6
Richert (L 3-2)	*1⅓	2	4-4	1	3
Brewer	†0	1	1-1	0	0
Bradley	‡4	8	6-5	0	0
Carrithers	§0	2	2-2	0	0
Willoughby	2	2	0-0	0	0
Moffitt	1	1	0-0	1	0
McMahon (W 2-0)	2	0	0-0	0	1

*faced three batters in ninth
†faced one batter in ninth
‡faced three batters in fifth
§faced three batters in fifth

Game-Winning RBI: Bonds
LOB: Los Angeles 8, San Francisco 2
BE: Los Angeles 1

2B: Speier, Bonds
3B: Crawford
HR: Buckner, Crawford, McCovey, Bonds
SH: Bradley, Rader, Sadek
SB: Joshua
CS: Matthews

HBP: by Carrithers (Garvey)

Time—2:48
Attendance—15,279
Umpires: E. Sudol, C. Pelekoudas, N. Colosi, & J. McSherry

The Dodgers were held to one hit the next day and lost to the Giants, 3-1. Since Cinncinnati won in Houston, Los Angeles fell to second place. There followed another loss in San Francisco, then four defeats at the hands of the San Diego Padres, running the Dodgers's losing streak to nine games and leaving Los Angeles 2½ games behind.

The Dodgers could not catch the Reds thereafter and finished 3½ games in back with a 95-66 final record.

1974 SUNDAY, SEPTEMBER 15TH, AT DODGER STADIUM

Wynn's Grand Slam Finishes Reds

Sutton Escapes Jams and Wins 6-Hitter, 7-1
L.A. Salvages Last Game of Series to Boost Lead to 2½

Today's Results			
LOS ANGELES 7-Cincinnati 1			
Atlanta 3-San Diego 1			
Houston 6-San Francisco 0 (1st game)			
San Francisco 8-Houston 4 (2nd game)			
Standings	**W-L**	**Pct.**	**GB**
LOS ANGELES	92-54	.630	—
Cincinnati	90-57	.612	2½
Atlanta	81-67	.547	12
Houston	74-73	.503	18½
San Francisco	67-81	.453	26
San Diego	53-95	.358	40

FACING THE TWIN SPECTRES OF THE surging Cincinnati Reds and of their own collapse down the stretch last season, the Los Angeles Dodgers laid a few ghosts to rest today by beating Cincinnati, 7-1. Don Sutton was the winning pitcher, and Jimmy Wynn clinched the victory with a grand slam home run in the seventh inning.

The Dodger victory definitely reversed the momentum in the race for the division pennant. Sure, Los Angeles had been in first place since April 14th. But the Dodgers had led the Reds by as much as 10½ games, and that margin had shrunk to just 1½ by this morning. And the memories of last season, when the Reds had come from 11 games behind to win out (aided by a 9-game Dodger losing streak) were growing in the minds of the fans. After the Reds had won the first two games of this three-game series, manager Walter Alston called a clubhouse meeting. He told his players that they were a better team than the Reds, and today was the time to go out and prove it.

The Reds, however, got the first run of the game and had chances to get more. With the bases loaded in the fifth inning, the league's leading RBI man, Johnny Bench, was called out on strikes. The Reds left the bases loaded again in the sixth and failed to score. Having thusly escaped disaster, the Dodgers stormed in and took the lead with two runs in the bottom of the sixth. Then they put the game out of reach with five in the seventh, Wynn hitting his grand slam and Steve Garvey following with a solo homer.

Sutton, winner of nine of his last ten decisions, was Alston's pitcher. Cincinnati manager Sparky Anderson chose little Freddie Norman. Neither hurler had much trouble in the early going. Norman had the Dodgers off balance with his off-speed screwballs and allowed just one hit and one walk in the first four innings. Sutton also allowed just one hit and one base on balls through four.

The Reds broke through for a run in the fifth, and Sutton nearly pitched himself out of the ballgame. Cesar Geronimo opened the inning by beating out a hit to shortstop. A steal and sacrifice put him on third. Ken Griffey lined to second baseman Dave Lopes for the second out. With pitcher Norman (a .122 hitter) at bat, it looked like Sutton would escape the jam. But Norman punched a hit over short, and Geronimo came home with the first run of the game.

Sutton then lost his control, walking Pete Rose and Joe Morgan to load the bases. He also fell behind on the count to the dangerous Bench, 3 balls and 1 strike. The next pitch was a high fastball, probably out of the strike zone. But Bench, a noted fastball hitter, swung at it and fouled it back. The count was now full, and Sutton did not risk another fastball. Instead he came in with a hard breaking ball, which caught Bench by surprise and nicked the plate for strike three.

Cincinnati missed another big chance in the next inning. Dan Driessen doubled to left with one out. Geronimo singled to the same field, and Driessen held third. Sutton pitched cautiously to Concepcion and issued a walk to load the bases. Rookie Ken Griffey needed only a ground ball or an outfield fly to add to the Reds' lead. But Sutton jammed him with a good fastball and got a pop out to short. Norman was called out on strikes, and the score remained 1-0.

Then the Dodgers finally got to the pesky Mr. Norman. With one out in the bottom of the sixth, Bill Buckner was nicked on the elbow by a screwball and trotted to first. He stole second by sliding in head-first just under Bench's throw. Wynn walked. Garvey hit a ground-rule double to left to drive Buckner home and tie the score.

Anderson decided that his lefthander would not fool the Dodgers any longer, and he replaced him with Pedro Borbon. An intentional pass to Ron Cey loaded the bases, and Joe Ferguson got a run home by hitting into a force play but beating the double play at first.

In the bottom of the seventh, Los Angeles put the game away. Steve Yeager slapped a hit past third base, and Sutton bunted him to second. Lopes popped one just beyond the reach of the infielders for a hit. Yeager advanced only one base, but Lopes streaked to second on the throw to third. After an intentional walk, Wynn came up with the bases loaded and one out. Borbon's first pitch was a sinker with not enough sink on it. Wynn jumped on it and crashed it well over the left field fence for a grand slam. Three runners danced home ahead of him, and Wynn received an enthusiastic reception in the dugout. He also got a standing ovation from the capacity crowd. The fans were still cheering when Garvey hit the second pitch to him 420 feet to center field for another homer.

The score was now 7-1. Given a lead, Sutton was sharp. He retired the Reds in order in the seventh and eighth and gave up only a two-out pinch double in the ninth. Rose flied out to right to end the game.

So the Dodgers had turned back the Reds, and all those ghosts of the past season, too.

Cincinnati	ab	r	h	bi	o	a	e
P. Rose, lf	4	0	1	0	3	0	0
J. Morgan, 2b	3	0	0	0	4	1	0
J. Bench, c	4	0	0	0	7	0	0
T. Perez, 1b	3	0	0	0	5	0	0
D. Driessen, 3b	3	0	1	0	0	1	0
D. Cheney, 3b6	1	0	0	0	0	0	0
C. Geronimo, cf	4	1	2	0	3	0	0
D. Concepcion, ss	2	0	0	0	1	3	0
K. Griffey, rf	4	0	0	0	1	0	0
F. Norman, p	3	0	1	1	0	0	0
P. Borbon, p6	0	0	0	0	0	1	0
W. McEnaney, p7	0	0	0	0	0	0	0
T. Crowley, ph9	1	0	1	0	-	-	-
	32	1	6	1	24	6	0

Los Angeles	ab	r	h	bi	o	a	e
D. Lopes, 2b	4	1	1	0	1	1	0
B. Buckner, lf	2	2	1	0	3	0	0
J. Wynn, cf	3	2	1	4	2	0	0
S. Garvey, 1b	3	1	2	2	7	0	0
R. Cey, 3b	3	0	0	0	1	2	1
J. Ferguson, rf	3	0	0	1	2	0	0
B. Russell, ss	4	0	0	0	1	2	0
S. Yeager, c	4	1	1	0	10	0	0
D. Sutton, p	3	0	0	0	0	0	0
	29	7	6	7	27	5	1

Cincinnati	000 010 000	= 1
Los Angeles	000 002 50x	= 7

	ip	h	r-er	bb	so
Norman (L 11-12)	5⅓	2	2-2	3	4
Borbon	1	4	5-5	2	0
McEnaney	1⅔	0	0-0	0	3
Sutton (W 16-9)	9	6	1-1	4	9

HBP: by Norman (Buckner)
Umpires: E. Sudol, L. Weyer, B. Engel & F. Pulli

Game-Winning RBI: Ferguson
LOB: Cincinnati 9, Los Angeles 5
BE: Cincinnati 1
DP: Garvey unassisted
2B: Driessen, Garvey, Crowley
HR: Wynn, Garvey
SH: Concepcion, Sutton
SB: Perez, Geronimo, Buckner
Time—2:35 Attendance: 52,116

The Reds lost five of their next seven games, while the Dodgers played more consistently, winning 10 of their remaining 16. A late rush by Cincinnati fell short, and Los Angeles captured the West Division championship by 4 games. Their final record was 102-60.

1974 WEDNESDAY, OCTOBER 9TH, AT DODGER STADIUM League Championship Series—Game #4

Crush Pirates 12-1 for Title

THE LOS ANGELES DODGERS' CHAMPIONSHIP JUGGERNAUT ROARED OVER THE DEfenseless Pittsburgh Pirates today, 12-1, and steamed to the National League championship by taking the playoff series, 3 games to 1. Leading the charge were the two heroes of the Dodger drive to the West Division pennant, pitcher Don Sutton and RBI man Steve Garvey. The victory came on owner Walter O'Malley's birthday.

Sutton, who had pitched a four-hit shutout in the first game of the series, pitched eight innings of three-hit ball today and got the win. It was his eleventh straight since his last loss back on August 16th. He left the game today because of a blister on the middle finger of his right hand. He was replaced by relief ace Mike Marshall, who set the Pirates down in order in the ninth.

Garvey, who had led the team in hits and RBIs during the regular season, pounded out four hits and drove in four runs today. He also scored four runs. Two of his hits were home runs.

But this was not just a two-man victory. On the contrary, seven Dodger players got hits, six drove in runs, and five scored. On defense, the team played errorless ball and made two double plays. And the Pittsburgh pitchers were kind enough to contribute eleven walks, Jimmy Wynn, Joe Ferguson, and Steve Yeager strolling three times each.

The Dodgers had won the two games played in Pittsburgh, 3-0 and 5-2. The Pirates had won in Los Angeles yesterday, 7-0. But the Dodgers were confident before today's game. For one thing, they had their hottest pitcher (Sutton) scheduled to work.

Jerry Reuss pitched for the Pirates. In the opening game he had pitched well for seven innings and left for a pinch-hitter trailing 1-0. But today he did not have his control. The lefty walked four men in less than three innings and was charged with three runs.

The Dodgers got their first run in the bottom of the first. Davey Lopes drew Reuss's first base on balls and stole second after Bill Buckner popped out. Jimmy Wynn then pounded a long drive to the center field fence for a run-scoring double. Wynn got to third on Garvey's ground out, and Ferguson walked. Ron Cey's long fly to left was caught, ending the inning.

Los Angeles waited until two were out in the third before getting the offense going again. Wynn then drew a pass. And Garvey ripped a vicious liner to right center that cleared the fence for a two-run homer. After Reuss walked Ferguson, Ken Brett was called in to pitch.

With Sutton shutting the Bucs out, Pittsburgh manager Danny Murtaugh thought something fishy was going on. In the top of the fifth, he asked the home plate umpire to inspect Sutton's glove for foreign substances. Nothing was found, and Don quickly disposed of three Pirate batters.

Garvey did his thing again in the bottom of the fifth. Wynn once again walked, this time with one out. Steve then pulled a long drive into the seats near the left field line for another two-run homer, this time off Brett.

Larry Demery was the Pittsburgh pitcher when the Dodgers scored two more runs in the sixth. Yeager opened with a walk and stole second. After Sutton went out, Lopes came through with a long drive to deep right. Yeager scored easily, and Lopes came home when the relay to third went wild.

Sutton was working on a two-hitter when he struck out Richie Hebner and Al Oliver in the top of the seventh. The third strike to Oliver broke sharply, and Murtaugh again came out to complain. Ump John McSherry again went to the mound and again pronounced Sutton fit to pitch. But the righty threw a fat one to the next batter, and Willie Stargell slugged a homer over the right field fence. That cut the

Los Angeles lead slightly, to 7-1, but it was also the last Pittsburgh hit of the season.

The home team upped its lead with another two-run rally in its half of the seventh. Garvey led off with a single, and Ferguson walked. Dave Giusti was brought in to replace Demery, and he retired the first man he faced. Then Bill Russell singled Garvey home. Yeager fanned, but Sutton contributed an RBI one-bagger.

The final three Los Angeles runs came in the eighth. Wynn again started things with a one-out walk. Garvey smashed an infield hit. And Ferguson drove Wynn home with a single to right. An intentional pass loaded the bases. A bloop single over the second baseman by Russell brought two men home.

With Sutton bothered by a slight blister, manager Walter Alston sent Marshall out to pitch the ninth. Iron Mike had worked in 106 regular-season games and had pitched two perfect innings in the second game of the playoff. Today he again set the Pirates down in order.

After the final out, fans leaped onto the field, and the players hustled to the dressing room for a wet celebration. They had given the man upstairs, Walter O'Malley, a little something extra to celebrate on his 71st birthday, too.

Pittsburgh	ab	r	h	bi	o	a	e
R. Stennett, 2b	4	0	0	0	2	5	1
R. Hebner, 3b	4	0	0	0	1	3	0
A. Oliver, cf	3	0	0	0	0	0	0
W. Stargell, lf	3	1	1	1	5	0	0
D. Parker, rf	3	0	1	0	1	1	0
M. Sanguillen, c	3	0	0	0	3	0	0
E. Kirkpatrick, 1b	2	0	0	0	8	0	0
M. Mendoza, ss	1	0	0	0	3	1	0
P. Popovich, ph6-ss	2	0	1	0	0	0	0
J. Reuss, p	0	0	0	0	0	0	0
K. Brett, p3	1	0	0	0	0	1	0
L. Demery, p6	0	0	0	0	0	1	0
D. Giusti, p7	0	0	0	0	1	0	0
J. Pizarro, p8	0	0	0	0	0	0	0
A. Howe, ph9	1	0	0	0	-	-	-
	27	1	3	1	24	12	1

Los Angeles	ab	r	h	bi	o	a	e
D. Lopes, 2b	4	2	2	1	1	2	0
B. Buckner, lf	5	0	0	0	1	0	0
J. Wynn, cf	2	3	1	1	2	0	0
S. Garvey, 1b	5	4	4	4	9	0	0
J. Ferguson, rf	2	2	1	1	3	0	0
R. Cey, 3b	4	0	1	0	1	1	0
B. Russell, ss	5	0	2	3	1	4	0
S. Yeager, c	2	1	0	0	8	0	0
D. Sutton, p	4	0	1	1	1	3	0
M. Mota, ph8	1	0	0	0	-	-	-
M. Marshall, p9	0	0	0	0	0	0	0
	34	12	12	11	27	10	0

Pittsburgh	000	000	100	=	1
Los Angeles	102	022	23x	=	12

	ip	h	r-er	bb	so
Reuss (L 0-2)	2⅔	2	3-3	4	0
Brett	2⅓	3	2-2	2	1
Demery	*1	2	4-4	2	0
Giusti	1⅓	5	3-3	2	1
Pizarro	⅔	0	0-0	1	0
Sutton (W 2-0)	8	3	1-1	1	7
Marshall	1	0	0-0	0	1

*faced two batters in seventh

Game-Winning RBI: Wynn
LOB: Pittsburgh 1, Los Angeles 9
BE: none
DP: Russell-Garvey (Sanguillen)
Sutton-Garvey
Hebner-Stennett-Kirkpatrick (Mota)
2B: Wynn, Cey
3B: Lopes
HR: Garvey 2, Stargell
SH: Reuss
SB: Lopes, Yeager
Time—2:36 Attendance—54,424

Umpires: J. McSherry, S. Crawford, S. Davidson, N. Colosi, P. Pryor, & L. Weyer

1974 SUNDAY, OCTOBER 13TH, AT DODGER STADIUM
World Series—Game #2

Pick Off A's to Even Series

USING THEIR ACE PITCHING COMBINATION, THE LOS ANGELES DODGERS TODAY WON the second game of the 1974 World Series, 3-2, to offset yesterday's victory by the defending-champion Oakland A's. There were many heroes today for the hometown Dodgers, but pitchers Don Sutton and Mike Marshall and slugger Joe Ferguson stood out.

Sutton won his twelfth consecutive decision, dating back to August 20th. He was touched for just five hits in eight-plus innings, and he had a shutout going when he left the game.

Bullpen star Marshall relieved Sutton with two men on and no outs in the ninth and the score 3-0. He allowed a two-run single to the first batter he faced. Then he saved the game by picking pinch-running specialist Herb Washington off base and striking out two batters.

Ferguson, who had been a defensive star in the first game, provided the biggest offensive blow today. He powdered a tremendous two-run home run off of A's pitcher Vida Blue in the sixth inning to give the Dodgers a 3-0 lead.

Oakland had won the first game of the series by the same score as today's game, 3-2. It had been a frustrating day for Los Angeles because the Dodgers outhit the A's 11 to 6, and Oakland made two errors as compared to one by Los Angeles.

Today's starting pitchers, Blue and Sutton, completely dominated the early going. The A's were unable to even hit a fair ball against Sutton in the first two innings, although they did get a man to second base on a walk and a wild pitch.

The Dodgers managed to scratch a run in the bottom of the second. With one out, Ron Cey walked on four pitches. Bill Russell popped one in back of first base. The ball landed just beyond the reach of right fielder Reggie Jackson and first baseman Gene Tenace, and Cey reached third on the hit easily. Steve Yeager then smashed one past shortstop and up the middle for an RBI single. Sutton and Lopes both struck out, leaving two men on base.

Bert Campaneris got the first Oakland hit with two out in the third, lining a double into the left field corner. Billy North then hit a high chopper toward shortstop and was retired on a fine play by Russell.

The score was 1-0 until the bottom of the sixth. Garvey beat out an infield hit with one gone. Ferguson, who had flied out twice, was the next batter. Blue served up a fastball, and Fergy got all of it, sending a drive high and deep and over the fence in straightaway center field for a two-run homer. When he returned to the outfield in the top of the seventh, Ferguson was given a standing ovation by the pavilion fans.

Jackson got the second Oakland hit in the seventh. But a force out and a double play quickly ended the inning.

Yeager opened the Los Angeles seventh with a hit, and he moved around to third on a bunt and a long fly out. But Bill Buckner bounced out to second base to end the inning.

A great fielding play by Garvey turned back a serious Oakland threat in the eighth. With one out, pinch-hitters Jim Holt and Claudell Washington grounded singles to right field. Campaneris grounded one toward the hole in left, and shortstop Russell fumbled it, loading the bases. North then hit one sharply past the mound. Russell ranged over to his left, gloved the ball, took one long stride to step on second base for a force out, and threw (somewhat off balance) to first. The sidearm sling was in the dirt and it bounced about two feet in front of Garvey. The ball took a high hop, but Steve stayed with it and made a pretty backhanded pickup to complete the double play and save at least one run.

Whereas Sutton had survived the eighth, he didn't get through the ninth. The first A's batter, Sal Bando, was hit by a pitch. Jackson then tried to duck out of the way on an inside pitch, and the ball caromed off his bat and down the left field line for a double, Bando stopping at third. Manager Walter Alston then brought in Marshall, who had finished eight of Sutton's 21 victories this season (including one in the playoffs).

The first man Iron Mike faced, Joe Rudi, dropped a liner into right field for a two-run single. With the score now 3-2, Tenace struck out trying for a home run.

Oakland skipper Alvin Dark then sent pinch-runner Herb Washington into the game to run for Rudi. Washington, a world-class sprinter with no previous baseball experience, was owner Charlie Finley's pet project. He had been in 92 games for Oakland without ever doing anything but pinch-run.

Marshall was familiar with Washington, who had been a student of his at Michigan State University. First baseman Garvey had also known Washington when Steve was at MSU. "The Professor" knew just what to do in this situation. First he lobbed a toss to first, and Washington got back easily. Then he stepped off the rubber and looked Washington back. Then he stepped off again without throwing. Then he stepped off yet again as Washington sauntered back to first. Now Marshall made his move, a quick pivot and hard throw to Garvey, and Washington was picked off easily for the second out.

Marshall then turned his attention to the batter, Angel Mangual, and struck him out.

So the Dodgers had the victory, 3-2, and the series went to Oakland all even.

Oakland (AL)	ab	r	h	bi	o	a	e
B. Campaneris, ss	4	0	1	0	0	1	0
B. North, cf	4	0	0	0	3	0	0
L. Haney, c8	0	0	0	0	2	0	0
S. Bando, 3b	3	1	0	0	0	1	0
R. Jackson, rf	3	1	2	0	2	0	0
J. Rudi, lf	4	0	1	2	3	0	0
H. Washington, pr9	0	0	0	0	-	-	-
G. Tenace, 1b	3	0	0	0	8	0	0
R. Fosse, c	2	0	0	0	5	0	0
J. Alou, ph8	1	0	0	0	-	-	-
B. Odom, p8	0	0	0	0	0	0	0
A. Mangual, ph9	1	0	0	0	-	-	-
D. Green, 2b	2	0	0	0	1	2	0
J. Holt, ph8	1	0	1	0	-	-	-
D. Maxvill, pr8-2b	0	0	0	0	0	0	0
V. Blue, p	2	0	0	0	0	1	0
C. Washington, ph8-cf	1	0	1	0	0	0	0
	31	2	6	2	24	5	0

Los Angeles (NL)	ab	r	h	bi	o	a	e
D. Lopes, 2b	4	0	0	0	3	2	0
B. Buckner, lf	4	0	0	0	3	0	0
J. Wynn, cf	3	0	0	0	0	0	0
S. Garvey, 1b	4	1	2	0	7	0	0
J. Ferguson, rf	3	1	1	2	0	0	0
R. Cey, 3b	3	1	0	0	2	1	0
B. Russell, ss	3	0	1	0	2	3	1
S. Yeager, c	3	0	2	1	10	1	0
D. Sutton, p	2	0	0	0	0	1	0
M. Marshall, p9	0	0	0	0	0	1	0
	29	3	6	3	27	9	1

Oakland	000 000 002	= 2
Los Angeles	010 002 00x	= 3

	ip	h	r-er	bb	so
Blue (L 0-1)	7	6	3-3	2	5
Odom	1	0	0-0	1	2
Sutton (W 1-0)	*8	5	2-2	2	9
Marshall (sv#1)	1	1	0-0	0	2

*faced two batters in ninth
HBP: by Sutton (Bando)
WP: Sutton

Game-Winning RBI: Yeager
LOB: Oakland 5, Los Angeles 6
BE: Oakland 1
DP: Sutton-Lopes-Garvey (Tenace)
Russell-Garvey (North)
2B: Campaneris, Jackson
HR: Ferguson
SH: Sutton
SB: Ferguson
Picked Off: H. Washington
Time—2:40 Attendance—55,989

Umpires: B. Kunkel, D. Harvey, D. Denkinger, A. Olsen, R. Luciano, & T. Gorman

The Dodgers could not match the A's in Oakland, losing three straight, tightly-fought games, 3-2, 5-2, & 3-2. That gave Oakland its third straight world championship.

1975 THURSDAY, APRIL 17TH, AT DODGER STADIUM

Win 4th Straight Thriller from Reds

Garvey Gets Five Hits, Marshall Picks up the Win
Seesaw Game Goes to L.A. in 11 Innings, 5-4

Today's Results

LOS ANGELES 5-Cincinnati 4 (11 innings)
Atlanta 2-Houston 1 (10 innings)
no other clubs scheduled

Standings	W-L	Pct.	GB
LOS ANGELES	6-4	.600	—
Atlanta	6-4	.600	—
San Diego	4-3	.571	½
San Francisco	4-4	.500	1
Cincinnati	4-6	.400	2
Houston	3-6	.333	2½

THOSE BIG NATIONAL LEAGUE WEST rivals, the Cincinnati Reds and Los Angeles Dodgers, staged another battle royal today at Dodger Stadium. Behind the heroic hitting of Steve Garvey, the home team came out on top again, this time 5-4 in 11 innings. That gave Los Angeles a sweep of the four-game series and revenge for three consecutive losses in Cincinnati to open the season.

There was still a very long way to go in the race, of course, but the seven games played between these two teams had all the tension and excitement of September battles for first place. In Cincinnati on April 7th, 9th, and 10th, the Reds squeaked out three come-from-behind, one-run victories. The Dodgers turned the tables by winning this Monday, Tuesday, Wednesday, and Thursday. In the Wednesday game, the Dodgers overcame a 5-0 deficit to pull out a 7-6 triumph.

This afternoon (Thursday), the two teams staged another barnburner. The lead changed hands three times, and the score was tied on three other occasions. After the Reds had scored two runs in the top of the ninth to go ahead, 4-3, Steve Garvey drove home a run in the bottom to send the game into extra innings. Two-out singles by Jimmy Wynn and Garvey and an error by the first baseman gave the home team the winning run in the eleventh. Garvey was 5-for-6 on the day. And Mike Marshall picked up his second win in less than 24 hours.

The Reds scored the first run of the game when Dave Concepcion blasted a solo home run in the second inning.

The Dodgers broke through for a run against Reds' starter Gary Nolan in the fifth. Ron Cey led off with a double and eventually scored on a two-out single by Davey Lopes. The inning ended with Jimmy Wynn, who had homered in four straight games, bouncing out with the bases loaded.

Garvey scored the go-ahead run for Los Angeles in the sixth. He doubled to left and came home on Willie Crawford's single to right.

Dodger pitcher Andy Messersmith had little trouble with the hard-hitting Cincinnati lineup until the eighth inning. Then pinch-hitters Terry Crowley and Dan Driessen and leadoff man Pete Rose erupted with consecutive singles to tie the game.

The Dodgers got one run off reliever Pedro Borbon in the bottom of the eighth but missed a chance to get more. Wynn walked leading off. Garvey naturally came through with a base knock to left. Crawford bunted the runners along, and Joe Ferguson was intentionally passed to fill the bases with one out. Ron Cey gave the fans a thrill with a deep drive to right. But the ball stayed in the park, and only one run scored on the sacrifice fly. Rick Auerbach then bounced out.

Los Angeles's lead did not last long. Cesar Geronimo opened the top of the ninth with a home run over the right field fence to tie the score.

After Concepcion walked, Dodger manager Walter Alston decided to remove the tiring Messersmith. Since the pitcher's spot was due to lead off the bottom of the ninth, Alston made two changes at once: he brought in pitcher Mike Marshall and replaced third baseman Cey with Ken McMullen. This put McMullen in the ninth slot in the order. McMullen wound up hitless in two trips to the plate, but he helped save the game with his fielding.

With the potential lead run on first, Cincinnati skipper Sparky Anderson ordered

Ken Griffey to bunt. His bunt was in the air, and McMullen raced in and grabbed it. Doug Flynn followed with a successful sacrifice. Driessen worked Marshall for a walk. Then Pete Rose pushed a single to left to drive Concepcion home. Joe Morgan walked, loading the bases for slugger Johnny Bench. Bench smashed one that looked line a sure two-run single to left. But McMullen dove to his left, knocked the ball down, and threw to second for a force out to end the inning.

It could have been worse, but the Dodgers were still trailing, 4-3, when they came to bat in the bottom of the ninth. McMullen grounded out. Lopes singled to center. With lefthanded hitting Bill Buckner due up, Anderson called southpaw Will McEnaney in to pitch. Alston countered by sending veteran Manny Mota, a righty, to the plate. Manny delivered an infield single. Anderson now called on Clay Carroll. He got Wynn on a fly ball to left for the second out. But Garvey delivered another key hit, driving Lopes home from second with a single to center, and the game was tied.

Carroll and Marshall pitched through the tenth inning without any trouble. And Marshall pitched around an error in the eleventh with the aid of a pickoff throw by catcher Ferguson.

In the home half of the eleventh, Wynn tapped a slow roller toward third and barely beat it out for a two-out single. Garvey got his fifth hit of the game, a hard grounder through the left side, sending Wynn to second. Crawford followed with a hot shot to first baseman Driessen, who couldn't handle it. The ball caromed into right field, and Wynn scored easily.

It was another victory for Los Angeles, completing a big sweep. Less than two weeks into the campaign, the season had already been filled with thrills.

Cincinnati	ab	r	h	bi	o	a	e
P. Rose, lf	6	0	2	2	2	0	0
J. Morgan, 2b	3	0	2	0	3	1	0
D. Chaney, 2b9	0	0	0	0	0	1	0
J. Bench, c	5	0	1	0	4	2	0
T. Perez, 1b	4	0	0	0	9	0	0
P. Borbon, p8	0	0	0	0	0	0	0
W. McEnaney, p9	0	0	0	0	0	0	0
C. Carroll, p9	1	0	0	0	0	1	0
C. Geronimo, cf	5	1	1	1	1	0	1
D. Concepcion, ss	4	2	1	1	2	3	0
K. Griffey, rf	5	0	2	0	3	0	0
J. Vukovich, 3b	2	0	0	0	1	2	0
T. Crowley, ph8	1	0	1	0	-	-	-
D. Flynn, pr8-3b	1	1	0	0	0	2	0
G. Nolan, p	2	0	0	0	0	4	0
D. Driessen, ph8-1b	2	0	2	0	7	0	1
	41	4	12	4	32	16	2

Los Angeles	ab	r	h	bi	o	a	e
D. Lopes, 2b	5	1	3	1	1	3	0
B. Buckner, lf	4	0	1	0	1	0	0
M. Mota, ph9	1	0	1	0	-	-	-
T. Paciorek, pr9-lf	1	0	0	0	0	0	0
J. Wynn, cf	5	2	1	0	3	0	0
S. Garvey, 1b	6	1	5	1	15	0	0
W. Crawford, rf	3	0	1	1	3	0	0
J. Ferguson, c	4	0	0	0	7	1	0
R. Cey, 3b	3	1	1	1	0	3	0
M. Marshall, p9	1	0	0	0	0	1	0
R. Auerbach, ss	4	0	0	0	1	4	1
A. Messersmith, p	2	0	0	0	0	2	0
K. McMullen, 3b9	2	0	0	0	2	2	0
	41	5	13	4	33	16	1

Cincinnati	010 000 012 00	=	4
Los Angeles	000 011 011 01	=	5

two out when winning run scored

	ip	h	r-er	bb	so
Nolan	7	7	2-2	3	1
Borbon	1⅓	2	2-2	2	0
McEnaney	*0	1	0-0	0	0
Carroll (L 1-2)	2⅓	3	1-0	1	0
Messersmith	†8	9	4-4	2	6
Marshall (W 2-1)	3	3	0-0	2	1

*faced one batter in ninth
†faced two batters in ninth
Umpires: T. Gorman, L. Weyer, D. Rennert, & F. Pulli

Game-Winning Run scored on Driessen's error
LOB: Cincinnati 9, Los Angeles 13
BE: Los Angeles 1, Cincinnati 0
DP: Messersmith-Auerbach-Garvey (Perez)
2B: Cey, Garvey
HR: Concepcion, Geronimo
SF: Cey
SH: Messersmith, Crawford, Flynn
SB: Lopes, Buckner, Morgan
CS: Auerbach, Crawford, Griffey
Picked Off: Morgan
Time—3:01
Attendance—27,835

Los Angeles opened up a 5½ game lead over Cincinnati and the rest of the division by May 16th. Then the Reds caught fire and won 43 of their next 53 to take a 12½ game lead by the All-Star break.

The Dodgers, hampered by injuries, were unable to make a race of it, finishing second, 20 games behind. Los Angeles had a final record of 88-74.

1976 WEDNESDAY, MAY 5TH, AT WRIGLEY FIELD, CHICAGO

Dodgers Win Chicago Windfest, 14-12

Gale Plays Havoc with All Fly Balls
Sutton Gets Win, Cruz Hits Two Homers

Today's Results			
LOS ANGELES 14-Chicago 12			
Cincinnati 2-New York 0 (11 innings)			
San Diego 6-Montreal 4			
Philadelphia 6-Houston 3			
St. Louis 4-Atlanta 0			
Pittsburgh 6-San Francisco 4			
Standings	**W-L**	**Pct.**	**GB**
LOS ANGELES	14- 9	.609	—
Cincinnati	12- 9	.571	1
San Diego	11-11	.500	2½
Houston	12-13	.480	3
Atlanta	8-14	.364	5½
San Francisco	8-14	.364	5½

QUICK SPORTS FANS, WHAT'S DON SUTTON's least-favorite spot on the major league map? And now another stumper: What's young Dodger outfielder Henry Cruz's favorite ballpark?

If you answered "Wrigley Field" to both of those questions, you go to the head of the class!

Today, in a bizarre game that could have happened only in the Chicago Cubs' quaint home stadium, the visiting Los Angeles Dodgers pounded out seven home runs and survived a rash of dropped fly balls to defeat the hometown Cubbies by the football score of 14-12. The victory was the eleventh in a row for the Dodgers. Sutton was roughed up for seven runs in less than six innings, but he got the win with relief help from three other pitchers. And Cruz, fighting for a regular berth in the Los Angeles outfield, hit two home runs, including the one that put the Dodgers into the lead for good. Henry had hit a homer here yesterday, too.

For the flu-ridden Cubs, Rick Monday hit two four-baggers and drove home six runs. Because of illness in the bullpen, starter Ray Burris stayed in through six innings and was charged with nine runs and the defeat.

Besides the home runs, the game featured seven errors (four by the Dodgers) and uncounted missed flies that were scored as hits. And there were 37 hits in all, 21 by the Cubs. And just to make the day complete at beautiful Wrigley Field, a ball got stuck in the ivy that covered the outfield wall.

The Dodgers' seven home runs set a new franchise record and was one short of the major league record. Los Angeles also fell one inning short of a record by scoring in eight of the nine innings in the game. Paul Reuschel set the visitors down in order in the ninth to after they had scored in every other inning. The Chicago fans gave Reuschel a standing ovation for his feat.

The game was a nightmare for the fielders as well as the pitchers. They spent much of the afternoon zigging and zagging around trying to get under fly balls. Dodger manager Walter Alston confessed after the game that he almost lost his cool over some of the dropped flies. He hurt his toe kicking the bat rack after one bad muff in the ninth. "Fans like these kinds of games," he said, "but they're sure tough on a manager."

Pitcher Sutton was of the same opinion. Talking about the vagaries of Wrigley Field, he quipped, "If I had to pitch here, I'd quit and sell Toyotas." Indeed, last Monday Sutton had vetoed a proposed deal that would have sent him to the Cubs. Today's victory gave him a lifetime record of just 4-9 in Chicago.

The Dodgers' Bill Buckner opened the scoring with a homer over the right field wall.

The Cubs tied the game in the bottom of the first on a single by Monday, Bill Madlock's double into the vines, and an infield out.

Davey Lopes drove in two Dodger runs in the second with a line triple to center after a booted ground ball had opened the gates.

Ron Cey homered in the third, and Bill Russell connected in the fourth.

A Dodger error on a pickoff play gave the Cubs a run in the third.

Rick Monday tied the game in the fourth with the longest home run of the day.

It was a three-run job that bounced onto the street beyond the right field fence and crashed into the building across the way. Two singles around a throwing error then put Chicago ahead, 6-5.

But Cruz put the Dodgers back on top with a fifth-inning drive into the center field seats with Steve Garvey on base.

Los Angeles managed two runs in the sixth without the aid of a homer.

Sutton was finally routed in the bottom of the sixth after a walk and two singles had pushed one run across.

Pinch-hitter Ed Goodson hit a three-run homer off Ken Crosby in the Dodger seventh. And Cruz and Steve Yeager hit back-to-back solo shots against Reuschel in the eighth. They put Los Angeles ahead by a touchdown, 14-7.

Charlie Hough, the third L.A. pitcher, was charged with a run in the last of the eighth when a two-out pop fell at the feet of shortstop Russell for a wind-aided RBI single.

In the ninth, the Cubs came close to pulling the game out. Manny Trillo led off with a double and scored on a single by Steve Swisher. Center fielder Dusty Baker caught one fly ball (by Dave Rosello) but dropped another (by Joe Wallis). Rick Monday then cracked a three-run homer, his second of the game.

Alston rushed Mike Marshall into take Hough's place. He got Jose Gardenal to fly to Baker, who made the catch with some difficulty. Madlock connected for this third double of the day. But Champ Summers, representing the tying run, was retired on a grounder to second to end the game.

It wasn't the prettiest victory in Dodger history, but it was a win. And even Don Sutton didn't complain about that.

Los Angeles	ab	r	h	bi	o	a	e
D. Lopes, 2b	4	0	1	2	1	3	2
B. Buckner, lf	5	1	1	2	2	0	0
J. Hale, rf9	0	0	0	0	0	0	0
D. Baker, cf	5	1	2	0	3	0	1
S. Garvey, 1b	5	1	2	1	6	0	0
R. Cey, 3b	5	1	1	1	0	0	0
H. Cruz, rf-lf9	5	3	2	3	4	0	0
S. Yeager, c	4	2	3	1	7	1	0
B. Russell, ss	5	3	2	1	4	4	1
D. Sutton, p	3	1	1	0	0	2	0
S. Wall, p6	0	0	0	0	0	0	0
E. Goodson, ph7	1	1	1	3	-	-	-
C. Hough, p7	1	0	0	0	0	0	0
M. Marshall, p9	0	0	0	0	0	0	0
	43	14	16	14	27	10	4

Chicago	ab	r	h	bi	o	a	e
R. Monday, cf	6	4	3	6	7	0	0
J. Cardenal, lf	6	1	3	0	3	0	0
B. Madlock, 3b	6	2	4	1	1	2	0
C. Summers, rf	6	0	3	4	2	0	1
P. LaCock, 1b	2	0	0	0	2	0	0
A. Thornton, ph6-1b	2	0	0	0	2	1	0
M. Trillo, 2b	5	1	2	0	3	3	0
S. Swisher, c	5	2	4	1	4	0	0
D. Rosello, ss	4	1	2	0	2	2	2
R. Burris, p	2	0	0	0	0	0	0
M. Adams, ph6	0	0	0	0	-	-	-
K. Crosby, p7	0	0	0	0	1	0	0
R. Hundley, ph7	1	0	0	0	-	-	-
P. Reuschel, p8	0	0	0	0	0	0	0
J. Wallis, ph9	1	1	0	0	-	-	-
	46	12	21	12	27	8	3

Los Angeles	121	122	320	=	14
Chicago	101	401	014	=	12

	ip	h	r-er	bb	so
Sutton (W 3-3)	5⅔	14	7-6	2	4
Wall	⅓	0	0-0	0	0
Hough	2⅓	6	5-3	1	1
Marshall (sv #5)	⅔	1	0-0	0	0
Burris (L 1-3)	6	11	9-6	2	2
Crosby	1	3	3-3	1	0
Reuschel	2	2	2-2	0	1

Time—2:50 Attendance—6,126

Game-Winning RBI: Cruz
LOB: Los Angeles 6, Chicago 10
BE: Los Angeles 2, Chicago 1
DP: Lopes-Russell-Garvey (Monday)
Rosello-Trillo-LaCock (Russell)
Russell-Garvey (Swisher)
2B: Madlock 3, Swisher, Sutton, Trillo
3B: Lopes
HR: Buckner, Cey, Russell, Cruz 2,
Goodson, Yeager, Monday 2
SF: Buckner
CS: Madlock

Umpires: T. Gorman, P. Pryor, J. McSherry, & A. Williams

The Dodgers won their twelfth straight game two days later in Philadelphia, 10-8.

But the powerful Cincinnati Reds overtook them during the Memorial Day weekend, and the Dodgers finished a distant second again. This time their final record was 92-70, which left them 10 games behind. Lack of hitting hurt them the most.

Sutton, however, enjoyed his first 20-win season, finishing with a 21-10 mark.

Walter Alston stepped down as manager after 23 years with the team. He was succeeded by Tommy Lasorda, who took over with four games left in the season.

Chapter XVII Lasorda's Dodger Bluebloods

1977 August 8th
Tommy John Hits a Home Run

1977 League Championship Series Game No. 3
Miracle Rally Tops Phils

1977 World Series Game No. 2
Beat Yanks with Hooton & Homers

1978 September 4th
Five-Run Rally Turns Giants Back

1978 League Championship Series Game No. 4
Russell's Single Follows Error to Win Flag

1978 World Series Game No. 2
Cey Drives in 4, Welch Fans Jackson

1979 May 25th
Seven L.A. Homers & One Fight with Cincinnati

1980 October 5th
Another Great Comeback Forces a Playoff

1980 Playoff
Dodger Pennant Dream Collapses

1981 May 14th
Fernando Wins 8th Straight

1981 Division Championship Series Game No. 5
Shutout by Reuss Completes Comeback

1981 League Championship Series Game No. 5
Monday's Homer Wins League Title

1981 World Series Game No. 6
"Comeback Dodgers" Crush Yanks for Championship

1982 August 8th
Eighth Straight Win Over Braves

AFTER MANAGING THE DODGERS FOR 23 YEARS, WALTER ALSTON STEPPED DOWN AT the end of the 1976 season and was succeeded by Thomas Charles Lasorda. Tommy's style was the antithesis of Walt's in many ways. Whereas Alston was a man of few words, Lasorda could talk for hours on end. And whereas Alston projected the image of an aloof father figure, his successor reveled in close contact with his players. When a Dodger hit a home run or completed pitching a good game, Lasorda was always ready to demonstrate his appreciation with a big hug and a hearty pat on the back. Even before he became manager, Lasorda had become famous for his claim that his veins ran with Dodger Blue blood. He emphasized loyalty to his players, and he practiced it in return.

Exhorting the spirit of the "Big Dodger in the Sky," Lasorda prepared for the 1977 season by psyching his players up. Dusty Baker, who had had a miserable season in 1976, was told emphatically that the left field job was his. He responded with a banner year. Lasorda told everyone that Bill Russell was the best shortstop on the planet, and Russell gave a top-notch effort to try and live up to the billing. Lasorda convinced team-player Steve Garvey that it would help everyone if he went for more home runs, even if it meant sacrificing Garvey's cherished 200 hits in a season. Garvey adapted his style and wound up with a career high in runs-batted-in.

The Dodger 30 Home Run Men of 1977:
(kneeling) Dusty Baker & Ron Cey; (standing) Steve Garvey & Reggie Smith

With the offense geared toward the long ball for the first time in Los Angeles Dodger history, the team ran away from the rest of the West Division early in the 1977 race. Through May 7th, the Dodgers had an eye-popping won-lost record of 22-4 and an incredible 10½-game lead. Ron Cey had the best batting statistics with a .372 average, 11 homers, and 38 RBIs. As a team Los Angeles had 25 homers in those first 26 gamers. By May 17th, the lead over the second-place Reds had bulged to 13 games, and the race was as good as over.

The pitching was very solid. Lasorda's five-man starting rotation (lefties Tommy John and Doug Rau and righties Don Sutton, Burt Hooton, and Rick Rhoden) started all but three of the team's games all season. In the bullpen, Charlie Hough was very effective in the first half, accumulating 19 saves. He slumped later on, but Mike Garman and Elias Sosa were there to pick up the slack.

John started the year more slowly than the rest. But after beating Tom Seaver in Cincinnati in late June, he emerged as the ace of the staff. He ran off eleven straight wins in the middle of the campaign and wound up with a 20-7 record. Because of his winning ways and the fact that he had a tendon from his right arm transplanted into his left elbow following a 1974 injury, he became a sports celebrity.

Cey, Garvey, Baker and Reggie Smith continued supplying home runs with regularity, and the Reds never mounted a serious pennant drive. The Dodger lead peaked at 14 games in late July, and the final margin was 10 games. The four big sluggers each hit 30 or more home runs, although it took Baker until the final game of the season to do it. And the club set a new all-time record by drawing 2,955,087 paying customers.

In the playoffs, Los Angeles was matched against a very tough Philadelphia Phillies team. In the first game, John was knocked out, and Los Angeles fell behind 5-1. Ron Cey then broke a 1-for-34 slump with a big grand slam off Steve Carlton to tie the score. But the Phils won out in the ninth, 7-5. In the second game, Baker

Tommy John in the Dodger dugout after hitting a home run, August 8, 1977

broke a 1-1 tie with a grand slam and Sutton went the distance to win 7-1. The third game was the most exciting. The Dodgers gave the Phillies five runs on three bases-loaded walks and two wild throws. Trailing with two out in the ninth, 5-3, old Vic Davalillo started a rally with a bunt single. Monny Mota, Davey Lopes, and Bill Russell followed with hits, the Phillies threw a couple away, and the Dodgers won 6-5. The fourth game was all Dodgers. Baker hit a two-run homer early, and John pitched masterfully to win 4-1 and cinch the series.

The World Series against the New York Yankees did not go so well. The Dodgers outhomered the Yanks, 9 to 8, but New York got better pitching, especially from Mike Torrez and Ron Guidry, and won in six games.

For 1978, the Dodgers signed their first high-priced free agent, reliever Terry Forster, but they made few other roster changes. Things started out well enough, with Los Angeles leading the West into mid-May. Then problems developed. The home runs of the previous year were just not coming as often, and all the starters except John got off to slower starts than in 1977.

By late June, the Dodgers trailed the surprising San Francisco Giants by 6 games. On June 30th, newcomer Bob Welch made his first pitching appearance, beating the Reds to help the Dodgers sweep a doubleheader. Welch soon proved himself effective both starting and relieving. In July, Los Angeles climbed back into the thick of the race. But as the calendar turned to August, the Dodgers dropped six in a row, including two to the Giants. On August 5th, Welch halted the skid with a 2-0 shutout in San Francisco, launching the Dodgers onto a seven-game winning streak that put them into the division lead.

On August 20th, the Dodger clubhouse was the scene of a scuffle between Don Sutton and Steve Garvey. Garvey had not been hitting and had resented some comment by Sutton. The incident blew over, and Garvey's bat soon started to ring out with hits.

San Francisco hung close going into September. On the 4th, the Giants came to L.A. trailing by only 1 game. They jumped out to a 4-0 lead, but the Dodgers scored five runs in the fifth inning and won 5-4. Los Angeles also won the next game, 9-2, and the Giants never threatened again. With a week to go in the season, the Dodgers clinched the pennant in their final home game. The season's attendance was an incredible 3,347,845. A slump on the road reduced the final margin to 2½ games over Cincinnati.

In the League Championship Series, the Phillies were again defeated 3 games to 1. The Dodgers won the first two games in Philadelphia with Garvey and Lopes being the hitting heroes. Steve Carlton prevented a sweep by winning the third game for Philadelphia. But the Dodgers wrapped up the series in Game #4, 4-3 in ten innings.

The World Series again matched Los Angeles against New York, and again the Yankees won 4 games to 2. The Dodgers won the first two games, the second being a dramatic, 4-3 affair in which Welch struck out Reggie Jackson for the final out. But the Yankees roared back and took the next four games in a row.

After helping pitch Los Angeles to two pennants in a row, Tommy John opted for free agency and signed with the Yankees. And in November, Terry Forster underwent elbow surgery, from which he did not fully rebound. After the 1979 season began, Doug Rau developed shoulder troubles and was lost after June 2nd. The sum of these developments was a collapse of the Dodgers' pitching. The bullpen was especially unreliable.

The team played erratically through the first two months. On May 25th, the Dodgers launched a modest spurt with a 17-6 victory over the Reds, and by the end of the month they were at .500. Then disaster struck in June. The team won only 7 of 27 games that month and fell completely out of the race. The skid lasted until the All-Star break in mid-July. When the vacation came, the Dodgers were deep in last place with a miserable 36-57 record. The staff ERA was an outsized 4.26, the second worst in the league. And the offense was only eighth in the circuit.

In the second game after the break, Reggie Smith injured his leg and was as good as through for the year. The offense improved only slightly in the second half. But the pitching came on strong, especially rookie Rick Sutcliffe, who was 9-2 in the last 2½ months. Another newcomer, veteran lefthander Jerry Reuss also improved dramatically in the second half, although his final record for the season was a lackluster 7-14.

By the end of the season, the ERA was down to 3.83, and the team was up to third place in the division with a 79-83 record.

The Dodgers opened the 1980 season with Forster and Rau still on the disabled list and six rookies on the 25-man roster. There were high hopes that free-agent acquisitions Don Stanhouse and Dave Goltz could set the pitching straight, but they were both big disappointments. Los Angeles won only 3 of its first 10 games and was already 6 games behind the defending champion Reds.

But suddenly the Dodgers won 10 in a row and leaped into the thick of the race. Reggie Smith was the leading hitter on the club for much of the summer. Jerry Reuss started out as the early-season bullpen stopper, then switched into the team's most consistent starter. Dusty Baker and Don Sutton also played well most of the season. The Dodgers alternated in the lead with the Astros, and the Reds stayed close behind most of the year. Rookie Steve Howe emerged as the ace relief pitcher, and the Dodger bullpen was strong down the stretch.

Smith suffered from a shoulder injury and started his last game on July 27th. The Dodgers missed his .323 hitting dearly. But the other players, particularly Ron Cey, picked up the slack. Bill Russell had a finger smashed at a critical time in September, but Derrel Thomas stepped in and did a credible job at shortstop.

Los Angeles and Houston were tied for the lead with just 10 games left to play. Then the Astros won six of seven while the Dodgers lost four of seven. The Astros came to L.A. with a 3-game lead and only three games left on the schedule. Needing to sweep the series and win a playoff game, the Dodgers won the first three games all by one run. Joe Ferguson, Steve Garvey, and Ron Cey all hit dramatic game-winning homers in successive games. That set up a one-game playoff. There the Dodger miracle came to an ignominious end one game too soon. Two errors helped the Astros to an early lead, and Joe Niekro held the Dodgers off to win easily, 7-1.

Rookie lefthander Fernando Valenzuela, a Mexican who spoke no English, had pitched in relief in 10 games down the stretch in 1980 without yielding an earned

Pedro Guerrero after hitting a home run in the sixth game of the 1981 World Series

run. With Don Sutton gone via free agency, Valenzuela won a spot in the starting rotation in 1981. And when Jerry Reuss and Burt Hooton both came up with minor injuries, Valenzuela got the assignment to pitch on opening day. He responded with a five-hit shutout against the Astros and was on his way to stardom. In his next seven starts, he allowed just four runs and ran his record to 8-0. This suddenly made him the hottest property in baseball. Everywhere he pitched, the fans jammed the parks. And nowhere more than in Los Angeles, where Fernando became the idol of the huge Chicano community.

Another youngster, Pedro Guerrero out of the Dominican Republic, was the Dodgers' leading slugger in the early going, and Los Angeles enjoyed leads as large as 6½ games. After some poor showings and some hard-luck defeats, Valenzuela's record was 9-4 when the season was interrupted by a players' strike on June 12th. At the time, the Dodgers' early lead had dwindled to just ½ game over the Reds.

After an eight-week walkout, the strike was ended and play was resumed. It was agreed that the season would be split, and the division leaders in the first half would qualify for a playoff with the winners in the second half. Thusly, the Dodgers were lame-duck champions for the second eight-week segment of the season. They played well until the final two weeks, when they dropped to fourth place due to a batting slump.

In the divisional playoff against Houston, the slump continued in the first two games. Valenzuela and Reuss each pitched well, but the Dodgers totalled only one run, and the Astros beat reliever Dave Stewart twice, 3-1 and 1-0. Trailing in the best-of-five series 2 games to 0, the Dodgers returned to Los Angeles and turned things round completely. A three-run first inning and a three-run ninth won the third game, 6-1. Valenzuela outpitched Vern Ruhle in the fourth game and won 2-1. In the decisive fifth game, Reuss hurled a 4-0 shutout, and the Dodgers advanced to the League Championship Series against the Montreal Expos.

In the opener of the league playoffs, Hooton, Welch, and Howe combined to win, 5-1. The Expos and Ray Burris beat Valenzuela in the second game, 3-0. Steve Rogers outpitched Reuss in the third game, and Montreal won again, 4-1. Facing elimination, the Dodgers battled back to win the fourth game, 7-1, with Garvey hitting the tie-breaking home run in the eighth inning. In the fifth game, Rick Monday homered in the ninth inning to make a winner out of Valenzuela and send the Dodgers into the World Series.

Los Angeles dropped the first two games of the series to the New York Yankees, 5-3 and 3-0. In the third game, Fernando survived a shaky start, and the Dodgers rallied to win, 5-4. A wild uphill battle won the fourth game for Los Angeles, 8-7; and Reuss beat Ron Guidry in the fifth game, 2-1, on back-to back home runs by Pedro Guerrero and Steve Yeager. The Dodgers then wrapped up the series in New York by taking the sixth game, 9-2.

The fabled infield of Garvey, Lopes, Russell, and Cey had finally won it all in its eighth year together. The combination was then broken up over the winter with the trade of Lopes to Oakland for a minor league infielder.

Young Steve Sax took over at second base, and he played rather well in the first half of 1982. But injuries and an ineffective bullpen kept the Dodgers from getting over .500 to stay until mid-June. As July was winding down, it appeared that the Atlanta Braves were running away with the division title. The Dodgers were trailing by 10½ games on July 30th. But they dramatically swept two four-game series in two weekends from the Braves and leaped into the lead by August 10th.

But the Braves snapped out of their slump and regained first place by the end of August. The Dodgers then rebounded and built up a 3-game lead with just twelve games to play. Then the bottom fell out of the Los Angeles pennant drive. The hitting stopped, especially with men on base, and the Dodgers lost eight games in a row to fall from the lead.

They won the next three and found themselves trailing by 1 game on the final day of the season. Although the Braves lost in San Diego, the Dodgers were beaten in San Francisco, 5-3, on a three-run homer by the Giants' Joe Morgan.

It had been a very exciting race, but second place was a very disappointing way to finish.

Tom Lasorda hugs the World Championship Trophy

1977 MONDAY EVENING, AUGUST 8TH, AT DODGER STADIUM

Tommy John Hits a Home Run

And Shuts Reds Out on Two Hits, 4-0
Retires Last 16 Batters in a Row

Today's Results

LOS ANGELES 4-Cincinnati 0
Montreal 6-San Diego 5
other clubs not scheduled

Standings	W-L	Pct.	GB
LOS ANGELES	68-43	.613	—
Cincinnati	55-55	.500	12½
Houston	52-60	.464	16½
San Francisco	50-61	.450	18
San Diego	48-67	.417	22
Atlanta	40-69	.367	27

LOS ANGELES'S TOMMY JOHN, THE MAN with the bionic elbow, did it to the Cincinnati Reds again tonight. He raised his record against the defending world champions to 3-0 for the season and 8-1 lifetime with a brilliant 4-0 victory. And not only did he pitch a two-hit shutout, he also connected for a home run to provide Los Angeles with its first run.

John missed half of the 1974 season and the entire 1975 campaign because of a torn ligament in his left (pitching) elbow. In September, 1974, he had an operation that took a tendon out of his right wrist and placed it in his left elbow to repair the damage to his pitching arm. He first tested his elbow in late 1975 in the Arizona Instructional League. In 1976, he pitched 207 innings for the Dodgers (with a 10-10 record) to prove that the surgery was successful. This season, relying on a natural sinker and good control, he has blossomed into an outstanding pitcher.

Today's victory moved the high-flying Dodgers to 12½ games ahead of the second-place Reds. Los Angeles took the division lead on April 16th. By May 6th, the Dodgers had a 22-4 record and a 10½ game advantage. The key players in the great getaway were sluggers Ron Cey and Steve Garvey (who combined for 17 homers and 60 RBIs in 26 games), starting pitchers Don Sutton, Rick Rhoden, and Don Rau (who were 13-0 with a cumulative ERA of 2.90), and reliever Charlie Hough (3-0 with 7 saves).

Tommy John, on the other hand, had only one decision in that period. As late as mid-June, his ERA was an unimpressive 4.10.

But starting on June 18th, he was undefeated in seven decisions (including tonight's), and the Dodgers had managed to win the other two games that he started but did not get a decision in. And his earned-run-average shrank to 2.74. And he won some big games in his streak. Probably the biggest came on June 24th, when he beat the Reds' newly-acquired pitching ace Tom Seaver before 51,000 in Cincinnati. On July 16th he stopped a three-game Dodger losing streak by beating the Padres 1-0. And tonight he snapped a four-game skid.

The game tonight, which started at 5:40 p.m. to accomodate national television, was typical of John's work. Using the sinker extensively, he got 17 outs on ground balls. His control was excellent, with only one walk charged against him. And he got more effective as the game progressed, retiring the last 16 batters in a row. The Dodger infield did not get its usual quota of double plays tonight, but that was because so few Reds got to first base.

Cincinnati managed just two hits, and one was of the infield variety. And only four men got to base at all. Their biggest scoring opportunity came in the second inning. George Foster led off with bouncing hit up the middle that Davey Lopes was unable to backhand cleanly. Johnny Bench grounded to first baseman Garvey, whose throwing error trying to force Foster put two men on base. Dave Concepcion bunted the runners to second and third. John got a big out by fanning Dan Driessen. And Lopes made a fine play to his left to flag down Cesar Geronimo's grounder and throw to first for the final out.

Ken Griffey got the other Cincinnati hit in the third, a two-out double to right. John struck out Joe Morgan to end the inning.

With one out in the bottom of the third, slugger John strode to the plate himself. He was carrying a .208 average (.161 lifetime), a one-game hitting streak, and 2 RBIs. Paul Moskau grooved a pitch, and John swung smoothly and connected with good wood. The ball sailed over the 370-mark and into the left field seats for a home run. Tommy looked a little out of place trotting around the bases, but he was mighty happy with his home run. And he got a rousing reception from his teammates in the dugout. It was his first National League homer and the fourth of his big league career. The last one came on May 19, 1968.

The Dodgers added two more runs in the inning. Bill Russell doubled past third base with two out. The ball looked foul to third baseman Pete Rose, and he argued enough about it to get kicked out of the game. Cincinnati manager Sparky Anderson also got ejected for his part in the discussion. Reggie Smith then pounded a two-run homer over the left field fence.

John only allowed one base runner after the third. That was Concepcion, who walked with two gone in the fourth. John got through the last five innings in one-two-three order. Thirteen of those last fifteen outs were made on grounders.

The Dodgers added a fourth run in the sixth on singles by Cey and Rick Monday around an infield out.

The game was completed in one hour and fifty-three minutes, and the Dodgers won by a final score of 4-0. Tommy John, whose left arm was raised from the dead by an implant operation, upped his pitching record to 13-4. And his slugging average soared from .208 to .275.

Cincinnati	ab	r	h	bi	o	a	e
P. Rose, 3b	2	0	0	0	0	0	0
R. Knight, 3b3	2	0	0	0	0	2	0
K. Griffey, rf	4	0	1	0	2	0	0
J. Morgan, 2b	4	0	0	0	2	2	0
G. Foster, lf	4	0	1	0	3	0	0
J. Bench, c	3	0	0	0	2	0	0
D. Concepcion, ss	1	0	0	0	2	6	0
D. Driessen, 1b	3	0	0	0	11	0	0
C. Geronimo, cf	3	0	0	0	2	0	0
P. Moskau, p	2	0	0	0	0	0	0
E. Armbrister, ph8	1	0	0	0	-	-	-
P. Borbon, p8	0	0	0	0	0	0	0
	29	0	2	0	24	10	0

Los Angeles	ab	r	h	bi	o	a	e
D. Lopes, 2b	4	0	0	0	0	5	0
B. Russell, ss	4	1	1	0	0	5	0
R. Smith, rf	4	1	1	2	3	0	0
R. Cey, 3b	4	1	3	0	0	2	0
S. Garvey, 1b	4	0	0	0	18	0	1
R. Monday, cf	2	0	1	1	1	0	0
G. Burke, pr6-cf	0	0	0	0	0	0	0
D. Baker, lf	3	0	0	0	0	0	0
S. Yeager, c	3	0	0	0	5	1	0
T. John, p	3	1	1	1	0	2	0
	31	4	7	4	27	15	1

Cincinnati	000	000	000	=	0
Los Angeles	003	001	00x	=	4

	ip	h	r-er	bb	so
Moskau (L 2-3)	7	6	4-4	1	2
Borbon	1	1	0-0	0	0
John (W 13-4)	9	2	0-0	1	5

Game-Winning RBI: John
LOB: Cinc 4, LA 4
BE: Cinc 1
2B: Griffey, Russell
HR: John, Smith
SH: Concepcion
Time—1:53 Attendance—48,242

Umpires: A. Williams, P. Runge, L. Weyer, & J. McSherry

The Dodgers played very steady ball the rest of the season, never losing more than two games in a row. The Reds never got closer than 8½ games behind. Los Angeles finished with a 98-64 record and a 10-game margin over second place.

Tommy John wound up with a 20-7 won-lost record.

The Dodgers had four players who hit 30 or more home runs for the season (Garvey, Smith, Cey, and Baker) and set a new Los Angeles record with 191 team homers. The pitching staff led the league in ERA by a wide margin as well.

1977 FRIDAY, OCTOBER 7TH, AT VETERANS STADIUM, PHILADELPHIA League Championship Series—Game #3

Miracle Rally Tops Phils

IN AN AGONIZINGLY CLOSE GAME, THE LOS ANGELES DODGERS RALLIED TO BEAT THE Philadelphia Phillies, 6-5, in the third game of the National League Championship Series this afternoon. The game had an incredible number of close plays and a large number of vigorous arguments with the umpires. Practically all the run-making was accompanied by controversy.

Amid close plays and harsh words, the Dodgers rallied with two out in the ninth inning for three runs to win the game and take a 2-games-to-1 lead in the best-of-five playoff. The Phillies won the opening game on Tuesday, 7-5, and the Dodgers bounced back on Wednesday to win 7-1.

After a day off to travel east, the rivals squared off today in Philadelphia. The starting pitchers were Larry Christenson for the Phils and Burt Hooton for the Dodgers.

The run-scoring and arguing started in the second inning. Steve Garvey singled with one out and tried to score the first run on a double to left center by Dusty Baker. Shortstop Larry Bowa's relay to the plate arrived at the same time as Garvey, who made a wide slide and was called safe by umpire Harry Wendelstedt. The Phillies argued the call, and there was some question as to whether Garvey ever touched home plate, but the run counted. After Rick Monday flied out, Steve Yeager singled Baker home. Hooton followed with a double into the left field corner, but this time the Phillies threw the man out at the plate, Luzinski to Bowa to Boone.

Undermined by bad fielding support, the umpire, the Philadelphia fans, and his own temper, Hootcn quickly let the 2-0 lead get away. Greg Luzinski opened the home half of the second with a hit to left. Richie Hebner followed with a double-play ball to second baseman Davey Lopes, who threw to shortstop Bill Russell for a force. But Russell dropped the ball before throwing to first, and Hebner was safe. Garry Maddox fanned, but Bob Boone singled. With the pitcher on deck, Hooton walked Ted Sizemore to load the bases. Christenson was allowed to bat for himself, and Hooton quickly got ahead on the count, one ball and two strikes. The Dodger hurler thought his next two pitches caught the corner for strike three, but ump Wendelstedt called them balls. After a foul, Hooton delivered ball four, forcing a run across the plate. Visibly upset by this, Hooton also walked Bake McBride to send another runner home. By now the fans were roaring with ever pitch, and Hooton had lost control of his emotions and his pitches. Another walk to Bowa gave the Phillies the lead and forced manager Tom Lasorda to remove his pitcher. Rick Rhoden came in and retired Mike Schmidt to end the inning.

The Dodgers routed Christenson and tied the score with a run in the fourth. Ron Cey got a double when center fielder Maddox missed a shoestring catch of his low liner. Baker's liner to right drove Cey home. A single by Monday sent Christenson to the showers. And a passed ball and an intentional pass loaded the bases. Rhoden then lined to right, and Baker was doubled at home trying to score after the catch.

The game remained tied until the bottom of the eighth. Lasorda sent Elias Sosa, his fourth pitcher of the day, to the mound at the start of the round. Hebner greeted Sosa with a ringing double off the wall in right. Maddox slapped a hit through the right side of the infield, and Hebner headed for home. Outfielder Reggie Smith uncorked a wild throw home, and Maddox got all the way to third. Boone followed with a grounder to third, which Cey fielded cleanly. After looking Maddox back to the base, Cey threw the ball away past first, allowing another run to score.

The Phillies were now leading 5-3 and needed only three outs to win the game. Reliever Gene Garber, who had pitched perfect ball in the seventh and eighth, got the first two outs in the ninth quickly. Down to his last chance, Lasorda sent 38-year-old Vic Davalillo up to bat for Yeager. The crafty veteran kept the Dodger hopes alive by dragging a bunt past the pitcher for a hit. Ace pinch-hitter Manny Mota, aged 39, was sent up to hit for the pitcher. With two strikes on him, Mota ripped a long fly to left. Luzinski went back to the wall and leaped. The ball went in and out of his glove, hit the fence, and caromed back into his glove again. Davalillo scored, and Mota made for second. When the throw to the base skipped past Sizemore, Mota scooted to third.

Suddenly the tying run was on third with two out, and Lopes was the batter. He cracked a hard one-hopper to third baseman Schmidt, who just got his glove up in time to deflect the ball. It ricocheted straight to shortstop Bowa. Although somewhat off balance, Bowa whipped a strong throw to first. The play was sooooo close . . ., and umpire Bruce Froemming called Lopes safe. The Phillies exploded, sure that they had made the play for the final out. The hot-tempered Bowa was still railing about the call long after the game.

With the ruling, the score was tied. Now it was Garber's turn to come unglued. He threw wildly trying to hold Lopes close to first, and the speedster went to second. Russell then smacked a grounder right through Garber's legs and into center field, and Lopes raced home to give the Dodgers a 6-5 lead.

Mike Garman pitched the bottom of the ninth. He hit Luzinski with a pitch with two out but had no real trouble retiring the side. So the Dodgers had managed to wade through the controversy, dodge a couple of bullets and win the game.

Los Angeles	ab	r	h	bi	o	a	e
D. Lopes, 2b	5	1	1	1	3	3	0
B. Russell, ss	5	0	2	1	5	2	0
R. Smith, rf	5	0	0	0	2	0	1
R. Cey, 3b	4	1	1	0	1	4	1
S. Garvey, 1b	4	1	1	0	9	0	0
D. Baker, lf	4	1	2	2	0	0	0
R. Monday, cf	3	0	1	0	3	0	0
J. Grote, c9	0	0	0	0	0	0	0
S. Yeager, c	2	0	1	1	3	0	0
V. Davalillo, ph0	1	1	1	0	-	-	-
G. Burke, cf9	0	0	0	0	1	0	0
B. Hooton, p	1	0	1	0	0	1	0
R. Rhoden, p2	1	0	0	0	0	0	0
E. Goodson, ph7	1	0	0	0	-	-	-
D. Rau, p7	0	0	0	0	0	0	0
E. Sosa, p8	0	0	0	0	0	1	0
L. Rautzhan, p8	0	0	0	0	0	0	0
M. Mota, ph9	1	1	1	0	-	-	-
M. Garman, p9	0	0	0	0	0	0	0
	37	6	12	5	27	11	2

Philadelphia	ab	r	h	bi	o	a	e
B. McBride, rf	4	0	0	1	1	1	0
L. Bowa, ss	4	0	0	1	0	5	0
M. Schmidt, 3b	4	0	0	0	1	6	0
G. Luzinski, lf	3	0	1	0	0	1	0
J. Martin, pr9	0	0	0	0	-	-	-
R. Hebner, 1b	5	2	1	0	14	0	0
G. Maddox, cf	4	1	1	1	3	0	0
B. Boone, c	4	1	2	0	6	0	0
T. Sizemore, 2b	3	1	1	0	2	3	1
L. Christenson, p	0	0	0	1	0	0	0
W. Brusstar, p4	0	0	0	0	0	0	0
T. Hutton, ph4	1	0	0	0	-	-	-
R. Reed, p5	0	0	0	0	0	0	0
T. McCarver, ph6	1	0	0	0	-	-	-
G. Garber, p7	0	0	0	0	0	1	1
	33	5	6	4	27	17	2

Los Angeles	020 100 003	= 6
Philadelphia	030 000 020	= 5

	ip	h	r-er	bb	so
Hooton	1⅔	2	3-3	4	1
Rhoden	4⅓	2	0-0	2	0
Rau	1	0	0-0	0	1
Sosa	⅔	2	2-1	0	0
Rautzhan (W 1-0)	⅓	0	0-0	0	0
Garman (sv #1)	1	0	0-0	0	0
Christenson	3⅓	7	3-3	0	2
Brusstar	⅔	0	0-0	1	0
Reed	2	1	0-0	1	2
Garber (L 1-1)	3	4	3-2	0	0

Game-Winning RBI: Russell
LOB: Los Angeles 6, Philadelphia 9
BE: Los Angeles 0, Philadelphia 1
DP: McBride-Boone

2B: Baker, Hooton, Cey, Russell, Hebner, Mota
SH: Garber

HBP: by Garman (Luzinski)
PB: Boone
Time—2:51 Attendance: 63,719
Umpires: H. Wendelstedt, B. Froemming, D. Rennert, P. Runge, P. Pryor, & B. Engel

The Dodgers wrapped up the series the next night with an easy 4-1 victory in the rain. Tommy John went the distance, and Dusty Baker got the game-winning hit, a two-run homer in the second inning off Steve Carlton.

1977 WEDNESDAY NIGHT, OCTOBER 12TH, AT YANKEE STADIUM, NEW YORK

1977 World Series—Game #2

Beat Yankees with Hooton & Homers

AFTER HIS EMBARRASSING EXPERIENCE LAST FRIDAY IN THE PLAYOFF GAME IN PHILAdelphia, people were wondering how Burt Hooton would perform in his next outing. Would he still be touchy about the umpiring? Would he again let the crowd get the better of him? Or would he bounce back with a good effort?

Last Friday, Hooton had lost his composure and his control following what he considered bad calls by the umpire; and he had walked four men in a row. After the game he got chewed out by both manager Tommy Lasorda and vice-president Al Campanis for his performance.

Tonight, in the zoo known as Yankee Stadium, he was in control all the way, however. He stopped the powerful New York Yankees on just five hits to win 6-1. The victory evened the World Series at one game apiece.

All the Los Angeles runs were sent across by home runs as the Dodger sluggers showed that even Yankee Stadium's fabled "Death Valley" could not contain their power. Ron Cey, Steve Yeager, and Steve Garvey all hit drives over the distant left field fence. Reggie Smith, batting lefthanded, chipped in with a very long homer into the bleachers in right center field. Smith's and Cey's homers each came with a runner aboard. Yeager and Garvey hit solo shots.

The first three homers, good for five runs, were hit against surprise Yankee starting pitcher Jim "Catfish" Hunter. Hunter, who had a reputation for serving up "gopher balls," had not pitched in a month. But the Yankee pitching was exhausted from a tough playoff series with Kansas City, and manager Billy Martin gambled on World Series veteran Hunter. Catfish had good stuff in the bullpen and threw harder than expected tonight. But he hung a couple of sliders, and the Dodgers hit them out.

It was apparent early that this would not be a great night for Hunter. Davey Lopes, the first batter of the game, hit a ball hard to center field, which was caught. Bill Russell also hit hard but out. Smith then blasted one to the wall in right center for a double. Hunter got two strikes on Cey, but then got a breaking ball too high. The Penguin crashed it over the 387-foot sign and into the left field bullpen for a two-run home run.

Hunter again got burned on a high slider with two out in the second. Although this pitch was about eye level, Yeager went after it and creamed it over the fence in left, a little closer to the line than Cey's shot. Outfielder Lou Pinella crashed his head into the wall trying in vain for a leaping catch, and the score went to 3-0.

With one out in the Dodger third, Russell lined a hit to left. The beleaguered Pinella charged the ball and made a diving pickup, but the umpire correctly ruled it a trap, and Russell was safely on base. Hunter then got a low fastball out over the plate to Smith. Reggie whipped around on it and sent it soaring into the bleachers in right center some 430 feet from the plate. The two-run homer gave Los Angeles five runs and sent Hunter to the showers.

Dick Tidrow came in in relief. The Dodgers hit him hard over the next three innings but failed to score. Hooton missed a sign on a squeeze play in the fourth inning to cost Los Angeles a run.

Ken Clay pitched the sixth, seventh, and eighth for New York, and he held the Dodgers hitless.

Bullpen ace Sparky Lyle pitched the ninth. The first man he faced, Garvey, lined a long drive over the left field wall for the fourth home run of the night.

In the meantime, Hooton had the Yankees under control. Using his baffling knuckle-curve, he struck out six batters in the first three innings. The only hit in that period was a check-swing blooper.

New York was able to score a run in the fourth. Willie Randolph led off with a single to deep short. Thurman Munson bounced a hit up the middle to send Randolph to third. Reggie Jackson hit a smash down the first base line, where Garvey made a fine pickup to start a double play. Randolph scored on the twin-killing. Chris Chambliss also hit the ball hard, but shortstop Russell had no trouble handling the grass cutter.

In the fifth inning, the Yankees again got a pair of singles. Pitching coach Red Adams went to the mound and suggested that Hooton use more fastballs, which he did thereafter. The Yankees were now looking for the knuckle-curve and not getting it, and they went hitless for the rest of the game. They hit some long flies, but the Dodger outfielders were always under them when they came down. Hooton issued his only walk of the game in the seventh inning, and he finished with a five-hitter.

With the game obviously lost by the home team, the New York fans became unruly and violent. Bottles, cans, fruit, and ice cubes were all thrown into the Dodger bullpen. In the ninth inning, four or five spectators jumped onto the field and ran around until corralled by the police. And as the last out was made, Reggie Smith was hit on the head by a hard rubber ball apparently thrown from the upper deck.

The Dodgers were glad to get out of Yankee Stadium in one piece. And they had beaten "Death Valley" to go back to Los Angeles with the series all even.

And Burt Hooton had shown that he could bounce back from adversity and pitch when it counted.

Los Angeles (NL)	ab	r	h	bi	o	a	e
D. Lopes, 2b	4	0	0	0	2	1	0
B. Russell, ss	4	1	1	0	0	4	0
R. Smith, rf	3	2	2	2	2	0	0
R. Cey, 3b	4	1	1	2	1	1	0
S. Garvey, 1b	4	1	2	1	6	1	0
D. Baker, lf	4	0	0	0	2	0	0
R. Monday, cf	3	0	1	0	0	0	0
G. Burke, cf7	1	0	0	0	5	0	0
S. Yeager, c	4	1	2	1	9	0	0
B. Hooton, p	3	0	0	0	0	0	0
	34	6	9	6	27	7	0

New York (AL)	ab	r	h	bi	o	a	e
M. Rivers, cf	4	0	0	0	4	0	0
W. Randolph, 2b	4	1	1	0	2	2	0
T. Munson, c	4	0	1	0	3	3	0
R. Jackson, rf	4	0	0	0	0	0	0
C. Chambliss, 1b	4	0	0	0	11	2	0
G. Nettles, 3b	2	0	1	0	0	6	0
L. Pinella, lf	3	0	1	0	4	0	0
B. Dent, ss	2	0	1	0	0	1	0
C. Johnson, ph7	1	0	0	0	-	-	-
F. Stanley, ss8	0	0	0	0	1	0	0
C. Hunter, p	0	0	0	0	1	0	0
D. Tidrow, p3	1	0	0	0	0	0	0
G. Zeber, ph5	1	0	0	0	-	-	-
K. Clay, p6	0	0	0	0	1	1	0
R. White, ph8	1	0	0	0	-	-	-
S. Lyle, p9	0	0	0	0	0	0	0
	31	1	5	0	27	15	0

Los Angeles	212 000 001	= 6
New York	000 100 000	= 1

	ip	h	r-er	bb	so
Hooton (W 1-0)	9	5	1-1	1	8
Hunter (L 0-1)	2⅓	5	5-5	0	0
Tidrow	2⅔	3	0-0	0	1
Clay	3	0	0-0	1	0
Lyle	1	1	1-1	0	0

Game-Winning RBI: Cey
LOB: LA 2, NY 4
DP: Garvey-Russell-Garvey (Jackson)
2B: Smith
HR: Cey, Yeager, Smith, Garvey
CS: Garvey, Monday
Time—2:27 Attendance—56,691
Umpires: E. Sudol, L. McCoy, J. Dale, J. Evans, J. McSherry, & N. Chylak

This was the high point of the series for the Dodgers.

Tommy John was beaten in Game #3, 5-3, by Mike Torrez.

Doug Rau was routed in Game #4, and Ron Guidry held onto the lead for the Yankees, winning 4-2.

Don Sutton salvaged the fifth game for Los Angeles with a 10-4 victory.

But in the sixth game, back in New York, Reggie Jackson hit three home runs. The Yankees won the game, 8-4, and took the series, 4 games to 2.

1978 MONDAY EVENING, SEPTEMBER 4TH, AT DODGER STADIUM

Five-Run Rally Turns Giants Back

Big Fifth Inning Overcomes 4-0 Deficit to Beat Halicki
Fielding by Lopes and Baker Robs S.F. of Runs

THE LOS ANGELES DODGERS RETAINED their hold on first place in the National League West Division today by turning back the second-place San Francisco Giants in a thriller, 5-4. A Giant victory would have put the two teams into a tie for the lead.

Today's Results			
LOS ANGELES 5-San Francisco 4			
Cincinnati 6-Houston 3			
San Diego 8-Atlanta 4			
Standings	**W-L**	**Pct.**	**GB**
LOS ANGELES	82-56	.594	—
San Francisco	80-58	.580	2
Cincinnati	75-62	.547	6½
San Diego	71-67	.514	11
Houston	63-74	.460	18½
Atlanta	59-78	.431	22½

San Francisco got out to a 4-0 lead with three runs in the second inning and one run in the top of the fifth. But Los Angeles bunched seven hits into the bottom of the fifth to score five runs. The Dodger relievers Lance Rautzhan and Terry Forster held onto the 5-4 lead for the rest of the game. Both teams made eleven hits, but the Dodgers won out on superior fielding. Second baseman Davey Lopes and left fielder Dusty Baker both robbed the Giants of runs with their gloves.

The starting pitchers were both righthanders, sidewinder Ed Halicki for the visitors and breaking-ball artist Don Sutton for the Dodgers.

Sutton pitched out of trouble in the first inning but was hit for three runs in the second. Hector "Heity" Cruz opened the rally for the Giants with a double down the third base line. Terry Whitfield's single sent Cruz to third. After Mark Hill popped out, Roger Metzger drove Cruz home with a solid single to right. Halicki struck out on a wild pitch, as the runners moved to second and third. Bill Madlock came up with a line single to left to drive the two men home.

In the fourth, the visitors were turned back by fine defense. With one out, Metzger hit a high hopper toward second. Lopes timed his leap perfectly, gloved the ball, and threw the batter out on a close play. Halicki then drove one to very deep left field. Baker backed up against the fence, leaped high, and made a one-handed catch to rob Halicki of a home run.

But the Dodgers made a couple of mistakes in the top of the fifth, and the Giants exploited them for a run. With one out, Jack Clark popped to shallow left. Baker came charging in but could not make the catch. The ball bounced past him, and Clark got to second base. Darrell Evans was walked intentionally. Then Sutton hung a breaking ball to Cruz, and the batter rammed it into center field for an RBI single. The Giants now led 4-0.

But that advantage did not last long. Rick Monday, leading off the bottom of the fifth, cracked a 3-and-2 pitch deep into the right field seats for a home run.

Then the San Francisco defense started to fall apart. Johnny Oates hit a check-swing dribbler past the mound, and second baseman Madlock juggled it just long enough to allow Oates to beat the throw to first for a hit. The Giants argued the call at first. Vic Davalillo, hitting for Sutton, grounded a single between first and second. Myron White, making his major league debut, was sent in as a pinch-runner for Davalillo. Lopes hit a grounder to third baseman Evans, who threw to Madlock at second for a force. Madlock tried for a double play, but White's hard slide caused the throw to first to be wild and in the dirt. It got past first baseman Jim Dwyer, and Oates came around third to score. While Dwyer was trying to decide what to do with the ball, Lopes ran down to second base without drawing a throw. Bill Russell followed with a soft single to right, and Lopes streaked home with the third run of the inning. As Reggie Smith was fanning on a 3-and-2 pitch, Russell stole second and continued to third on a throwing error by the catcher.

Now Giant manager Joe Altobelli had to make a decision about his pitcher. The tying run was on third with two out, and ace reliever Gary Lavelle, a lefthander, was ready in the bullpen. But the pitcher's spot was due to bat next for San Francisco, and the next three Dodger batters were all righthanded. So Altobelli stuck with Halicki. The decision cost him the game.

Steve Garvey pulled a double down the left field line to tie the score. Ron Cey hit a hot one to third, where Evans knocked it down but could make no play, Garvey advancing to third. Baker lined a single to center, and Garvey came home with a go-ahead run. Now that it was too late, Altobelli removed Halicki and brought in Lavelle. The new pitcher walked Monday to load the bases, then got pinch-batter Lee Lacy to fly out to end the inning.

Rautzhan, the new Dodger pitcher, allowed one base runner in each of the next two innings, but they did not get as far as second base.

In the eighth inning, San Francisco made its bid to tie. Rob Andrews, pinch-hitting, hit a difficult grounder up the middle and reached second when shortstop Russell's throw went into the dugout. Andrews went to third on Hill's ground out.

Big Mike Ivie came up to hit, the Dodger infield came in to cut off the run at the plate, and Forster relieved Rautzhan on the mound. Ivie hit a hard grasser past the mound, but Lopes had a fine backhanded stop, looked the runner back to third, and threw Ivie out at first. Larry Herndon then hit another hard one toward center. Lopes angled back to cut the ball off, but it took a tricky hop off the edge of the outfield grass. Davey stayed in front of the ball, however, fielded it at his waist, and got the man at first for the third out.

In the ninth, slugger Clark beat out a two-out bunt. But Evans lined out to right to end the game. Los Angeles was still in first place, and San Francisco had slipped back another length.

San Francisco	ab	r	h	bi	o	a	e
B. Madlock, 2b	5	0	2	2	2	2	1
J. Dwyer, 1b	3	0	0	0	1	0	0
Heintzelman, ph7-1b	2	0	0	0	1	0	0
J. Clark, rf	5	1	3	0	1	0	0
A. Gardner, pr9	0	0	0	0	-	-	-
D. Evans, 3b	3	0	0	0	2	1	0
H. Cruz, cf-lf5	4	1	2	1	3	0	0
T. Whitfield, lf	3	1	1	0	2	0	0
G. Lavelle, p5	0	0	0	0	0	0	0
R. Andrews, ph8	1	0	1	0	-	-	-
J. LeMaster, ss8	0	0	0	0	0	0	0
M. Hill, c	4	0	0	0	6	1	1
R. Metzger, ss	3	1	2	1	2	1	0
M. Ivie, ph8	1	0	0	0	-	-	-
R. Moffitt, p8	0	0	0	0	0	0	0
E. Halicki, p	2	0	0	0	0	0	0
L. Herndon, cf5	2	0	0	0	4	0	0
	38	4	11	4	24	5	2

Los Angeles	ab	r	h	bi	o	a	e
D. Lopes, 2b	4	1	0	0	1	4	0
B. Russell, ss	5	1	2	1	0	0	1
R. Smith, rf	4	0	0	0	5	0	0
S. Garvey, 1b	4	1	2	1	11	0	0
R. Cey, 3b	2	0	1	0	1	3	0
D. Baker, lf	4	0	2	1	5	0	0
R. Monday, cf	3	1	1	1	0	0	0
B. North, cf9	0	0	0	0	0	0	0
J. Oates, c	2	1	1	0	2	0	0
L. Lacy, ph5	1	0	0	0	-	-	-
L. Rautzhan, p6	0	0	0	0	1	1	0
T. Forster, p8	1	0	1	0	0	0	0
D. Sutton, p	1	0	0	0	0	0	0
V. Davalillo, ph5	1	0	1	0	-	-	-
M. White, pr5	0	0	0	0	-	-	-
S. Yeager, c6	2	0	0	0	1	0	0
	34	5	11	4	27	8	1

San Francisco	030	010	000	=	4
Los Angeles	000	050	00x	=	5

	ip	h	r-er	bb	so
Halicki (L8-7)	4⅔	10	5-5	1	3
Lavelle	2⅓	0	0-0	2	2
Moffitt	1	1	0-0	1	1
Sutton (W 13-10)	5	8	4-4	1	2
Rautzhan	2⅓	2	0-0	1	1
Forster (sv #17)	1⅔	1	0-0	0	0

WP: Sutton

Game-Winning RBI: Baker
LOB: SF 9, LA 9
BE: none
2B: Cruz, Clark 2, Garvey, Forster
HR: Monday
SB: Madlock, Russell
CS: Russell
Time—2:42
Attendance—52,589
Umpires: B. Froemming, J. West, B. Williams, & D. Stello

The Dodgers won the second game of the two-game series, 9-2. Then they won eight of the next ten games. Meanwhile, the Giants lost eight of nine to drop to third place.

Los Angeles clinched the pennant with a week to go and finished with a record of 95-67.

1978 SATURDAY, OCTOBER 7TH, AT DODGER STADIUM League Championship Series—Game #4

Russell's Single Follows Error to Win Flag

IN A TENSION-PACKED, CLOSELY-FOUGHT GAME, THE LOS ANGELES DODGERS TOOK advantage of an error by the Philadelphia Phillies to pull off a ten-inning, 4-3 victory today and capture the National League Championship Series, 3 games to 1.

The winning run was manufactured with two outs on a base on balls to Ron Cey, and line drive that was dropped by the usually sure-handed Garry Maddox, and a clutch single by Bill Russell.

Previous to the final tally, the game had featured big home runs (two by each team) and missed scoring opportunities. Seventeen runners in all were left on base, and each side had men on third with less than two out and failed to score.

The series opened with two games in Philadelphia, and the Dodgers won them both. In the opener, they clubbed four home runs, Steve Garvey leading the attack with two round-trippers and a triple. Bob Welch got the win in a 9-5 victory. Tommy John held the Phillies to four singles in the second game and won, 4-0. Davey Lopes drove in three of the runs with a home run, a triple, and a single.

The series shifted to Los Angeles, where the third game was played yesterday. Philadelphia delayed the Dodger victory party by winning, 9-4. Philly hurler Steve Carlton pitched a complete game and drove in four runs with a home run and a single.

This afternoon, the Phillies got off to a good start, loading the bases with none out in the first inning. But Dodger pitcher Doug Rau pitched out of the jam.

Los Angeles scored the first run of the game in the bottom of the second. With one out, Cey bounced a double into the left field corner. Pitcher Randy Lerch then jammed Dusty Baker with a fastball on the fists. But Baker muscled the ball over the third baseman for a hit, and Cey came in to score. Russell also dropped a hit into left. But Steve Yeager lined out, and Rau fouled out, leaving two men on.

The Los Angeles lead did not last long. The Phillies came in and scored twice in the third to go ahead. With one out, Larry Bowa placed a soft liner over the second baseman for a hit. After Maddox flied out, Greg Luzinski unloaded a drive six rows deep into the left field pavilion seats for a two-run homer.

The Phils left a man on third in the fourth inning. With two out, Ted Sizemore lined a hit to right. Reggie Smith made a diving try for the catch, but the ball got past him for a triple. Lerch, a good-hitting pitcher, drove one to deepest center field, but outfielder Billy North caught it on the warning track for the third out.

Cey tied the game with a home run into the left field seats down toward the line in the Dodger fourth. Baker followed with a single, but Russell bounced into a double play.

Rick Rhoden succeeded Rau as the Dodger pitcher in the sixth inning. His first pitch was hit to the fence in center, but North made the catch. Rhoden then struck out the next two batters.

Garvey hit one over the fence in left in the home half to give the Dodgers the lead, 3-2, and to send Lerch to the showers. Warren Brusstar relieved and allowed a double and a walk before retiring the side.

Bake McBride pinch-hit for Brusstar with two out and none on in the Phillies' seventh. Rhoden put one over the heart of the plate, and McBride wristed it into the visitors' bullpen for a home run, tying the score, 3-3.

Ron Reed took over on the hill for the Phils in the bottom of the seventh. With one out, Lopes slapped a hit past the mound. After holding on two pitchouts, Lopes stole second and continued to third as the throw skipped past the shortstop. It was golden opportunity for the home team, but Rick Monday struck out, and Smith grounded to the first baseman.

A walk and a single with two out put Phillies on first and second in the eighth. But Rhoden fanned Jerry Martin on a good slider.

The Dodgers got three hits in the bottom of the eighth but did not score because Garvey, who led off with a hit, was caught stealing.

Neither side got a runner on base in the ninth.

Terry Forster shut the Phils out in the tenth, despite a single by Bowa.

Tug McGraw got the first two Dodgers out quickly enough in the home half of the tenth. Then he walked Cey. Baker, who already had four hits on the day, sent a sinking liner to center. Maddox, a perennial Gold Glove outfielder, came striding in for the ball and tried for a belt-high catch. But the ball kicked out if his hands and fell safely for an error, Cey stopping at second. Bill Russell, a fine hitter in the clutch, picked on a curveball and lined a hit to center. With Cey rounding third in his inimitable straight-backed, penguin style, Maddox's only chance was to charge hard and make a perfect pickup and throw. But in his desperation, he again allowed the ball to bounce off his glove, and Cey came home unmolestedly with the pennant-winning run.

The Dodgers burst out of the dugout and began a wild celebration, while Maddox and the rest of the crestfallen Phillies trudged off the field. They had given a good fight, but the better team had won.

Philadelphia	ab	r	h	bi	o	a	e
M. Schmidt, 3b	4	0	1	0	0	5	0
L. Bowa, ss	4	1	2	0	2	3	0
G. Maddox, cf	5	0	1	0	4	0	1
G. Luzinski, lf	4	1	1	2	1	0	0
J. Cardenal, 1b	4	0	1	0	11	0	0
J. Martin, rf	4	0	0	0	5	0	0
B. Boone, c	4	0	0	0	5	1	1
T. Sizemore, 2b	4	0	1	0	1	2	0
R. Lerch, p	2	0	0	0	0	1	0
W. Brusstar, p6	0	0	0	0	0	0	0
B. McBride, ph7	1	1	1	1	-	-	-
R. Reed, p7	0	0	0	0	0	0	0
R. Hebner, ph9	1	0	0	0	-	-	-
T. McGraw, p9	0	0	0	0	0	0	0
	37	3	8	3	29	12	2

Los Angeles	ab	r	h	bi	o	a	e
D. Lopes, 2b	5	0	1	0	1	1	0
B. North, cf	3	0	0	0	7	0	0
R. Monday, ph7-cf	2	0	0	0	0	0	0
R. Smith, rf	5	0	0	0	2	0	0
S. Garvey, 1b	5	1	2	1	6	2	0
R. Cey, 3b	4	3	2	1	0	2	0
D. Baker, lf	5	0	4	1	4	0	0
B. Russell, ss	4	0	3	1	2	1	0
S. Yeager, c	3	0	1	0	5	1	0
L. Lacy, ph8	1	0	0	0	-	-	-
J. Grote, c9	0	0	0	0	2	0	0
D. Rau, p	1	0	0	0	1	0	0
M. Mota, ph5	0	0	0	0	-	-	-
R. Rhoden, p6	1	0	0	0	0	2	0
J. Ferguson, ph9	1	0	0	0	-	-	-
T. Forster, p10	0	0	0	0	0	0	0
	40	4	13	4	30	9	0

Philadelphia	002 000 100 0	= 3
Los Angeles	010 101 000 1	= 4

two out when winning run scored

	ip	h	r-er	bb	so
Lerch	5⅓	7	3-3	0	0
Brusstar	⅔	1	0-0	1	0
Reed	2	4	0-0	0	1
McGraw (L 0-1)	1⅔	1	1-0	1	2
Rau	5	5	2-2	2	1
Rhoden	4	2	1-1	1	3
Forster (W 1-0)	1	1	0-0	0	2

Game-Winning RBI: Russell
LOB: Philadelphia 7, Los Angeles 10
BE: Los Angeles 1
DP: Sizemore-Bowa-Cardenal (Russell)
2B: Schmidt, Cey, Baker
3B: Sizemore
HR: Luzinski, Cey, Garvey, McBride
SH: Mota
SB: Lopes
CS: Schmidt, Garvey
Time—2:53
Attendance—55,124

Umpires: S. Davidson, B. Williams, J. McSherry, L. Weyer, N. Colosi, & A. Olsen

1978 WEDNESDAY EVENING, OCTOBER 11TH, AT DODGER STADIUM

World Series—Game #2

Cey Drives in 4, Welch Fans Jackson

THE LOS ANGELES DODGERS TONIGHT TOOK A TWO GAMES-TO-NONE LEAD IN THE 1978 World Series with a storybook, 4-3 victory over the New York Yankees. The game was climaxed by rookie pitcher Bob Welch striking out Yankee slugger Reggie Jackson with the tying and leading runs on base. Ron Cey provided the Dodger offense with four runs-batted-in. Burt Hooton was the winning pitcher, but relievers Terry Forster and Welch were the pitching heroes for the victors. They each retired the biggest New York hitters, Jackson and Thurman Munson, with the game on the line.

The triumph was all the more meaningful for Los Angeles because most of the members of the club had attended the funeral of much-respected coach Jim Gilliam earlier in the day.

While the Dodgers entered the game with a grim emotional bond uniting them, the Yankees were engaged in their proverbial squabbling. Before the game, center fielder Mickey Rivers had scuffled with team officials on the bus to the stadium. Rivers, who had complained of a bad leg earlier in the week, did not play tonight. Neither did injured regulars Willie Randolph and Chris Chambliss.

A makeshift Yankee lineup produced eleven hits, compared to just seven for the Dodgers. But Los Angeles bunched three hits into each of two innings, while New York never got more than two hits in any round. As a result, the Dodgers got more runs.

New York opened the scoring with two runs in the third. Roy White got a one-out hit to right center. After Gary Thomasson flied out, White stole second. Hooton walked Munson on a 3-and-2 pitch. Jackson then pulled a double down the right field line, and both runners scored. Graig Nettles struck out, but the Yanks had a 2-0 lead.

Los Angeles broke into the scoring column in the fourth. Bill Russell opened with a hit to left, but he was forced on Reggie Smith's grounder to third. Nettles robbed Garvey of extra bases with a diving stop behind third, but he could not throw the batter out. Cey delivered a single to center, and Smith scored. Baker bounced into a double play, and the inning ended with the score 2-1.

Los Angeles took the lead in the sixth on a big home run by Cey. Lopes opened with a single past Nettles. Russell fouled out trying to sacrifice. But Smith lined a hit to right, and Lopes went to third. Garvey failed in the RBI situation, fouling out behind the plate. With a count of 2-and-0, Cey came through by driving a high slider from Catfish Hunter into the middle of the left field pavilion for a three-run homer. The blow put the Dodgers ahead, 4-2.

Hunter got the final out in the sixth, then he was replaced by relief ace Rich Gossage. "The Goose" set the Dodgers down in order in the seventh and eighth.

In the meantime, the Yankees threatened to tie the game.

In the seventh, White led off with a hit to left. Manager Tom Lasorda yanked Hooton out and brought Forster in. Paul Blair, pinch-hitting for Thomasson, greeted the Dodger lefty with a ground-rule double to left center. Forster muscled up and fanned Munson with men on second and third. Jackson grounded out to second as White scored and Blair went to third. With the lead now only 4-3, Nettles struck out in the clutch.

Lou Pinella led off the New York eighth with a hit. But Forster blew a third strike past Jim Spencer and got pinch-hitter Cliff Johnson to hit into a double play.

The score was still 4-3 as the game went into the dramatic ninth inning. The Yankees again started with a hit, this one by Bucky Dent. White fouled off two bunt attempts. Then he advanced the runner with a "swinging bunt" to the pitcher. Blair worked a walk, and once again the tying and winning runs were on base for New York.

Lasorda went to the mound to call in rookie Welch. The 21-year-old righthander had started the season with Albuquerque but had pitched quite a few big games for Los Angeles during the summer. Although he had shown a good curve and changeup in the past, tonight he threw nothing but fastballs.

His first pitch to Munson was a swinging strike. The next one was lined to short right field, where Smith caught it for the second out of the inning.

The next batter was Reggie Jackson, "Mr. October." He had wrecked the Dodgers in the 1977 World Series with five home runs and had homered in the first game this year. Fifty-five thousand fans were on their feet in the stands, and fifty million more were watching on television.

Welch's first pitch was right down the pipe, but Jackson missed it with a big swing. The next one was high and inside, sending Reggie into the dirt.

Three more fastballs came over, with Jackson only able to foul them back.

The next pitch missed for a ball. After another foul to the screen, Welch missed again to run the count to 3-and-2.

With the runners running, Welch put a little bit extra on the next pitch, a fastball up and in. Jackson took a big swing and missed, corkscrewing himself into the ground in his effort.

Strike Three!

The crowd went crazy. Jackson stomped back to the dugout in frustration as the Dodgers raced to the mound to congratulate Welch. The rookie took it all in stride and seemed to be about the calmest person in the whole stadium.

New York (AL)	ab	r	h	bi	o	a	e
R. White, lf	5	2	2	0	1	0	0
G. Thomasson, cf	3	0	1	0	2	0	0
P. Blair, ph7-cf	1	0	1	0	2	0	0
T. Munson, c	4	1	1	0	3	1	0
R. Jackson, dh	4	0	1	3	-	-	-
G. Nettles, 3b	4	0	0	0	3	3	0
L. Pinella, rf	4	0	2	0	2	0	0
J. Spencer, 1b	4	0	1	0	8	1	0
B. Doyle, 2b	3	0	1	0	2	1	0
C. Johnson, ph8	1	0	0	0	-	-	-
F. Stanley, 2b8	0	0	0	0	0	0	0
B. Dent, ss	4	0	1	0	0	1	0
C. Hunter, p	-	-	-	-	1	0	0
R. Gossage, p7	-	-	-	-	0	0	0
	37	3	11	3	24	7	0

Los Angeles (NL)	ab	r	h	bi	o	a	e
D. Lopes, 2b	4	1	1	0	3	4	0
B. Russell, ss	4	0	1	0	2	1	0
R. Smith, rf	4	2	1	0	3	0	0
S. Garvey, 1b	3	0	1	0	6	1	0
R. Cey, 3b	3	1	2	4	1	1	0
D. Baker, lf	3	0	0	0	2	0	0
R. Monday, cf	3	0	0	0	1	0	0
B. North, cf8	0	0	0	0	0	0	0
L. Lacy, dh	3	0	0	0	-	-	-
S. Yeager, c	3	0	1	0	8	1	0
B. Hooton, p	-	-	-	-	1	0	0
T. Forster, p7	-	-	-	-	0	1	0
B. Welch, p9	-	-	-	-	0	0	0
	30	4	7	4	27	9	0

New York	002	000	100	=	3
Los Angeles	000	103	00x	=	4

	ip	h	r-er	bb	so
Hunter (L 0-1)	6	7	4-4	0	2
Gossage	2	0	0-0	0	0
Hooton (W 1-0)	*6	8	3-3	1	5
Forster	2⅓	3	0-0	1	3
Welch (sv #1)	⅔	0	0-0	0	1

*faced one batter in seventh
WP: Hooton
HBP: by Hooton (Jackson)

Game-Winning RBI: Cey
LOB: New York 10, Los Angeles 2
Base on Missed 3rd Strike: New York 1
DP: Nettles-Spencer (Baker)
Cey-Lopes-Garvey (Johnson)
2B: Munson, Jackson, Blair
HR: Cey
SB: White
CS: Thomasson
Time—2:37 Attendance—55,982
Umpires: B. Haller, J. Kibler, M. Springstead, F. Pulli, J. Brinkman, & E. Vargo

The Yankees won the third game, 5-1, thanks to some incredible fielding by Nettles.

A throw that glanced off Jackson's hip in the fourth game helped New York come from behind to win in ten innings, 4-3.

The the Yankees pounded out 29 hits in the next two games to win, 12-2 & 7-2, and take the series in six games.

1979 FRIDAY NIGHT, MAY 25TH AT DODGER STADIUM

Seven L.A. Home Runs & One Fight with Cincinnati

Seven Different Dodgers Hit for Circuit
Brawl Starts in 8th Inning after Lopes is Decked

THE LOS ANGELES DODGERS HIT SEVEN home runs tonight to trounce the Cincinnati Reds, 17-6. But not all the slugging was done with baseball bats. A brawl erupted in the bottom of the eighth inning after Reds' pitcher Dave Tomlin had low-bridged Davey Lopes on four consecutive pitches. The fight had no material effect on the outcome of the game, but it did show the bad blood that had developed between these two traditional rivals.

Today's Results

LOS ANGELES 17-Cincinnati 6
San Francisco 6-Atlanta 4
San Diego 2-Houston 1 (10 innings)

Standings	W-L	Pct.	GB
Cincinnati	24-18	.571	—
San Francisco	25-20	.556	½
Houston	24-22	.522	2
LOS ANGELES	22-24	.478	4
San Diego	19-27	.413	7
Atlanta	15-27	.357	9

The triumph was badly needed by Los Angeles. The team had been struggling all season to reach the .500 mark, and tonight's victory inched it to within two games of even. The Dodgers' biggest problem was pitching. Tommy John, the team's top winner in both 1977 and 1978, left the club as a free agent, leaving a void in the pitching rotation. Equally damaging was the absence of relief ace Terry Forster, who saved 22 games last season. He underwent elbow surgery over the winter and had been unable to pitch until tonight, when he was given his initial test of the year in the ninth inning.

For this one night, at least, the Dodgers had it all together. Pitcher Rick Sutcliffe held the powerful Cincinnati lineup in check until the game was well in hand. The Dodger fielding was excellent, and their hitting was tremendous. Seven different Los Angeles players hit home runs, setting a new National League record. And the seven homers tied the club record set in Chicago in 1976. Eleven different men got base hits, nine scored, and eight drove in runs.

Rookie Sutcliffe showed good stuff in the first inning but was charged with a run. After Ken Griffey struck out to open the game, Junior Kennedy beat out an infield hit. Dave Concepcion singled Kennedy to third. Sutcliffe balked him home. It was the second time in his two starts since the end of the umpires' strike that Sutcliffe had balked with a man on third. He ended the inning by fanning both Dan Driessen and Johnny Bench.

The Dodgers got the run back in their half of the first against Cincinnati starter Tom Seaver. Lopes led off with a base on balls and stole second. He took third on a ground out and scored on a hit by Reggie Smith.

A leaping catch at the fence by center fielder Gary Thomasson robbed the Reds' Ray Knight of a home run in the top of the second.

The Dodgers took the lead for good in the bottom. Dusty Baker opened with a home run over the left field wall. Two outs later, Sutcliffe, a righthanded pitcher but lefthanded batter, unloaded his first major league homer over the right field fence.

Ken Griffey got a homer for the Reds in the third to cut the Los Angeles lead to 3-2.

But the Dodgers routed Seaver with four runs in the bottom of the inning. Steve Garvey, Ron Cey, and Baker singled in succession for a run. Thomasson then scratched a hit off the first baseman's glove to load the bases. Joe Ferguson quickly unloaded them with a three-run double to left, knocking Seaver out of the game. Tom Hume came in and retired the side.

Hume went out for a pinch-hitter in the fourth, and Frank Pastore took over on the mound for Cincinnati in that inning. He was to bear the brunt of the Los Angeles assault, giving up five homers and ten runs in less than three innings pitched.

The Dodgers got to him for five runs in the fourth. Garvey and Thomasson hit two-run homers, and Ferguson added a solo shot.

Los Angeles scored five more runs in the sixth inning. Derrel Thomas led off with a homer to right. Baker walked. Johnny Oates singled with one out, and Sutcliffe hit a shot past shortstop for an RBI single. Pastore fell behind on the count to Lopes, 3-and-0. He grooved the next pitch, and Lopes parked it into the seats in left for a three-run homer. That was the last of Pastore, who was replaced by Tomlin.

With the score 17-2, Sutcliffe let up in his work and allowed one run in the seventh and three in the eighth.

Lopes came to bat in the bottom of the eighth with one on and none out. Tomlin's first pitch was aimed just behind Davey's head, and he barely managed to avoid getting beaned. The next three pitches were also well in on him, and Lopes yelled angrily at Tomlin before trotting toward first. Both benches emptied as the players gathered around the mound.

Just as it seemed that the storm had passed, Thomas and the Reds' Rick Auerbach starting punching one another. Soon there were many players scuffling. Johnny Bench landed one big punch before disappearing under a herd of Dodger bodies. In all, about 15 minutes was required to restore order. The only players ejected were Thomas and Auerbach.

Play finally resumed, and the game was finished quickly. The main features of the final inning were the appearances of Forster on the mound (he worked a perfect inning), and Manny Mota in the outfield (for the first time since July 12, 1977).

The final score was 17-6, and what was left of the big crowd went home happy. They had gotten to see plenty of slugging. And seven Dodger home runs, too.

Cincinnati	ab	r	h	bi	o	a	e
K. Griffey, rf	5	1	2	2	0	0	0
J. Kennedy, 2b	5	1	2	1	3	2	0
D. Concepcion, ss	5	0	1	0	1	6	1
D. Driessen, 1b	5	1	1	0	12	0	0
J. Bench, c	3	0	2	0	2	0	0
V. Correll, c6	2	1	1	0	2	0	0
R. Knight, 3b	4	0	1	0	0	1	0
D. Collins, lf	3	0	1	0	0	0	0
D. Tomlin, p6	1	0	0	0	0	0	0
C. Geronimo, cf	4	2	2	1	3	0	0
T. Seaver, p	1	0	0	0	0	0	0
T. Hume, p3	0	0	0	0	0	1	0
K. Henderson, ph4	1	0	0	0	-	-	-
F. Pastore, p4	0	0	0	0	0	1	0
P. Blair, lf6	2	0	1	1	1	0	0
	41	6	14	5	24	11	1

Los Angeles	ab	r	h	bi	o	a	e
D. Lopes, 2b	4	2	1	3	2	5	0
B. Russell, ss	5	0	2	0	2	2	0
T. Martinez, pr6-ss	1	0	0	0	1	1	0
R. Smith, rf	5	1	2	1	4	0	0
S. Garvey, 1b	4	2	2	2	5	0	0
P. Guerrero, 1b6-3b9	1	0	0	0	2	0	0
R. Cey, 3b	2	0	1	0	0	0	0
D. Thomas, pr3-3b	3	2	1	1	1	0	0
T. Forster, p9	0	0	0	0	0	1	0
D. Baker, lf	4	4	3	2	1	0	0
V. Joshua, lf8-cf9	0	0	0	0	0	0	0
G. Thomasson, cf-1b9	5	2	3	2	3	0	0
J. Ferguson, c	3	1	2	4	5	1	0
J. Oates, ph6-c	2	1	1	0	1	0	0
R. Sutcliffe, p	4	2	2	2	0	0	0
M. Mota, ph8-lf	0	0	0	0	0	0	0
	43	17	20	17	27	10	0

Cincinnati	101 000 130	= 6
Los Angeles	124 505 00x	= 17

	ip	h	r-er	bb	so
Seaver (L 2-3)	*2	10	7-7	1	1
Hume	1	0	0-0	0	0
Pastore	2⅓	9	10-10	1	2
Tomlin	2⅔	1	0-0	3	1
Sutcliffe (W 5-3)	8	14	6-6	0	7
Forster	1	0	0-0	0	0

*faced five batters in third

WP: Tomlin Balk: Sutcliffe

Game-Winning RBI: Baker
LOB: Cincinnati 8, Los Angeles 7
BE: Los Angeles 1
DP: Concepcion-Kennedy-Driessen (Ferguson) Kennedy-Driessen (Russell)
2B: Ferguson, Geronimo, Driessen
HR: Baker, Sutcliffe, Griffey, Garvey, Thomasson, Ferguson, Thomas, Lopes
SB: Lopes
Time—3:11 Attendance—49,372
Umpires: J. McSherry, P. Runge, B. Engel, & D. Stello

Plagued by lack of pitching, inconsistent offense, and poor execution, the Dodgers won only 7 of 27 games in June. By the All-Star break they were deep in last place, 17½ games out of first. This all contributed to some internal dissension.

But the team turned itself around in the second half, winning 43 and losing only 26. That still left them below .500 (79-83) at the end of the season. Their final position was third place, 11½ games behind the division-champion Reds.

1980 SUNDAY, OCTOBER 5TH, AT DODGER STADIUM
Another Great Comeback Forces a Playoff

Dodgers Complete Dramatic Series Sweep Over Astros with 4-3 Win
Cey's Homer in 8th Puts L.A. on Top

Today's Results			
LOS ANGELES 4-Houston 3			
Cincinnati 1-Atlanta 0			
San Diego 7-San Francisco 3			
Standings	**W-L**	**Pct.**	**GB**
LOS ANGELES	92-70	.568	—
Houston	92-70	.568	—
Cincinnati	89-73	.549	3
Atlanta	81-80	.503	10½
San Francisco	75-86	.466	16½
San Diego	73-89	.451	19

COMPLETING ONE OF THE MOST DRAMATIC series sweeps in baseball history, the Los Angeles Dodgers kept their championship hopes alive today with another come-from-behind victory over the Houston Astros, 4-3. The victory completed a three-game sweep by the Dodgers and left Los Angeles and Houston with identical 92-70 records at the end of the 162-game schedule. So they would have to play a one-game playoff to decide the West Division pennant.

The Astros had come to town for the final three games of the season with a 3-game lead. But the Dodgers thrilled their fans with three dramatic victories. All three games were nail-biters, and each triumph turned Dodger Stadium into a madhouse.

On Friday night, the Dodgers rallied from behind to tie the game with two out in the ninth on a single by Ron Cey. Then they won it in the tenth on a homer by Joe Ferguson.

On Saturday, they edged the Astros, 2-1, with Steve Garvey scoring both Dodger runs, one on a homer. Jerry Reuss was the winning pitcher over Nolan Ryan.

Today they won another thriller. Houston got out to a 3-0 lead by the fourth inning. The Dodgers were inspired to come back. They scored single runs in the fifth and seventh. Then in the eighth, Ron Cey clubbed a dramatic two-run home run to give Los Angeles the lead, 4-3. Houston threatened in the ninth, but Don Sutton came out of the bullpen to get the last out and record the very first save of his pitching career.

The starting pitchers were Vern Ruhle for the visitors and Burt Hooton for the home team. Ruhle had cut his right index finger on Friday and was pitching with two stitches on his pitching hand.

Hooton was knocked out of the game in the second inning. Cesar Cedeno opened with a bunt single and stole second. Art Howe also bunted and Hooton muffed a barehanded pickup for an error. Alan Ashby lined a hit to left center, Cedeno scoring. Craig Reynolds lined a single to right, and Howe scored.

Dodger manager Tommy Lasorda hustled reliever Bobby Castillo into the game. The new pitcher walked a man but pitched out of a bases-loaded jam.

Ruhle's stitches forced him to leave the game in the bottom of the third, and Joaquin Andujar took over on the hill.

Houston added a run to its lead in the fourth. Ashby led off with a solid single, and Reynolds sacrificed. After Andujar fanned, Terry Puhl stroked a double past the diving left fielder for a run-batted-in.

The Dodgers scored their first run in the fifth on consecutive singles with one out by Derrel Thomas, Gary Thomasson, and Davey Lopes. Joe Sambito was called in to replace Andujar, and he quickly squelched the rally by getting a double play.

The Dodgers scored another run in the seventh but left the bases loaded. Pedro Guerrero led off with a soft liner over second base for a hit. Ferguson's long single to left sent Guerrero to second. Thomas bunted the runners to second and third. With the pitcher due up, Lasorda called Manny Mota in from his post as first base coach to pinch-hit. The 42-year-old bat magician swatted a hard single to right, driving Guerrero in. Houston manager Bill Virdon brought Frank LaCorte into pitch, and he eventually got Dusty Baker to foul out with the bases loaded.

But the Dodgers took the lead in classic fashion in the eighth. Garvey, first up, hit a hopper down to third base. Third sacker Enos Cabell got caught between hops, and the ball kicked off the heel of his glove for an error. Cey was the next batter, and he had instructions to bunt. But he failed twice and the count went to 3-and-2. With Garvey running, Cey fouled one pitch off his left ankle. Ron was already hobbled by a pulled hamstring muscle, and now he was in pain from the foul. But he stayed in and fouled off two more fastballs in on his fists. Finally LaCorte got a pitch out over the plate, and Cey blasted it over the 385-foot marker and into the left field pavilion for a two-run home run. The Dodgers suddenly had the lead, and the stands went crazy.

But the Astros still had one last chance. Jeff Leonard opened the ninth with a foul fly down the right field line. Jay Johnstone made a spectacular catch just before tumbling over the rail. Gary Woods lined a hit to right center. Puhl sent a slow roller toward the hole in the right side, which Lopes converted into a force out at second with a fine whirling play. Two out. Cabell delayed the celebration by lacing a pitch from Steve Howe to left center for a single, sending Puhl to third.

Having exhausted his bullpen, Lasorda called upon starting pitcher Don Sutton in this emergency. Sutton's second pitch to Denny Walling was rolled to Lopes, who threw to Garvey for the final out.

The crowd, which had been cheering all weekend, outdid itself with noise. The big heroes, Cey and Sutton, were called out for several "curtain calls." In the clubhouse, the Dodgers were exuberant. After three stirring victories in a row, they were confident they would win the playoff tomorrow.

Houston	ab	r	h	bi	o	a	e
T. Puhl, rf	2	0	1	1	4	0	0
E. Cabell, 3b	5	0	1	0	1	2	1
J. Morgan, 2b	4	0	0	0	3	1	0
R. Landestoy, 2b7	0	0	0	0	2	0	0
D. Walling, ph9	1	0	0	0	-	-	-
J. Cruz, lf	4	0	0	0	1	0	0
C. Cedeno, cf	4	1	2	0	1	0	0
A. Howe, 1b	3	1	0	0	4	0	0
D. Bergman, 1b8	0	0	0	0	1	0	0
A. Ashby, c	4	1	2	1	7	1	0
C. Reynolds, ss	2	0	1	1	0	5	0
J. Leonard, ph9	1	0	0	0	-	-	-
V. Ruhle, p	1	0	0	0	0	0	0
J. Andujar, p3	1	0	0	0	0	0	0
J. Sambito, p5	1	0	0	0	0	0	0
F. LaCorte, p7	0	0	0	0	0	0	0
G. Woods, ph9	1	0	1	0	-	-	-
	34	3	8	3	24	9	1

Los Angeles	ab	r	h	bi	o	a	e
D. Lopes, 2b	3	0	1	1	0	3	0
R. Monday, rf	2	0	0	0	2	0	0
M. Hatcher, ph5-rf	1	0	0	0	1	0	0
J. Johnstone, ph7-rf	0	0	0	0	1	0	0
D. Baker, lf	4	0	1	0	1	0	0
S. Garvey, 1b	4	1	1	0	5	0	0
R. Cey, 3b	4	1	1	2	2	1	0
P. Guerrero, cf	4	1	1	0	4	0	0
P. Frias, ss9	0	0	0	0	1	0	0
J. Ferguson, c	3	0	1	0	8	0	0
R. Law, pr7	0	0	0	0	-	-	-
S. Yeager, c8	1	0	1	0	2	0	0
D. Thomas, ss-cf9	3	1	2	0	0	0	0
B. Hooton, p	0	0	0	0	0	0	1
B. Castillo, p2	1	0	0	0	0	2	0
G. Thomasson, ph5	1	0	1	0	-	-	-
F. Valenzuela, p6	0	0	0	0	0	0	0
M. Mota, ph7	1	0	1	1	-	-	-
G. Weiss, pr7	0	0	0	0	-	-	-
S. Howe, p8	1	0	0	0	0	0	0
D. Sutton, p9	0	0	0	0	0	0	0
	33	4	11	4	27	6	1

Houston	020 100 000	=	3
Los Angeles	000 010 12x	=	4

	ip	h	r-er	bb	so
Ruhle	*2	2	0-0	0	1
Andujar	2⅓	4	1-1	1	3
Sambito	2	3	1-1	0	1
LaCorte (L 8-5)	1⅔	2	2-1	1	1
Hooton	†1	3	2-1	1	2
Castillo	4	2	1-1	1	4
Valenzuela	2	0	0-0	1	1
S. Howe (W 7-9)	1⅔	3	0-0	0	1
Sutton (sv #1)	⅓	0	0-0	0	0

*faced two batters in third
†faced four batters in second

Game-Winning RBI: Cey
LOB: Houston 9, Los Angeles 8
BE: Houston 1, Los Angeles 1
DP: Reynolds-Morgan-A. Howe (Hatcher)
2B: Puhl
HR: Cey
SH: A. Howe, Reynolds, Thomas
SB: Puhl 2, Cedeno
CS: Thomas

Time—3:33
Attendance—52,339

Umpires: D. Harvey, A. Olsen, N. Colosi, & J. Crawford

1980 PLAYOFF

MONDAY, OCTOBER 6TH, AT DODGER STADIUM

Dodger Pennant Dream Collapses

Houston Wins West Division Title in Playoff Game
Two Dodger Errors in 1st Inning Start the 7-1 Rout

Today's Results

Houston 7-LOS ANGELES 1
(Houston wins one-game playoff for division championship)

Standings	W-L	Pct.	GB
Houston	93-70	.571	—
LOS ANGELES	92-71	.564	1
Cincinnati	89-73	.549	3½
Atlanta	81-80	.503	11
San Francisco	75-86	.466	17
San Diego	73-89	.451	19½

IT WAS GREAT WHILE IT LASTED! BUT couldn't it have lasted just one more day? The Los Angeles Dodgers had turned the whole town on with their three rousing victories over the Houston Astros to tie for first place at the end of the season. But in today's playoff to decide the division champion, with seemingly everyone in L.A. watching or listening, the Dodgers' dream finish was rudely shattered as the Astros won easily, 7-1.

The game was one-sided from the start. In the first inning, the Dodgers committed two errors to hand the Astros two runs. Houston scored two more in the third and another three in the fourth. Los Angeles got its run in the bottom of the fourth and only threatened to score once after that. Astro knuckleballer Joe Niekro pitched a complete-game six-hitter for his 20th win of the season.

As a result, Houston and not Los Angeles would represent the West Division in the National League Championship Series.

The first indication that it might not be the Dodgers' day came before the game. Ron Cey, yesterday's big hero, was taken out of the lineup because of a painfully swollen ankle. The injury was the result of a foul ball he hit Sunday.

The air was pretty smoggy today, but the fans didn't care. They were confident that the Dodgers would pull out another big victory. The stadium was sold out, despite the fact that the game was unscheduled, and scalpers did a brisk business. Mayor Tom Bradley threw out the first ball. After singing "The Star-Spangled Banner," Toni Tenille called the Los Angeles fans "the greatest in the world."

But the festive mood changed quickly. Terry Puhl, the first Astro batter, hit pitcher Dave Goltz's third pitch to second base, and Davey Lopes booted it for an error. Enos Cabell lunged for a low fastball and lined it over Lopes for a single, sending Puhl to third. Cabell stole second as Joe Morgan was striking out. Jose Cruz grounded to third baseman Mickey Hatcher, whose throw home had Puhl beaten. But the runner knocked the ball out of catcher Joe Ferguson's grasp with his shoulder, and Houston had a run. Lopes backpedalled to field Cesar Cedeno's grounder, and Cabell scored on the out at first. Hatcher saved a run with a diving stop of Art Howe's hit, and Alan Ashby flied out. Houston led 2-0.

The Astros pounded Goltz for five straight hits in the third, and the pitcher was lucky to get through the inning with just two runs scored against him. With one out, Cruz grounded a hit through the left side. He was then caught trying to steal second. Cedeno bounced a single up the middle. He stole successfully. With a full count on Howe, Goltz hung a slider, and Howe hit it over the fence in left center for a two-run homer. Ashby lined the next pitch to center for a single. And Craig Reynolds hit the one after that into the gap in right center for a double. But Rick Monday cut the ball off before it got to the fence, and Ashby was thrown out at home by plenty. The runner tried to bowl catcher Ferguson over. Fergy held onto the ball and knocked Ashby down, adding a knee to the ribs for good measure. Players from both dugouts came out to the scene but no fighting took place.

Houston cinched the game in the fourth with three runs against relievers Rick Sutcliffe and Joe Beckwith. With one out, Puhl beat out a bunt, and Cabell and Morgan walked to load the base. Lasorda derricked Sutcliffe in favor of Beckwith.

The new pitcher was also unable to get out of the inning. Cruz hit a liner to left center, which Monday caught with a fine diving effort. Puhl trotted home after the catch. Cedeno was given a base on balls to load the bases again. Howe then looped a hit to center, driving two more runs home and knocking Beckwith out of the box.

Bobby Castillo came in and gave up the fourth walk of the inning before fanning Reynolds to end the rally.

With the score 7-0, the crowd became unruly. Stuff was thrown onto the field from the pavilion. Dusty Baker opened the bottom of the fourth with a shot off Cabell's chest and took second on a wild throw past first base. Garvey struck out. Monday bounced a hit up the middle to score Baker and make it 7-1. The barrage in left field crept dangerously close to outfielder Cruz, and the umpires pulled the Astros off the field until emotions subsided. After a short delay, play resumed and the inning was ended.

In the final five innings there was no more scoring and each side made only two hits. The only scoring threat was mounted in the sixth, when the Dodgers loaded the bases with two out. But Derrel Thomas lined out to center fielder Cedeno, and Los Angeles failed to score.

Many spectators started to leave in the eighth inning, but most stayed until the bitter end.

In the bottom of the ninth, the Astros' bullpen crew had to come into the dugout to escape the missiles from the stands. Thomas's two-out bloop single gave the Dodgers one last, forlorn hope. But Jack Perconte rolled out to first base, and the Dodgers' season was over.

The year had seen many injuries and many setbacks. Yet the final three-game sweep against the Astros had lent a magical tone to the season. Too bad Los Angeles had not won the playoff, too.

Houston	ab	r	h	bi	o	a	e
T. Puhl, rf	5	2	1	0	1	0	0
E. Cabell, 3b	4	2	2	0	1	2	1
D. Bergman, 1b8	0	0	0	0	3	0	0
J. Morgan, 2b	2	1	0	0	1	2	0
R. Landestoy, 2b4	2	0	0	0	1	1	0
J. Cruz, lf	4	0	1	1	3	0	0
C. Cedeno, cf	4	1	1	1	4	0	0
A. Howe, 1b-3b8	5	1	3	4	8	0	0
A. Ashby, c	4	0	1	0	5	1	0
C. Reynolds, ss	4	0	3	0	0	1	0
J. Niekro, p	2	0	0	0	0	2	0
	36	7	12	6	27	9	1

Los Angeles	ab	r	h	bi	o	a	e
D. Lopes, 2b	4	0	0	0	2	3	1
S. Howe, p8	0	0	0	0	0	0	0
J. Johnstone, rf	4	0	0	0	2	0	0
D. Baker, lf	4	1	1	0	4	0	0
S. Garvey, 1b	4	0	0	0	7	0	0
R. Monday, cf	3	0	1	1	3	1	0
J. Ferguson, c	4	0	1	0	5	3	1
M. Hatcher, 3b	3	0	1	0	3	3	0
G. Thomasson, ph9	1	0	0	0	-	-	-
D. Thomas, ss	3	0	2	0	1	0	0
D. Goltz, p	0	0	0	0	0	0	0
R. Law, ph3	1	0	0	0	-	-	-
R. Sutcliffe, p4	0	0	0	0	0	0	0
J. Beckwith, p4	0	0	0	0	0	0	0
B. Castillo, p4	0	0	0	0	0	0	0
V. Davalillo, ph5	1	0	0	0	-	-	-
F. Valenzuela, p6	0	0	0	0	0	1	0
J. Perconte, ph7-2b	2	0	0	0	0	1	0
	34	1	6	1	27	12	2

Houston	202	300	000 =	7
Los Angeles	000	100	000 =	1

	ip	h	r-er	bb	so
Niekro (W 20-12)	9	6	1-0	2	6
Goltz (L 7-11)	3	8	4-2	0	2
Sutcliffe	⅓	1	3-3	2	0
Beckwith	⅓	1	0-0	1	0
Castillo	1⅓	1	0-0	1	2
Valenzuela	2	1	0-0	0	1
S. Howe	2	0	0-0	0	0

PB: Ashby

Game-Winning Run scored on catcher's error
LOB: Houston 9, Los Angeles 8
BE: Houston 2, Los Angeles 0
Base on Missed 3rd Strike: Los Angeles 1
2B: Reynolds, Cabell
HR: A. Howe
SH: Niekro 2. SF: Cruz
SB: Cabell, Cedeno, Puhl 2
CS: Cruz
Time—3:10 Attendance—51,127
Umpires: D. Harvey, N. Colosi, P. Runge, & J. Dale

1981 THURSDAY NIGHT, MAY 14TH, AT DODGER STADIUM

Fernando Wins 8th Straight

Capacity Crowd Cheers Dodger Rookie

Jomrón de Guerrero en la Novena Dio Los Angeles la Victoria, 3-2

ANOTHER TRIUMPHANT CHAPTER WAS added to the incredible saga of Fernando Valenzuela tonight at Dodger Stadium. Before an absolutely packed house, the 20-year-old Mexican rookie scored his eighth consecutive victory of the season, beating the Montreal Expos, 3-2. In his eight starts this year, Valenzuela had five shutouts and had allowed a total of just four runs.

Today's Results

LOS ANGELES 3-Montreal 2
Cincinnati 6-Chicago 1
Philadelphia 3-San Francisco 1
St. Louis 7-Houston 6
San Diego 10-New York 6
no other game scheduled

Standings	W-L	Pct.	GB
LOS ANGELES	23- 9	.719	—
Cincinnati	17-14	.548	5½
Atlanta	17-14	.548	5½
San Francisco	17-18	.486	7½
Houston	15-18	.455	8½
San Diego	13-20	.394	10½

Both Montreal runs came on home runs, the first that Fernando ever yielded in the National League. But teammate Pedro Guerrero hit a homer for the Dodgers in the bottom of the ninth to win the game. The blow sent the festive crowd of 55,806 home happy.

Many of the fans were of Mexican parentage, as Fernando was already established as a superhero among Spanish-speaking fans. Bus loads came from south of the Mexican border to cheer Valenzuela, their countryman. But the most significant portion of the ticket-buyers were Mexican-Americans from north of the border.

An ingenuous demeanor and incredible pitching ability have made the youngster from the northwest Mexican state of Sonora an international star. There was even a television crew from Sweden at the game tonight! And the Dodger organization catered to the Mexican flavor of the evening by serving enchiladas and refried beans in the press room. Outside the park, hawkers sold an array of Fernando T-shirts, phonograph records, and other memorabilia.

The youngest of 12 children of a poor family, Fernando learned to play baseball under the tutelage of his older brothers. He signed his first professional contract (with Los Mayos de Navajoa in his native Sonora) at age 15. After working his way up a few rungs on the ladder of Mexican professional baseball, his contract was purchased by the Dodgers in July, 1979. He began the 1980 season with San Antonio in the Texas League and was called up to Los Angeles in September.

In the final weeks of the 1980 National League season, Valenzuela pitched in ten games, all as a reliever. He allowed two unearned runs in his first appearance but was unscored upon in the next nine.

He won a spot in the Dodgers' starting rotation in spring training this year and got the assignment to pitch on opening day after Jerry Reuss came down with a minor injury. He pitched a five-hit shutout to beat Houston, 2-0, before over 50,000 fans.

That alone might have been enough to make him a hero in Southern California. But Valenzuela was just getting started. He won his next start, 7-1, in San Francisco. In San Diego he won his third, another 2-0 five-hitter. In Houston he beat ex-Dodger Don Sutton 1-0 and drove in the game's only run himself.

By the time he pitched in Los Angeles again, the whole city was stricken with "Fernandomania." A near-sellout crowd of 49,478 cheered him as he won his fifth game, a 5-0 shutout of the Giants. Valenzuela got three hits himself in the game, including the game-winner.

His next two games were on the road in front of big crowds. In Montreal he pitched nine innings and got the win in a 6-1, ten-inning Dodger victory. In New York he beat the Mets 1-0.

So he entered his next start (tonight) with a perfect 7-0 record and the city of Los Angeles at his feet.

He gave the Expos only three hits in winning his eighth tonight. But two of the blows were home runs. The first came in the third inning with one out. Chris Speier, who had not hit a homer in nearly a year, connected with a hanging breaking ball and sent it into the left field seats just barely fair.

The Dodgers were lucky to get their first two runs in the sixth. Davey Lopes led off with a single and moved to second on Dusty Baker's one-out hit. Expo pitcher Bill Gullickson then unfurled a costly wild pitch. With "el Zurdo de Oro" (the Golden Lefthander) pitching for Los Angeles, Montreal manager Dick Williams decided that he had to try and keep the Dodgers scoreless. So he ordered the infield in for a play at the plate. The next batter, Steve Garvey, hit a dying blooper off the fists just over the drawn-in second baseman. The ball did not even carry to the outfield grass on the fly, but it fell safely, and both Lopes and Baker raced home.

Valenzuela protected the 2-1 lead until the ninth. He pitched around a bunt single in the seventh and a walk and a stolen base in the eighth. Fernando retired the first two batters in the ninth, and Dodger Stadium was rocking in celebration. But Montreal's best hitter, Andre Dawson, suddenly silenced the crowd by powdering a low screwball over the center field fence to tie the game. Gary Carter flied out deep to left, but the game was not over yet.

It ended soon enough. Guerrero, the young slugger from the Dominican Republic, was the first batter in the bottom of the ninth. Expo reliever Steve Ratzer got a 1-and-1 pitch too high, and Guerrero sent it soaring over the left field fence for the game-winning homer. Pedro danced around the bases and was met by joyous "high-five" hand slaps from his teammates.

The fans were once again delirious, and the phenomenal Senõr Valenzuela was now "ocho y cero" (8 and 0). It had been a perfect evening. Now the question was, would Fernando have a perfect season?

Montreal	ab	r	h	bi	o	a	e
J. White, lf	4	0	0	0	0	0	1
R. Scott, 2b	4	0	1	0	2	2	0
A. Dawson, cf	4	1	1	1	3	0	0
G. Carter, c	4	0	0	0	7	0	0
W. Cromartie, 1b	3	0	0	0	7	0	0
T. Wallach, rf	3	0	0	0	2	0	0
L. Parrish, 3b	3	0	0	0	1	3	1
C. Speier, ss	2	1	1	1	2	1	0
T. Raines, pr8	0	0	0	0	-	-	-
M. Phillips, ss8	0	0	0	0	0	1	0
B. Gullickson, p	2	0	0	0	0	0	0
C. Smith, ph8	1	0	0	0	-	-	-
S. Ratzer, p8	0	0	0	0	0	0	0
	30	2	3	2	24	7	2

Los Angeles	ab	r	h	bi	o	a	e
D. Lopes, 2b	4	1	1	0	3	2	0
K. Landreaux, cf	4	0	0	0	4	0	0
D. Baker, lf	4	1	1	0	3	0	0
S. Garvey, 1b	4	0	1	2	7	0	0
R. Cey, 3b	4	0	0	0	0	2	0
P. Guerrero, rf	4	1	1	1	2	0	0
M. Sciosia, c	3	0	1	0	7	0	0
B. Russell, ss	3	0	1	0	1	1	0
D. Thomas, ss8	0	0	0	0	0	0	0
F. Valenzuela, p	3	0	2	0	0	1	0
	33	3	8	3	27	6	0

Montreal	001 000 001	= 2
Los Angeles	000 002 001	= 3

none out when winning run scored

	ip	h	r-er	bb	so
Gullickson	7	7	2-2	0	6
Ratzer (L 1-1)	*1	1	1-1	0	1
Valenzuela (W 8-0)	9	3	2-2	1	7

*faced one batter in ninth
WP: Gullickson

Game-Winning RBI: Guerrero
LOB: Mont 2, LA 6
BE: LA 1
2B: Sciosia, Russell
HR: Speier, Dawson, Guerrero
SB: Raines
Time—2:22
Attendance—53,906 paid, 55,806 total
Umpires: L. Weyer, H. Wendelstedt, D. Rennert, & E. Montague

Valenzuela was finally beaten in his next start (on May 18th) by the Phillies, 4-0. He finished the season with a 13-7 record.

The season was interrupted on June 12th by a players' strike. At the time the Dodgers were still in first place, although the Cincinnati Reds were just ½ game behind.

After eight weeks, play resumed with a contingency plan that divided the season into two halves, with the winners of each half qualifying for the playoffs. As a result, the Dodgers were guaranteed a post-season berth. Their second half record was just 27-26 (a fourth-place finish), and their overall record was 63-47.

1981 SUNDAY, OCTOBER 11TH, AT DODGER STADIUM
Division Championship Series—Game #5

Shutout by Reuss Completes Comeback

THE LOS ANGELES DODGERS TODAY COMPLETED THE MOST REMARKABLE COMEBACK possible in a best-of-five-game championship series by defeating the Houston Astros for the third straight time after losing the first two games of the playoff. Today's score was 4-0, with Jerry Reuss pitching the shutout. So the Dodgers became the first team in major league history to come back from a two game deficit to win a series 3 games to 2. The comeback gave them the National League West Division championship in the special playoff arranged between the winners of the two halves of the split season caused by the players' strike.

In the final analysis, Los Angeles won the title by outpitching the vaulted Astro staff. Houston held Los Angeles to just eleven runs in the five games, but the Astros were only able to manage six tallies in the series against the Dodgers pitchers.

The first two games, played in the Astrodome in Houston, were classic pitchers' battles. Fernando Valenzuela and Nolan Ryan were locked in a 1-1 tie through eight innings in the first game. Valenzuela was removed for a pinch-hitter in the ninth. Alan Ashby then hit a two-run home run off reliever Dave Stewart in the bottom of the ninth to win the game for Houston, 3-1. Game #2 was scoreless until the eleventh, when three Astro singles won the game 1-0.

The Dodgers returned home with their backs to the wall, trailing 2 games to 0. But manager Tommy Lasorda proclaimed his confidence. His pitching was strong, and he felt sure that his hitters would do better. And the Astros had been able to win only 2 of the last 12 games they had played in Los Angeles, so they were undoubtedly wary of the Dodger Stadium jinx.

In the first inning in Game #3, the Dodgers scored three runs, two more than they had scored in 20 innings in Houston. Los Angeles won the game, 6-1, with Burt Hooton, Steve Howe, and Bob Welch doing the pitching.

Valenzuela came back with three days of rest to pitch the fourth game. Pedro Guerrero's home run in the fifth gave the Dodgers the first run, and they added another in the seventh. Valenzuela had a two-hit shutout until the ninth. Then the Astros got one run on two hits. But Fernando did not allow the tying run to get past first base and won the game, 2-1.

That sent the series into the fifth and deciding game today. Lasorda came back with Reuss, who had allowed no runs in nine innings in the second game on Wednesday. In the regular season, Jerry had held the Astros to two runs in 17 innings pitched. Houston manager Bill Virdon chose Ryan, who had allowed the Dodgers one run on two hits on Tuesday night and had pitched a no-hit shutout in his only other start against them this season.

As expected, the game started out as a pitching duel. Although the fielding was shaky (there were five errors and two dropped foul pops in all), the game was scoreless through five innings. Houston got three singles and one walk in that time, and Los Angeles managed just one hit and one walk.

Reuss had his most serious difficulty in the sixth. He walked Tony Scott leading off on four pitches. But catcher Mike Sciosia cut Scott down trying to steal second. Art Howe then lined a soft hit to right field. Jose Cruz worked Reuss for another walk, putting men on first and second. But Denny Walling fouled out, and Dickie Thon hit into a force out.

Ryan had been having trouble with his curveball in the early going but had held the Dodgers off. Finally, Los Angeles broke through against him in the sixth. With one out, Dusty Baker's foul fly fell on the warning track because second baseman Phil Garner lost the ball in the sun. On the next pitch, Baker walked. With a count of 2-and-2 on Steve Garvey, Lasorda called for the hit-and-run play. Garvey executed it perfectly, grounding a hit to left as Baker raced to third. Rick Monday lined a low fastball to right for a hit, scoring Baker with the first run and sending Garvey to second. Guerrero popped out. Sciosia then smacked a pitch past Ryan and up the middle for a run-scoring single. Russell followed with a slow hopper toward third. The throw to first was off line toward the plate, and Russell knocked the ball out of the first baseman's glove, allowing Monday to steam home from second. Reuss fanned, but he now had a 3-0 lead.

Ryan was removed for a pinch-batter in the seventh, and Dave Smith took over as the Houston pitcher. With one out in the bottom of the inning, Ken Landreaux smashed one off Smith's shin that bounced all the way to the grandstand for a double. Smith limped off the field, and Frank LaCorte came in. He retired the first man he faced, but then Garvey tripled to left center for a run.

Reuss got through the seventh and eight while allowing one runner in each round. And he got the first two men out in the ninth without any trouble. Dave Roberts was sent up as the last Houston hope. Reuss got him to swing at a third strike, but the ball got past catcher Sciosia and went to the screen. Roberts, however, was unaware of the fact that he was not out yet, and he turned disconsolately to the dugout. Finally he realized his mistake and lit out for first base. Sciosia had chased the ball down, and he threw to first. Roberts dove for the bag, but first baseman Garvey stretched and dug the ball out of the dirt just in time to make the putout and end the game.

Reuss jumped up and down on the mound like a kangaroo, and he was soon surrounded by happy teammates and fans. The Dodgers had done it! They had come from two games back in a best-of-five series to win the National League West Division's special split-season championship playoff and advance a big step toward the World Series.

Houston	ab	r	h	bi	o	a	e
T. Puhl, rf	4	0	0	0	1	0	0
P. Garner, 2b	4	0	0	0	1	0	1
T. Scott, cf	3	0	0	0	2	0	0
A. Howe, 3b	4	0	1	0	1	3	0
J. Cruz, lf	3	0	2	0	2	0	0
D. Walling, 1b	4	0	1	0	3	1	1
D. Thon, ss	4	0	0	0	1	1	1
A. Ashby, c	4	0	0	0	12	0	0
N. Ryan, p	1	0	1	0	1	0	0
J. Pittman, ph7	1	0	0	0	-	-	-
D. Smith, p7	0	0	0	0	0	0	0
F. LaCorte, p7	0	0	0	0	0	0	0
D. Roberts, ph9	1	0	0	0	-	-	-
	33	0	5	0	24	5	3

Los Angeles	ab	r	h	bi	o	a	e
D. Lopes, 2b	5	0	1	0	2	1	0
K. Landreaux, cf	4	1	1	0	4	0	0
D. Baker, lf	3	1	0	0	4	0	0
S. Garvey, 1b	4	1	2	1	7	0	0
R. Monday, rf	3	1	1	1	3	0	0
D. Thomas, pr7-rf	0	0	0	0	0	0	0
P. Guerrero, 3b	3	0	0	0	0	5	1
M. Sciosia, c	4	0	1	1	4	2	0
B. Russell, ss	4	0	1	0	3	2	1
J. Reuss, p	4	0	0	0	0	1	0
	34	4	7	3	27	11	2

Houston	000 000 000	=	0
Los Angeles	000 003 10x	=	4

	ip	h	r-er	bb	so
Ryan (L 1-1)	6	4	3-2	2	7
Smith	⅓	1	1-1	0	1
LaCorte	1⅔	2	0-0	1	3
Reuss (W 1-0)	9	5	0-0	3	4

Game-Winning RBI: Monday
LOB: Houston 9, Los Angeles 9
BE: Houston 2, Los Angeles 3
2B: Landreaux, Russell
3B: Garvey
SB: Guerrero, Puhl, Lopes
CS: Scott
Time—2:52 Attendance—55,979

Umpires: L. Weyer, E. Montague, J. Dale, J. Quick, S. Davidson, & J. McSherry

1981 MONDAY, OCTOBER 19TH, AT OLYMPIC STADIUM, MONTREAL League Championship Series—Game #5

Monday's Homer Wins League Title

THE DODGERS DID IT AGAIN! THEY CAME BACK FROM THE BRINK OF ELIMINATION TO win another best-of-five series, 3 games to 2. This time they won the National League Championship playoff against the Montreal Expos after having fallen behind in the series, 2 games to 1.

Today's victory was one of the most dramatic in the long history of the Dodger franchise. Ace rookie Fernando Valenzuela was nicked for a run in the first inning, then he pitched brilliantly and drove in the tying run with a ground out in the fifth. With the score still 1-1 in the ninth, Rick Monday hit a two-out home run to put the Dodgers on top. Valenzuela needed last-out relief help from Bob Welch, but the Dodgers came away winners, 2-1.

The series had opened in Los Angeles with Burt Hooton combining with Steve Howe and Welch to stop Montreal 5-1. It was the Expos' tenth loss in a row in Dodger Stadium. Montreal broke the streak in the second game with a 3-0 victory. Ray Burris outpitched Valenzuela in that one.

The series switched from sunny California to chilly Quebec for the final three games (if necessary). Expo ace Steve Rogers beat Jerry Reuss in Game #3, 4-1, thanks to a three-run homer by Jerry White. The Montreal fans were all set to celebrate a league championship the next day, but the Dodgers won, 7-1. Hooton, Welch, and Howe once again combined to stop the Expos' hitters, and Steve Garvey's two-run homer in the eight inning broke a 1-1 tie.

The fifth game was scheduled for Sunday afternoon, and many hearty Canadian fans sat through 3½ hours of freezing rain hoping for the game to begin. But the weather did not clear up, and the game was postponed.

Today the rain was still coming down at game time, and the start was delayed 25 minutes. The temperature was a chilly 7° celcius (45° F). And the crowd was only 36,491, about 18,000 below capacity. The starting pitchers were Valenzuela and Burris.

The Dodgers got a one-out triple into the right field corner by Bill Russell in the first inning. But he had to hold on Dusty Baker's ground out to third and was left when Garvey went out on a check-swing bouncer to the mound.

Montreal leadoff man Tim Raines worked the count full before driving a double into the gap in left center. Rodney Scott laid down a bunt; Valenzuela pounced on it and threw to third. The play was very close, but the speedy Raines was just barely safe. Andre Dawson faked a bunt, and Scott was hung up between first and second. Catcher Mike Sciosia threw to shortstop Russell, who looked Raines back to third before throwing to first, allowing Scott to beat the tag by an eyelash. Dawson then swung away and hit a grounder to the right side. Second baseman Davey Lopes made a nice pickup and started a double play, while Raines scored. Gary Carter flied out to end the inning.

Valenzuela settled down to some remarkable pitching. Spotting his screwballs and fastballs beautifully, he allowed only one Expo to reach base in the next five innings. In the second and third, he got six outs on only twelve pitches.

Burris was also pitching great ball. He walked Ron Cey in the second but got Pedro Guerrero to bounce into a double play. He set the Dodgers down in order in the third. In the fourth, Russell opened with a single and moved to third on two outs before being left when Cey fouled out.

Los Angeles finally put two hits together in the fifth and tied the score. Monday, leading off, barely missed a home run when a long drive curled foul. Then he bounced a single up the middle. With the count full, Burris got a pitch too high to Guerrero, and Pedro hit a long single to center to send Monday to third. Sciosia lined out to second. A pitch to Valenzuela bounced away from catcher Carter, and although Monday had to hold at third, Guerrero took second. The infield came in for a play at the plate. Fernando hit a grounder toward the hole in right. Second baseman Scott got to the ball but had no chance to get Monday at home and had to settle for the out at first. That tied the game, 1-1.

The Expos got a two-out double by Lance Parrish in the seventh, but nothing came of it.

In the eighth, manager Jim Fanning decided to send Tim Wallach up to hit for Burris. Wallach was an easy out.

Ace starter Rogers was brought in to pitch the ninth. He got Garvey to pop out on the first pitch. He fell behind Cey, 3-and-0, before coming back to get a fly out to the warning track. The first pitch to Monday was right down the pipe, but Rick could only foul it back. The next three serves missed for balls. The 3-and-1 pitch was over the heart of the plate almost waist high. Monday got his arms extended and sent a high liner to deep center. The ball carried over the fence for the tie-breaking home run. Monday jubilantly hustled around the bases to a hero's welcome in the Dodger dugout.

All that was left was for Fernando to get three more outs. Scott went out quickly trying to bunt his way on. Dawson was retired on an easy fly to center. Valenzuela got ahead of Carter, one ball and two strikes, but then walked him. He also walked Parrish on seven pitches.

Lasorda decided his rookie had worked enough and called Bob Welch in from the bullpen. Welch threw just one pitch, and White grounded it toward second. Lopes played back on the ball, but his snap throw to Garvey was in time for the out.

The Dodgers were National League champions! After a short but raucous clubhouse celebration, the team flew to New York to start the World Series.

Los Angeles	ab	r	h	bi	o	a	e
D. Lopes, 2b	4	0	1	0	3	3	0
B. Russell, ss	4	0	2	0	2	3	0
D. Baker, lf	4	0	0	0	0	0	0
S. Garvey, 1b	4	0	0	0	10	0	0
R. Cey, 3b	3	0	0	0	0	2	0
R. Monday, rf	4	2	2	1	0	0	0
K. Landreaux, cf9	0	0	0	0	0	0	0
P. Guerrero, cf-rf9	4	0	1	0	5	0	0
M. Sciosia, c	3	0	0	0	7	0	0
F. Valenzuela, p	3	0	0	1	0	1	0
B. Welch, p9	0	0	0	0	0	0	0
	33	2	6	2	27	9	0

Montreal	ab	r	h	bi	o	a	e
T. Raines, lf	4	1	1	0	2	0	0
R. Scott, 2b	3	0	0	0	4	4	0
A. Dawson, cf	4	0	0	0	4	0	0
G. Carter, c	3	0	1	0	3	1	0
J. Manuel, pr9	0	0	0	0	-	-	-
L. Parrish, 3b	3	0	1	0	0	1	0
J. White, rf	3	0	0	0	2	0	0
W. Cromartie, 1b	3	0	0	0	12	0	0
C. Speier, ss	3	0	0	0	0	5	1
R. Burris, p	2	0	0	0	0	1	0
T. Wallach, ph8	1	0	0	0	-	-	-
S. Rogers, p9	0	0	0	0	0	0	0
	29	1	3	0	27	12	1

Los Angeles	000	010	001	= 2
Montreal	100	000	000	= 1

	ip	h	r-er	bb	so
Valenzuela (W 1-1)	8⅔	3	1-1	3	6
Welch (sv #1)	⅓	0	0-0	0	0
Burris	8	5	1-1	1	1
Rogers (L 1-1)	1	1	1-1	0	1

WP: Burris
Time—2:41 Attendance—36,491

Game-Winning RBI: Monday
LOB: Los Angeles 5, Montreal 5
BE: Los Angeles 1
DP: Lopes-Russell-Garvey (Dawson)
Speier-Scott-Cromartie (Guerrero)
2B: Raines, Parrish
3B: Russell
HR: Monday
SH: Scott
SB: Lopes

Umpires: H. Wendelstedt, J. West, P. Pryor, E. Gregg, P. Runge, & D. Rennert

1981 WEDNESDAY NIGHT, OCTOBER 28TH, AT YANKEE STADIUM
World Series—Game #6

"Comeback Dodgers" Crush Yanks for Championship

AFTER FALLING BEHIND IN YET ANOTHER SERIES IN THE POST-SEASON CHAMPIONships, the Los Angeles Dodgers again came back and tonight wrapped up the world championship of baseball. In the best-of-seven World Series against the New York Yankees, the Dodgers lost the first two games. But then they bounced back to win four in a row and take the series without having to go to a seventh game.

Tonight's heroes were many. Pitchers Burt Hooton and Steve Howe held the hard-hitting American League champs to just seven hits and two runs. Pedro Guerrero drove in five runs for the Dodgers with a triple, a single, and a home run. And Ron Cey's fifth-inning single provided the game-winning RBI.

Heroes in the series also included Jerry Reuss (who bested Yankee ace Ron Guidry in the pivotal fifth game, 2-1), Fernando Valenzuela (whose gutty complete-game victory in Game #3 picked the Dodgers up off the floor), Steve Garvey (who had 10 hits and a .417 batting average), Steve Yeager (who had two game-winning ribbies), Jay Johnstone (who had two hits and 3 RBIs as a pinch-hitter), and many more.

For the Yankees, the goats included Dave Winfield (who was 1-for-22 in the number-three slot in the batting order), George Frazier (who was charged with three losses as a pitcher), and the management (which removed Tommy John from tonight's game with the score tied 1-1 in the fourth inning).

Beating the Yankees, who had beaten his Dodgers in the series in both 1977 and 1978, made the victory all the sweeter for Los Angeles manager Tommy Lasorda.

The fifth game had been played in Los Angeles on Sunday. But a travel day and a rain-out postponed the sixth game until Wednesday night. The delay gave Ron Cey some extra time to recover from being hit in the head by a Rich Gossage fastball in the Sunday game. Although still a little bit woozy, Cey started tonight.

The pitching pairing was a rematch of Game #2: Burt Hooton vs. Tommy John. The Yankees had won the last time, 3-0, although Hooton was only charged with one run and John only pitched seven innings of the shutout.

Tonight the Dodgers had a base runner or two in each inning against John but did not score until the fourth.

New York was held hitless in the first two innings, thanks to fine plays by Cey and Dusty Baker.

Then the Yankees got a run in the third on a two-out home run into the left field bleachers by Willie Randolph.

The Dodgers tied the game in the top of the fourth. Baker lined a solid single to right center with one out. Guerrero's shot to left was caught for the second out. Then Rick Monday hit a shot that went right between the first baseman's legs for a hit. Yeager bounced one sharply past the third baseman, and Baker came home from second.

Graig Nettles doubled for New York with one out in the home half of the fourth. Rick Cerone struck out, and the Dodgers gave Larry Milbourne an intentional pass to get to Tommy John. Yankee manager Bob Lemon shocked the crowd, not to mention John himself, by sending pinch-hitter Bobby Murcer to bat. Murcer flied out to the warning track in right.

Frazier, who had had tough luck in losing Games #3 and #4, was the new pitcher in the top of the fifth. Davey Lopes greeted him with a ground single to left. Bill Russell bunted Lopes to second. Garvey flied out. Cey then bounced one past the mound and up the middle. Second baseman Randolph ranged over for the ball, but it took a tricky hop off the edge of the outfield grass and skidded past for a hit as Lopes ran home with the go-ahead run. Baker blooped another hit just beyond the reach of Randolph. Thus far, Frazier had not been hit too hard. But Guerrero then blasted a big drive into the wide-open spaces in left center for a two-run triple, and the Dodgers led 4-1.

The Dodgers racked up four more runs against Yankee relievers Ron Davis and Rick Reuschel in the sixth. Davis got in trouble by walking Hooton and Lopes, and Russell knocked him out with an RBI single. With Reuschel on the mound, a double steal, a walk, an infield out, an error and a two-run single by Guerrero rounded out the rally.

Hooton suddenly lost his effectiveness with one out in the Yankee sixth. He gave up a single and walked two men. Lasorda removed his starter and brought in lefty Steve Howe.

The first batter Howe faced, Lou Pinella, singled a run home. But after that, the Yankees never threatened the big Dodger lead. Howe gave up just one more hit during the rest of the game.

Guerrero capped his big day with a home run against Rudy May in the eighth inning, making the score 9-2.

A walk and an error put two Yankees on in the ninth. But when Bob Watson flied out to Ken Landreaux in center for the third out, the Dodgers were world champions.

The veteran infield of Cey, Russell, Lopes, and Garvey had been working together for a long time for this, as had people like Lasorda, Hooton, Yeager, vice-president Al Campanis, and the rest. It had been a long time coming, and it certainly hadn't been done the easy way this year, but now they could all savor the ultimate baseball triumph: winning the World Series.

Los Angeles (NL)	ab	r	h	bi	o	a	e
D. Lopes, 2b	4	2	1	0	1	2	1
B. Russell, ss	4	0	2	1	0	5	0
S. Garvey, 1b	4	1	1	0	9	0	0
R. Cey, 3b	3	1	2	1	1	1	0
D. Thomas, ph6-3b	2	1	0	1	0	0	0
D. Baker, lf	5	2	2	0	2	0	0
P. Guerrero, cf-rf6	5	1	3	5	6	0	0
R. Monday, rf	3	0	1	0	1	0	0
K. Landreaux, cf6	1	0	0	0	1	0	0
S. Yeager, c	5	0	1	1	6	0	0
B. Hooton, p	2	1	0	0	0	0	0
S. Howe, p6	2	0	0	0	0	0	0
	40	9	13	9	27	8	1

New York (AL)	ab	r	h	bi	o	a	e
W. Randolph, 2b	3	1	2	1	2	2	0
J. Mumphrey, cf	5	0	1	0	2	0	0
D. Winfield, lf	4	0	0	0	2	0	0
R. Jackson, rf	5	0	0	0	3	0	0
B. Watson, 1b	5	0	0	0	10	0	0
G. Nettles, 3b	3	0	2	0	1	2	1
A. Rodriguez, pr6-3b	1	1	1	0	0	0	0
R. Cerone, c	3	0	0	0	7	2	0
L. Milbourne, ss	2	0	0	0	0	3	1
T. John, p	1	0	0	0	0	1	0
B. Murcer, ph4	1	0	0	0	-	-	-
G. Frazier, p5	0	0	0	0	0	0	0
R. Davis, p6	0	0	0	0	0	0	0
R. Reuschel, p6	0	0	0	0	0	0	0
O. Gamble, ph6	0	0	0	0	-	-	-
L. Pinella, ph6	1	0	1	1	-	-	-
R. May, p7	0	0	0	0	0	0	0
B. Brown, ph8	1	0	0	0	-	-	-
D. LaRoche, p9	0	0	0	0	0	0	0
	35	2	7	2	27	10	2

Los Angeles	000	134	010	= 9
New York	001	001	000	= 2

	ip	h	r-er	bb	so
Hooton (W 1-1)	5⅓	5	2-2	5	2
Howe (sv#1)	3⅔	2	0-0	1	3
John	4	6	1-1	0	2
Frazier (L 0-3)	1	4	3-3	0	1
Davis	⅓	1	3-2	2	1
Reuschel	⅔	1	1-0	2	0
May	2	1	1-1	1	2
LaRoche	1	0	0-0	0	2

Game-Winning RBI: Cey
LOB: Los Angeles 10, New York 12
BE: Los Angeles 2, New York 1
2B: Nettles, Randolph
3B: Guerrero
HR: Randolph, Guerrero
SH: Russell
SB: Randolph, Lopes, Russell
CS: Russell
Time—3:09 Attendance—56,513
Umpires: D. Stello, L. Barnett, N. Colosi, T. Cooney, D. Harvey, & R. Garcia

1982 SUNDAY, AUGUST 8TH, AT DODGER STADIUM

Eighth Straight Win Over Braves

Welch & Niedenfuer Combine for 2-0 Shutout
L.A. Has Gained 9 Games in Ten Days, Now Trails by 1½

BY WINNING ANOTHER TIGHT GAME from the first-place Atlanta Braves, the Los Angeles Dodgers closed to within 1½ games of the National League West Division lead today. The 2-0 triumph was the Dodgers' eighth over the Braves in ten days. In those ten days, they have closed the gap between themselves and the leaders from 10½ games to the present 1½. No team in major league history ever gained more ground on the league leaders faster.

Today's Results			
LOS ANGELES 2-Atlanta 0			
San Diego 3-Cincinnati 1			
San Francisco 3-Houston 2 (1st game)			
San Francisco 8-Houston 3 (2nd game)			

Standings	W-L	Pct.	GB
Atlanta	62-47	.569	—
LOS ANGELES	62-50	.554	1½
San Diego	60-51	.541	3
San Francisco	57-55	.509	6½
Houston	48-62	.436	14½
Cincinnati	40-71	.360	23

The Los Angeles team arrived in Atlanta a week ago Friday with a record of 52-49. Atlanta had just completed a four-game sweep of second- place San Diego and had a 61-37 log. The situation was desperate for the Dodgers, who practically had to sweep the series to even stay in the pennant race.

The series began with a twi-night doubleheader. The Braves took a 6-1 lead in the first game, but the Dodgers staged a great rally and won, 10-9. Then Los Angeles pounded out an 8-2 victory in the second game. With momentum suddenly on their side, the Dodgers easily wrapped up the next two games, 3-0 and 9-4, to sweep the series.

The Braves then lost two out of three to San Francisco, while the Dodgers won two of three in Cincinnati.

The Braves arrived in Los Angeles on Thursday for a four-game series at Dodger Stadium. The first three games were all extra-inning thrillers, and the home team won them all. The opening game saw the Dodgers tie the score in the ninth and win the game, 3-2, in the tenth. In the second game, the Braves rallied in the eighth to tie. Then they got the go-ahead run in the top of the tenth on a home run by Claudell Washington. But the Atlanta defense handed Los Angeles two unearned runs in the bottom of the tenth, and the Dodgers won again, this time 5-4. Yesterday's game was again marked by errors, five by Los Angeles and two by Atlanta. The Braves managed to tie the score with two unearned runs in the ninth. But in the eleventh, Dusty Baker singled, stole second, and scored the winning run on a pinch single by Mike Marshall to give Los Angeles the victory, 7-6.

Today the Dodger fans were primed for the second sweep in two weekends. A total of 51,494 fans paid to see the game, bringing the total for the series to 202,997. There was an Old-Timers' Game on the program, but the sudden resurgence of the 1982 Dodgers overshadowed the stars of yesteryear.

Rick Camp was Atlanta manager Joe Torre's choice to try and stem the tide. The sinkerballer pitched a very good game, but he was undermined by a questionable call by the first base umpire. Fastballer Bob Welch started for the Dodgers, and he shut the Braves out for eight innings. The offensive star was Ken Landreaux, who scored both runs after two steals of second base. The goat was Atlanta catcher Biff Pocoroba, against whom the Dodgers had been running with inpunity.

The first run came in the bottom of the first inning. With one out, Landreaux punched a bouncer toward the mound. Camp deflected the ball, but shortstop Rafael Ramirez made a remarkable play in front of second base and gunned the ball to first. Umpire Billy Williams called the batter safe, although even many of the Dodger partisans thought he was out. Landreaux proceeded to steal second. A long fly by Baker sent him to third, and Guerrero's line single to right center brought him home.

Guerrero was picked off between first and second.

Atlanta did not get a man to first against Welch until one was out in the fifth, when Bob Horner pulled a hit through the infield. Glenn Hubbard followed by grounding into a double play.

The Braves finally mounted a threat in the seventh but lost their chance to score through poor judgement on the bases. Terry Harper, substituting for the injured Washington, led off with a hit to center. Ramirez rapped neat hit-and-run single to left, and Harper reached third. Chris Chambliss lined one toward the pitcher's mound. Welch got a glove on it, but it ricocheted off him. Harper took a couple of steps toward the plate, then made a fatal hesitation. Shortstop Mark Belanger, meanwhile, had scooped the ball up. When Harper finally broke for home, Belanger threw him out. Dale Murphy followed with another rap off Welch's glove, which second baseman Steve Sax converted into an out at first. With runners on second and third, Horner hit a dangerous liner toward the gap in right center. But the ball stayed up long enough for Guerrero to chase it down for the third out.

The tiring Welch walked two batters with two out in the eighth, but he retired Harper on a fly ball to end the inning.

With Camp out of the game to make way for a pinch-hitter, Gene Garber pitched for Atlanta in the bottom of the eighth. With one out, Sax got a hit. Landreaux forced him at second. Kenny stole second again and scored on a hit to left by Baker.

Tom Niedenfuer was called in to protect the 2-0 lead for Los Angeles. Ramirez led off the ninth with a hit to center. Chambliss flied out, and Murphy forced Ramirez at second. Horner walked, putting the tying runs on base. But Hubbard ended the game by lining out to right field.

So Atlanta's division lead, which just ten days before had seemed insurmountable, was reduced to a very manageable 1½ games. The Dodgers and their fans were confident that Los Angeles would be in first place before too much longer.

Atlanta	ab	r	h	bi	o	a	e
T. Harper, rf	4	0	1	0	1	0	0
R. Ramirez, ss	4	0	2	0	1	2	0
C. Chambliss, 1b	4	0	0	0	9	0	0
D. Murphy, cf	4	0	0	0	6	0	0
B. Horner, 3b	3	0	1	0	2	2	0
C. Washington, pr9	0	0	0	0	-	-	-
G. Hubbard, 2b	4	0	0	0	1	4	0
B. Pocoroba, c	3	0	0	0	4	0	0
L. Whisenton, lf	2	0	0	0	0	0	0
R. Camp, p	2	0	0	0	0	1	0
B. Porter, ph8	0	0	0	0	-	-	-
G. Garber, p8	0	0	0	0	0	0	0
	30	0	4	0	24	9	0

Los Angeles	ab	r	h	bi	o	a	e
S. Sax, 2b	4	0	1	0	1	2	0
K. Landreaux, cf	4	2	1	0	6	0	0
D. Baker, lf	4	0	2	1	2	0	0
T. Niedenfuer, p9	0	0	0	0	0	0	0
P. Guerrero, rf	3	0	1	1	6	0	0
R. Cey, 3b	4	0	0	0	1	1	0
S. Garvey, 1b	3	0	1	0	3	0	0
M. Sciosia, c	3	0	1	0	5	0	0
M. Belanger, ss	3	0	1	0	1	2	0
B. Welch, p	2	0	0	0	1	2	0
R. Roenicke, ph8-lf	1	0	0	0	1	0	0
	31	2	8	2	27	7	0

Atlanta	000	000	000	= 0
Los Angeles	100	000	01x	= 2

	ip	h	r-er	bb	so
Camp (L 8-5)	7	6	1-1	0	4
Garber	1	2	1-1	1	0
Welch (W 13-7)	8	3	0-0	2	4
Niedenfuer (sv #6)	1	1	0-0	1	0

WP: Garber, Niedenfuer

Game-Winning RBI: Guerrero
LOB: Atlanta 6, Los Angeles 6
DP: Sax-Belanger-Garvey (Hubbard)
SB: Landreaux 2
CS: Guerrero
Time—2:09
Attendance—51,494
Umpires: J. West, B. Williams, J. Davis, & T. Tata

Los Angeles won its next two games while Atlanta was losing two, and the Dodgers took over first place on August 10th.

The lead seesawed back and forth, but with twelve games to play, Los Angeles had a 3-game lead. The Dodgers then lost eight in a row (six of them by one run) to fall behind. They fought back only to lose the last game of the season (5-3 in San Francisco) and miss a chance to tie the race. Los Angeles finished second, 1 game behind Atlanta, with an 88-74 record.

The tight pennant race helped the club set yet another all-time major league attendance record with 3,608,881.

Chapter XVIII Retooling a Winner in 1983

1983 September 11th
4-Run 9th-Inning Rally Sends Braves Reeling

1983 League Championship Series Game No. 2
Fernando & Dodgers Even Series With 4-1 Victory

AFTER NARROWLY MISSING THE DIVISION PENNANT IN 1982, THE DODGERS UNDERWENT some changes over the winter. Veterans Steve Garvey and Terry Forster were lost to free agency, and Ron Cey was traded to the Cubs for two minor leaguers. The rebuilding plan called for shifting Pedro Guerrero from right field to third base, installing young Mike Marshall (a first baseman in the minors) in right, and placing rookie Greg Brock at first. Overall, the Dodgers appeared to be substantially weakened compared to 1982.

The other winter news included salary arbitration for Fernando Valenzuela (he was awarded a $1,000,000 salary) and drug and alcohol rehabilitation for Ken Landreaux and Steve Howe.

There seemed to be no consensus about a favorite in the N. L. West race before the season started, with Los Angeles, Atlanta, San Francisco, and San Diego all thought to be potential winners. The Dodgers' biggest question marks seemed to be the bullpen and the ability of Brock and Marshall to pick up the slack left by the departure of Garvey and Cey. Despite a lackluster Grapefruit League record (11-17), Dodger manager Tom Lasorda was confident, as always, about his team's chances.

The Dodgers opened the season in Houston with four runs in the very first inning, but Valenzuela was knocked out of the box in the third, and Los Angeles had to rally again to win going away, 16-7. Rookie Brock got off to a hot start, and the bullpen showed surprising strength and depth. By the time the season was ten games old, a two-team race had developed between the Dodgers and Braves. It remained that way all year.

Los Angeles encountered some ominous problems in May. Brock and Marshall both slumped at bat. Utility standout Derrel Thomas suffered a thumb injury and was out for a month. And catcher Mike Sciosia, who seemed to be rebounding from a poor 1982, suffered a shoulder injury on May 14th and was out for the year.

But the team grabbed first place on May 6th with a sloppy 16-10 victory over St. Louis and held it for nearly two months. It was quite evident that pitching was carrying the club, and Lasorda skillfully utilized all ten men on his staff to good effect. Bob Welch, Fernando Valenzuela, and Alejandro Pena pitched consecutive shutouts on May 22nd, 23rd, and 24th, and Welch came back on June 1st and pitched a one-hit, 1-0 shutout.

But more clouds were on the horizon. Steve Howe, who had not allowed an earned run in the first two months, went onto the disabled list in late May after lapsing into drug use again. He was out for a month and fined $54,000 by the commissioner. And the catching situation was very delicate with Sciosia out. Steve Yeager, 34 years old and suffering from painfully sore knees, had to do the backstopping nearly every day. He performed heroically well into the summer, but his first two backups, Dave Sax and Gilberto Reyes, left something to be desired.

As June wore on, the big story became the strange inability of second baseman Steve Sax to make routine throws to first. And the rest of the Dodger fielding also seemed to be substandard. But at least Sax continued to perform effectively as a leadoff hitter, and cleanup man Pedro Guerrero came through with lots of big home runs.

The pitching was outstanding. On June 17th, Bob Welch beat Cincinnati Reds' ace Mario Soto 1-0 by hitting the first home run of his professional career and pitching his third shutout in four weeks. Two days later, Burt Hooton pitched a three-

Bob Welch

Fernando Valenzuela

hitter to beat the Reds 5-1 and lower the Dodgers' staff ERA to 2.57. The victory also increased Los Angeles's lead over Atlanta to 5½ games.

Then the bottom fell out of the Dodger pennant drive. The team lost four straight to San Diego, then six of the next ten to fall 1 game behind the Braves just before the All-Star Game.

At the break, the Dodgers led the league in errors with 92 (24 by Steve Sax). And the offense ranked eighth in batting average and seventh in runs-per-game. Dusty Baker, so long a mainstay of the Los Angeles attack, was batting only .231. Mike Marshall carried a .242 mark, and Greg Brock was down at .219. Steve Yeager was hitting only .233, but he had hit 13 home runs. Only Pedro Guerrero (.301), Sax (.271), and Ken Landreaux (.267) were producing up to standard. Still, the Dodgers led the league in homers (79) and earned-run-average (2.81).

Baker got hot after the break, and Marshall showed signs of coming out of the doldrums. Guerrero continued to slug the ball for ten days or so, then he succumbed to a slump. Worse still, the starting pitching was faltering. The staff had only one complete game in July, and the team fell to 4½ games behind by the end of the month.

On July 31st, Steve Yeager suffered a fractured wrist, and Jack Fimple, just up from Albuquerque, became the number one catcher by default. Luckily, he turned out to be pretty good. On August 5th, he hit a double and a triple and scored both runs in a big 2-1 triumpth over Atlanta.

Still, the Dodgers found themselves 6½ games behind after losing in Cincinnati on August 10th. Lasorda, who had handled his youngsters with patience and skill, had finally had enough. He closed the clubhouse doors and gave his men a scorching lecture. Then the veteran players took over the meeting and took some of the younger ones to task. The next day, Brock hit a three-run homer, and the Dodgers beat the Reds 4-3.

The team traveled to Atlanta and won two out of three despite a heartbreaking, 8-7 loss in the middle game of the series. Sax keyed the two victories with five leadoff singles and some nice fielding. In fact, Steve made his last throwing error of the season on August 5th.

It was about this time that a silly but morale-boosting ritual was instituted following each victory: the presentation of the ''Mr. Potatohead Award'' to the star of the game.

Other things were starting to come around, too. Landreaux and Marshall had boosted their averages into the .280's with good clutch hitting. On August 15th, the Braves suffered a telling blow when their slugging third baseman, Bob Horner, suffered a broken wrist. Starting the next day, the Dodgers reeled off eight straight victories at home. Jerry Reuss, who had missed a start in early August due to a sore elbow, came back with seven strong outings in a row. And on August 19th, Los Angeles announced the acquisition of lefthanded pitcher Rick Honeycutt, who was leading the American League in ERA at the time. Honeycutt beat the Phillies in each of his first two starts for the Dodgers.

On August 29th, the Dodgers leaped into first place by winning a doubleheader in New York. Pedro Guerrero, who was just coming out of a mild five-week slump, was 5-for-10 on the night.

When the rosters were expanded on September 1st, the Dodgers called up eight minor leaguers, and Lasorda fearlessly threw them into the pennant race with some gratifying results. R. J. Reynolds, a .337 hitter with San Antonio, clubbed a three-run homer on September 6th for his first major-league hit. The next night, Sid Bream, who had led the Pacific Coast League with 118 RBIs, tied a game with his first major league hit with two out in the ninth inning.

The Dodger lead was 2 games when the Braves came to town on September 9th to start a three-game set. Reynolds started all three games in center field because of an ankle injury to Landreaux. In the first game, Alejandro Pena pitched seven shutout innings and smacked a two-run single, and the Dodgers held on to win, 3-2. The next night, Reynolds went 3-for-4, and Fimple drove in two runs, but the Braves eventually won in ten innings, 6-3. In the rubber game of the series, Atlanta routed Honeycutt in four innings and held a 6-3 lead going into the bottom of the ninth. Then the Dodgers staged one of the best rallies of the year, scoring four runs to win, 7-6, with Reynolds bringing home the winner with a squeeze bunt. The defeat sent the Braves out of town trailing by 3 games.

Although the Dodgers won only 8 games while losing 11 and tying 1 over the final three weeks, they finished the year with a 3-game margin over the Braves. The most discouraging development in this stretch run was the suspension of Steve Howe for missing a plane. The pennant was clinched on Friday, September 30th, when the Braves lost to the Padres while the Dodgers were playing the Giants.

Despite the injuries and slumps, Lasorda had somehow managed to guide the Dodgers to the division championship. In the League Championship Series, their opponents were the Philadelphia Phillies, who had finished the season with 14 victories in their final 16 games. But the Dodgers had beaten the Phils in 11 of 12 meetings during the year and were, therefore, declared favorites.

To take advantage of the Dodgers' weakness against lefthanded pitching (9-21 during the regular season), the Phillies bypassed hot righthander John Denny (19-6) in favor of lefty Steve Carlton (15-16) in the first game. Jerry Reuss (12-11 overall and 6-1 in the last two months) was the starting pitcher for Los Angeles. He gave up a home run to Mike Schmidt in the first inning, and Carlton and southpaw reliever Al Holland made that run stand up for a 1-0 Philly victory.

In the second game, the Dodgers scratched three unearned runs off of Denny, and Fernando Valenzuela and Tom Neidenfuer pitched Los Angeles to a 4-1 victory.

Then the series shifted to Philadelphia, and the Dodgers suddenly could not do anything right. Bob Welch (15-12) started the third game, but nagging hip trouble flared up, and he was removed after walking two batters in the second inning. Alejandro Pena was brought in to pitch, and he and catcher Jack Fimple quickly handed the Phils a run on a wild pitch and a passed ball. A second run scored when third baseman Pedro Guerrero threw to first base when he had an easy chance to retire a runner at home. Gary Matthews drove in four additional runs for Philadelphia,

Jerry Reuss

Burt Hooton

and rookie righthander Charles Hudson limited the Dodgers to four hits in the game. The final score was Phillies 7-Dodgers 2.

Facing elimination, the Dodgers came back with Reuss in the fourth game, and the Phils countered with Carlton again. In the bottom of the first, Reuss gave up two ground-ball singles with two out, and the red-hot Mr. Matthews followed with a long three-run homer. Los Angeles got a solo homer from Dusty Baker, but poor base running by Steve Sax and Mike Marshall squelched a couple of promising rallies, and the Dodgers again lost by a 7-2 final score.

After the last out was made and the Phillies had won the series 3 games to 1, the Dodgers sat in the dugout dumbfounded, while the video screen in the scoreboard showed the Phillies spraying champagne in their clubhouse. It was a bitter defeat for Los Angeles, and it had pointed out painfully the weaknesses of the team. There was the inability to beat lefthanders. And the youngsters, notably Marshall, Brock, Sax, and Fimple, had performed poorly in the pinches.

But despite the playoff defeat, the year had to be rated as a success. The club had drawn over 3½ million paying fans at home. And in what was in many respects a rebuilding year, manager Tom Lasorda had successfully exploited the depth of talent provided by vice-president Al Campanis and the player development department and had won the West Division title. Mike Marshall, Greg Brock, and Jack Fimple were established as big leaguers, and R. J. Reynolds, Dave Anderson, German Rivera, and half a dozen others had shown that they deserved a chance to establish themselves. Pedro Guerrero had solidified his reputation as one of the game's leading sluggers. And the team's pitching was solid.

The National League and World championships had eluded the Dodgers in 1983. But as they used to say in Brooklyn, "Wait until next year!"

1983 SUNDAY, SEPTEMBER 11TH, AT DODGER STADIUM

4-Run Rally Sends Braves Reeling

7-6 Victory Boosts Dodgers' Lead to 3 Games
Squeeze Bunt by Rookie Reynolds Brings in Winning Run

Today's Results

LOS ANGELES 7-Atlanta 6
San Francisco 3-Houston 2
Cincinnati 4-San Diego 2

Standings	W-L	Pct.	GB
LOS ANGELES	83-60	.580	—
Atlanta	80-63	.559	3
Houston	75-67	.528	7½
San Diego	71-73	.493	12½
San Francisco	68-76	.472	15½
Cincinnati	65-79	.451	18½

FACED WITH THE PROSPECT OF SEEING their lead in the pennant race reduced to just one game, the Los Angeles Dodgers today came up with four runs in the ninth inning to defeat the second-place Atlanta Braves, 7-6, and send the visitors out of town 3 games behind with 19 games to play.

It was a very hot and smoggy day in Los Angeles, and the crowd at the game was below capacity. And of the nearly 50,000 who came to the park, about half had left before the Dodgers staged their dramatic rally.

It was not a good day for pitchers, and each team employed six different hurlers, including one man who was not even warming up before he got into the game. Fourteen batters were walked, and six of them came around to score. The starting pitchers, Rick Honeycutt for Los Angeles and Len Barker for Atlanta, had both been plucked from the American League within the last four weeks, and each had been given a fat five-year contract. Neither one did particularly well, although Barker outlasted Honeycutt by a couple of innings.

The Dodgers got the first runs of the day in the bottom of the second on a two-out, two-run double down the right field line by Jack Fimple.

But the Braves' big gun, Dale Murphy, quickly turned the game around in the third inning. Not only did he hit a long three-run homer in the top of the inning, he robbed Pedro Guerrero of a two-run homer with a great catch in the bottom of the round.

Honeycutt was knocked out of the box in the fourth, and it took three more pitchers to finally get the Braves out in the inning. Atlanta scored three runs, the last two coming on a two-run single by Brad Komminsk, to up their lead to 6-2.

The Braves used four hurlers in the bottom of the sixth, but they held the Dodgers to one run. With one gone, Barker gave up a walk and a single and was removed from the game. Tommy Boggs came on and struck out one pinch-hitter before walking another one to load the bases. At this juncture, manager Joe Torre called for a fresh righthander to face Steve Sax. Unfortunately, lefty Terry Forster was the only pitcher loose in the bullpen. After some confusion, righty Tony Brizzolara came in, even though he had not warmed up. He quickly walked Sax on four pitches to force home a run. Lefty Forster was then hustled in to finally retire the side.

Forster aggrevated a muscle pull in his leg with his first pitch in the seventh inning, and Donnie Moore took his place.

Moore was able to protect the 6-3 lead until the ninth. Then veteran pinch-hitter Jose Morales led off with a double to left. After Moore walked Sax, Gene Garber was called in to pitch. He struck Bill Russell out. Dusty Baker followed with a little pop that fell safely in short right field for a hit, loading the bases. Garber got a couple of strikes on Guerrero, but Pedro fouled off at least four pitches and wound up with a walk, forcing pinch-runner Dave Anderson across the plate.

With the winning runs on base, Mike Marshall came to the plate. Earlier in the year, the youngster had trouble in the clutch because he got too excited. But by now he had gained enough confidence to keep his cool in such situations. This time he went with an outside slider and lined it to deep right. Outfielder Claudell Washington had trouble with the sun, and the ball sailed over his head and to the fence for a game-tying double. An intentional walk loaded the bases again.

The batter was rookie R. J. Reynolds. Only one man was out, so manager Tom Lasorda contemplated a squeeze bunt, even though he had never seen Reynolds bunt before. Bob Welch, sitting next to Lasorda on the bench, advised letting the kid swing away. Since the guys on the bench had been wrong all day, Lasorda decided to call for a squeeze on the second pitch. With Guerrero breaking for home, Reynolds dropped a neat bunt down the first base line. The runner galloped home with the winning tally as the pitcher was tagging Reynolds out, and the Dodgers had won the game, 7-6.

In the jubilant Dodger clubhouse after the game, Marshall was presented with the Mr. Potatohead Award, symbolic of the star of the game. And an informal poll revealed that everyone on the bench except Lasorda had been in favor of Reynolds swinging away. The manager confessed that he had been mighty nervous ordering a bunt, but he was mighty happy now.

Over in the visitors' clubhouse, no one was happy. The usually cooperative Torre locked himself in the managers' office and finally issued a statement which began, "I have nothing to say. . ." After a loss like that, there really wasn't much the Braves could say. The Dodger rally had said it all.

Atlanta	**ab**	**r**	**h**	**bi**	**o**	**a**	**e**
B. Butler, lf	4	0	1	0	3	0	0
J. Royster, 2b	5	2	2	0	1	4	0
R. Ramirez, ss	4	2	2	0	1	2	1
D. Murphy, cf	3	2	1	3	3	0	0
C. Chambliss, 1b	4	0	1	0	6	1	0
B. Komminsk, rf	3	0	1	2	0	0	0
C. Washington, rf5	2	0	0	0	3	0	0
B. Benedict, c	4	0	2	0	5	0	0
R. Johnson, 3b	4	0	1	0	2	0	0
L. Barker, p	3	0	0	0	1	0	0
T. Boggs, p6	0	0	0	0	0	0	0
T. Brizzolara, p6	0	0	0	0	0	0	0
T. Forster, p6	1	0	0	0	0	0	0
D. Moore, p7	0	0	0	0	0	0	0
G. Garber, p9	0	0	0	0	1	0	0
	37	6	11	5	26	7	1

Los Angeles	**ab**	**r**	**h**	**bi**	**o**	**a**	**e**
S. Sax, 2b	3	1	0	1	2	4	0
B. Russell, ss	5	0	1	0	0	5	0
D. Baker, lf	5	0	1	0	1	0	0
C. Espy, pr9	0	1	0	0	-	-	-
P. Guerrero, 3b	4	1	0	1	1	2	0
M. Marshall, rf	5	1	3	2	0	0	0
G. Brock, 1b	2	2	1	0	14	0	0
R. Reynolds, cf	4	0	1	1	3	1	0
J. Fimple, c	1	0	1	2	3	0	1
R. Monday, ph6	1	0	0	0	-	-	-
S. Yeager, c7	1	0	0	0	3	0	0
R. Honeycutt, p	1	0	0	0	0	2	0
P. Zachry, p4	0	0	0	0	0	0	0
R. Rodas, p4	0	0	0	0	0	0	0
O. Hershiser, p4	0	0	0	0	0	0	0
S. Bream, ph4	1	0	0	0	-	-	-
B. Hooton, p5	0	0	0	0	0	0	0
K. Landreaux, ph6	0	0	0	0	-	-	-
R. Landestoy, pr6	0	0	0	0	-	-	-
J. Beckwith, p7	0	0	0	0	0	0	0
J. Morales, ph9	1	0	1	0	-	-	-
D. Anderson, pr9	0	1	0	0	-	-	-
	34	7	9	7	27	14	1

Atlanta	003 300 000	=	6
Los Angeles	020 001 004	=	7

two out when winning run scored

	ip	**h**	**r-er**	**bb**	**so**
Barker	5⅓	6	3-3	3	1
Boggs	⅓	0	0-0	1	1
Brizzolara	*0	0	0-0	1	0
Forster	⅓	0	0-0	0	1
Moore	†2	1	2-2	1	0
Garber (L 3-5)	⅔	2	2-2	2	1
Honeycutt	3⅔	7	5-5	2	1
Zachry	‡0	0	1-1	1	0
Rodas	§0	1	0-0	1	0
Hershiser	⅓	0	0-0	1	0
Hooton	2	1	0-0	0	2
Beckwith (W 2-3)	3	2	0-0	1	3

Game-Winning RBI: Reynolds
LOB: Atlanta 11, Los Angeles 10
BE: Atlanta 0, Los Angeles 1
DP: Royster-Ramirez-Chambliss (Reynolds) Reynolds-Brock
2B: Fimple, Morales, Marshall
HR: Murphy
SH: Reynolds
SB: Ramirez

HBP: by Honeycutt (Butler)

*faced one batter in sixth
†faced two batters in ninth
‡faced one batter in fourth
§faced two batters in fourth
Time-3:48 Attendance—45,269

Umpires: D. Stello, S. Davidson, E. Vargo, & J. West

The Dodgers split their next ten games, while the Braves were losing seven of nine. That stretched the Los Angeles lead to 5½ games. The Dodgers won only three of their final nine decisions but still wound up in first place with a 3-game margin over the Braves.

1983 WEDNESDAY EVENING, OCTOBER 5TH, AT DODGER STADIUM
League Championship Series—Game #2

Fernando & Dodgers Even Series with 4-1 Victory

IT HAD NOT BEEN A PARTICULARLY GREAT YEAR FOR LOS ANGELES DODGER PITCHER Fernando Valenzuela. Although his won-lost record for the regular season was a respectable 15-10, he had finished just 7-8 after a good 8-2 start. And his earned-run-average this season was 3.75, compared to a career ERA of 2.62 at the start of the year. But at least today Fernando came through with a clutch victory to get the Dodgers even in the best-of-five playoff series versus the Philadelphia Phillies.

Valenzuela's lackluster finish had caused manager Tom Lasorda to bypass him in favor of veteran Jerry Reuss in the first game of the League Championship Series yesterday. Reuss pitched a strong game, but the Dodgers were unable to score againt lefthanders Steve Carlton and Al Holland and lost a heartbreaker, 1-0.

Today it was Fernando's turn. He was matched against a very tough opponent, John Denny, who had led the league in victories with 19 and finished second in ERA at 2.37. Denny limited the Dodgers to just five hits and no earned runs in six innings of work. But Los Angeles exploited two Philly errors for three unearned runs and scratched an earned run off of reliever Ron Reed. Valenzuela, with last inning relief from Tom Niedenfuer, held the Phillies to one run and seven hits, and Los Angeles won by a final score of 4-1. Valenzuela added to these laurels by slugging a long drive to center field to start the game-winning rally in the fifth inning.

Fernando had good velocity on his fastball tonight, which helped compensate for his inability to get his screwball over the plate consistently. When he was taken out of the game in the ninth inning, he showed uncharacteristic irritation as he came off the field. But it turned out that he was mad that the official scorers had not given him a triple in the fifth inning and was not complaining about being removed in favor of Niedenfuer.

The Phillies got a walk in the top of the first but failed to score.

In the bottom, Philadelphia handed Los Angeles a run after the first two batters were out. Dusty Baker, batting third, hit a ground ball that went under shortstop Ivan DeJesus's glove for an error. Denny then hit Pedro Guerrero in the seat of the pants with a curveball, putting men on first and second. Ken Landreaux delivered a sharp ground single up the middle, and Baker scored without drawing a throw.

Gary Matthews tied the game with a leadoff home run in the top of the second. Garry Maddox followed with a single, but Valenzuela fooled Bo Diaz on a screwball and got a double play. DeJesus walked with two gone, but Denny lined out to left.

Maddox doubled with two down in the fourth, but Diaz grounded out again, this time on a fastball.

Poor execution on a double steal killed a Dodger rally in the last of the fourth.

Another double play turned the Phillies back in the top of the fifth.

In the bottom half, Valenzuela whaled the first pitch high and deep to right center. Outfielder Maddox was able to get under it, but just as he gloved the ball he tripped on the grass and fell to the ground, allowing the ball to squirt out of his grasp. Huffing and puffing, Fernando slid safely into third base. It was rightly ruled an error on Maddox, much to the chagrin of Valenzuela.

The Dodgers almost failed to cash in on this big opportunity. Steve Sax grounded out, with Valenzula holding. Greg Brock then bounced to third base, and Fernando was thrown out at the plate. With two down and a man on first, Denny walked Baker. Guerrero then came through with the key hit. It was not very impressive, just a flare down the right field line, but the ball landed safely and took a crazy hop behind the right fielder, allowing two runs to score and giving Guerrero a triple.

With a 3-1 lead, Valenzuela retired the next five Phillies before allowing two two-out singles in the seventh inning. Joe Morgan followed these with a liner toward the right field line. Outfielder Mike Marshall misjudged the ball at first, but he recovered just in time to make a diving catch near the line to preserve the lead.

Mike Schmidt dropped a bunt single down the third base line with one out in the eighth. But Bill Russell and Steve Sax turned their third double play of the game to end the inning.

The Dodgers added an insurance run in the last of the eighth on a two-out walk to Russell, a stolen base, and a single by Jack Fimple.

The Phillies mounted one more threat in the ninth. Matthews got a hit deep in the shortstop hole and took second on a wild throw by Russell. After delivering two balls to Maddox, Valenzuela was removed in favor of Niedenfuer. Greg Gross pinch hit for Maddox and drew two more balls for a walk. But then Niedenfuer turned on the heat. He fanned Joe Lefebvre, jammed Von Hayes for a pop out to short, and got Ozzie Virgil on a called third strike to end the game.

So Los Angeles was even in the series. Most of the Dodgers were happy with the victory and it was a mighty big win for Valenzuela. But Fernando still couldn't get over the ruling of the official scorers that gave Maddox an error instead of giving Valenzuela a triple.

Philadelphia	ab	r	h	bi	o	a	e
J. Morgan, 2b	3	0	0	0	4	3	0
P. Rose, 1b	3	0	0	0	7	0	0
M. Schmidt, 3b	4	0	1	0	1	3	0
S. Lezcano, rf	4	0	0	0	1	0	0
G. Matthews, lf	4	1	2	1	1	0	0
G. Maddox, cf	3	0	2	0	4	0	1
G. Gross, ph9	0	0	0	0	-	-	-
B. Diaz, c	3	0	0	0	5	1	0
J. Lefebvre, ph9	1	0	0	0	-	-	-
I. DeJesus, ss	2	0	1	0	1	3	1
V. Hayes, ph9	1	0	0	0	-	-	-
J. Denny, p	1	0	0	0	0	0	0
T. Perez, ph7	1	0	1	0	-	-	-
J. Samuel, pr7	0	0	0	0	-	-	-
R. Reed, p7	0	0	0	0	0	1	0
O. Virgil, ph9	1	0	0	0	-	-	-
	31	1	7	1	24	11	2

Los Angeles	ab	r	h	bi	o	a	e
S. Sax, 2b	4	0	0	0	4	4	0
G. Brock, 1b	4	1	0	0	7	0	0
D. Thomas, rf8	0	0	0	0	0	0	0
D. Baker, lf	3	2	0	0	3	0	0
P. Guerrero, 3b	3	0	1	2	0	2	0
K. Landreaux, cf	3	0	2	1	3	0	0
M. Marshall, rf-1b8	4	0	0	0	2	0	0
B. Russell, ss	3	1	2	0	1	5	1
J. Fimple, c	4	0	1	1	6	1	0
F. Valenzuela, p	3	0	0	0	1	0	0
T. Niedenfuer, p9	0	0	0	0	0	0	0
	31	4	6	4	27	12	1

Philadelphia	010 000 000	=	1
Los Angeles	100 020 01x	=	4

	ip	h	r-er	bb	so
Denny (L 0-1)	6	5	3-0	3	3
Reed	2	1	1-1	1	1
Valenzuela (W 1-0)	*8	7	1-1	4	5
Niedenfuer (sv #1)	1	0	0-0	0	2

*faced two batters in ninth
WP: Valenzuela
HBP: by Denny (Guerrero)
Time—2:44
Attendance—55,967

Game-Winning RBI: Guerrero
LOB: Philadelphia 8, Los Angeles 8
BE: Philadelphia 0, Los Angeles 2
Base on Missed 3rd Strike: Phila 1
DP: Russell-Sax-Brock (Diaz)
Russell-Sax-Brock (Rose)
Russell-Sax-Marshall (Lezcano)
2B: Maddox
3B: Guerrero
HR: Matthews
SH: Denny
SB: Rose, Russell
CS: Marshall

Umpires: D. Stello, J. McSherry, L. Weyer, D. Harvey, J. Crawford, & T. Tata

After a day for travel, the series resumed in Philadelphia, where the Dodgers could not seem to do anything right. They lost two straight games by identical 7-2 scores, and the Phillies won the series, three games to one.

Appendix A Season Statistics

Year	(Teams in League-Games Scheduled)	Final Standing	W-L	Pct.	GB	(Ties)	Record at home	Home Attendance	Days in first + days tied for first
BROOKLYN—INTERSTATE ASSOCIATION									
1883	(96-7)	First	44-28	.611	+ 2	(1)	27-13-1	—	29
BROOKLYN—AMERICAN ASSOCIATION									
1884	(110-12)	Ninth	40-64	.485	33½	(5)	23-25-3	—	0
1885	(112-8)	Fifth (tie)	53-59	.473	26		36-22	—	0+2
1886	(140-8)	Third	76-61	.555	16	(4)	44-25-1	—	5
1887	(140-8)	Sixth	60-74	.448	34½	(4)	36-38-1	—	6+8
1888	(140-8)	Second	88-52	.629	6½	(3)	53-20-3	—	42+6
1889	(140-8)	First	93-44	.679	+ 2	(3)	50-19-2	353,690	45+1
BROOKLYN—NATIONAL LEAGUE									
1890	(140-8)	First	86-43	.667	+ 6		58-16	121,412	70
1891	(140-8)	Sixth	61-76	.445	25½		41-31	181,477	0
1892A	(77-12)	Second	51-26	.662	2½	(1)	26- 8-1	183,727	0+4
1892B	(77-12)	Third	44-33	.571	9½	(3)	25-16-2		2+11
1893	(132-12)	Sixth (tie)	65-63	.508	20½	(2)	43-24	175,000	4+9
1894	(132-12)	Fifth	70-61	.534	20½	(3)	42-24-2	137,000	0
1895	(132-12)	Fifth (tie)	71-60	.542	16½	(2)	43-22-1	230,000	0+2
1896	(132-12)	Ninth (tie)	58-73	.443	33	(2)	35-28-2	200,000	0+5
1897	(132-12)	Sixth (tie)	61-71	.462	32	(4)	38-29-3	220,831	0+2
1898	(154-12)	Tenth	54-91	.372	46	(4)	30-41-3	122,514	0+2
1899	(154-12)	First	101-47	.682	+ 8	(2)	61-16-1	269,641	146
1900	(140-8)	First	82-54	.603	+ 4½	(6)	43-26-4	183,000	116+1
1901	(140-8)	Third	79-57	.581	9½	(1)	43-25	198,200	1+6
1902	(140-8)	Second	75-63	.543	27½	(3)	45-23-1	199,868	0+2
1903	(140-8)	Fifth	70-66	.515	19	(3)	40-33	224,670	0+1
1904	(154-8)	Sixth	56-97	.366	50	(1)	31-44-1	214,600	0
1905	(154-8)	Eighth	48-104	.316	56½	(3)	29-47-1	227,924	0
1906	(154-8)	Fifth	66-86	.434	50	(1)	31-44-1	227,400	0
1907	(154-8)	Fifth	65-83	.439	40	(5)	38-38-2	312,500	0
1908	(154-8)	Seventh	53-101	.344	46		27-50	275,600	0
1909	(154-8)	Sixth	55-98	.359	55½	(2)	34-45	321,300	0+1
1910	(154-8)	Sixth	64-90	.416	40	(2)	39-39-2	279,321	0+1
1911	(154-8)	Seventh	64-86	.427	33½	(4)	31-42-1	269,000	0
1912	(154-8)	Seventh	58-95	.379	46		33-43	243,000	0
1913	(154-8)	Sixth	65-84	.436	34½	(3)	29-47-1	347,000	0+1
1914	(154-8)	Fifth	75-79	.487	19½		45-34	122,671	0+7
1915	(154-8)	Third	80-72	.526	10	(2)	51-26-1	297,766	0
1916	(154-8)	First	94-60	.610	+ 2½	(2)	50-27	447,747	149+3
1917	(154-8)	Seventh	70-81	.464	26½	(5)	36-38-4	221,619	0
1918	(*WW-8)	Fifth	57-69	.452	25½		33-21	83,831	0
1919	(140-8)	Fifth	69-71	.493	27	(1)	36-34	360,721	14+7
1920	(154-8)	First	93-61	.604	+ 7	(1)	49-29	808,722	80+7
1921	(154-8)	Fifth	77-75	.507	16½		41-37	613,245	0+1
1922	(154-8)	Sixth	76-78	.494	17	(1)	44-34	498,856	0+1
1923	(154-8)	Sixth	76-78	.494	19½	(1)	37-40-1	564,666	0
1924	(154-8)	Second	92-62	.597	1½		46-31	818,883	0+1
1925	(154-8)	Sixth (tie)	68-85	.444	27		40-37	659,435	0+2
1926	(154-8)	Sixth	71-82	.464	17½	(2)	38-38	650,819	15+1
1927	(154-8)	Sixth	65-88	.425	28½	(1)	34-39-1	637,230	0+1
1928	(154-8)	Sixth	77-76	.503	17½	(2)	41-35-1	664,863	4
1929	(154-8)	Sixth	70-83	.458	28½		42-35	731,886	0
1930	(154-8)	Fourth	86-68	.558	6		49-28	1,097,339	74+2
1931	(154-8)	Fourth	79-73	.520	21	(1)	46-29-1	753,133	0

Year	(Teams in League-Games Scheduled)	Final Standing	W-L	Pct.	GB	(Ties)	Record at home	Home Attendance	Days in first + days tied for first
1932	(154-8)	Third	81-73	.526	9		44-34	681,827	0+1
1933	(154-8)	Sixth	65-88	.425	26½	(4)	36-41-3	526,815	0+2
1934	(154-8)	Sixth	71-81	.467	23½	(1)	43-33-1	434,188	0+1
1935	(154-8)	Fifth	70-83	.458	29½	(1)	38-38-1	470,517	4+6
1936	(154-8)	Seventh	67-87	.435	25	(2)	37-40-2	489,618	0
1937	(154-8)	Sixth	62-91	.405	33½	(2)	36-39-1	482,481	0
1938	(154-8)	Seventh	69-80	.463	18½	(2)	30-41-2	663,087	0+1
1939	(154-8)	Third	84-69	.549	12½	(4)	51-27	955,668	0
1940	(154-8)	Second	88-65	.575	12	(3)	41-37-3	975,978	38+12
1941	(154-8)	First	100-54	.649	+ 2½	(3)	52-25-2	1,214,910	77+8
1942	(154-8)	Second	104-50	.675	2	(1)	57-21	1,037,765	145+3
1943	(154-8)	Third	81-72	.529	23½		46-31	661,739	42+2
1944	(154-8)	Seventh	63-91	.409	42	(1)	37-39-1	605,905	0
1945	(154-8)	Third	87-67	.565	11	(1)	49-30	1,059,220	21+1
1946	(154-8)	Second†	96-60	.615	2	(1)	56-22-1	1,796,824	97+25
1947	(154-8)	First	94-60	.610	+ 5	(1)	52-25-1	1,807,526	110+3
1948	(154-8)	Third	84-70	.545	7½	(1)	36-42-1	1,398,967	5+3
1949	(154-8)	First	97-57	.630	+ 1	(2)	48-29-1	1,633,747	57+14
1950	(154-8)	Second	89-65	.578	2	(1)	48-30	1,185,896	33+8
1951	(154-8)	Second†	97-60	.618	1	(1)	49-29	1,282,628	142+5
1952	(154-8)	First	96-57	.627	+ 4½	(2)	45-33-2	1,088,704	146+8
1953	(154-8)	First	105-49	.682	+13	(1)	60-17-1	1,163,419	106+6
1954	(154-8)	Second	92-62	.597	5		45-32	1,020,531	16+10
1955	(154-8)	First	98-55	.641	+13½	(1)	56-21	1,033,589	163+3
1956	(154-8)	First	93-61	.604	+ 1		52-25	1,213,562	14+3
1957	(154-8)	Third	84-70	.545	11		43-34	1,028,258	1+8
		LOS ANGELES—NATIONAL LEAGUE							
1958	(154-8)	Seventh	71-83	.461	21		39-38	1,845,556	0
1959	(154-8)	First†	88-68	.564	+ 2		46-32	2,071,045	8+7
1960	(154-8)	Fourth	82-72	.532	13		42-35	2,253,887	1+8
1961	(154-8)	Second	89-65	.578	4		45-32	1,804,250	24+4
1962	(162-10)	Second†	102-63	.618	1		54-29	2,755,184	108+3
1963	(162-10)	First	99-63	.611	+ 6	(1)	50-31	2,538,602	96+2
1964	(162-10)	Sixth (tie)	80-82	.494	13	(2)	41-40	2,228,751	0+1
1965	(162-10)	First	97-65	.599	+ 2		50-31	2,553,577	130+6
1966	(162-10)	First	95-67	.586	+ 1½		53-38	2,617,029	28+1
1967	(162-10)	Eighth	73-89	.451	28½		42-39	1,664,362	0
1968	(162-10)	Seventh (tie)	76-86	.469	21		41-40	1,581,093	0
		LOS ANGELES—NATIONAL LEAGUE WEST DIVISION							
1969	(162-6)	Fourth	85-77	.525	8		50-31	1,784,527	22+11
1970	(162-6)	Second	87-74	.540	14½		39-42	1,697,142	0
1971	(162-6)	Second	89-73	.549	1		42-39	2,064,594	0
1972	(*PS-6)	Third	85-70	.548	10½		41-34	1,860,858	23+6
1973	(162-6)	Second	95-66	.590	3½	(1)	50-31	2,136,192	78+1
1974	(162-6)	First	102-60	.630	+ 4		52-29	2,632,474	172+5
1975	(162-6)	Second	88-74	.543	20		49-32	2,539,349	39+1
1976	(162-6)	Second	92-70	.568	10		49-32	2,386,301	20
1977	(162-6)	First	98-64	.605	+10		51-30	2,955,087	170+5
1978	(162-6)	First	95-67	.586	+ 2½		54-27	3,347,845	66+9
1979	(162-6)	Third	79-83	.488	11½		46-35	2,860,954	1
1980	(162-6)	Second†	92-71	.564	1		55-27	3,249,287	44+13
1981A	(*PS-6)	First	36-21	.632	+ ½		17- 8	2,381,292	62+2
1981B	(*PS-6)	Fourth	27-26	.509	6		16-15		2+3
1982	(162-6)	Second	88-74	.543	1		43-38	3,608,881	32+4
1983	(162-6)	First	91-71	.562	+ 3	(1)	43-32	3,510,313	97+5

*WW 1918 season ended on Labor Day due to World War I

*PS 1972 and 1981 seasons shortened by player's strikes

A,B 1892A & 1892B, 1981A & 1981B denote first and second halves of split seasons

† **Playoffs** to determine first place after teams finished the schedule tied for first. (These games counted in season statistics). See Appendix B for summation of playoffs.

Attendance figures for 1902 thru 1982 are from *The Sporting News Official Baseball Dope Book.* Reprinted with permission of *The Sporting News.*

Appendix B Playoffs and Post-Season Championship Play

1889 Brooklyn (AA) **lost** best-of-eleven **World Series** to New York (NL), 6 games to 3

1890 Brooklyn **tied** best-of-nine **World Series** with Louisville (AA), 3 games to 3 with one game tied. The series was called off before being completed.

1900 Brooklyn (NL) **won** best-of five **Cup Series** from second-place Pittsburgh (NL), 3 games to 1

1916 Brooklyn (NL) **lost** best-of-seven **World Series** to Boston (AL), 4 games to 1

1920 Brooklyn (NL) **lost** best-of-nine **World Series** to Cleveland (AL), 5 games to 2

1941 Brooklyn (NL) **lost** best-of-seven **World Series** to New York (AL), 4 games to 1

1946 Brooklyn (NL) **lost** best-of-three **Playoff** to St. Louis (NL), 2 games to 0.

1947 Brooklyn (NL) **lost** best-of-seven **World Series** to New York (AL), 4 games to 3

1949 Brooklyn (NL) **lost** best-of-seven **World Series** to New York (AL), 4 games to 1

1951 Brooklyn (NL) **lost** best-of-three **Playoff** to New York (NL), 2 games to 1

1952 Brooklyn (NL) **lost** best-of-seven **World Series** to New York (AL), 4 games to 3

1953 Brooklyn (NL) **lost** best-of-seven **World Series** to New York (AL), 4 games to 2

1955 Brooklyn (NL) **won** best-of-seven **World Series** from New York (AL), 4 games to 3

1956 Brooklyn (NL) **lost** best-of-seven **World Series** to New York (AL), 4 games to 3

1959 Los Angeles (NL) **won** best-of-three **Playoff** from Milwaukee (NL), 2 games to 0; then

Los Angeles (NL) **won** best-of-seven **World Series** from Chicago (AL), 4 games to 2

1962 Los Angeles (NL) **lost** best-of-three **Playoff** to San Francisco (NL), 2 games to 1

1963 Los Angeles (NL) **won** best-of-seven **World Series** from New York (AL), 4 games to 0

1965 Los Angeles (NL) **won** best-of seven **World Series** from Minnesota (AL), 4 games to 3

1966 Los Angeles (NL) **lost** best-of-seven **World Series** to Baltimore (AL), 4 games to 0

1974 Los Angeles (NLW) **won** best-of-five **League Championship Series** from Pittsburgh (NLE), 3 games to 1; then

Los Angeles (NL) **lost** best-of-seven **World Series** to Oakland (AL), 4 games to 1

1977 Los Angeles (NLW) **won** best-of-five **League Championship Series** from Philadelphia (NLE), 3 games to 1; then

Los Angeles (NL) **lost** best-of-seven **World Series** to New York (AL), 4 games to 2

1978 Los Angeles (NLW) **won** best-of-five **League Championship Series** from Philadelphia (NLE), 3 games to 1; then

Los Angeles (NL) **lost** best-of-seven **World Series** to New York (AL), 4 games to 2

1980 Los Angeles (NLW) **lost** one-game **Playoff** to Houston (NLW)

1981 Los Angeles **won** best-of-five **West Division Championship Series** from Houston, 3 games to 2; then

Los Angeles (NLW) **won** best-of-five **League Championship Series** from Montreal, 3 games to 2; then

Los Angeles (NL) **won** best-of-seven **World Series** from New York (AL), 4 games to 2

1983 Los Angeles (NLW) **lost** best-of-five **League Championship Series** to Philadelphia (NLE), 3 games to 1

Appendix C Ballparks

THE FOLLOWING BALLPARKS WERE USED BY THE BROOKLYN CLUB FOR MOST OF ITS home games in the years listed:

1883-1890 **Washington Park**—on the block bounded by Fifth Street, Fourth Avenue, Third Street, and Fifth Avenue.

1891-1897 **Eastern Park**—on the block bounded by present-day Pitkin Avenue, Powell Street, Sutter Avenue, and Van Sinderen Avenue.

1898-1912 **Washington Park**—on the block bounded by Fourth Avenue, Third Street, Third Avenue, and First Street.

1913-1957 **Ebbets Field**—on the block bounded by present-day Sullivan Place, McKeever Place, Montgomery Street, and Bedford Avenue.

The Brooklyn club also used a number of other parks for its "home" games. The games played in these parks are included in the "Record at home" column in Appendix A.

Domestic Club Grounds, Newark, New Jersey, for one game in 1883 (won by Brooklyn).

Prospect Park, Brooklyn, for one game in 1883. The Brooklyn club won the game.

Ridgewood Park, Queens—located in the area bounded by Irving Avenue, Hancock Street, Wyckoff Avenue, and Covert Street. This area is now in Brooklyn, but in the 1880's it was in Queens County, and the Brooklyn club used it to stage Sunday games. The team's won-lost record at Ridgewood was: 1886, 8-5 with one tie; 1887, 6-9; 1888, 12-8; and 1889, 9-5.

West New York Field Club Grounds, Weehawken, N.J., which was used for two Sunday games in 1898. Brooklyn won 1 and lost 1.

Roosevelt Stadium, Jersey City, N.J. The Dodgers were 6-1 here in 1956 and 5-3 in 1957.

The Los Angeles Dodgers played their home games in two stadiums:

From 1958 through 1961 in **Memorial Coliseum** —located in Exposition Park.

Since 1962 in **Dodger Stadium**—in Chavez Ravine, south of Elysian Park.

Photo Credits

Courtesy of *The Sporting News*: Pages 24, 27 (Kennedy), 47 (both), 65, 66 (both), 67, 85, 86, 87 (both), 105 (both), 124, 125, 139, 140, 141, 155, 157, 172, 173, 185, 186, 187, 207 (both), 208, and 232

Courtesy of the Los Angeles Dodgers: Pages 26 (both), 27 (Foutz), 45, 46, 103, 123, 156, 171, 231, 233, 247, 248, 249, 271, 273, 287, 288, 289, 303, 304, 306, 307, 337 (both), and 339 (both)